I0882650

Corporate Standardization Management and Innovation

Kai Jakobs
RWTH Aachen University, Germany

A volume in the Advances in Human Resources Management and Organizational Development (AHRMOD) Book Series

IGI Global
DISSEMINATOR OF KNOWLEDGE

Published in the United States of America by
IGI Global
Business Science Reference (an imprint of IGI Global)
701 E. Chocolate Avenue
Hershey PA, USA 17033
Tel: 717-533-8845
Fax: 717-533-8661
E-mail: cust@igi-global.com
Web site: http://www.igi-global.com

Copyright © 2019 by IGI Global. All rights reserved. No part of this publication may be reproduced, stored or distributed in any form or by any means, electronic or mechanical, including photocopying, without written permission from the publisher. Product or company names used in this set are for identification purposes only. Inclusion of the names of the products or companies does not indicate a claim of ownership by IGI Global of the trademark or registered trademark.

Library of Congress Cataloging-in-Publication Data

Names: Jakobs, Kai, 1957- editor.
Title: Corporate standardization management and innovation / Kai Jakobs, editor.
Description: Hershey, PA : Business Science Reference, [2019] | Includes bibliographical references and index.
Identifiers: LCCN 2019005243| ISBN 9781522590088 (hardcover : alk. paper) | ISBN 9781522590101 (ebook) | ISBN 9781522590095 (softcover : alk. paper)
Subjects: LCSH: Organizational effectiveness. | Management. | Information technology--Management.
Classification: LCC HD58.9 .M3554 2019 | DDC 658.4/013--dc23 LC record available at https://lccn.loc.gov/2019005243

This book is published in the IGI Global book series Advances in Human Resources Management and Organizational Development (AHRMOD) (ISSN: 2327-3372; eISSN: 2327-3380)

British Cataloguing in Publication Data
A Cataloguing in Publication record for this book is available from the British Library.

The views expressed in this book are those of the authors, but not necessarily of the publisher.

For electronic access to this publication, please contact: eresources@igi-global.com.

Advances in Human Resources Management and Organizational Development (AHRMOD) Book Series

Patricia Ordóñez de Pablos
Universidad de Oviedo, Spain

ISSN:2327-3372
EISSN:2327-3380

Mission

A solid foundation is essential to the development and success of any organization and can be accomplished through the effective and careful management of an organization's human capital. Research in human resources management and organizational development is necessary in providing business leaders with the tools and methodologies which will assist in the development and maintenance of their organizational structure.

The **Advances in Human Resources Management and Organizational Development (AHRMOD) Book Series** aims to publish the latest research on all aspects of human resources as well as the latest methodologies, tools, and theories regarding organizational development and sustainability. The **AHRMOD Book Series** intends to provide business professionals, managers, researchers, and students with the necessary resources to effectively develop and implement organizational strategies.

Coverage

- Job Enrichment
- Diversity in the Workplace
- Training and Development
- Succession Planning
- Entrepreneurialism
- Human Resources Development
- Workplace Culture
- Personnel Policies
- Work-Life Balance
- Outsourcing HR

IGI Global is currently accepting manuscripts for publication within this series. To submit a proposal for a volume in this series, please contact our Acquisition Editors at Acquisitions@igi-global.com or visit: http://www.igi-global.com/publish/.

The Advances in Human Resources Management and Organizational Development (AHRMOD) Book Series (ISSN 2327-3372) is published by IGI Global, 701 E. Chocolate Avenue, Hershey, PA 17033-1240, USA, www.igi-global.com. This series is composed of titles available for purchase individually; each title is edited to be contextually exclusive from any other title within the series. For pricing and ordering information please visit http://www.igi-global.com/book-series/advances-human-resources-management-organizational/73670. Postmaster: Send all address changes to above address. Copyright © 2019 IGI Global. All rights, including translation in other languages reserved by the publisher. No part of this series may be reproduced or used in any form or by any means – graphics, electronic, or mechanical, including photocopying, recording, taping, or information and retrieval systems – without written permission from the publisher, except for non commercial, educational use, including classroom teaching purposes. The views expressed in this series are those of the authors, but not necessarily of IGI Global.

Titles in this Series

For a list of additional titles in this series, please visit: www.igi-global.com/book-series

Handbook of Research on Strategic Communication, Leadership, and Conflict Management in Modern Organizations
Anthony Normore (California State University – Dominguez Hills, USA) Mitch Javidi (International Academy of Public Safety (IAPS), USA) and Larry Long (Illinois State University, USA)
Business Science Reference • copyright 2019 • 400pp • H/C (ISBN: 9781522585169) • US $245.00 (our price)

Management Techniques for Employee Engagement in Contemporary Organizations
Naman Sharma (Entrepreneurship Development Institute of India, India) Narendra Chaudhary (Symbiosis International University, India) and Vinod Kumar Singh (Gurukul Kangri Vishwavidyalaya, India)
Business Science Reference • copyright 2019 • 339pp • H/C (ISBN: 9781522577997) • US $225.00 (our price)

Emotion-Based Approaches to Personnel Management Emerging Research and Opportunities
Sara Fazzin (Niccolò Cusano Italian University in London, UK)
Business Science Reference • copyright 2019 • 235pp • H/C (ISBN: 9781522583981) • US $165.00 (our price)

Corporate Social Responsibility and Opportunities for Sustainable Financial Success
Julia Margarete Puaschunder (Columbia University, USA & The New School, USA)
Business Science Reference • copyright 2019 • 300pp • H/C (ISBN: 9781522576198) • US $200.00 (our price)

Contemporary Human Resources Management in the Tourism Industry
Demet Tüzünkan (Okan University, Turkey) and Volkan Altıntaş (Izmir Katip Celebi University, Turkey)
Business Science Reference • copyright 2019 • 405pp • H/C (ISBN: 9781522557609) • US $205.00 (our price)

Managing Diversity, Innovation, and Infrastructure in Digital Business
Nilanjan Ray (Adamas University, India)
Business Science Reference • copyright 2019 • 287pp • H/C (ISBN: 9781522559931) • US $195.00 (our price)

Managerial Competencies for Multinational Businesses
Macarena López-Fernández (University of Cádiz, Spain) and Pedro M. Romero-Fernández (University of Cádiz, Spain)
Business Science Reference • copyright 2019 • 364pp • H/C (ISBN: 9781522557814) • US $215.00 (our price)

Organizational Culture and Behavioral Shifts in the Green Economy
Violeta Sima (Petroleum-Gas University of Ploiesti, Romania)
Business Science Reference • copyright 2018 • 334pp • H/C (ISBN: 9781522529651) • US $205.00 (our price)

IGI Global
DISSEMINATOR OF KNOWLEDGE

701 East Chocolate Avenue, Hershey, PA 17033, USA
Tel: 717-533-8845 x100 • Fax: 717-533-8661
E-Mail: cust@igi-global.com • www.igi-global.com

Editorial Advisory Board

Knut Blind, *TU Berlin, Germany & FhG FOKUS, Germany*
Carl Cargill, *Independent Researcher, USA*
Tineke Egyedi, *DIRoS, The Netherlands*
Vladislav Fomin, *Vytautas Magnus University, Lithuania*
Richard Hawkins, *University of Calgary, Canada*
Geerten van de Kaa, *TU Delft, The Netherlands*
Kalle Lyytinen, *Case-Western Reserve Univeresity, USA*
Mostafa Hashem Sherif, *Independent Researcher, USA*
Jan Smits, *TU Eindhoven, The Netherlands*
Henk de Vries, *Erasmus University, The Netherlands*
Robert van Wessel, *ApexIS, The Netherlands*

Table of Contents

Detailed Table of Contents

It has been observed that standards (and implicitly, standardization) are a hallmark of an industrialized society, since standards provide the necessary interconnections to make things interoperate. As the world tends increasingly towards a "global economy," just-in-time supply chains, and massive interdependencies, standards and standardization forms the infrastructure of these agreements. And yet, standardization is not well understood. This chapter explores standardization.

Corporate standardization coordinates and supports experts involved in standardization bodies. It sets up standardization strategy in alignment with global strategy of the company. In this chapter, the authors illustrate how a company can embrace standardization and leverage it to increase its position in a competitive business environment. The authors first present an overview of corporate standardization strategy: how is standardization considered in a private company; how to capture the ins and outs of a corporate standardization; how to define, implement, and manage standardization strategy; etc. Then the authors present the benefits of standardization development for a company. Finally, an example of commitment in ISO TC 279 innovation management is presented.

It is widely recognized that we are in rapid transition to the so-called fourth industrial revolution, a world of digitalization and mass interconnectedness enabled by a plethora of emergent powerful technologies including artificial intelligence (AI), internet of things (IoT), and distributed ledgers (DLT). A key element of this "revolution" is the move to digital manufacturing. While undoubtedly exciting, this transition presents challenges to policymakers, industry, and societal stakeholders alike. One such challenge is defining an optimum level for any market intervention measure(s), such that a balance is struck between ensuring a pro-industrial and economic innovation-friendly approach and guaranteeing adequate levels of consumer-focused protection. Standardization can be leveraged as one element of interventionary policy designed to help strike the required balance, both in its well-proven bottom-up and industry-led voluntary application and as a tool to support implementation of regulations. With a focus on digital transformation, this chapter will analyze the readiness of the current standardization system to support this significant transition focusing on strengths and challenges to be addressed from the perspective of industry, policymakers, and standards-setting organizations.

This chapter examines the organizational capabilities that firms develop in order to influence and adapt to standards. Standards are voluntary rules or guidelines developed by standard-setting organizations or consortia in order to promote compatibility/interoperability, minimum quality, variety reduction, and information. The authors argue that firms develop specific capabilities for assessing which emerging standards are likely to become dominant, and in order to successfully influence the development of new standards. The argument is illustrated by a case study of a global player in the information and communication technology sector.

Many companies have embarked on IT standardization initiatives with specific benefits in mind, but some projects fail dramatically whereas others are very successful. The research suggests that successful company standardization projects require good governance and management across distinct lifecycle phases: selection, implementation, and use and change. The authors present a case study from a financial services company to demonstrate effective practices that have led to significant financial benefits, to improved service delivery and support, and to a more stable IT environment. In addition, the authors discuss how an agile way of working could further improve standardization initiatives in organizations.

This chapter aims to contribute to the nascent, but expanding, body of literature concerned with sociologies of standards and standardization. Specifically, this chapter focuses on the creation of standardized forensic "products" within the marketized forensic science sector in England and Wales. This "menu" of standardized forensic products emerged during a period of significant economic and organizational disruption. The implementation of these codified products created further tensions, demonstrating the unintended consequences, which may flow from incomplete application of standards, incomplete understanding of their effect, and the instrumental use of these same standards, not to achieve efficiencies or harmonization but to affect particular institutional goals, and which are not shared across the wider community of practice.

In standards wars, FUD (fear, uncertainty, and doubt) is sometimes created to weaken an opponent's market position. Little is known about these strategies, their use in committee standardization settings, and how to respond to them. This chapter explores this phenomenon. It (1) identifies various FUD strategies, (2) their context of emergence, and (3) their effect on the dynamics of a standards war in a historical case study: the European standards war on digital mobile radio communication in the 1990s. The study highlights the need to distinguish "FUD as perceived" from "FUD as intended." FUD strategies and case-specific characteristics of their emergence are illustrated. The chapter shows that perceived FUD polarizes and entrenches positions of warring parties thereby affecting the course of the standards war. The authors conclude that, given its impact, reflection by corporate standardization managers on (perceived) FUD, preclusion, counter-strategies, and the downscaling of standards wars is warranted.

Among open innovations, standardization activities that do not cause some souse of profits, such as issuing standard essential patents for standardized technologies, can be said to be offering-type outbound open innovations. Technology providers require a careful strategy to make a profit from standardization activities. The core of this is to determine in what state the technology in the target product itself will be kept, which is the technology control strategy. What is particularly important is to determine what information will be proactively disclosed based on the theory, utility, and implementation of the technology, and what information will be kept secret. In this chapter, the author examines several cases of standardization and, by focusing on those that earned profits, presents technology management strategies that generate profits using standardization.

Preface

Quite a bit has changed in the world of standardisation in general, and in standardisation management in particular, since the 'predecessor' to this book was published in 2015. Probably most notably, the standardisation of 'smart' systems has become much more prominent; I'll come back to that further below. Prior to that, I will briefly outline some other recent papers that address various aspects standardisation management.

Spring (2016) argues that standards and standardisation are not normally managed centrally. Rather, important processes and procedures evolve from the community of (potential) standards users. The paper explores more recent developments in the information and communication technologies (ICT) sector highlighting pressures and forces on ICT standardisation and asks if there is a need for more management of ICT standards development. Some suggestions are made for management activities that might help enhance ICT standards development, in particular in relation to security and privacy of digital information.

Along similar lines, Kuhlmann et al. (2016) argue that the development of standards for ICT security poses new challenges for the management of standardisation processes in this field. They discuss some deficiencies of the current management of these standards and argue that most importantly trust in, and legitimacy of, standardisation have to be (re)gained. To this end they also call for some independent self-reflection in this area

With a focus on public administrations, Balta et al. (2016a) present a conceptual framework for the analysis of co-ordination mechanisms based on resource dependencies. The underlying goal is an effective stakeholder management in standardisation. An exemplary application of the theory-based framework is discussed in a case study of a standardisation project in German public administration.

Balta et al. (2016b) present first results of a review of standardisation activities in e-Government. They argue that actors, activities, contextual factors, effects, co-ordination mechanisms and evaluation approaches shape standardisation in a rather context-specific way. Therefore, they distinguish between public administrations and private organisations due to these major differences in economic regimes, political influence and legitimacy.

Balta et al. (2018a) present a model that defines three levels of interoperability and five categories of standardisation artefacts. Applying this framework to an e-government project shows that said project almost exclusively focuses on the technical/syntactic layer rather than the semantic concepts, which are much more complex.

The analysis framework applied in Balta et al. (2018b) identifies three types of standardisation strategies ('anticipatory standardisation', 'integrated solutions', 'flexible generification'; with increasing level of pragmatism), three categories of determinants and three categories of potential benefits. In addition, three standards development stages are identified. It turns out that most standardisation projects implement a mixture of strategy types and that standards are adapted pragmatically if and when necessary. They also show that the lack of external pressure on government entities significantly contributes to the lack of proper standardisation (management).

Applying integration-responsiveness theory to internationalisation strategies of companies, Müller (2016) shows that companies involved in standardisation assign different level of importance to national, international and internal company standards, respectively; the assignments are based on a company's business strategy. Company standards are more relevant for highly integrated firms which are part of a transnational group or co-operation. In such cases they foster the establishment of a global network and the transfer of knowledge within the group. The more the products are adapted to local markets, the more they conform to national formal standards, which then are more important than multi-domestic and transnational ones. If a product is sold globally, international standards will become relatively more relevant.

Naveh (2018) discusses how tensions that result from different and potentially contradicting company-internal priorities may affect process standardisation in organisations. Focussing on the potential conflict between standardisation and innovation, he shows how firms can manage and possibly even benefit from such conflicts. Specifically, he discusses a number of approaches from the literature how standardisation and innovation may be balanced.

Although Foukaki (2017) does not focus on the ICT sector (but on the automotive one), her work is certainly of relevance for this field as well. Her in-depth comparative case study of two heavy-truck manufacturers finds at least two very different approaches to voluntary consensus-driven standardisation, the assertive one and the vigilant one[1]. The former aims to lead and to influence standardisation efforts, the latter aims primarily at intelligence gathering. The study's findings also indicate that active engagement in standardisation may serve as an effective way to manage an organisation's resource dependence and environmental uncertainties, thus linking standardisation to Resource Dependence Theory (RDT). Finally, and looking at corporate standardisation management from a co-opetitive angle the study reveals that to some degree inter-organisational tensions within standardisation may be resolved by demonstrating the possibilities of "win-win strategies" (which is what co-opetition is all about).

As already mentioned, smart systems represent one of the most important – and most challenging and complex – areas for standardisation efforts. This complexity is owed to, on the one hand, the necessary multi-disciplinarity of the work. On the other hand, the still totally unclear socio-economic ramification of this technology (should) mandate the consideration of these aspects also during standardisation. It should be noted that this further contributes to the multi-disciplinarity of the work.

One of smart systems' most prominent characteristics is their true ubiquity. These days, the Internet is frequently associated with this term. However, on the one hand this holds only for the access network (not necessarily for applications), on the other hand even today we still see numerous white spots on a connectivity map (certainly in Germany). In contrast, smart applications 'promise' 100% coverage not just of an access network, but of applications. The vision is that billions (the British variety, not the US one) of interconnected sensors (part of the Internet of Things; IoT) collect data and transmit them to some central entity, which computes them, draws conclusions and makes recommendations or takes action.

Depending on your point of view, this ubiquity borders on inescapability (think George Orwell and Aldous Huxley). The IoT in combination with big data analytics and machine learning approaches has the inherent potential for both fostering the good of humankind and enabling the emergence of a surveillance society. Smart applications will also have considerable legal ramifications; Stuurman (2019) discusses them against the background of the new European General Data Protection Regulation (GDPR).

Despite the above – so far, literature's coverage of smart systems standardisation, let alone of the associated management aspects, is still limited. In the following some exceptions will be briefly summarized.

The standardisation of smart applications and their underlying smart communication infrastructure pose new challenges on standardisation in general and for the European Standardisation System (ESS) in particular. Jakobs (2017) identifies and discusses a number of policy issues that the ESS faces or is likely to face in the not-too-distant future. A number of potential steps that the ESS could take to help resolve these issues are sketched.

Jakobs (2018) discusses some aspects of the standardisation of the IoT and of some of its application areas. He shows that the standardisation environment has changed quite considerably over the past 20 years. During this period a mushrooming of specialised standardisation entities working in the field (including Standards Setting Organisations (SSOs) but also Technical Committees and Working Groups) may be observed. A closer look reveals that the establishments of these entities or the individual domains follow very similar patterns over time. The paper suggests that the number of these entities will continue to increase for a while, albeit a much slower pace (a fairly steep decline in the number of newly founded standardisation entities may be observed for the past 2 years). It will probably reach saturation in the not too distant future. Nevertheless, the need for co-operation and co-ordination will increase with these numbers.

Jakobs (2019a) looks at some issues that need to be considered in the context of the standardisation of smart applications and the underlying communication infrastructure at a rather more general level. Based on theoretical deliberations and on a small study it argues that the inherent multi-disciplinarity of smart systems, their future true ubiquity and the resulting diversity of their stakeholders call for dedicated standardisation efforts, which also need to include societal and other non-technical aspects, as erll as stakeholders from these areas.

de Vries et al. (2018) name standardisation management one of the most important research topics in the field. They identify three levels at which additional research will be necessary – the firm level, the level of intra-/inter-organisational standardisation projects and the level of technological sectors that are in need of standardisation (think smart systems) – how to manage it?

The papers in this volume address issues and problems from each of these three levels.

The first three chapters present the views of invited experts from industry. I am absolutely convinced that standardisation research in general and research into standardisation management in particular must not just be *l'art pour l'art*, but should have practical relevance. This requires some form of dialogue between research and industry, with the latter informing the former about open problems and the former offering practicable solutions (in the ideal case). So, let us start with papers written by practitioners.

The first chapter, titled 'Standardization, Not Standards Matters', by Carl Cargill, looks at how to use standardisation within a commercial organisation in the ICT sector. That is, the chapter is not about standards but about managing (some might say manipulating) co-operative action. This, in turn, should somehow enable standardisation to further a defined policy or legal, social, or business management goals. Against this background, Carl also bemoans the lack of adequate education in this field.

Chapter 2 was written by Alice de Casanove and is titled 'How Corporate Standardization Shapes Tomorrows Business'. It provides an overview of corporate standardisation activities, their main stakeholders and how these activities internally link to other corporate entities. This connectivity makes standardisation a central corporate function. The chapter provides a toolbox how to leverage this position. However, the individual tools have to be adapted to the respective company culture.

In Chapter 3, 'Challenges Facing Technology Standardization in the Age of Digital Transformation', Brian McAuliffe looks at digital manufacturing, one of the new 'smart' applications enabled by the ongoing digitalisation. He observes that this transition presents the challenge to strike a balance between an innovation-friendly approach and the guarantee of an adequate level of consumer-focused protection. Standardisation can be leveraged to help actually strike this balance. To this end, the chapter analyses whether or not the current standardisation system is ready to support this transition. The conclusion is that the disruption caused by the digitalisation of industries will require a parallel disruption in the standardisation system.

Chapter 4 examines the organisational capabilities that firms develop in order to influence and adapt standards. The authors argue that firms develop specific capabilities to, on the one hand, assess which emerging standards are likely to become dominant. On the other hand, they may also aim successfully influence the development of new standards. Their argument is illustrated by a case study of a global player in the information and communication technology sector.

Chapter 5 suggests that successful company standardisation projects require good governance and management across the different lifecycle phases: selection, implementation, use and change. A case study from the financial sector demonstrates that effective practices will lead to significant financial benefits, improved service delivery and support, and to a more stable IT environment. The paper also discusses how agile working may further improve internal standardisation initiatives in organisations.

Chapter 6 applies Dooyeweerd's theory of modal aspects to gain a better understanding why employees may resist company standardisation initiatives. The authors identify a set of causes for resistance to standardisation and develop an approach to overcome this resistance.

Chapter 7 focuses on the role of internal standardisation in business models. The authors show how internal standardisation efforts may be related to – and enable – value creation and innovation. They also discuss how business models relate to internal and external standardisation. With regard to business model innovation, this chapter may aid in identifying shifts in the firm's internal standardisation focus associated with changes in its business model.

In e-government, the deployment of international standards often suffers from e.g. complex administrative procedures, jurisdiction and stakeholders with diverging needs. Chapter 8 argues that, therefore, the transfer of findings from private organisations is rarely a viable approach, due to the different boundary conditions. The authors apply co-ordination theory to standardisation in e-government. It matches the identified challenges to standardisation onto co-ordination modes and derives co-ordination mechanisms that contribute to effective standardisation in e-government.

With the growing societal concern for ethical conduct by companies and markets alike, the important relationship between ethics and standardisation must be explored. In Chapter 9 the authors claim that ethics and standardisation are deeply interwoven concepts and should be seen as conjoined twins. They examine a variety of standards that can contribute to more ethical market transactions by reducing uncertainty and enhancing trust among anonymous market participants and suggest some approaches to make international standards development follow higher ethical norms,

Chapter 10 looks at two issues that are associated with the standardisation of smart systems and the ramifications they may have for standardisation management. These issues include a) the necessary multi-disciplinarity of the standards setting process and the resulting diversity of stakeholders to be involved and b) the need to standardise responsibly, i.e. to also take into account various societal aspects. The complexity of proper standardisation management will increase because of these needs.

Against the background of 5G and IoT standardisation Chapter 11 discusses 'license for all' vs. 'end-user licensing' and the recent associated communication by the EU Commission, from an SME perspective. Given the importance of the participation of SMEs in the standardisation process it is argued that the EU Commission and the European Court of Justice should offer more guidance on their preferences regarding licensing models

Using the provision of forensic science services in England and Wales as an example, Chapter 12 critically examines the associated standards-making process, emphasising the complex negotiations required. Further, it exposes the material, historical, and organisational contingencies, which led to the creation of standardised forensic products, surveys their implementation and explores the ways in which these standards became subverted in site-specific contexts.

Chapter 13 discusses the use of predatory strategies by firms. Typically, such strategies are deployed by dominant firms to keep potential new marker entrants at bay. The authors show that such strategies have also been deployed in standardisation. Specifically, this includes behaviour like discreditation, misrepresentation and legal actions. This behaviour is illustrated by a case study on the standards battle between TETRA and Tetrapol

Chapter 14 observes that standardisation activities may be seen as a form of outbound open innovation. In order to benefit from standardisation activities technology providers need to put particular emphasis on the deliberation which information to proactively disclose during standards setting and which to keep secret. The author analyses several cases of standardisation, focusing on those that made a profit. Based on these analyses he presents technology management strategies that may be applied to generate profits through standardisation.

Chapter 15 summarises the Spanish experience with the management of new standards. It shows how the development of national standards was triggered by needs and requirements not addressed by international standards. It also shows how the collaboration with international bodies has created new opportunities for businesses. On the other hand, the chapter also addresses the gap between industry's need for people used to understand standards and the lack of university graduates actually prepared for that task.

REFERENCES

Balta, D. (2016a). Stakeholder Management in Standardisation – A Framework for Analysis of Coordination Mechanisms based on Resource Dependencies. In *Enterprise Interoperability in the Digitized and Networked Factory of the Future* (pp. 52–57). ISTE.

Balta, D. (2016b). The Shape of Standardisation in the eGovernment Research Landscape. In *Enterprise Interoperability in the Digitized and Networked Factory of the Future* (pp. 66–72). ISTE.

Balta, D. (2018a). Managing IT Standardization in Government: Towards a Descriptive Reference Model. In *Enterprise Interoperability: Smart Services and Business Impact of Enterprise Interoperability* (pp. 137–142). Wiley. doi:10.1002/9781119564034.ch17

Balta, D. (2018b). *What are the Strategies for and Benefits of Effective IT Standardization in Government? In Enterprise Interoperability: Smart Services and Business Impact of Enterprise Interoperability* (pp. 143–149). Wiley. doi:10.1002/9781119564034.ch18

De Vries, H., Jakobs, K., Egyedi, T. M., Eto, M., Fertig, S., Kanevskaia, O., ... Scaramuzzino, G. (2018). Standardization: Towards an agenda for research. *International Journal of Standardization Research, 16*(1), 52–59. doi:10.4018/IJSR.2018010104

Foukaki, A. (2017). *Corporate Standardization Management – A Case Study of the Automotive Industry* (Dissertation). Lund University. Retrieved from http://portal.research.lu.se/portal/files/21522119/Corporate_Standardization_Management_A_Case_Study_of_the_Automotive_Industry_Dissertation_2017.pdf

Jakobs, K. (2017). Emerging Smart Technologies and the European Standardisation System. Proc. 30th Bled eConference: Digital Transformation – From Connecting Things to Transforming Our Lives, 231 – 244. doi:10.18690/978-961-286-043-1.17

Jakobs, K. (2018). Standardizing the IoT and its Applications – Learning from the Past?! In *Internet of Things – Concepts, Technologies, Applications, and Implementations* (pp. 191–218). IEEE. doi:10.1002/9781119456735.ch7

Jakobs, K. (2019). *'Smart' Standardisation.* Presented at the *82nd IEC General Meeting.*

Kuhlmann, D., Chen, L., & Mitchell, C. (2016). Trust and Legitimacy in Security Standardization–a new Management Issue? Interoperability for Enterprise Systems and Applications (I-ESA 16), Guimaraes, Portugal.

Müller, J. A. (2016). Subsidiary Strategy and Importance of Standards: Re-interpreting the integration-responsiveness framework. In *Annual Conference 2016.* Verein für Socialpolitik/German Economic Association.

Naveh, E. (2018). Standardization and Innovation: a Multipriority Approach. *Enterprise Interoperability: Smart Services and Business Impact of Enterprise Interoperability*, 125-130.

Spring, M. B. (2016). Standards management in the twenty-first century: Architectural challenges and management opportunities. *International Journal of Standardization Research, 14*(1), 34–44. doi:10.4018/IJSR.2016010103

Stuurman, K. (2017). The Digitisation Driven Impact of Data Protection Regulation on the Standardisation Process. In *Digitalisation: Challenge and Opportunity for Standardisation. Proc. 22nd EURAS Annual Standardisation Conference. EURAS contributions to standardisation research* (vol. 12). Mainz Publishers.

Updegrove, A. (2006). The Essential Guide to Standards. In *Participating In Standard Setting Organizations: Value Propositions, Roles And Strategies.* Academic Press. Retrieved from http://www.consortiuminfo.org/essentialguide/participating1.php

ENDNOTE

1 These approaches correspond with the 'leader' and the 'follower' approach identified in (Updegrove, 2006) for the ICT sector.

Acknowledgment

I would like to thank Jan Travers and IGI Global for their enduring patience and their valuable support throughout the editing process.

Section 1
Invited Papers

Chapter 1
Standardization, Not Standards Matter

Carl Cargill
Sun Microsystems, USA

ABSTRACT

It has been observed that standards (and implicitly, standardization) are a hallmark of an industrialized society, since standards provide the necessary interconnections to make things interoperate. As the world tends increasingly towards a "global economy," just-in-time supply chains, and massive interdependencies, standards and standardization forms the infrastructure of these agreements. And yet, standardization is not well understood. This chapter explores standardization.

BACKGROUND

Simply, standardization is one method of controlling a market, either politically, economically, legally, technically or in any combination of these areas. Generally, standardization is an unappreciated art because the signal product of standardization - a standard - is usually a boring document and as such, suffers from business, academic, and policy neglect. (Parenthetically, when standards are brought up for discussion, they are usually brought up as contentious issues. One need only look at the current [late 2018] arguments over BREXIT and food standards in policy discussions. "Britain's trade minister will 'categorically' deny on Wednesday that the government plans to lower foods standards to win trade deals after Brexit[1]" is an example of standards being important only when contentious – they were safely invisible until they were used to define a policy direction.) But this is the nature of standards and standardization; they are invisible until something goes wrong or something blows up. Then, and only then, do they gain a larger share of public awareness.

Standardization can be seen and used as a social policy tool, a public policy tool, and as a business management tool. There is very little literature (academic, legal, or otherwise) that describes how to pursue standardization within a corporation or other commercial organization to accomplish these activities (policy, social control, or business management) except in a retrospective view. The reason this is important is simple – nearly all standards (and many regulations based on standards) are the product

DOI: 10.4018/978-1-5225-9008-8.ch001

Copyright © 2019, IGI Global. Copying or distributing in print or electronic forms without written permission of IGI Global is prohibited.

of commercial business organizations - they fund and populate the standards organizations that create standards and they are also charged with implementing these standards in products.

This chapter looks at ways to actually use the art of standardization (since there is not enough data to make this a discipline yet) within the Information Technology sector and within a commercial organization[2] to effect change of some type. Note that this is not about standards - which are relatively sterile documents - but rather a description of how to manage (some might say manipulate) cooperative action which will result, in some manner, in a standard which can be used to create standardization to further a defined policy, legal, social, or business management goal.

The author is, and has been, involved in standardization in a multitude of U.S. software based IT companies, and this biases my view of standardization. The first and most critical bias derives from the fact that, unlike many other industries, the software industry is characterized as a low capital, high intellectual property activity. It is an industry that has been characterized as "IP Intensive". Facebook, Alibaba, e-Bay and Amazon and multiple other multi-billion organizations are all examples of software based firms that started with little or low capital investments and continue to operate in high Intellectual Property, as opposed to real property, investment arenas. As an example, when Alibaba wants to add another 100,000 customers, it adds a server and possibly several more systems administrators; when a brick-and-mortar store seeks to add a 100,000 customers, it needs warehouses, property, stores, and retail associates. This difference is especially critical in IT standardization, since it drives a more transient standard, less influenced by the standardization process[3] than it is by immediacy and deployment. It is not an approach that is recommended when dealing with something like a nuclear power plant, where tried and tested standards are much more valued.

INTRODUCTION

Standards, and standardization, are now a fact of life in all industries globally. With the growth of the linked global economy, and with the dependence of industry on the World Wide Web and the Internet for information, the importance of standards has increased substantially over the last 20 years. While it can be argued that telecommunications (with their implicit standards and standardization) have been present since the early 1900s, I would argue that the use of the web for everything from retail to supply chain management to personal entertainment devices has dwarfed the importance of the earlier telecommunications standardization activity.

Most importantly, nearly all of the Information Technology standards which are the basis of current computing are voluntary standards created by the IT industry. There is a deliberate exclusion of telecommunications standards here, since many of them, although created by a voluntary process, end up being utilized in a regulatory (or at least highly regulated) telecommunications environment. It is this distinction – the use and creation of voluntary, industry led, consensus standards as opposed to regulated or governmentally influenced standards – that has made standards less than a discipline and more of an art form, leading, in turn, to a lack of both predictability and serious academic study.

To understand the whole issue, it is first necessary to look at the document called a "standard". In this article, I will ignore "management standards" and similar types of documents, since they tend to describe best practices garnered from participants in a singular practice (quality, environment, security). What I'd like to look at is "technical specifications" – that is, documents that describe some specific technology. As an example, the following is part of a technical specification (W3C HTML 5 specification):

The Style Attribute

All HTML elements may have the style content attribute set. This is a CSS styling attribute as defined by the CSS Styling Attribute Syntax specification. [CSSATTR]

In user agents that support CSS, the attribute's value must be parsed when the attribute is added or has its value changed, according to the rules given for CSS styling attributes. [CSSATTR]

Documents that use style attributes on any of their elements must still be comprehensible and usable if those attributes were removed.

In particular, using the style attribute to hide and show content, or to convey meaning that is otherwise not included in the document, is non-conforming. (To hide and show content, use the hidden attribute.)

element . style

Returns a CSSStyleDeclaration object for the element's style attribute.

The *style* IDL attribute is defined in the CSS Object Model (CSSOM) specification. [CSSOM]

In the following example, the words that refer to colors are marked up using the span element and the style attribute to make those words show up in the relevant colors in visual media.

```
<p>My sweat suit is <span style="color: green; background:
transparent">green</span> and my eyes are <span style="color: blue;
background: transparent">blue</span>.</p>4
```

This is a part of a technical specification. It is meant to give instructions to software designers on how to manage the style element in the global attributes section of HTML 5. It is the result of a the activities of a group of technical experts who worked for several years putting together an entire specification on how the HTML 5 language was to be encoded to that it would work across multiple platforms and multiple languages.

I have chosen the HTML 5 specification for a reason. Unlike many specifications referred to by academics and others who research standards, the HTML5 spec was created by the World Wide Web Consortium (W3C). W3C operates outside of the aegis of the International Organization for Standardization (ISO) and the International Electrotechnical Committee's (IEC) Joint Technical Committee 1 (JTC1). It is a consortia that produces specifications at the behest of its members. It is focused on specifications and technologies that are web-centric. The consortium is of interest to and populated by developers, providers, and organizations which have an interest in the World Wide Web, whether technical, policy, or legal. And it was created and funded extensively by companies who are willing to commit significant human and monetary resources to producing web standardization.

Notice that the majority of executives in these companies never see – or even want to see – a "standard". A standard, and the arcane trivia about the process to create one, are of little or no interest to a tremendously large majority of corporate executives. Most don't care about the creation of a standard, the complexities and checks and balances of the process, the many ways to resolve conflict, or any of the other issues which so fascinate people who study standards. They don't understand the time honored process that is so beloved by standards people and standards researchers.

But, what they do understand (mostly) is their business. They understand products. They understand the concept of path dependence (Puffert, 2009), which is a core rationale for business to engage in standardization. They understand interoperation, and they understand the power of joint development activities which are at the heart of standardization – in the business world. And here is where there is the tremendous disconnect between the "world of standards" and the "world of standardization".

THE PRACTICE OF STANDARDIZATION FROM A COMMERCIAL ORGANIZATIONAL PERSPECTIVE

To begin, it is necessary to bifurcate the argument for a moment into two separate streams. The first stream is a look at the actual management of the entire standardization process by the "commercial sector", and the second is the utility of standardization in a commercial setting and how organizations manage standardization to accomplish a business goal.

Management of the Standards Setting System

One of the unspoken truths about standardization is that it is structured to serve industry – the producers of goods and services. While there is always the myth that balance exists[5], the reality is that the vast majority of members of any IT standards committee are members of the IT industry or consultants who are paid by the companies comprising the IT industry. The exception to this rule (since every strong opinion must have an exception) are those committees such as biometrics or security, where governmental representation increases slightly since some governmental organizations have a legal mandate for implementing these standards. However, generally, the bulk of the participants and the bulk of the technology are contributed by the commercial segment. This is especially true in consortia, where the membership is generally comprised primarily of producers.

Complicating the issue further (and lessening the battle for balance) is the fact that larger companies tend to predominate in these organizations – or at least they tend to be the dominant voice in many of the administrative arguments. Larger companies can generally afford to populate multiple opposing or complementary standardization activities. As an example, there are numerous standardization activities occurring in the "Cloud". ISO/IEC JTC1 has an activity, as do many national bodies (with mirror committees), and there are at least a dozen or so consortia who are creating specifications (or at least marketing) around the idea of the cloud.[6] Most of these standardization organizations have representation from the major providers of cloud services and members of the IT community (except where the provider believes that they are a market dominant and have no need to participation). However, with this number of organizations, a public sector or even a NGO would be hard pressed to track all of the activities. And it in the ability to create standardization group after standardization group that the private sector - especially the companies with deep pockets – have an advantage.

The private sector engages in venue shopping – that is the use of a standardization body that is most likely to produce the results desired by the sponsoring company/companies. To complicate the discussion further, consortia do not have to model their structures on those of formal ISO/IEC/ITU Standards Developing Organizations (SDOs), and it is this ability to create a structure that meets user demands (the law of "form follows function")[7] which allow consortia to differ so radically from the formal ISO/IEC Standards Developing Organization (including the ISO National Bodies). As an example, the W3C is composed not just of technical standardizers, but also a host of other groups that an SDO does not have. Because the Web has social, cultural, and political significance, W3C has a Technology and Society Domain, in which activities that have social impact are gathered, systematized, and eventually, standardized. There is a Patent and Standards Interest Group that looks after the issues of patents within the W3C, and is responsible for guidance of the consortia Intellectual Property matters as they relate to the Royalty Free licensing of the consortium. There are liaisons with multiple other groups (not uncommon in SDOs), but there is also a close and deliberate liaison with governments and NGOs who have an interest in the development of the World Wide Web.

The consortium – as a standardization body - has its own unique processes for operating which adhere to the general guidelines for standardization (openness, transparence, right of appeal, and so on), but it has one advantage that ISO derived bodies do not; it can refuse to take a standardization program on. Because it is an organization which has entrance fees, and those members who pay to join have the right of governance. This gives the members the right to reject (or possibly not consider) standardization outside the interests of the members. Finally, the consortium members alone have the right to pass on the goodness of a standard; it is subject to no higher appeal (excepting judicial or legal review) than the members of the consortium. There is no requirement to subject it to a national or international review. Finally, because of their very nature, consortia tend to operate as international entities. There are no German or American or Chinese national consortia standards; consortia specifications are meant to be deployed globally, usually for use by all IT producers in the IT arena.

This ability to accept or reject standardization – driven by the paying membership – and the international nature of their specifications are two of the distinguishing characteristics of a consortium. The ability to create unique processes, the right to limit or grant membership, the right to establish and mandate Intellectual Property structures and strictures on members, and finally, the right to more completely control the results of process are all specialized attributes that make consortia a preferred venue for IT standardization.

In so far as I am aware, there have been few studies of the percentage of IT standards actually being created by as a percentage of the total number of IT standards being created. The only data that I've seen suggested that over 90 percent of all standards that are being developed for the IT industry are driven through consortia – data on this would be gratefully accepted. However, to complicate this quest for quantification, there is no exact count of the consortia that exist. Absent this data base, it is difficult to actually know how many consortia standards there are[8]. The latest authoritative list was published in 1996[9]; I've seen no "official" update since then. However, I believe that the 90% number is probably moderately accurate, given the amount of continuing consortia spending that is occurring in the industry.

The privatization of standards is a phenomena that has not gone unnoticed. It was illustrated at length by Timothy Schoechle (2009). Schoechle calls this privatization by the private sector and by governmental forces (who recognize that standards are an element of international economic policy) a reshaping of the standardization world. Rebecca McKinnon (2012) sounded a similar note of concern when she pointed out that the standards that drive the internet – indeed, all technical standards for interconnection – are a new form of legislative mandate in which the general public has little say. "The reality is that the corporations and governments that build, operate, and govern cyberspace are not being held sufficiently accountable for the exercise of their power over the lives and identities of the people who use digital networks". (McKinnon, 2013, p.xxi). She goes on to state, citing Larry Lessig, that "… software code and technical standards are for all practical purposes a new form of law, because just like laws, they shape what people and can cannot do". (McKinnon, 2013, p.25).

If Schoechle, McKinnon, and Lessig are correct, corporations (and lately governments) have basically taken over the creation and management of technical standards – and with it, standardization. This poses two questions – how did they get away with doing this, and why did they think it necessary?

The "How" of Standards Takeover

As H.L. Mencken observed "For every complex problem there is an answer that is clear, simple, and wrong." The simple (and probably very wrong) answer lies in conspiracy theory – it was a multi-year plot by industrialists to put themselves above the law, or to at least make the law subservient to them. In reality, the gradual takeover of standardization was a complex and multi-year happening. It occurred because of a series of intertwined events happened in the industrial and post-industrial societies of the United States and Europe. It is necessary to differentiate between the IT sector and other industrial sectors her, because the IT sector was the bellwether segment from approximately 1980 onwards – but by that time, much of the groundwork for the current standardization system had been laid in the US.

Much of the credit for the standardization system as it is currently practiced in the US goes back to the unwillingness of the US government to intervene in the making of standards outside of metrology and similar commercial infrastructure standards. In the US (as much of the industrialized world) the growth of a science and technology based society replacing the rural and agrarian economy which marked the first Industrial Revolution was in turn followed by the intense innovation and expansion of the production sector in the Second Industrial Revolution. The Second Industrial Revolution saw mass production in a supply chain environment which changed the entire nature of industry. You need to ensure that your suppliers (who may also serve your competitors) provide you material that "you" need.

So, the first standards organizations were based on trade organizations, but with a technical twist. These standards organizations were based upon a particular technology knowledge set. The "experts" - usually gatherings of professional men - who were knowledgeable in a particular field (boilers, civil engineering, mechanical engineering, electrical engineering, railroads, or other applied technical discipline) gathered to pool knowledge and expand their common knowledge. They documented their knowledge with best practices or standards, specifications embodying their wisdom for the sake of their colleagues. They created societies such as the American Society of Mechanical Engineers (ASME), the Institute of Electrical and Electronics Engineers (IEEE), and The American Society for Testing and Materials (ASTM. These groups were directly responsible for technical practices which could impact their industries as a whole, and needed to ensure that the specifications which they published were correct (or at least creditable). Peer review was not only desirable, it was necessary and expected.

Douglas Puffert, in the study of the standardization of rail gauges, describes the issues that helped determine which rail gauge would be used where. One of the common activities was the use of "technical publications" to justify the choice of a rail gauge. All gauges had their learned proponents who championed their specific gauge. And all studies were used to influence a sympathetic public and legislators into mandating a particular gauge. But standardize the railroads did – but not for reasons of "science". Railroads standardized because transshipment costs where discontinuous lines met finally became too much of an economic burden, and the benefits of a single gauge outweighed the economic costs of switching gauges. And this, I believe, became more and more common as industrialization continued. For a manufacturer, a standard was no guarantee of a superior product – it was merely the guarantee of a saleable product that worked with other products. Similarly, for a consumer, a "standard" product was one that met **expectations that had been set in the market** and therefore meant that you were safe to buy it. (The setting consumer expectations will be examined later).

But this collective work of standardization had a second and less obvious purpose. These standards were part of commoditizing the supply chain. By providing their suppliers – from ballast providers to tie makers to rail forgers – with precise specifications the rail lines knew exactly what to expect and how much their lines would cost. By using standards, they began to commoditize the education of the people who built the track and who ran the trains. To return to guilds – and the Ogilvie statement, railroad management "...was an enduring corporate association, usually of practitioners of a particular occupation, which was legally endowed with the exclusive right to practice certain economic activities in a certain area by **virtue of privileges granted by the political authorities** (Ogilvie, 2004) [Emphasis the author's]". And, like the guilds, they worked for their own interests. A good companion piece to Puffert (2009) is Walter Borneman's volume 'Rail Rivals' (Borneman, 2010), which describes the business of building a railway, where the real prize was not the successful construction of rail as much as it was getting the public financing by whatever method necessary. Standards legitimized the rails and made the Second Industrial Revolution really accelerate, but it was basic greed (and the right to nearly coin money) that the leaders of the rail industry sought.

In the case of the early rail industry, standards were used when other business methods (bribery, technology, or marketing) were either inappropriate or when a different approach was needed. These organizations were based upon a particular technology knowledge set. The "experts" - usually gatherings of professional men - who were knowledgeable in a particular field (boilers, civil engineering, mechanical engineering, electrical engineering, railroads, or other applied technical discipline) gathered to pool knowledge and expand their common knowledge. They documented their knowledge with best practices or standards, specifications embodying their wisdom for the sake of their colleagues. They created societies such as the American Society of Mechanical Engineers (ASME), the Institute of Electrical and Electronics Engineers (IEEE), and The American Society for Testing and Materials (ASTM. These groups were directly responsible for technical practices which could impact their industries as a whole, and needed to ensure that the specifications which they published were correct (or at least creditable). Peer review was not only desirable, it was necessary and expected.

Note, however, that these standards were not generated by public requirements. Rather, they were generated by a self-selected group of professionals who decided – for their companies and industry – what a good solution would be. In the case of boiler standards, there was public outcry about exploding boilers[10] as early as 1860. It would be one subject of the first standards the ASME would publish[11]. But, again, it was in response to a general outcry about the results of not having the standard, not about the need for a specific standard. The founders of ASME realized that standardization would solve significant problems for them as producers as the Second Industrial revolution continued.

While this is a simplified account of how the standardization system was changed in the US, it should be understood within the context of the US industrial experience. At the time that this was occurring, the legislative process was in the midst of probably the largest laissez faire mindset seen in the industrial era. Unlike Europe and the United Kingdom, there was no history of industrial control or social good in US industrialization. These would not arrive until the reform movements of the Progressive era (circa 1890 -1920.) But by this time, the "professional society" had become established as the source for industrial standards – and the societies were created to serve their creators, not the public's, interests.

Within the US, there have been several attempts to assert more governmental control – Hoover in the 1920s and the Department of Commerce/Department of Justice in the 1960s-1970s. In both cases, the resistance to change and the promises to "self-police" made externally imposed significant reform difficult. In both cases, the reform was a restructuring and changing of process and requirements that ostensibly opened the organizations – while the parties that were most vested lost little of their clout. Generally, the standards associations that make up the American National Standards Institute (ANSI) are very sensitive to governmental influence, and maintain a significant presence on the US Capitol Hill.

However, in the mid-1980s, the US semiconductor industry came under extreme pressure from the Japanese. In searching for a way to strengthen domestic industry (while avoiding any possible inference of industrial policy), the US legislature passed National Cooperative Research Act (NCRA) of 1984 (15 U.S.C. §§ 4301 – 4305), which allowed common research and development activities to be undertaken by US industry. By 1986, over a dozen US semiconductor manufacturers had come together (with Department of Defense and their own funding) to create an organization called Sematech.

This was all well and good for a few years. Then, in 1993, a new legislative effort created the National Cooperative Production Amendments of 1993, Pub. L. No. 103-42, which amended the National Cooperative Research Act of 1984, Pub L. No. 98-462, renamed it the National Cooperative Research and Production Act (NCRPA) of 1993, and extended its provisions to joint ventures for production. Probably, there was little thought given to this particular bill by the lobbyists of the standardization agencies – it appeared benign and reasonably irrelevant to the activities of ANSI and its members. This was to be a grave miscalculation.

The NCRPA, while ostensibly focused on joint research and production ventures, was quickly recognized as an ideal tool for the legitimization and creation of non-ANSI standardization organizations. The ostensible reason for the creation and use of consortia was that the formal ISO based process, requiring as it did multiple layers of approval for an international standard, was too slow and too out of phase with the Information Technology industry. An international standard, from conception to completion and publication as a national standard, took up to five years, and possibly longer if the issue was contentious or novel. At the same time, the pace of technological change was increasing in the high technology industry and new models of computing began to emerge.

The Open Systems Interconnection model – the protocol to connect all devices to a common net – was undertaken simultaneously by ISO and the CCITT, which ended up being a monstrous disaster for the IT industry. It was slow, contentious, and much given to compromise. While in and of itself it was worthy, it became the poster child for why consortia were needed. And consortia began to proliferate. There were consortia for objects, operating systems, peripherals, communications schemes, structured languages, artificial intelligence, internationalization, and almost anything else in the IT panoply of technology.

The rationale for these consortia was simple. Despite the claims that consortia were faster, they probably weren't tremendously quicker. What they were was louder, and more aggressive in their standardization activities. And they caught the attention of the business and marketing community in the US and elsewhere. Standardization became a marketing tool – and the major standards bodies in the world were ill equipped to deal with the influx of marketing hype, lawyers, marketing people, and above all, publicity. Very few standards organization could then (and can, even now) describe quickly and coherently the impact of standardization on an industry they served, let alone the contribution that their organization made to the success of products and productization in that industry. Consortia, however, could, because these were the very reasons for their creation. They could make significant claims for their specifications and how these specifications would be used by the industry – because the users of these specifications belonged to the consortia.

Setting Customer Expectations

And this field of publicity quickly took entirely new meaning when consortia realized that proposing a standardized specification (or the use of standardization) could shape the market and the user expectations. At the same time claiming benefits for the use of the specification could also shape the market –

and favorably incline the market to the product that claimed to instantiate the specification. In consortia, the marketers found full reign for their skill set.

And this left traditional standards bodies at a loss. They were not composed of similarly minded organizations – noir were they necessarily able to quickly produce documents that described what they were doing. All they could do was try to prepare a consensus document that described – in vague and non-threatening terms – what they were doing.[12] And, of course, it was usually too little, too late when compared with what the consortia were doing.

At the same time, the external environment was changing. The internet, and then the World Wide Web, emerged, opening the area of software creation and deployment to entirely new audiences and developers, At the same time vendor proprietary operating systems became less and less viable, being replaced by universal proprietary systems (such as UNIX), which in turn was replaced by LINUX, more completely open than its predecessors. And this change, along with the increasing popularization of computers (thanks to Microsoft and other PC makers) led to an increasing demand for software that could "do customer things" that people could use. And these applications needed to be able to run against a certain set of standards – but there was no demand for the standards to go through other than perfunctory market validation. The emphasis – as I said earlier – was on speed and deployment. The rate of change in the market drove a different set of expectations for vendors and users.

Consortia could manage to change their processes – or they could be created anew – to meet these market expectations; formal organizations could not. And this led to the consortia gaining the upper hand in IT standardization; they were able to better adapt to market needs and requirements more quickly than could the formal organizations.

However, even consortia could not meet market requirements for the speed of change and ease of evolution. As the computing environment changed with the addition of mobile apps and walled garden apps, standards development (that is, where standards were developed in more or less structured environments) has begun to decline in favor of community (either actual open source community or informal developer communities). This development – while offensive to many who believe that standards as standards should be developed in formal organizations, represents merely another evolution of standardization within the IT industry. Speed, time to product and time to profit are the drivers of this movement; large scale (or even medium scale review) is too time consuming in this environment. Additionally, most of these products are transitory (with a limited life and impact.) However, the model of develop quickly, implement, and deploy has become a new norm, and even things that becoming standards are the result of this new standardization. Things like the Google developed SPDY protocol morphed into HTTP2 in the Internet Engineering Task Force, and elements of the Webkit Open Source development activity have been introduced into various W3C and other standards.

Hence, the title of this article. To industry, the practice of standardization – that is, collective acceptance and deployment of a technology in products – is more important than are formal codified and compiled standards. The standard (and the processes that produce them) that is written and agonized over in committees and produced by complex processes is becoming an increasingly passé artifact in the Web environment. That being said, however, fundamental infrastructure standards (documented and stable) as well as hardware (connector, media, and display, for example) standards continue to be necessary and developed. However, they too are beginning to driven by the time and competitive pressures; standardization has become a competitive activity, with venue shopping and consortia creation becoming more and more common as a response to a market, rather than a technical, need. And the push of the market for faster and more standards (whether to capture a market or to protect intellectual property of to create entry barriers) is rapidly becoming "the standard" for standardization.

Managing a Corporate Standardization Effort

To begin, commercial organizations use standardization for a host of different reasons. All too often in the literature about standardization, one gets the impression participants are creatures of good will, gathering to harmoniously craft a standard that serves the greater glory of their industry, technology, and their nation.

The reality is that most professionals who are there are there to defend their corporate or business position. Consultants are there angling for business and an exploitable niche; market leaders are there to stop or mitigate the impact of adverse technology or craft barriers to entry; some companies are there to insert technology for the purpose of garnering royalties. Sometimes participants are there to "do the right thing", although this is rare. If one participates correctly, you go armed with a corporate position of goals. The goal may be to promote your technology, intellectual property, or other corporate asset. Or the rationale for attendance might be to learn what your competition is doing so that you can either mimic or leap-frog, or begin a similar or competing product/implementation/standard. Finally, you could be attending because it is in your organizations purpose to delay, modify, or otherwise impede a standard, allowing your technology/product time to survive, gain or increase market share. The politics in a standardization effort start the minute that an activity is first proposed and continue throughout the life of the activity.

The most important "thing" that a standards participant can possess when going to a standards meeting is a knowledge of their own corporate requirement for the standardization activity. If he or she knows what their organization needs to achieve in the committee, they have a basis for planning how they will respond to others on the committee. With respect to others on the committee, it is also important to know if there are potential allies who are participating, and if you are capable of "making a deal". In many instances, knowledge of the potential partner's last activity is known (in varying degrees) by all of the members of the committee or work group, so that the willingness to form coalitions or partnerships varies depending on the company, the committee, and even the participant. The potential for intrigue (and betrayal) is significant.

Once the friend(s)/foe(s) issues are settled, the contributions and participation levels of the members clarified or disguised, and the direction of the group decided, the work starts. This is where the real politics begins. Disruption, accusation, and general other disingenuous methods are used to slow a group or to disadvantage competition. Intellectual property is submitted with or without notification.[13] The committee officer roles are crucial (as might be expected), but all too often the selection of a committee chair can become a partisan issue, leading to recrimination. As the work progresses, there are various tactics that can be used to slow or stop the work or to modify it with "creeping elegance."[14]

The important take away is that standardization is not the technical love-fest of cooperating technologists. It is a business – and, as with all complex human interactions, there are always multiple agendas, multiple personalities, and multiple opportunities for unintended consequences. It would tax the skills of the three princes of Serendip to understand how a standard managed to emerge from a standardization process.

With this as a background on the way that organizations **can** participate in standardization, the question is – how often are these behaviors seen? Based on experiential data, my response would be "nearly always". There is very little actual information on this type of activity, since most of the participants either won't admit that they are doing this or they fail to see that the activities in which they participate partake of these characteristics. It is all too easy to join a coalition to modify a spec – if that specification disrupts your product planning, or your architectural vision. The problem is that if you join a standard merely to stop or "change" it, you are in fact, engaging in a disruptive and essentially negative activity.

This type of activity gives lie to the idea that standardization is a technical cooperative activity – rather, it is a multi-billion dollar business activity couched in technical guise that is used as an extension of a corporate business or marketing strategy. And, to make clear, standardization is a strategy. It requires careful planning and (usually) good execution. Because standardization fundamentally acts as a change agent, it should involve careful planning and well thought out activities. (Since the exception proves the rule, a transient commitment to a standardization activity can be used to provide temporary relief from market pressure. The benefits can be short lived if the press and industry are interested enough to track the story, however. Microsoft's pseudo-standardization of Active X is a classic example of such a gambit.[15])

Standardization as Policy

Of course, the success of businesses in regulating a market using standards has not gone unnoticed in the geo-political world. The European Union has a long history of using standardization in a significant way to smooth the functioning of the single market, for the protection of health and safety, and as a way of increasing the competitiveness of industry and the promotion of international trade. China has an even older tradition of using standardization as a unification tool, probably starting with Li Si, who argued (successfully) for weights, coinage, and character standardization as a method of unifying the Warring Kingdoms.[16]

While the use of standardization and standards is not unusual within a country or region, its use in a "global economy" creates a bit of a complication. A standardization regime that is successful in Europe for achieving unification of divergent national entities would be anathema in the United States which has a laissez faire approach to governmental interference in standardization (unless it serves to advance someone's agenda.) At the same time, standardization can be used to push an industrial objective (i.e. capturing the secretariat or chairmanship of a standardization committee such as wool, heavy earth moving equipment, or similar committees), or imposing unique IP requirements on standardization. All of these methods are used in the world as nations strive to achieve industrial parity (or possibly hegemony) through use of "non-tariff trade activities". Using standards as a non-tariff trade barrier is passé these days; it too easily caught out. Using other methods (committee control, IPR, standardization regimes that fall outside of the WTO [such as consortia]) is more opaque and more effective, since there is no effective recourse if other nations need to interoperate/interface with you. The more economically powerful the nation is, the more likely it is to be able to dominate or manage standardization to fit its own policy objectives.

The European Union has been using standards and has passed enabling legislation to create European Standards Organizations and to harmonize pan-European standards. The United States created consortia with the NCRPA, at first to strengthen its semi-conductor industry and then to allow US industries an alternative to a formal standardization system. China is rewriting its standards laws to encourage "social groups" to create voluntary industry technical specifications, with the intent of creating a more innovative and open process. All of these acts are recognition that nations (and sometimes regional bodies) are using standardization in trade policy and social engineering, much as businesses have, in the past, used them to control a market.

In the past ten years (2008 forward), the Chinese government has also begun to exploit standardization as a national policy. The creation of new categories of standards setting organizations – analogous to but not the same as consortia in the US and Europe – is aimed at opening up China's domestic to standardized competition and structure, and then secondarily aimed at the international market. The recognition by the Chinese government that standardization is a key to coherent and efficient economic development has been ongoing since Deng Xiaoping launched China's modernization; the process of putting a standardization taxonomy in place that is crafted for the Chinese society and governance model took a bit longer. It was obvious to Chinese scholars that the Western model, with its emphasis on a capitalistic model of competition, was inappropriate. They built their own model which meets their needs (Liu & Cargill, 2017). My personal belief is that this model of standardization (based upon the idea of the "social organization" will be exported to multiple countries as part of the Chinese Belt and Road Initiative (BRI), since the model is useful in developing and growing countries.

Unfortunately, there are very few other relevant precedents to guide nations in their efforts to use standardization successfully. Previously, many nations could act in an independent fashion – what one did with steel or cotton depended upon market conditions internally or externally rather than whether or not the cotton or steel could interface with another set of steel or cotton. The difference in IT standards is that they are interdependent – there is no such thing as a German Internet of Things and a Chinese HTML5 or a US Cloud Standard. All of these activities – the IoT, HTML5, and Cloud Computing standards – require invisibility of borders. The value of IT standards is that they allow, even encourage, borderless computing. And this is what keeps politicians awake at night. The idea that they cannot mandate either for their producers or their citizens a safe and simple solution to these complex issues which does not disadvantage their citizens or their put their careers at risk must seem grossly unfair.

The key issue is the lack of a good understanding of what "standardization", not standards, is both in practice and theory. Standardization, especially in the IT fields, is an interdisciplinary, cross functional study. It is not enough to know technology and what makes a good standard. One needs to know what makes good standardization practice. This would include understanding the legal rationale for standardization across various jurisdictions, understanding the social and policy implications of a standard, understanding the market impact of standardization, and finally, the impact of standardization in the long term. All too often, the "strategy of unplanned change" (or the doctrine of unanticipated consequences) rears its head because some aspect of policy or technology or social consequence was overlooked by the originator of the activity – when it would have been easy to predict the outcome **if** there had been someone familiar with the specific discipline. And it is in this lack of interdisciplinary study and understanding that the greatest danger to standardization resides.

CONCLUSION

The major problem that I've found with standards and standardization in the 35 some years I've been involved is the lack of education about standardization. Many commercial organizations (ANSI, DIN,

AFNOR, ISO)[17] are willing to tell you about how their or their processes are superior for the production of specifications; very few can tell you why or how their specifications benefit individuals, businesses, or society. From a commercial or business point of view, all of these organizations appear to be selling a commodity product – like nails or glue – to hold things together. This approach – selling a commodity - works well for nails and glue, but it really fails when you're dealing with an interface that is trying to describe how complex information systems interoperate or function. Standardization – in its structure, utility, and implications – is not simple. Treating it like it is a unique and separate discipline does a disservice to those who must use it.

Compounding the problem is the fact that education in this area, when it is available, rarely recognizes the cross disciplinary necessity. It's as if marketing classes were taught without any reference to how a product was to be distributed, promoted, or priced – but only on how it was to be produced. Standardization has all the attributes of a marketing plan – there is a product, a distribution plan, a price (there's always a price for standardization), and a promotional campaign. There are also competitive issues for standardization – from the lack of standardization to an overabundance of standards. But these aren't taught; rather the focus is on how to run a committee, or how to make sure the committee is balanced, or how to create an equitable IPR policy. All are important – but all are a subset of the far larger and more fascinating arena of standardization.

And hence, I repeat – it's about standardization, not standards.

REFERENCES

ANSI. (2015). *Essential Requirements: Due process requirements for American National Standards.* Retrieved 15 January 2018 from https://www.ansi.org/essentialrequirements/

Borneman, W. R. (2010). *Rival Rails: The Race to Build America's Greatest Transcontinental Railroad.* Old Saybrook, CT: Tantor.

Liu, H., & Cargill, C. F. (2017). *Setting standards for industry: comparing the emerging Chinese standardization system and the current US system.* Honolulu, HI: East-West Center.

McKinnon, R. (2013). *Consent of the Networked: The Worldwide Struggle For Internet Freedom.* New York, NY: Basic Books.

Ogilvie, S. (2004). Guilds, efficiency, and social capital: Evidence from German proto-industry. *The Economic History Review, 57*(2), 286–333. doi:10.1111/j.1468-0289.2004.00279.x

Puffert, D. (2009). *Tracks across Continents, Paths through History: The Economic Dynamics of Standardization in Railway Gauge.* Chicago, IL: University of Chicago Press.

Ralston, A., & Reilly, E. D. (Eds.). (1993). *Encyclopedia of Computer Science* (3rd ed.). New York, NY: Van Nostrand Reinhold.

Schoechle, T. (2009). *Standardization and Digital Enclosure: The Privatization of Standards, Knowledge, and Policy in the Age of Global Information Technology.* Hershey, PA: IGI Global. doi:10.4018/978-1-60566-334-0

Sullivan, L. H. (1896). The Tall Office Building Artistically Considered. *Lippincott's Magazine*, *57*, 403–409.

Toth, R. B. (1996). *Standards Activities of Organizations in the United States*. Retrieved 16 October 2018 from https://nvlpubs.nist.gov/nistpubs/Legacy/SP/nistspecialpublication806e1996.pdf

ENDNOTES

1 https://uk.reuters.com/article/us-britain-eu-fox-food/uk-wont-lower-food-standards-to-win-post-brexit-trade-deals-minister-idUKKCN1MQ33Q, retrieved 18 October 2018.

2 This description could also probably apply to Non-Governmental Organizations (NGOs) as well; however, the author does not have enough familiarity with NGOs to make a positive case.

3 A note here for clarification. Standards are usually the result of an arcane process (each unique to its specific organization) which is supposed to mitigate the possibility of anti-competitive or monopolistic accusations against those creating the standards. The author has seen some efforts that – because of process requirements – have taken up to eight years to complete, making them a successful standard and a commercial failure.

4 http://www.w3.org/html/wg/drafts/html/master/dom.html#the-style-attribute, retrieved Feb 6, 2015

5 "The standards development process should have a balance of interests. Participants from diverse interest
categories shall be sought with the objective of achieving balance." (ANSI, 2019, page 4).

6 A partial list includes: European Union Agency for Network and Information Security; European Telecommunications Standards Institute; Global Inter-Cloud Technology Forum; Institute for Electrical and Electronics Engineers; Internet Engineering Task Force; International Organization for Standardization; International Telecommunication Union; ITU Telecommunication Standardization Sector; Organization for the Advancement of Structured Information Standards; Open Data Center Alliance; Open Grid Forum; Operations Support System/Business Support System; Quality Excellence for Suppliers of Telecommunications; Storage Networking Industry Association; Telecommunications Industry Association; TeleManagement Forum; The Open Group

7 "It is the pervading law of all things organic and inorganic, of all things physical and metaphysical, of all things human and all things superhuman, of all true manifestations of the head, of the heart, of the soul, that the life is recognizable in its expression, that form ever follows function. This is the law." (Sullivan, 1896)

8 ANSI, the official voice of US standardization, makes the following absurd statement: "ANSI is often asked about the total number of standards (and standards setting bodies) in the United States. It is estimated that in the U.S. today there are hundreds of "traditional" standards developing organizations - with the 20 largest SDOs producing 90% of the standards - and hundreds more "non-traditional" standards development bodies, such as consortia." Basically, ANSI is admitting that they have no idea about the size or importance of the US standards industry. http://www.ansi.org/about_ansi/introduction/introduction.aspx?menuid=1, retrieved 8 April 2015

9 According to data provided in (Toth, 1996), there are more than 93,000 standards produced and nearly 700 organizations. Data shown is as of 1996; newer statistics are not available.

10 http://www.nytimes.com/1860/11/08/news/steam-boiler-explosions.html, retrieved 2 March 2015

11 https://www.asme.org/getmedia/1adfc3df-7dab-44bf-a078-8b1c7d60bf0d/ASME_BPVC_2013-Brochure.aspx retrieved 2 March 2015

12 It was the author's unfortunate experience to try to write a brief (two page) pamphlet describing how ASC X3 worked and why it was significant to its members. The draft was sent to the subcommittee that was to approve it. Two years later, it emerged from the subcommittee. The group could not agree that standards changed the market (this might upset entrenched interests), that standards activities required meetings (this might upset finance officers who approved travel budgets), that standards were good (this might upset those with proprietary offerings), or that standards set strategy (this would upset market leaders.) It was a shambles and taught me a valuable lesson in consensus standards when dealing with non-technical ideas.

13 Most standardization committees require that all members commit to RAND licensing of technology – but only in the final three months (or thereabouts) of a standardization creation life cycle. This late identification of embedded technology penalizes those who implement the standard before final call – which is common practice. You can imagine someone's shock at finding that the new interface they are designing has suddenly become burdened with a royalty which had not been considered in the original business plan.

14 Technologists are especially susceptible to the creeping elegance gambit, since nearly every technologist wants to "...add that one little feature that hadn't been thought of before but which now is absolutely vital". Needless to say, creeping elegance has slowed or destroyed more standards that it has helped.

15 "Microsoft appears to be in the full-flush of damage control brought on by what Microsoft EVP Steve Ballmer last week called a naive move to thrust ActiveX into an independent standards body, reports sister paper ClieNT Server News ." http://www.cbronline.com/news/microsoft_back_pedals_activex_standardization

16 Li Si was also the official to whom the "burning of books and burial of scholars" was also ascribed, showing that there can be an occasional nasty side to standardizers.

17 I consider all standards organizations to be commercial enterprises – they sell a product, usually a specification, receiving payment in some form or another. (The exception might be the IETF, but that's only because the organization is sort of anti-organization.) They are all devoted to ensuring their continued commercial success and employ large numbers of people. They can fail when revenue fails to meet expenditures, or when the market no longer cares for their product.

Chapter 2
How Corporate Standardization Shapes Tomorrow's Business

Alice de Casanove
Airbus Defence and Space, France

ABSTRACT

Corporate standardization coordinates and supports experts involved in standardization bodies. It sets up standardization strategy in alignment with global strategy of the company. In this chapter, the authors illustrate how a company can embrace standardization and leverage it to increase its position in a competitive business environment. The authors first present an overview of corporate standardization strategy: how is standardization considered in a private company; how to capture the ins and outs of a corporate standardization; how to define, implement, and manage standardization strategy; etc. Then the authors present the benefits of standardization development for a company. Finally, an example of commitment in ISO TC 279 innovation management is presented.

INTRODUCTION

Because standards frame our daily life, because standards make the world safer and more interoperable, because standards try to solve babel tower issues, they impact strongly businesses.

When the word "standard" is pronounced in a company, a lot of questions arise on the actual scope and acceptation of the word standards. Actually, a lot of concepts are covered under this concept: does "standard" make reference to internal standards, policies or a regulation or a certification, product standardisation (especially in lean management), interfaces standards (technical specifications…). Standard can also be the assessment of the customer perception. We note there are common and usual thinking about standards: about their usefulness, representatively or applicability. Henceforth, it is relevant to report on what is perceived behind each of these notions; and analyse how corporate standardisation manage these (sometimes wrong) perceptions of standardisation purpose.

DOI: 10.4018/978-1-5225-9008-8.ch002

Copyright © 2019, IGI Global. Copying or distributing in print or electronic forms without written permission of IGI Global is prohibited.

Defining every used term can be considered as an obsession of standardisation staff but understanding how the word "standard" is used in business is mandatory to develop a standardisation development strategy. In the first part, the authors sum up typical perception of standard and standardization activities in a company. Then they recall actual objectives of standardisations, how to set up a standardization corporate function, how to efficiently benefit from standard to implement a company strategic plan. Finally, the authors introduce the current work on the standardization on innovation management. In each section, a set of questions are raised and answered to guide the reader through all the reasoning and questioning associated with the set up of a standardization activity.

HOW IS STANDARDISATION PERCEIVED IN A COMPANY?

"Standards" have different declination in a company. They all revolve on the concept of defining and agreeing upon a set of practice so as to improve business or facilitate communication. Here is a collection of the notion of "standards", ranging from internal practice up to customer-oriented needs.

Internal Standards or Policies

Companies use internal policies to harmonise their internal practices, so as to facilitates interaction across and among their departments. Even if these policies are internal, they have a huge impact on company's external image. Indeed, as these policies regulate the whole company life, they create the values of the company. The values conveyed by a company can become only marketing words to create an image if they do not have any footprints on employees and their internal processes; or become iconic and representative of a set of values customers want to share (and buy).

Setting an internal policy has many impacts on other policies up to the whole organization of a company. For example if one of the company values is green compliancy (ecology, preservation or resources, etc.), then one can expect there will be an internal policy specifically for this topic. But all other policies gravitating around this topic will be impacted (e.g. general procurement, company building) and an emphasis on this topic will be put. Generally the creation or the update of new policies is accompanied with a communication plan to aware employees. Hence, company policies are a bridge between management standards and their implementation in the company.

Certification

Certification moves internal policies one step further and confirm to external parties – customer or business partners – which particular policies are effectively in place in a company. A typical example is the ISO9001 standard that is being associated with certification activities. As a matter of fact, since the 1980's most of the company wants or has to be ISO9001 certified given its importance in quality assessment process. As the needs for quality were huge, the ISO9001 certification has been an amazing success. CQO (Chief Quality Officer) function has been created to manage this topic and create a quality culture across companies.

However, this strong link between a standard and its certification process blurred the lines on the actual intent of standards. They are now mostly considered as a topic for quality department, and induce regular audits. But only few standards generate a certification process, and standards use is always a deliberate process except for the ones references in regulations.

Regulation

The general public connect standards to regulations; they prescribe acceptable or allowed practices in an industry. These are a part of "de jure" standards, enforced by national laws. They are usually transcribed from general agreement at various scales. They are defined and enforced so as to increase the safety of goods and services, as it is the case for instance in the food industry and the management of temperature for dairy products, or safety in airplane and airport.

Yet, they are perceived as a set of complex norms limiting the business development. People are generally complaining about these regulations, stating that "everything is standardised" like if originality or out of the box thinking was killed by a unified and harmonised world. But most of the time this unification is a fertile soil for innovation development: it eases testing and rapid prototyping; it generates new ecosystem and increase the interaction between different organisations by creating a common set of knowledge and objectives. Regulation is also beneficial to the final customer: it increases trust in a product, e.g. safety regulations for food or transport.

Product Standardisation

Standard applied to goods and products complement industry-level regulation. It is a way to rationalise product life management: efficient management of configuration instead of "make-to-the-measures", savings on big volumes of material to assemble products, communication rationalization based on standardised family products, etc. A company with an efficient standardisation development strategy can make these products become the reference for the market. Large Internet-based companies demonstrated how to enforce such product standardization for smartphones or social networks, and have it accepted by its customer base.

Customers

Conversely to product standardization, customers may also favour some products. Again, the telecommunication industry showed how products could be massively adopted. When a product is successful and adopted by a large part of the population, it becomes a reference, a standard "de facto". If a new product does not fulfil the same needs as the "standards" it would be disregarded by the market and considered as below the expectations. These standards are not necessary "open" but they are at least product specifications than can be translated in a performances standard. Products or services compliant with a service are considered as safe and secure and with up to date technologies.

From Informal Standards to Standards on Standards

In the previous list, we summarized regular occurrences of standards in daily or professional life. They arise in various aspects. For instance, business standards are also key elements of request for proposal or call for tender, they speed up the creation of these Request for Proposals (RFPs) and guarantee a good communication with the potential providers. These are in place to establish customer-provider relationships across most industries, but also between state operators and the industry

Similarly, interface standards provide technical specification, creating interoperability among different systems. Hence, cars can be refuelled thanks to standards in oil industries defining characteristics of gasoline. When standards are not widely adopted they bring inconvenience, for example the electric outlet

International standardization that created multiple heterogeneous form factors.

We have presented several aspects of standards. Let us not that most of the standards are used on a deliberate way and are not supporting any regulation, but instead increase business value. If they are used wisely, they may represent a strategic asset in a company roadmap. In the following sections, the authors will discuss International standardisation and the management of this standardisation process. The corporate standardisation department usually operates this function. In the following, the authors do no discuss internal company standards, as these are not externally visible.

WHAT IS THE REAL PURPOSE OF STANDARDISATION?

Standardisation is a voluntary and deliberate process of developing specifications based on consensus among all interested parties (industry including SMEs, consumers, trade unions, public authorities, etc.). They shape our daily live by providing minimal performance levels for services, such as safety or energy; management policies for organisation; or support for interoperability like in telecommunication.

Standardisation process is regulated by independent standard bodies, acting at national (ANSI – US, BSI – UK, AFNOR – France, DIN – Germany, etc.), European (CEN) or international (ISO, ITU, etc.) levels. They provide standards by law, which can support regulations (example in European market with CE marking).

As standardisation is based on consensus principle, it involves several levels of discussions at national, regional and then international levels. National standardisation bodies harmonies position of national stakeholders. Later, this position has to be defended at international level (regional or intergovernmental levels). Corporate standardisation has to consider this geopolitical landscape in standardisation strategy.

The organization of a standardization body follows the following pattern: the steering committee gives the long-term strategy of the standardisation organism and represents authority of standardisation process. All the technical committees report to the steering committee and are focused on a given topic. A technical committee sets the global vision, defines the framework and coordinates the different working groups that pertain to its area of interest. Finally, the working group gathers the experts and develops standards – its technical content.

It can be also be carried out by an industrial or domain-focused consortium. In this case, such standards would not be recognised by the states but if they are widely used they are become de facto standards adopted by the industry, like ECSS standards for the European Space standards; IETF or ECMA for the computer and network industry.

Figure 1. Organization of an international standardization body

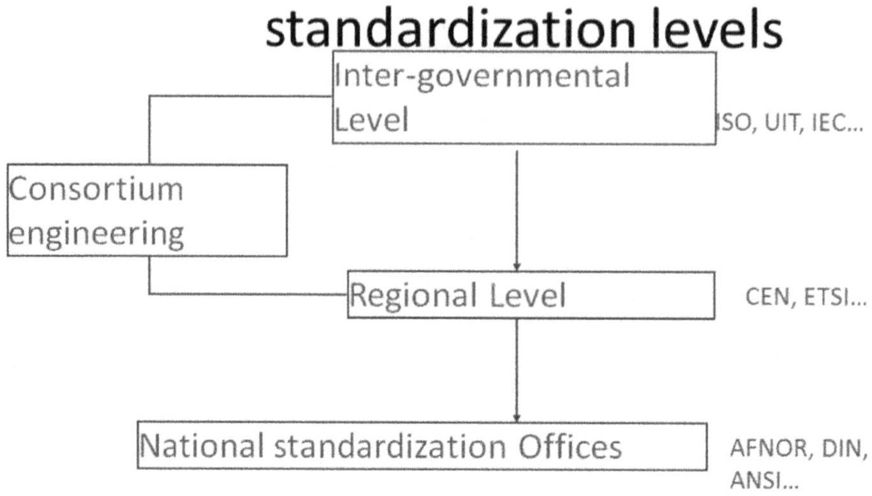

What Are the Different Kinds of Industrial Standards?

There are different kinds of standards, with different objectives:

- Fundamental standards are terminology standards, their primary objective is to build a common understanding for a given domain;
- Specification standards are technical specifications. They define interfaces standards, or performances standards; and the associated requirements for interoperability;
- Test and methods standards focus on ensuring a minimum level of quality or safety. These are achieved through defined testing methods;
- Management standards provide guidelines for organization, they precise how decision chains are managed through recommendations or requirements.

These terms are defined below and the impacts on standardisation strategies are described.

- Terminology standards are generally the first step of standardization. Sharing the same vocabulary is mandatory prior to any works. It clarifies the concept behind each word and then obviously limits misunderstanding behind two parties having different backgrounds. This first step is also necessary to define the standardisation perimeter: it will support the development of the standards documents but also mobilise the stakeholder. Indeed as the terminology is one of the first documents published, this document gives visibility to the working group and then generally new members are joining.
- Technical specifications like interfaces standards concentrate on technologies and technical works. All the stakeholders have to be around the table to debate, share, and establish relevant specifications, which would be widely adopted. This family of document requires the involvement of an efficient rapporteur to drive the agenda, moderate the discussions and coordinate the writing activities.

They are big stakes behind this kind of document, each company or consortium of companies wanted to see his in-house technology adopted by the community to capture any potential market, including significant portion of key patents necessary to implement the standard.

An efficient rapporteur will be able to keep the fundamental direction and make a standard that can be widely adopted by the community. Its key mission is to maintain the energy and commitment of all standards developers. Hence, there is a difficult but mandatory balance to find.

- Performance standards describe the minimum set of performance that a product or a service may fulfil to be compliant. This family of standards can also crystallise some market frictions. A company wanting to penalise a competitor may propose (and see enforced) unreachable, non-relevant or out of scope performances.
- Management standards are nowadays often known as management system, and support companies in the creation of their internal policies. They facilitate the relationships between different partners for co-development, research (common technical interfaces), procurement relationship (decision chain clearly identified), or supply chain management (common quality control) etc. They are also a powerful tool to disseminate good practices, and to improve the efficiency in organisations. Let us note they are also mandatory for consultants: these management standards support and legitimate their activity

How to Select the Kind of Standard to Develop?

As the authors underlined in the previous section, standard can have a dual role of market enabler, and competitor neutralizer. Hence, corporate standardisation strategy has to define the type of standard to develop. This mostly depends on the market maturity: new technology or new management method requires a clear terminology to guarantees a efficient development market position; to become leader on a market a performance standard can eliminate less valuable competing solution.

Most of standard practitioners acknowledge that standards are nothing else than tools in a toolbox. Hence, one has to understand the purpose of each standard element, and how they can be components of a company toolbox. Furthermore, standards are embraced by the community only if they are efficient. The screwdriver with a star pattern is generally less used than the flat or cross screw because most of the screws have a flat or cross pattern. That is the same for standards, if the document does not fulfil a need efficiently; it is forgotten in the history oubliettes.

A standard is worthless without a community promoting it, using it, and maintaining it. The core of the community has generally created the seed of the standards and has grown in parallel of the development of the standard. But assembling a set of high-level experts around the table is not a guarantee of success: all the stakeholders have to be involved in the standardisation process. Generally the less represented party is the end users, even if at the end they contribute to the adoption (or not) of a standard.

Standards require also a lot of resources to be developed. Yet, one can note that standards are emerging from everywhere. The standardization landscape has become some kind of a jungle. This creates risks for a company to miss new business opportunities emerging from standards (think USB stack taking over most traditional communication buses), or updates that would impact performances of new products (e.g. certification authorities changing regulation, for instance the FAA allowing twin-jets for long haul flight across oceans), or disrupt an established market.

Hence, it might be difficult for companies to identify where to put some efforts, resources and how to get involved. So as company management resources cannot be deployed on every standardisation field, a selection has to be done and effort put on standardisation have to be coordinated and optimized.

As a matter of fact, big companies have set up during the past decades a department for "Corporate standardisation". This Corporate standardisation department ensures consistency in company participation to Standardisation bodies. It has to ensure that the company business and technology roadmap benefit from external standardisation works, and the return on investment of these activities is acceptable to compensate fees, delegated personnel, etc. Nowadays, this function exists in big group as well as in start-ups and SMEs. In the latter case, it can be merged with innovation CIO or CTO functions.

In the next section, the author emphasises the main activities and role of the stakeholders in the construction of a standardisation department in a large group.

FIRST ACTIONS FOR A NEW CORPORATE STANDARDISATION DEPARTMENT

When a corporate standardisation department is created, there are two key actions to lead: 1) depict the landscape, e.g. the standardisation bodies impacting company business, relevant standard in preparation or already in place; 2) and know who goes where: who are the experts already involved in standardisation activities. Generally this department reports to CEO in the frame of institutional relationships functions or report to CTO in the frame of engineering functions.

Several inputs are required to map relevantly the standardisation landscape: company global strategy, technology roadmap, competitive landscape, and product portfolio. Based on these data, the corporate standardisation team can identify relevant standardisation bodies, technical committees and working groups to monitor or to contribute to. This identification can be supported either by the company experts who are aware of the well know standards, or by the national standardisation bodies who are in charge of awareness actions.

Awareness and networking are key elements in the definition of this strategy. Hence, national standardisation bodies are easy to identify, but private and consortium initiatives may be less visible. It is highly advised to follow newsletters from national, regional and international standardisation offices, and also attend awareness events organised by actors and supports of standardisation. Also, standardisation coordination is also a matter of networking. The more your network across standardisation body is spread, the easier standardisation watch is.

As the landscape is complex, it may be interesting to have a visual representation. A chart or mind map assessing by influence zones the standardisation groups may help. The following picture provides an example of standardisation landscape of the European space industry. It is built across formal standardization bodies (ISO, IEC, ARINC), industry consortium (Eurospace, ECSS) in connection with other consortia like ETSI or CENELEC. All work is closely monitored by space agencies at the national or European levels, and the corresponding standardization bodies (BSI, BNAE on behalf of AFNOR, DIN, etc.). Given the various interaction levels, such mind map is crucial to share a common vision of all stakeholders, their role and prerogative in the decision taking process.

The second action consists in identifying experts among the company who are already involved in standardisation activities, or are willing to join one. This data collection is not easy and has to be always on going. Experts can be involved in multiple ways, most of the time as part of opportunities

Figure 2. Standardisation organisation in the space sector

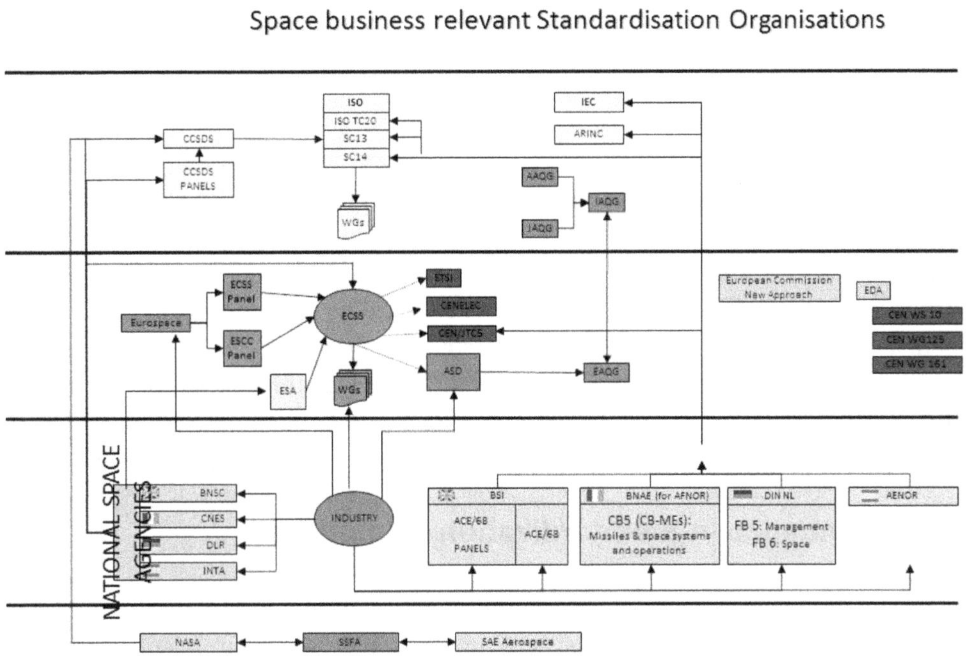

in a project. It is thus important to closely monitor any new participation, and to evaluate its potential benefits in the long term.

These data can be collected trough company internal networking. Generally top experts in a technical area are recognised and well known. Attending standardisation meetings is a way to confirm, have recognised and maintain this expertise. This identification work can also be made in contacting standardisation body offices; they can provide a list of people registered in their committees. At last finance department or procurement that is fully aware of the expenses related to standardisation activities can support this work.

This information is fundamental to coordinate standards development: from a management point of view several aspects have to be considered in corporate standardisation such as budget management, optimised attendance in standardisation committees, valorisation of experts (careers, training, etc.). The authors review each of these activities in the forthcoming paragraphs.

To Control the Budget Dedicated to Standards Development

There are three main approaches to manage standardization budget: centralized or decentralized budget, or a balanced mix. The three approached have advantages and drawbacks but depending on the company structure, there are preferred approaches:

- A centralized budget owned by the corporate structure will create a strict control of the expenses and the attendance strategy will be intimately bounded to the corporate strategy and will support the long-term vision of the company. Nevertheless it creates a bottleneck in the management of experts' attendance and slows down new membership in emerging consortium where it might be key to be in particular for innovation dissemination.

- A decentralized budget, which is owned by the operational level of the company, will ensure an attendance to standardization bodies developing standards that impact today business. This is connected to the fact that operational teams generally adopt a short-term approach. The expected benefits from standards development are mainly networking (with potential customers, suppliers, or partners), market intelligence (competitors watch) and notoriety (especially for the introduction of new product into the market). Nevertheless, operational teams may cut first standards development budget in case of finance issues.
- A balanced approach, with a part of the budget in both the operational and the corporate levels, may seem a way to mitigate the pros and cons detailed previously. Yet, the main issue with this approach consists in the coordination of the experts. There is nothing worst than having two experts from the same company having opposite opinion in a standardization meeting: it duplicates company expenses for standardization activities, and most of all it creates a bad image of the company.

To Optimize Attendance in Standardization Committees

Optimizing experts' attendance to the meeting means having a clear view of the famous "who goes where?" and maintaining this mapping consistent and accurate over time. A subsequent activity is to keep it updated with a network of focal points at different operational levels (business lines, project teams, programme teams).

Generally, the corporate standardization function is in charge of the animation of this community: it has to organize regularly coordination meetings where focal point exchange information from standardization bodies works, new bodies created, experts leaving, new comers, etc. These internal communities uses also company social network tools (or intranet) to share, keep and track standardisation works.

To Valorise Internal Expertise and Develop International Influence

From a technical point of view other aspects have to be considered in corporate standardization such as company notoriety, expertise development inside and outside of the company; maintain the knowledge of company top experts, spread of technical innovation and the backward and forward compliance of company products with future standards

The best way to guarantee the compliance of today product with future standards is to turn internal standards into external standards. However, this is possible if the company has an efficient footprint on both state-of-the-art technology and standards development.

Let us recall that the standardization landscape is a kind of map with isolated islands (young consortia gathering some stakeholders of a given business) and hyper linked land. (Well-established standardization offices). If we keep the geography analogy, the role of corporate standardization is to identify relevant soil for the development of standards promoting business. Standardization coordinators are like pioneers who test the value of the soil before sending the experts who will develop the standards.

Identify Where the Company Should Be

Several aspects have to be taken into account: the strength of the standardization body, the level of relevance of the standardization body with the company business and technology, the involvement of other stakeholders in this standardization bodies, the legal landscape (which kind of standards are produced: consortium standards, de jure standards, standards supporting a regulation etc.).

Standards consortia are perceived as efficient bodies but with too flexible rules to guarantee a strong consensus in the community (One usually says that "he, who has the pencil has the power"). If they gather a representative community of stakeholders they produce powerful documents, superseding de jure standards. So they are agile but might be also fragile.

On the other hand, formal Standardisation bodies (such as ISO, CEN, ITU-T…) are perceived as huge machinery, difficult to penetrate with complicated rules. Yet, they are strong enough and reliable, trying to reach a consensus, with all points of view being respected. The consensus is key to guarantee a wide adoption of the standards. It is also part of the manifesto of these bodies.

As there are several levels of standardisation development (national, regional, international), the right levels has to be identified in considering several aspects: working group dynamism (if for instance all activities are at the regional levels and no more at national ones); company strategy to identify whether company stakes are at national or international levels and then to decide commitment at the corresponding levels either as basic participants, or as a leader.

Once relevant standardization bodies are identified, working groups have to be assessed. Company generally builds a grid with its own assessment criteria such as competitiveness, working group's reactivity, works relevance, required resources, and competitor position. Nevertheless, the involvement in some working groups can benefit from a "golden token", in particular when the said working groups publish standards supporting a regulation impacting business.

To Decide Whether to Develop Proprietary Solution or Implement an External Standard

There are different degrees of involvement in standardization working groups: no involvement (proprietary solution), follower (undergo a standard), contributor (contribute to the definition of standards), and lead (contribute, create new standards, involved in steering committees).

R&D units generally consider that developing an in-house technology is three time more expensive than implementing a standard. Furthermore, standard solutions are considered safe and secure by the customers, who can considerer the technology as being open, with binding to a given provider. Finally, the manufacturer is reassured that a community shares the technical solutions; and these solutions represent the state of the art.

In-house solutions are preferred especially when they are disruptive technical choices. These solutions are generally standardised later in order to disseminate and make these solutions adopted once early adopters have recognized the value of the solution.

Hence, the degree of involvement depends on both the capability to support the development of a standard (budget for the development), and its strategic interest for the company.

Standardisation Development Budget

In most of the cases, the company reviews yearly the benefits of standardization activities during membership renewal. That's why it's important to have a clear vision of the entities in the company in charge of membership fees, but also the delegation of experts to plenary sessions.

The mission of corporate standardization is to

1. Analyse company engagements in standardization bodies, review value for business, coordinate and align contributors
2. Monitor and assess standardization bodies to identify spots where further engagement from company may be beneficial to business
3. Align company standardization strategy with company technology road map and global strategy
4. Influence key standardization bodies trough steering committees

How to Develop and Maintain a Standardisation Strategy?

Standardisation strategy is linked with the R&D roadmap and company strategy. Hence, the standardisation strategy is the mapping of these two strategies on the future standardization landscape. The strategy elaboration consists then in 3 phases:

- Identify the future standardisation landscape, in anticipating which are the working groups or committees to be closed, the ones to be created by third parties. This identification requires being aware of the standardization Working Group activities and also steering group decisions.
- Identify the new topics of standardization that emerges in the company; and check if there is a working group, which can host this activity. If no working group exists then it is necessary to find a technical committee able to host this new working group.
- Define the level of involvement of each working groups. This is done using several criteria to evaluate adequacy to the company roadmap, such as interest for the business, competition position, in-house development, etc.

Hence, the efficiency of the corporate standardisation strategy reflects the effectiveness of standards culture by company stakeholders, their commitment in standardisation bodies or their support in this participation, and the associated RoI. The RoI of the development of standards -- and not the usage of standards -- will be detailed in the next section.

HOW TO BENEFIT FROM STANDARDS DEVELOPMENT?

There are two main obvious motivations in standards development: support the spread of new technology or working methods, and guarantee the compliance of company products with the standards through active monitoring of forthcoming revisions. The authors want to emphasize the many other benefits: such as develop standards to enable new markets, to give visibility to existing or emerging topics, to build lifelong training, to build technology watch and market intelligence, to foster company expertise, to build company social network and branding, etc.

Business Enabler or Trigger

However, one of the key issues is to demonstrate the relevance of standardization to the company roadmap, and have it well understood by the top management so as to support it. The Standardization corporate function has to demonstrate the importance of standards to CEO and CTO top management.

The authors already presented that standards development has several added values to the company. One has to turn them into strategic elements to the top management. This is performed each time a new standard is in development: the ecosystem behind this standard has to be presented and the impact of this standard on the business has also to be enlightened. Standards can have multiple impacts:

- Standardization can create or trigger new markets. For instance, when they introduce a new regulation. Such standard has to specify how to be compliant with this regulation. In turn, customers will update or renew their product base or systems, organisation to become compliant to the new regulation. Hence, these new constraints can be source of innovation, e.g. to meet new performance standards, and then create or renew markets.
- Standards can also enable a new market. For example Interface standards define interconnection mechanisms between systems. In making integration simpler, new business can be developed by economic actors who can enlarge their activity scopes. Standards create interfaces among different technologies and create even a new ecosystem.
- Standards also facilitate the relationship among partners. For example, a terminology standard will allow for a partnership between two companies, as sharing the same vocabulary is mandatory for an efficient collaboration. Terminology standard also favours innovation: one usually acknowledges that innovation comes from the collision of two different worlds. Should these companies have different backgrounds, these partnerships would produce new solution and lead to innovation at large.
- Performances standards can also purge a market. It gives customers a grid to assess the cost/performances ratio. If this ratio is not acceptable, a company may decide to exit this market, or on the contrary invest on it. Similarly, performances standards are scrutinized by customers to define their baseline for requirements

In the following, the authors report on three examples where standards were essential for the development of or participation in a market, and how the authors initiated the development of new standards.

- The first one is an application market place, in which images from Spot images are available on for map application, e.g. a GPS or an imaginary application. To bring updated images, we need interface standards to connect to the application provider image repository. Such general interoperability standard is in the portfolio of the OGC, the Open Geospatial Consortium, but also at ISO in the technical committee ISO/TC 211.
- Our second example is attached to regulation standards. Power plants are required to have communication means capable of working whatever the situation is. This is necessary to keep the distribution grid running, but also in case of disaster to know the situation in remote sites. In case of major disasters, part of the general infrastructure is destroyed, including land communications. Satellite-based communication is resilient to such default. They could provide an alternative solu-

tion to land lines. Yet, the industry has to show that using regular communication means and satellite communication means provide the same quality of service. Hence, a performance standard and a regulation standard have been defined: the first one describes how the performance required to support requirements for bandwidth, availability, etc.; the second one indicates how to combine satellite and land-line communication infrastructure to increase safety in the operation of power plants, and how to be compliant with these new rules of operation. This is done as part of the French BNAE standard body on behalf of the French electricity providers.

- The third example concerns certification. Let us consider issues faced by helicopters during rescue missions under bad weather condition: fog, snow, wind, etc. In such situation, the pilot requires assistance to land, but also to avoid obstacles (tree, power line, building, etc.). Using a helicopter-mounted radar, one can build in real-time a 3-D model of the local environment, and combine it with a more general 3-D map of the local area from an external database. This information can be provided through an enhanced, synthetic vision of the environment to increase the safety of the mission. In order to move forward such services, one needs to define performance standards, and associated certification process that that both the radar and the database can be used on-board an aircraft. Let us recall that the operation of aircraft is one of the most stringent standardization domains, whose main purpose is to reach the maximum level of safety in all operations. The EUROCAE and RTCA standardization bodies, in charge of the whole aeronautics industry standards, perform this work.

Hence, standards are closely related to product definition and innovation, providing various insights. First, standards can be considered as the state-of-the-art, the soil of your seed for your project. Then, when you are in development phase, you need to establish partnerships and thus you need agreement on some terminology or interfaces. Again, standards provide some elements on these topics. Finally, the authors illustrated in the previous examples how standards help organizing or shaping a market, in line with a valorisation strategy. The later usage of standard can be a strong competitive asset for a company.

Conditions to Use Standards Development as Business Trigger

A company can benefit from standardization activities only if corporate standards strategy and is aligned with the global strategy of the company, in particular with the Business development strategy and the Intellectual property strategy. It is the reason why the standards department is integrated to corporate functions. However, being in corporate functions should never imply being disconnected from operational teams. Standardization strategy has to be fed and led by company business. Market and business indicators provide insights on the degree of involvement required in standardization working group. Conversely, the attendance or involvement to standardization activities by experts from operational or business entities depends on the expected value added from operational teams.

Hence, tools and methods to capture and valorise information caught during standardization meeting have to be put in place. Information captured during standardization meeting (informal talking, or early announcement) can be shared with marketing intelligence department through regular report from standardization experts. The most relevant information for top management has also to be gathered and spread in quarterly report. It shows the importance of standardization activities but also interrogate Top management on strategy (impact of company strategy on standardization strategy).

Participation to a standardization activity is tangible evidence of company values and engagement. Also, since standardization of a topic creates buzz around a particular domain, it can be used as a communication vector to increase employees' commitment at large. They can witness the national, regional or international influence of their company. Standardization development also impacts company branding towards external customers or the general public.

Standardisation Activities Alignment With Overall Business Strategy

To assess the alignment of standards development with the business strategy, it is mandatory to set up in advance an internal community of practitioners, to educate this community so that its members are aware of the standards development, and can react rapidly to comment or to reorient the standards.

This internal communication is significant at key point, for instance when a milestone of the standards development is passed: the community may provide valuable feedbacks and comments. Agility is also mandatory to be an efficient actor in the standards development.

There are three main kinds of actors to mobilize to coordinate across all companies division:

- The experts in a given area, who generally attend standardization meetings, or follow remotely development of standard documents,
- The business team, capturing customers' requirements, partners' participation in standardization bodies, competitors' watch,
- The standardization coordinators, who are in contact with standardization bodies' management and steering committees.

There are different period of time for communicating with this community:

- When the community is assembled, confirming the commitments of the members is mandatory. It can be obtained through their management or the natural curiosity of experts.
- To convene this community, regular activity reports have to be sent as newsletter or update on internal corporate sites, and regular meetings to develop the commitments have to be organized.

Given the wealth of information exchange, these reports and meetings must provide minimal yet relevant information, such as: main standardisation steps, impacts of the company involvements (business and technical point of view), marketing intelligence, etc.

How to Use Standardisation to Develop Employees' Competences?

As standards address various topics most functions are impacted by standards. It turns out standardisation development can be used to develop employee's competences. As a matter of fact, standardization development and adoption impacts training for all kind of employees and in particular experts.

Experts who attend standardization committees can meet their peers in a non-competitive atmosphere. They can have open discussions on their preferred topic and challenge their views on their core expertise. The informal discussions with the other experts make their expertise grow and support technology watch

Generally company experts participating to standard development is also seen as an internal expert of the topic. Its position and role is thus increased. Hence, when a company decides to develop training in this area, this expert is a natural stakeholder, to be mobilized to participate in the realization of the learning solution. Hence, standards become a basis, frame and reference to design training towards all teams: business, legal, marketing, operational, etc.

A key issue remains: the selection of the right expert to participate actively in standards development. This choice has to be made after the decision has been taken to join a working group, and not before so as to maximize the efficiency of the decision. Actually, the following points should be considered: efficiency, visibility, and availability. One may consider the following points for selecting the right profile:

- **Efficiency:** Working experience of 5 to 10 years or more depending on the technical domain,
- **Visibility:** A woman may be more visible, especially if the area is generally lead by men. Women are better remembered by WG attendees, and may have more impact in decisions,
- **Availability:** Someone connected to both operational activities (to have enough availabilities), and to the business and company strategy.

A mission letter must be established to precise an expert code of conduct. This mission letter will frame the work of the experts in the working group. It must precisely define the limits in the topics to be discussed, recall basic principles of IP protection when considering the disclosure of technical details to be included in a standard, etc.

One of the other issues that might be solved by this mission letter is the commitment of the expert's manager. Indeed experts mission in standardisation may not be properly recognized: standardisation is generally a long-term action, time to standardize is longer than time to market with an uncertain return on investment. This mission letter will formalize the commitment of management in allocating time and budget for standardisation activities. Mission letter can also contain the different objectives that can be used as key performance indicator during employee yearly review. Hence, standardisation activities can be valorised during employee careers.

The population of standardisation experts has to be regularly trained to efficiently represent company interest during standardisation meetings. They have to be trained on three main aspects:

- To be aware of the main standardisation rules (consensus rules, types of standards, mode or operation of a standardization committee, etc.),
- To make a contribution, to obtain internal consensus to elaborate the contribution,
- To disseminate in the company information captured during meeting.

This training must allow for interaction with other domains. The authors already mentioned connections with the marketing, business development or operation teams. Intellectual Property (IPR) should also be an integral part of the strategy. IPR management department has a philosophy of confidentiality whereas corporate standardisation has a philosophy of disclosure. Nevertheless, they share a common goal to reinforce competitiveness and protect innovations. A close coordination of these both departments is essential to drive standard development. IPR may oppose the participation in a standard body if there is a risk of disclosing key technologies for which the company as a strong competitive asset to defend.

INNOVATION MANAGEMENT ISO TC 279: CHAIRMANSHIP – BENEFITS FOR A LARGE CORPORATIONS - INNOVATING IS DISOBEYING THE STANDARDS

As the authors reported in this chapter, standard are closely related to the creation of new products and markets. By extension, it is also connected to innovation, which is also a matter for standardization.

Innovation is a powerful driver for creating value, competitiveness and profitable growth.

Innovation management helps organizations to grasp innovation opportunities to create and introduce new business models, organizations, products or services into the market. Innovation is a pillar of global competitiveness as well as human progress over the coming decades. In other words innovation management means not leaving innovation to chance for outperforming competitors and differentiating from them, but innovation management is a systematic approach to make innovation a guarantee of business sustainability.

Then Innovation has become a must-have in most of large sustainable organizations. Many organizations are today striving towards becoming more innovative to answer the paradigm: disrupt or being disrupted.

How Can an Organization Take Steps to Becoming More Innovative?

ISO 50500 series provides guidance, tools and methods dedicated to the field of innovation and in interaction between all actors in the innovation, for industrial, environmental and social benefits to allow to:

- Share a common understanding of innovation and its concepts, thanks to the elaboration of a shared glossary of the concepts, tools and methods built and implemented
- Ensure common practices of innovation fostering the innovation capabilities, the performance and effectiveness of the innovation process thus facilitating partnerships with all actors of the chain of innovation and create business opportunities,
- Integrate sustainable development issues in the management practices of innovation,
- Ensure coherence and links with existing international standards (such as ISO 9001, ISO 31000, ISO 26000) to explain the specificities related to innovation management in relation to the processes or methods described.

The following documents will be published in 2019 (see Table 1).

Table 1.

• ISO 56000	Innovation management -- Fundamentals and vocabulary
• ISO 56002	Innovation management -- Innovation management system -- Guidance
• ISO 56003	Innovation management -- Assessment -- Guidance
• ISO 56004	Innovation management - Tools and methods for innovation partnership --Guidance
• ISO 56005	Innovation management -- Strategic intelligence management -- Guidance
• ISO 56506	Innovation management -- Intellectual property management – Guidance
• ISO 56507	Innovation management – Idea Management – Guidance

The ISO 56000 series provide an innovation management system plug-able on all existing management systems from the ISO family. It supports the setup, deployment and improvement of organizations and processes dedicated to innovation. For example, they provide a shared understanding of what innovation, innovation management and invention are, as well as tools and methods to open the innovation to other partners, assess the impact of a deployed innovation management system.

Innovation management standards are also used as a basis for innovation training, which are key to foster innovation culture. Standards and innovation are rarely in the same sentence, Innovation management is perceived as an oxymora then having a standard on innovation management is an impossible wager.

But all innovation practitioners agree on the fact that there is a need to use specific methodologies to manage innovations regarding aspects such as intellectual property, funding, marketing, dissemination, user education, which is a good incitation to build a standard.

About Chairing an ISO TC Committee

Since 2013 Airbus Defence and Space chairs ISO TC 279 on innovation management. The authors are involved in this undertaking. These standards will not standardize what is innovation but provide guidelines and good practices to support innovation management in organisations (from public research centres, universities to SMEs, big group, etc.).

AFNOR has proposed this chairmanship to different experts already involved in Innovation management standardization at French and European level. Before accepting or declining the proposition, the company compared the RoI because Company directly supports both personnel and travel costs. Strong benefits have been identified such as the image of an innovative company, the lead of the standards development. Similarly to mandate given to experts, the company prepared an internal mandate for his representative. It contains the mission to develop pragmatic guidelines to support innovation management and share the results not only in the standardization community but also in the innovation community of the group.

Which Are the First Benefits?

After the 5 first years of chairmanship of his technical committee Airbus D&S confirmed some of its expected benefits. First in term of image, Airbus Defence and Space has been invited to several conferences about innovation and/or standardization and has extended his network and his notoriety. This image facilitates the recruitment of employees with an innovation mind-set and the creation of partnership with innovative start-ups. It's also a way to network and develop partnership with world top experts and also with public policy representatives in innovation. Furthermore, this notoriety in the governmental institutions makes the company an unavoidable actor to be consulted for governmental studies on national policies impact on the industry.

Also, being part of the Technical committee allows the company to make an easy and relevant benchmark on existing tools and methods deployed to foster innovation and also to be aware of new available tools. These results have to be shared inside the company through an animation of an internal community. As for expert reports, this activity summarizes standardization activity but also list emerging topics addressed in the standards development. Hence, it helps the group to challenge its good practices and also give a benchmark for a reasonable cost with other international groups or disruptive SMEs.

What Are the Main International Impacts?

The OECD working group NESTI and ISO TC 279 developed jointly the terminology and structure on innovation. In 2014, OECD started Oslo manual revision in parallel with ISO initiating Technical committee on innovation management.

In parallel to the third revision of the Oslo Manual, OECD has established a relationship with the International Organisation for Standardisation (ISO) that initiated a technical committee on Innovation Management in to develop standards related to innovation management (ISO 56000 series). The exchange between the two organisations helped to include the different perspectives from expert groups and to develop the definitions related to the topic of innovation and innovation management. Discussion of the definition of innovation for statistical measurement purposes by the OECD and for application to innovation management in the context of standardization led to an alignment of the definitions taking into account the different objectives of the Oslo Manual and of the ISO standards.

CONCLUSION

In this chapter, the authors provided an overview on corporate standardization activities, the main stakeholders and how standardization activities are internally connected to other corporate functions, and could lead to the emergence of new markets, new products but also innovation. The definition of involvement in standardization activities goes in high-level of management, in line with strategic roadmap; but also deeply connected to the operational activities. Such level of connectivity makes standardisation corporate functions central in multiple decision paths. Authors illustrated how to leverage this position through various examples: leveraging standards to keep or create a position; to gather experts to participate in standard development. In this chapter, the authors did not aim at providing definite answers, but rather a toolbox for setting standard corporate functions. Actually, they have to be adapted to each company culture.

Chapter 3
Challenges Facing Technology Standardization in the Age of Digital Transformation

Brian McAuliffe
HP Inc., Ireland

ABSTRACT

It is widely recognized that we are in rapid transition to the so-called fourth industrial revolution, a world of digitalization and mass interconnectedness enabled by a plethora of emergent powerful technologies including artificial intelligence (AI), internet of things (IoT), and distributed ledgers (DLT). A key element of this "revolution" is the move to digital manufacturing. While undoubtedly exciting, this transition presents challenges to policymakers, industry, and societal stakeholders alike. One such challenge is defining an optimum level for any market intervention measure(s), such that a balance is struck between ensuring a pro-industrial and economic innovation-friendly approach and guaranteeing adequate levels of consumer-focused protection. Standardization can be leveraged as one element of interventionary policy designed to help strike the required balance, both in its well-proven bottom-up and industry-led voluntary application and as a tool to support implementation of regulations. With a focus on digital transformation, this chapter will analyze the readiness of the current standardization system to support this significant transition focusing on strengths and challenges to be addressed from the perspective of industry, policymakers, and standards-setting organizations.

INTRODUCTION

According to most observers we are now entering the fourth industrial revolution. This latest era will probably best characterised as being that which introduced the digitalization and interconnectedness of everything, enabled by a plethora of emergent powerful technologies including artificial intelligence (AI), internet of things (IoT), and distributed ledgers (DLT), all supported by enhanced and distributed networking platforms.

DOI: 10.4018/978-1-5225-9008-8.ch003

Copyright © 2019, IGI Global. Copying or distributing in print or electronic forms without written permission of IGI Global is prohibited.

While very exciting, the rapid pace of innovation in the underlying information and communication technology (ICT), together with previously unimagined application areas that impact all aspects of modern life, present many challenges to policy makers, industry, and societal stakeholders alike. One such challenge lies in establishing the optimum level of market intervention, for example with legislative & regulatory initiatives, the aim being - as should be the case with any intervention - to strike a balance between a pro-industrial & economic innovation-friendly approach and an adequate level of consumer-focused protectionary measures. Standardization, as one such interventionary policy instrument, both in a voluntary capacity and as a tool to support implementation of regulations, can be leveraged in this regard.

Standardization indeed has been used extensively in the past to play a key role in ensuring sustainable market development and technology adoption. However, as this paper will show, to meet the needs of this fourth industrial revolution, there are some challenges with the system of technology standardization that will need to be addressed - internally in private organisations, in the way policy makers leverage the standards system (including the interplay between private industry and public authorities), and, as important, in how incumbent standards development organisations (SDOs) will be forced to change as they strive to stay relevant, for example in how they interact with sector and technology specific industry consortia.

TECHNOLOGY AND STANDARDIZATION UP TO NOW

Mostly technological innovation takes the form of discrete and incremental developments in the area of a product or service – for example how computers have gone from mainframe to tablets over many decades. Accordingly, the focus of technology SDOs was in well-defined silos, for example at ITU (telecommunications)[1], IEC (eletrotechnical)[2], and ISO (technology specific technical committees (TCs) e.g. on health informatics)[3], and standards were developed that focused on individual products or product categories (think telephones, washing machines) or on interfaces enabling interconnection of products, such as the IEEE 802.3[4] series of ethernet standards.

This highly segmented standardization structure enabled suppliers develop products to comply with one or more relevant product-specific standards, with some differences depending on market geography. Once the appropriate product and interface-specific standards were implemented, the result was a well-functioning market with an interoperable set of products and services that leveraged them.

As well as benefitting the consumer, it also meant that manufacturing companies could specify standards-based procurement requirements for machines, products, and services they required for the production process.

Disruptive Technology Developments

However, with recent advances in technology – abundantly more computing power at a fraction of the cost together with the advent of the smartphone ecosystem and the rise of social media - we are now witnessing the 'digitalization of (almost) everything'. While not so welcomed by some incumbents - digitalization has enabled the disintermediation and disruption of many tried and tested service models: travel agents (think SkyScanner™), hotel/guest accommodations (think AirBnB™) - it is certainly a development that garners huge mass consumer appeal.

Once more mature, and some important issues such as trustworthiness of the technology are addressed, digitalization-based disruption will also surely impact some of the more traditional business-related areas e.g. the legal profession. If the smartphone and app ecosystem have enabled massive disruption with solutions such as Uber™, surely it is only a matter of time before a country's land registry could be implemented using DLT, potentially eliminating the need for a solicitor to perform a title check during house or land sales. There is also much discourse underway relating to cryptocurrency eliminating the trusted system of trading based on cash. And, of course, one of the biggest sectors yet to be truly digitized is manufacturing - the 12 trillion USD global industry[5] that in many ways is still rooted in mid-20th century models of limited automation and lengthy complex supply chains, both inbound and outbound.

However, over the past decade, in addition to the advances in computing power mentioned above, several technological innovations have really awakened industry to the paradigm shift that is 'digital manufacturing': miniaturised & low-power sensor development, ultra-high rate wireless communications infrastructure, big data, and artificial intelligence-based machine learning to name a few. These developments, together with the recent explosion in functionality and application areas for additive manufacturing (also referred to as '3D Printing'), indicate that a truly 'digital' manufacturing environment is not so far away. This digital manufacturing ecosystem is seen as a key enabler of the Fourth Industrial Revolution[6], and is becoming an important focus area for government supported research, as can be seem from initiatives such as the European Commission's 'Factory of the Future' project (EFFRA, 2018)[7].

CHALLENGES FOR STANDARDIZATION

Using the concept of digital manufacturing as a case study and focusing on the implications for three key actors in the standardization ecosystem - industry, SDOs, and policy makers - the challenges that 'digitalization of everything' presents to how that ecosystem operates, and potentially must change to stay relevant, are well-illustrated.

There are many challenges to be considered, the entirety of which analysis goes far beyond the purpose of this paper. Some of the more pressing challenges however will be presented, namely those focusing on:

- The acceleration in pace of innovation cycles in a context of relatively slower standards development lifecycles;
- Societal concerns introduced by digitalization;
- Increasing trend of more regional/national policy approaches; and
- A fragmented SDO landscape – digital manufacturing covers a vast technology and process area footprint

THE INDUSTRY VIEW

The technology industry has many years' experience engaging with the standardization system, through both formal SDOs and industry consortia. For example, you will find many of the key technology industry players actively engaged globally in 'ISO/IEC JTC 1 Information technology', the TC responsible for most IT related standards produced by ISO/IEC, which was formed in 1987[8] as an amalgamation, or joint technical committee (JTC), of separate ISO and IEC TCs[9] . This committee has produced and continues to develop many well-known and utilised standards including those used in the areas of SQL, RFID, programming languages, JPEG formats, cybersecurity and more recently standards for cloud & distributed platforms, AI, and IoT[10]. At the same time many industry players also engage in the specifications development work of consortia such as the World Wide Web Consortium (W3C)[11], which was established in 1994, and produces many of the specifications and protocols that are core to the operation of the world wide web, such as HTTP, and, consortia established more recently, and more relevant in the context of digital manufacturing such as the Industrial Internet of Things (IIoT) Consortium[12].

Though formal standardization bodies, such as ISO, which are national member body driven, out of necessity operate differently to the approach utilized in industry consortia such as W3C, it is clear that industry recognises the need for both - amongst the W3C's 475 members[13], is a list of many significant technology companies, whom also take part via national member bodies in countries around the world in the formal standards system[14].

Resource Utilization

In fact, in recognition of the importance of the role played by both SDO and consortia, there are examples of formal links between both entities whereby the specifications developed by consortia can be adopted by SDOs through a well-defined process and published as international standards. The ISO/IEC JTC 1 Publicly Available Specifications (PAS) Process is a good example of this, whereby currently thirteen consortia have been approved by JTC 1 as PAS Submitters, resulting in 100's of consortia specifications being published as ISO/IEC standards. Implementation of this process means that ISO/IEC JTC 1 can identify and embrace specifications that are complimentary to its work program and thereby avoid duplication of effort.

While embraced by ISO/IEC JTC 1, endorsement of consortia specifications by other international standards organisations is not as common place. As both consortia and SDOs begin to engage more in development of specifications/standards in areas relevant to digital manufacturing e.g. machine learning, defining interfaces between factory floor, office & supply chain, MES and ERP[15], such collaboration will become more important. In its absence, there will be significant challenges around resource allocation for industry subject matter experts (SMEs), and as illustrated below, gaining the support of senior management for any such engagement is always a challenge. And without such SMEs engaged, standards will simply not be produced, or at least will not be produced in a timely fashion with optimum quality. In recognition of this fact it is encouraging to see the recent establishment of a strategic group within the IEC (SG 13)[16] to investigate how IEC can structure itself to work more closely with consortia. At the same time ETSI has agreed to re-visit its policy on working with consortia[17].

Broader Internal Engagement Required

By definition, as digitalization expands into more and more aspects of business, the range of stakeholders that need to be engaged in its implementation widens. It would make sense, for example, that a smart contract with a key component supplier implemented via a DLT would involve experts from many teams across a company – legal, procurement, IT, finance, production operations, etc.

While early innovators in this area are experimenting with DLT and piloting use cases in many sectors, there is also standardization work ongoing on smart contracts. One of the most active groups on smart contracts is in WG X of 'ISO/TC 307 Blockchain & DLT'[18]. While it is encouraging to see such initiatives take off it is critical that industry representation in the working group is representative of the cross-section of relevant functional areas. This can be a challenge internally for some companies, whereby functions typically not engaged in external standards activity need to be convinced of the benefit to such engagement. Traditionally, for technology-focused companies, standards departments needed to only engage SMEs from engineering or IT as the standards being developed were firmly in the technology domain. With digitalization, as the example above illustrates, the stakeholder group constituency is much broader. Standardization professionals will now and in the future need to produce more compelling company-wide strategic positions demonstrating why executives across multiple functions in the company need to resource staff to participate in standards development activity. Both SDOs and industry standards professionals need to work to develop persuasive and compelling value-based propositions for when and why management need to resource participation in standards development.

Standards Advocacy

What of course what would help when making any external resourcing decision is a recognition by the wider industry, policy makers, and the ecosystem at large of the valuable role that standards play. With the increasingly negative noise around 'tech', and in particular technology companies engaged in generation and processing of large amounts of personal data, this is becoming increasingly important[19].

It is widely recognised, and previously highlighted in this paper, that digitalization has been and continues to disrupt many sectors and is core to the concept of digital manufacturing. Key to the enablement of digitalization is the availability of masses of data – both personal and non-personal. With such reliance on significant amounts of personal data the concerns around privacy, security, ethics, and trustworthiness inevitably are to the fore. While it is important that policy makers where necessary introduce legislation & regulations to ensure such personal data are adequately protected, it is key that such initiatives leverage the standardization system where relevant.

Unfortunately, this is not always the case. For example, in early drafts of the recent European Commission proposal for an EU Cybersecurity Act (European Commission, 2018) there were provisions in the Act whereby ENISA[20] could codify technical specifications into sector specific certification schemes rather than refer to already published standards. And this system, the way it was initially envisaged, did not provide for a direct industry participation mechanism in the drafting of any such technical specifications. After consultation with relevant stakeholders, the final version of the Act has been modified to support participation of industry experts in the development of certification schemes.

While of course industry and other participants in the development of standards should do everything they can to ensure timely delivery of relevant cybersecurity standards (so that they may be referenced by certifcation schemes), it is also critical that industry continues to work to advocate with policy makers to illustrate both the benefits of the existing standardization system, and, how it is vital that industry has the ability to participate directly in any discussions around technical specification and standards for this and any future certifcation schemes.

STANDARDS SETTERS

As discussed in the previous section, formal SDOs and consortia have co-existed for many years now, sometimes working together and other times effectively competing to develop relevant standards for the same target audience. One of the main differentiators is that consortia always operate in a bottom-up mode working on standardizing topics only of interest to members., those areas, in some cases, being of interest to as little as a handful of founding member companies. At the same time the work programs of SDOs such as ISO and IEC (or CEN and CENELEC in Europe) is decided by agreement amongst the global national member body participants (of which there can be up to 160 but typically at least 40-50 active countries on a given topic), or sometimes in the case of CEN/CENELEC in response to European Commission mandates for standards to support legislation[21].

This difference in mode of operation between SDO and consortia, by definition, means that consortia have traditionally been nimbler and more efficient at producing standardisation deliverables. As SDOs did not have as much focus on hi-tech areas (compared to consortia) this efficiency difference has not mattered so much and industry participants engaged with both depending on their needs. It has been generally acceptable, and some would say necessary, for IEC to take many years to develop a complex standard related to electromagnetic compatibility test methods for electronic equipment[22] such as laptop computers. However, on the other hand, it is critical that consortia such as the Bluetooth SIG[23] exist to (relatively) rapidly develop new interface specifications each time that Bluetooth technology advances to the next iteration. Industry must, and do, take part in both activities.

Mode of Operation

The infiltration of digitalization across all vertical application areas will, and is, requiring a fresh look at this status quo. Technologies used to enable digitalization are no longer niche and are relevant right across the digital manufacturing lifecycle e.g. cloud computing, IoT, and more recently still AI/ML. Three to five-year standards development lifecycles that are typical for some projects at SDOs such as ISO and IEC will not be adequate to support the rapid pace of development in digital manufacturing industry requirements[24].

One challenge is the current model of standards development where experts from around the globe meet face-to-face two or three times a year for a week, or even longer in some cases. This has advantages, not least in building rapport amongst team members. However, it proves very challenging for many experts especially from small and medium enterprises to fund this travel and dedicate time away from the office. To address this, SDOs will most likely be faced with introducing some mix of face-to-face and remote meetings.

The ISO Technical Management Board (TMB) has recognised this fact and is undertaking a number of initiatives in an attempt to address the challenge. One such initiative is a pilot project at 'ISO/TC 301 Energy management and energy savings', whereby a standard will be developed from start to finish using only electronic virtual meeting methods. It will be interesting to see how this develops as it will introduce a new dynamic around participant engagement and behaviour when everybody is not physically in the same room; perhaps it will impact on efficiency when trying to establish consensus. ISO is not alone in this regard with ETSI reporting in 2018 that is was also instigating discussions around potential for use of new standardisation tools 'for direct online collaboration (beyond) direct participation'. The TMB has also established a task force on project management aimed at reducing the development time for standards, and is focusing for example on training material for experts on methodology for how to introduce new work, often a source of delay by many months before a project can get started.

And recognising the need for more participation by innovators in digital transformation, perhaps one of the more relevant panel discussions in this context at this year's ISO General Assembly was around the challenge of how to engage younger experts and start-ups form the tech field – these are key stakeholders in terms of digital transformation. It was recognised that ISO needs to improve its image and some suggestions tabled were around getting younger participants to speak on panels, promoting same more heavily on social media, and maybe 'repackaging' standards content into digestible video clips.

Embracing Open Source?

Outside of these operational challenges, another topic that has been escalating in the recent past is should and how SDOs embrace the significant expansion in open source initiatives that are operating in the digital transformation space.

Recognizing this needs to be discussed and analysed, ISO/IEC JTC 1 resolved in November at its Plenary meeting to establish a study group on Open Source Software (OSS). The study group will investigate amongst the JTC 1 sub-committees, many of which are working on topics that enable digitalization (for example cloud, IoT, cybersecurity & privacy, AI) if the experts can identify requirements/needs/opportunities with regard to OSS in the context of the work programs they envisage in their technical areas. Part of the study will also investigate where OSS has been utilised in standardization previously, both within and beyond JTC 1.

One of the key friction points when it comes to discussions around OSS and standardization is the topic of intellectual property rights (IPR). Open source initiatives, by definition, operate on a royalty free (RF) basis, and so the (patent) licensing and copyright issues surrounding inclusion of OSS in formal published standards is a complication yet to be successfully addressed. There are two contentious aspects: firstly, unlike with the RF IPR policy applying to OSS, both ISO and IEC IPR policies operate the FRAND[25] model (Contreras, 2017), whereby essential patent holders can charge reasonable licensing fees to implementors of a standard containing a standard essential patent (SEP); and, secondly, a significant portion of the revenue generated by ISO and IEC is via publication sales.[26] Striking a balance between these competing objectives is needed if the potential benefit to utilising OSS where relevant is desirable, whereby, for example, some limited number of RF projects could take place at ISO, IEC. For now, however, the JTC 1 study group will not address IPR matters, but rather defer them until the study group first reports on the existing or nascent need for integrating OSS.

From the example of both this JTC 1 OSS study group, and the operational issues mentioned in the previous section, it is clear that SDOs are aware of the need to continuously innovate. ISO and IEC will therefore be studying with interest the discussions ongoing around 'Standards-As-A-Service', or put another way, a 'pay-per-use' model. Very relevant for digital manufacturing, the concept is that a machine can 'pay' (or rent if you like) for each use/implementation of a standard, or even part of one. This idea, amongst many other innovation topics, are under discussion at IEC's Market Strategy Board (MSB)[27]

STANDARDS AND POLICY MAKERS

Policy makers have historically recognised the benefits standards bring to developing markets and international trade, and, conversely, how the absence of common technical specifications has a detrimental effect on global trade.

International Trade

It was just after World War II in 1947 that both GATT (since renamed to the World Trade Organisation[28] (WTO)) and ISO were founded. It was at that time recognised that world peace needs international trade, and international trade can only work if supported by international standards – while import tariffs can slow down trade, lack of standards can stop it dead. And while there is now an increasing trend towards regionalism/nationalism it is encouraging to know that there are 22 countries currently applying to become WTO members.

There is however a challenge in relation to a lack of understanding amongst policy makers and regulators of the role that standards play in global trade. In a keynote address at the 2018 ISO GA the WTO Director General, Mr. Alan Wolf, strongly encouraged SDOs and industry to play a more proactive role in reaching out to regulators demonstrating to them the success stories around standards, and for industry – through educating its senior executives – to support WTO in negotiations on multilateral trading policy efforts. Mr. Wolf also highlighted the Standards for Trade Development Fund (STDF)[29], and that there where would be merit in promoting this instrument to help develop quality in-country standards-based product assessment infrastructures particularly in developing countries

Ensuring a Broad Stakeholder Base

In addition to fostering trade, a key objective for policy makers is balancing the needs of all societal stakeholders and achieving this balance in the standardization sphere is no different. While in most developed countries the government does not directly develop standards, it is incumbent on them to introduce and promote policies that encourage the widest possible stakeholder engagement in a bottom-up industry-led system.

A good example of this stakeholder collaboration can be seen via the European Union's (EU) Multi-stakeholder Platform (MSP). The MSP was established under the provisions of the so-called standardization regulation in Europe in 2012 (European Parliament and Council, 2012). The MSP is a key forum for dialogue between multiple stakeholders - policy makers, EU member states, industry, SDOs, consortia, consumer organisations - to engage in standardization discussions around ICT-related topics in the context of EU policy objectives. Recently on the agenda has been discussion relating to standardization in the area of AI. One of the significant achievements of the MSP is that it enables consortia specifications to be 'identified'[30] and therefore classified as suitable for use in public procurement specifications throughout Europe.

The US standardization infrastructure is predominantly a bottom-up system whereby ANSI effectively sub-contracts standards development activity to technical advisory groups (TAGs). These TAGs are ANSI accredited which ensures the integrity of the system and adherence to the normal WTO-based principles of SDO operation – transparency, openness, coherence, consensus, voluntary application, independence from special interests and efficiency. Membership of TAGs is open to all stakeholder types.

And in China, which has traditionally been a very top-down approach controlled by government, the introduction of the China Standardisation Law (CSL) in 2017 (Standardization Administration of China, 2017)[31] has introduced some reforms that enable a wider stakeholder constituency. With the introduction of the CSL, foreign multinational companies may become members of TCs and working groups within the Standards Administration of China (SAC). However, voting rights are still heavily influenced by Chinese companies in the TC structure. On another positive note the practice of mandatory local and regional standards has been ceased, with only national standards now being considered as candidates for mandatory application. The introduction of 'social organizations' (effectively akin to consortia) is also seen as positive, though some concern exists with the potential for fast-tracking standards produced by social organisations that may have embedded IP owned by China companies into the international standards system.

Policy Approaches Around Digitalization

As has been illustrated, the major regional and national governments are mostly cognisant of the role that standards can play. However, as digitalization continues to disrupt more and more, and consumers are becoming more concerned with the trustworthiness of digital products and services, there is a tendency for policy makers to rush to regulation as a solution. As mentioned earlier, the EU Cybersecurity Act introduces the development of sector specific certification schemes, led by ENISA. But early drafts, which did not allow for direct industry engagement, potentially allowed for ENISA to codify technical specifications in the provisions of a certification scheme(s) rather than referring to published standards for technical requirements. This despite many years' successful experience with the EU's New Approach and latterly the New Legislative Framework[32], enabling market access across the EU single market (28 Member States & 500 million citizens) for products, and founded on the principle of presumption of conformity based on published harmonised standards.

On a positive note, in the context of the European Commission initiative 'Digitising European Industry' (DEI) the MSP has proven yet again to be a useful forum for standards discussion. In this case a working group of the MSP was established to produce a roadmap of standards needs in support of DEI (the DEI-WG). DEI-WG is made up of interested parties from industry, SDOs, consortia, and alliances. The first phase of this work was recently completed, where the standardisation needs for supporting DEI were identified and, secondly, based on these needs, the gaps in the body of published standards also identified[33]. The DEI-WG is now working on producing a roadmap to address these gaps and working on a synchronisation model between participants to avoid duplication of effort.

Though more hands-off in the direct development of standards, through policy measures the US Government can and does also indirectly influence the standardisation system. In the context of digital manufacturing this can be seen via the recent publication of a standardisation roadmap by the America Makes & ANSI Additive Manufacturing Standardization Collaborative (AMSC)[34] – America Makes essentially comes under the auspices of the National Center for Defense Manufacturing and Machining (NCDMM). This roadmap identifies gaps in both the research required and standards development activity needed to support the expansion of the additive manufacturing sector in the US.

And with China's 'Made in China 2025' policy approach hoping to bring Chinese-based manufacturing up the value chain also focusing on standardisation of digitalization topics (including AI and additive manufacturing), it is important that these three major geographies of EU, US, and China work together at international SDOs such as ISO and IEC to develop standards that can be leveraged in multilateral trade agreements between them.

One of the criticisms of the current standardization system is that it moves too slowly. From initiation of a new work item to final publication of a standard it is not uncommon for a four-year development period to have elapsed. While there are valid reasons, in some cases, for such a lengthy development lifecycle – producing a standard of 100s of pages of technical content that has been agreed by up to 160 countries is no mean feat – this process simply will not suffice in a world of ever decreasing innovation cycles. Promotion by government of policies that leverage further the work of industry consortia involved in producing standards would almost certainly be beneficial[35]. To help with promoting these policies it would also be beneficial for governments to promote efforts in the area of 'education in standardization', in both formal education curricula – aimed at the next batch of innovators, standardizers, and policy makers - and with current policy makers. One of the actions in the EU's Joint Initiative on Standardisation (JIS) focused on this aspect (European Commission, 2016).

CONCLUSION AND NEXT STEPS

It is widely accepted that traditional methods of raw material distribution, manufacturing, and product delivery to the customer are contributing to the ongoing impact on the environment and that more sustainable solutions are desirable, if not indeed an imperative. While demand-side policy initiatives aimed at reduced consumption, and, where such reduction is difficult or not possible, initiatives aimed at reuse, are beneficial it is difficult to see with the projected rise in global population allied with growing consumerism in the developing world, how demand can be maintained at sustainable levels. It is therefore incumbent upon us to devise new methods for fulfilling this demand with sustainable methods.

'Digital manufacturing' has the potential to contribute in a significant way to the goal of a sustainable production-consumption model by driving a paradigm-shift in the way goods are produced and delivered: eliminating waste though mass customization; none or greatly reduced requirement for inventory holding; drastic reduction in supply chain footprint (inbound & outbound). Digital manufacturing will most likely also contribute greatly to achieving the objectives of Goal 12 'Responsible Consumption and Production'[36] of the UN Sustainable Development Goals[37] initiative.

While additive manufacturing (or 3D printing) is at the core of this manufacturing renaissance, essentially enabling the democratization of manufacturing, allowing product to be produced effectively at the point of consumption, it is only a subset of the necessary digital manufacturing ecosystem. To make digital manufacturing a reality, and hence realise the desirable benefits around sustainability, in addition to the innovation required in the additive manufacturing process itself (more materials needed, improved part quality, speed etc.) there is a need to redefine the way products are envisaged, manufactured, and tested – this is what 'digital manufacturing' can deliver on.

Standards are key to making this happen and there are some activities underway for example at ASTM (F42)[38], at ISO (TC 261)[39], and on file formats at the 3MF Consortium[40]. But to really drive the transformation this will require industry, standards setters, and policy makers to think differently. Standardization gaps have been identified, (see reference to AMSC Roadmap highlighted earlier in this paper), now coordination is required between all parties concerned.

As well as coordinating with each other, each of these entities needs to review its own internal operations. Industry will need to engage, in addition to its technology SMEs, SMEs from all aspects of its business (e.g. legal, procurement, finance) in the standards setting process. SDOs used to protracted development lifecycles will need to devise new ways of deciding on which standards are required (including coordination with consortia) and how to accelerate development lifecycles. And, policy makers need to continuously optimise standardization frameworks, including those in support of regulatory frameworks, such that innovation and coherence across industry sectors and geographies are possible.

In summary, the disruption that is digital manufacturing, if it's to be realised, will require a parallel disruption in the system of standardization.

REFERENCES

Contreras, J. L. (2017). *Technical Standards, Standards-Setting Organizations and Intellectual Property: A Survey of the Literature (with an Emphasis on Empirical Approaches).* Retrieved 10 January 2019 from https://papers.ssrn.com/sol3/Delivery.cfm/SSRN_ID3034557_code1335192.pdf?abstractid=2900540&mirid=1

EFFRA (Ed.). (2018). *Factories of the Future Public-Private Partnership. Progress Monitoring Report for 2017.* Retrieved from https://www.effra.eu/sites/default/files/fof_cppp_progress_monitoring_report_for_2017_online.pdf

European Commission (Ed.). (2016). *Joint Initiative on Standardisation.* Retrieved on 12 January 2019 from http://ec.europa.eu/DocsRoom/documents/22722/attachments/1/translations/en/renditions/native

European Commission (Ed.). (2018). *Proposal for a Regulation of the European Parliament and of the Council.* COM(2018) 630 final. Retrieved 15 January 2019 from http://ec.europa.eu/newsroom/dae/document.cfm?doc_id=54252

European Parliament and Council (Eds). (2012). *Regulation (EU) No 1025/2012 of the European Parliament and of the Council of 25 October 2012 on European standardisation.* Retrieved 22 December 2018 from https://eur-lex.europa.eu/legal-content/EN/TXT/PDF/?uri=CELEX:32012R1025&from=EN

Standardization Administration of China. (2017). *Standardization Law of the People's Republic of China.* Retrieved 12 December 2018 from http://www.sesec.eu/app/uploads/2017/09/SESEC-III-translation-China-Standardization-Law-2nd-reading-20170905.pdf

ENDNOTES

1 https://www.itu.int/en/Pages/default.aspx
2 https://www.iec.ch/
3 https://www.iso.org/technical-committees.html
4 http://www.ieee802.org/
5 As of 2014 https://www.nam.org/newsroom/top-20-facts-about-manufacturing/

6 https://www.forbes.com/sites/bernardmarr/2018/08/13/the-4th-industrial-revolution-is-here-are-you-ready/#50f4802d628b

7 See also http://ec.europa.eu/research/industrial_technologies/factories-of-the-future_en.html

8 JTC 1 history page https://jtc1historyblog.wordpress.com/

9 ISO/TC 97 and IEC/TC 83

10 As of January 2019 JTC 1 has published 3175 standards and currently has 517 under development https://www.iso.org/committee/45020.html

11 https://www.w3.org/

12 https://www.iiconsortium.org/about-us.htm

13 https://www.w3.org/Consortium/Member/List#xA

14 Companies such as Microsoft, Apple, Google, Huawei, IBM

15 Manufacturing Execution Systems & Enterprise Resource Planning

16 https://www.iec.ch/dyn/www/f?p=103:85:16738408798351::::FSP_ORG_ID,FSP_LANG_ID:22292,25

17 https://www.etsi.org/about/our-partnerships

18 https://www.iso.org/committee/6266604.html

19 https://www.theguardian.com/technology/2018/jan/28/tech-backlash-facebook-google-fake-news-business-monopoly-regulation

20 European Union Agency for Network and Information Security (https://www.enisa.europa.eu/)

21 For example, standards for GSM radio performance under the Radio Equipment Directive

22 CISPR 32 is an example that took 7 years to develop and publish (https://webstore.iec.ch/publication/22046)

23 https://www.bluetooth.com/

24 ISO reported at is General Assembly in September 2018 that the average time over past twelve months for development of deliverables is 33.1 months

25 See e.g. (Contreras, 2017).

26 https://www.iso.org/files/live/sites/isoorg/files/about%20ISO/annual_reports/en/annual_report_2017_en.pdf

27 https://www.iec.ch/dyn/www/f?p=103:47:0::::FSP_ORG_ID,FSP_LANG_ID:3261,25

28 https://www.wto.org/

29 http://www.standardsfacility.org/

30 Articles 13 and 14 of Regulation 1025/2012

31 The official Chinese version may be found at http://www.npc.gov.cn/npc/xinwen/2017-11/04/content_2031446.htm

32 https://ec.europa.eu/growth/single-market/goods/new-legislative-framework_en

33 https://ec.europa.eu/digital-single-market/en/news/communication-digitising-european-industry-reaping-full-benefits-digital-single-market

34 https://www.ansi.org/standards_activities/standards_boards_panels/amsc/Default

35 This is already done via JTC 1 PAS and by Regulation 1025/2012 identification process

36 https://www.iso.org/sdg12.html

37 https://www.un.org/sustainabledevelopment/

38 https://www.astm.org/COMMITTEE/F42.htm

39 https://www.iso.org/committee/629086.html

40 https://3mf.io/

Section 2

Internal Standardization Management in Industry and Administration

Chapter 4
Standardization as an Organizational Capability:
Examples From a Global Player in the Information and Communication Technology Industry

Magnus Johansson
Lund University, Sweden

Niklas L. Hallberg
Lund University, Sweden

ABSTRACT

This chapter examines the organizational capabilities that firms develop in order to influence and adapt to standards. Standards are voluntary rules or guidelines developed by standard-setting organizations or consortia in order to promote compatibility/interoperability, minimum quality, variety reduction, and information. The authors argue that firms develop specific capabilities for assessing which emerging standards are likely to become dominant, and in order to successfully influence the development of new standards. The argument is illustrated by a case study of a global player in the information and communication technology sector.

INTRODUCTION

Is standardization an organizational capability? If so, how is a standardization capability organized? Standards are voluntary (consensus-oriented) rules or guidelines developed by standard-developing organizations (SDOs) or consortia in order to promote compatibility/interoperability, minimum quality, variety reduction, and information (Blind, 2004). Standards constitute the main output of SDOs, but may also arise as output from industry consortia. Famous standards battles between rival consortia include Blu-ray versus HD-DVD, USB versus Firewire, and WiFi versus HomeRF (see van den Ende, van de

DOI: 10.4018/978-1-5225-9008-8.ch004

Copyright © 2019, IGI Global. Copying or distributing in print or electronic forms without written permission of IGI Global is prohibited.

Kaa, den Uijl, and de Vries, 2012). Standardization activity is often described as driven by individual employees with a personal interest in the focal technology. While this is true in certain industries, where standardization does not have a very large effect on firms' competitiveness, we argue that firms in many industries are forced by competition to develop specific organizational capabilities in order to assess which emerging standards are likely to become dominant, to successfully influence the development of new standards, and to implement new standards when in place. To illustrate and support our argument, we present an empirical example describing the standardization activities and organization of a global firm in the information and communication technology (ICT) industry.

We argue that firms face two key challenges related to standardization: First, industries subject to technological change place high demands on incumbents in terms of the efficient adoption of, and adaptation to, new or emerging standards. The challenge for firms involves early spotting of technological trajectories and identifying competing interests in the industry, as well as having the ability to judge who is likely to succeed in making their standard dominant. These activities are not costless, requiring extensive investments in specific processes, routines, information technology, and organization. Second, firms are not just passive recipients of externally imposed standards (for instance, by SDOs), but are also active participants in the development and implementation of these standards. Whether standards evolve through technical committees in SDOs or through the work of consortia formed by some subset of the industry incumbents, the potential competitive impact of standards once in place creates pressures on the individual firm to devote resources, and develop specific routines and processes, to influence the emerging standard in ways that are beneficial to the focal firm (for example, to promote technology that is complementary to patents or other forms of assets owned by the firm [see Teece, 1986]). We refer to the ability of firms to efficiently perform these sets of activities as having a standardization capability.

BACKGROUND

What Is an Organizational Capability?

There is a large body of literature on the nature and dynamics of organizational capabilities (see Dosi, Nelson, & Winter, 2000, for an overview). Capability typically refers to a "high-level routine (or collection of routines) that, together with its implementing input flows, confers upon an organization's management a set of decision options for producing significant outputs of a particular type" (Winter, 2003: 991). While so-called *zero-level capabilities* include normal functional capabilities, such as logistics, manufacturing, sales, etc., that "permit a firm to 'make a living' in the short term" (Winter, 2003: 991), scholars have also recognized that firms may be more or less skilled at activities that are important for their survival in the medium to long term. Such capabilities include *dynamic capabilities* that allow firms to adapt and change their zero-level capabilities in response to dynamic environmental conditions (Collis, 1994; Teece, Pisano, and Shuen, 1997; Winter, 2003). Closely related to dynamism of capabilities are integrative capabilities. These integrate external knowledge into the organization, or integrate internal resources or capabilities of the organization, which differentiates them from lower-level day-to-day problem-solving capabilities (Yeoh & Roth, 1999). In addition, the notion of capabilities has more recently been extended to include activities related to strategic alliances (Anand & Khanna, 2000; Heimeriks & Duysters, 2007; Kale, Singh, Perlmutter, 2000), contract design (Mayer & Argyres, 2004), and governance (Argyres, Felin, Foss, & Zenger, 2012). Generally, this extant research has shown that firms exhibit differential learning (or capabilities) in identifying and implementing an efficient institutional structure for economic relationships. We argue that this also translates into the area of standardization. Hence, in industries where standards are important for economic performance, it is reasonable to conjecture that firms will develop specific capabilities to deal with the competitive challenges that are associated with the standardization process.

Standards, Economic Effects, and Gaining Competitive Advantage

A standard is a published document that sets specifications and processes to ensure that a product or service functions as it was meant to, fulfills the purpose it was intended for, and reliably performs according to intentions (National Standards Advisory Committee Australia, 2006). Standards may be either formal or informal. An often-applied distinction claims that formal standards originate from SDOs and committees, and are based on negotiation processes and voluntary consensus, whereas informal standards are initiated by industry consortia or even individual companies, and achieve market dominance through market selection and competition (Blind, 2004, 2011; see also Farrell & Saloner, 1988 for a discussion on the differences in selection processes).[1] We adopt a slightly different distinction in order to delimit the focus of this research. In this study, we consider both standards of a formal nature and standards resulting from other types of consensus-oriented organizations, such as consortia. These are contrasted by *de facto* standards, which are widely adopted products, services, and practices that have not been subject to a consensus-based adoption decision (see Egyedi & Blind, 2008). The focus on formal SDOs as well as consortia (henceforth, we refer to all consensus-based standardization bodies as *standardization organizations*) reflects the changes in standardization settings of industries in the ICT sector. In such industries, the traditional standardization structure dominated by official standardization organizations has been challenged by a multitude of regional SDOs, as well as private standardization consortia and forums (Werle, 2011).

Why are standards useful in some contexts? According to Blind (2004) and Swann (2000), different types of standards can have particular positive and negative economic effects. First, standards may help to ensure compatibility and interoperability among different components, products, or systems (see Suarez, 2004). Relevant examples are IT or telecom standards that allow for the creation of direct or indirect network effects between, for instance, operating systems, applications, and hardware. In these situations, direct network effects (or network externalities) materialize when a technology becomes more valuable to the individual user as the number of users increases, while indirect network effects are present when the product becomes more valuable as the number of available complementary products increases (Katz & Shapiro, 1985; Farrell & Saloner, 1985). In addition, the creation of compatible systems has been shown to reduce switching costs and lock-in effects, and improve supply chain coordination (Stigzelius & Mark-Herbert, 2009). Second, there are minimum quality and safety standards that set the necessary requirements of products and signal these requirements to buyers. For example, standards on the minimum requirements for health and adult social care serve as a guarantee to the potential user or customer (Care Quality Commission, 2010). Such standards may reduce information asymmetries, adverse selection, and transaction costs (Den Butter, Groot, and Lazrak, 2007; Blind, 2004). Third, there are also variety reduction standards that reduce the variety of inputs to enable mass production, efficient distribution, and economies of scale (Blind, 2004; Farrell & Saloner, 1985). One example is engineering standards that describe the materials that should be used as inputs in a production process. The adoption of variety reduction standards makes it easier for firms to communicate with suppliers by preventing conflicts related to desired input characteristics (ANSI, 2018). On the downside, this reduction of variety might discourage product innovation and increase market concentration (Matutes & Regibeau, 1996). Fourth and finally, there are information standards that are created to reduce information asymmetries and transaction costs (Blind, 2004; Tassey, 2000).

A firm's success can in turn vary depending on these economic effects. Schilling (1999) has emphasized firm involvement in standards and standardization as a way to gain competitive advantages. Although standards establish uniformity in markets and among firms, exploitation of the benefits of standards can depend on heterogeneity among other types of resources and capabilities that in turn are interlinked with standards implemented within the market or within the firm. Standardization is therefore in itself not just a collaborative but also a competitive arena. Involvement in standardization is an opportunity for firms to influence industry standards (Leiponen, 2008), which can be highly rewarding; for instance, the firm can influence a standard-setting consensus process to adopt the firm's particular system (Farrell & Saloner, 1988), or try to shape industry technological development in a direction that favors its technological capabilities (Rosenkopf et al., 2001). One example that directly illustrates the link to economic effects of standards is how high-quality producers promote minimum quality standards in order to exclude low-cost/low-quality players from the market—in other words, by raising rivals' costs (Swann, 2000).

Firm Resources and Influencing the Standardization Process

Recognizing the process by which standardization evolves through various structures (SDOs, consortia, etc.) is particularly important in order to understand how the firm can adapt to and influence standardization. As Blind (2004) noted, innovation and standardization processes are linearly related. He further emphasized that *development*-related standardization in particular entails interaction with development processes. It serves the purpose of enabling standardization where needed and of providing information to potential suppliers and customers during the innovation process to prepare them for the market being created.

Rosenkopf et al. (2001) outlined the costs and benefits for firms of participating in cooperative technical organizations, of which standardization organizations are prime examples. Participation requires membership fees, occasional hosting, time and travel of engineers and managers, but also the risk of having to share valuable proprietary information with competitors. The benefits include access to information and knowledge and an opportunity to influence technological development in the industry. For the firm to take advantage of these benefits and influence standard setting in its own interest requires the appropriate resources. For instance, the process of standardization in standardization organizations does not rely solely on technical evaluation but also on resources in the form of social capital. According to Tushman and Rosenkopf (1992), the development and adoption of standards depend on social factors. Dokko and Rosenkopf (2010) distinguished between the role of social capital (in the form of resources embedded in relationships) related to individuals and related to the firm. First, they found that individuals can carry social capital with them to a new firm. Therefore, in addition to interacting with their current human resources in standard setting, such as a standard-setting committee, a firm can hire individuals with resources embedded in their relationships to increase their influence. This is one way of strengthening the social capital of the firm. However, Dokko and Rosenkopf (2010) also found that an outflow of human resources may not necessarily reduce the influence of all firms in the standard setting to the same extent. Participating in technical committee work is not just an arena for influencing standards, but provides access to an interfirm network that stretches beyond the standard-setting context (Dokko & Rosenkopf, 2010). Inversely, other relationships than those based on committee interaction and the resulting social capital may exert influence on the standard setting, such as in the relationship between supplier and buyer. Closer interfirm collaboration is also a possible outcome, as participation in technical organizations can bring about alliance formation between firms (Rosenkopf et al., 2001).

Shapiro and Varian (1999) conducted a wider discussion on resources and capabilities in association with innovation, standard emergence, and dominance. They did not limit their consideration to formal standardization, but provided a broad view of standards wars—that is, the battle between rival technologies to become the industry standard. Of particular interest here are the assets that they identified as crucial to winning a standards war. They mentioned user install base, intellectual property rights (IPR), innovation ability, first-mover advantage, manufacturing capabilities, strength in complements, brand name, and reputation. Suarez (2004) focused specifically on the *ex ante* dynamics of dominant design establishment and standard formation. Similar to Shapiro and Varian (1999), Suarez recognized the role of the firm's technological superiority (which is close to Shapiro and Varian's focus on innovation), complementary assets (complements), credibility (brand and reputation), and install base. Under these headings, Suarez also listed strategic maneuvering factors: entry timing, pricing, licensing, and relationships with complementors, marketing, and PR. Suarez made the environmental factors explicit and viewed these as directly and indirectly affecting technological dominance (the dependent variable).

STRUCTURE AND CHARACTERISTICS OF STANDARDIZATION CAPABILITY

The previous section showed that extant research has outlined how generic resources and capabilities of the firm affect standard setting and technological dominance. This section aims to outline a specific standardization capability based on the routines the firm employs to influence and adapt standardization. The benefits of standardization are normally assumed to affect whole sectors of the economy in a relatively homogeneous way. In addition to these system-wide effects of standards, we conjecture that firms are heterogeneous in their standardization capability, and, as a result, gain differential benefits (and costs) from standards.

Standardization Capability as Routinized Activities

Capabilities can be seen as a collection of routinized activities (Nelson & Winter, 1982; Winter, 2003) or processes (Felin, Foss, Heimeriks & Madsen, 2012). Based on prior research, we can identify three main types of activities of standardization. The first type is of an outside-in nature, channeling information and knowledge towards the firm. According to Rosenkopf et al. (2001), participation in cooperative technical organizations, such as standardization organizations, provides the firm with access to knowledge of standardization, but also to general technical and strategic knowledge within the industry. Rosenkopf et al. emphasized the role of the individual representative in such activities as a carrier of information and knowledge back to the firm.

The second type of activity relates to influencing the interorganizational standardization process in the interest of the firm. This type of activity is directed from the inside-out—that is, from the firm towards the standardization environment. Dokko and Rosenkopf (2010) mentioned two main reasons for the firm to perform activities that influence standard setting in the committees of SDOs. First, the

IPR included in standards can require firms to pay royalties to the license holder. Therefore, influencing standard setting to be in line with the firm's IPR position becomes important. Second, standards aligned with the technological capabilities of a firm may provide long-term competitive advantage as the firm does not have to invest in new technological capabilities. Performing inside-out activities can also help position the firm in the industry and increase awareness from major players. Taking leadership roles in the technical organizations can further increase influence in the industry (Rosenkopf et al., 2001).

The third type of activity is more long term and concerns more fundamental influence on the standardization organizations that surround the firm. One aspect concerns the long-term positioning in the industry via existing standardization organizations, similar to the short-term, inside-out activities mentioned above. Another concerns influencing the overall structure of the standardization landscape, contributing to changes in existing standardization organizations, altering the level or participation in various standardization organizations. This may be particularly important in an environment where an increasing number of consortia and other forums are being established as alternatives to formal SDOs (cf. Werle, 2011).

In order to gain an empirically workable definition and operationalization of standardization capability, we build on Winter's definition of capabilities as a "high-level routine (or collection of routines) that, together with its implementing input flows, confers upon an organization's management a set of decision options for producing significant outputs of a particular type" (Winter, 2003: 991). We also recognize that capabilities are collective constructs (Nelson & Winter, 1982) that coordinate and integrate individual resources (Felin et al., 2012). The routinized activities that substantiate capabilities can also be supported by structures of the organization. Depending on the level of dynamism of a capability, such support can be more or less valid (Felin et al., 2012).

Our definition of standardization capability relies on the following: First, through the definition of capabilities as a routine, or a collection of routines, it follows that standardization capability essentially refers to activities that are directed towards influencing standards (inside-out activities) and adopting standards (outside-in activities). Second, in order for these activities to constitute a capability, they must form a repetitive pattern that ensures a high level of reliability in the performance of activities (Helfat & Peteraf, 2003). Third, the identified standardization activity must be significant for management and the conversion of inputs to outputs (Winter, 2003). The following sections elaborate on the character of standardization capability by considering research in fields relating to an integrative nature of capabilities and capabilities that influence the institutional setting of the firm.

Integrative Character of Standardization Capability

The capabilities literature has provided several examples of distinctions between capabilities that are of an integrative versus a local nature (for instance, integrative versus component capabilities [Henderson & Cockburn, 1994; Yeoh & Roth, 1999] and integrative versus technological capabilities [Verona, 1999]). Integrative capabilities can absorb knowledge from external sources, as well as blend competencies from various internal departments (Verona, 1999), use resources and local (component) capabilities (Yeoh & Roth, 1999), or integrate activities, capabilities, and products across internal and external vertical chains (Helfat & Raubitscheck, 2000). Thus, a key dimension among integrative capabilities is the integration of external knowledge and internal resources and local capabilities. According to Yeoh and Roth (1999), this differentiates them from local capabilities, which are concerned with day-to-day problem solving and regular patterns of activity (Nelson & Winter, 1982).

As can be seen in discussions conducted by Rosenkopf et al. (2001) and Dokko and Rosenkopf (2010), a key aspect of standardization is the transfer of knowledge and information back to the firm from the standardization organization. Thus, a standardization capability can be of an external, integrative nature, following Verona's (1999) outline with respect to the routinized outside-in activities. Regarding the internally integrative aspect, we can turn to previous studies of resources and capabilities in association with standardization. A standardization capability would then serve the purpose of integrating resources and capabilities, such as those outlined in Shapiro and Varian (1999) and Suarez (2004), and in that sense be *internally* integrating (cf. Verona, 1999) with regard to routinized inside-out activities.

Another dimension of integrative capabilities concerns dynamism. For instance, Yeoh and Roth (1999) explicitly stated that integrative capabilities refer to those that support organizational renewal. Verona (1999) was less concerned with dynamism, instead distinguishing between external and internal integrative capabilities, mainly with a focus on product development. The external integrative capabilities include managerial processes (external communication, socialization), managerial systems (empowerment, incentives, recruitment), absorptive structures (networks of collaborations), culture, and values for external absorption. The internal integrative capabilities outlined by Verona are similar to their external counterparts, but instead of absorptive structures they include integrative structures. Verona (1999) provided a relevant view of the distinction between functional and local capabilities due to his focus on product development. Product development represents a type of function and activity that has potential interaction with interorganizational standardization processes in their formative phases—that is, the phases in which standards evolve and contribute to formation of the market.

Although it seems likely that a standardization capability has integrative features, whether it also has dynamic (see the description of integrative and dynamic capabilities in Yeoh & Roth, 1999) or managerial features (see the description of integrative as managerial capabilities in Fortune & Mitchell, 2012) is less certain at first sight. It is possible to imagine higher-level managerial involvement for important IPR or technology issues that threatens product acceptance in the market or leads to vast changes in the structure of the standardization environment. To some extent, standardization capabilities may be more dynamic regarding organizational renewal (Yeoh & Roth, 1999) when it comes to the ability of the firm to renew or alter external organizational entities, such as standardization organizations, in its own interest rather than that of the internal organization. In addition, higher-level managerial participation may very well come indirectly through other resources and capabilities, such as those listed by Shapiro and Varian (1999) or Suarez (2004).

Influencing Institutional Structure

As mentioned in the Introduction, research on capabilities related to contracting, alliances, and governance describe firm capabilities directed at identifying and implementing the institutional structure for economic relationships. The key role of social capital in cooperative technical organizations (Rosenkopf et al., 2001), such as standardization organizations, resembles the role of relational capital in association with alliance capabilities (Kale et al., 2000). However, Kale et al. (2000) and Mayer and Argyres (2004) stressed the role of organizational learning in affecting the institutional structure within which the firm acts. Thus, such a perspective emphasizes an iterative situation in which the firm learns to influence the institutional setting through interchange with it over time. This strong focus on learning makes it slightly different from the idea of integrative capabilities, as it highlights the long-term implications of learning from the environment in order to influence it.

As discussed previously, participating in cooperative technical implementation, such as via standardization organizations, influences technological development and opportunities to position the firm in the industry (Rosenkopf et al., 2001). Such effects of standardization organization participation can be seen as examples of influencing the institutional setting. This can be particularly important in a standardization landscape with an increased presence of alternative standardization organizations such as consortia, as described by Werle (2011). Here, it is important to recognize that compared to, for instance, alliance and contracting capabilities, such an aspect of a standardization capability would be associated with the industry-wide economic outcomes of standardization that the firm sees as beneficial from its own perspective.

A Preliminary Standardization Capability Framework

To sum up the probable character of a standardization capability we can conclude that, in line with influence and adoption, it is likely to consist of three main types of activities: inside-out influencing activities, outside-in adoption activities, and long-term activities in which the firm learns to influence the standardization environment. It will also have an integrative character. Outside-in activities will be externally integrative in that they channel knowledge from the environment, such as through standardization participation. Inside-out activities will be internally integrative in bringing together resources from various functions and local capabilities; for instance, in laying out firm direction of standardization efforts. Dynamism is mainly directed at changes in the organization in relation to external institutions and organizations, such as standardization organizations. Higher-level managerial participation and influence will depend on whether influence is exerted through the activities that provide the foundations of a standardization capability or through other capabilities. In addition, it is important to consider the longer-term standardization influencing aspects of a standardization capability, where the firm learns in order to position itself and influence the industry. The preliminary standardization capability framework is shown in Table 1.

Table 1. Standardization capability framework

	Outside-in activities	Inside-out activities	Longer term activities
Relevance	Significant for Management & Conversion	Significant for Management & Conversion	Significant for Management & Conversion
Routinization	Repetitiveness & Structures	Repetitiveness & Structures	Repetitiveness
Internally integrative		Integrating firm resources and capabilities to influence standardization environment	Integrating firm resources and capabilities to influence standardization environment
Externally integrative	Providing standardization information and knowledge to the firm		Learning to influence the standardization environment
Integrative dynamism		Support of org. renewal - alliances in standardization organizations.	Support of organizational renewal - networks.
Integrative managerial		For strategically relevant standardization decisions (IPR and vast technology changes)	For strategically relevant changes in standardization environment
Organizational learning for institutional influence		Short-term influencing	Long-term altering and creating standardization structures

Standardization capability is theorized as a set of routinized activities that are repetitive and relevant from a managerial and conversion perspective. However, a few question marks remain with regard to the nature and function of standardization capability. To what extent does standardization capability vary in terms of level of integration, dynamism, and managerial influence? To what extent is standardization capability routinized and independent of human capital? For example, while Rosenkopf et al. (2001) highlighted the role of individuals in standardization, others, such as Dokko and Rosenkopf (2010), have recognized the role of collective social capital in the interaction with technology and standardization organizations. In addition, the level of dynamism for each activity type is likely to vary, and with it the number of structures supporting it (Felin et al., 2012). For instance, it is likely that the longer-term influencing activities are more dynamic in nature as they will renew the organization's network resources.

Further, similar to Suarez (2004), we acknowledge that environmental and industry factors will directly influence standard setting and the role of standardization capabilities (such as the character of standardization effects, the network, transaction cost reduction, scale effects, etc.). However, our primary focus in this chapter is to establish the existence and generic character of standardization capability. Hence, limited attention will be paid to environmental and industry contingencies and their potential effect on standardization capability (although we acknowledge that they may be significant). To this end, the following sections apply the framework to an empirical example in order to illustrate and develop the framework further. Of particular interest in these sections is the extent to which activities are routinized and the significance of the performed activities for converting inputs to outputs.

STANDARDIZATION CAPABILITY AT TECHCOMP

Our empirical example covers the standardization activities, organization, and individual skills involved in standardization at a global technology-intensive firm with approximately 5000 employees. The studied firm has been anonymized as "TechComp," and was chosen as an illustration because of its innovative products and its membership in an industry that is known for strong network effects and compatibility requirements that elevate the importance of standards (Blind, 2004). The data was collected in five semi-structured interviews with managers and professionals at TechComp, with each interview lasting between two and four hours. All the interviews were conducted onsite in three different locations, apart from one that was carried out offsite. All interviews were recorded, transcribed, and categorized according to the concepts included in the framework (see Table 1). The respondents and their respective positions in TechComp are shown in Table 2.

Table 2. Respondents at techcomp

Respondent	Position
Alpha	Head of standardization and industry networks
Beta	Standardization Responsible, technology area 1
Gamma	Standardization Responsible, technology area 2
Delta	Strategy Analyst

Empirical Background

TechComp is a member of several standardization organizations, roughly 50 in total. In some cases, the membership is combined with an active role in standardization (technical) committees, and in other instances the position pertains more to monitoring. The chosen position depends on the role that the technology being subject to standardization plays in relation to TechComp's product development. Further, TechComp is mainly focused on developing products by utilizing technologies advanced by research-oriented parts of the industry. It is partly involved in basic technology research, but primarily with the application of technologies, and turning them into new and innovative products. Among the 50 standardization organizations of which TechComp is a member, 10 are subject to more active participation.

Influencing the industry standardization process involves informal alliance building with other players within standardization committees, and finding common ground that can serve as a basis for countering other firms' attempts to influence the standardization process. The standardization may be influenced in a certain direction in order to minimize additional internal development costs by certifying that the standardization follows the same track. Another approach is to exploit weaknesses of competitors by pushing standardization in line with the firm's technological position.

The employees involved in standardization (approximately 30 people) are typically senior, experienced engineers who combine their tasks within the development organization with representing TechComp in standardization committees. They are primarily recruited from the firm's engineering staff, and combine a role within the development organization with their standardization tasks. These employees, besides being senior, have rather extensive social skills that enable them to handle formal and informal interaction in association with the work taking place in the committees. Employees are largely expected to be able to handle their internal and external tasks in an independent fashion. Their tasks are twofold: First, to constantly monitor the standardization process and inform the internal development projects of the direction of standardization and what specifications to adhere to. Second, to influence the standardization process in favor of TechComp and align it with the technological path upon which TechComp has already embarked (where TechComp has a patent advantage).

The standardization staff combines presence in standardization with commitment to and participation in the development organization. The head of standardization has three main standardization group managers reporting to him. They are responsible for different technological areas with which a number of SDOs and consortia are associated. In turn, the group managers have a number of standardization professionals reporting to them. These individuals, as discussed above, work closely with the development organization and participate in day-to-day work contributing to development activities. From a budgetary perspective, they are also part of the development organization.

Standardization Activities

Bringing standards inside the firm. Standardization representatives of TechComp interact with representatives of competitors, suppliers, customers, and other industry players in standardization committee work. This primarily involves coordinative action during formal meetings of the standardization organizations. Staff involved in standardization inform and influence the development of TechComp while participating in such activities. The following quote, from Beta, illustrates the importance of being present in the committee work from the perspective of the firm and its product development: "you always have the advantage of having been there at the meeting, having access to first-hand information, and having heard the discussion. This allows you to read between the lines in the standard, which is of great help."

A further quote from Beta illustrates how staff working with standardization and R&D (Research and Development) bring knowledge and information back to the R&D activities: "For me, and this is what I explain to people, we do not want a big organization for standardization. It is very important for us that the people who derive the standardization are the ones [that are] also involved in R&D projects. Because if you want to be active … for something not just for fun, you must be part of the activity. … There is a big difference between being active and passive in the specification. [By being] active in developing standardization you do understand the spec. You know why these parameters [equal] this one and so on. You know all the tricks for your product. So you will go very fast. If you have been passive somebody will give you the spec and you start to read it, it is very complex, trying to understand each chapter … For me, standardization is part of innovation and R&D. If you keep your engineers behind the computers doing the job and so on it is not good. You must expose your engineer to competitors, to other people."

Alpha also emphasized the role of staff combining their R&D tasks with standardization tasks: "One of the advantages of this … organization is that the individuals who work with standardization have one foot in the development organization and one foot in standardization operations. [In that way] they are very good information carriers. Because standardization is a two-way street; to be efficient in standardization meetings requires a hell of a lot of knowledge. You need to be able to judge in a moment if a proposal is good or bad for us."

This is in line with the channeling of information and knowledge as described by Rosenkopf et al. (2001) and the preliminary framework. It particularly shows the importance of continuously following the industry innovation process taking place in association with standardization in order to keep up with other players. Thus, outside-in-oriented activities certify the alignment between the internal development process and the interorganizational standardization process in order to adapt to industry standards. Such activities involve coordination among internal parties, as well as towards external parties.

Influencing standard setting. The inside-out-oriented activities reveal that TechComp influences the standardization process as far as possible in its own interest so that it aligns with internal development and the IPR to which TechComp has access, and thus reduces costs. Of particular importance here are activities that enable escalating standardization issues internally in order to influence the standardization process at a higher level, beyond the workgroup and development level. These activities are also of an integrative nature. They involve gathering information as a participant in development around the technological development trajectory and the solutions chosen by TechComp. Externally, they involve coordinated action both during formal meetings as well as in informal settings outside of the arrangements of the standardization organizations. Another internal integrative activity is of an internal, vertical nature: that of evaluating key standardization issues with the inclusion of more senior standardization staff and of escalating and anchoring, and thus enabling, cooperative action with other industry players. `

Longer-term influencing activities. The case also illustrates the need for activities oriented toward the long-term. We can divide these into two parts based on the empirical case: (1) activities related to resource acquisition that primarily certify that standardization professionals can be recruited to the organization, and (2) activities related to evaluating, prioritizing among, and, when needed, creating or influencing the structure of standardization organizations. We will address the third category in more detail in the section titled "Influencing standardization organization structure and learning."

Routinization

The standardization organization of TechComp indicates a certain stability in the way in which activities are performed. The standardization organization, which is a hierarchical structure in which the standardization professionals double as development staff, thus facilitates activities and communication of issues that require cooperation among standardization staff within the firm. Although budget-wise the majority of the standardization staff are associated with development, the standardization hierarchy certifies a certain level of reporting and cooperation stability.

In addition, the structure of the work streams within one of the key technological areas of TechComp reveal a specific way of working and of controlling short- and long-term directions on an organizational level. Therefore, the organization displays standardization activities that are repetitive enough to formalize ways of working over a longer time period. The activities thus seem to be coordinative (involving several individuals within and outside of standardization), as well as repetitive enough to certify reliability. Structures are also in place to support the activities directed towards participation in standard setting in standardization organizations, and of influencing it and bringing knowledge back into the firm, as described by Alpha:

"We have a work model for that. If we take [one of the prime technological areas] we have four work streams with slightly different emphasis. Here there are a number individuals working with this. It is typically one to two [people] who go to meetings and some of them that work back office. Back office may be those who work at home with analysis and suggestions and help to formulate input papers to meetings, help to analyze the suggestions of others to see what we think of them … So, it looks like this in all of these four. For each [standardization] work stream there is a small steering committee. In the steering committee there are people from the standardization organization, development organization, and from R&D. … To guide the work in each workstream, once a year a statement is written. It is a document that controls and sets guidelines for what to do in this kind of work stream for the next 12 months."

Relevance

Standardization activities at TechComp directly influence product development, either through enabling adoption and adherence to evolving standards or through affecting creation of the market through standardization by bringing key technical development items of TechComp to the standardization process. Therefore, standardization activities have a strong bearing on the conversion of input to output of TechComp, as well as the firm's value-capture opportunities. Standards set in the most important standardization organization have a huge impact on products developed not just by TechComp but by all players in the industry. The following quote, from Gamma, illustrates the importance of aligning with the standards of the most important standardization organization: "Of course, the main issue and the main topic most of the time is [standardization organization 2]. And actually, that's the organization that more or less defines the system specification that your implementation needs to be compliant with." Another quote, from Beta, also illustrates the need for, and the reasons for being present in, standardization organizations: "Sure, cost is a reason, but it is not the first one. You cannot jeopardize your business because of cost. There is a list of standardization organizations where you cannot go out, no way. There is no way. For example … [standardization organizations 3–6], because they are impacting so many business units that you would screw up everybody. Because you would have no more access to the spec, no more access to certification."

Thus, standardization is highly relevant for the products developed and also, since TechComp is heavily dependent on R&D activities, for the input to output conversion. Another indication of the importance of compliance with standards comes from the way in which customers express their view on standard-compliant versus proprietary products. Alpha stated: "[Customer A] would not accept [it] if we had proprietary solutions. They would just tell us to stop that: 'It's not ok that a player like you [has] your own solutions with their own interface.'" But the firm also has a certain freedom in association with the standard as Alpha states: "Many of the features defined in the default release are optional. There is an opportunity there to differentiate by fulfilling more or less of the standard."

The relevance for product competitiveness can be seen in the following statement by Alpha: "For instance, if a competitor finds out that we have a weakness in our product they will try to exploit that as far as possible through standardization, by coming up with specifications for the standard that hinders us." The relevance of standardization for products can also be viewed from the perspective of IPR. The following statement, by Delta, provides some additional detail on the role of IPR compared to how it has been described by Dokko and Rosenkopf (2010):

I think that you can not avoid discussing IPR mechanisms in a standardization argument. I think it's fundamental. On the one hand you see companies buying other companies just to get hold of the IPRs. And then you often buy IPRs of an implementation nature. ... It's very good to have a lot of IPR in the standard but it is perhaps not optimal to have your best IPRs there.

Since getting the right IPR into the standard is important, relevance seems to be a matter not only of passively complying with the emerging standards or differentiating within boundaries, but also of influencing standard setting in line with ongoing product development (and thereby with IPR and technological capabilities of the firm [Dokko & Rosenkopf, 2010]). This is illustrated by Beta, who described two approaches to committee participation:

Or you want to be monitoring. So we do not deploy big efforts to contribute and so on. But you will be monitoring in case somebody will not go in the direction that you want things to go. ... Then it's proactive, or active as I would say. Here you will contribute or block. You could be in standardization just to give time to your product. ... Because you have the technology. You are in advance of your competitors. And you see new technology being standardized which is good. But for the time being you are able to succeed on the market. So what to do, you just create a lot of technical discussion in the standardization to delay the outcome of the spec. Contribute. To push your development as being the standard.

The managerial and strategic relevance can also be seen in the following statements. First, consider the following view on the strategic relevance of being active in standard setting:

Interviewer: "So if you compare TechComp with competitors do you think that it is an area where you can gain an advantage towards competitors? Or is it just more of a hygiene factor to reach above the bar in the industry?"

Beta: "You say being active in standardization makes you more competitive than [others]?"

Interviewer: "Yes, do you think this is an area where you could potentially be so good that you gain an advantage?"

Beta: "Yes definitely."

Managerial relevance is present indirectly through the importance of standard setting in R&D activities, but sometimes standardization also explicitly reaches higher management decision-making levels. If issues of larger strategic importance appear, such as when one player is trying to control a standardization committee entirely to their advantage, such issues are escalated—first to the head of standardization, and possibly higher in the organization if necessary. Alpha provided details on how often standardization issues were escalated beyond the standardization organization to higher-level management: "Last year we have had three to four escalations that have gone up to division management level." The routinization of these occasional high-level escalations is less clear than other managerial involvement. This is discussed further in the later section titled *Managerial involvement and dynamism*.

Externally Integrative Character

A standardization capability will have an integrating nature towards external sources of information. An obvious example of an external integrating characteristic is the way in which the outside-in activities provide information and knowledge to R&D. Similar to what Rosenkopf et al. (2001) noted, participating in standardization organizations also generates networks, which is one of Verona's (1999) examples of an integrative capability. Here, we interpret this capability as part of the routinized activities that serve to support the establishment of such networks and social capital. As Dokko and Rosenkopf (2010) noted, this social capital can be attributed to the organization, and not solely to the individuals.

The following statement, from Beta, also shows that networks established through standardization participation, and thus supported by the standardization capability, serve purposes beyond the specific standardization setting: "Yet because sometimes with all this stuff you see your competitor, there is stuff that you can discuss as being under the standard umbrella. And after you could decide for example that something happening in standardization is going wrong or, and you need to be in a one on one with your competitor and say: 'look, we have a problem here' … Or from the point of [standardization organization 4] we do it also because we know the people participating in the standardization. So we have a separate meeting to understand the time schedule. There we are speaking roadmap and so on. So we do this also, for sure. You need to be able to use your contacts also for business purposes."

The externally integrative character shows itself in carrying knowledge and information from standardization organizations not only to R&D, but also to marketing. The following quote, from Alpha, shows how information from standardization organizations are used by marketing in order to highlight compliance with standards, but also differentiation.

It is often in the form of feature lists. If you take the [standards specifications], they contain a number of main features, it could be a dozen. And then in the marketing process you make sure that you talk about what these are and that you have a good story [as to] why we've skipped some of them that you do not include. But it's something that we negotiate. Negotiation of the product's functional content begins before the product is ready. You start probing quite far ahead of seeing the finished product and then you get feedback and you start to adjust.

This shows that the integrative nature is present in the outside-in process of bringing information into the marketing process of communicating with customers. It also shows how this lays the groundwork for further integration and thereby, potentially, for later stages where the firm needs to affect standardization; in other words, it lays the groundwork for future inside-out activities.

Internally Integrative Character

The internally integrative nature of the standardization process can be seen in the way that the organization utilizes resources and knowledge from several different functions (cf. Verona, 1999). The following quote shows how representatives from various parts of the organization are involved in making strategic decisions regarding the position to take in the interorganizational standardization process. Alpha stated: "For each [standardization] work stream there is a small steering committee. In the steering committee there are people from the standardization organization, development organization, and from R&D. So there you have that interdisciplinary link."

Managerial Involvement and Dynamism

As discussed in the section above on *Relevance*, managerial involvement in standardization at TechComp only includes top-level managers a few times a year. In addition, when it happens it is primarily related to the firm trying to influence standard setting in the standardization organization. Therefore, top-level managerial involvement mainly concerns inside-out activities.

Dynamism in the form of organizational renewal as part of an integrative capability (Yeoh & Roth, 1999) is limited in the TechComp example. Renewal can primarily be seen in the form of changes in firm networks and how they depend on standardization organizations and changes in the standardization environment. For instance, the firm can influence the standardization organization structures and establish new standardization consortia:

Interviewer: "I just want to come back to the discussion before about [whether] you have several different standardization organizations up and running. … Do you do reviews of them and look at: do we want to, do we have to choose between some?"
Beta: "Yes, for some companies we stop some alliances."
Interviewer: "So you have processes for this? To do that kind of review?"
Beta: "Normally it is on a quarterly basis. But for sure, it is done regularly. I receive the bill to pay. But some stuff we stop because, I stopped one last year. It was [standardization organization 6]. It was an alliance to define an interface for an [IPR]. We did it for one customer specifically. We do not have it anymore, this customer, so we stopped. Sometimes we realize that there is no added value for us. … But there is a review."

Such changes will affect firm network structures and firm representation in the standardization environment. It is in these situations that it is most relevant to talk about dynamism in the form of organizational renewal as being part of the integrative character of a capability.

Influencing Standardization Organization Structure and Learning

Finally, we deal specifically with the more profound and long-term influencing character of a standardization capability. The previous section showed how the organization regularly reviews its participation in various standardization organizations. Such activities are more long-term in character than day-to-day participation and standard setting in standardization organizations. Another example of more profound influence on the standardization organization environment can be found in the following statement, in which Beta described the initiation of a new standardization organization:

A lot of times what happens is that you have four or five companies who form a club. They discuss together and so on, 'what do we want to do?'

The question in the case considered here is whether it is possible to also claim that organizational learning takes place in association with such activities. In addition, these activities seem to recur less and be less repetitive, and in our example rely more on individual efforts. There is also a difference in how learning is handled in different technological areas. Within one technological area TechComp has a slightly more structured approach. However, this might be due to the fact that standardization within this area is more structured on an industry level.

CONCLUDING DISCUSSION

In the above example we have shown how standardization activities of TechComp are coordinative (among individuals), routinized, and of significant relevance to the organization as they influence the conversion of input to output and contribute to the decision-making map that managers must navigate. Therefore, the example displays that the organization does not solely depend on individuals and their isolated activities, but does indeed show signs of standardization routines that constitute a standardization capability. This is especially the case for the outside-in and inside-out activities of the organization. Affecting the short-term perspective of setting the market context for a specific technology through a standard takes place in the day-to-day standardization work through interaction with TechComp's development function. Although individuals play a key role, it is also indicated that routines are established to facilitate inside-out and outside-in efforts in association with standardization. This is most evident for the routinized inside-out activities where TechComp has established clear structures and routines for reviewing and planning its future standardization efforts within existing standardization organizations.

The case also highlights the importance of standardization activities to influence and adapt to institutional structures on various levels and based on different time perspectives. Affecting the long-term institutional structures typically entails influencing various standardization organizations. However, the level of routinization in the example case is difficult to determine fully.

Furthermore, the example illustrates that standardization capabilities are of an integrative nature in that they carry external knowledge and information to the firm, especially towards R&D functions but also towards marketing. The example also shows how structures are formed to support routines that integrate internal resources and capabilities in order to establish firm strategies towards standard setting.

Within the proposed framework one dimension is evident: the difference between adoption and influence of standards. In adoption, information and knowledge flows towards the firm. In influencing standards, information and firm action flows from the firm towards the standardization organization environment. This is evident in the routinized activities laid out in the framework and illustrated in the example. It is also shown in the externally and internally integrating capabilities, where the internally integrating serve to support the influencing of the standardization organization environment. The other dimension concerns the time perspective. We can distinguish between short-term influencing and adoption of standards within the existing firm and standardization environment versus longer-term reshaping of the standardization environment and the part of the organization involved in standardization. Further research should also attempt to clarify these differences.

It is of interest to note that managerial involvement is more significant when it comes to influencing the standard setting, as opposed to the adoption of standards. Managerial involvement is most likely when interorganizational standardization decisions with substantial strategic impact are made. In the example case, this could have involved escalating standardization issues to higher management levels, though it is difficult to fully determine whether such escalation was routinized and could be seen as part of a standardization capability. In addition, managerial involvement in the case firm seemed to be stronger when the firm was about to change its network within the sphere of standardization and actively change the standardization organization structures, such as through contributing to the establishment of new standardization organizations. This type of activity was at least partly indicated as routinized in the example case.

Changing the standardization organization structures, and thus the network of the firm, is also the prime example of integrative dynamism in our case. It may be that in other firms or industries dynamism in the form of organizational renewal is also stronger in association with standardization adoption. For instance, profound technological innovation in an emerging standard that deviates from the technological capabilities of the focal firm may spur radical organizational renewal. However, our case did not display these features very strongly. Thus, our example indicates that there is a difference in the level of dynamism and managerial involvement between the inside-out, the outside-in and the long-term activities of a standardization capability.

Thus, instead of talking about a single standardization capability, should we talk about several standardization capabilities, where one mainly certifies efficient adoption of standards, another certifies efficient short-term influencing of standard setting, and a third certifies long-term influence on the standardization environment? Further research should be directed at these distinctions, and in particular should consider them based on various time perspectives and within different industries, with different standardization settings, environmental factors (see Suarez, 2004), and firm sizes. For instance, what role does firm size play for the existence of a standardization capability? What role does the degree of network effects in association with standardization in the industry play for the presence of firm standardization capability?

This study identifies a standardization capability as consisting of routines that connect firm resources and capabilities with its standardization environment. Other researchers (e.g. Shapiro & Varian, 1999; Suarez, 2004) have pointed to other types of resources and capabilities as the sources of a dominating standards position. Further research should try to clarify the difference between a standardization capability and other resources and capabilities in explaining a firm's dominant position in standardization.

Participation in standardization organizations relies on social or relational capital; in addition, to some extent the proposed standardization capability resembles, for example, alliance capabilities. However, whereas alliance capabilities largely focus on close collaborations with other firms, often, in order to generate learning across firm boundaries, a standardization capability is primarily intended to generate industry economic effects that align with the resources and capabilities of the focal firm. Although this may involve cross-organizational learning via standards it is not the main purpose, and, as Rosenkopf et al. (2001) noted, committee participation mainly serves to *identify* potential alliance partners. Nevertheless, further studies should outline the difference between standardization capabilities and alliance capabilities. For instance, the empirical example of this study shows that participation in standardization organizations can be a starting point for identifying alliance partners and taking the first steps towards forming alliances beyond the normal consensus processes of standardization organizations.

In this study, we have argued that standardization capability is essential for facilitating efficient governance choices and the configuration of key aspects of the firm's institutional environment. In our empirical example, the firm employed specific routines to align its development activities with the industry standardization process and to influence the standardization organization environment for its own benefit. In more practical terms, our findings indicate that firms should recognize the role of standardization for realizing strategic objectives. When doing so, firms should pay close consideration to how they organize efforts aimed at exploiting the part of their institutional environment made up of standardization organizations such as formal standardization organizations and industry consortia. Hence, a better understanding of the concept of standardization capability, and its proposed components, may help firms design routines that will establish and maintain a favorable position *vis-à-vis* standardization organizations, thereby securing both influence and adaptability.

It is important to note the limitations of this study, especially concerning the empirical example. The example comes from a setting in which innovation and product development play a substantial role in the value creation of the focal firm and its competitors. In such a setting, firms will influence technology standard creation mainly in alignment with their development activities. In other markets, where other types of standards are involved, the link to the development functions of the firm may be less important. In addition, as discussed above, parameters such as firm size may correlate with the capability of the firm in relation to influencing standard setting.

REFERENCES

Anand, B. N., & Khanna, T. (2000). Do firms learn to create value? The case of alliances. *Strategic Management Journal*, *21*(3), 295–315. doi:10.1002/(SICI)1097-0266(200003)21:3<295::AID-SMJ91>3.0.CO;2-O

ANSI. (2018). *American National Standards Institute.* Retrieved from http://www.craftechind.com/ansi-standards-everything-need-know/

Argyres, N., Felin, T., Foss, N., & Zenger, T. (2012). Organizational economics of capability and heterogeneity. *Organization Science*, *23*(5), 1213–1226. doi:10.1287/orsc.1120.0746

Blind, K. (2004). *The economics of standards: Theory, evidence, policy.* Cheltenham, UK: Edward Elgar.

Blind, K. (2011). An economic analysis of standards competition: The example of the standardization organization ODF and OOXML standards. *Telecommunications Policy*, *35*, 373–381. doi:10.1016/j.telpol.2011.02.007

Care Quality Commission. (2010). Retrieved from https://www.cqc.org.uk/sites/default/files/documents/guidance_about_compliance_summary.pdf

Collis, D. J. (1994). Research note: How valuable are organizational capabilities? *Strategic Management Journal*, *15*(S1), 143–152. doi:10.1002mj.4250150910

Den Butter, F. A. G., Groot, S. P. T., & Lazrak, F. (2007). *The transaction costs perspective on standards as a source of trade and productivity growth.* Tinbergen Institute Discussion Papers, 07-090/3. Available at: http://www.tinbergen.nl/discussionpapers/07090.pdf

Dokko, G., Nigam, A., & Rosenkopf, L. (2012). Keeping steady as she goes: A negotiated order perspective on technological evolution. *Organization Studies*, *33*(5-6), 681–703. doi:10.1177/0170840612443624

Dokko, G., & Rosenkopf, L. (2010). Social capital for hire? Mobility of technical professionals and firm influence in wireless standards committees. *Organization Science*, *21*(3), 677–695. doi:10.1287/orsc.1090.0470

Dosi, G., Nelson, R. R., & Winter, S. G. (2001). *The nature and dynamics of organizational capabilities*. Oxford University Press.

Egyedi, T. M., & Blind, K. (2008). General introduction. In T. Egyedi & K. Blind (Eds.), *The dynamics of standards*. Cheltenham, UK: Edward Elgar.

Farrell, J., & Saloner, G. (1985). Standardization, compatibility, and innovation. *The Rand Journal of Economics*, *16*(1), 70–83. doi:10.2307/2555589

Farrell, J., & Saloner, G. (1988). Coordination through committees and markets. *The Rand Journal of Economics*, *19*(2), 235–252. doi:10.2307/2555702

Felin, T., Foss, N. J., Heimeriks, K. H., & Madsen, T. L. (2012). Microfoundations of routines and capabilities: Individuals, processes, and structures. *Journal of Management Studies*, *49*(8), 1351–1374. doi:10.1111/j.1467-6486.2012.01052.x

Fortune, A., & Mitchell, W. (2012). Unpacking firm exit at the firm and industry levels: The adaptation and selection of firm capabilities. *Strategic Management Journal*, *33*, 794–819.

Heimeriks, K. H., & Duysters, G. (2007). Alliance capability as a mediator between experience and alliance performance: An empirical investigation into the alliance capability development process. *Journal of Management Studies*, *44*(1), 25–49. doi:10.1111/j.1467-6486.2006.00639.x

Helfat, C., & Peteraf, M. A. (2003). The dynamic resource-based view: Capability lifecycles. *Strategic Management Journal*, *24*(10), 997–1010. doi:10.1002mj.332

Helfat, C., & Raubitscheck, R. S. (2000). Product sequencing: Co-evolution of knowledge, capabilities and products. *Strategic Management Journal*, *21*(10-11), 961–979. doi:10.1002/1097-0266(200010/11)21:10/11<961::AID-SMJ132>3.0.CO;2-E

Henderson, R. E., & Cockburn, I. (1994). Measuring competence? Exploring firm effects in pharmaceutical research. *Strategic Management Journal*, *15*(S1), 63–84. doi:10.1002mj.4250150906

Kale, P., Singh, H., & Perlmutter, H. (2000). Learning and protection of proprietary assets in strategic alliances: Building relational capital. *Strategic Management Journal*, *21*(Special Issue), 217–237. doi:10.1002/(SICI)1097-0266(200003)21:3<217::AID-SMJ95>3.0.CO;2-Y

Katz, M. L., & Shapiro, C. (1985). Network externalities, competition, and compatibility. *The American Economic Review*, *75*, 424–440.

Leiponen, A. E. (2008). Competing through cooperation: The organization of standard setting in wireless telecommunications. *Management Science*, *54*(11), 1904–1919. doi:10.1287/mnsc.1080.0912

Matutes, C., & Regibeau, P. (1996). A selective review of the economics of standardization. Entry deterrence, technological progress and international competition. *European Journal of Political Economy, 12*(2), 183–209. doi:10.1016/0176-2680(95)00013-5

Mayer, K., & Argyres, N. (2004). Learning to contract: Evidence from the personal computer industry. *Organization Science, 15*(4), 394–410. doi:10.1287/orsc.1040.0074

National Standards Advisory Committee, Standards Australia. (2006). Available at: http://www.standards.org.au/Pages/FAQ.aspx

Nelson, R., & Winter, S. (1982). *The evolutionary theory of the firm*. Cambridge, MA: Harvard University Press.

Rosenkopf, L., Metiu, A., & George, V. P. (2001). From the Bottom Up? Technical Committee Activity and Alliance Formation. *Administrative Science Quarterly, 46*(4), 748–772. doi:10.2307/3094830

Schilling, M. (1999). Winning the standards race: Building installed base and the availability of complementary goods. *European Management Journal, 17*(3), 265–274. doi:10.1016/S0263-2373(99)00005-5

Shapiro, C., & Varian, H. R. (1999). The art of standards wars. *California Management Review, 41*(2), 8–32. doi:10.2307/41165984

Stigzelius, I., & Mark-Herbert, C. (2009). Tailoring corporate responsibility to suppliers: Managing SA8000 in Indian garment industry. *Scandinavian Journal of Management, 25*(1), 46–56. doi:10.1016/j.scaman.2008.04.003

Suarez, F. F. (2004). Battles for technological dominance: An integrative framework. *Research Policy, 33*(2), 271–286. doi:10.1016/j.respol.2003.07.001

Swann, G. P. (2000). *The economics of standardization: Final report for standards and technical regulations directorate*. Manchester, UK: Department of Trade and Industry, Manchester Business School.

Tassey, G. (2000). Standardization in technology based markets. *Research Policy, 27*, 273–284.

Teece, D. (1986). Profiting from technological innovation: Implications for integration, collaboration, licensing and public policy. *Research Policy, 15*(6), 785–805. doi:10.1016/0048-7333(86)90027-2

Teece, D. J., Pisano, G., & Shuen, A. (1997). Dynamic capabilities and strategic management. *Strategic Management Journal, 18*(7), 509–533. doi:10.1002/(SICI)1097-0266(199708)18:7<509::AID-SMJ882>3.0.CO;2-Z

Tushman, M. L., & Rosenkopf, L. (1992). Organizational determinants of technological change: Toward a sociology of technological evolution. In L. L. Cummings & B. M. Staw (Eds.), *Research in organizational behavior* (pp. 311–347). Greenwich, CT: JAI Press.

van den Ende, J., van de Kaa, G., den Uijl, S., & de Vries, H. J. (2012). The paradox of standard flexibility: The effects of co-evolution between standard and interorganizational networks. *Organization Studies, 33*(5-6), 705–736. doi:10.1177/0170840612443625

Verona, G. (1999). A resource-based view of product development. *Academy of Management Review, 24*(1), 132–142. doi:10.5465/amr.1999.1580445

Werle, R. (2011). Institutional aspects of standardization—Jurisdictional conflicts and the choice of standardization organizations. *Journal of European Public Policy*, *8*(3), 392–410. doi:10.1080/13501760110056031

Winter, S.G., (2003). "Understanding dynamic capabilities." *Strategic Management Journal,* October Special Issue, 24, 991–996.

Yeoh, P.-L., & Roth, K. (1999). An empirical analysis of sustained advantage in the U.S. pharmaceutical industry: Impact of firm resources and capabilities. *Strategic Management Journal*, *20*(7), 637–653. doi:10.1002/(SICI)1097-0266(199907)20:7<637::AID-SMJ42>3.0.CO;2-Z

ENDNOTE

1 The above dichotomy of formal and informal standardization may also be characterized as *de jure* and *de facto*, respectively (Dokko, Nigam, & Rosenkopf, 2012).

Chapter 5
Company IT Standardization:
Anticipated Agile Benefits

Robert M. van Wessel
ApexIS, The Netherlands

Henk J. de Vries
Erasmus University, The Netherlands & Delft University of Technology, The Netherlands

ABSTRACT

Many companies have embarked on IT standardization initiatives with specific benefits in mind, but some projects fail dramatically whereas others are very successful. The research suggests that successful company standardization projects require good governance and management across distinct lifecycle phases: selection, implementation, and use and change. The authors present a case study from a financial services company to demonstrate effective practices that have led to significant financial benefits, to improved service delivery and support, and to a more stable IT environment. In addition, the authors discuss how an agile way of working could further improve standardization initiatives in organizations.

INTRODUCTION[1]

Many companies try to converge on particular IT processes and/or IT products to gain business benefits such as quality improvements, cost reductions or obtaining strategic advantage (Swaminathan, 2001; Boh and Yellin, 2007; Mueller et al., 2015). These efforts can be described as standardization activities since the parties involved *".... have the intention and expectation that the established solutions will be used within a certain period by a substantial number of the parties for which the solutions are meant.*" (De Vries, 1999, p. 162). The result of such an initiative is called a company IT standard (Van Wessel, 2010). De Vries (1999) argues that a company standard may have the form of:

1. A reference to one or more external standards officially adopted by the company;
2. A company modification of an external standard;

DOI: 10.4018/978-1-5225-9008-8.ch005

Copyright © 2019, IGI Global. Copying or distributing in print or electronic forms without written permission of IGI Global is prohibited.

3. A subset of an external standard (for instance, a description of the company's choice of competing possibilities offered in an external standard, or a subset of the topics covered in the external standard);
4. A standard reproduced from (parts of) other external documents, for instance, suppliers' documents;
5. A self-written standard.

We define a company IT standard as: "*A specification of an IT product or process to be repeatedly and consistently used in the company*" and the company IT standards in this chapter relate to category 4. in the above list.

Typically, a company standardization process encompasses a number of sequential steps: selection, implementation, and use (including changes and withdrawals) of the standard, which together comprise the lifecycle of the company's IT standards. These internal IT standards are not necessarily restricted to formal standards created by official standard setting organizations, but may also include standards set by consortia or even specifications of propriety products and processes. Some of such standardization initiatives fail dramatically whereas others are very successful, and the reasons are not clear. Companies have to make choices among numerous IT products and processes to arrive at company standards, but how should they do so effectively and efficiently? Who should be involved? How should they plan and control? How should they measure their effects? What are the pros and cons, and the costs and benefits? This paper aims to find empirical evidence of the business impact of a company's IT standard and of the effective governance and management mechanisms for successful company standardization initiatives.

Since the 1980s, scholars have studied the economic aspects of standardization, such as network effects and switching costs (Van de Kaa et al., 2011). The majority of standardization studies focus on the effects of (IT) standards on a macro-economic scale (Blind, 2004; WTO, 2005), on the development of standards by industry, consortia, and international standards bodies (Backhouse, 2006; Nickerson and zur Muehlen, 2006; Teichmann, 2010; Jain, 2012), and on battles between competing standards (overview of studies in Van de Kaa et al., 2011). Others apply the diffusion of innovation theory (Rogers, 2003) to the field of standardization (Poba-Nzaou and Raymond, 2011), or a combination of diffusion of innovation and economic theories (West and Dedrick, 2006; Mendoza and Ravichandran, 2011). At the company level Wiegman (2019) investigated, among others, how firms managed standards for micro Combined Heat and Power (mCHP) technology while developing their mCHP products. Yet, the number of academic studies on standardization in companies remains limited and fragmented and this book forms an exception. The professional literature on IT standards seems to have adopted an almost exclusively technical point of view.

One of the classic problems facing standardization and standards usage in companies is demonstrating its contribution to the company's total success (Hesser and Inklaar, 1997). Typically, in standardization there are significant uncertainties about the factual costs and benefits and about adequate planning and control strategies (Weitzel, 2003). Kayworth and Sambamurthy (2000) show that the organizational context in which IT infrastructure standards are used is an important success factor with respect to the satisfaction of specific local needs and the degree to which the standards are integrated in the whole company. Swaminathan (2001) describes the issues that companies face when they consider mass customization to meet the needs of their businesses. He identifies four operational strategies for standardization employed by firms to minimize the increase of variability in the operating environment. These include part standardization, process standardization, product standardization, and procurement standardization.

De Vries and Slob (2006) investigate a 'best practice' for company standardization at six chemical and petrochemical industries in the Netherlands by comparing the standardization activities and, subsequently, by choosing the best way to execute them. They define success of the company standardization process as "a standard that is known to the users and that is used in practice" and identify factors that positively influence the use of such standards. Despite the difficulty of measuring the real usage of a standard, they identify a set of best practices for company standardization, grouped under the headings Standardization Policy (at strategic, tactical and operational level), Prioritization Process, Company Standard Development Process, Company Standard Introduction Process, Distribution Process, Facility Management, and Funding.

In a survey research on the use of such standards, Boh and Yellin (2007) investigate to what extent the use of IT infrastructure standards facilitates organizations to improve the sharing and integration of IT resources across the enterprise and how different mechanisms affect their usage. Their results show that the use of enterprise architecture standards is significant in helping organizations to effectively manage IT resources. Hesser (2010) presents the effects of company standardization on competitive and functional strategies in design and development, procurement, and production with direct relevance to industrial processes. Company standardization includes: numbering systems, size range systems, unit assembly systems, modularization, quality management systems, and environmental management. However, company standards are often only introduced after cost or complexity targets have been missed. He argues that company standardization must be part of corporate and competitive strategies. Li and Chen (2012) examine company standardization within corporations and its impact on sellers' incentives to invest in IT compatibility. Their research suggests that exclusive purchase commitment by a company is dependent on the degree of horizontal differentiation among sellers, its product compatibility and the relative competitive advantages. Meuller et al. (2015) describe factors that influence the intention to accept and use company standards at an employee level, and Manders (2015) investigates the implementation and impact of ISO 9001 at the country, company, and employee level. Interestingly, despite the surge in agile practices (VersionOne, 2018), its application for company standardization remains fully unclear. To the best of our knowledge no attempts have been made so far to test agile approaches in company standardization initiatives.

Because the number of scholarly articles on company standardization is so limited, our paper investigates how organizations can achieve business benefits from company IT standardization. This research expands on this scarce theoretical base and uses insights from practice. For this purpose, case study research is an appropriate research method (Yin, 2009). We present a case study from a financial services company, ABN AMRO. Data were gathered from ABN AMRO's headquarters, and included official company records such as project plans, project reports, presentations, policy documents, memoranda, and leaflets. We evaluated the financial, organizational, and technical objectives of the company and examined their effects on efficiency and effectiveness. We conducted semi-structured interviews, lasting an average of 90 minutes, aimed at discussing the selection, implementation, and usage of IT process and/or product standards. The interviewees ranged from senior executives to IT experts. Most interviews were taped and subsequently transcribed within 24 hours. Only a few interviewees did not give permission for the interview to be audio-taped. The interviews focused on how the bank could achieve the intended business performance from IT standardization, and in particular on the governance and management practices across the entire lifecycle of the company's IT standards.

The term *governance* (Weill and Ross, 2004) in relation to company IT standards refers to which decisions must be taken, who should take these decisions, and how they are taken and monitored to ensure the effective management of the standardized IT environment. *Management* (Boynton and Zmud, 1987) means actually taking decisions on planning, organizing, directing, and controlling the company IT standard. The results of the IT standardization project have led to significant financial benefits, but also better IT service delivery and support. For this study, we use a company IT standardization management framework, as depicted in Figure 1, which was successfully validated in a number of case studies (Van Wessel, 2010).

Governance and Management impact Selection, Implementation, and ultimately Use of company IT standards, which should result in Business Benefits. The arrow from Governance to Management indicates that adequate management presupposes effective governance. The feedback loop from Business Benefits to Governance and Management symbolizes the dynamic character of the framework. If Business Benefits are not achieved, changes to governance and/or management of company IT standards should be considered.

ESTABLISHING COMPANY IT STANDARDS AT ABN AMRO

Rationale for a New IT Architecture

Our case study was carried out at ABN AMRO, a Dutch financial service company with a presence in 21 countries worldwide. At one of ABN AMRO's business units, the IT environment consisted of a plethora of different hardware and software products. Managing this environment was difficult and resulted in high support costs and long resolution times. Upgrades were difficult to implement. A lack of standardization was a root cause of these problems. Therefore, a two-year IT standardization project affecting 10,000 users was carried out in this business unit. The business unit's management set project targets for cost savings and also set functional requirements, which made the project business-oriented

Figure 1. Company IT standardization management framework

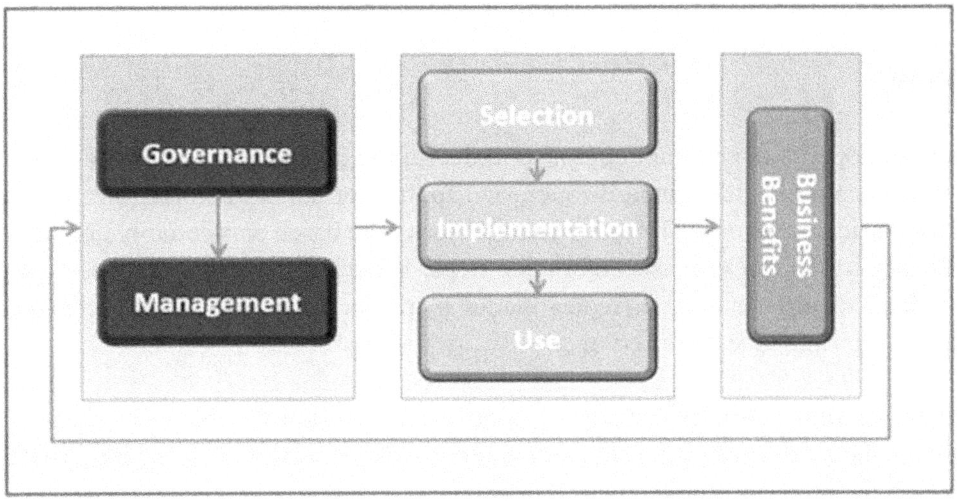

rather than technology-focused. The scope of the project, which included the choice and implementation of hardware and software at both the front-end and the back-end of the business unit, ranged from desktop productivity tools to cost accounting applications.

The main objectives of the standardization project were to reduce the total cost of ownership or TCO[2] by 18% (calculated against industry benchmarks) and to increase flexibility by implementing a set of company standards. Cost reductions were particularly needed in the fields of procurement and support, and were expected to be achieved by reducing the complexity of the IT environment by limiting the variety at both the hardware and software levels. Greater flexibility was needed to allow for 'hot desking', and to roll out changes seamlessly. The project was completed successfully in time and with a marginal cost overrun.

The next sub-section provides a discussion of the successful accomplishment of this company IT standardization initiative.

SELECTING THE COMPANY IT STANDARDS

Governance

The business unit's senior management initiated the standardization project. It had two main reasons to do so: increasing flexibility and reducing costs. These two goals had to be reached by rationalizing the number of IT applications used by the business unit, and by simplifying their maintenance. These objectives, in turn, were to be achieved through standardizing the IT infrastructure. The business unit and its IT department worked in close cooperation to specify and select the IT products in the new set of company IT standards. However, this rationalization and standardization process was not easy. It required much effort, and it took time to convince all stakeholders of its added value. At the start of the initiative to standardize the IT environment, the IT department asked the business unit what kind of functionalities it required (not which applications it wanted). The answer was a 300-page document with requirements that would have cost a significant amount of money to implement. To deal with this issue, the business unit asked the IT department how the IT environment could be rationalized. The IT department suggested to script applications for browser-based access if technically possible and financially feasible, and to introduce terminal servers for applications that could not be ported.

Management

Management developed a three-tiered approach to devise the company's new IT standards: hardware standardization, system software standardization, and application software standardization. Alternatives were carefully considered for each IT product, and choices were based on a combination of functionality and costs. The selection process consisted of three steps: 1) request for proposal focusing on functional and non-functional requirements; 2) price negotiation by reversed auction; and 3) acceptance testing of two products, to determine the preferred one.

- **Hardware standardization:** To decrease complexity and allow flexible workplaces (with the aim of reducing the number of staff workplaces), an environment known as 'server-based computing' was chosen. It consisted of three main elements:

- Thin clients (PCs with a minimum of local applications)
- Web servers and terminal servers hosting applications
- Back-end servers hosting all user data.

- **System Software Standardization:** Managing the original desktop environment was difficult since it consisted of a large collection of locally installed applications on fat client desktops, and implementing changes could take as long as three to four months. Whenever technically possible, therefore, the new system software was not installed on desktops. Instead, users used browsers to access applications from their PCs. The browser-based applications ran on the web servers in a multi-application hosting environment on an AS/390 mainframe using products called Websphere, and Java Virtual Machine. Applications that were not browser-based were installed on terminal servers running on Wintel, also using Websphere. To minimize interdependencies between these logical nodes, no multi-application hosting was allowed on terminal servers.
- **Application Software Standardization:** The 'server-based computing' approach was stretched as far as technically possible, but some bandwidth issues were encountered, and it was decided to install a few applications on the workstations instead of on the servers to prevent network overload. Some of these applications were remaining legacy software, whereas some such as a word processor, spreadsheet, and presentation software and groupware were used daily by the majority of staff. After inventorying, the number of applications was reduced from more than 6,000 to 265 – more than twenty-two[3] times less!

This set-up minimized dependencies among the system's hardware components. The new environment consisted of 10,000 thin client workstations, 1,000 laptops, 1,000 terminal servers, a dozen of web servers, and around 300 back-end servers. User and group data were stored on the terminal servers which were replicated daily to a central storage.

Interestingly, the biggest savings were achieved by a reduction of license fees. In the past, several hundreds of licenses had been purchased – some for very few users or even no users at all – simply because no-one could keep track of the installed software on thousands of locally run PCs. So the guiding principle in this standardization project phase was that only one type of software was allowed – preferably the latest version – unless it considerably degraded business functionality. In a tendering process, proposals were requested from several suppliers. The key criterion for selecting applications, and subsequently listing that as preferred software, was the balance between functionality, support, and license costs. But other criteria, such as manufacturer or vendor strategy and track record, were also taken into account. The lists were drawn up per department, subject to approval of business management. The final set of specifications of IT products, the company IT standards, is listed in Table 1.

IMPLEMENTING THE COMPANY IT STANDARDS

Governance

A program organization carried out the implementation of the company standardization initiative (Figure 2). Project groups with a specific assignment reported to a program manager, who reported to a steering group that consisted of members from the business unit and the IT department. The steering group was accountable for managing project costs and progress, for approving project changes, monitoring the qual-

Table 1. Set of standard IT products (from a user perspective)

IT products	Remarks
Desktops and Laptops	Multi-language MS Windows and Office; Web browser; PDF Reader; Winzip; Lotus Notes; Anti-Virus Software
Monitors	17" LCD
Printers	Network printers (no personal printers allowed)
Work-at-home facilities	Browser via Internet/SSL, replacing most company laptops
RSI prevention tools	Special computer mouses and software
Smartcard readers	Integrated with keyboard
Specials	On demand, like scanners, or Braille for the poorly sighted

ity of the implementation through progress reports, deciding on organizational changes, and controlling the type and number of applications. The program manager was supported by a project office.

Management

To manage the complexity of the standardization initiative, the program involved many people, processes and technological changes, five separate projects were set up that each covered specific aspects of the program (Table 2). A total of 51 FTEs (Full Time Equivalent), including the program manager and the project office, were involved for 19 months.

Implementing the set of standards was vital to achieve the required flexibility of the new hardware and system software. Because of its modular structure, with only one hardware and software type allowed, the new IT environment had maximum flexibility at both client-end and server-end. Strict adherence to project management processes was another key element in the successful implementation. Moreover,

Figure 2. Program organization

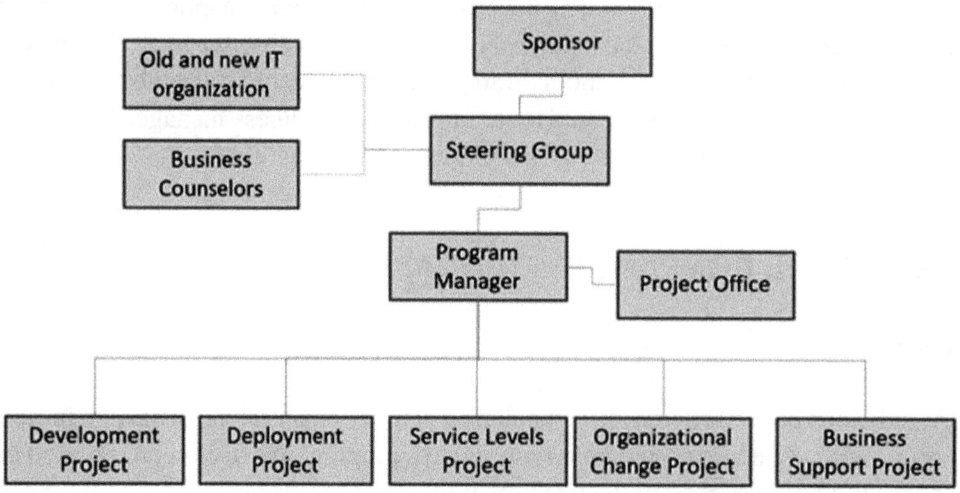

Table 2. Projects of the server-based computing program

Project	Objective	FTEs
Development	Preparing applications for terminal servers; scripting, conversion, testing	29
Deployment	Rolling out the new infrastructure in each department	8
Service Levels	Setting up service level agreements with the business unit	7
Organizational Change	Managing the IT department's organizational change caused by the project	3
Business Support	Counseling and liaising with the business departments	2

the project was carried out as a joint effort by the business unit and its IT department, which increased the buy-in at both sides.

A number of potential risks were identified that could cause the project to fail in the implementation phase. These consisted of organizational and HR risks because the IT support organization had to be dismantled and its staff relocated in order to set up a new centralized IT support department. Also financial risks were taken because the estimates of operational revenues and expenditures were exactly that: estimates. The most important project risks are listed in Table 3, including the countermeasures taken to prevent these risks.

USE AND CHANGE OF THE COMPANY IT STANDARD

Governance

An IT review team, consisting of four IT staff with clear responsibilities in governing the use of the set of standards, was appointed (Table 4). The IT product coordinator was the primary point of contact for functional changes. Their core tasks were to assess requests for changes and deviations from the standards, and to make recommendations to an IT policy board.

This IT policy board approved changes and deviations to the set of IT standards. Approval was based on four policies:

1. The application level and the operating system level should be uncoupled to ensure minimum dependence between developments at these two levels.

Table 3. Project risks, impact, and countermeasures

Risk	Possible impact	Countermeasure
Organizational change is carried out without any consideration to staff.	IT staff morale deteriorates, which is reflected in lower service quality.	Pay special attention to staff involvement and open and honest communication.
The business unit's management shows no commitment to the project.	Business units do not commit to the new company IT standard. The costs reductions and flexibility required are not achieved.	Maintain close contact between the business unit's managers and the company's general management.
The reduction of the number of applications is not achieved.	Potential benefits of scale are not fully exploited. More licenses and terminal servers are needed. Support remains costly and complex.	Continuously monitor and enforce the maximum number of applications.

Table 4. Staff responsible for managing the Company IT Standard

Function	Accountability
IT architect	Preserves IT infrastructure consistency and evaluates the overall impact of deviation requests.
IT product manager	Manages costs and charging the business departments, reduces expenses, and improves cost transparency. Calculates the financial impact of deviation requests. Accountable for all assets, budget-responsible for infrastructure deprecations, and owner of all support contracts.
IT product coordinator	Translates functional and technical requirements into specifications of IT products and assesses deviation requests from a technical point of view.
IT support coordinator	Plans and controls the IT operations and reviews change requests from an IT operations viewpoint.

2. Upgrades to the computing platform must be possible without large investments to update in-house developed applications.
3. Only COTS products (Commercial Of The Shelf) are allowed. This prevents legacy applications from remaining operational, which would cause security and stability problems, and high support and license costs.
4. No business-specific applications are allowed on workstations, and workstations must be completely de-personalized to ease maintenance and increase security.

When a deviation request was granted, there were two options. The preferred one was to incorporate the specification of the requested product into the set of company IT standards. The alternative was to grant the deviation, but only on a temporary basis. After a year, the IT review team re-evaluated the deviation request.

Conformance testing of proposed IT products (e.g., by individual staff or by projects members) to the applicable IT standard by specific IT teams is a practice that was found in other companies as well (Rada and Craparo, 2000; Boh and Yellin, 2007). The review team also assessed any upgrades, replacements, or patching needed. A full review process was carried out every two years. This often resulted in a new product, the specification of which was then incorporated into the set of company standards, reflecting developments in technological and business environments.

Management

There are several ways in which company standards can be enforced once they are implemented (Cargill, 1989) and these can be classified into three categories: the regulatory style, the *laissez faire*, or a combination of these two. This business unit adopted the first style, which was expressed in their maxim 'each and every desktop must have the same configuration'. Consequently, the company IT standards were strictly applied. As discussed earlier, the business unit's objectives were to achieve cost reductions and increase flexibility. The business unit's IT department fully supported these goals but realized that the costs of IT delivery and support would sometimes not be a convincing argument for business staff. In some cases, business departments were willing to pay substantially more, rather than less, for products that did not conform to company IT standards. The deviation process, therefore, had to be very strict to ensure that only requests with a sound business rationale would be made. Any such requests were then assessed by the IT review team and approved by the IT policy board, taking both business and technological considerations into account. Very serious arguments were needed to convince this group to allow deviations, and these would then have to be reported to IT management on a monthly basis.

The choice was limited to the applications and hardware that were specified in the list of company IT standards. Changes to these standards were relatively easy to make because of the modular structure of the new IT environment. But anyone requesting modifications to functionality first had to try to realize those within the company's current standards. Failing that, the IT team would only make structural changes on the basis of a sound business rationale with indicators such as added value, the number of users affected, the possibility of charging someone for it, the vendor's track record, and the total costs involved. Planning and controlling the company IT standards was the task of staff as listed in Table 4. Strict adherence to "IT service management processes", such as those specified in ISO/IEC 20000, was another key element in using the company standard successfully.

BENEFITS ACHIEVED

The new standardized IT environment was assessed by analyzing the project's financial results and by evaluating operational aspects of IT service delivery and support obtained from the Finance unit.

Financial Results

With the introduction of the standardized IT environment, many costs were eliminated. The most important savings were achieved by reducing the number of licensed applications, by removing local installations resulting in an easier process of application support, and by eliminating hardware relocations (formerly approximately 25% of total desktop costs). As a result, the costs for IT support and development were considerably lower than before the standardization initiative. In addition, less specific staff expertise was needed, and re-use of IT processes and products was easier. The resulting economies of scale enabled the company to negotiate significant global purchase discounts from its suppliers. Staff used their web browsers to acquire any additional applications needed on their thin client. The extent to which they used them determined the variable costs of those workstations. Authorization was obtained through an application also used for license management, which gave the business unit maximum transparency and cost control.

The project's investments ran to a total of €32 million (€17M hardware and software transitions costs and €15M project staff outlays), which was 5% more than budgeted. The direct costs of the old and new IT environments, calculated as of January 1st of the year of the project and again exactly one year later, fell from € 4,600 per desktop per year to € 2,392 (Figure 3). Calculating on the basis of 10,000 desktops and a four-year life span, the payback period[4] was 1.45 years. The return on investment rate[5] was 176% and the internal rate of return[6] 58%. Figure 4 shows the cash flow for four years. The initiative resulted in a positive cash flow of + €56M in the fourth year. The bottom line was that the new IT environment costs were reduced by about 50%.

IT Service and Support Benefits

Significant organizational improvements were achieved, from decreased time to process service requests to the implementation of the standardized IT environment for a whole department. New projects showed

Figure 3. Direct costs per desktop per year (before and after standardization)

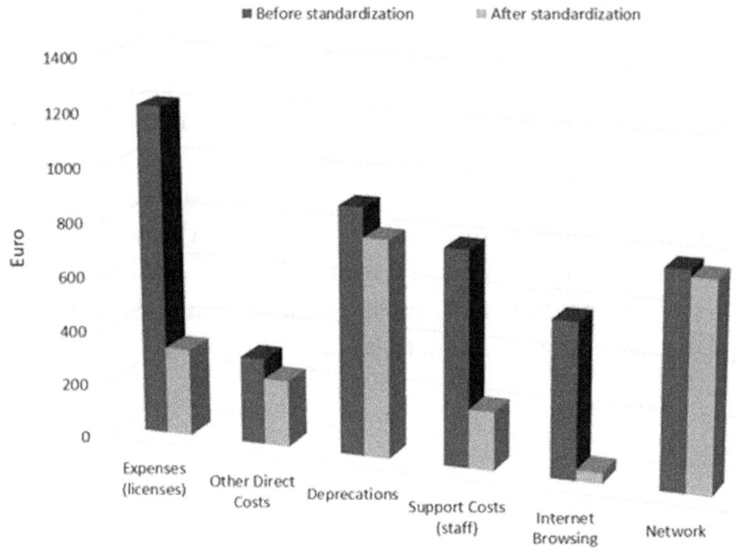

Figure 4. Cash flow following investment in the standardized IT environment

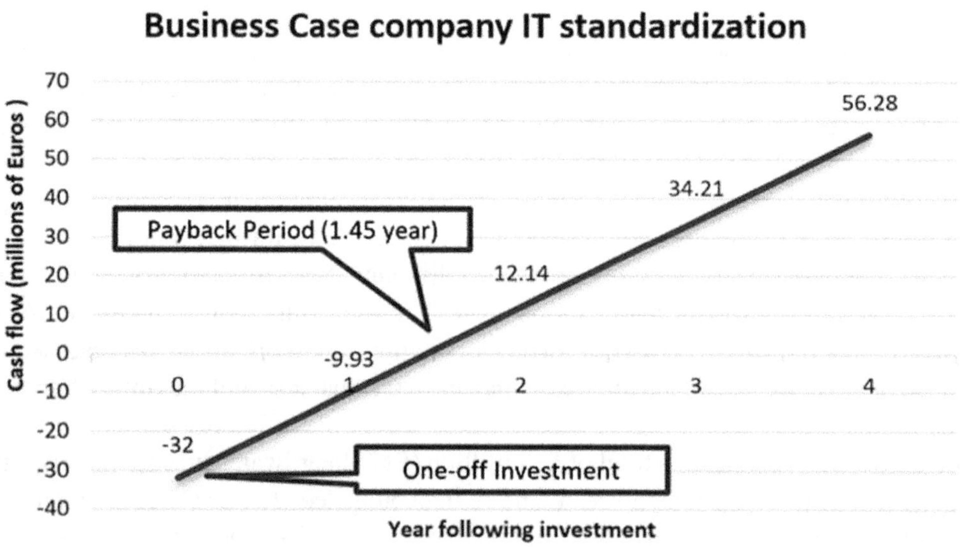

lead time decreases of up to 75%. New applications were made operational within a few weeks and deploying the standardized IT environment typically took no more than a month. So service performance increased from both the development and the support point of view. The area in which no significant improvements were achieved related to error and rework rates, as the former organization was already responsive in this respect.

In addition, the information security was improved through automated anti-virus updates and the uniform patching of the applications and operating system. Smartcards were used for application single sign-on. Desktop downtime became negligible since instability was predominantly application-related, not hardware-related. Moreover, the impact of IT failures dropped because of the modular setup of server-based computing with one application per terminal server. Altogether, the new IT environment proved to be very robust.

The standardized IT environment facilitated improved technical, organizational, and financial flexibility. Technical flexibility was achieved in terms of adaptability, scalability, and robustness. The ATMs used by customers of ABN AMRO, for example, were incorporated in this environment as essentially just another peripheral. Furthermore, the IT environment allowed several versions of an application such as Lotus Notes 6 and 8 to run simultaneously on a single desktop, because the software was installed on separate and independent terminal servers. Organizational flexibility was exemplified by a department using a dedicated Local Area Network. The new IT environment allowed the department's staff to work anywhere, irrespective of their physical location. This meant its business functionality could be spread over several locations. Financial flexibility was achieved because application and hardware usage were charged based on the actual number of subscriptions. Users were charged for access to the system's web and terminal servers, so when a department reduced or increased its staff, the IT costs changed automatically. Of course, this kind of flexibility caused some financial uncertainty for the IT organization, but flexibility was considered necessary to achieve a more effective environment for users.

How the Users Perceived the Changes

The business unit staff needed some time to become familiar with the new IT environment. Initially, there were some negative reactions such as 'We will lose all flexibility...' but this changed for the better and most of the staff perceived the new environment as quite acceptable. The interviewees reported that the majority of business unit staff considered the change an improvement, 30% were indifferent, and some 10% were less satisfied with IT delivery and support than before – and those, interestingly, were predominantly IT staff. Generally speaking, the users were satisfied. With just a few clicks they could select from more than 250 applications that were made available within a quarter of an hour. Staff could use more applications more easily, and since almost all of the applications conformed to a standard look and feel, staff training costs were only marginal. Incidents and requests for new hardware and software were logged using a web-application. The hot desking concept allowed staff to use workstations with exactly the same features at other locations. The fact that all workstations were the same also made the business unit less dependent on delivery and support. For the business unit as a whole, this meant decreased costs. For its staff, it meant less hassle and therefore an improved working environment.

Other Benefits

The organization learned that a strict way of dealing with deviations from IT standards proved to be worthwhile. First and foremost, it provided signs of changing business needs from users, and secondly, only genuine requests entered the process. In this case, the business unit chose *de facto* standard software products from Microsoft. It was aware of the danger of potential lock-in effects by being bound to a single supplier of hardware or software. But this presented no real problems, although adaptability and interoperability became more difficult when applications that deviated from Microsoft's products had to be integrated. However, these lock-in effects were considered far less important than the benefits. Hardware seemed to present almost no such risks at all. And it was considered even less important for system software, since the modular set-up of the environment allowed changing front-end or back-end software relatively easily.

LESSONS LEARNED

Governance and Management Arrangements

This case study showed us that the standardized IT environment resulted in several advantages:

- An up-to-date set of IT products, aligned with business requirements and technical developments
- Significant cost reductions and improved transparency and control
- Satisfied customers through improved service delivery and support
- Deliverables of projects in conformance to the set of IT standards
- A stable and fully modular IT environment with better reusability and change flexibility

The following governance and management mechanisms facilitated these changes.

Governance

- **Selection:** The business decision to standardize the IT environment was taken in collaboration with the IT department, with business departments taking the lead. Key objectives were cost reductions and increased flexibility. This resulted in a formalized organizational setting: an IT policy board with senior representatives from the business units and from IT.
- **Implementation:** A program management organization was established. Key players included a program manager and a steering group with members from both the business units and the IT department.
- **Use:** In the operational phase, an IT review team carries out refinement and updates of the standard with input from business and IT. This team assesses specified IT products and processes for projects, and evaluates changes and deviation requests to the set of IT standards. Decisions concerning the standardized IT environment are taken on the basis of functionality, not on specific software packages. Four key players were appointed to ensure the effective management of the standardized IT environment: an IT architect, an IT product manager, an IT product coordinator, and an IT support coordinator. In addition, an IT policy board approves or rejects changes and deviations by taking business and technological considerations into account. Ratification is based on infrastructure consistency policies. Approved requests are expected to be incorporated in the standardized IT environment.

In terms of archetypal IT governance decision-making (Weill and Ross, 2004), the arrangement described above is an 'IT Duopoly': "two party decision-making involving IT executives and one group of business leaders". This governance mechanism is in contrast to an 'IT monarchy' in which an individual or a group of IT executives are the decision makers. Our case company uses a duopoly arrangement between business units (involved mostly in the selection and implementation phase) and the IT department (involved mostly in the implementation and use phase) as shown in Figure 5.

Figure 5. IT governance arrangement in the case company: duopoly

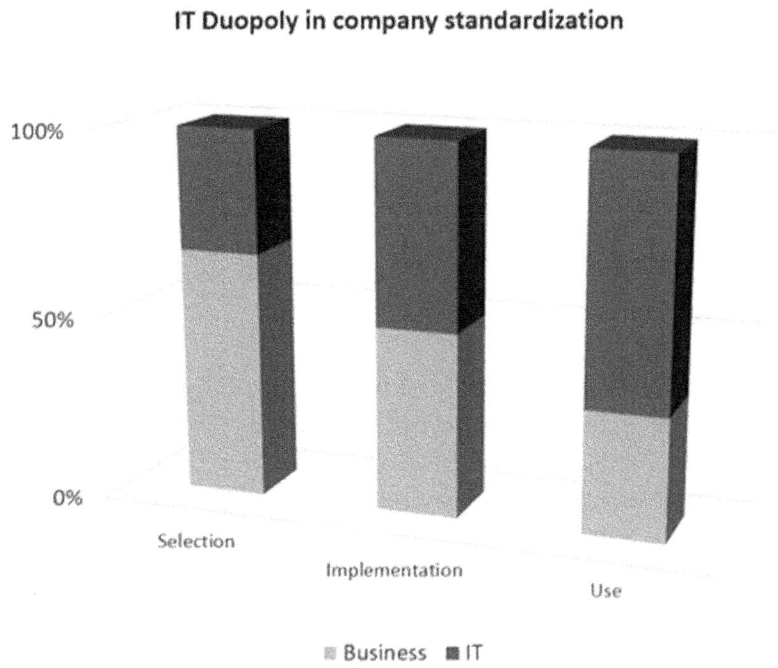

Management

- **Selection:** The primary selection criterion was based on finding a balance between functionality and support/license costs. The selection of products was simplified by subdividing the IT infrastructure into three architectural layers (hardware, system software, and application software).
- **Implementation:** Formalized project management was essential for the successful implementation of the standardized IT environment. This included managing progress and costs, approving project changes, and monitoring the quality of implementation. In addition, risk management was carried out, notably deciding on organizational changes, and controlling the number and type of applications.
- **Use:** Once implemented, the company's IT standards are updated according to requests for changes and deviations from the business department (e.g., from projects) and technical considerations from the IT department. There is strict control on usage and enforcement of the IT standards via the slogan 'comply or explain', and the process of making exceptions to policy and standards is restrictive. Formalized processes for IT service management are also essential for the success of the standardized IT environment. User impact and number of users involved, the possibility to charge costs, the contribution to a reduction of expenses, and the vendor's track record are the main considerations when allowing changes to company IT standards. Table 5 summarizes the governance and management of this set of company IT standards.

Table 5. Effective governance and management of company IT standards – key elements

Phase	Governance	Management
Selection	• Business and IT (evolved into IT Policy Board)	• Selection criteria • Consider three IT architectural layers (hardware, system, and application software)
Implementation	• Steering group (evolved into IT Policy Board) • Program Manager	• Project Management • Risk Management
Use (incl. changes)	• IT Policy Board • IT Review Team	• 'Comply or explain' slogan • Service management • Change criteria

The concepts of governance and management have been successfully applied in this case study. These proved to be essential in realizing the anticipated Business Benefits from company IT standardization as suggested by Weill and Ross (2004) and later investigated in detail by Van Wessel (2010). The project resulted in a low-cost and fully standardized IT environment that was successfully selected, implemented, and used.

CONCLUSION AND DISCUSSION

This study adds empirical evidence to the scarce academic literature on the effects of company IT standards on organizational performance and the influence of its governance and management arrangements. Furthermore, it provides practical insights for companies how to effectively set up governance and management in company standardization initiatives.

Contribution to Theory

The number of studies related to company standardization and standards is still very limited. Some key success factors such as standard enforcement, institutionalized mechanisms to involve key stakeholders, commitment from top management and ensuring that company standardization is part of corporate strategy (Kayworth and Sambamurthy, 2000; De Vries and Slob, 2006; Boh and Yellin, 2007, Dey et al., 2009; Hesser, 2010) have been acknowledged in this study on product standardization. However, we have added some specific aspects to the body of knowledge which relate to the way the benefits have been assessed, and the involvement of stakeholders during the lifecycle of the company standards. Due to the explicit distinction between governance and management, as part of the company IT standardization Management Framework (Figure 1), we were able to elaborate on specific governance arrangements between Business and IT stakeholders. In addition, we have described financial, service-and-support, and user-related benefits, whereas others (such as Boh and Yellin, 2007) have not addressed these benefits from a business point of view, or have related the success of company standards only to the actual "use of the standards" (De Vries and Slob, 2006). Because of our explicit distinction between governance and management, we were able to describe an efficient and effective company standardization initiative. Although this study deals with a single case, this chapter can be used as a basis of further academic studies.

Contribution to Practice

Companies carry out numerous standardization initiatives aimed at creating value by converging on particular software, hardware, or processes, but often with mixed success. The company studied here has shown that two practices in particular have contributed to the achievement of the intended benefits of the IT product standardization project. *First*, it is important to recognize the life cycle of a company standard and its phases of selection, implementation, and use. *Second*, it is essential to set up good governance and management mechanisms throughout each of these distinct phases.

Key to the success of company standardization, as far as governance is concerned, is the manner in which both business and IT stakeholders are involved in the selection, implementation, and use phases. These business stakeholders are the internal end-users of the standards, and ultimately well-functioning company processes are beneficial for the company's customers. During the lifecycle of a company standard, involvement of stakeholders may vary depending on the type. In our case, business stakeholders took the lead. Typically, representatives from (Business and IT) management, subject matter experts and the end-user community should be involved. Furthermore, decisions regarding deviations, changes, withdrawals, and renewals of company IT standards must be dealt with seriously to ensure standards reflect up-to-date requirements, and to prevent users from bypassing these standards. Senior business and IT representatives make and monitor such decisions through program management during the implementation phase, and policy boards are involved in the use phase.

In the selection phase, each decision should be based on preserving a balance between functionality, user impact, and the costs of implementation and maintenance. To minimize costs, the chosen IT standards have to be aligned with the IT architecture of the company. During the implementation phase, adequate project management must be in place to mitigate risk, and to track that the selected company standard is implemented as intended. In the use phase, proper IT service management processes and change management procedures must be in place. This includes enforcing the use of company standards and effectively managing changes in case of changed business requirements. It is more important for an organization to repeatedly and consistently use a company standard, than to aim for the "perfect" one, but not use it consequently. The described governance and management arrangements of company IT standardization may inspire IT executives and others to successfully adopt company standards in their enterprise.

An Agile Company Standardization Approach?

With the maturing of agile methodologies, based on the "*The Manifesto for Agile Software Development*" (Beck et al., 2001), working agile has gained much traction in many organizations around the globe. The Agile Manifesto was originally intended to reinvent traditional, waterfall-oriented software development methods. Agile is an umbrella term that covers frameworks adhering to the Agile manifesto. Meanwhile, the concept of working agile has been adopted in more and more settings. Therefore, the question arises what would be the impact if one applies an agile approach to a company standardization process? Are all process steps described in this chapter consisting of 'selection', 'implementation', and 'use' equally suited? Or is this an old-fashioned waterfall approach? Will the efficiency and effectiveness of the process be significantly impacted by an agile approach? And will governance and management mechanisms for successful company standardization initiatives, such as which stakeholders should be involved, be different when using an agile approach?

Agile Manifesto

To seek answers to these questions, we will first look into the Agile Manifesto's four Values and twelve Principles. The Agile Manifesto was triggered as part of iterative software development, to provide an alternative for the documentation driven, heavy-weight and waterfall-based software development processes (Beck et al., 2001). To investigate the potential applicability of this approach to a company standardization process, the wording of the Agile Manifesto's four values and twelve principles has not been changed, *except for the replacement of "software" in "company standards".*

The Agile Manifesto's Four Values

1. Individuals and interactions over processes and tools.
2. Working *company standards* over comprehensive documentation.
3. Customer collaboration over contract negotiation.
4. Responding to change over following a plan.

De Vries (1999, p. 156) argues developing a standard and creating standard software resemble each other to a large extent: 'The manufacturer of the standard software may have the intention and expectation that its software will be "the standard" in the market. In depends on the market situation whether or not this expectation is realistic and the software becomes "the standard". But then, what is the standard? In fact the product is not the standard, but its specifications are the standard. They are the "solutions for general use" from the definition. (...) Standardization is not the professional process of creating software, but it is the determination and recording of the software specifications."

What would these four values mean for a potential agile company standardization approach? Of the Agile Manifesto's four values, one can argue whether value 2 holds true for company standards as standards are typically "documented" specifications (ISO/IEC (2004)). It feels out of touch given this context as company standards are "*specifications*" pur sang. The other three values seem to be fitting as these relate to interactive and responsive collaborations with stakeholders of company standards.

The Agile Manifesto's 12 Principles

1. Our highest priority is to satisfy the customer through early and continuous delivery of valuable *company standards*.
2. Welcome changing requirements, even late in development. Agile processes harness change for the customer's competitive advantage.
3. Deliver working *company standards* frequently, from a couple of weeks to a couple of months, with a preference to the shorter timescale.
4. Business people and developers work together daily throughout the project.
5. Build projects around motivated individuals. Give them the environment and support they need and trust them to get the job done.
6. The most efficient and effective method of conveying information to and within a development team is face-to-face conversation
7. Working *company standards* is the primary measure of progress

8. Agile processes promote sustainable development. The sponsors, developers and users should be able to maintain a constant pace indefinitely.
9. Continuous attention to technical excellence and good design enhances agility.
10. Simplicity--the art of maximizing the amount of work not done--is essential
11. The best architectures, requirements and designs emerge from self-organizing teams.
12. At regular intervals, the team reflects on how to become more effective, then tunes and adjusts its behavior accordingly.

Regarding these twelve Agile Manifesto's principles numbers 1, 3 and 7 now directly reference company standards. Whereas these no. s 1 and 7 seem quite appropriate given the context of company standards as it refers to customer satisfaction, no. 3 is not applicable as company standards are "*to be repeatedly and consistently used*". Other agile principles also hold in the company standardization context, since they include a focus on change even late in development (no. 2), involving a broad range of motivated stakeholders in face-to-face sessions (nos. 4, 5, 6), considerations regarding simplicity, technical excellence and architectures and self-organizing teams that regularly reflect on its performance (nos. 11 and 12).

Based on the Agile Manifesto, various agile methods and practises have been developed. By far the most commonly adopted method is SCRUM, developed by Schwaber and Sutherland[7]. SCRUM is an agile framework for developing, delivering, and sustaining complex products. It was originally designed for small software development teams (Schwaber, 1996; Schwaber and Beedle, 2002), who break-up their work into actions that can be completed within timeboxed iterations (so called sprints). SCRUM has been adapted for multiple SCRUM teams in larger organizations in and in various contexts. To date, 56% of organisations worldwide that have adopted agile practices are using SCRUM-like methods with the Scaled Agile Framework (*SAFe*[8]) the most popular scaling method (VersionOne, 2018).

Anticipated Application of Agile Principles

The remainder of this sections reflects on the ABN AMRO case study with regard to possible application of these agile principles. For the three process steps, the observed governance and management arrangements and its potential adjustments will be considered.

Selection Phase

Governance (This Case Study)

In the selection phase, senior management initiated the standardization project in close collaboration with the IT department. However, it took time to convince all business stakeholders of its added value.

Governance (Agile Approach)

With an agile approach, business stakeholders could be convinced earlier of the added value of valuable company standards as they are typically more motivated (no. 5) and have face-to-face discussions (no.6).

Management (This Case Study)

Each decision should be based on preserving a balance between functionality, user impact, and the costs of implementation and maintenance (support/license costs).

Management (Agile Approach)

Decision making in the selection phase could be made more efficient as the stakeholders work closely together (no. 4) and focus on simplicity, good design and technical excellence (no. 10, 9).

Implementation Phase

Governance (This Case Study)

Key stakeholders during the implementation of the company standard included a program manager and a steering group with members from both the business unit and the IT department. Project groups reported to a program manager as part of this hierarchical program structure.

Governance (Agile Approach)

In an agile context, SCRUM-like methods have been developed to coordinate the work of multiple scrum teams in larger organizations with the Scaled Agile Framework (*SAFe*) as the most popular scaling method using. In such settings project members work in self-organizing teams (no. 11) allowing fast, decentralized decision-making in the implementation phase.

Management (This Case Study)

Strict adherence to project management processes was instrumental to manage progress and costs, approving project changes, mitigate risks (e.g. controlling the number and type of applications) and to track that the selected company standard was implemented as intended.

Management (Agile Approach)

Alternatively, agile project management methods can be applied which allow changing requirements late in development (no. 2) and let project members reflect on performance and risks and act accordingly (no. 12). Examples of such agile project delivery frameworks include the DSDM Agile Project Framework[9] and PRINCE2® Agile[10].

Use Phase

Governance (This Case Study)

Requests regarding deviations, changes, withdrawals, and renewals of company IT standards were assessed by the IT review team and approved by the IT policy board, taking both business and technological considerations into account.

Governance (Agile Approach)

In an agile context sustainable development is promoted (no. 8). Requests regarding deviations, changes, withdrawals, and renewals of company standards will be jointly processed by IT and Business representatives (no. 4) instead of IT staff only. This should result in better functional suitability and technical feasibility.

Management (This Case Study)

A full review process was carried out every two years and is based on provided functionality of the set of company standards. Formalized processes for IT service management are also essential for the success of the standardized IT environment. This includes enforcing the use of company standards and effectively managing changes in case of changed business requirements.

Management (Agile Approach)

Reviews will occur more frequently to tune and adjust the set of company standards (no. 12) since working company standards are the primary measure of progress (no. 7). Enforcing the use of company standards and effectively managing changed business requirements by means of IT service management processes, are dealt with on the premise of customer satisfaction through early and continuous delivery of valuable company standards (no.1).

Based on this anticipated application of agile principles the following picture emerges. In all phases of the IT company standardization process the added value of an agile approach is projected. This is true for the section phase as close collaboration of Business and IT departments, which is key to the success of company standardization, is an integral aspect of working agile. Therefore, an agile approach provides added value in the development/selection of the standard as well as the decisions making about it. Also, in the implementation and use phase the agile approach could add value, such as short reporting lines, effective decision making and prompt follow-up on proposed changes to the company standards. However, replacing a company standard too quickly with a new version or even something completely different could lead to problems. At least backwards compatibility and good version management is required. This is not different from the traditional approach as described in this case study.

As a rule, one could argue that the more business involvement is required in a company standardization process, the more agile practices seem to make sense. However, no predictions can be made, nor can one say something on the results from such an agile approach compared to the result in this case study. Therefore, we intend to carry out action research to learn how an agile way of working impacts company standardization in practice. This should add to the current literature on 'standard dynamics' (Egyedi & Blind, 2008).

ACKNOWLEDGMENT

The authors would like to thank ABN AMRO and in particular those staff that took part in this case study. Moreover, we thank four anonymous reviewers for all improvements they suggested.

REFERENCES

Backhouse, J., Hsu, C. W., & Silva, L. (2006). Circuits of Power in Creating de jure Standards: Shaping an International Information Systems Security Standard. *Management Information Systems Quarterly, 30*(Special Issue), 413–438. doi:10.2307/25148767

Beck, K., Beedle, M., Van Bennekum, A., Cockburn, A., Cunningham, W., Fowler, M., & Kern, J. (2001). *Manifesto for agile software development*. Academic Press.

Blind, K. (2004). *The Economics of Standards – Theory, Evidence, Policy*. Cheltenham, UK: Edward Elgar.

Boh, W. F., & Yellin, D. (2007). Using Enterprise Architecture Standards in Managing Information Technology. *Journal of Management Information Systems, 23*(3), 163–207. doi:10.2753/MIS0742-1222230307

Boynton, A. C., & Zmud, R. W. (1987). Information Technology Planning in the 1990s. *Management Information Systems Quarterly, 11*(1), 59–71. doi:10.2307/248826

Cargill, C. F. (1989). *Information Technology Standardization: Theory, Process, and Organizations*. Bedford, MA: Digital Press.

De Vries, H. J. (1999). *Standardization – A Business Approach to the Role of National Standardization Organisations*. Boston: Kluwer Academic Publishers. doi:10.1007/978-1-4757-3042-5

De Vries, H. J., & Slob, F. J. (2006). Best practice in company standardization. *International Journal of IT Standards and Standardization Research, 4*(1), 62–85. doi:10.4018/jitsr.2006010104

Dey, P. K., Clegg, B., & Bennett, D. (2009). Managing implementation issues in enterprise resource planning projects. In M. H. Sherif (Ed.), *Handbook of enterprise integration*. Boca Raton, FL: Auerbach. doi:10.1201/9781420078220-c24

Egyedi, T. M., & Blind, K. (Eds.). (2008). *The Dynamics of Standards*. Cheltenham, UK: Edward Elgar.

Hesser, W. (2010). Standardisation within a company – A strategic perspective. In W. Hesser (Ed.), *Standardisation in companies and markets* (3rd ed., pp. 215–258). Hamburg: Helmut Schmidt University.

Hesser, W., & Inklaar, A. (1997). *An introduction to Standards and Standardization, DIN-Normungskunde* (Vol. 36). Berlin: Beuth Verlag GmbH.

Jain, S. (2012). Pragmatic agency in technology standards setting: The case of Ethernet. *Research Policy*, *41*(9), 1643–1654. doi:10.1016/j.respol.2012.03.025

Kayworth, T., & Sambamurthy, V. (2000). Facilitating localized exploitation and enterprise-wide integration in the use of IT infrastructures: The role of PC/LAN infrastructure standard. *The Data Base for Advances in Information Systems*, *31*(4), 54–81. doi:10.1145/506760.506765

Li, X., & Chen, Y. (2012). Corporate IT Standardization: Product Compatibility, Exclusive Purchase Commitment, and Competition Effects. *Information Systems Research*, *23*(4), 1158–1174. doi:10.1287/isre.1110.0412

Manders, N. B. (2015). Implementation and Impact of ISO 9001. ERIM Ph.D. Series Research in Management (Vol. 337). Rotterdam, The Netherlands: Erasmus Research Institute of Management (ERIM).

Mendoza, R. A., & Ravichandran, T. (2011). An Exploratory Analysis of the Relationship Between Organizational and Institutional Factors Shaping the Assimilation of Vertical Standards. *International Journal of IT Standards and Standardization Research*, *9*(1), 24–51. doi:10.4018/jitsr.2011010102

Mueller, T., Dittes, S., Ahlemann, F., Urbach, N., & Smolnik, S. (2015). Because Everybody is Different Towards Understanding the Acceptance of Organizational IT Standards. *Proceedings of the 48th Hawaii International Conference on System Sciences*. 10.1109/HICSS.2015.487

Nickerson, J. V., & zur Muehlen, M. (2006). The ecology of standards processes: Insights from Internet standards making. *Management Information Systems Quarterly*, *30*(1), 476–488.

Poba-Nzaou, P., & Raymond, L. (2011). Managing ERP system risk in SMEs: A multiple case study. *Journal of Information Technology*, *26*(3), 170–192. doi:10.1057/jit.2010.34

Rada, R., & Craparo, J. (2000). Standardizing Software Projects. *Communications of the ACM*, *43*(12), 21–25. doi:10.1145/355112.355117

Rogers, E. M. (2003). *Diffusion of innovations* (5th ed.). New York: Simon & Schuster International.

Schwaber, K. (1996). SCRUM development process. *Proceedings of ACM SIGPLAN on Objected-Oriented Programming, Systems, Languages, & Applications (OOPSLA '96).*

Schwaber, K., & Beedle, M. (2002). *Agile software development with Scrum*. Upper Saddle River, NJ: Prentice Hall.

Swaminathan, J. M. (2001). Using Standardized Operations. *California Management Review*, *43*(3), 125–135. doi:10.2307/41166092

Teichmann, H. (2010). *Global Standardization: Coping with Multilingualism, EURAS contributions to standardisation research 3*. Aachen, Germany: Verlag Mainz.

Van de Kaa, G., Van den Ende, J., De Vries, H. J., & Van Heck, E. (2011). Factors for winning interface format battles: A review and synthesis of the literature. *Technological Forecasting and Social Change*, *78*(8), 1397–1411. doi:10.1016/j.techfore.2011.03.011

Van Wessel, R., De Vries, H., & Ribbers, P. (2016), Business Benefits through Company IT Standardization. In K. Jakobs (Ed.) Effective Standardization Management in Corporate Settings (pp. 34-52). Hershey, PA: IGI Global. doi:10.4018/978-1-4666-9737-9.ch003

van Wessel, R., Ribbers, P., & de Vries, H. (2006). Effects of IS Standardization on Business Process Performance: A Case in HR IS Company Standardization. *Proceedings of the 39th Annual Hawaii International Conference on System Sciences*, 6. 10.1109/HICSS.2006.141

VersionOne. (2018). *The 12th annual state of agile report*. VersionOne Inc. Retrieved from http://stateofagile.versionone.com/

Weill, P., & Ross, J. (2004). *IT Governance – How Top Performers Manage IT decision Rights for Superior Results*. Boston, MA: Harvard Business School Press.

Weitzel, T. (2003). A Network ROI", MISQ Special Issue Workshop Standard Making: A Critical Research Frontier for Information Systems. *Pre-Conference Workshop, International Conference on Information Systems*, 62-79.

van Wessel, R. (2010). Toward Corporate IT Standardization Management: Frameworks and Solutions. Hershey, PA: IGI Global.

West, J., & Dedrick, J. (2006). Scope and Timing of Deployment: Moderators of Organizational Adoption of the Linux Server Platform. *International Journal of IT Standards and Standardization Research*, *4*(2), 1–23. doi:10.4018/jitsr.2006070101

Wiegmann, P. M. (2019). *Managing Innovation and Standards: A Case in the European Heating Industry*. Springer. doi:10.1007/978-3-030-01532-9

WTO. (2005). *World Trade Report 2005: Standards, 'offshoring' and air transport*. Geneva: World Trade Organization.

Yin, R. K. (2009). *Case Study Research – Design and Methods* (4th ed.). Thousand Oaks, CA: SAGE.

KEY TERMS AND DEFINITIONS

Agility: Ability to act quickly and easily on changing circumstances.

Business Benefits: An outcome of an action or decision that contributes towards meeting one or more business objectives.

Business IT Alignment: The continuous, mutual coordination of business departments and the IT department to optimize the value that information technology contributes to an enterprise.

Business Performance: The efficiency and effectiveness of an organization reflected in the business objectives set by management.

Company Standard: A specification of a product or process to be repeatedly and consistently used in the company.

Company Standardization: The activity of establishing and recording a limited set of solutions to actual or potential matching problems, directed at benefits for the party or parties involved, balancing their needs, and intending and expecting that these solutions will be repeatedly or continuously used, during a certain period, by a substantial number of the parties for whom they are meant.

Company Standardization Process: A set of sequential process steps, a) selection, b) implementation, c) use (including changes and withdrawals) that comprise the lifecycle of a company standard.

Governance of Company Standards: Specifying the decision rights and accountability framework to encourage desirable behavior in the selection, implementation and use of standards within an organization.

Management of Company Standards: The decision-making efforts associated with planning, organizing, controlling, and directing the selection, implementation and use of standards within an organization.

ENDNOTES

1. An earlier version of this book chapter appeared in Van Wessel et al. (2016). The main difference is in the addition of the discussion on agility.
2. Total cost of ownership is an indicator of IT efficiency, introduced by Gartner in 1987.
3. Calculated on the basis of functional equivalents
4. Payback period = 32,000,000 / {(4,600-2,392) x 10,000} = 1.45 year
5. ROI = {(4,600-2,392) x 10,000 – 32,000,000} / 32,000,000 = 176%
6. $32,000,000 = \sum_{j=1}^{4} \frac{(4,600 - 2,392)x10,000}{(1+i)^j} \Rightarrow i = 0.5759$
7. https://www.scrum.org/resources/scrum-guide
8. https://www.scaledagileframework.com/
9. https://www.dsdm.org/sites/default/files/essentializing_the_dsdm_agile_project_framework.pdf
10. https://www.axelos.com/best-practice-solutions/prince2-agile

Chapter 6
Managing In-Company Standardization While Avoiding Resistance:
A Philosophical-Empirical Approach

Ries Haverkamp
Interface, The Netherlands

Henk de Vries
Erasmus University, The Netherlands & Delft University of Technology, The Netherlands

ABSTRACT

Standards may be an advantage for a company, but employees often resist them because they feel they are forced to behave in a certain way. Even a broad approach like TQM seems to have to too little focus on the "human aspects" to prevent resistance and failure during change projects like in-company standardization. This chapter uses a philosophical approach to study why staff tend to resist company standardization initiatives. Foucault and Habermas provide insights into the reasons for this resistance but do not solve the tension between freedom and control. Dooyeweerd's philosophy seems to be more promising. This chapter uses a company standardization project of an automotive supplier to examine these three philosophical approaches to understand resistance to standards and to investigate how this resistance can be avoided by managing in-company standardization in a more holistic way.

INTRODUCTION[1]

'Conforming to standards means following the advice of others, relinquishing a certain degree of one's freedom of choice and self-control to others, and often becoming more similar to many others as well – none of which is very consistent with the concept of an actor. We may therefore expect a certain reluctance to follow standards – in particular those that are well known and followed by many – from individuals and organizations seeking to be highly autonomous, innovative, and different' (Brunsson and Jacobsson, 2000, p. 134). Actors may view standards negatively because these can limit responsibility, prevent them

DOI: 10.4018/978-1-5225-9008-8.ch006

Copyright © 2019, IGI Global. Copying or distributing in print or electronic forms without written permission of IGI Global is prohibited.

from doing or saying what they want, and incur high costs during conversion from current practice to the practice prescribed in the standards. Moreover, standards may lead to uniformity (Brunsson and Jacobsson, 2000, p. 136). 'Many of the objections to standards are similar to the objections to rules and regulation in general. Standardization is often seen as an unwelcome, unnecessary, and harmful intrusion into a world of free, distinct individuals and organizations that are wise enough to decide for themselves, or into the world of civil society or free markets. Standardization, it is felt, will mean regulation from outside, whereby actors, things, and conditions are now to be shaped in a uniform manner' (Brunsson, 2000, p. 171). Standardization is the activity of establishing and recording a limited set of solutions to actual or potential matching problems, directed at benefits for the party or parties involved, balancing their needs, and intending and expecting that these solutions will be used repeatedly or continuously, during a certain period, by a substantial number of the parties for whom they are meant (De Vries, 1997). In the case of in-company standardization, the activity is carried out fully or mainly within the company, the standard may be used outside the company as well.

The issue of resistance to standards has received little attention in the literature on managing standardization within a company. Even studies that provide a broad managerial approach ignore it (Adolphi, 1997; AFNOR, 1967; Boh & Yellin, 2007; Wenström et at., 2000; Van Wessel, 2010). These objections may apply to all standards but probably in particular to management system standards because these affect human behavior in a more direct way than technical standards. Therefore, this chapter starts by discussing management standards and examining the paradox between benefits of implementation on the one hand, and resistance to this implementation on the other hand. We discuss that broad implementation approaches like TQM and BPR fall short in avoiding resistance and/or failure. Inspired by Lelong and Mallard (1995) who referred to Foucault in their introduction to a special issue of Réseaux on standardization, and by a study by Van Veldhuisen (1996), we analyze resistance to such standards using Foucault's (1977) analysis of anonymous power systems. This analysis provides an explanation for resistance but not for benefits. Habermas' (1987) concept of communicative action provides additional insights but does not solve the problem of the tension between control and freedom. Dooyeweerd's (1955, 1957) philosophy overcomes this tension and provides the basis for a holistic management approach. We apply this approach in the case of a standardization project in a company. This project was related to the company's quality management system which was based on an international quality management standard. We evaluate the company standardization project and the resistance to it during a six-year period, using quality management literature and philosophical studies by Foucault, Habermas and Dooyeweerd.

THEORETICAL BACKGROUND

The Paradox: Benefits of Standards and Resistance to Them

The paradox of benefits of standards and resistance to them may be related to the difference between common and individual benefits of standards mentioned by Arthur (1989). Psychologists emphasize human resistance to control – freedom versus order (Brehm and Brehm, 1981). The same terms are used by David (1995, p. 18): 'The kernel of the problem posed for private and public decision-making with regard to the setting of technology standards may be construed to be nothing more and nothing less than the fundamental issue with which all social organizations are confronted: where to position themselves on the terrain between the poles of 'order' and 'freedom'.'

In this chapter we focus on management system standards. More than one million organizations have obtained a certificate showing that their quality management systems meet the requirements in the international standard ISO 9001 (ISO, 2008, ISO 2015 and ISO, 2018). Several researchers report positive impacts of implementation of ISO 9001 (Cadadesús and Karapetrovic, 2005; Corbett et al., 2005; Lo and Chang, 2007; Nicolau and Sellers, 2002; Padma et al., 2008), others find hardly any or no positive impact (Dick et al., 2008; Martínez-Costa et al., 2009; Terziovski et al., 1997; Tzelepis et al., 2006), and some report mixed positive/neutral effects (Benner and Veloso, 2008; Boiral and Roy, 2007; Nair and Prajogo, 2009; Naveh et al., 2004; Yeung et al., 2003). The best explanation for these differences seems to be the motivation to implement the standard. Is the company internally motivated to implement the standard because it is a tool to improve performance, or is it just implementing it because it needs the certificate for their position in the market? (Nair and Prajogo, 2009; Terziovski et al., 2003; Yeung et al., 2003). Boiral and Roy (2007) find a positive effect of internal motivation on performance improvements related to ISO 9001 implementation. However, in case of low internal motivation, external pressure does not necessarily lead to more human resource problems and a sort of iron cage of bureaucracy (Weber, 1922; Boiral, 2003), and external pressure can encourage a better integration of ISO 9001 (Boiral and Roy, 2007, p. 240). In these studies, 'motivation' refers primarily to the motivation of the organization's management but few studies take employee motivation into account. Some address the internalization of practices related to ISO 9001 (Nair and Prajogo, 2009; more references in their paper) but they focus on the measures prescribed by the standard rather than on the attitude of the employees. Lazaric and Denis (2005) report that implementation of ISO 9001 may lead to stress because of a change in routines and consequent broadening of tasks, and an aversion to writing and recording the majority of tasks. Surprisingly, literature about organizational routines (Becker, 2008) pays little attention to resistance. However, Connor (1997) noted the importance of employees in achieving quality management objectives.

Van Kemenade et al. (2011) focuses on the employees themselves (his case is not about ISO 9001 implementation but about a more or less similar situation of accreditation of universities of applied sciences in Flanders (Belgium) and the Netherlands). He reports that professionals in these organizations are willing to contribute to the process of obtaining accreditation if this process has internal added value, has a motivating object, has procedure and subject, has simple rules, and does not have control as its dominant value. He also states that willingness to contribute also depends on employee characteristics (is loyal to the organization, sees self-interest, and relates to the organization and does not delegate to others) and organization characteristics (does not have quality experts to do all the work, gives enough management support, and has its internal quality management system in place). In other words, the basic attitude is positive, but many conditions have to be fulfilled. If this is not the case, professionals may react with 'dramaturgical compliance' (just pretending to comply, fooling the auditor). Involvement of employees is found to contribute to the success of ISO 9001 implementation (Brown et al.,1998; Mahadevappa and Kotreshwar, 2004).

Some studies report a positive impact of ISO 9001 on employees. In Egyptian manufacturing firms, ISO 9001 implementation improved employee motivation (Magd, 2008). Almost 50% of registered Spanish firms reported an increase in employee satisfaction (Casadesús and Karapetrovic, 2005). However, the information in these studies comes from respondents at management level, not from employees. Brown et al. (1998) report that ISO 9000 certification did not bring any significant improvements in staff motivation and staff retention within Australian SMEs. Employee commitment was the most often (50%) mentioned problem in these companies. In a Swedish study, several quality management approaches were compared. Users of ISO 9001 reported fewer improvements in the organization than non-users (Lagrosen and Lagrosen, 2005).

ISO 9001 views the organization as a network of manageable processes designed to satisfy customers and includes measurable objectives, management control, and documentation (Furusten, 2000). ISO 9001 has codified the layman's conception of a successful organization. It sees organizations as manageable and controllable units which can be used by management as instruments for fulfilling predetermined goals, strategies, and visions. It ignores the scholars that find fault with rational models for control and management of organizations or that cast doubt on the whole conception of being modern (Furusten, 2000, pp. 83-84). In a study on the implementation of the 1994 predecessor version of ISO 9001:2008, Naveh and Erez (2004) found that the implementation of the standard focuses workers on documentation, standardization and conformity to rules and procedures and not on a culture of innovation.

In the 2000 and 2008 version of ISO 9001, the number of compulsory procedures was reduced from 19 to six. The 2015 version only refers to the requirement of 'documented information', the extent depending on the size of the organization, the complexity of processes and competence of persons (ISO, 2015, paragraph 7.5). Although the standards do not prescribe a lot of paper work, in practice, this is often different. Manders (2015) shows that this practice may differ per employee. The attitude towards actual use of control measures depends on awareness, perceived usefulness and ease of use, and the willingness to contribute to continuous improvement depends on the extent they feel responsible for the functioning of the ISO 9001 system. If these conditions do not apply, employees may ignore the system or show resistance. The process approach prescribed in the 2000, 2008 and 2015 versions of ISO 9001 'forces' people to behave in a way prescribed by the system; in fact, they are part of the system. Its approach resembles the 'cybernetic' view as described by Hofstede (1978). ISO 9001:2008 and ISO 9001:2015 refer to employees as 'human resources,' next to other resources such as equipment and money and this is exactly the consequence mentioned by Hofstede (1978, p. 460). It is not surprising that such a system may cause concern and unrest among employees. Different theoretical lenses may be used to study this: theory of planned behavior (Ajzen, 1991; Manders, 2015), innovation diffusion theory (Rogers 2003), and the technology acceptance model (Davis, 1989; Davis et al., 1989). Theories on change management (e.g. Bevan, 2011; Carnall, 2007) provide approaches to involve employees in change projects.

TQM

An approach that pretends to involve people during change projects is Total Quality Management (TQM). TQM involves the application of quality management principles to all aspects of the organization, including customers and suppliers, and their integration with the key business processes (Dale et al., 2007: 29). It is an integrated approach, consisting of principles and practices, whose goal is to improve the quality of an organization's goods and services through continuously meeting and exceeding customer's needs in most competitive ways (Talib et al., 2010).

The concept of TQM is often confused with other practices such as quality circles and ISO 9000. Although similarities exist between TQM and other business process improvement practices, the TQM philosophy pretends to be all-encompassing. Dale and Cooper (1992, p. 11) state that TQM is a much broader concept than the initiatives which have gone before, encompassing not only product, service and process quality improvements but also those relating to costs and productivity, and people involved and development. To put it in Spencer's words: it blurs the boundaries between the organization and the environment. Entities previously regarded as outsiders (e.g. suppliers, customers) are now considered part of the organizational processes (Spencer, 1994). Although different quality experts emphasize different aspects, TQM can be summarized as a systematic approach to the practice of management, requiring changes in organizational processes, strategic priorities, individual beliefs, individual attitudes, and individual behaviors (Olian and Rynes, 1991; Zink, 2007). Spencer (1994) states that TQM is not a cut-and-dried reality but an amorphous philosophy that is continuously enacted by managers, consultants, and researchers who make choices based on their own conceptual frameworks concerning the nature of organizations.

Due to its amorphous character, TQM has been defined in different ways. For example, Kanji (1990) defined it as 'the way of life of an organization committed to customer satisfaction through continuous improvement. This way of life varies from organization to organization and from country to country to another but has certain principles which can be implemented to secure market share, increase profits and reduce costs'. Berry (1991) defined the TQM process as a total corporate focus on meeting and exceeding customers' expectations and significantly reducing costs resulting from poor quality by adopting a new management system and corporate culture. The British Standards Authority (1971) defined TQM as follows (BS 47778, Part 2): *A management philosophy embracing all activities through which the needs and expectations of the customer and the community, and the objectives of the organization are satisfied in the most efficient and cost-effective way by maximizing the potential of all employees in a continuing drive for improvement.* This definition, as van der Wiele (1998) mentioned: *'...seems to fit with the broader views in quality management, in which quality management becomes synonymous with 'good management' and the focus is no longer on the specific quality activities, but on all aspects of managing the business.'*

Talib *et al.* (2011) define TQM as a set of management practices applicable throughout the organization and geared to ensure the organization consistently meets or exceeds customer requirements. Based on a literature review of research papers on TQM practices they extracted the following major practices of TQM: '(1) Top-management commitment (includes leadership, management support and management commitment), (2) Customer focus (includes customer satisfaction and orientation), (3) Training and education, (4) Continuous improvement and innovation, (5) Supplier management (includes supplier relationship, supplier quality and supplier partnership, collaboration), (6) Employee involvement'.

However, despite its emphasis on employee involvement, literature indicate for some time some limitations of TQM as well. Based on a literature review, Reed *et al.* (2000) noticed a direct relationship between the adoption of TQM and improved firm performance. However, Zink (2007) pointed out that the first reports of failures in the implementation of TQM appeared in the early 1990s, and first surveys by US and UK consultancy firms showed that two-third of the implementation processes have been given up (Brown *et al.*, 1994). The primary reasons for failures (or success) are leadership, management commitment and involvement, established need and strategic view (long term). Similar experiences have been made in Europe (Dahlgaard *et al.*, 1997; Zink, 1997). However, for companies taking a more 'structured way' in introducing TQM by using the models of the international quality awards based on self-assessment approaches, such as the American Malcolm Baldrige National Quality Award or the European Quality Award (EFQM, 1992), the situation seems to be partly different. Some studies show that especially the award-winning companies achieved – among others – improvements in their financial performance (Zink, 2007). But here too the success rates have to be considered as mentioned above: regarding any major change of an organization like business re-engineering or lean management or the realization of a Toyota like production system *no more than a third of the companies gain the success they have intended (Zink, 1997).* In summary, failures have been related to inadequate implementation of TQM mainly caused by a lack of leadership or the willingness and ability to change the culture.

BPR

Similarly, we may learn lessons from the success factors of other concepts that has been implemented in businesses. One of these is Business Process re-engineering (BPR), popularized as a formal concept by Hammer (1990), Davenport and Short (1990) and Hammer and Champy (1993), but with earlier roots: Harrington (1987) emphasized process improvement in action. BPR has been defined in different ways with different terms (e.g. business improvement, business process redesign or business process re-engineering) which roughly all refer to the same type of activity: pointing out that gains in performance can be achieved by taking a holistic and objective view of business processes (Macdonald and Dale, 2007). Macdonald and Dale (2007) report that in general TQM and BPR do not exclude each other but rather complement each other and both are integral approaches. In fact, several fundamental principles and themes of BPR, such as the integration of people and technical aspects, are similar to those which are related to TQM. One of the key differences is that BPR places more emphasis on equipment and technology and TQM more emphasis on people.

Some organizations have been able to achieve good results with Business Process Reengineering (BPR). For example, Caterpillar, Inc. reported cost savings between $10 and $20 million over a five-year period from BPR initiatives (Paper et al., 2001). However, in many cases, BPR has failed repeatedly to deliver its promised results (Al-Mashari et al., 2001). Hammer and Champy (1993) claim a failure rate of 70%, Al-Mashari et al. (2001) show in an international BPR survey that the success rate of BPR is higher (55.46%).

Paper et al. (2001) conducted a BPR case study at Honeywell Inc., USA, for the purpose of uncovering the success factors of BPR. From this case study they developed a set of general lessons. In line with Al-Mashari et al. (2001), who state that many of the reported failures are thought to be due to the primary focus of BPR on 'technical aspects', the majority of these ten formulated lessons in the case study at Honeywell are not about BPR 'tools' and/or 'techniques. Almost all lessons are directly related to (the management of) 'human aspects'. For example, the very first lesson they report is that people are the key enablers of change. People do the work and therefore must be trained, facilitated, and nurtured. In short, the lessons learned for BPR concern mainly 'soft' issues about encouragement, involvement, communication, dedication and ownership. Further, support from the top is critical, but the actual implementation should be carried out bottom-up. Finally, if the managerial attitude remains that of 'command and control' and/or their behavior does not change, transformation will most likely fail.

In summary, a TQM approach is broader and more encompassing than ISO 9001 and BPR. However, it is not obvious that a TQM approach is always successful. And also the improvement approach of BPR can fail if not implemented right. The success factors of TQM and BPR illustrate the importance of interdisciplinarity. Too much focus on technical aspects while not recognizing or ignoring the more 'human aspects' might lead to failures in business practices such as in-company standardization.

However, will ISO 9001, TQM and BPR be successful by just focusing more on the 'human aspects' of improvement or change processes? Which human aspects? Are there more aspects relevant? To answer these questions, we will investigate these standards / approaches in a deeper way. Because of the diversity of angles and the need to combine these, a holistic approach is needed. Such a search for a holistic view and diagnosis, combining disciplines, triggered us to make use of the discipline of all disciplines: philosophy (Strauss, 2009), to address these limitations of TQM and BPR. In this chapter, we therefore intend to focus on resistance to standards in a broad and fundamental way by taking a philosophical approach.

Foucault and ISO 9001

Philosophers that studied man in relation to power systems include Michel Foucault and Jürgen Habermas. Both Foucault and Habermas criticize the historical transformations of modern forms of rationality (Kelly, 1994, p. 372). Foucault did not develop a complete theory but rather studied several domains that have been shaped by power relations (Foucault, 1976, p. 109). His objective was to create a history of different modes by which human beings are made subjects (Foucault, 1982, p. 208). Foucault (1977) studied the domain of torture, punishment, and prisons which can serve as an example for other systems of anonymous power. The emergence of the prison marks the institutionalization of the power to punish. Traditionally, the focus was on the body, with the ultimate punishment of public torture and execution, to be seen by all almost as a triumph (Foucault, 1977, p. 34). This changed in punishing the soul instead, following a penal judgement (Foucault, 1977, p. 19). This soul is shaped by methods of punishment, supervision and constraints (Foucault, 1977, p. 29). The object of control is 'the economy, the efficiency of movements, their internal organization. (…) Finally, there is the modality: it implies an uninterrupted, constant coercion, supervising the processes of the activity rather than its result and it is exercised according to a codification that partitions time, space, movement as closely as possible. These methods allowed the meticulous control of the operations of the body, which assured the constant subjection of its forces and imposed upon them a relation of docility-utility, might be called 'disciplines'' (Foucault, 1977, p. 137). The success of disciplinary power derives from the instruments of hierarchical observation (eyes that must see without being seen), normalizing judgement (a combination of comparing, differentiating, hierarchizing, homogenizing and excluding), and examination (Foucault, 1977, pp. 170-187). Examination transforms the economy of visibility into the exercise of power. (…) It is the fact of being constantly seen, of always being able to be seen, that maintains the disciplined individual in his subjection (Foucault, 1977, p. 187). The examination that places individuals in a field of surveillance also situates them in a network of writing; it engages them in a mass of documents that captures and fixes them (Foucault, 1977, p. 189). The examination opens up the possibility of the constitution of a comparative system of measurements, description and registrations (Foucault, 1977, p. 190). It makes each individual a 'case'. The individual may be described, judged, measured and compared to others, in his very individuality; and it is also the individual who has to be trained or corrected, classified, normalized and excluded, etc. (Foucault, 1977, p. 191). Finally, the examination is at the centre of the procedures that constitute the individual as effect and object of power and as effect and object of knowledge (Foucault, 1977, p. 192). Public execution was replaced by penal detention as a calculated technique for altering individual behavior (Foucault, 1977, p. 264).

Foucault refers to Bentham's (1838) Panopticon: a prison in the form of a circle, with a tower in the middle. The prisoners live in cells in this circle. These cells have barred windows in the outside of the building and in the inside of the circle so that the supervisors in the tower can observe them. The prisoners, however, cannot see whether they are observed or not. 'The surveillance is permanent in its effects even if it is discontinuous in its action. (…) The power relation is independent of the person who exercises it' (Foucault, 1977, p. 201). 'The side walls prevent each individual from coming into contact with his companions. He is seen, but he does not see; he is the object of information, never a subject in communication' (Foucault, 1977, p. 200). The Panopticon was also a laboratory; it could be used as a machine to carry out experiments, to alter behavior, to train or correct individuals (Foucault, 1977, p. 203). 'Whenever one is dealing with a multiplicity of individuals on whom a task or a particular form of behavior must be imposed, the panoptic schema may be used' (Foucault, 1977, p. 205). Moreover, the level of use may be extended from individuals to organizations: 'The seeing machine was once a sort of dark room into which individuals spied; it has become a transparent building in which the exercise of power may be supervised by society as a whole' (Foucault, 1977, p. 207).

The prison system has not been successful. 'Prisons do not diminish the crime rate, detention causes recidivism, the prison produces delinquents, encourages the organization of a milieu of delinquents' (Foucault, 1977, pp. 265-268). As a result, initiatives to reform of the prison system have been taken at the national level. Illegal activities remain but society uses them or even needs them to show the limits of legality and to make illegality less dangerous. 'The carceral 'naturalizes' the legal power to punish, as it 'legalizes' the technical power to discipline' (Foucault, 1977, p. 303). The prison is 'linked to a series of 'carceral' mechanisms which seem distinct enough – since they are intended to alleviate pain, to cure and to comfort but which all tend to exercise a power of normalization' (Foucault, 1977, p. 308).

Foucault is the co-founder of the Groupe de l'Information de les Prisons, a prison information group that provides a channel for prisoners to voice their concerns, and such protest is, in fact, Foucault's "solution" for those who suffer from the exercise of power. He "walked his talk" by joining students in occupying administration buildings and fighting with the police.

An ISO 9001 quality management system is a system of control to assure that the organization's products (which may include services) meet the expressed or unexpressed requirements of the customer. This control is achieved through process management with a set of measures including policy development and deployment, written procedures, registrations, measuring of product characteristics against requirements, measuring customer satisfaction, corrective and preventive actions, internal and external audits, and management reviews. The 'human resources' are managed by providing them education. Employees have to behave in the way prescribed in the written instructions and procedures of the quality management system. Manders (2015, chapter 4) investigated the involvement of individual employees in their company's ISO 9001 system. She found a diversity of attitudes towards the system, from very negative to very positive, with some employees showing the kind of resistance described by Foucault. Others had a positive attitude to the system, acknowledging its usefulness and perceived ease of use. Only those who had a specific role within the system, for example, internal auditors, were also involved in improving the system, provided they felt responsible to do so. The manager or management team is not the 'sovereign king' of the organization but, instead, part of the system. Management observes (management review) but is observed as well through internal and external audits.

We can see the similarities with Foucault's systems. Once established, the quality management system exercises normalizing power. It is an instrument of discipline. This power is exercised rather than possessed, it comes from the bottom up rather than from the top to the bottom, and it is not repressive (backed by sanctions) but productive (Kelly, 1994, p. 374). The prescriptions of behavior related to described processes and the subsequent measurements, evaluations and audits make employee behavior transparent. This does not mean that employees cannot take any initiative. On the contrary, but such initiatives are prescribed by the system as well because it defines their responsibilities, authorities and tasks which include corrective and preventive actions and even improvements of the quality management system. In forcing them to further strengthen the system, ISO 9001 even goes a step further than the old prison systems. Anyhow, the employee as well as his manager is captured by the system. It is not surprising that they may have feelings of resistance. At the end of the day, Foucault would have advised them to escape. This is indeed what Gouldner (1954) already observed: a discrepancy between official procedures and actual behavior. This discrepancy is problematic for organizations striving for quality or being more or less forced by customers or government to implement ISO 9001. So Foucault helps us to understand resistance to standards but does not offer an acceptable solution.

Habermas and ISO 9001

Habermas (1987) distinguishes between 'System' and 'Lifeworld'. The lifeworld is 'that province of reality which the wide-awake and normal adult simply takes for granted in the attitude of common sense. By this taken-for-grantedness, we designate everything which we experience as unquestionable; every state of affairs is for us unproblematic until further notice' (Habermas, 1987, p. 130). 'The lifeworld is the intuitively present, in this sense familiar and transparent, and at the same time a vast and incalculable web of presuppositions that have to be satisfied if an actual utterance is to be at all meaningful, that is, valid *or* invalid' (Habermas, 1987, p. 131). Systems, on the other hand, are characterized by economy (resources), polity (goals), pattern-maintaining systems (values) and integrative subsystems (norms) (Habermas, 1987, p. 244). Society is in crisis because of the "colonization" of the lifeworld by systems (Habermas, 1987, p. 394). Systems are fully rationalized and are related to material reproduction, rationality of money and power, and achievement of results. Principles of rationalization are efficiency, calculability, predictability and control.

Conflicts are about defending and restoring endangered ways of life. (…) The new problems are related to quality of life, equal rights, individual self-realization, participation, and human rights (Habermas, 1987, p. 392). The lifeworld consists of 'communicative action' and therefore Habermas proposes such communicative action that 'decodes the deformations of the lifeworld' (Habermas, 1987, p. 403). Communication has three functions: (1) reaching understanding (communicative action serves to transmit culturally stored knowledge), (2) coordinating action (it serves the fulfilment of norms in the form of social integration and establishment of solidarity), and (3) socializing actors (it serves the formation of personality structures) (Habermas, 1987, pp. 63, 137). The concept of consensus is important: 'participants in communication reach an agreement concerning the validity of an utterance; agreement is the validity claim the speaker raises for it' (Habermas, 1987, p. 120).

Implementing TQM or a quality management system based on ISO 9001 can be regarded as the introduction of a 'system' in the lifeworld of an organization, and consequently, it is logical that feelings of resistance may surface. Organizations are more than just units for material reproduction; they are important for the identity and wellbeing of individuals. Habermas would protest against ISO 9001 implementation and in particular against the reduction of human beings to 'human resources'. If such a system is inevitable, Habermas would probably advise the lifeworld to penetrate into the system. This should be done through communicative action. Employees should discuss and negotiate all elements of the quality management system and the necessity of the system itself, taking into account both the external (market) situation and the lifeworld within the organization. If they reach consensus, the system will better satisfy their needs or the system is no longer needed because common understanding provides an alternative way of coordination.

If Foucault had been confronted with this fictitious advice, he would have argued that the necessity to communicate and arrive at consensus becomes an element of the system. 'The problem is not of trying to dissolve them [relations of power] in the utopia of a perfectly transparent communication, but to give oneself the rules of law, the techniques of management, and also the ethics, the ethos, the practices of the self, which would allow these games of power to be played with a minimum of domination' (Foucault, cited by Kelly, 1994, p. 391). Habermas focuses on moral-practical relations between modern, autonomous subjects but that regime exists alongside a second regime, analyzed by Foucault, determined by practices, institutions, and knowledge (Kelly, 1994, p. 376). Therefore, their approaches are complementary in their application to ISO 9001, and in both cases, there is a conflict between freedom and control. The organization's management, or even the entire organization, uses its freedom to opt for a (quality management) system, but, once established, this system restricts individual freedom, including that of the management.

Addressing the Conflict Between Freedom and Control

Freedom and control are essential values in Western culture. Goudzwaard (1979) argues that freedom and control are the two main ideals of Humanism which originate from the Renaissance. Exercising individual freedom includes controlling one's environment including the creation of systems of control but this may affect the freedom of other people. How can this problem be solved?

Erasmus, one of the founding fathers of humanism, talks about individual freedom in a way uncommon in our days: 'Nobody obeys more (…) than he who has drunk in the Spirit of Christ and starts getting free' (Allen, 1913, p. 374). He links freedom to Christianity. The Christian source document, the Bible, addresses the tension between freedom and control but uses different terms. The basic assumption in Renaissance and Humanism is man's autonomy, whereas man, according to the Bible, was created and, therefore, is in a subordinate position to his Creator. Man has been given freedom, but this freedom gets a purpose. 'Everything is permissible, but not everything is beneficial or constructive' (1 Corinthians 10:23). Man has been set free to love his neighbors and to look after creation and develop culture. His freedom includes the option to choose to go against his Creator. The latter is called 'sin' which means 'miss the goal'. Sin is related to autonomy: deciding for yourself what to do instead of being dependent on your Creator and respecting the structures of creation and God's commandments. So in the positive sense, man's freedom gets a purpose of serving, which includes the creation of artefacts, organizations and systems, and thus measures and systems of control. Such control, embedded in the attitude of serving neighbors, is claimed to be of benefit to other people and to creation. However, sin affects behavior and man, seeking his autonomy, may use his freedom to control in a way that affects his environment. Such behavior may lead to a system of control in which man is both offender and victim. This may include systems at societal level. The first biblical example is the tower of Babel, it has numerous similarities with the systems described by Foucault (Ellul, 1970). Foucault provides a thorough analysis of such systems and its inherent reasons for resistance. However, his view is too negative. Reality shows a mixture of positive and negative developments, of emancipation and of oppression.

Standards imply control, which may result in organizational benefits but can cause employee resistance as well. We will now explore the feasibility of a Christian-philosophical approach to the control that is inherent to standards. Again, we take the case of ISO 9001 implementation and explore if such an alternative way of control may avoid resistance. This topic can be addressed using ideas by Dooyeweerd.

Dooyeweerd and the Freedom vs. Control Issue

The Christian philosopher Herman Dooyeweerd (1955; 1957; see for an introduction Basden, 2010 and Kalsbeek, 1975) addresses the issue of freedom versus control more indirectly (Basden, 2004). Dooyeweerd understands 'freedom' in another way than common in our culture. Freedom should be 'meaningful', otherwise it is no real freedom. For instance, we are free to design a car with square wheels, but it makes little sense to do so. Meaningful freedom constitutes response to norms. Such norms apply to entities, such as organizations, and to aspects. We will focus on the diversity of aspects. Freedom is 'free to' rather than 'free from': free to do something meaningful, which our Creator granted us. For instance, if we had not been given the ability to communicate in common symbols, we would have had no freedom in that area (Basden, 2004).

Aspects Related to ISO 9001 / TQM

We can distinguish several aspects of phenomena in reality. A table, for instance, may have four legs – a numerical aspect. It may have a certain economic value – an economic aspect. It may be beautifully designed – an aesthetical aspect. Dooyeweerd lists 15 aspects which are distinct ways in which reality can be meaningful and good, and can exist and occur. These are: the numerical, spatial, kinematic, physical, biotic (organic life), psychic (sensitive), analytical (logical), historical, lingual, social, economic, aesthetic, juridical, ethical and pistic (trust, faith) aspect. There are laws related to each aspect that should be honored. For the first six aspects, these are natural laws which are generally obeyed without opposition. For instance, mathematical laws of adding, subtracting, multiplying, etc., apply to the numerical aspect. For the other nine aspects, these 'laws' are normative principles that man, in his freedom, can obey or violate, unintentionally (not being aware of certain normative principles) or intentionally. Much of the dissatisfaction with TQM or ISO 9001 quality systems may be explained by violating the 'human' side of quality management. This will not come as a surprise. Therefore, we examine two less evident aspects: the lingual aspect and the pistic aspect.

According to Dooyeweerd, the lingual aspect concerns symbolic signification. It is related to more than just language. For example, reserving the best parking place, next to the company's main entrance, for the general manager is a form of non-verbal communication that reveals something about the organization's internal relationships. According to Dooyeweerd, each aspect has a normative component. Clarity is the normative component for the lingual aspect. In quality management practice, the lingual aspect is related to communication about establishing and using the system, and the system's description in the form of quality handbooks, procedures, and instructions. Violating the lingual aspect is a source of unnecessary dissatisfaction. Examples include:

- The organization's management that does not clearly communicate their quality management policy or show their commitment. Perhaps there is a well-written and verbally expressed policy, but the absence of top management at meetings of the steering committee for quality, signals a lack of commitment.
- Quality management systems that are designed by an 'expert' such as the organization's quality management officer or an external consultant, instead of resulting from a joint effort of all employees. The latter has proven to be better (Brown et al.,1998; Mahadevappa and Kotreshwar, 2004). Involvement creates enthusiasm for quality management and lack of involvement is a source

of dissatisfaction. 'Listening to employees' can be improved, for instance, by using interview techniques.

- The quality system's documentation that is often an impressive folio in the cupboard instead of a practical guide for the employees working on the shop floor. Sometimes, integration of a procedure into, for instance, software applications may replace a written instruction. In other cases, the process descriptions can be improved using clear text, or flow charts.
- One-way communication. Using feedback systems can eliminate dissatisfaction and improve customer service.

The pistic aspect is not related to a religion but to the possibility to believe. Reliability is the normative principle for this aspect. The organization's mission statement is its 'confession' and its quality policy should be in line with this, otherwise both are untrustworthy. To be reliable, the organization's actions should support its policy. In order to achieve this, quality management is needed. It is characterized as: 'say what you do and do what you say.' (Grimes, 2003, p. 11), sometimes with the addition 'and (be in a position to) prove it' (Dale, 2007, p. 293). Quality assurance should ensure that the organization is able to promise only what it is able to fulfil, and, once promised, to deliver what was promised. Reliability can be honored by a certification audit. However, is the certificate itself reliable? The above findings suggest that an ISO 9001 system can have little impact, no impact or a positive impact, and the main reason for this difference is the internal motivation. However, this implies that it is possible to achieve a certificate for a quality management system that has little or no added value. This questions the trustworthiness of the certification. Even ISO's own journal reports about lack of trust. An Italian survey revealed that 45% of the quality management systems of suppliers of an energy company did not sufficiently conform to the standard (Nicoloso, 2007). This problem does not only affect the energy company. Employees of the unreliable suppliers may feel uncomfortable with the window-dressing in their organization and may prefer to have reasons to be proud of their employer.

The examples of these two aspects show that these normative 'laws' do not reflect an esoteric activity but common wisdom and issues addressed in professional and scientific literature. However, it is difficult and time consuming to examine all 15 aspects of an entire system. Therefore, the empirical part of our study will focus on one process only instead of studying the entire implementation of a quality management system. We will address the management decision to standardize one of the processes to enhance efficiency, and examine employee resistance, if any, to this standardization.

RESEARCH APPROACH

During 2003 and 2004, we developed an approach based on the philosophy of Dooyeweerd to analyze a standardization project in the company Voestalpine Polynorm. We offered solutions and recommendations. Six years later, we evaluated the results of this approach, and focused on how resistance to standardization developed during the years. We make a case reconstruction and then analyze the case using quality management literature and the ideas of Foucault, Habermas and Dooyeweerd (see Figure 1).

During 2003 and 2004, we applied Dooyeweerd's philosophy in the real-life case of a standardization project in a company. Scientific research tends to focus on one or a few aspects, running the risk of remaining unaware of other aspects and not seeing reality as it is. Dooyeweerd emphasizes the importance of what he calls 'naïve experience': an unprejudiced experience of the situation, similar with

Figure 1. Research approach

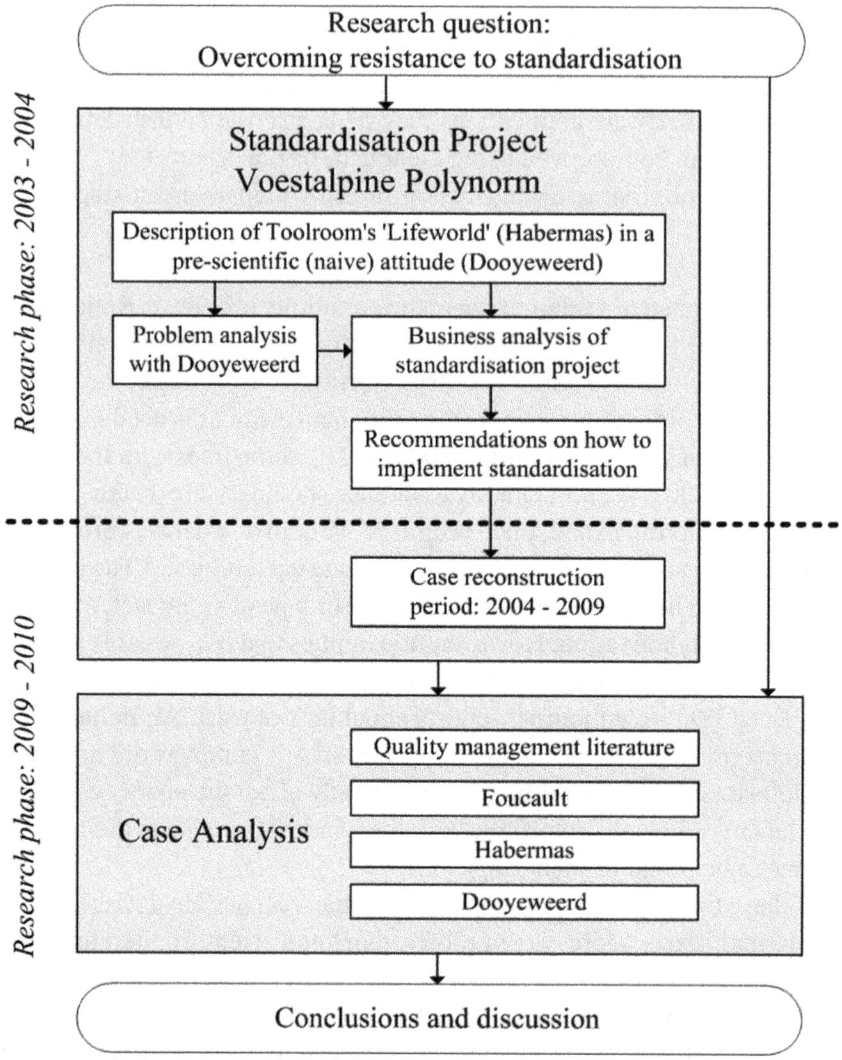

what Habermas (1987, p. 130) names the taken-for-grantedness typical for the 'lifeworld'. Therefore, we started our research with a 'lifeworld' approach which is also common in social-constructivist research. We evaluated the situation by being on the shop floor, talking informally to people involved in the process and conducting unstructured interviews. We further analyzed the situation by examining the organizational embedding of the standardization project, and the various aspects described by Dooyeweerd. For this purpose, we studied internal documents, observed behavior and held interviews. This fieldwork, carried out in 2003, resulted in a report, which describes and analyses the situation and provides recommendations for the company (Haverkamp, 2004, summarized in Haverkamp, 2006). In 2009 and 2010, we conducted ten new interviews, mainly with people also interviewed in 2003, and studied new internal documents in order to see what had changed since then. As part of the interview protocol, we developed a measurement protocol for identifying, selecting, and accessing sources of evidence, and for generating a valid and reliable score for each of the variables, which were measured through the interviews. We measured the following concepts: efficiency of work in terms of time, work standardization in terms of implemented standard working methods, and satisfaction. In particular, we addressed the concept of satisfaction related to the standardization initiatives. The degree of satisfaction was defined as the extent to which workers perceived their daily work related to the project as satisfying, and refers to a value attributed to work by the workers. It is a characteristic of people's opinions, and the value of this variable ranges from 'not satisfying at all' to 'very satisfying'. The interview evidence was recorded and transcribed, and we analyzed and evaluated the contents of these transcriptions. We were able to graphically visualize the (relative) degree of resistance to the standardization activities in time (see Figure 4). The interviewees reviewed the case reconstruction and visualization of resistance in time and agreed with our description and analysis.

Below, we first describe the company, the department, the problem and the reasons for standardization. Then, we give a chronological description including the extent to which our recommendations were implemented, and we relate resistance to the phases of the project. Next, we analyze the case and discuss whether Dooyeweerd's approach was feasible to tackle the standardization problem.

STANDARDIZATION PROJECT VOESTALPINE POLYNORM

Case Company and Department

The case company Voestalpine Polynorm Automotive in Bunschoten, the Netherlands, develops and produces automobile body parts, such as doors, bonnets and roofs for the automotive industry. The company is a preferred supplier of major automobile manufacturers in Europe. The production requires specific tools that determine the shape of the parts. These tools are made, maintained and, if necessary, repaired or adapted by the company's Toolroom. Professional technical skills are a prerequisite for accurate 'formability', the degree in which a sheet-metal is formed in the required shape.

The parts are made by a process called deep drawing, in which a punch forces a flat sheet-metal into a die cavity. A sheet-metal blank is placed over a die opening, and is held in place with a blank holder. The punch travels downward and forces the blank into the die cavity. The important variables in deep drawing are the properties of the sheet metal, the ratio of blank diameter to punch diameter, the clearance between punch and die, the punch radius and die-corner radius, the blank holder force, friction, and lubrication (Kalpakjian, 1995, p. 472). Especially deep drawing of non-symmetric parts can present significant difficulties in practice (Kalpakjian, 1995, p. 476). For example, various regions of a part undergo different types of deformation during drawing. In order to avoid sheet metal during forming, it is important to consider and control all relevant factors. In our research, we examined the Toolroom's activities regarding the control of these relevant factors of formability in the deep drawing process.

Voestalpine Polynorm had a certified quality management system based on the international standard ISO TS 16949 (the predecessor of IATF 16949:2016), which is an extension of ISO 9001 with additional requirements for the automotive supply chain. One of the additional prescriptive requirements of this standard is that management shall review the product realization processes and the support processes to assure their effectiveness and efficiency (ISO, 2009a, p. 7).

The Problem

The Toolroom had already successfully implemented a standardized process for formability, as part of the quality management system. As a result, the lead times in getting tools ready for production had decreased and scrap percentages had reduced significantly. However, the process description (procedure) allowed different working methods and, indeed, the teams differed in the method they used. Management thought that they could achieve more efficiency by standardizing working methods. They would modify the standard as soon as further improvements to the working methods were found. It would reflect 'best practices', see Figure 2.

Interestingly, this project can be seen as a standardization project in two ways. It is part of the company implementation of an international standard, but it also leads to the development and implementation of a new in-company standard. A researcher (first author of this chapter) was asked to investigate how the working methods in the Toolroom could be standardized.

First Impression: Resistance to Intended Standardization Project

The researcher joined the Toolroom for 10 months and was accepted by the workers immediately, partly because of his technical background. The first impressions and rather informal interviews with 12 employees (Toolroom manager, shift leader, team leaders (4), toolmakers (3), welder, project leader and formability specialist), revealed that the older employees expressed more resistance to the standardization initiative than the younger generation. The following quote of a very experienced toolmaker is exemplary for the older generations 'Craftsmen are not clonable' (Haverkamp, 2004, p. 26). The younger generation, both toolmakers and team leaders, were more positive about standardization. 'Our methods can and need to be standard; we could benefit considerably. However, it is important that everything remains understandable for everybody. Everything needs to be explainable.' (Haverkamp, 2004, p. 27).

Aspectual Analysis

Next, the researcher analyzed the organizational embedding of the process and the aspects more systematically. The aspectual analysis was mainly based on many interviews on the shop floor, logbooks, internal documents, and observations (during meetings and on the shop floor). The functioning of the

Figure 2. Standardization project in toolroom of voestalpine polynorm

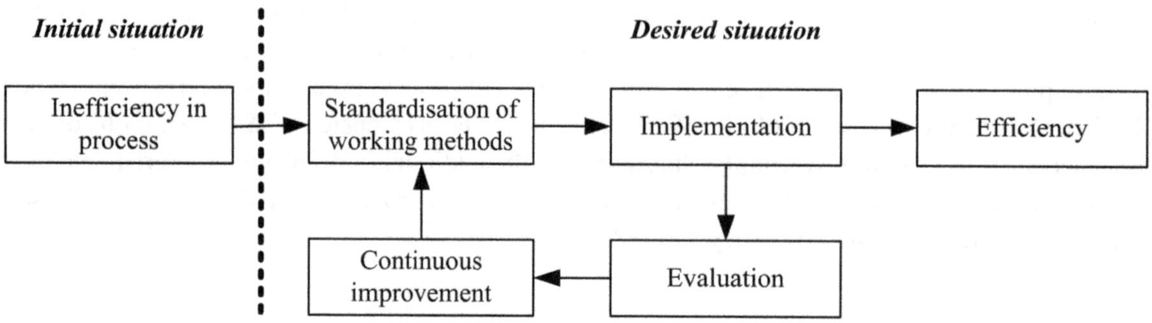

Toolroom was analyzed using each of Dooyeweerd's 15 aspects. For example, the process of tool reparation relates to the numerical aspect in the form of several different working methods. The tools are located in the Toolroom (spatial aspect) and consist of a punch which travels down (kinematic aspect) to transform a blank (physical aspect) into a die cavity, in accordance with ergonomic standards (biotic aspect). However, standardization of this process may lead to resistance (psychic aspect) and requires an investigation of practices and the choice of a best practice (analytical aspect). The current standard was developed and implemented in the past (historical aspect). However, it was expected that a written (lingual aspect) standard for working methods, implemented in an acceptable way (social aspect), would lead to more efficiency (economic aspect). The description has a certain format (aesthetical aspect). It should meet customer specifications (juridical aspect). The Toolroom's mission (pistic aspect) is to serve customers (ethical aspect) in a flexible way. Next, the researcher determined to which extent the functioning was in line with the specific (normative) 'laws' for each aspect.

A similar analysis was made for the change process and for the desired (standardized) situation. For each aspect, the researcher predicted the positive and negative consequences of process standardization by investigating all possible changes in functioning in relation to the corresponding 'laws' of all aspects. For example, standardizing existing working methods (numerical aspect) might lead to a more efficient way of working, which is in line with the norm of 'efficiency' in the economic aspect.

The aspectual analysis of the initial situation, change process and desired situation resulted in an overview of relevant aspects related to the research question. Although all aspects are relevant, some, for example, the psychic aspect were found to be more prominent, whereas others, such as the aesthetic aspect, were less apparent. The applicable normative requirements for each of these aspects should be found and honored. From Dooyeweerd's point of view, this is a necessary condition for the success of the project. For example, the normative component of the analytical aspect is the ability to distinguish one thing from another and to abstract something from the concrete reality. Applied to the Toolroom, knowledge is required to be able to analyze a tool. Insufficient knowledge could (unconsciously) lead to a wrong analysis, which is an example of not functioning in line with the norms for the analytical aspect. Standardizing a 'best practice' assumes that everybody has the same skills and knowledge to be able to 'analyze' according to this 'best practice'. The empirical data showed that this was not the case, and that more attention should focus on the analytical aspect. In a similar way, the researcher determined whether special attention was required for each aspect during the standardization process. The following aspects needed special attention:

- Psychic aspect; in which the *motivation* of employees is crucial.
- Social aspect: in which the condition of true *respect* for each other is important.
- Lingual aspect; in which verbal and non-verbal *communication* is important.
- Pistic aspect; in which *trust and commitment* are important.
- Analytical aspect; in which homogeneous *knowledge* and *skills* are required.
- Historical aspect; in which *events and managerial behavior in the past* partly explain current resistance to standardization, and therefore need to be addressed.

Following Dooyeweerd, it is especially important to consider whether everything is in line with the normative requirements for these aspects in order to avoid resistance to the standardization project.

Pragmatic business administration insights can help businesses to function in compliance with the normative requirements because these reflect experiences in what 'works' and what does not. The 'norms' in the psychic, social, lingual and pistic aspects can be understood and managed by insights about motivation. The 'norms' in the analytical aspect can be understood and managed by applying knowledge management concepts. Normative requirements in the historical aspect can be honored by notions of willingness to change, see Figure 3.

Business Analysis of the Standardization Project

We investigated the relation between the numerical (number of methods) and the economic aspect (efficiency) with insights related to standardization. Notions such as 'standardization', 'standards' and 'continuous improving standards', as described in the problem field, were applied to the Toolroom. We used the ideas of Nakamura (2000), who sees continuous improvement as one of the key concepts of in-company standardization. We applied a model of Slob and De Vries (2001) to understand how such standards can be developed. Furthermore, we determined how these standards can be developed and maintained, based on Simons and De Vries (2002), Kondo (2000) and Imai (1986).

In order to function in line with the norms in the analytical aspect in the standardized situation, knowledge management is required; employees first need to learn from each other. Different types of knowledge apply: implicit and explicit (Nonaka, 1994), and subject, method, social and acting knowledge (Sprenger & Ten Have, 1996). We used Buckler's model for learning to understand learning as a continuous process – a prerequisite for the Toolroom. Buckler (1996) sees learning as a process which requires three ingredients: focus, a stimulating environment and the right techniques. Because Buckler does not distinguish the different types of knowledge that need to be transferred, we used the notions of knowledge conversion (Nonaka, 1994) to get insight into the 'how' of learning. Nonaka distinguishes four types of knowledge conversion: socializing (from tacit knowledge to tacit knowledge), internal-

Figure 3. Problem analysis based on Dooyeweerd's philosophy

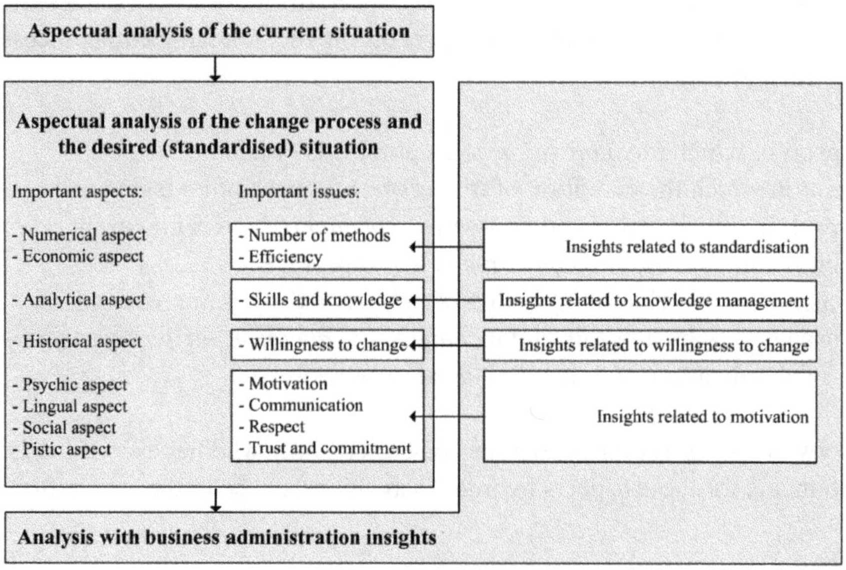

izing (from explicit to implicit), externalizing (from implicit to explicit) and combining (from explicit to explicit). Mom et al. (2002) conclude that there are three phases in knowledge conversion processes: decision, transfer, and integration. Also according to Buckler (1996), learning requires a transition through different phases or stadiums (ignorance, awareness, understanding, commitment, enactment and reflection). We applied these insights in our recommendations for the Toolroom.

The psychic aspect relates to understanding and managing the feelings of employees during the standardization process. In order to function in line with the psychic norms, people should remain (or become) motivated. Motivation originates in the introduction and unfolding of human aspects in daily work, such as creativity (the pleasure of thinking) and sociality (the pleasure of sharing things with colleagues) (Kondo, 1996). We applied this vision to the Toolroom.

The historical aspect relates to willingness to change. This willingness stems from employee motivation, whereas resistance to change originates from incomprehension regarding what, why and how management wants to do something (Wissema et al., 1991). Thus, in combination with Kondo's findings, the success of standardization in the Toolroom depends on the willingness to change, which in turn depends on the amount of attention on the human aspects in this process.

This conclusion is in line with Dooyeweerd – all norms in the 'human aspects' need to be honored to function successfully. In addition to the findings of Wissema et al. (1991) and Kondo (1996), Dooyeweerd's philosophy helped us to describe exactly *which* human aspects needed special attention.

Recommendations for Implementation

We concluded that the Toolroom could benefit from standardizing their working methods, but that the organization was not fully prepared for the proposed standardization project. First, the above-mentioned insights (described in detail in the report (Haverkamp, 2004, pp. 91-134)) were needed to help the Toolroom to function in line with the norms of the indicated aspects. Therefore, the researcher made the following recommendations to Toolroom's management:

- Establish a common goal and vision. The purpose of the standardization needs to be crystal clear and should be communicated regularly (lingual aspect). This is important for an effective learning process (analytical aspect), motivation (psychic aspect) and the willingness to change (historical aspect).
- Invest in mitigating individual differences in relevant knowledge and skills (analytical aspect), because this allows all employees to meet agreed-upon standards.
- Strengthen social knowledge through which employees can learn from each other (Sprenger & Ten Have, 1996). Social knowledge gives insight in the communicative processes and is required to support and coach one another (analytical aspect). It gives access to the knowledge others obtain. Awareness and understanding of the need to learn are fundamental for this (Buckler, 1996). A decentralized and informal structure stimulates the development of social knowledge.
- Stimulate employees to express (verbally or non-verbally) their ideas, concerns or feelings about the standardization project and give them feedback (lingual aspect). This increases understanding (analytical aspect) and, as a result, commitment (pistic aspect) and action.
- Pay attention to commitment ("Yes, we can") (psychic aspect).
- Give employees time to get used to the idea that change is needed (historical aspect).

- Be flexible – employees need freedom to influence changes in their work and want to be taken seriously, so adjustments during the process should be possible. This increases involvement (social aspect) and commitment (pistic aspect).
- Adopt a decentralized approach with a clear project structure (historical aspect).

Case Reconstruction 2004-2009

During the last quarter of 2009 and the beginning of 2010, we investigated if and how our recommendations had been implemented, and whether there had been any resistance among staff. We interviewed the Toolroom manager who described the changes and activities since 2004. The manager started the change project just after the researcher had left the company. The recommendations were implemented implicitly rather than explicitly and systematically. The Toolroom manager hired a consultant who applied a human-centered approach, founded in social constructivism. She did not receive the researcher's report with analyses and recommendations, and started from scratch and interviewed people again to gather data. She focused on knowledge management rather than on standardization. However, part of this knowledge management was to make implicit knowledge explicit (Nonaka and Takeuchi, 1995) with the intention to use this explicit knowledge repeatedly, which is standardization as well (De Vries and Van Delden, 2006). Important elements of her approach were: how to learn from each other, how to make implicit knowledge explicit, how to write down practices, and how to standardize and implement a best practice.

The start-up phase of the project involved examining the working methods in the Toolroom. The consultant arranged workshops and investigated how people perceived their job, which other departments needed to be involved and what was important to the employees. Central questions were 'who' 'what', 'where', 'why' and 'how'. Other questions included 'what are we good at?', 'what do you think is important?', 'when is standardization successful?' and 'how can you contribute to the project?' The employees expressed their expectations and points of views, after which a common view was created by and for the Toolroom.

Next, an abstract level content of the standard was defined through mind mapping techniques. However, the project became much more extensive and complex than initially foreseen due to the company's ambition to further increase performance and lower cost because of fierce competition in the automotive market. Instead of just a standardization project, it became a project to transform the Toolroom in a streamlined and mature organization, in which working, learning and innovating were to be key elements. The more complex project continued with an emphasis on knowledge management. Knowledge 'pilot production teams' were formed and 'experts' per specific area were nominated to produce teaching content to educate their colleagues. The teaching materials could be seen as standards. However, it was not successful because even the motivated leaders of the pilot teams did not understand the structure and complexity of the project. The rules and guidelines of the project were too complex and vague and, in their perception, unnecessary and therefore ineffective. The external consultant failed to clearly explain the objectives of the project, partly because the manager wanted to restrict her contact with Toolroom employees. As a result, the employees lost confidence and enthusiasm and no longer supported the project. Shortly afterwards, the external consultant was replaced by an internal project leader. This new project leader, a professional and experienced teacher, had other (didactic) ideas regarding the project. He discontinued the trial with the pilot production teams and tried to implement his own views and insights. However, Toolroom management did not support his initiatives, and consequently, the project made very little progress.

However, Toolroom employees acknowledged the need for more efficiency because of increased international competition. Together with one of production teams, the new project leader started bottom-up activities in developing the standard in a way he thought was right. According to the production team, the manager was not aware of this and they pretended to act in line with his original ideas in case he suddenly attended one of their meetings. This 'dramaturgical compliance' (Van Kemenade et al., 2011) continued until the manager left in April 2009. From then on, Toolroom employees openly continued their standardization activity. They decided to keep it simple and defined three levels of craftsmanship. They used pictures rather than text in their descriptions. Training was provided group by group instead of the whole department at once. As a result, the lead time for writing these knowledge standards decreased considerably.

Resistance During the Standardization Project

In this chapter, we analyzed resistance to standards by applying the philosophical ideas of Foucault, Habermas and Dooyeweerd. In the empirical part of the chapter, we focused on the standardization process at the case company Voestalpine Polynorm. We used insights from our philosophical analysis in our recommendations to the company. Six years later, we evaluated the results of this intervention by analyzing internal reports related to the project and by conducting six in-depth interviews. These interviews had an 'open' character and were aimed at retrieving real feelings and opinions from the respondents. Based on a systematic questionnaire, we measured whether (1) the initial philosophical diagnosis of the problem field and the practical conclusions and recommendations were effective and adequate and (2) whether the Dooyeweerd approach of implementing company standards was effective in overcoming resistance to standardization. The amount of resistance was determined by measuring the degree of satisfaction for each stage in the standardization process. The objects of measurement were the evaluation of the project as formulated in the project management reports and the judgements, opinions and recollections of individual persons (face-to face in-depth interviews). Several ways of recording the interview evidence were applied. We used voice recording and made notes of verbal and non-verbal communication. The interview evidence (comments, experiences and suggestions) was recorded and transcribed (reviewed and approved by the respondents). The content of these transcriptions and the project reports were analyzed, evaluated and used for a reconstruction. Based on the evaluation and reconstruction, we could visualize the relative amount of resistance during each project phase (Figure 4). This tentative visualization was approved and confirmed by the respondents.

1. Initial resistance to the Toolroom management's plan to standardize.
2. Resistance decreases during the initial project phase.
3. Resistance increases during the project.
4. Resistance peaks during the phase of implementation of the standard.
5. Resistance decreases in the final stage of the project.

We now explain these five changes in resistance.

Figure 4. Resistance to standardization 2003-2009

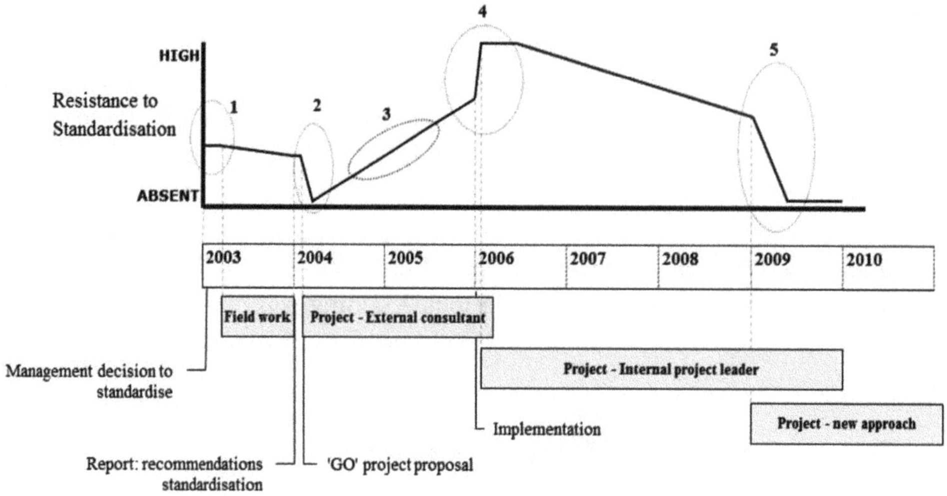

1. In 2003, particularly older employees were unhappy with the management decision to standardize. The subsequent involvement of the researcher reduced this resistance slightly.
2. The project that started in 2004 had a multi-sided approach. Implicitly, most of the researcher's recommendations were applied. A common goal and vision were established in the workshops, the purpose was clearly communicated, and knowledge management became an (important) element of the project. Everyone understood the need to change, the project was managed on commitment, and a gradual implementation strategy was developed in which the role of the employees seemed to be important. During this start-up phase, employees were enthusiastic, satisfied and, as a consequence, cooperative.
3. However, the last recommendation was not implemented. The project was not decentralized or clearly structured. The project team changed its bottom-up approach into a top-down approach in which several of the other recommendations (unintentionally) were ignored. It developed a project structure which was only clear to the team itself. The common goal and vision became unclear and the standard became too complex. The possibilities for employees to propose or make adjustments seemed very limited, and feedback and communication were lacking. As a consequence, key employees lost confidence and enthusiasm, their commitment decreased, and resistance to the standardization initiative grew.
4. Resistance reached a peak during the implementation phase. Employees no longer supported the project and the standard was not implemented.
5. However, team leaders were convinced that the Toolroom could benefit from standardization. After a while (in Figure 4: between 4 and 5), a small team started to convert implicit practical knowledge into explicit knowledge in the form of a standard. By providing employees with standard packages of knowledge, it was assumed that the tool maintenance process could be made more efficient. The implementation of this new standard was successful. The standard was easy to understand and pictures rather than text were used. Communicating about the relevance of the standard and verifying whether it was understood became important elements. Moreover, the standard was now seen as a new way to approach a certain problem, rather than a prescribed way to control the behavior

of the toolmakers. As a result of standardizing knowledge and skills, toolmakers automatically adopted the most efficient working method for similar problems. They were free to adopt other methods and were not forced to use the standard. As a result, in their perception the standard was not a limitation of their freedom, but a necessary tool to become mature craftsmen. The initial goal was achieved: efficiency in terms of quicker repair times and shorter lead times to get tools ready for series production.

CASE ANALYSIS

In this section, we analyze the case and in particular the five events that mark changes in resistance by using standardization and quality management literature and by applying the insights of the philosophers Foucault, Habermas and Dooyeweerd.

Standardization and Quality Management Literature

As mentioned, most literature on the adoption and use of standards in a company ignores possible staff resistance to standards. Van Wessel's (2010) main message is that proper governance and management of standardization projects in the phases of standard selection, implementation and use lead to success. The best practice for company standardization provided by De Vries (2006) addresses policies, processes, facility management and funding, but does not include individual employees. In this sense, some studies related to management system standards (Boiral, 2003; Manders, 2015) are an exception. They notice differences between employees, whereas in our case, all employees share a certain amount of resistance, only age seems to make a small difference. Boiral (2003) and Manders (2015) interviewed employees and show patterns in employee perceptions but they do not provide an in-depth diagnosis of their resistance, and as a consequence, they cannot provide fundamental solutions. This in-depth diagnosis might be a research area for psychologists (Brehm & Brehm, 1981) but then the relation to standards management is missing.

In our case company, Toolroom management was highly motivated to start the standardization project for economic reasons: they were convinced it could improve their competitiveness. Such motivation is a good starting point for achieving results. However, their commitment did not avoid resistance. Resistance grew, in particular, due to lack of communication. In line with Brown et al. (1998) and Mahadevappa and Kotreshwar (2004), the initial enthusiasm and satisfaction disappeared because the normative requirements of the 'human' aspects, especially the lingual aspect, were violated.

Van Kemenade et al.'s (2011) findings are helpful in sharpening our diagnosis of resistance. They developed criteria for professionals' willingness to contribute to quality assurance. (1) A main reason for the initial resistance to standardization was the limitation of the toolmakers' freedom. However, as we have seen in the aspectual analysis, there were more reasons for this initial resistance. It slowly decreased due to better communication. The absence of resistance in the start-up and final phase of the project (2 and 5) can be understood using Van Kemenade et al.'s prerequisites as well. The criteria were met both times, but in different ways. The growing resistance after the start-up phase (3 and 4) was because two of Van Kemenade et al.'s criteria were not satisfied: the rules and templates were too complex and needed to be followed strictly. This rigidity caused control, rather than freedom as the dominant factor during implementation. Moreover, there was a decrease in ownership by Toolroom professionals since the work was done by a small development team directed by an external expert. Since management was part of this development team, support for management decreased as well. Although Van Kemenade et al.'s prerequisites were met in phases 2 and 5, this was not sufficient to avoid resistance to the standard. An explanation is that Van Kemenade et al.'s prerequisites do not cover all of Dooyeweerd's (human) aspects. For example, Van Kemenade et al. do not mention the lingual aspect, which proved to be important in this case.

Foucault

Foucault's findings on power systems can be used to analyze quality management systems such as the case company's ISO TS 16949 system (Van Veldhuisen, 1996) but for the employees in the Toolroom, it is not the system as such which is of interest but its impact on their department. Our case description shows that in line with the ISO TS 16949 (and its successor IATF 16949:2016) requirements, the Toolroom management intended to standardize processes on the shop floor. Employees were expected to behave according to predefined rules and guidelines. The plan to implement this (1) caused resistance. The more concrete the plan became (3 and 4), the stronger the resistance. The attempt to force production teams to use the standard (4) resulted in the strongest resistance. Foucault helps us to understand this resistance. Interestingly, the revolt against the standard is also in line with Foucault. The employees revolted against the proposed way of working and, finally, escaped from the 'system' by no longer supporting it. However, their voluntary decision to develop another standard (5) and the lack of resistance in phase 2 are not in line with Foucault.

Habermas

Resistance to this standardization project can also be understood with Habermas' insights. (1) The initial resistance in 2003 decreased due to communicative action. (2) The absence of resistance in the start-up phase can partly be understood by this communicative action as well. However, as mentioned earlier, this successful project start was not only dependent on honoring the normative requirements regarding communication. (3) Next, besides the Toolroom's 'lifeworld', a 'system' was being developed which the workers perceived as questionable, it was not taken for granted in the attitude of common sense. (4) This system had to be implemented into the lifeworld of the Toolroom which resulted in strong resistance because it was seen as too complex and too theoretical. Apart from the lingual aspect, Habermas does not mention any of Dooyeweerd's other human aspects and these, as we have seen, in this case, the economic, analytical, historical, psychic, social and pistic aspects are important for success as well. On the other hand, it seems that violating the norms of only the lingual aspect, the one Habermas mentions, could be enough for the project to fail.

Dooyeweerd

According to Dooyeweerd, all of the sides, or aspects, of the project are important and all corresponding normative requirements should be honored. Our problem analysis using Dooyeweerd's philosophy showed which aspects required additional attention. This philosophical analysis was fundamental for the selected combination of business-administrational approaches and, as a result, the recommendations for standardization. As we have seen in the systematic inventory of the Toolroom, not all the normative requirements of the (human) aspects were honored, which explains the initial resistance to the standardization plan (1). In the start-up phase (2), most of our recommendations were implicitly implemented. Attention focused on the 'human' side of standardization. As expected, there was no resistance to the proposal and even the older employees were cooperative. However, soon these normative requirements were violated. Due to inadequate communication (lingual aspect) and ignoring the comments of the employees (social aspect), the motivation (psychic aspect) and trust (pistic aspect) in standardization eroded. Also, commitment (pistic aspect) and the willingness to change to the unintelligible standard (analytical aspect) decreased dramatically (3 and 4). In the new project approach (5), all recommendations were implicitly implemented again. Instead of resistance, a form of standardization was achieved in which the tension between control and freedom seemed to have been eliminated.

Common Case Analysis

In general, the Polynorm case can be indicated as a small BPR activity that failed due to an overemphasis of the 'technical' aspects of the standardization project while having too little regard for the more 'human' aspects. Foucault and Habermas help us to understand staff resistance to the standardization project. However, they fail to explain the initial lack of resistance and do not offer an acceptable solution to overcome resistance to the project. Habermas' call for communicative action and Foucault's advice to escape do not solve the conflict between control (of the development team) and freedom (of the production team).

The analysis based on Van Kemenade et al. and Dooyeweerd considers the economic necessity for standardization which is ignored by Foucault and Habermas. According to Dooyeweerd, the economic aspect is the leading aspect for a company. 'Frugality in managing scarce goods' is fundamental for this aspect (Kalsbeek, 1975, p. 100, based on Dooyeweerd, 1955, p. 66). By planning and executing a standardization project, Toolroom management acknowledged this. Toolroom employees also seemed to recognize the leading role of this aspect. Toolmakers perceived the quality management system as a 'necessary evil' which ensured that customers received the right products. Moreover, without ISO TS 16949 certificate, Voestalpine Polynorm would be out of business. This explains both the absence of resistance and the strongest resistance in Figure 4 (2, 4 and 5). The strongest resistance occurred in phase 4 when Toolroom employees perceived the standard to be unnecessarily complex, ineffective, and therefore not in line with 'frugality in managing scarce goods'. The economic aspect also shows an additional explanation for the increasing resistance in phase 3. The company hired an external consultant who was unsuccessful in implementing the project. The employees felt they could have achieved more for the company without these extra costs.

The resistance during the project can partly be explained from a TQM perspective as well. For example, the case indicated that the resistance was low during the start of the project (Figure 4, phase 2) when employee involvement and management commitment were high; two major practices for a successful TQM approach. However, the increasing resistance in phase 3 is more difficult to explain from a TQM perspective. Management was committed and people were involved but key employees lost confidence in the project and developed resistance to the standardization initiative. Unlike a diagnosis and analysis based on Dooyeweerd's philosophy, a TQM approach would not have been able to identity the required attention to, for example, the analytical and historical aspect during this project. TQM stresses the importance of attention to 'human aspects' but does not define which aspects and norms need to be fulfilled in order to be successful. A BPR approach is even less encompassing than a TQM approach and tends to under-appreciate the 'human aspects'.

We can conclude that the philosophy of Dooyeweerd provides a better explanation for (1) staff resistance to Toolroom management's plan to standardize, (2) the decreasing resistance when the recommendations based on Dooyeweerd's philosophy were implicitly implemented, (3 and 4) the increasing resistance when the 'laws' related to the aspects were increasingly violated and (5) the decreasing resistance in the final stage.

CONCLUSION AND DISCUSSION

Standards can generate benefits but may cause resistance as well because they may impact human behavior directly. This applies in particular to management system standards. The implementation of such standards in an organization leads to process standardization in the form of written procedures and work instructions. Resistance to this form of standardization can be partly explained using standardization and quality management literature. In particular, the prerequisites as formulated by Van Kemenade et al. (2011) appear to be useful.

The paradox of the benefits of standards and the resistance to them may be related to the fundamental tension between the poles of 'order' and 'freedom' in a social organization. To get a deeper understanding of this issue, we applied some concepts of philosophers that study man in relation to power systems. We found that Foucault's analysis of systems and Habermas' notions of communicative action give us a deeper understanding of resistance, but their approaches are not of help in understanding the benefits of standards. Moreover, neither Foucault nor Habermas provide a solution for the tension between freedom and control, two essential ideals of Humanism. Exercising individual freedom includes controlling one's environment, and this may involve the creation of systems of control which may affect the freedom of other people. We explored how this problem can be solved by following Erasmus, one of the founding fathers of Humanism, in linking the notion of freedom to Christianity. In Dooyeweerd's Christian-philosophical approach, freedom is not absolute, but it should be 'meaningful', otherwise it is not real. Meaningful freedom constitutes response to norms. These norms can be related to (organizational and other) structures and to the 15 aspects in which 'things' (e.g., processes) function.

In this study, we focused on these aspects and applied them in a company standardization project. We found that the economic goals of standardization can be achieved without resistance from employees. Our analysis shows that social needs are not necessarily detrimental to economic goals. On the contrary, they can support these and have a beneficial influence. However, too much focus on human aspects can undermine the leading economic aspect of an organization. By addressing all relevant aspects and associated norms, Dooyeweerd's philosophy has helped us to determine the interrelated set of causes for resistance to standardization, and to develop an approach to overcome this resistance. We found that Dooyeweerd's theory of modal aspects was especially useful for analyzing the problem, for systematically selecting relevant business theories for the project, and for giving a holistic analysis as a basis for recommendations. This was done by linking insights from the field of business administration to those aspects that were most prominent in the case. These aspects relate to the original situation, the intended new situation, and the transition from the existing to the desired situation. Our findings suggest that such an approach can be applied in other standardization cases as well, but we expect that modifications will be required due to situational differences. Moreover, it is a holistic approach and not just a management tool, and rigid application would create rather than solve problems because it would mean forcing employees to accept a system. Therefore, the solution is not to prescribe but rather to familiarize managers with the approach. Then they will learn that business issues can be seen from different angles and that by doing so rigid solutions that may harm rather than benefit the organization can be avoided. By becoming sensitive to the multitude of aspects and getting a feeling which are the most relevant ones, they may also look for – case-specific – managerial and quality management approaches and tools to support them in finding sustainable solutions. It illustrates that standardization is a multidisciplinary field of research and that contributions from many disciplines are needed for a solid understanding, and that a business approach fed by philosophy may help to interrelate these contributions (De Vries, 2015).

Our approach differs from 'best practice' approaches for in-company standardization (De Vries, 2006; Van Wessel, 2010) or for ISO 9001 implementation (Briscoe et al., 2005; Lin & Jang, 2008). First, this is a single case study and replication studies might show whether certain patterns apply that distinguish good from worse practices. However, assuming that indeed a best practice model can be developed, then this model as such might serve as a system which would be implemented in another organization. This as such may cause resistance (Foucault) and affect the 'life world' (Habermas). Following Dooyeweerd, a best practice may be of help because it provides insights into what helps in similar situations, and the more aspects covered in this best practice the more informative the model, but each situation is unique as well and may deserve other emphasis, also depending on the people involved. So, our approach would help researchers as well as managers to not forget aspects that might be important, but we think it does not make sense to see the 'model' developed for our case company as a general model to be applied in other companies as well.

We encourage researchers to replicate our study. A longitudinal multiple case study would be best but requires a substantial amount of time and research capacity. Action-research in which our approach is applied to one or more cases would be a feasible alternative. It seems that our findings reach beyond the area of in-company standardization and can be beneficial to organizational areas as well. Our approach may be used to combine insights from mono-disciplinary studies of organizations into a balanced multidisciplinary approach which is relevant for both research and practice.

REFERENCES

Adolphi, H. (1997). *Strategische Konzepte zur Organisation der betrieblichen Standardisierung. In DIN Normungskunde* (Vol. 38). Berlin: Beuth Verlag.

AFNOR. (1967). *La normalisation dans l'entreprise*. Paris: AFNOR.

Ajzen, I. (1991). The theory of planned behavior. *Organizational Behavior and Human Decision Processes*, *50*(2), 179–211. doi:10.1016/0749-5978(91)90020-T

Al-Mashari, M., Irani, Z., & Zairi, M. (2001). Business process reengineering: A survey of international experience. *Business Process Management Journal*, *7*(5), 437–455. doi:10.1108/14637150110406812

Allen, P. S. (Ed.). (1913). *Opus Epistolarum Des Erasmi Roterodami* (Vol. 2, pp. 1517–1519). Oxford, UK: Oxford University Press.

Arthur, W. B. (1989). Competing Technologies, Increasing Returns, and Lock-in by Historical Events. *Economic Journal (London), 394*(99), 116–131. doi:10.2307/2234208

Basden, A. (2004). Dooyeweerd and Freedom. In *The Dooyeweerd Pages*. Retrieved January 7, 2010, from http://www.dooy.salford.ac.uk/freedom.html

Basden, A. (2010). *The Dooyeweerd Pages*. Retrieved January 7, 2010, from http://www.dooy.salford.ac.uk/index.html

Becker, M. C. (Ed.). (2008). *Handbook of organisational routines*. Cheltenham, UK: Edward Elgar. doi:10.4337/9781848442702

Benner, M. J., & Veloso, F. M. (2008). ISO 9000 practices and financial performance: A technology coherence perspective. *Journal of Operations Management, 26*(5), 611–629. doi:10.1016/j.jom.2007.10.005

Bentham, J. (1838). Plan of the Panopticon. In J. Bowring (Ed.), *The Works of Jeremy Bentham* (Vol. 4, pp. 172–173). Edinburgh, UK: William Tait.

Berry, T. H. (1991). *Managing the Total Quality Transformation*. New York, NY: McGraw-Hill.

Bevan, R. (2011). *Changemaking: Tactics and Resources for Managing Organizational Change*. Seattle, WA: ChangeStart Press.

Boh, W. F., & Yellin, D. (2007). Using Enterprise Architecture Standards in Managing Information Technology. *Journal of Management Information Systems, 23*(3), 163–207. doi:10.2753/MIS0742-1222230307

Boiral, O. (2003). ISO 9000: Outside the iron case. *Management Science, 14*(6), 720–737.

Boiral, O., & Roy, M. (2007). ISO 9000: Integration rationales and organisational impacts. *International Journal of Operations & Production Management, 27*(2), 226–247. doi:10.1108/01443570710720630

Brehm, S., & Brehm, J. W. (1981). *Psychological Reactance – a Theory of Freedom and Control*. New York: Academic Press.

Briscoe, J., Fawcett, S., & Tood, R. (2005). The Implementation and Impact of ISO 9000 among Small Manufacturing Enterprises. *Journal of Small Business Management, 43*(3), 309–330. doi:10.1111/j.1540-627X.2005.00139.x

Brown, A., Van der Wiele, T., & Loughton, K. (1998). 'Smaller enterprises' experiences with ISO 9000. *International Journal of Quality & Reliability Management, 15*(3), 273–285. doi:10.1108/02656719810198935

Brown, M., Hitchkock, D., & Willard, M. (1994). *Why TQM Fails and What to Do About It*. Burr Ridge, IL: Irvin.

Brunsson, N. (2000). The Pros and Cons of Standardisation – An Epilogue. In *A World of Standards* (pp. 169–173). Oxford, UK: Oxford University Press.

Brunsson, N., & Jacobsson, B. (2000). Following Standards. In *A World of Standards* (pp. 125–137). Oxford, UK: Oxford University Press.

Buckler, B. (1996). A learning process mode to achieve continuous improvement and innovation. *The Learning Organization*, *3*(3), 31–39. doi:10.1108/09696479610119660

Carnall, C., & Todnem, R. (2007). *Managing Change in Organizations* (6th ed.). Harlow, UK: Pearson Education.

Casadesús, M., & Karapetrovic, S. (2005). Has ISO 9000 lost some of its lustre? *International Journal of Operations & Production Management*, *25*(6), 580–596. doi:10.1108/01443570510599737

Connor, P. E. (1997). Total quality management: A selective commentary on its human dimensions, with special reference to its downside. *Public Administration Review*, *57*(6), 501–509. doi:10.2307/976961

Corbett, C. J., Montes-Sancho, M. J., & Kitsch, D. A. (2005). The Financial impact of ISO 9000 Certification in the United States: An Empirical Analysis. *Management Science*, *51*(7), 1046–1059. doi:10.1287/mnsc.1040.0358

Dahlgaard, J., Larsen, H. Z., & Norgaard, A. (1997). Leadership profiles in quality management: A Danish perspective. *Total Quality Management*, *8*(2/3), 16–30. doi:10.1080/0954412979659

Dale, B. G. (2007). Quality Management Systems. In B. G. Dale, T. Van der Wiele, & J. Van Iwaarden (Eds.), *Managing Quality* (pp. 279–309). Malden, MA: Blackwell Publishing.

Dale, B. G., & Cooper, C. (1992). *Total Quality and Human Resources: An Executive Guide*. Oxford, UK: Blackwell.

Dale, B. G., Van der Wiele, A., & Van Iwaarden, J. D. (2007). TQM: An Overview. In B. G. Dale, T. Van der Wiele, & J. Van Iwaarden (Eds.), *Managing Quality (5)*. Malden, MA: Blackwell Publishing.

Davenport, T. H., & Short, J. E. (1990). The new industrial engineering: Information technology and business process re-design. *Sloan Management Review*, *31*(4), 11–27.

David, P. A. (1995). Standardisation policies for network technologies: the flux between freedom and order revisited. In Standards, Innovation and Competitiveness – The Politics and Economics of Standards in Natural and Technical Environments (pp. 15-35). Aldershot, UK: Edward Elgar.

Davis, F. D. (1989). Perceived usefulness, perceived ease of use, and user acceptance of information technology. *Management Information Systems Quarterly*, *13*(3), 319–340. doi:10.2307/249008

Davis, F. D., Bagozzi, R. P., & Warsaw, P. R. (1989). User acceptance of computer technology: A comparison of two theoretical models. *Management Science*, *35*(8), 982–1003. doi:10.1287/mnsc.35.8.982

De Vries, H.J. (1997) Standardization – What's in a name? *Terminology – International Journal of Theoretical and Applied Issues in Specialized Communication*, *4*(1), 55-83.

De Vries, H. J. (2015). Standardisation – A Developing Field of Research. In P. Delimatsis (Ed.), *The Law, Economics and Politics of International Standardsation*. Cambridge, UK: Cambridge University Press. doi:10.1017/CBO9781316423240.002

De Vries, H. J., & Slob, F. J. C. (2006). Best Practice in Company Standardization. *International Journal of IT Standards and Standardization Research*, *4*(1), 62–85. doi:10.4018/jitsr.2006010104

De Vries, H. J., & Van Delden, M. (2006). How to integrate standardisation in knowledge management. *ISO Focus*, *3*(3), 37–40.

Dick, G. P. M., Heras, I., & Casedesús, M. (2008). Shedding light on causation between ISO 9001 and improved business performance. *International Journal of Operations & Production Management*, *28*(9), 687–708. doi:10.1108/01443570810881811

Dooyeweerd, H. (1955). A new critique of theoretical thought. In The general theory of the modal spheres (vol. 2). Amsterdam: H.J. Paris, and Philadelphia: The Presbyterian and Reformed Publishing Company.

Dooyeweerd, H. (1957). The structures of individuality of temporal reality. In A new critique of theoretical thought (vol. 3). Amsterdam; H.J. Paris, and Philadelphia: The Presbyterian and Reformed Publishing Company.

Elkington, J. (1997). *Canibals with Forks: The triple bottom line of the 21st century business*. Oxford, UK: Capstone.

Ellul, J. (1970). *The meaning of the city*. Grand Rapids, MI: Eerdmans.

Foucault, M. (1976). *Histoire de la sexualité I – La volonté de savoir*. Paris: Éditions Gallimard.

Foucault, M. (1977). *Discipline and Punish; Birth of the Prison* (A. Sheridan, Trans.). London: Penguin. (Original work published 1975)

Foucault, M. (1982). Afterword. The subject and power. In H. L. Dreyfus & P. Rabinov (Eds.), *Michel Foucault. Beyond structuralism and hermeneutics* (pp. 208–226). Chicago, IL: University of Chicago Press.

Furusten, S. (2000). The Knowledge Base of Standards. In *A World of Standards* (pp. 71–84). Oxford, UK: Oxford University Press.

Goudzwaard, B. (1979). *Capitalism and Progress: A Diagnosis of Western Society*. Toronto: Wedge.

Gouldner, A. W. (1954). *Patterns of industrial Bureaucracy – A case study of modern factory administration*. New York: The Free Press.

Grimes, K. R. (2003). *ISO 9001:2000: a practical quality manual explained*. Milwaukee, WI: ASQ Quality Press.

Habermas, J. (1987). The Theory of Communicative Action: Lifeworld and System: A Critique of Functionalist Reason (vol. 2; T. *McCarthy, Trans.*). Boston: Beacon. (Original work published 1981)

Hammer, M. (1990). Re-engineering work: Don't automate, obliterate. *Harvard Business Review*, *68*(4), 104–112.

Hammer, M., & Champy, J. (1993). *Re-engineering the corporation: a manifesto for business revolution*. New York, NY: Harper Business.

Harrington, H. J. (1987). *The Improvement Process*. New York: McGraw-Hill.

Haverkamp, A. (2004). *Bezint eer gij begint – Standaardisatie van werkmethoden bij Polynorm Automotive – Onderzoek op basis van een christelijk-filosofische analyse*. Rotterdam: Erasmus Universiteit, Faculteit Bedrijfskunde.

Haverkamp, A. (2006). Een veelzijdig kwaliteitsverbeteringsproject. *Synaps, 4*(20), 21–26.

Hesser, W. (2010). Standardisation within a Comnpany – a Strategic Perspective. In W. Hesser (Ed.), Standardisation in Companies and Markets (3rd ed.; pp. 215–258). Hamburg: Academic Press.

Hofstede, G. (1978). The Poverty of Management Control Philosophy. *Academy of Management Review, 3*(3), 450–461. doi:10.5465/amr.1978.4305727

IATF. (2016). Quality management system for organizations in the automotive industry. *IATF, 16949*, 2016.

Imai, M. (1986). *Kaizen – the key to Japan's competitive success.* New York: Random House.

ISO. (2008). *ISO 9001:2008 Quality management systems – Requirements.* Geneva: International Organization for Standardisation.

ISO. (2009). *ISO/TS 16949:2009 Quality management systems – Particular requirements for the application of ISO 9001:2008 for automotive production and relevant service part organizations.* Geneva: International Organization for Standardisation.

ISO. (2015). *ISO 9001:2015 Quality management systems – Requirements.* Geneva: International Organization for Standardisation.

ISO. (2018). *The ISO Survey of Management System Standard Certifications 2017.* Retrieved November 1, 2018, from https://isotc.iso.org/livelink/livelink/fetch/-8853493/8853511/8853520/18808772/00._Overall_results_and_explanatory_note_on_2017_Survey_results.pdf?nodeid=19208898&vernum=-2

Kalpakjian, S. (1995). *Manufacturing Engineering and Technology* (3rd ed.). Reading, MA: Addison-Wesley.

Kalsbeek, L. (1975). *Contours of a Christian Philosophy: An Introduction to Herman Dooyeweerd's Thought.* Toronto: Wedge.

Kanji, G. K. (1990). Total quality management: The second industrial revolution. *Total Quality Management, 1*(1), 3–12. doi:10.1080/09544129000000001

Kelly, M. (1994). Foucault, Habermas and the Self-Referentiality of Critique. In M. Kelly (Ed.), *Critique and Power – Recasting the Foucault/Habermas Debate.* Cambridge, MA: The MIT Press.

Kondo, Y. (1996). Are creative ability and work standardisation in contradictory relationship? *Training for Quality, 4*(3), 35–39. doi:10.1108/09684879610125734

Kondo, Y. (2000). Innovation versus standardisation. *The TQM Magazine, 12*(1), 6–10. doi:10.1108/09544780010287177

Lagrosen, Y., & Lagrosen, S. (2005). The effects of quality management – A survey of Swedish quality professionals. *International Journal of Operations & Production Management, 25*(10), 940–952. doi:10.1108/01443570510619464

Lazaric, N., & Denis, B. (1995). Routinization and memorization of tasks in a workshop: The case of the introduction of ISO norms. *Industrial and Corporate Change, 15*(5), 873–896. doi:10.1093/icc/dth074

Lelong, B., & Mallard, A. (1995). Presentation. *Reseaux, 18*(102), 9–34.

Lin, Ch.-I., & Jang, W.-Y. (2008). Successful ISO 9000 implementation in Taiwan: How can we achieve it, and what does it mean? *International Journal of Productivity and Performance Management, 57*(8), 600–622. doi:10.1108/17410400810916044

Lo, L. K., & Chang, D. S. (2007). The difference in the perceived benefits between firms that maintain ISO certification and those that do not. *International Journal of Production Research, 48*(5), 1881–1897. doi:10.1080/00207540600733709

Macdonald, J., & Dale, B. G. (2007). Business Process Re-engineering. In Managing Quality (5). Malden, MA: Blackwell Publishing.

Magd, H. A. E. (2008). ISO 9001:2000 in the Egyptian manufacturing sector: perceptions and perspectives. *International Journal of Quality & Reliability Management, 25*(2), 173–200. doi:10.1108/02656710810846934

Mahadevappa, B., & Kotreshwar, G. (2004). Quality Management Practices in Indian ISO 9000 Certified Companies: An Empirical Evaluation. *Total Quality Management, 15*(3), 295–305. doi:10.1080/1478336042000183389

Manders, B. (2015). *Implementation and Impact of ISO 9001. ERIM PhD Series Research in Management.* Rotterdam: Erasmus Research Institute of Management – ERIM.

Manders, B. (2015). *Implementation and Impact of ISO 9001. ERIM PhD Series in Research in Management 337.* Rotterdam: Erasmus Research Institute of Management – ERIM.

Martínez-Costa, M., Choi, T. Y., Martinez, J. A., & Martínez-Lorente, A. R. (2009). ISO 9000/1994, ISO 9001/2000 and TQM: The performance debate revisited. *Journal of Operations Management, 27*(6), 495–511. doi:10.1016/j.jom.2009.04.002

Mom, T. J. M., Van den Bosch, F. A. J., & Volberda, H. W. (2002). Exploratie en exploitatie van kennis - Het managen van de determinanten van horizontale kennisuitwisseling. *Management en Organisatie, 56*(5), 23–43.

Nair, A., & Prajogo, D. (2009). Internalisation of ISO 9000 standards: The antecedent role of functionalist and institutionalist drivers and performance implications. *International Journal of Production Research, 47*(16), 4545–4568. doi:10.1080/00207540701871069

Nakamura, S. (2000). *The new standardisation: Keystone of continuous improvement in manufacturing.* Portland, OR: Productivity Press.

Naveh, E., & Erez, M. (2004). Innovation and Attention to Detail in the Quality Improvement Paradigm. *Management Science, 50*(11), 1576–1586. doi:10.1287/mnsc.1040.0272

Naveh, E., Marcus, A., & Moon, H. K. (2004). Implementing ISO 9000: Performance improvement by first or second movers. *International Journal of Production Research*, *42*(9), 1843–1863. doi:10.1080/00207540410001662912

Nicolau, J. L., & Sellers, R. (2002). The stock market's reaction to quality certification: Empirical evidence from Spain. *European Journal of Operational Research*, *142*(3), 632–641. doi:10.1016/S0377-2217(01)00312-5

Nicoloso, E. (2007). Bridging the gap between quality management systems and product quality. *ISO Management Systems*, *7*(1), 7–11.

Nonaka, I. (1994). A Dynamic Theory of Organisational Knowledge Creation. *Organization Science*, *5*(1), 14–37. doi:10.1287/orsc.5.1.14

Nonaka, I., & Takeuchi, H. (1995). *The knowledge creating company: how Japanese companies create the dynamics of innovation*. New York: Oxford University Press.

Olian, J. P., & Ryness, S. L. (1991). Making total quality work: Aligning organizations, performance measures, and stakeholders. *Human Resource Management*, *30*(3), 303–333. doi:10.1002/hrm.3930300303

Padma, P., Ganesh, L. S., & Rajendran, C. (2008). A study on the critical factors of ISO 9001:2000 and organisational performance of Indian manufacturing firms. *International Journal of Production Research*, *46*(18), 4981–5011. doi:10.1080/00207540600793299

Paper, D., Rodger, J., & Pendharkar, P. C. (2001). A BPR case study at Honeywell. *Business Process Management Journal*, *7*(2), 85–99. doi:10.1108/14637150110389416

Reed, R., Lemak, D. J., & Mero, N. P. (2000). Total quality management and sustainable competitive advantage. *Journal of Quality Management*, *5*(1), 5–26. doi:10.1016/S1084-8568(00)00010-9

Rogers, E. M. (2003). *Diffusion of innovations* (5th ed.). New York: Simon & Schuster.

Simons, C. A. J., & De Vries, H. J. (2002). *Standaard of maatwerk – Bedrijfskeuzes tussen uniformiteit en verscheidenheid*. Schoonhoven, The Netherlands: Academic Service.

Slob, F. J. C., & De Vries, H. J. (2001). Wie die (petro)chemische Industrie von Normen profitiert. *DIN-Miteilungen*, *80*(6), 440–442.

Spencer, B. A. (1994). Models of organization and total quality management: A comparison and critical evaluation. *Academy of Management Review*, *19*(3), 446–471. doi:10.5465/amr.1994.9412271807

Sprenger, C. C., & Ten Have, S. (1996). Kennismanagement als motor van de lerende organisatie. *Holland Management Review*, *51*, 69–76.

Strauss, D. F. M. (2009). *Philosophy: Disciplines of the Disciplines*. Paideia Press.

Talib, F., & Zillur, R. (2010). A study of total quality managent and supply chain management practices. *International Journal of Productivity and Performance Management, 60*(3), 268–288. doi:10.1108/17410401111111998

Tamm-Halström, K. (2004). *Organizing International Standardization – ISO and the IASC in Quest of Authority*. Cheltenham, UK: Edward Elgar.

Terziovski, M., Power, D., & Sohal, A. S. (2003). The longitudinal effects of the ISO 9000 certification process on business performance. *European Journal of Operational Research, 146*(3), 580–595. doi:10.1016/S0377-2217(02)00252-7

Terziovski, M., Samson, D., & Dow, D. (1997). The business value of quality management systems certification – Evidence from Australia and New Zealand. *Journal of Operations Management, 15*(1), 1–18. doi:10.1016/S0272-6963(96)00103-9

Tzelepis, D., Tsekjouras, K., Skuras, D., & Dimara, E. (2006). The effects of ISO 9001 on firms' productive efficiency. *International Journal of Operations & Production Management, 26*(10), 1146–1165. doi:10.1108/01443570610691111

Van Kemenade, E. A., Hardjono, T. W., & De Vries, H. J. (2011). The willingness of professionals to contribute to their organisation's certification. *International Journal of Quality & Reliability Management, 28*(1), 27–42. doi:10.1108/02656711111097535

Van Veldhuisen, A. (1996). *De Macht van het Systeem – Een studie naar kwaliteitssystemen gebaseerd op het werk van Michael Foucault*. Rotterdam: Erasmus Universiteit, Faculteit Bedrijfskunde.

Van Wessel, R. (2010). *Toward Corporate IT Standardization Management: Frameworks and Solutions*. Hershey, PA: IGI Global. doi:10.4018/978-1-61520-759-6

Weber, M. (1922). *Wirtschaft und Gesellschaft.* Tübingen: J.C.B. Mohr.

Wenström, H., Ollner, J., & Wenström, J. (2010). *Focus on Industry and Standards – An Integrated Approach*. Stockholm: SIS.

Wissema, J. G., Messer, H. M., & Wijers, G. J. (1991). *Angst voor veranderen? Een mythe! – Of: Hoe u veranderingsbereidheid op de werkvloer vergroot*. Assen: Van Gorcum.

Yeung, A. C. L., Lee, T. S., & Chan, L. Y. (2003). Senior management perspectives and ISO 9000 effectiveness: An empirical research. *International Journal of Production Research, 41*(3), 545–569. doi:10.1080/0020754021000033896

Zink, K. J. (1997). *Total Quality Management as a Holistic Management Concept*. Berlin: Springer.

Zink, K. J. (2007). From total quality management to corporate sustainability based on a stakeholder management. *Journal of Management History, 13*(4), 394–401. doi:10.1108/17511340710819615

ENDNOTE

1. This chapter is an extended and updated version of an earlier paper in the book *Effective Standardization Management in Corporate Settings* edited by K. Jakobs (2016, Advances in IT Standards and Standardization Research. Hershey, PA: IGI Global, pp. 184-213). That chapter adapted the paper Overcoming resistance against quality control – A philosophical-empirical approach (De Vries, H. J. & Haverkamp, A. (2015). *International Journal of Quality and Reliability Management* 32(1), 18-41), written for the domain of quality management, to make it fit for the domain of standardization research.

Chapter 7
The Role of Internal Standardization in Business Models:
An Activity Configurations Perspective

Magnus Johansson
Lund University, Sweden

Matts Kärreman
Lund University, Sweden

Amalia Foukaki
Lund University, Sweden

ABSTRACT

This chapter focuses on business models and the role of internal standardization in business models. The authors develop a typology that outlines the role of internal standardization for a set of value configurations that serve as representations of generic business models. The topic is of importance for both managers and researchers in relation to firm level innovation and strategy, as well as how business models relate to internal and external standardization. With regard to business model innovation, this chapter can aid in identifying shifts in the firm's internal standardization focus associated with changes in its business model.

INTRODUCTION

Interest in the business model concept has surged during the last twenty years (Ghaziani & Ventresca, 2005; Zott, Amit & Massa, 2011). The increased attention of management scholars in business models and the relation to strategy stems from the attempt to explain value creation in the arising digital economy and increasingly important networked markets (Zott et al, 2011), both in the form of markets with single-side as well as multiple-side network effects (stemming from complementarity).

DOI: 10.4018/978-1-5225-9008-8.ch007

Copyright © 2019, IGI Global. Copying or distributing in print or electronic forms without written permission of IGI Global is prohibited.

A business model can be viewed as a system of activities which is not delimited to the firm itself but includes a system-level approach to how the firm interacts with its environment and does business (Zott et al, 2011). Developing a successful business model is often insufficient to assure competitive advantages as imitation might be easy. Business model innovation can, however, be a pathway to competitive advantage and limit the risks of imitation (Teece, 2010). Christensen, Grossman and Hwang (2009) have addressed the topic of business model innovation by utilizing activity configurations (Stabell & Fjeldstad, 1998; Porter, 1985) as descriptions of generic business models.

The network configuration (Stabell & Fjeldstad, 1998) is of particular interest. It relies on standardization to facilitate a networked market. The creation of networked markets and complementarity between them depends on the ability of standards to provide compatibility (Gallagher, 2007; Tassey, 2000), and networked markets have been of certain interest for research on standardization due to the fierce standardization competition they can entail (Besen & Farrel, 1994). The network configuration can rely on proprietary standards to facilitate a networked market, but also on industry standardization to facilitate inter-network connections. Diffusion of industry standards is critical on networked markets (Stabell & Fjeldstad, 1998) and consequently the firm's business model depends on its proprietary standards as well as their relation to industry standards.

In general, standards enforce conformity requirements (Tassey, 2000) and serve as rules of key activities, resulting from consensus between agents (Narayanan & Chen, 2012)). The chain (Porter, 1985; Stabell & Fjeldstad, 1998) and package (Johansson & Jonsson, 2012) configurations also rely on standardization to realize value creation, for instance by reducing transaction costs of firm products in the market (Foss, 1996).

Hence, standardization seems to play an important role in activity configurations for value creation, but its more precise nature in association with each of generic configurations above has not been treated as a key topic in the literature. This chapter aims at elucidating the particular use of internal standardization in enabling different business models in the form of generic activity configurations. Hence, this chapter links the field of standardization with the fields of activity configurations as business models. By development of a typology, the main internal standardization nature of the chain, network, package and shop configurations is outlined. The focus is on internal standardization, but we also recognize that internal and external standardization are interrelated (Botzem & Dobusch, 2012; Okhomatovskiy & David, 2012; Schilling, 1999; Boiral, 2012; Narayanan & Chen, 2012), and thus our findings are of importance also in relation to external standardization, activity configurations, and the value of external standards (Mione, 2015). In particular, our findings can serve as an antecedent or partial explanation to coopetitive strategies in association with standardization, as standardization can be seen as a specific type of coopetition (Blind and Mangelsdorf, 2016).

BACKGROUND

Activity Configurations as Business Models

During the 1990s, research pursued alternatives to the value chain (Porter, 1985) by focusing on interrelationships and complementarity, but also by focusing on various types of scale effects. For instance, Normann and Ramirez (1993;1994), through their concept of value constellations, pay specific attention to co-creation of value between players. Stabell and Fjeldstad's (1998) value configurations, on the other hand, focus more on the internal activity configuration of an organization. Stabell and Fjeldstad extend Porter's value chain by relating activity configurations to generic strategies associated with particular economic effects. This is discussed by Christensen et al. (2009) when they illustrate moves from one configuration to another as business model innovation paths along which firms can transform their ways of working and interacting with the market. Therefore, activity configurations are considered in this chapter as business models in the form of systems of activities (Zott et al, 2011).

Stabell and Fjeldstad (1998) proposed three activity configurations: the chain, shop and network configuration. At the center of each configuration they have placed value creation logics inspired by Thompson's (1967) technologies. These alternative configurations emphasize integration and interrelations of activities, internally and externally, and that these can be radically different from what we associate with the value chain. The value chain configuration, according to Stabell and Fjeldstad, utilizes long-linked technologies (Thompson, 1967), which are associated with the mass production assembly line and the transformation of input to output. The focus of mass production is the perfection of the production of a standard output, repetitively and at a constant rate.

The value shop configuration utilizes intensive technology to solve customer unique problems through iterative problem solving (Stabell & Fjeldstad, 1998). Thompson also states: "The intensive technology is a custom technology. Its successful employment rests in part on the availability of all the capacities potentially needed, but equally on the appropriate custom combination of selected capacities as required by the individual case or project." (Thompson, 1967, p. 18). Typical examples of shop configurations are professional services firms, such as consulting firms or medical practice.

Finally, the network configuration relies on linking customers through mediating technologies (Thompson, 1967). Stabell and Fjeldstad (1998) describe the role of the firm as a network service supplier and a mediator between customers. The network logic utilizes network externalities (Katz & Shapiro, 1985) to create value. A classic example of a network dependent firm is a telecom network operator, bringing multiple subscribers together. Furthermore, in Johansson and Jonsson (2012) the set of three activity configurations (and logics) is extended with a fourth, the package configuration. The package logic is, similarly to the shop logic, centered on problem-solving. However, this is problem-solving across a range of potential customers, with the goal of making such common problem-solving efficient through underlying solutions. Typical examples are firms producing designs for licensing, such as hardware IPs for the semiconductor industry. The four activity configurations and their logics are summarized in Table 1. Despite the fact that Stabell and Fjeldstad (1998) proposed three activity configurations[1] - the chain, shop and network- they also recognized the relevance of their hybrid versions (cf. Miller, 1996).

Christensen et al. (2009) have linked these configurations to business model innovation by considering them to be generic descriptions of business models. One of the main views of business models in research addresses them as firm-centric but at the same time as boundary-spanning systems of activities (Zott et al, 2011). Christensen et al. emphasize the importance of innovating the firm's business model, and essentially the value creation logic of the firm, by moving from one configuration to another. Thus, business model innovation concerns innovation regarding the set of activities, their configuration, or the parties involved in performing them (cf. Amit & Zott, 2012).

Activity configurations can, in addition to being considered as business models (Christensen et al, 2009) and value creating entities, be understood from a governance perspective. For particular transaction attributes the costs of governing activities differ, depending on whether these activities are governed through markets or in organizations (Masten, 1991). Boundaries for activities, and consequently activity configurations, are results of governance-costs minimization attempts. Sources of governance-cost dif-

Table 1. Typology of value configurations. (Stabell & Fjeldstad, 1998, p. 415 and Johansson & Jonsson, 2012, p. 548)

	Network	Package	Chain	Shop
Value creation logic	Linking customers	Solving common problems	Transformation of inputs to products	(Re)solving customer problems
Primary technology	Mediating	Intensive	Long-linked	Intensive
Primary activity technologies	Network promotion and contract management Service provisioning Infrastructure operation	Problem gathering Problem prioritization Problem decomposition Problem solving Control of parallel development Marketing and support	Inbound logistics Operations Outbound logistics	Problem finding and acquisition Problem solving Choice Execution Control/evaluation
Main interactivity relationship logic	Simultaneous, parallel	Single to multiple point packaging funnel	Sequential	Cyclical, spiraling
Primary activity interdependence	Pooled Reciprocal	Pooled Sequential Reciprocal	Pooled Sequential	Pooled Sequential Reciprocal
Key cost drivers	Scale Capacity utilization	Scale/Development Capacity utilization	Scale Capacity utilization	Efficiency in referral Reuse of human resources
Key value drivers	Scale Capacity utilization	Quality		Reputation
Business value system structure	Layered and interconnected networks	Packaging funnels in tree structure	Interlinked chains	Referred shops

ferences can be understood from three streams of thought, those being transaction costs, measurement difficulties and knowledge differences (Santos & Eisenhart, 2005), all of which will be discussed in the next section.

From a transaction cost economics perspective, structures for defining, monitoring and enforcing activities and activity configurations are consequences of firms striving to minimize transactions costs. While measurement costs are caused by information problems (Holmstrom, 1999; Williamson, 1985), these, in turn, change over time through organizational learning. Supervision of activities, alignment of incentives and collecting information are simpler within an organization than in the market. Different activity configurations come with different challenges regarding measurement costs. Costs derived from idiosyncrasies in knowledge include coordination costs. Individuals bring and develop different knowledge and will practice or argue for different solutions to organizational tasks if not coordinated. The extent of the need for coordination more than likely varies among activity configurations, and routines developed in order to reduce costs will be aligned to the specific activity configuration.

Of particular interest during the last decades has been the network configuration, which provides a business model perspective on the deployment of network effects (Katz & Shapiro, 1985; 1994), and thus, also relates to the role of industry platforms (Eisenmann, Parker & Van Alstyne, 2006; Parker & Van Alstyne, 2003; Rochet & Tirole, 2003). A fundamental aspect of realizing network effects of an industry platform is the utilization of standardization in order to enable compatibility across players accessing the network (Cusumano, 2010; Ulrich, 1995).

Moreover, in the activity configurations proposed by Stabell and Fjeldstad (1998), we see great consideration made to cooperative aspects, which is in line with the systemic view of business models (Zott et al, 2011). For instance, the shop configuration may include joint, iterative execution together with a customer, where the outcome may very well also depend on the efforts of the customer. This results in the firm's iterative problem-solving activity sequences. The network configuration also relies on cooperative actions by players participating in the network facilitated by the focal firm. In the following section, standards and standardization are defined; before we move on to outline the role of standardization in the configurations.

Internal and External Standards and Standardization

Standardization codifies and diffuses state of the art technology and best practice (Swann, 2010; Krechmer 2000, 2005; Blind & Grupp, 2000), essentially establishing conformity requirements on products and processes (Naryanan and Chen, 2012; Tassey, 2000) - and thus can be seen as the outcome of consensus among agents on how to perform certain key activities according to specific rules (Naryanan & Chen, 2012). Several scholars have pointed to how agents try to influence the standardization process in their own interests (Blind & Mangelsdorf, 2012; Dokko & Rosenkopf, 2010). Therefore, we view industry standards as reducing variety in artefacts and activities within an industry. Also, we recognize that industry standardization may very well encompass varying degrees of influence from the various agents that try to promote their own interests, for instance within consensus based committee work.

Consequently, we view internal standards as internally based variety reduction, and especially that internal standards have a variety reducing effect across products and production processes for instance, and as a consequence between intraorganizational entities, such as divisions, functions or teams. . This is the internal equivalent of industry codification and diffusion of technology and best practices. In many instances the development and implementation of these follow internal consensus processes, analogous to external standardization (Grossman, 2013). These internal standards can be deployed internally as well as externally, i.e. utilized for the output and input markets, as is the case for private standards (Vandemoortele & Deconinck, 2013).

External standardization depends on the input from several participating firms. Such input may originate from internal standardization (of processes, products or sub-deliveries). At the same time, internal standardization might be the result of adoption of external standards if they need to be accustomed to serve the firm's needs. Therefore, standardization is not a far-away industry matter, but is interdependent on firm internal standardization. For instance, in Okhomatovskiy and David (2012) the firm responds to industry standardization by creating its own internal standard. However, this internal standard does not only serve internal purposes, but also signals certain organizational traits to the external environment. Thus, the firm has several strategic options related to standardization and these involve internal and external standardization and their interdependence.

Since a firm centric view is applied in this chapter, the role of standards needs to be considered from the input and output market perspectives, rather than those from the demand and supply side, as is common for external standards (Naryanan & Chen, 2012). An internal standard may be applied to suppliers of the firm (as in Grossman, 2013). The use of internal standards on the output market, i.e. the suppliers, means that standardization occurs through an internal process and then its outcome has consequences for other firms as well at the input or output markets of the firm. One example of standards that are of an internal origin, but with external effects, is private standards, a type of standard mainly associated with minimum quality certification within the food and agricultural sector (Henson & Hooker, 2001; Vandemoortele & Deconinck, 2013). Private standards controlled by an intermediary in a market can have an effect on the input as well as the output market of the firm but can only under certain circumstances be optimal for both buyers and suppliers (Vandemoortele & Deconinck, 2013).

Standardization is often associated with the process by which external standards emerge (Tassey, 2000; Blind, 2004; Greenstein & Stango, 2007). For instance, Tassey (2000) distinguishes between the process of standardization, which enables the conformity associated with standards, and standards themselves, which are denoted as a set of specifications. In several instances, research on standardization has focused on the consensus processes of standards developing entities (cf. Botzem & Dobusch, 2012), such as Standards Developing Organizations (SDOs) or Consortia. The emphasis in the aforementioned cases is primarily placed upon the inter-organizational rather than the intra-organizational processes. Also, external standards and their economic effects are often discussed from the perspective of the impact they have on market establishment and efficiency (Blind, 2004; David, 1987). However, several of the economic effects associated with external standardization are also relevant from a firm perspective, or from that of inter-firm relations, e.g. between a firm and its supplier network. For instance, variety reduction of components, resulting in scale effects, has been referred to as internal standardization (Ulrich, 1995). The firm frequently faces a situation of standards-related alternative choices, such as keeping its standardization internal or diffusing it among a number of other firms (through consortia or SDOs), or adopting external standards for internal variety reduction. At its most basic level, standardization concerns "reducing the infinite number of things in the world … to a moderate number of well-defined varieties" (March & Simon, 1958, p 181). The key question for the firm is on what level this reduction of varieties should occur, i.e. internally or externally.

A firm is not isolated from industry structures and their changes, even if outside its boundaries (Sheehan & Foss, 2007). Boundaries of the firm and its standardization activities arguably intertwine and mutually affect organizations in terms of efficiency, competence, identity and influence (Santos & Eisenhardt, 2005). Firm boundaries are a central phenomenon that has been examined from various perspectives. Firstly, as a demarcation of the social structure that forms an organization, and as such, activities operate under a particular logic of identity that shapes how things are done in the organization and sets the rules for inclusion (Kogut, 2000). Secondly, boundaries are the demarcation of the resources controlled by the firm, thus shaping the development of the organization (Helfat, 1997). Thirdly, boundaries can be seen as the determinants for organizational influence, including the degree of industry control and power over external forces (Santos & Eisenhart, 2005). Porter (1985) points to the reciprocal relationship between industry structure and the chain of activities of the players in an industry, while claiming that "potential sources of competitive advantage are everywhere in a firm" (Porter, 1985, p. 3). Thus, standardization influences the firm and its activities via the effects it has on industry structures and vice versa.

On the other hand, the firm can also influence standardization and in turn the industry. Schilling (1999) presents standards as means to gain competitive advantage, determining success or failure, depending on how a firm employs them. For instance, she stipulates how a firm could promote and influence a specific standard, thereby affecting the evolution of the industry in a manner advantageous to the firm. Furthermore, the firm must perform variety-reducing and conformity-enabling activities while at the same time considering other players involved in a standardization process, be it of a consensus or strictly competitive nature.

INTERNAL STANDARDIZATION AND STANDARDS

Internally and Externally Applied Standardization of Products and Processes

Viewing standardization as the process by which standards emerge is one way of addressing the difference between the standards' development procedure and its outcome. However, the processes taking place within an organization might also be standardized. That is, the process of standardization may lead to an outcome, the standards, being either for processes (Perez-Aleman, 2011) or for products (Warner, Fairbank, & Steensma, 2006). Brunson and Jacobsson (2000) distinguish between standardization of processes on the one hand and services and products on the other. Similarly, Blind (2011) makes a distinction between standardization of products, procedures and practice. Here, a distinction will be made between standardization of products (including internal and external parts and sub-deliveries, and changes to those stemming from service execution) versus standardization of processes (within which are included procedures and practices).

Another distinction relates to organizational boundaries. A standard can originate internally as well as externally (Okhmatovskiy & David, 2012), i.e. it can stem from within an organization as well as from an external standardization body. Following this line of argument, a standard can also be applied internally or externally. An illustration is seen in Figure 1, where we also highlight the interdependence between internal and external standards.

As an example, it is possible to distinguish between process standards applied internally and standards that are applied externally. Process standards are closely linked to procedures, practices and actions (cf. Brunson & Jacobsson, 2000; Perez-Aleman, 2011) and thus the internal aspects of process standards relate to the way that work is done in an organization. From the internal perspective, process standardization can play a role in enabling modularity (Tu, Vonderembse, Ragu-Nathan, & Ragu-Nathan, 2004), thus representing the internal application. However, as Okhomatovskiy and David (2012) have shown; an internally developed process standard can also be communicated externally in order to convey certain practices.

Figure 1. Origin and application of standards from the firm perspective.

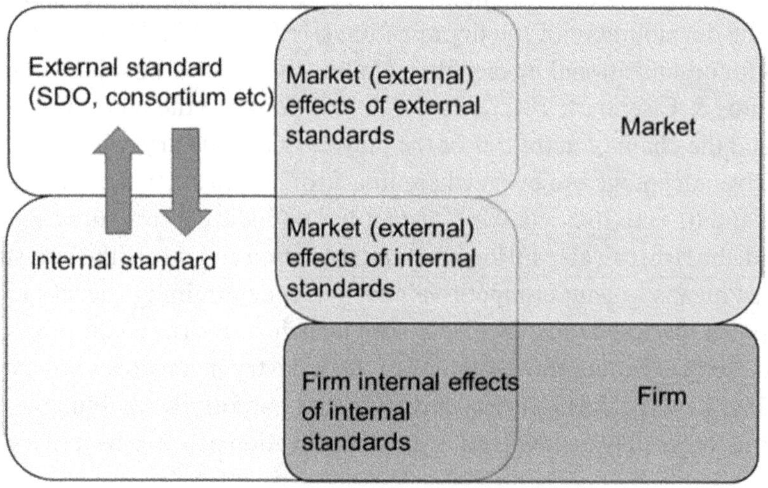

Product standards can even be viewed from the perspective of their application, internal or external. An internally developed standard can be *applied* internally in order to reduce variety or facilitate compatibility between components such as internal sub-deliveries. Internal application of product standards is fundamental for enabling modularity of components (cf. Argyres & Bigelow, 2010) within the firm. An internally developed product standard can also be *applied* externally as part of an offering in a market. As a standardized item it can communicate certain characteristics (such as minimum quality in the case of private standards (Vandemoortele & Deconinck, 2013)) on the output market compared to other products from the same firm or from other firms, i.e. it relies on a certain level of uniformity vis-à-vis the environment. This is important from a transaction cost perspective as it affects search and control costs related to products. (cf. Barzel, 1982; Foss, 1996). It can also be applied externally to the input market, for instance in order to control supplies from subcontractors (Ulrich, 1995).

Some standards reduce variety resulting in, for instance, transaction cost reduction, as well as providing compatibility, leading to, for example, network effects across firms or customers (Blind, Gauch, & Hawkins, 2010; Blind, 2004). As an example, consumers might receive utility from using arrangements containing a variety of compatible components (Matutes & Regibeau, 1996) while for firms, modularity enabled by standardization can play a role beyond the boundaries of the firm when the development and production of components is outsourced. The above-mentioned externally and internally applied standards may relate to both processes and products.

- **Internal Standardization for Efficiency:** Here the focus is either on standardization of a type of process, enabling a certain level of efficiency, or efficiency due to more precise interaction between several internal processes. An example would be time-critical deliveries from several sub-processes to fit into each other, thus requiring precise execution according to an internal standard.
- **Internal Standardization:** This box encompasses internal standardization of sub-deliveries and components that often serves to facilitate efficient utilization of interfaces between modules and sub-deliveries and consequently their production processes. For instance, a product is made up of several components from separate production lines that require clearly defined and standardized interfaces to fit together. This includes interoperability as well as minimum quality aspects.
- **Standard Services Execution:** Standardization of externally oriented processes that constitute services fall under this category. One example is services execution through software systems or service execution with human interfaces fulfilling requirements of an internal standard.
- **Product Standardization:** This box encompasses the standardization and homogeneity of products to the output market resulting in transaction cost reduction among the firm's offerings. This section can also include results of services; i.e. the changes that services incur on goods and products of the customer.

Table 2. Outline of internal standardization

	Input market			Output market	
	Compatibility	**Uniformity**	**Internal**	**Uniformity**	**Compatibility**
Process	Time dep Supply Platform	Services Supply Timing	Internal for efficiency	Services Execution	Time dep Platform
Product	Supply Platform	Supply Product and Tech	Internal	Output Product	Platform

- **Time Dependent Platform Standardization:** Here the focus is on the timing aspect, making sure that processes are standardized to facilitate interaction between users. For instance, online sales and auction sites need not only certify the right information in its systems but also through standardized processes ensure that counterparts supply information and act with the timing required.
- **Platform Standardization:** From a firm perspective this section includes standardization to ensure compatibility between products, technologies and users on the output market. Thus, an example would be online platforms such as Facebook.

Analogously as the categories on the output market we can imagine internally developed standards applied to the input market to facilitate certain economic effects vis-á-vis suppliers. Thus, the firm through its internally developed standards introduces conformity requirements on its suppliers. In Table 2 they are called *Time Dependent Supply Platform, Supply Platform, Services Supply Timing* and *Supply Product and Technology*.

Platform standardization requires additional consideration. Platforms that enable double-sided network effects between several players can stretch beyond the input and output market border through vertical standardization of interfaces. Thus, for platforms the input and output distinction is, in some instances, not relevant as all players joining the platform can be seen as customers to some extent.

Processes are considered as internal if they predominantly concern activities that can be performed without direct interaction with the environment. That is not to say that external input is unnecessary but that direct interaction in day-to-day execution is limited. Processes of external application, however, are related to activities in direct interaction with the environment in the form of customers, suppliers etc. In the literature on standards, *standardization for internal efficiency* is seldom discussed in-depth. From the perspective of the strategic management and organization theory literature this area is mostly associated with terms such as practices (cf. Brown & Duguid, 1991) and routines as part of the evolutionary perspective (Nelson & Winter, 1982).

However, the standardization literature[2] may stretch into the internal aspects of reducing variety and providing compatibility concerning *products and parts* but rarely as far as applying the concept of standards on internal *processes*, unless they are a result of internalizing externally specified process standards (such as Boiral, 2012; Narayanan & Chen, 2012; Sandholtz, 2012; Perez-Aleman, 2010). Here internal processes will be included in the analysis in order to point to differences between the activity configurations. Also, whereas extensive parts of the standardization literature deal only with standards that diffuse a substantial share of a market, this chapter also includes standardization of output or processes from one firm, i.e. variety reduction for, and across, firm products (Foss, 1996) or services (Tether, Hipp, & Miles, 2001). This can be argued to be an important aspect since a standard on the single firm level can provide a reduction in transaction costs (cf. Barzel, 1982; Foss, 1996).

STANDARDIZATION IN ACTIVITY CONFIGURATIONS AND ITS ANTECEDENTS

Externally Applied Standardization

Stabell and Fjeldstad (1998) make an explicit reference to Katz and Shapiro (1985) and direct network effects, i.e. single-side effects. Since then the field of network effects has advanced through the definition of indirect network effects (Katz & Shapiro, 1994), two-sided markets (Eisenmann et al, 2006; Parker

& Van Alstyne, 2003; Rochet & Tirole, 2003) and the role of platforms as multi-sided market enablers (Gawer & Cusmano, 2008). In turn, industry platforms rely on standardization. Not all standards are platforms (Cusumano, 2010) but all platforms contain an aspect of standardization to enable network effects. This dependence on standards is noted by Stabell and Fjeldstad (1998) and has its origin in a fundamental aspect of the mediating technology to ensure compatibility (Thompson, 1967). Thus, standards also play a role in enabling collaboration simultaneous with collaboration, i.e. coopetition (cf. Blind and Mangelsdorf, 2016). How a firm shares its technology in association with standards depends on several different aspects. In addition, when firms decide to engage in coopetition, exercising selectiveness in knowledge sharing becomes vital for realizing or sustaining competitiveness (Alexy, George, and Salter, 2013). On the other hand, Saltzman, Chatterjee, and Raman (2008) argued that there can be several different combinations of rivalry and excludability tactics among competitors—and hence, different combinations of availability and sharing among competitors as well. Chesbrough (2003), von Hippel (2005) and Laursen and Salter (2014) problematized "the paradox of openness," stressing the need for firms to open up (to external actors) so that they do not "miss opportunities to exchange knowledge with different actors" (Laursen and Salter, 2014, p.876). On the other hand, protecting a technology will dramatically decrease the likelihood—or at least delay the process—of this technology being diffused in the market (Schilling, 1999). Chandler and Hikino (2009) argued that in technologically advanced industries, improvement of products and processes becomes the key competitive weapon—rather than, necessarily, the uniqueness or heterogeneity of products and processes.

Another discussion on standardization revolves around the level of standardization of a firm's products from the internal perspective, and not in relation to offerings from other players in the output market. To what extent does the firm deliver similar products or services to multiple customers versus tailoring for each customer's needs? In Stabell and Fjeldstad (1998, p. 416) the value chain has standardized output: "Consider assembly line-based manufacturing as an example of a long-linked value creation technology. The assembly line is designed to produce standard products at low cost per unit by exploiting cost economies of scale." Stabell and Fjeldstad mention that value shop deliveries may include standardized solutions but the value creation process is essentially designed to handle unique cases. Johansson and Jonsson (2012) deal specifically with this, claiming that the value creation associated with the standardized solution is the basis for a unique activity configuration, the package configuration (see the consequences of this in Table 1, outlining four activity configurations), thus facilitating standardized solutions that form a basis for internal and, in some cases, external output. The package configuration is also interesting as it emphasizes activities such as those of research and development as primary, especially in combination with value capture models built on licensing. This in turn has close connections to external standardization in innovative industries (cf. Blind, 2002; 2004).

Internally Applied Standardization

The use of the label standardization can, however, also have an internal character as in Thompson (1967),. Although Thompson includes an external perspective in association with defining different technologies, standardization is in the sections related to interdependence internal, as it is inspired by the definitions in March and Simon (1958). These authors claim standardization to concern three devices: Homogenization of semi-manufactured products for subsequent steps, interchangeability between parts, and coordination of timing between subprocesses. These three are all aspects of "reducing the infinite number of things in the world, potential and actual – to a moderate number of well-defined varieties" (March & Simon, 1958, p. 181). Standardization, as described by March and Simon. serves the purpose of enabling process specialization and in turn efficiency. Whereas in March and Simon standardization is a general means of enabling process specialization, it is according to Thompson (1967) a distinct way of coordinating activities. Furthermore, Thompson, in the case of standardization, stresses the aspects of pooled interdependence, i.e. what may involve several units or processes and not only successive processes. Successive processes, however, is the key example in March and Simon (1958) with regard to device three of standardization: coordinated timing.

The tampering of labels (and the tampering to some extent of their content) by Thompson is beneficial in the sense that it enriches the typology with situations of stronger and more diverse mutual dependence but it also switches the role of standardization from a process specialization enabler into an activity coordination mechanism. Thus, independent of March and Simon's or Thompson's take on the labels, standardization is present from an internal perspective in all types of organizations.

Another internal application of standardization by Thompson (1967) can be found in the repetitive nature of processes in association with the long-linked technologies and that "proportions of resources involved can be standardized" (p. 15). Also, criteria can be established with regard to the resources involved. Thus, for the value chain, internal standardization takes place with regard to the process, the involvement of resources and the homogeneity of resources. Standardization of the process in the internal sense is similar to the concept of practices and to some extent routines.

Nelson and Winter (1982) argue for routines as the fundamental units of analysis in an organization, though unanimous definition of organizational routines – or agreement regarding their origins – is still lacking (Cohen, Burkhart, Dosi, Egidi, Marengo, Warglien & Winter, 1996; Felin & Foss, 2005). The issue is then how standardization of internal processes, with limited direct external interdependence, relates to routines. The concept of routines has its roots partly in *standard operating procedures* (Cyert & March, 1963; Felin & Foss, 2009). Thus, from the internal perspective it is worth recognizing the aspect of routines that relates to repetitive behavior in a standardized fashion, which is also evident in the above discussion on standardization by March and Simon (1958). When the literature focusing on routines discusses standardization it can also do so from a design perspective where standards set the framework for routines. Felin and Foss (2005) discuss this taking the individual level into consideration. Standard operating procedures are first set and within these individuals interact and gradually change the rules and procedures, and thus the routines. Thus, standards and routines are different concepts and as indicated above, routines concern variety reduction across a temporal dimension. Standards, on the other hand, fulfil their function across the spatial dimension, i.e. reducing variety across a population, be it technologies, products or processes.

It is vital to acknowledge the differing views on standardization from the perspective of routines as well as the way it is displayed by Thompson (1967). When Thompson discusses standardization in association with technologies, he places the organization in its environmental context. On the other hand, when he discusses structure, the focus is primarily internal. Thus, whereas compatibility in the first case is inter-organizational in association with the mediating technology, it is in the latter case intra-organizational. However, with the wide definition Thompson applies to standardization for pooled resources it pretty much encompasses any instances where an organization makes any shared commitments or shares any resources. This chapter requires a slightly more distinct use of the term standardization and thus requires viewing standards in relation to the process or product, as in Table 2.

Internally developed standardization can therefore help the firm increase internal efficiency or generate a number of effects in its input or output market. Another opportunity is to diffuse an internally developed standard to the industry (Botzem & Dobusch, 2012; Guler, Guillen & Muir Macpherson, 2002) through consensus processes such as those administered by standardization organizations, or adopt an external standard. In either case, internal standardization is interrelated with external standardization.

STANDARDIZATION IN ACTIVITY CONFIGURATIONS

Service vs. Product Character and Processes

Before summarizing the role of internally controlled standardization in activity configurations in detail it is relevant to consider the most common distinction of deliveries of various organizations, i.e. products versus services. The importance of recognizing this distinction here stems from the fact that aspects of it reside also in the disparity between product and process standards. Furthermore, both of these distinctions are inherent in the activity configurations. As Rathmell (1966) points out, services are acts or processes, or as Parasurman, Zeithaml and Berry (1985) put it: performances, rather than tangible items. (This does not mean that services cannot have market characteristics that resemble those of tangibles.) Thus, service organizations will rely more strongly on processes directed at the market or individual customers, than on goods and products. And therefore, standardization of processes will play a specific role in the case of services, as services themselves are processes.

In Parasuraman, Zeithaml and Berry (1985) two more characteristics of services besides intangibility are mentioned: heterogeneity and inseparability. These are also inherent in some of the activity configurations, and especially the shop configuration where deliveries are customized (and thus highly heterogeneous) and considerably iterative vis-à-vis the customer (and therefore production and consumption are inseparable). The heterogeneity aspect is difficult to relate to standardization, as the goal of standardization is the opposite: to reduce heterogeneity. The issue of inseparability can to some extent be captured explicitly by considering those instances where standardization is involved in externally applied processes.

A final distinction can be made, which relates to the result of service processes. Hill (1999) argues that the output of service processes can consist of material changes in goods or persons that the service supplier works with (the client or customer). Thus, in our discussion with regard to standardization, we separate such changes from the processes that produce them. Thus in Table 2 we see them as part of the *product* category.

By taking the nature of services versus products into account, the implications for services versus product firms are clarified. However, the prime distinction here is, as depicted in Table 2, between products and processes. Delivery characteristics are to some extent inherent in the specific activity configurations. Also, economic products are positioned somewhere along a continuum between products (goods) and services.

The following section summarizes the utilization of internal standardization in each of the activity configurations as defined by Stabell and Fjeldstad (1998) and with the addition by Johansson and Jonsson (2012). The summary will include externally as well as internally applied standardization (but not diffused into the industry level) in an attempt to provide an overview of the role of standardization in association with each activity configuration. For external application the overview will be more detailed as it will distinguish between uniformity and compatibility. Implications for services, due to their intangible nature, will be mentioned specifically in association with standardization of processes. The concept of processes in this section refers to the way it is used in the standardization literature (Botzem & Dobusch, 2012; Perez-Aleman, 2011). It refers to sequences that can be standardized, for instance a specific way of executing a service in order to certify a standardized minimum quality level. This delimited nature makes a process narrower than activities in most instances and consequently narrower than activity configurations that are systems of interlinked activities. Although a process may cut across a set of interlinked activities it most often does not encompass all the aspects of an activity configuration so that it entails the whole of a business model in the form of an activity system.

The Role of Standardization Types in the Network Configuration

Product standardization for the *network configuration* appears primarily for external application with a compatibility dimension in order to facilitate network effects and reduce transaction costs. As an example, consider the Android operating system, including application development software, an output that is utilized by handset providers and application developers and thus enables a network effect by functioning as a platform, but still largely controlled by Google. Therefore, the prime focus of internal standardization for the output market in accordance with Table 2 is *Platform standardization*. Also for the input market the prime type of standardization will be *Supply platform standardization*. However, when providing platforms that facilitate network effects, and especially double-sided network effects, the distinction between supplier and customer is not that necessarily clear. Players connecting to the network can be both suppliers and customers simultaneously.

Process standardization in association with the *network configuration* is most prominent for service organizations as externally applied services with a compatibility dimension to enable network effects, i.e. execution follows a standardized pattern which enables several customers and several sides of a market to access the network. The main types in accordance with Table 2 are *Time dependent platform standardization and Time dependent supply platform.*

The Role of Standardization Types in the Package Configuration

The prime type of standardization is product standardization for external application with high uniformity, either in the form of a product or service concept (the package configuration also includes signalling of offerings, rather than actual deliveries, to the environment such as through marketing, see Johansson & Jonsson, 2012). Also, the package configuration may involve internal interface standardization in order to enable modularity (cf. Sanchez & Mahoney, 1996) of a concept. In addition, an internally developed process, guiding execution, may serve a purpose of sending signals to external observers (Okhomotovskiy & David, 2012). This is the case when signalling a standardized service delivery, i.e. what is signalled is the promise of the delivery. When it comes to diffusion, the firm may very well contribute to diffusion of its own standards or adopt external standards within a delimited area. However the prime outcome of the package logic, i.e. the packaged offering (or standardized solution) will most often retain some firm uniqueness unless the firm has internal cost advantages versus its competitors (which are then a result of uniqueness from its chain logic aspects) or if uniqueness can be protected through other means, such as unique access to other sources of value capture which benefit from complementarity (cf. Teece, 1986). Thus, the prime type of standardization is *Output Product standardization*.

Process standardization for the *package configuration* may appear through internal application to enable problem solving (although the character of activities within the configuration will always contain some uniqueness as it involves solving a problem which is new or unique). This is different from the signaling described above, as it relates to the actual execution. An example of this is the way consulting firms standardize their approaches (internal standardization or adaptation stemming from external standards) to assist client organizations (Werr, Stjernberg, & Docherty, 1997; Wright et al, 2012). Standardization may also appear in external application, in particular for services, as the package logic may facilitate development of a standardized services execution concept. Thus, process standardization in association with the package configuration is relevant for facilitation of service execution, i.e. *Services execution stadardization* in Table 2.

The Role of Standardization Types in the Chain Configuration

Product standardization for the *chain configuration* occurs through sub-deliveries within the organization (the extent depends on whether execution is broken down into subsets which require uniformity and compatibility; compare Thompson, 1967 and March & Simon, 1958) to produce a single kind of output. Thus, the prime area of internally controlled standardization of output for the chain configuration is: *Internal interface standardization* and *Output Product standardization* but also *Supply Product Standardization* to optimize input conformity with internal execution. The difference from the package configuration lies in the static view of the output. The package configuration focuses on the creation of new concepts with innovation value but standardized over a population of customers.

Process standardization for the chain configuration appears to facilitate repetitive execution and internal efficiency. High diffusion of process standardization may be favourable if uniqueness can be protected by other means, such as unique access to other sources of value capture which benefit from complementarity (here without network effects). For instance, if a firm benefits from adhering to (or diffusing its own) process standards in an industry while maintaining uniqueness in other aspects of its processes or its offerings, and thus maintaining cost advantages, differentiation, or advantages through complementarity, diffusion may be favourable. Therefore, the main types of standardization are related to *Internal standardization for efficiency* and *Services Supply Timing* to align input, and due to the single type output also *Services execution standardization*.

The Role of Standardization Types in the Shop Configuration

The prime character of the value *shop configuration* is the solving of customer and temporally unique problems. The level of externally applied standardization is by definition low and thus this section will only highlight a few items rather than go through all the sections of Table 2. Although internal processes and subdeliveries may have some common traits over time they also tend to have a high level of uniqueness from time to time and from project to project. In Stabell and Fjeldstad (1998), standardized solutions, are included in the value shop but this chapter recognizes the central role of such as a key part of its own value creation logic and configuration in accordance with Johansson and Jonsson (2012). This is also in line with the way that Christensen et al (2009) view a standardized execution within healthcare (although they directly categorize this as a chain logic example without recognizing the importance of creating standardized solutions). An important exception to the above standardized solutions in Stabell and Fjeldstad can be mentioned, though, and that is the standardized process on the individual level,

Table 3. Internal standardization for each business model/activity configuration

		Network	Package	Chain	Shop
Process	Input Compatibility	Time Dep. Supply Platform	-	-	-
	Input Uniformity	-	Services Supply Timing	Services Supply Timing	
	Internal application	-	-	Internal for efficiency	Internal for efficency (individual)
	Output Uniformity	-	Services Execution	Services execution	-
	Output Compatibility	Time Dep. Platform	-	-	-
Product	Compatibility	Supply Platform	-	-	-
	Uniformity	-	Supply Product and Tech	Supply Product and Tech	-
	Internal application	-	-	Internal	-
	Uniformity	-	Output Product	Ouput Product	-
	Compatibility	Platform	-	-	-

i.e. the individual professional has a standard procedure for approaching a variety of problems through the information acquisition phase. This can be viewed as *Internal efficiency standardization* on the individual level.

Internal and External Standardization Interrelations

To illustrate more in-depth how value configurations involve internal standards and how these interrelate with external standards we provide two examples. The first one is Camfil, a developer and producer of filters and systems for air cleaning. Camfil relies on continuous development of the technology that is included in its products but which is also submitted to external standardization in order to set minimum quality levels for systems (Freyschuss, 2015). Camfil has a long history of this way of working with standardization. However, it is also evident that the approach relies on investments in improved or new product technology, which would correspond to a significant part of value creation relying on the package configuration.

Thus for Camfil, presence in external standardization is important to influence external standards setting to create minimum quality standards and thus raising rivals' costs (Swann, 2000), as well as to align external standards with its own internal standards which could potentially provide first mover advantages and temporary monopoly rents. This is based on the ability to refine or develop new technologies, concepts and products, which is the essence of the package configuration. This can then serve as a basis for setting the industry standardization agenda.

Another example comes from the Volvo Group, where internal standardization is approached as a problem-solving mechanism, yet it is often triggered proactively and relates to early phase research and external stimulus. Here, the company is taking a product output standard from internal to external in order to direct standard setting within external standardization committees and influence the external standardization in the firm preference (proprietary innovation (Laursen & Salter, 2014; Leiponen, 2008;

Rosenkopf, Metiu, & George, 2001)). That is, Volvo tries to influence external standards and hence promote internal standards as private standards towards suppliers and customers (Vandemoortele & Deconinck, 2013).

This is a case linking to chain configuration, where influence of external standardization becomes crucial in order to discipline sub-deliveries, e.g. input from suppliers. In agreement with Stabell and Fjeldstad (1998) and Thompson (1967), the company's aim is to utilize long-linked technologies for the mass production assembly line, by ensuring standardized input (through external standards) aligned with the company's internal preferences.

The above-mentioned examples indicate that firm strategies versus industry level standardization, depend on firm internal standardization in relation to the business model of the firm(s). Thus, to certify successful firm participation in external standardization requires being able to develop internal standards that when appropriate can provide additional cost reduction or market value creation by being included in an industry standard.

FUTURE RESEARCH DIRECTIONS

Further research should try to expand the above typology into external standards and outline in detail how these vary with each activity configuration. As a consequence of such studies, further research could also apply the perspective of activity configurations to shed light on the relationship between internal and external standardization from the perspective of the firm. For managers, understanding how the firm reduces variety through firm controlled action, and how this is related to value creation, should be a highly important input to firm participation in external standardization. How do we standardize internally? What type of value and cost effects does it have? Understanding this in detail should provide a better basis for involvement in external standardization and an ability to decide what to share with other players, and in particular competitors, and what external standardization the firm should try to hinder in order to protect capture of its created value (cf. Mione, 2015).

Such insights are thus fundamental in relation to coopetitive strategies in association with standardization. External standardization as a specific type of coopetition has for recently been discussed by Blind and Mangelsdorf (2016). The increaseingly coopetitive character of standardization has also been noted by Besen and Farrell (1994) and Mione (2015),

Through the discussion on standards in association with activity configurations the use of the terms *standard* and *standardization* in organizational theory and in association with business models as activity systems is highlighted. Due to the interdependence with the concepts of practices and routines it is apparent that the basic function of reducing variety (across populations) and enabling compatibility are central to intra- as well as inter-organizational effects. Thus, in order to develop our understanding of standards and standardization further, more studies bridging these fields and clarifying the use of the concepts related to standards in each setting (and determining commonalities and differences) should be pursued.

CONCLUSION

This chapter highlights the areas in which internal standardization is prominently associated with activity configurations (Johansson & Jonsson; 2012; Stabell & Fjeldstad, 1998) as business models (Christensen et al, 2008; Zott et al, 2011). This is important in the sense that it provides a map that guides internal standardization efforts related to value creation logic design and innovation.

For most organizations it is a matter of integrating two or several value creation logics into what Stabell and Fjeldstad (1998) call *hybrid* value configurations. Thus, from a standardization perspective, the firm often has to combine its standardization efforts in several areas. Similarly, firms in transition of their activity configuration dependence have to consider multiple types of standardization. Innovating through value creation transformation, as described in Christensen et al (2009), i.e. a shift in its set of activities, their configuration or the parties involved, could be accompanied by an alteration of standardization efforts. Christensen et al show how moves from reliance on a shop configuration via a chain and finally a network configuration can be seen as a disruptive innovation of the business model as opposed to disruptive innovation within the current business model. The typology proposed here of internal standardization in association with each configuration shows in what way standardization will have to change.

ACKNOWLEDGMENT

This research was made possible through the funding provided by the Swedish Standardization Association. We would also like to thank the discussants and the reviewers at the 18th EURAS conference, Brussels 2013 and the EURAM conference, Valencia 2014 for insightful and valuable feedback.

REFERENCES

Alexy, O., George, G., & Salter, A. J. (2013). Cui bono? "The selective revealing of knowledge and its implications for innovative activity." *Academy of Management Review*, *38*(2), 270–291. doi:10.5465/amr.2011.0193

Amit, R., & Zott, C. (2012). Creating Value Through Business Model Innovation. *MIT Sloan Management Review*, *53*(3), 41–49.

Argyres, N., Bigelow, L., (2010). Innovation, modularity, and vertical de-integration: Evidence from the early US auto industry. *Organization Science, 21*(4), 842-853.doi:10.1287/orsc.1090.0493

Barzel, Y. (1982). Measurement Cost and the Organization of Markets. *The Journal of Law & Economics*, *25*(1), 27–48. doi:10.1086/467005

Besen, S. M., & Farrell, J. (1994). Choosing How to Compete: Strategies and Tactics in Standardization. *The Journal of Economic Perspectives*, *8*(2), 117–131. doi:10.1257/jep.8.2.117

Blind, K. (2002). Driving forces for standardization at standardization development organizations. *Applied Economics*, *34*(16), 1985–1998. doi:10.1080/00036840110111158

Blind, K. (2004). *The economics of standards: Theory, Evidence, Policy*. Northampton, MA: Edward Elgar Publishing.

Blind, K. (2011). An economics analysis of standards competition: The example of the ISO ODF and OOXML standards. *Telecommunications Policy*, *35*(4), 373–381. doi:10.1016/j.telpol.2011.02.007

Blind, K., Gauch, S., & Hawkins, R. (2010). How stakeholders view the impacts of international ICT standards. *Telecommunications Policy*, *34*(3), 162–174. doi:10.1016/j.telpol.2009.11.016

Blind, K., & Grupp, H. (2000). *Standards Statistics as New Indicators for the Diffusion of Technology*. Paper presented to the International JA Schumpeter Conference, Manchester, UK.

Blind, K., & Mangelsdorf, A. (2016). Motives to standardize: Empirical evidence from Germany. *Technovation*, *48–49*, 13–24. doi:10.1016/j.technovation.2016.01.001

Boiral, O. (2012). ISO certificates as organizational degrees? Beyond the rational myths of the certification process. *Organization Studies*, *33*(5-6), 633–654. doi:10.1177/0170840612443622

Botzem, S., & Dobusch, L. (2012). Standardization cycles: A process perspective on the formation and diffusion of transnational standards. *Organization Studies*, *33*(5-6), 737–762. doi:10.1177/0170840612443626

Brown, J. S., & Duguid, P. (1991). Organizational learning and communities of practice: Toward a unified view of working, learning and innovation. *Organization Science*, *2*(1), 40–56. doi:10.1287/orsc.2.1.40

Brunson, N., & Jacobsson, B. (2000). The contemporary expansion of standardization. In N. Brunson & B. Jacobsson (Eds.), *A world of standards*. New York: Oxford University Press.

Chandler, A. D., & Hikino, T. (2009). *Scale and scope: The dynamics of industrial capitalism*. Harvard University Press.

Chesbrough, H. (2003). The logic of open innovation: Managing intellectual property. *California Management Review*, *45*(3), 33–58. doi:10.2307/41166175

Christensen, C. M., Grossman, J. H., & Hwang, J. (2009). *The innovator's prescription: A disruptive solution for healthcare*. New York: McGraw-Hill.

Cohen, M. D., Burkhart, R., Dosi, G., Egidi, M., Marengo, L., Warglien, M., & Winter, S. (1996). Routines and Other Recurrent Action Patterns of Organizations: Contemporary Research Issues. *Industrial and Corporate Change*, *5*(3), 653–698. doi:10.1093/icc/5.3.653

Cusumano, M. (2010). Technology Strategy and Management – The Evolution of Platform Thinking. *Communications of the ACM*, *53*(1), 32–34. doi:10.1145/1629175.1629189

Cyert, R. M., & March, J. G. (1963). *A behavioral theory of the firm*. Prentice Hall.

David, P. A. (1987). Some new standards for the economics of standardization in the information age. Economic policy and technological performance, 206-239. doi:10.1017/CBO9780511559938.010

Dokko, G., & Rosenkopf, L. (2010). Social capital for hire? Mobility of technical professionals and firm influence in wireless standards committees. *Organization Science, 21*(3), 677–695. doi:10.1287/orsc.1090.0470

Eisenmann, T., Parker, G., & Van Alstyne, M. W. (2006). Strategies for two-sided markets. *Harvard Business Review, 84*(10), 92–101. PMID:16649701

Felin, T., & Foss, N. J. (2005). Strategic organization: A field in search of micro-foundations. *Strategic Organization, 3*(4), 441–455. doi:10.1177/1476127005055796

Felin, T., & Foss, N. J. (2009). Experience and Repetition as Antecedents of Organizational Routines and Capabilities: A Critique of Behaviorist and Empiricist Approaches. *SMG WP, 9*, 2009.

Foss, K. (1996). *A transaction cost perspective on the influence of standards on product development: Examples for the fruit and vegetable market.* Working paper No 96-9. DRUID working paper series, Copenhagen.

Freyschuss, A. (2015). Så blev en svensk koncern världsledande med hjälp av standarder. *SIS.* Retrieved from http://www.sis.se/Global/Om%20SIS/kundseminarium%202011/camfil_ppt.pdf

Gallagher, S. (2007). The complementary role of dominant designs and industry standards. *IEEE Transactions on Engineering Management, 54*(2), 371–379. doi:10.1109/TEM.2007.893991

Gawer, A., & Cusumano, M. A. (2008). How Companies Become Platform Leaders. *MIT Sloan Management Review, 49*(2), 29–30.

Ghaziani, A., & Ventresca, M. J. (2005). Keywords and Cultural Change: Frame Analysis of Business Model Public Talk, 1975–2000. *Sociological Forum, 20*(4), 523–559. doi:10.100711206-005-9057-0

Grossmann, A.-M. (2013). Suppliers' motives for applying company standards – How company standards can affect the buyer-supplier relationship. In *EURAS Proceedings 2013. The Euras board series.* Verlagshaus Mainz.

Guler, I., Guillén, M., Macpherson, J., & Guillen, M. F. (2002). Global competition, institutions, and the diffusion of organizational practices: The international spread of ISO 9000 quality certificates. *Administrative Science Quarterly, 47*(2), 207–232. doi:10.2307/3094804

Helfat, C. E. (1997). Know-how and asset complementarity and dynamic capability accumulation: The case of R&D. *Strategic Management Journal, 18*(5), 339–360. doi:10.1002/(SICI)1097-0266(199705)18:5<339::AID-SMJ883>3.0.CO;2-7

Henson, S. J., & Hooker, N. H. (2001). Private Sector Management of Food Safety: Public Regulation and the Role of Private Controls. *The International Food and Agribusiness Management Review, 4*(1), 7–17. doi:10.1016/S1096-7508(01)00067-2

Hill, P. (1999). Tangibles, intangibles and services: A new taxonomy for classification of output. *The Canadian Journal of Economics. Revue Canadienne d'Economique, 32*(2), 426–447. doi:10.2307/136430

Holmstrom, B. (1999). The Firm as a Subeconomy. *Journal of Law Economics and Organization*, *15*(1), 74–102. doi:10.1093/jleo/15.1.74

Johansson, M., & Jonsson, A. (2012). The package logic: A study on value creation and knowledge flows. *European Management Journal*, *30*(6), 535–551. doi:10.1016/j.emj.2012.04.003

Katz, M., & Shapiro, C. (1985). Network Externalities, Competition, and Compatibility. *The American Economic Review*, *75*, 424–440.

Katz, M., & Shapiro, C. (1994). Systems competition and Network effects. *The Journal of Economic Perspectives*, *8*(2), 93–115. doi:10.1257/jep.8.2.93

Kogut, B. (2000). The network as knowledge: Generative rules and the emergence of structure. *Strategic Management Journal*, *21*(3), 405–425. doi:10.1002/(SICI)1097-0266(200003)21:3<405::AID-SMJ103>3.0.CO;2-5

Krechmer, K. (2000). *The Fundamental Nature of Standards: Economics Perspective*. Paper to the International JA Schumpeter Conference, Manchester, UK.

Krechmer, K. (2005). *Standards Mark the Course of Economic Progress* (Unpublished paper). Academic Press.

Laursen, K., & Salter, A. J. (2014). The paradox of openness: Appropriability, external search and collaboration. *Research Policy*, *43*(5), 867–878. doi:10.1016/j.respol.2013.10.004

Leiponen, A. E. (2008). Competing through cooperation: The organization of standard setting in wireless telecommunications. *Management Science*, *54*(11), 1904–1919. doi:10.1287/mnsc.1080.0912

March, J. G., & Simon, H. A. (1958). *Organizations*. Cambridge, MA: Blackwell publishers.

Masten, S. E. (1991). A legal basis for the firm. In O. E. Williamson & S. G. Winter (Eds.), *The Nature of the Firm: Origins, Evolution and Development* (pp. 196–212). New York: Oxford University Press.

Matutes, C., & Regibeau, P. (1996). A selective review of the economics of standardization. Entry deterrence, technological progress and international competition. *European Journal of Political Economy*, *12*(2), 183–209. doi:10.1016/0176-2680(95)00013-5

Miller, D. (1996). Configurations revisited. *Strategic Management Journal*, *17*(7), 505–512. doi:10.1002/(SICI)1097-0266(199607)17:7<505::AID-SMJ852>3.0.CO;2-I

Mione, A. (2015). The value of intangibles in a situation of innovation: Questions raised by the case of standards. *Journal of Innovation Economics & Management*, *2*(17), 49–68. doi:10.3917/jie.017.0049

Narayanan, V., & Chen, T. (2012). Research on technology standards: Accomplishment and challenges. *Research Policy*, *41*(8), 1375–1406. doi:10.1016/j.respol.2012.02.006

Nelson, R. R., & Winter, S. G. (1982). *An evolutionary theory of economic change*. Cambridge, MA: Belknap press/Harvard University Press.

Normann, R., & Ramirez, R. (1993). From value chain to value constellation: Designing interactive strategy. *Harvard Business Review*, *71*, 65–78. PMID:10127040

Normann, R., & Ramirez, R. (1994). *Designing interactive strategy – from value chain to value constellation*. Chichester, UK: Wiley & Sons.

Okhomatovskiy, I., & David, R. J. (2012). Setting your own standards: Internal corporate governance codes as a response to institutional pressure. *Organization Science*, *23*(1), 155–176. doi:10.1287/orsc.1100.0642

Parasuraman, A., Zeithaml, V. A., & Berry, L. L. (1985). A conceptual model of service quality and its implications for future research. *Journal of Marketing*, *49*(4), 41–50. doi:10.1177/002224298504900403

Parker, G., & Van Alstyne, M. W. (2003). Two sided networks: A theory of information product design. *Management Science*, *51*(10), 1494–1504. doi:10.1287/mnsc.1050.0400

Perez-Aleman, P. (2011). Collective learning in global diffusion: Spreading quality standards in a developing country cluster. *Organization Science*, *22*(1), 173–189. doi:10.1287/orsc.1090.0514

Porter, M. (1980). *Competitive strategy*. New York: Free Press.

Porter, M. E. (1985). *Competitive advantage: creating and sustaining superior performance*. New York: Free Press.

Rathmell, J. M. (1966). What is meant by services? *Journal of Marketing*, *4*(4), 32–36. doi:10.1177/002224296603000407

Ray, G., Barey, J. B., & Muhanna, W. A. (2004). Capabilities, business processes, and competitive advantage: Choosing the dependent variable in empirical tests of the resources based view. *Strategic Management Journal*, *25*(1), 23–38. doi:10.1002mj.366

Reimers, K., & Li, M. (2005). Effectiveness of governance structures for 3G standardization and implications for China's 3G policy. In P. Cunningham & M. Cunningham (Eds.), eAdoption and the knowledge economy: Issues, applications, case studies (pp. 256-263). IOS Press.

Rochet, J.-C., & Tirole, J. (2003). Platform competition in two-sided markets. *Journal of the European Economic Association*, *1*(4), 990–1029. doi:10.1162/154247603322493212

Rosenkopf, L., Metiu, A., & George, V. P. (2001). From the Bottom Up? Technical Committee Activity and Alliance Formation. *Administrative Science Quarterly*, *46*(4), 748–772. doi:10.2307/3094830

Salop, S.C., & Sheffman, D.T. (1983). Raising Rivals' Costs. *The American Economic Review*, *73*(2), 267-271.

Saltzman, J., Chatterjee, S., & Raman, M. (2008). A framework for ICT standards creation: The case of ITU-T standard H. 350. *Information Systems*, *33*(3), 285–299. doi:10.1016/j.is.2007.10.001

Sanchez, R., & Mahoney, J. T. (1996). Modularity, flexibility, and knowledge management in product and organizational design. *Strategic Management Journal*, *17*(S2), 63–76. doi:10.1002mj.4250171107

Sandholtz, K. W. (2012). Making standards stick: A theory of coupled vs. Decoupled compliance. *Organization Studies*, *33*(5-6), 655–679. doi:10.1177/0170840612443623

Santos, F. M., & Eisenhardt, K. M. (2005). Organizational Boundaries and Theories of Organization. *Organization Science*, *16*(5), 491–508. doi:10.1287/orsc.1050.0152

Schilling, M. (1999). Winning the standards race: Building installed base and the availability of complementary goods. *European Management Journal*, *17*(3), 265–274. doi:10.1016/S0263-2373(99)00005-5

Schumpeter, J. (1934). *The theory of economic development*. London: Transaction publishers.

Shapiro, C., & Varian, H. R. (1999). The art of standards wars. *California Management Review*, *41*(2), 8–32. doi:10.2307/41165984

Sheehan, N. T., & Foss, N. J. (2007). Enhancing the prescriptiveness of the resource-based view through Porterian activity analysis. *Management Decision*, *2*(3), 240–260.

Stabell, C. B., & Fjeldstad, Ø. D. (1998). Configuring value for competitive advantage: On chains, shops, and networks. *Strategic Management Journal*, *19*(5), 413–437. doi:10.1002/(SICI)1097-0266(199805)19:5<413::AID-SMJ946>3.0.CO;2-C

Swann, G. P. (2000). *The economics of standardization*. Manchester, UK: University of Manchester.

Swann, G. P. (2010). *The economics of standardization: an update. Report for the UK Department of Business, Innovation and Skills*. BIS.

Tassey, G. (2000). Standardization in technology-based markets. *Research Policy*, *29*(4-5), 587–602. doi:10.1016/S0048-7333(99)00091-8

Teece, D. J. (1986). Profiting from technological innovation: Implications for integration, collaboration, licensing and public policy. *Research Policy*, *15*(6), 285–305. doi:10.1016/0048-7333(86)90027-2

Teece, D. J. (2010). Business Models, Business Strategy and Innovation. *Long Range Planning*, *43*(2-3), 172–194. doi:10.1016/j.lrp.2009.07.003

Tether, B. S., Hipp, C., & Miles, I. (2001). Standardisation and particularization in services: Evidence from Germany. *Research Policy*, *30*(7), 1115–1138. doi:10.1016/S0048-7333(00)00133-5

Thompson, J. D. (1967). *Organizations in action*. New York: McGraw-Hill.

Tu, Q., Vonderembse, M. A., Ragu-Nathan, T. S., & Ragu-Nathan, B. (2004). Measuring modularity-based manufacturing practices and their impact on mass customization capability: A customer-driven perspective. *Decision Sciences*, *35*(2), 147–168. doi:10.1111/j.00117315.2004.02663.x

Ulrich, K. (1995). The role of product architecture in the manufacturing firm. *Research Policy*, *24*(3), 419–440. doi:10.1016/0048-7333(94)00775-3

Vandemoortele, T., & Deconinck, K. (2013). When are private Standards more Stringent than Public Standards? *American Journal of Agricultural Economics*, *96*(1), 154–171. doi:10.1093/ajae/aat064

Warner, A., Fairbank, J., & Steensma, H. (2006). Managing uncertainty in a formal standards-based industry: A real options perspective on acquisition timing. *Journal of Management*, *32*(2), 279–298. doi:10.1177/0149206305280108

Werr, A., Stjernberg, T., & Docherty, P. (1997). The functions of methods of change in management consulting. *Journal of Organizational Change Management*, *10*(4), 288–307. doi:10.1108/09534819710175839

Williamson, O. E. (1985). *The economic institutions of capitalism: firms, markets, relational contracting*. New York: Free Press.

Wright, C., Sturdy, A., & Wylie, N. (2012). Management innovation through standardization: Consultants as standardizers or organizational practice. *Research Policy*, *41*(3), 652–662. doi:10.1016/j.respol.2011.12.004

Zott, C., Amit, R., & Massa, L. (2011). The business model: Recent developments and future research. *Journal of Management*, *37*(4), 1019–1042. doi:10.1177/0149206311406265

KEY TERMS AND DEFINITIONS

Business Model: A system of activities not delimited to the firm itself but includes a system-level approach to how the firm interacts with its environment and does business.

Chain Configuration: Utilizes long-linked technologies in the transformation of input to output.

Internal Standard: Serve to reduce variety internally across products and production processes and as a consequence between intraorganizational entities. In many instances these follow internal consensus processes.

Network Configuration: Links customers through mediating technologies.

Package Configuration: Solves problems across a range of potential customers, with the goal of making such common problem-solving efficient through underlying solutions.

Shop Configuration: Utilizes intensive technology to solve customer unique problems through iterative problem solving.

Standard: Serve to reduce variety across for instance products, processes and technologies.

Standardization: The process of creating and spreading standards.

Value/activity Configuration: Activity organization of a firm for value creation.

ENDNOTES

1. Stabell and Fjeldstad's original label is *value configurations* since what Stabell and Fjeldstad call the *value creation logic* is at the center of each configuration. This focus on value is in line with Porter's original idea of value created by the things that firms do, the activities (Porter, 1985; Sheehan and Foss, 2009). Here the focus is on the configurations as generic models of activity organization.
2. The standardization literature is defined here as management oriented literature that uses the word standard or standardization in the title, in the keywords or the abstract of the article or book.

Chapter 8
Effective Management of Standardizing in E-Government

Dian Balta
fortiss GmbH, Germany

ABSTRACT

Standards play an important role in the interoperable exchange of information among actors with different business functions. Particularly in government, standards enhance communication between public administrations and lay the ground of interoperability in e-government service provision. Still, practice often struggles with numerous challenges such as complex administrative procedures, jurisdiction, numerous stakeholders with diverging wants and needs and the ultimate goal of social welfare. At the same time, academia provides a limited number of approaches to address existing challenges and transferring findings from a private organizations' context is rarely a viable approach. The authors introduce effective management of standardization in e-government by describing the shape of standardization in that specific domain and by encompassing suitable coordination mechanisms. They follow a qualitative explorative research approach and apply coordination theory to pragmatically interpret our findings, offering implications for both theory and practice.

INTRODUCTION

Standards play an important role in the interoperable exchange of information—for example, master data management, software system interoperability and integration, service delivery (Krcmar, 2015)—among actors with different business functions (International Organization for Standardization, 2015). Particularly in government, standards enhance communication between public administrations (European Commission, 2010). For instance, standards are a way to secure and correct information exchanged at the right time with the right people and in the right quality (Radack, 1990) by enabling the interconnectivity of the information systems that underlie the execution of administrative procedures and, ultimately, the provision of services to citizens (Borras, 2004b). With the rise of electronic government (e-government) and corresponding digitalization efforts, standards for managing information technology are a necessity in improving the maturity of digitalized government services (Lam, 2006), so standardization has gained

DOI: 10.4018/978-1-5225-9008-8.ch008

Copyright © 2019, IGI Global. Copying or distributing in print or electronic forms without written permission of IGI Global is prohibited.

increased attention in government (Blind & Gauch, 2009), (Charalabidis, Lampathaki, & Askounis, 2009),(A. S. Hellberg & Å. Grönlund, 2013).

Given the importance of IT standardization and the complexity of its effective management (Jakobs, 2005, 2007, 2009), extant research on standardization in organizations (Brunsson, Rasche, & Seidl, 2012) and information systems management (Lyytinen & King, 2006b) has emphasized measures to counter complexity challenges (e.g.(Ole Hanseth, Jacucci, Grisot, & Aanestad, 2006)). Still, the applicability of the provided measures in an e-government context is limited by differences between private organizations and government bodies (Jurisch, 2014b; Rainey, Ronquillo, & Avellaneda, 2010). In particular, IT standardization management is challenged by the complexity of government procedures (Bharosa, Lee, & Janssen, 2009),(Janssen, 2011), stakeholder dependencies and their benefit expectations is often ineffective in practice (Blum, 2005; Hans Jochen Scholl, Kubicek, Cimander, & Klischewski, 2012). To address those issues, various approaches to IT management tailored to the context of e-government have been developed (Guijarro, 2007),(Büttner et al., 2014). Examples standardization artefacts include SAGA (Federal Government Commissioner for Information Technology, 2011) with its focus on software specifications and development methods in the context of government bodies in Germany and the European Interoperability Framework (European Commission, 2010) for public administration in the European Union. Still, their application in practice has not led to the expected results and our understanding of further approaches has yet to advance in theory and practice in order to successfully mediate the process of standardization.

With respect to the addressed challenges, the objective of this paper is to introduce effective management of standardization in e-government by describing the shape of standardization in that specific domain and by encompassing suitable coordination mechanisms. In regard to the shape of standardization in the context of complex administrative procedures, our approach consists of addressing the following two questions by studying literature and surveying cases using secondary data of standardization projects in the e-government context: (i) What are determinants, strategies and outcomes of standardization in e-government? (ii) What types of standardization artefacts are in focus of research and practice in the e-government context? Finally, based on that descriptive approach to shedding light on standardization, we adopt coordination theory to address: What are coordination mechanisms for effective standardization management in the e-government context?

This article is structured as follows. First, we present the research background and describe our research method. Next, we describe the shape of standardization in e-government as well as effective coordination mechanisms for standardization management. Finally, we discuss our findings in regard to implications for theory and practice as well as conclude on limitations and future research.

RESEARCH BACKGROUND

E-Government

Electronic Government ('e-government') is the execution of any kind of processes with the help of information and communication technology within the public sector (Reinermann & Von Lucke, 2002, p. 1). Public administrations can either communicate with each other, with private organizations and with citizens, while one party either consumes or provides a service based on an administrative procedure predefined in law and regulations. Still, e-government is not only about the administration providing services via internet (Layne & Lee, 2001). Restructuring internal processes (Olbrich, 2008, p. 12) and consolidating existing IT infrastructure (Layne & Lee, 2001) are important factors to guarantee a better coordination of public administrations and the administrative procedures in their jurisdiction. Therefore, common goals of e-government are an increased efficiency, cost reduction as well as a better participation through citizens, a boost in economy (Boehme-Nessler, 2001; Olbrich, 2008, p. 12) and a higher quality of government services (Gil-Garcia & Pardo, 2005). Though different challenges hamper the development of e-government: technological incompatibility, technology topicality, restrictive laws and regulations, privacy and security issues as well as the autonomy of public administrations, lack of technological skill and low budgets (Gil-Garcia & Pardo, 2005).

Since e-government might have an indirect impact on responsibilities and types of collaboration between public administration, administrative procedures and their underlying information systems are forced to change, which increases their complexity in terms of *number* and *variety* of *components* and of their *interactions* to be managed (Cilliers 1998; Jacucci et al. 2006; Benbya & McKelvey 2006). First, an adaption to environmentally imposed tensions has to take place (Benbya & McKelvey 2006), e.g. innovation tensions through digitalization of paper-based documents have to be considered (Dunleavy et al. 2005; Brown 2005; Moon 2002). Second, a modular design (Simon 1962; Benbya & McKelvey 2006) has to be implemented in procedures, e.g. an encapsulation of the execution logic of an administrative procedures, and a focus on customer orientation (Ho 2002; Schedler & Summermatter 2007; Korunka et al. 2007). Third, multiple causes of complexity have to be effectively managed in a context where organizational structures are extended into a network (Benbya & McKelvey 2006; Lindblom 1959), e.g. the output in one step of a procedure's execution process is input for one or more actors (different public administrations, citizens, companies) and a strive for efficiency in processing the execution is present (Afonso et al. 2010; Houy et al. 2010; Greiling 2006; Kalb et al. 2012; Fraefel et al. 2013). Consequently, there is a need for e-government standardization based on different artefacts and including multiple perspectives and goals.

Standardization

We define a standard as "a uniform set of measures, agreements, conditions, or specifications between parties" (Spivak & Brenner, 2001). The process of reaching a standard encompasses stabilizing and solidifying its definition and boundaries (David & Greenstein, 1990; Ole Hanseth et al., 2006), i. e. standardization represents "the activity of establishing and recording a limited set of solutions to actual or potential matching problems directed at benefits for the party or parties involved balancing their needs and intending and expecting that these solutions will be repeatedly or continuously used during a certain period by a substantial number of the parties for whom they are meant" (De Vries, 1999). In regard to e-government, standardization might lead to different artefacts.

Since standardization in e-government involves information systems, process and organizations and different federal layers (Janssen, Charalabidis, Kuk, & Cresswell, 2011; Janssen, Snijders, & Herkemij, 2011; Misuraca, Alfano, & Viscusi, 2011a), standards at different levels as solutions for managing information and underlying systems are a necessity for improving the maturity of digitalized government services (Lam, 2006). Although this necessity represents one of the drivers for an increased attention to standardization in government (Charalabidis et al., 2009; A.-S. Hellberg & Å. Grönlund, 2013), standardization in e-government practice is challenging. In particular, standardization is challenged by the complexity of government procedures (Bharosa et al., 2009), (Janssen, Charalabidis, et al., 2011) and is often ineffective in practice (Blum, 2005), (Hans J. Scholl & Klischewski, 2007).

Various approaches to information management that are tailored to the context of government bodies through standardization have been developed in response (Guijarro, 2007),(Büttner et al., 2014), following the aim of interoperability at different levels (Hans Jochen Scholl et al., 2012). For example, frameworks like SAGA in Germany (Federal Government Commissioner for Information Technology, 2011), with its focus on software specifications and development methods in the context of government bodies, and the European Interoperability Framework (European Commission, 2010) have been proposed to management practice. With regard to the latter framework, interoperability can be defined as "[..] the ability of disparate and diverse organizations to interact towards mutually beneficial and agreed common goals, involving the sharing of information and knowledge between the organizations, through the business processes they support, by means of the exchange of data between their respective ICT systems".

We focus on standardization that aims at interoperability along three layers (Gascó, 2012; Gottschalk, 2009; Kubicek & Cimander, 2009b; Ojo, Janowski, & Estevez, 2009; Saekow & Boonmee, 2009): (i) the organizational layer focuses on interoperability of business processes applied in delivering public service; (ii) the semantic layer states that information and data exchanged should be interoperable also in regard to its meaning between parties involved; (iii) the technical / syntactic layer is responsible for enabling interoperability regarding structure and format of data, communication protocols for sending and receiving data, electronic mechanisms to store data as well as software and hardware. Further, we define standardization strategy as an approach to development, choice and use of standards (Ole Hanseth & Bygstad, 2015) along the described interoperability levels.

Coordination Modes and Mechanisms

With regard to extant literature and the numerous perspectives on coordination (Alexander, 1993; Malone & Crowston, 1994; Okhuysen & Bechky, 2009; Williams & Karahanna, 2013), this paper addresses *coordination* as a means for "*managing dependencies between activities*" (Malone & Crowston, 1994) and, in particular, we use the term *coordination of standardization* to denote the management of dependencies between activities involving persons and the resources (e.g. information, knowledge) they exchange in regarding to e-government standardization. Further, coordination is exerted through different mechanisms that can be predefined or emerge based on the context there are applied in (March & Simon, 1958; Melin & Axelsson, 2005; Mintzberg, 1993).

Three complementary *modes of coordination*[1] can be distinguished (Baltta & Krcmar, 2018), (Srikanth & Puranam, 2011, 2014), (Kotlarsky, Scarbrough, & Oshri, 2014). The first mode, *explicit coordination by planning*, involves a designer, who partitions activities into capsuled modules and builds interfaces between the modules (Simon, 1969; Srikanth & Puranam, 2011, 2014). Applicable planning mechanisms involve pre-established plans, schedules, forecasts, formalized rules, policies etc. (e.g. electronic data interchange (EDI) protocol). The second mode, *explicit coordination by feedback*, represents "mutual adjustments" between the individuals that take place "upon new information" (Thompson, 1967; Van De Ven, Delbecq, & Koenig Jr, 1976). Applicable mechanisms in this mode involve ongoing communication such as an on-demand face-to-face (or virtual) personal or group meeting. The third mode, *tacit coordination by knowledge exchange*, involves the notion that coordination takes place in a tacit manner with mechanisms that build or leverage shared knowledge (Schelling, 1980; Srikanth & Puranam, 2011, 2014). Sharing knowledge is accomplished through boundary objects (Okhuysen & Bechky, 2009; Srikanth &

Puranam, 2014; Star & Griesemer, 1989) and can span across organizational (Kellogg, Orlikowski, & Yates, 2006; Pawlowski & Robey, 2004; Tanriverdi, 2005). For example, a team can be staffed with an experienced member from another team who is able to transfer context based knowledge into the task at hand in the new team such as a software codebase (Bolici, Howison, & Crowston, 2016).

For each of the three modes, the coordination involves an analysis of the situation it takes place in (Malone & Crowston, 1994). The situation comprises an understanding of which activities and dependencies should be coordinated (Malone & Crowston, 1994) and can be studied along four dimensions (Baltta & Krcmar, 2018). The first dimension common ground is denoted as knowledge that is or will be shared in order to allow for reciprocal predictability of action (Clark, 1996; Schelling, 1980; Srikanth & Puranam, 2014). The second dimension–communication–considers how the actors involved exchange information upon coordinating task accomplishment (Reich & Benbasat, 2000), (Galbraith, 1977). Environment is the third dimension and it includes external factors that influence the actors and their activities. It can be dynamic or stable, i.e. (i) it accounts for innovative tasks that require novel common ground and do not rest upon pre-established plans or responsibilities or (ii) it accounts for common well-known tasks that can be accomplished based on pre-defined modules and interfaces. The fourth dimension is interdependency type and addresses how each actor depends on the other actors during task accomplishment, namely: pooled and sequential (suitable for coordination by planning), reciprocal (suitable for coordination by feedback) as well as team (suitable for coordination by knowledge exchange) interdependencies (Henningsson, Rukanova, & Hrastinski, 2010; Kuldeep & van Dissel Han, 1996; Pfeffer & Salancik, 1978).

RESEARCH METHOD

We follow a qualitative analysis approach to explorative research that aims at developing descriptive artefacts that can be categorized as a theory for analyzing (Gregor, 2006) rooted in the paradigm of pragmatism (Goles & Hirschheim, 2000), (Goldkuhl, 2012). In consequence, our approach is built upon two pillars: the first pillar is focused on the shape of standardization and is based on studying extant literature as well as secondary data on cases of successful standardization projects in e-government. The second pillar is focused on studying effective coordination mechanisms involves incorporation of coordination theory into an in-depth single case study. Research in both pillars was conducted separately and the findings of both pillars were finally merged.

During our research in the first pillar, we applied the following methodological approach. We reviewed extant literature on standardization in e-government based on a list of relevant context-specific outlets (Hans J. Scholl & Dwivedi, 2014) as well as information systems outlets (Lowry et al., 2013) and additionally searching backwards and forwards for relevant articles (Webster & Watson, 2002). The search and analysis was based on a predefined protocol that was developed in regard to a set of contours (based on (Lyytinen & King, 2006a)) including concepts and relationships adapted from (Flak & Solli-Saether, 2012; Sæbø, Rose, & Flak, 2008) as well as a differentiation between e-government and private organizations contexts. In particular, we developed two separate protocols that included search keywords and criteria for two streams of research: (i) determinants (e.g. financial resources), strategies (e.g. top-down approach) and outcomes (e.g. service innovation) as well as (ii) standardization artefacts (e.g. business process definition or data format)[2] and interoperability levels. The search and analysis were performed by two researchers independently who structured the results based on iteratively developed categories for each corresponding stream of research. The results of the analysis were reviewed by a third researcher, which led to adjusting the initial frameworks. Next, we applied the developed framework on secondary empirical data of standardization projects in e-government based on the case survey method (Jurisch, 2014b). In regard to the first stream of research, we applied the corresponding framework on 18 projects[3] of successful standardization in government that were selected as a purposive sample (Hans Jochen Scholl et al., 2012). In regard to the second stream of research, we selected 10 cases according to predefined characteristics, analyzed the cases with our framework and refined it. The cases We selected different sets of cases, since the analysis requires different amount and level of detail of information in the two streams of reearch we focus on. The applied cases analysis–although applied on a small case sample–has had the ultimative purpose of evaluating the applicability of the developed shape of standardization.

During our research in the second pillar, our research was conducted as a qualitative study of coordination in information systems (Myers, 1997; Myers & Avison, 2002), epistemologically rooted in two paradigms: interpretation (Walsham, 1993),(Klein & Myers, 1999) as well as pragmatism (Goles & Hirschheim, 2000), (Goldkuhl, 2012) with research results communicated to corresponding research community in the e-government domain.This approach was chosen in accordance with (Goldkuhl, 2012), (Cole, Purao, Rossi, & Sein, 2005) for two reasons. On the one hand, the authors were involved in dialogical action during the project under study in their role as scientific consultants (Mårtensson & Lee, 2004). This allowed for an in-depth study of a single case. On the other hand, we aim at the development of a theory based artifact combining interpretation of work (Klein & Myers, 1999) well as practical inquiry (Goldkuhl, 2012).

Finally, we studied the findings of both pillars in an interpretative phase through an argumentative-deductive analysis (Wilde & Hess, 2007). Thus, we incrementally adjusted our interpretation (Boell & Cecez-Kecmanovic, 2014), (Klein & Myers, 1999) by reframing our findings. Thus, we were able to learn and enhance our understanding of the shape of as well as coordination mechanisms for effective standardization in e-government considering different coordination modes.

THE SHAPE OF STANDARDIZATION IN E-GOVERNMENT

To study the shape of standardization in e-government, we address two research questions: (i) What are determinants, strategies and outcomes of standardization in e-government? (ii) What types of standardization artefacts are in focus of research and practice in the e-government context? To clarify the relations between the concepts applied, we present the following overview (cf. Figure 1). This overview has purely narrative purposes, since our research does not focus on studying any causality relationships (e.g. explanations or predictions) between the concepts.

Determinants (e.g. financial resources or stakeholder influence) have an impact the standardization process. In particular, they impact the analysis and selection of a particular standardization strategy or a mix of strategies. The standardization strategies would lead to a set of outcomes for each standardization project. Since strategies are not always explicitly defined or linked to particular outcomes or expectations for the latter, this relation can be described as intentional to a limited extent. Standardization artefacts are related to all other concepts. They may represent a determinant (e.g. installed software base), they are particular subjects of the strategy applied (e.g. the development or application of a specific standard) and they are palpable results of standardization that are linked to reaching expected outcomes. Finally,

Figure 1. Overview of the concepts applied to describe the shape of standardization in e-government

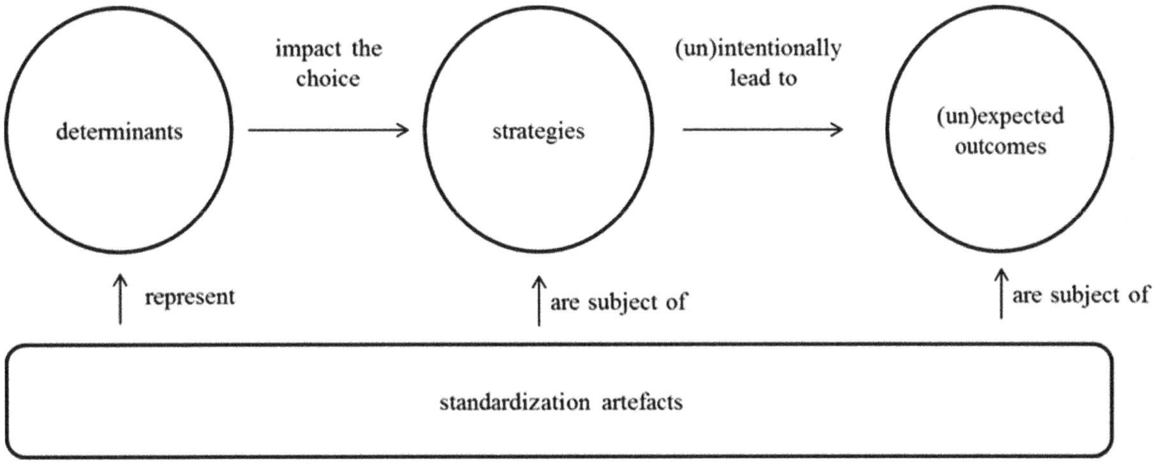

it is of importance for this study to put all concepts in the context of e-government, since it has major differences compared to a private organizations setting and thus impacts the shape of standardization on its own.

Differences Between Public and Private Context

In order to shed more light on standardization in e-government, we begin by describing what are differences between public administrations and private organizations along four perspectives: economic regime, political influence, legitimacy and governance system. In regard to the economic regime, e-government standardization in public administrations takes place in a nonmarket context. In that case, (i) objectives are directed by the implementation of and compliance to laws and regulations (Jurisch, 2014a; Rainey et al., 2010), (ii) governance is limited through law and divisions of power (e.g. coordination trough centralization might not be feasible) (Kubicek & Cimander, 2009a), (iii) "wants and needs" of stakeholders (Hans Jochen Scholl et al., 2012) have to be considered with focus on social welfare (e.g. needs of a small group of citizens cannot be neglected, since government has to serve everyone). In contrast, private organizations standardize in a market context. In that contrasting case, (i) economics of standards direct the objectives setting (e.g. optimizing switching cost (P. Y. Chen & Forman, 2006)), (ii) governance is more relaxed in constraints, i.e. industry coordination mechanisms can be freely defined by the actors involved (e.g. through centralized hubs as intermediaries (Markus & Bui, 2012; Markus, Steinfield, & Wigand, 2006)), (iii) customer requirements (and further market-driven forces) have to be considered (e.g. "standard wars" (Shapiro & Varian, 1999)).

Political influence is another dimension to differentiate between the context of public administrations and private organizations. In a private organization context an internal and indirect political influence takes place, while in a public administrations context there is an external and direct political influence (Jurisch, 2014a; Rainey et al., 2010). For example, in the former case, influence is more likely bounded to the boundaries of an organization. In the latter case, politicians–external to a public administrations–can directly influence standardization.

Legitimacy of standardization (Botzem & Dobusch, 2012) is the third dimension of differentiation between the context of public administrations and private organizations. Legitimacy can be defined as "a generalized perception or assumption that the actions of an entity are desirable, proper, or appropriate within some socially constructed system of norms, values, beliefs, and definitions" (Suchman, 1995, p. 574). Hence, we argue that the socially constructed systems in both contexts are quite different – with respect to institutional pressures, resource dependencies and stakeholder management (J. C. Chen & Roberts, 2010). In the context of public administrations, legitimacy–of the standards developed as well as of the actors involved–is shaped by political accountability and democratic processes (Bruner, 2008; Mena & Palazzo, 2012). In the context of private organizations, standardization is shaped by reputation, stockholder, contracts as well as "capitalist" economy (Mena & Palazzo, 2012; Mitchell, Agle, & Wood, 1997).

The state governance system (e.g. unitary state, federal state) rooted specific cultural administrative traditions (e.g. Anglo-Saxon, Germanic etc.) (Misuraca et al., 2011a) is a fourth dimension of differentiation between public administrations and private organizations. For instance in a federal state, jurisdiction is defined along vertical federal layers (Scharpf 1988) and horizontal functional departments (Layne and Lee 2001) driven by a constitutionally guaranteed sharing of power and sovereignty across distinct layers and departments (Wheare 1946; Hueglin and Fenna 2015). This leads to a relatively high number of public administrations that independently deliver e-government services to citizens and companies. For example, in Germany there are over 11,000 local governments with similar service portfolios (Algermissen et al. 2005) accompanied by 16 partly independent state governments with various independent departments as well as a federal government with varying departmental structure. Still, all organizations should cooperate instead of competing and should jointly develop and use e-government standards, which leads to an increased coordination effort.

Determinants, Strategies and Outcomes

Our analysis resulted in a framework that is structured in three categories of determinants, three types of strategies and standardization stages as well as three categories of expected outcomes. The determinants are categorized as organizational, technical and environmental. The organizational determinants result directly from the setup of public administrations and further actors involved in standardization and include factors that we grouped as follows: (i) stakeholder interactions and integration (e.g. attention paid to standardization efforts at community level (Vaezi, 2008) or management of the relationships to local government representatives (Hovav, Patnayakuni, & Schuff, 2004)), (ii) organization resources (e.g. employees skillset (Gil-Garcia & Pardo, 2005) or complexity management capabilities (Saekow & Boonmee, 2009)) as well as (iii) governance (e.g. leadership skills (Henning, 2016) or coping with needs and wants (Galasso, Aresu, Luppi, Campisi, & Garbasso, 2016)).

Environmental determinants include factors that cannot be influenced by an organization and are grouped as follows: (i) economic factors (e.g. market structure (Wang & Kim, 2007)), (ii) law and regulation factors (e.g. jurisdiction (Hans Jochen Scholl et al., 2012) or directives (Henning, 2016)) as well as (iii) government mindset (e.g. perceived role in the standardization process (Wang & Kim, 2007)). The technical determinants include factors are grouped as follows: (i) properties of the standards (e.g. complexity of the standard (Gil-Garcia & Pardo, 2005) or compatibility with other standards (Hovav et al., 2004)) and (ii) installed standards base (e.g. adaptability (King, 2013) or heterogeneity of the existing IT (Hans J. Scholl & Klischewski, 2007; Hans Jochen Scholl et al., 2012)). Interestingly, we were able to identify concurrent standards only as an environmental factor, i.e. standardization of e-government seems to focus on cooperation and mutual agreement between standardization actors and does not seem to consider "standard wars" (Shapiro & Varian, 1999).

We distinguish three types of strategies (Ole Hanseth & Bygstad, 2015). The first strategy, anticipatory standardization, represents a top-down process that is "worked out as detailed compromises". Next, the diffusion of standardization artefacts takes place in a centralized, top-down manner. Finally, implementation solutions based on the proposed standards takes place. The second strategy is named integrated solutions. It involves standardization efforts driven by user-needs and standards can be recognized as parts of requirements specifications. In contrast to anticipatory standardization, the result is a particular solution that fits the standards. The third strategy is named flexible generification. IT involves dynamic work processes that start with innovation activities and lead to the development of particular solutions, which is the basis for deriving standards. Additionally, we distinguish between three stages of development and use of a standard (Lyytinen & King, 2006b): (i) development and design, (ii) acceptance and enforcement as well as (iii) choice and diffusion.

Our analysis shows that a strategy mix is the common approach instead of focusing on one single strategy and the process of standardization presented spans over one or two stages of development and use of a standard. For instance, the FreESBee-SP standardization project (Mecca, Santomauro, Santoro, & Veltri, 2016) aimed at improving existing system architecture and further develop IT systems. On one hand, it is categorized as anticipatory standardization, since it was organized top-down. On the other hand, it had components of flexible generification, since it allowed reusing existing standards. Finally, it focused on design and development of a standard as well as on acceptance and enforcement, since it aims at deploying performance test of the newly developed standard to increase acceptance. In summary, we were able to identify each of the strategies or a mixture of two strategies applied. Interestingly, we were not able to find a single study that focused on the choice and diffusion standardization stage, which is a clear contrast to the body of literature in the private organizations domain (e.g. (Weitzel, Beimborn, & König, 2006)).

The expected benefits are structured in the following groups: efficient consumption of resources, process enhancement and innovation. The group efficient consumption of resources includes expected benefits such as cost reduction (Ole Hanseth & Bygstad, 2015) or time savings and reduced red tape (Hans Jochen Scholl et al., 2012). The group process enhancement includes expected benefits such as transparency between actors involved in a standardized IT system (King, 2013), avoiding lock-in (Galasso et al., 2016) or effective data exchange (Hans Jochen Scholl et al., 2012). The group innovation includes expected benefits such as support of innovative service provision (Ole Hanseth & Bygstad, 2015). In summary, the expected benefits in the e-government context are similar to benefits in a private organizations context in regard to efficient consumption of benefits, but miss aspects such as increasing competitiveness, driving market segmentation or pricing strategies.

Types of Standardization Artefacts

We structured the findings of our analysis of standardization artefacts in e-government in two dimensions (cf. Table 1). The first dimensions represent the three layers of interoperability at which standards are targeted: organizational, semantic as well as technical and syntactic. The second dimension differentiates between standards in regard to their functional view that is taken in terms of the purpose and or target users.

In regard to the first dimension of our analysis, we structure the types of standardization artefacts as follows. Standards at the organizational interoperability layer consider business processes as well as relations between organizations. The impact of business processes for the interoperability between public administrations is considered high (Chourabi, Bouslama, & Mellouli, 2008), especially when process are dependent on each out: output of a process might be used by multiple other processes (Scherer, Liotas, Wimmer, Tambouris, & Tarabanis, 2011, p. 106). This requires common data definitions as well as common protocols and practices (Gottschalk & Saether, 2008; Scherer et al., 2011, p. 106). Additionally, for many public services, multiple organizations must work together and become part of a process chain and challenges such as jurisdiction and authority (Janssen, Snijders, et al., 2011, p. 165) as well as harmonization of processes (Hulstijn et al., 2011) have to be managed. Standardization of the relations between organizations would include examples such as service level agreements.

To guarantee that transmitted data is interpreted and processed correctly, standards at the semantic level of interoperability are needed. They assign a meaning to data and allow different actors to interpret the data the same way (Davies, Harris, Crichton, Shukla, & Gibbson, 2008; Gottschalk & Saether, 2008; Misuraca, Alfano, & Viscusi, 2011b). This 'data' can either be transmitted packages that need to be interpreted by another information system (Gottschalk & Saether, 2008), or a term (Craig & Schriar, 2001). The technical and syntactic interoperability level includes standards that link systems and networks (Moen, 1994), define the structure and language of data (Gottschalk & Saether, 2008) or the syntax of data (Misuraca et al., 2011b). Examples include software standards, middleware services and network protocols (Gottschalk & Saether, 2008) as well as data formats. For instance, the latter represent a type of standards for communication and interaction. Data formats are represented by data definitions and data types (Borras, 2004a; Kubicek & Cimander, 2009b; Moen, 1994; Su et al., 2005).

In regard to the second dimension of our analysis, we recognize five different functional views. The administration view consists of mostly non-technical standards that affect personnel and process aspects as well as communication within or between public administrations. The second view is the modeling view, which includes models and reference architectures as well as modelling languages for each interoperability level. The processing view contains standards that focus the computation of data and is often materialized through specific software. The communication and interaction view handles the data and information exchange between different public administrations. Finally, the security and privacy view contains standards that aim at addressing issues such as managing access policy, using cryptography approaches or requesting a minimum of person's data in order to respect her or his privacy.

Table 1. Types of standardization artefacts in e-government[4]

	Administration	Modeling	Processing	Communication & Interaction	Security & Privacy
Organizational	six types, e. g. Business Process	two types, e.g. Process Reference Architecture	Business Process Modeling Tool	two types, e.g. Process Model Exchange Format	three types, e.g. Information Access Policy
Semantic	Shared Terminology	Ontology	Information Search Service	four types, e.g. Common Metadata Definition	
Technical / Syntactic	Reporting	six types, e.g. Application Architecture	seven types, e.g. Software Application	fourteen types, e.g. Data Format	three types, e.g. Encryption Algorithm

In summary, our findings show that extant research and practice spans over each interoperability level and addresses each of the five functional views. Interestingly, there are communication and interaction standards in e-government developed at the technical and syntactic level such as the Latin character encoding in Unicode (Coordination Site for IT-Standards (KoSIT), 2012, p. 1). Still, it is argued (e.g. (Kubicek & Cimander, 2009b)) that standards on the technical and syntactic level should not pose a challenge to standardization in e-government anymore, since they are quite well developed and might only slightly differ from a private organizations context. Instead, focus should be put more intensively on semantic and organizational standards. Especially the latter seem to be quite challenging for both theory and practice (Kubicek & Cimander, 2009b), since they appear to be very context specific and require relatively high coordination effort to bring all involved actors together in a cooperation.

COORDINATION OF E-GOVERNMENT STANDARDIZATION

Our study of the shape of standardization in e-government provides hints that the specifics of the context as well as the heterogeneity of standards and actors involved lead to a challenging endeavor. Since actors aim at cooperation instead of competition, specific coordination mechanisms should be applied. In order to present what are coordination mechanisms of effective e-government standardization, we apply the previously introduced coordination theory to an exemplary case as suggested by (Balta & Krcmar, 2018)..

Case Background and Shape of Standardization

In Germany, administrative procedures are situated on federal, state and community level and, with regard to administrative traditions (Misuraca et al., 2011a), can be described as quiet heterogeneous between the levels, which impacts e-government equally. In particular, the existing structures of jurisdiction and authority have impact on business process and their execution in and between public administrations situated at different federal levels. Moreover, business processes differ in their design and execution in public administrations situated at the same level, e.g. two communities in the same state could exchange information with involved actors during a procedure in a totally different way depending on public administration size or the information technology landscape of the community.

In an effort to manage the complexity of numerous and heterogeneous administrative procedures towards a standardized e-government, the federal and state public administrations in Germany started in 2012 the project FIM to standardize procedures at all federal layers on a reference model level and is currently applied in the design of an interoperable government service platform. Consequently, the shape of standardization of FIM can be described as follows. In terms of organizational determinants, (i) FIM had to handle a large number of stakeholder interactions and integration at federal and state levels that included different departments, (ii) the employees' skillset was limited regarding the aim at providing unified models of business processes and forms and (iii) in terms of governance, FIM had to cope with needs and wants of actors inside and outside public administrations such as domain experts is particular laws and regulations as well as software vendors and form publishers.

In regard to environmental determinants, (i) an oligopoly market structure was recognized, where a number of companies provided software products and data models which were not standardized, (ii) jurisdiction had to be considered without exception (e.g. who is responsible for defining the data forma of an address on a form) and (iii) the government perceived its role a driving force in the standardization process, since there was obviously insufficient pressure on established actors to standardize. As technical determinants, FIM had to face heterogeneity of the existing (often incompatible) installed based as well as existing data and process models or even the lack of any models at all.

Since FIM was commissioned in consent of responsible bodies and federal and state level, it started as an anticipatory standardization strategy. Still, it also implemented integrated solutions as a strategy, since the requirements specifications led to deriving specific standards (reference models of forms and processes) that represented particular solutions. Moreover, FIM focused on the phases development and design and analyzed means for acceptance and enforcement (e.g. as a part of the planned government service platform) of the standards. It expected outcomes were to deliver standardization artefacts that were open to all software providers and public administrations (i.e. avoid lock-in effects) that would allow for effective and efficient data exchange. Finally, FIM helped to develop a number of standardization artefacts: shared terminology, a library for reusable elements of forms and processes as well as numerous particular models of forms and processes that can be applied as references.

Coordination Mechanisms: An Exemplary Application

We analyze the project FIM (cf. Table 2) and emphasize what mechanisms were applied towards effective standardization given the need of coordination in different modes.

In the planning mode of coordination regarding FIM, the common ground between the actors involved were predefined laws and application forms (e.g. registering a business). The communication regarding this common ground was expected to be minimal, since FIM was expected to have only a minimal impact and lead to a minimal impact of existing processes and forms, since some laws did change quite seldom. The interdependency was sequential, since the federal structure led to quite strict definitions of processes and forms that had to be implemented without any (or only with minor) changes at state and community levels. In that particular situation of coordination, our analysis showed a need for action in terms of introducing an editorial process as a planning mode of communication. Since each standard for an administrative procedure represents a reference model and cannot be defined in great detail, the strictly predefined process allows for keeping the standardization effective and with a minimal effort (Van De Ven et al., 1976).

Table 2. Analysis of coordination mechanisms for the FIM project (based on (Balta & Krcmar, 2018))

	Planning mode (explicit)	Feedback mode (explicit)	Knowledge exchange mode (tacit)
Common ground between actors	laws and predefined application forms	newly established or updated laws	a common library of models of form models, processes and services
Communication	minimal, only regarding the FIM approach	update on changes of a law	update on change in laws and the models
Environment	laws that change rare	laws that change yearly	laws that change yearly
Interdependency type	federal structure	reciprocal in working groups based on specific topics	team-based regarding external consultants and domain experts according to jurisdiction
Mechanism applied	editorial process	working groups consisting of experts	introduce model owner to the design process

In the feedback mode of coordination regarding FIM, the common ground between the actors involved were newly established or updated laws. Communication found place in meetings called upon updates. This mode was applicable to a set of laws that changed often (e.g. specific social services such as housing benefit). Since there was a need for intensive knowledge exchange between corresponding departments at federal and state levels, there was a reciprocal dependency that was coordinated by the mechanisms working groups. In each working group, domain experts as well as FIM experts were introduced to the updates and would come up with suggestions for adjusting the standards developed by FIM.

The common ground between the actors in the tacit mode of coordination was a common library of models of form models, processes and services that represented particular standardization artefacts. Communication and environment were similar to the feedback mode. Still, the interdependencies were much tighter: it was the case of a team-based interdependency between external consultants from software companies and domain experts according to jurisdiction. This was the case, since the common ground had to be adjusted to both existing software base and updated laws and integrated with FIM. In that situation of coordination, the library would allow for reusing elements without strictly limiting the standardization process, i. e. we suggest a suitable level of standard flexibility (O. Hanseth, Monteiro, & Hatling, 1996). As a suitable coordination mechanism, a new role needed during the design process–referred to as model designer–was introduced. This role should allow for transporting existing artefact knowledge between different application domains and mediate the development of new or updated reference models.

DISCUSSION AND CONCLUSION

Our research aimed at presenting means for an effective standardization of e-government. Therefore, we addressed three research questions: (i) What are determinants, strategies and outcomes of standardization in e-government? (ii) What types of standardization artefacts are in focus of research and practice in the e-government context? (iii) What are coordination mechanisms for effective standardization management in the e-government context? Following a qualitative analysis approach to explorative research, we studied literature, secondary data on e-government standardization cases as well as an in-depth case study, where were interpreted results from a pragmatism perspective. Hence, our study can be described as an analytical and descriptive theoretical contribution (Gregor, 2006) that has particular implication for practice.

In regard to the first and second research questions, we demonstrated the differences between a government and a private organizations context. Then, we presented a set of determinants, strategies and outcomes of standardization in e-government that allows for analysing and structuring standardization efforts. As a further tool for analysis, we presented a two dimensional framework that allows for navigating through different types of standardization artefacts. Put together, the tools for analysis shed light on the characteristics of standardization in e-government and emphasized the coordination challenges towards standardizing in cooperation between public administration that act according to their jurisdiction. In regard to the third question, we demonstrated the application of coordination theory to standardization in e-government. In particular, we demonstrated the analysis of specific coordination mechanisms to an exemplary case where the understanding of the shape of standardization was a prerequisite to define the specific situation of coordination. This, in turn, allowed for matching the standardization challenges to coordination modes and normatively deriving suitable mechanisms of coordination towards effective standardization in e-government.

Our study has a number of limitations. First, we rely on a limited set of secondary data for deriving the shape of IT standardization in government that does not allow for a quantitative evaluation. A further limitation exists regarding the conjecture made in terms of the importance of management of standardization. Although results in extant research support this conjecture (e. g. (Sherif, Jakobs, & Egyedi, 2007)), we have no clear evidence from the data available. A third limitation is our suggestion that management challenges can be addressed by coordination mechanisms, although there might be other approaches not emphasized by the theoretical perspective taken in our study.

Still, we believe that our contribution is of value for both academia and practice. On the one hand, the findings presented offer a number of possibilities for future research. For instance, future work could relax the first limitation by adding cases of (un)successful standardization in order to derive a model of (in)dependent variables or even patterns of successful standardization. On the other hand, practitioners can apply the shape of standardization to analyze their standardization determinants and expected benefits as well as the potential strategic fit. Moreover, they can apply the proposed framework of coordination mechanisms for an effective standardization management that is based on the analysis of the shape of standardization there are confronted with.

REFERENCES

Alexander, E. R. (1993). Interorganizational Coordination: Theory and Practice. *Journal of Planning Literature*, *7*(4), 328–343. doi:10.1177/088541229300700403

Balta, D., Harders, N. M., & Krcmar, H. (2018). Managing IT Standardization in Government: Towards a Descriptive Reference Model. In *Proc. Enterprise Interoperability: Smart Services and Business Impact of Enterprise Interoperability*. London: ISTE. doi:10.1002/9781119564034.ch17

Balta, D., & Krcmar, H. (2018). Managing Standardization in eGovernment: A Coordination Theory based Analysis Framework. In *Proc. International Conference on Electronic Government*. Cham: Springer. 10.1007/978-3-319-98690-6_6

Bharosa, N., Lee, J., & Janssen, M. (2009). Challenges and obstacles in sharing and coordinating information during multi-agency disaster response: Propositions from field exercises. *Information Systems Frontiers*, *12*(1), 49–65. doi:10.100710796-009-9174-z

Blind, K., & Gauch, S. (2009). The Demand for E-Government Standards. In *Information Communication Technology Standardization for E-Business Sectors: Integrating Supply and Demand Factors* (pp. 9-23). IGI Global.

Blum, U. (2005). Lessons from the Past: Public Standardization in the Spotlight. *International Journal of IT Standards and Standardization Research*, *3*(1), 1–20. doi:10.4018/jitsr.2005010101

Boehme-Nessler, V. (2001). Electronic Government: Internet und Verwaltung. *NVwZ, 374.*

Boell, S., & Cecez-Kecmanovic, D. (2014). A Hermeneutic Approach for Conducting Literature Reviews and Literature Searches. *Communications of the Association for Information Systems*, *34*(1), 257–286.

Bolici, F., Howison, J., & Crowston, K. (2016). Stigmergic coordination in FLOSS development teams: Integrating explicit and implicit mechanisms. *Cognitive Systems Research*, *38*, 14–22. doi:10.1016/j.cogsys.2015.12.003

Borras, J. (2004a). International Technical Standards for e-Government. *Electronic. Journal of E-Government*, *2*(2), 75–80.

Borras, J. (2004b). International Technical Standards for e-Government. *Electronic. Journal of E-Government*, *2*, 75–80. doi:10.3109/14992020209090412

Botzem, S., & Dobusch, L. (2012). Standardization Cycles: A Process Perspective on the Formation and Diffusion of Transnational Standards. *Organization Studies*, *33*(5/6), 737-762. doi:10.1177/0170840612443626

Bruner, C. M. (2008). States, Markets, and Gatekeepers: Public-Private Regulatory Regimes in an Era of Economic Globalization. *Michigan Journal of International Law*, *30*(1).

Brunsson, N., Rasche, A., & Seidl, D. (2012). The Dynamics of Standardization: Three Perspectives on Standards in Organization Studies. *Organization Studies*, *33*, 613-632. doi:10.1177/0170840612450120

Büttner, F., Bartels, U., Hamann, L., Hofrichter, O., Kuhlmann, M., Gogolla, M., . . . Stosiek, A. (2014). Model-driven standardization of public authority data interchange. *Science of Computer Programming*, *89*(B), 162-175. doi:10.1016/j.scico.2013.03.009

Charalabidis, Y., Lampathaki, F., & Askounis, D. (2009). A Comparative Analysis of National Interoperability Frameworks. *15th Americas Conference on Information Systems (AMCIS 2009)*, 1-10.

Chen, J. C., & Roberts, R. W. (2010). Toward a More Coherent Understanding of the Organization–Society Relationship: A Theoretical Consideration for Social and Environmental Accounting Research. *Journal of Business Ethics*, *97*(4), 651–665. doi:10.100710551-010-0531-0

Chen, P. Y., & Forman, C. (2006). Can vendors influence switching costs and compatibility in an environment with open standards? *MIS Quarterly: Management Information Systems*, *30*(SPEC. ISS.), 541–562. doi:10.2307/25148772

Chourabi, H., Bouslama, F., & Mellouli, S. (2008). *BPMapping and UMM in Business Process Modeling for e-Government Processes.* Paper presented at the International Conference on Digital Government Research, Montreal, Canada.

Clark, H. H. (1996). *Using Language* (Vol. 23). Academic Press.

Cole, R., Purao, S., Rossi, M., & Sein, M. K. (2005). Being Proactive: Where Action Research meets Design Research. *ICIS 2005 Proceedings*, 1-21.

Coordination Site for IT-Standards (KoSIT). (2012). *Lateinische Zeichen im Unicode Version 1.1.1 vom 27. 01. 2012.* Retrieved from http://xoev.de/latinchars/1_1/latinchars.pdfv

Craig, A., & Schriar, S. (2001). The Find-It! Illinois controlled vocabulary: Improving access to government information through the Jessica subject tree. *Government Information Quarterly*, *18*(3), 195–208. doi:10.1016/S0740-624X(01)00077-6

David, P. A., & Greenstein, S. (1990). The Economics of Compatibility Standards: An Introduction To Recent Research. *Economics of Innovation and New Technology*, *1*(1-2), 3–41. doi:10.1080/10438599000000002

Davies, J., Harris, S., Crichton, C., Shukla, A., & Gibbson, J. (2008). *Metadata Standards for Semantic Interoperability in Electronic Government*. Paper presented at the international conference on Theory and practice of electronic governance, Cairo, Egypt. 10.1145/1509096.1509111

De Vries, H. J. (1999). *Standardization: A business approach to the role of national standardization organizations*. Springer. doi:10.1007/978-1-4757-3042-5

European Commission. (2010). European Interoperability Framework (EIF) for European public services. Brussels: Academic Press.

Federal Government Commissioner for Information Technology. (2011). *SAGA-Modul Grundlagen Version de.bund 5.1.0*. Berlin: Author. Retrieved from http://www.cio.bund.de/SharedDocs/Publikationen/DE/Architekturen-und-Standards/SAGA/saga_modul_grundlagen_de_bund_5_1_0_download.pdf?__blob=publicationFile

Flak, L. S., & Solli-Saether, H. (2012). *The Shape of Interoperability: Reviewing and Characterizing a Central Area within eGovernment Research*. Paper presented at the 2012 45th Hawaii International Conference on System Science (HICSS).

Galasso, G., Aresu, F., Luppi, M., Campisi, C., & Garbasso, G. (2016). *Study on best practices for ICT procurement based on standards in order to promote efficiency and reduce lock-in*. PwC.

Galbraith, J. R. (1977). Organization design: An information processing view. *Organizational Effectiveness Center and School*, *21*, 21–26. doi:10.1287/inte.4.3.28

Gascó, M. (2012). Approaching E-Government Interoperability. *Social Science Computer Review*, *30*(1), 3–6. doi:10.1177/0894439310392181

Gil-Garcia, J. R., & Pardo, T. A. (2005). E-government success factors: Mapping practical tools to theoretical foundations. *Government Information Quarterly*, *22*(2), 187–216. doi:10.1016/j.giq.2005.02.001

Goldkuhl, G. (2012). Pragmatism vs interpretivism in qualitative information systems research. *European Journal of Information Systems*, *21*(2), 135–146. doi:10.1057/ejis.2011.54

Goles, T., & Hirschheim, R. (2000). The paradigm is dead, the paradigm is dead…long live the paradigm: The legacy of Burrell and Morgan. *Omega*, *28*(3), 249–268. doi:10.1016/S0305-0483(99)00042-0

Gottschalk, P. (2009). Maturity levels for interoperability in digital government. *Government Information Quarterly*, *26*(1), 75–81. doi:10.1016/j.giq.2008.03.003

Gottschalk, P., & Saether, H. S. (2008). Stages of e-government interoperability. *Electronic Government, an International Journal*, *5*, 310. doi:10.1504/EG.2008.018877

Gregor, S. (2006). The nature of theory in information systems. *Management Information Systems Quarterly*, *30*(3), 611–642. doi:10.2307/25148742

Guijarro, L. (2007). Interoperability frameworks and enterprise architectures in e-government initiatives in Europe and the United States. *Government Information Quarterly*, *24*(1), 89–101. doi:10.1016/j.giq.2006.05.003

Hanseth, O., & Bygstad, B. (2015). Flexible generification: ICT standardization strategies and service innovation in health care. *European Journal of Information Systems*, *24*(6), 645–663. doi:10.1057/ejis.2015.1

Hanseth, O., Jacucci, E., Grisot, M., & Aanestad, M. (2006). Reflexive Standardization: Side Effects and Complexity in Standard Making. *Management Information Systems Quarterly*, *30*, 563–581. doi:10.2307/25148773

Hanseth, O., Monteiro, E., & Hatling, M. (1996). Developing Information Infrastructure: The Tension Between Standardization and Flexibility. *Science, Technology & Human Values*, *21*(4), 407–426. doi:10.1177/016224399602100402

Hellberg, A.-S., & Grönlund, Å. (2013). Conflicts in implementing interoperability: Re-operationalizing basic values. *Government Information Quarterly*, *30*(2), 154–162. doi:10.1016/j.giq.2012.10.006

Henning, F. (2016). A theoretical framework on the determinants of organisational adoption of interoperability standards in Government Information Networks. *Government Information Quarterly*.

Henningsson, S., Rukanova, B., & Hrastinski, S. (2010). Resource dependencies in socio-technical information systems design research. *Communications of the AIS*, *27*(42), 777–802.

Hovav, A., Patnayakuni, R., & Schuff, D. (2004). A model of Internet standards adoption: The case of IPv6. *Information Systems Journal*, *14*(3), 265–294. doi:10.1111/j.1365-2575.2004.00170.x

Hulstijn, J., van Wijk, R., de Winne, N., Bharosa, N., Janssen, M., & Tan, Y.-H. (2011). *Public Process Management: A Method for Introducing Standard Business Reporting*. Paper presented at the 12th Annual International Conference on Digital Government Research, New York, NY. 10.1145/2037556.2037577

International Organization for Standardization. (2015). *ISO/IEC 2382:2015 Information technology -- Vocabulary*. Fundamental Terms.

Jakobs, K. (2005). *Advanced Topics in Information Technology Standards and Standardization Research* (Vol. 1). IGI Global.

Jakobs, K. (2007). *Standardization Research in Information Technology: New Perspectives*. Hershey, PA: IGI Global.

Jakobs, K. (2009). *Information Communication Technology Standardization for E-Business Sectors: Integrating Supply and Demand Factors*. IGI Global.

Janssen, M. (2011). Sociopolitical Aspects of Interoperability and Enterprise Architecture in E-Government. *Social Science Computer Review*. doi:10.1177/0894439310392187

Janssen, M., Charalabidis, Y., Kuk, G., & Cresswell, T. (2011). Guest Editors' Introduction: E-government Interoperability, Infrastructure and Architecture: State-of-the-art and Challenges. *Journal of Theoretical and Applied Electronic Commerce Research*, *6*(1), i–viii. doi:10.4067/S0718-18762011000100001

Janssen, M., Snijders, B., & Herkemij, F. (2011). A Reference Architecture for Interoperable and Adaptive Processes. In Y. Charalabidis (Ed.), *Interoperability in Digital Public Services and Administrations: Bridging E-Government and E-Business* (pp. 162–179). Information Science Reference. doi:10.4018/978-1-61520-887-6.ch009

Jurisch, M. C. (2014). *IT-enabled business process change in private and in public sector organizations*. Academic Press.

Kellogg, K. C., Orlikowski, W. J., & Yates, J. (2006). Life in the trading zone: Structuring coordination across boundaries in postbureaucratic organizations. *Organization Science*, *17*(1), 22–44. doi:10.1287/orsc.1050.0157

King, N. (2013). Exploring the impact of operating model choice on the governance of inter-organizational workflow: The U.S. e-prescribing network. *European Journal of Information Systems*, *22*(5), 548–568. doi:10.1057/ejis.2012.47

Klein, H. K., & Myers, M. D. (1999). A Set of Principles for Conducting and Evaluating Interpretive Field Studies in Information Systems. *Management Information Systems Quarterly*, *23*(1), 67–93. doi:10.2307/249410

Kotlarsky, J., Scarbrough, H., & Oshri, I. (2014). Coordinating expertise across knowledge boundaries in offshore-outsourcing projects: The role of codification. *Management Information Systems Quarterly*, *38*(2), 607–627. doi:10.25300/MISQ/2014/38.2.13

Krcmar, H. (2015). *Informationsmanagement* (6th ed.). Berlin: Springer-Verlag.

Kubicek, H., & Cimander, R. (2009). Three dimensions of organizational interoperability. *European Journal of ePractice, 6*, 3-14.

Kuldeep, K., & van Dissel Han, G. (1996). Sustainable Collaboration: Managing Conflict and Cooperation in Interorganizational Systems. *Management Information Systems Quarterly*, *20*(3), 279–300. doi:10.2307/249657

Lam, W. (2006). Barriers to e-government integration. *Journal of Enterprise Information Management*, *18*(5), 511–530. doi:10.1108/17410390510623981

Layne, K., & Lee, J. (2001). Developing fully functional E-government: A four stage model. *Government Information Quarterly*, *18*(2), 122–136. doi:10.1016/S0740-624X(01)00066-1

Lowry, P. B., Moody, G., Gaskin, J., Galletta, D. F., Humphreys, S., Barlow, J. B., & Wilson, D. (2013). *Evaluating Journal Quality and the Association for Information Systems (AIS) Senior Scholars' Journal Basket Via Bibliometric Measures: Do Expert Journal Assessments Add Value?* Rochester, NY: Social Science Research Network.

Lyytinen, K., & King, J. L. (2006a). Standard making: A critical research frontier for information systems research. *Management Information Systems Quarterly*, *30*, 405–411. doi:10.2307/25148766

Lyytinen, K., & King, J. L. (2006b). Standard Making: A Critical Research Frontier for Information Systems Research. *Management Information Systems Quarterly*, *30*(August), 405–411. doi:10.2307/25148766

Malone, T. W., & Crowston, K. (1994). The interdisciplinary study of coordination. *ACM Computing Surveys*, *26*(1), 87–119. doi:10.1145/174666.174668

March, J. G., & Simon, H. A. (1958). Organizations. Academic Press.

Markus, M. L., & Bui, Q. N. (2012). Going Concerns: The Governance of Interorganizational Coordination Hubs. *Journal of Management Information Systems*, *28*(4), 163–198. doi:10.2753/MIS0742-1222280407

Markus, M. L., Steinfield, C. W., & Wigand, R. T. (2006). Industry-wide information systems standardization as collective action: The case of the US residential mortgage industry. *Management Information Systems Quarterly*, *30*, 439–465. doi:10.2307/25148768

Mårtensson, P., & Lee, A. S. (2004). Dialogical action research at omega corporation. *Management Information Systems Quarterly*, *28*(3), 507–536. doi:10.2307/25148648

Mecca, G., Santomauro, M., Santoro, D., & Veltri, E. (2016). On federated single sign-on in e-government interoperability frameworks. *International Journal of Electronic Governance*, *8*(1), 6. doi:10.1504/IJEG.2016.076684

Melin, U., & Axelsson, K. (2005). Understanding Organizational Coordination and Information Systems-Mintzberg's Coordination Mechanisms Revisited and Evaluated. *ECIS 2005 Proceedings*, 115.

Mena, S., & Palazzo, G. (2012). Input and Output Legitimacy of Multi-Stakeholder Initiatives. *Business Ethics Quarterly*, *22*(3), 527–556. doi:10.5840/beq201222333

Mintzberg, H. (1993). *Structure in fives: Designing effective organizations*. Prentice-Hall, Inc.

Misuraca, G., Alfano, G., & Viscusi, G. (2011a). Interoperability Challenges for ICT-enabled Governance: Towards a pan-European Conceptual Framework. *Journal of Theoretical and Applied Electronic Commerce Research*, *6*(1), 95–111. doi:10.4067/S0718-18762011000100007

Misuraca, G., Alfano, G., & Viscusi, G. (2011b). A Multi-Level Framework for ICT-Enabled Governance: Assessing the Non-Technical Dimensions of 'Government openness". *Electronic. Journal of E-Government*, *9*(2), 152–165.

Mitchell, R. K., Agle, B. R., & Wood, D. J. (1997). Toward a theory of stakeholder identification and salience: Defining the principle of who and what really counts. *Academy of Management Review*, *22*(4), 853–886. doi:10.5465/amr.1997.9711022105

Moen, W. E. (1994). Information technology standards: A component of federal information policy. *Government Information Quarterly*, *11*(4), 357–371. doi:10.1016/0740-624X(94)90015-9

Myers, M. D. (1997). Qualitative research in information systems. *Management Information Systems Quarterly*, *21*(June), 1–18. doi:10.2307/249422

Myers, M. D., & Avison, D. E. (2002). Qualitative Research in Information Systems. *A Reader*, 328–328.

Ojo, A., Janowski, T., & Estevez, E. (2009). *Semantic Interoperability Architecture for Electronic Government.* Paper presented at the 10th Annual International Conference on Digital Government Research, Puebla, Mexico.

Okhuysen, G. A., & Bechky, B. A. (2009). Coordination in Organizations: An Integrative Perspective. *The Academy of Management Annals, 3*(1), 463–502. doi:10.5465/19416520903047533

Olbrich, S. (2008). *Modellierung von E-Government-Prozessen. In Modellierung gesetzlicher Rahmenbedingungen für Verwaltungsprozesse aus dem E-Government* (pp. 47–86). Wiesbaden: Gabler.

Pawlowski, S. D., & Robey, D. (2004). Bridging user organizations: Knowledge brokering and the work of information technology professionals. *Management Information Systems Quarterly, 28*(4), 645–672. doi:10.2307/25148658

Pfeffer, J., & Salancik, G. R. (1978). *The External Control of Organizations: A Resource Dependence Perspective.* New York: Harper & Row.

Radack, S. M. (1990). More effective federal computer systems: The role of NIST and standards. *Government Information Quarterly, 7*(1), 37–49. doi:10.1016/0740-624X(90)90005-9

Rainey, H. G., Ronquillo, J. C., & Avellaneda, C. N. (2010). Decision making in public organizations. Handbook of Decision Making, 6, 349-349.

Reich, B. H., & Benbasat, I. (2000). Factors that influence the social dimension of alignment between business and information technology objectives. *Management Information Systems Quarterly, 24*(1), 81–113. doi:10.2307/3250980

Reinermann, H., & Von Lucke, J. (2002). *Electronic Government in Deutschland, Ziele - Stand - Barrieren - Beispiele - Umsetzung Speyerer Forschungsberichte 226.* Speyer: Forschungsinst. für Öffentliche Verwaltung.

Sæbø, Ø., Rose, J., & Flak, L. S. (2008). The shape of eParticipation: Characterizing an emerging research area. *Government Information Quarterly, 25*(3), 400–428. doi:10.1016/j.giq.2007.04.007

Saekow, A., & Boonmee, C. (2009). A Pragmatic Approach to Interoperability Practical Implementation Support (IPIS) for e-Government Interoperability. *Electronic. Journal of E-Government, 7*(4), 403–414.

Schelling, T. C. (1980). *The strategy of conflict.* Harvard university press.

Scherer, S., Liotas, N., Wimmer, M. A., Tambouris, E., & Tarabanis, K. (2011). Interoperability Requirements, Recommendations and Standards in e-Participation. In Y. Charalabidis (Ed.), *Interoperability in Digital Public Services and Administrations: Bridging E-Government and E-Business* (pp. 95–117). Information Science Reference. doi:10.4018/978-1-61520-887-6.ch006

Scholl, H. J., & Dwivedi, Y. K. (2014). Forums for electronic government scholars: Insights from a 2012/2013 study. *Government Information Quarterly, 31*(2), 229–242. doi:10.1016/j.giq.2013.10.008

Scholl, H. J., & Klischewski, R. (2007). E-Government Integration and Interoperability: Framing the Research Agenda. *International Journal of Public Administration, 30*(8-9), 889–920. doi:10.1080/01900690701402668

Scholl, H. J., Kubicek, H., Cimander, R., & Klischewski, R. (2012). Process integration, information sharing, and system interoperation in government: A comparative case analysis. *Government Information Quarterly*, *29*(3), 313–323. doi:10.1016/j.giq.2012.02.009

Shapiro, C., & Varian, H. R. (1999). The art of standards wars. *California Management Review*, *41*(2), 8–32. doi:10.2307/41165984

Sherif, M. H., Jakobs, K., & Egyedi, T. M. (2007). *Standards of quality and quality of standards for telecommunications and information technologies. In Challenges in the Management of New Technologies* (pp. 427–447). World Scientific.

Simon, H. A. (1969). *The Sciences of the Artificial* (Vol. 1). Academic Press.

Spivak, S. M., & Brenner, F. C. (2001). *Standardization essentials: Principles and practice*. CRC Press. doi:10.1201/9781482277388

Srikanth, K., & Puranam, P. (2011). Integrating distributed work: Comparing task design, communication, and tacit coordination mechanisms. *Strategic Management Journal*, *32*(8), 849–875. doi:10.1002mj.908

Srikanth, K., & Puranam, P. (2014). The firm as a coordination system: Evidence from software services offshoring. *Organization Science*, *25*(4), 1253–1271. doi:10.1287/orsc.2013.0886

Star, S. L., & Griesemer, J. R. (1989). Institutional Ecology, 'Translations' and Boundary Objects: Amateurs and Professionals in Berkeley's Museum of Vertebrate Zoology, 1907-39. *Social Studies of Science*, *19*(3), 387–420. doi:10.1177/030631289019003001

Su, S., Fortes, J., Kasad, T. R., Patil, M., Matsunaga, A., Tsugawa, M., ... Herrera, M. (2005). Transnational Information Sharing, Event Notification, Rule Enforcement and Process Coordination. *International Journal of Electronic Government Research*, *1*(2), 1–26. doi:10.4018/jegr.2005040101

Suchman, M. C. (1995). Managing legitimacy: Strategic and institutional approaches. *Academy of Management Review*, *20*(3), 571–610. doi:10.5465/amr.1995.9508080331

Tanriverdi, H. (2005). Information technology relatedness, knowledge management capability, and performance of multibusiness firms. *Management Information Systems Quarterly*, *29*(2), 311–334. doi:10.2307/25148681

Thompson, J. D. (1967). *Organizations in action: Social science bases of administration*. Academic Press.

Vaezi, S. K. (2008). Critical Success Factors for Implementing Knowledge Based Models for Electronic Public Services (EPS). In T. Janowski & T. A. Pardo (Eds.), *ICEGOV '08: Proceedings of the 2Nd International Conference on Theory and Practice of Electronic Governance* (pp. 471–473). New York: ACM.

Van De Ven, A. H., Delbecq, A. L., & Koenig, R. Jr. (1976). Determinants of Coordination Modes within Organizations. *American Sociological Review*, *41*(2), 322–338. doi:10.2307/2094477

Walsham, G. (1993). Interpreting Information Systems in Organizations. *Organization Studies*, *15*, 269–269. doi:10.1177/017084069401500614

Wang, J., & Kim, S. (2007). Time to get in: The contrasting stories about government interventions in information technology standards (the case of CDMA and IMT-2000 in Korea). *Government Information Quarterly*, *24*(1), 115–134. doi:10.1016/j.giq.2006.04.001

Webster, J., & Watson, R. T. (2002). Analyzing the Past to Prepare for the Future: Writing a Literature Review. *Management Information Systems Quarterly*, *26*(2), 13–23.

Weitzel, T., Beimborn, D., & König, W. (2006). A unified economic model of standard diffusion: The impact of standardization cost, network effects, and network topology. *Management Information Systems Quarterly*, *30*, 489–514. doi:10.2307/25148770

Wilde, T., & Hess, T. (2007). Forschungsmethoden der Wirtschaftsinformatik Eine empirische Untersuchung. *Wirtschaftsinformatik*, *49*(4), 280–287. doi:10.100711576-007-0064-z

Williams, C. K., & Karahanna, E. (2013). Causal Explanation In The Coordinating Process: A Critical Realist Case Study Of Federated It Governance Structures. *Management Information Systems Quarterly*, *37*(3), 933–A938. doi:10.25300/MISQ/2013/37.3.12

ENDNOTES

1 cf. Appendix C for an overview.

2 cf. Appendix A for an overview of the results of the search for types of standardization artefacts.

3 cf. Appendix A for an overview of selected projects.

4 cf. Appendix B for a detailed overview of the types of artefacts found.

APPENDIX A

Table 3. An overview of the 18 projects under study

#	Project name	Country	URL
1	HamburgGateway	Germany	http://www.ifib.de/publikationsdateien/Interoperability_in_HamburgGateway.pdf
2	eBourgogne	France	http://www.ifib.de/publikationsdateien/GPC_Shared_IOP_in_Bourgogne.pdf
3	Social Security Benefits	Belgium	http://www.ifib.de/publikationsdateien/GPC_IOP_in_soc_sec_in_Belgium.pdf
4	e-Enabled Child Benefit	Irland	http://www.ifib.de/publikationsdateien/GPC_IOP_in_Child_Benefit_Ireland.pdf
5	Kadaster-on-line	Netherlands	http://www.ifib.de/publikationsdateien/GPC_IOP_in_cadastral_services_Netherlands.pdf
6	eID	Estonia	http://www.ifib.de/publikationsdateien/Interoperability_in_eID_in_Estonia.pdf
7	Finnish Address System	Finnland	http://www.ifib.de/publikationsdateien/GPC_IOP_in_Finnish_Address_System.pdf
8	e-Form exchange	Austria	http://www.ifib.de/publikationsdateien/GPC_IOP_in_EDIAKT2_Austria.pdf
9	Interoperability Valencia	Spain	http://www.ifib.de/publikationsdateien/Interoperability_Platform_of_Valencia.pdf
10	eInvoicing	Finnland	http://www.ifib.de/publikationsdateien/GPC_IOP_in_eInvoicing_in_Finland.pdf
11	eInvoicing Denmark	Denmark	http://www.ifib.de/publikationsdateien/Interoperability_in_eInvoicing_in_Denmark.pdf
12	Civil Registration	Germany	http://www.ifib.de/publikationsdateien/GPC_IOP_in_civil_registration_in_Germany.pdf
13	Civil Registration	Austria	http://www.ifib.de/publikationsdateien/GPC_IOP_in_civil_registration_in_Austria.pdf
14	Company Registration	Sweden	http://www.ifib.de/publikationsdateien/GPC_IOP_in_Company_Registration_in_Sweden_final.pdf
15	Health services Friuli Venezia	Italy	http://www.ifib.de/publikationsdateien/GPC_IOP_in_health_services_FriuliVeneziaGiulia.pdf
16	Danish OIO-XML Project	Denmark	http://www.ifib.de/publikationsdateien/GPC_IOP_in_PA_in_Denmark.pdf
17	ICAR	Italy	http://www.ifib.de/publikationsdateien/GPC_ICAR_Italy.pdf
18	Road Traffic Accident	UK	http://www.ifib.de/publikationsdateien/GPC_IOP_in_RTA_automation_project_in_UK.pdf

Table 4. Overview of types of standardization artefacts resulting from the literature analysis

Dimension	References
Archiving	Moen (1994), Borras (2004b)
Authentication	Charalabidis et al. (2009b), Kefallinos et al. (2006), Stefanova et al. (2010)
Business Process	Scherer et al. (2011), Janssen et al. (2011b), Becker et al. (2007), Charalabidis et al. (2009b), Chourabi et al. (2008), Gottschalk and Saether (2008), Hulstijn et al. (2011), Kubicek and Cimander (2009b)
Business Reporting	Guilloux et al. (2012), Hulstijn et al. (2011)
Code List	Charalabidis et al. (2009b), Kubicek and Cimander (2009b)
Common Search Service	Borras (2004b), Craig and Schriar (2001)
Common Terminology and Vocabulary	Bettahar et al. (2009), Borras (2004b), Charalabidis et al. (2009b), Craig and Schriar (2001), Davies et al. (2007)
Data Format	Borras (2004b), Kubicek and Cimander (2009b), Moen (1994), Su et al. (2005), Peristeras et al. (2007)
Data Modelling Rules	Borras (2004b)
Data Modelling Tool	Saekow and Boonmee (2009)
File Format	Fairchild and de Vuyust (2007), Shah and Kesan (2009), Shah and Kesan (2007)
Information Access	Sarathy and Muralidhar (2006), Su et al. (2005)
Law and Regulation	Su et al. (2005)
Message Format	Guilloux et al. (2012), Lee et al. (2009)
Messaging	Gottschalk and Saether (2008), Stefanova et al. (2010)
Metadata Definition	Alasem (2009), Davies et al. (2007), Davies et al. (2008), Landsbergen Jr. and Wolken Jr. (2001), Ojo et al. (2009)
Ontology	Bettahar et al. (2009), Charalabidis et al. (2009b), Kubicek and Cimander (2009b), Saekow and Boonmee (2009)
Operating System	Su et al. (2005)
Process Modelling Language	Becker et al. (2007), Chourabi et al. (2008), Gionis et al. (2011)
Process Modelling Tool	Saekow and Boonmee (2009)
Protocol	Gottschalk and Saether (2008), Misuraca et al. (2011b), Kubicek and Cimander (2009b), Shah and Kesan (2007), Sarathy and Muralidhar (2006)
Record	Borras (2004b)
Reference Architecture	Janssen et al. (2011b)
Repository	Charalabidis et al. (2009b), Davies et al. (2007), Lee et al. (2009), Saekow and Boonmee (2009)
Security and Privacy Mechanism	Charalabidis et al. (2009b), dos Santos and Reinhard (2008), Gottschalk and Saether (2008), Moen (1994), Stefanova et al. (2010)
Service Oriented Architecture	Stefanova et al. (2010), Kubicek and Cimander (2009b)
Software	Su et al. (2005), Misuraca et al. (2011b), Saekow and Boonmee (2009), Moen (1994)
Web Service	Bettahar et al. (2009), Lee et al. (2009), Stefanova et al. (2010), Saekow and Boonmee (2009)

APPENDIX B

Table 5. Detailed overview of types of artefacts

	Administration	Modeling	Processing	Communication and Interaction		Security & Privacy
Organizational	Business Process	Business Process Modelling Language	Business Process Modeling Tool	Process Model Exchange Format	Web Forms	Information Access Policy
	Record					
	Form					
	Law/Regulation	Process Reference Architecture				Document Integrity
	Information Service					
Technical/ Syntactic	Business Reporting	Application Architecture	Operating System	Messaging	User-Portal	Authentication
			Logging	Geo-Referencing		
			Archiving	Web Service/ API		
			SDK	Protocol	Website	
		Computing Language	Database	Network		Data Encryption
		Design Patterns	Software Application	Directory Service		Communication Security
		Data Modelling Language	Data Modelling Tool	Data Format	Barrier-free representation	
				Message Format	Representation Formats	
				File Format		
				Character Set		
Semantic	Shared Terminology	Ontology	Information Search Service	Metadata Definition	Micro Format	
				Repository		
				Code List		

The different types of artefacts are described as follows (Balta et al., 2018).

- Semantic Interoperability
- **Code List:** Commonly agreed list that assigns a number to an entity
- **Information Search Service:** Service to guarantee every organization has access to shared, common knowledge
- **Metadata Definition:** Assigns meaning to data so every organization knows how to interpret a received data item
- **Ontology:** Model to represent the knowledge and connect the terms of the shared vocabulary

- **Repository:** Space to share and store knowledge to be available for every organization
- **Shared Terminology:** All organizations use the same vocabulary and assign the same meaning to a term
- Technical and Syntactic Interoperability
- **Archiving:** Defines how and which documents have to be archived in order to connect the archive to other IT systems for automated archiving
- **Authentication:** Technical implementation to verify a software's or a user's identity
- **Business Reporting:** Technical aspects to simplify the communication between administrations and enterprises for the purpose of business reporting
- **Data Format:** Common format for data items, like address or date, which can be sent and received by every organization
- **Data Modelling Language:** Language for modelling common data items that every organization can receive and send
- **Data Modelling Tool:** Tool for modelling data items based on the common modelling language so every organization has the same functionality and builds interoperable models
- **File Format:** File format for defined documents, like .PDF or .CSV, to ensure every organization can open the file and get an expected representation of the content
- **Message Format:** Common format for messages sent and received with a messaging tool
- **Messaging:** Defines a method to exchange messages on network level between different organization, only works when both parties have implemented the respecting software and know the message format
- **Network Protocol:** Defines a specific way of communication on any level of a network model
- **Operating System:** Defines the preferred operating system on the computers of a public administration, which influences the choice of tools and file formats
- **Security and Privacy Mechanisms:** Defines any technical mechanism to make communication or other technical components more secure. It is split in two classes: Data Encryption and Communication Security
- **Service Oriented Architecture:** Paradigm for how to connect several IT components to a composed service, which leads to more flexibility and reusability
- **Web Service:** Tool to connect IT components to each other, one implementation of a service oriented architecture
- Organizational Interoperability
- **Business Process Modelling Language:** Defines the language for modelling processes to guarantee a common syntax and semantic
- **Business Process Modelling Tool:** Tool for modelling business processes based on the common modelling language so every organization has the same functionality and builds interoperable models
- **Business Process:** Defines the processes behind every public service, both, within one organization and between different organizations

- **Document Integrity:** Defines how to treat a document
- **Information Access Policy:** Restricts access to information, tools or services to specific user groups at a certain time
- **Law/Regulation:** Determines what methods or standards have to be used for an e-government application
- **Process Reference Architecture:** Defines an architecture for processes that is reusable and enables high interoperability between different organizations
- **Record:** Defines the content and format of a record to ensure every organization requires the same information for a certain service

APPENDIX C

Table 6. Overview of coordination modes based on the situation of coordination (source: (Balta & Krcmar, 2018)

	Planning mode (explicit)	Feedback mode (explicit)	Knowledge exchange mode (tacit)
General mechanism	partitioning of tasks into modules and defining interfaces	establishment of an on-demand, face-to-face (or virtual) ongoing communication	exchange and adaption of boundary objects, transfer of resources
Common ground between actors	minimal, constant level	constant updates	knowledge transfer and updates by adaptation to context
Communication	impersonal, "one-time" communication, modules and interfaces	personal or in group ongoing communication	different possible ways to communicate, but explicit communication is not a prerequisite
Environment	stable, pre-established tasks and responsibilities	dynamic, innovative tasks under volatile conditions	dynamic, innovative tasks under volatile conditions
Interdepen-dency type	pooled or sequential interdependency	reciprocal interdependency	reciprocal or team interdependency
Example	Public administrations in the EU using the eIDAS message format	a telephone call or a meeting, an online video conference	a software codebase (Bolici et al., 2016), team staffing with an experienced member from another team (Srikanth & Puranam, 2011)

Section 3

Ethics and Responsibility in Standards Setting

Chapter 9
Ethics and Standardization

John-Stewart Gordon
Vytautas Magnus University, Lithuania

Vladislav V. Fomin
https://orcid.org/0000-0001-8423-2500
Vytautas Magnus University, Lithuania & Vilnius University, Lithuania

ABSTRACT

This chapter examines the important relationship between ethics and standardization. This issue has never been among the most prominent issues in the context of standardization, even though it has been extensively discussed in the context of ethics and the economy. Nonetheless, it is important to properly understand the development of standards in the first place and why standards are indeed ethically relevant. The main claim is that ethics and standardization are deeply interwoven concepts and should be seen as conjoined twins. There is no ethics without standards and there is no standardization without ethics, because the market—the exchange of goods among people—is part of the normative realm.

INTRODUCTION

This chapter examines the important relationship between ethics and standardization. This issue has never been among the most prominent issues in the context of standardization, even though it has been extensively discussed in the context of ethics and the economy. Nonetheless, it is important to properly understand the development of standards in the first place and why standards are indeed ethically relevant.

Our main claim is that ethics and standardization are deeply interwoven concepts and should be seen as conjoined twins. There is no ethics without standards and there is no standardization without ethics, because the market—the exchange of goods among people—is part of the normative realm. The idea that the market as such is independent from ethics (e.g. Robbins 2007/1932; Baumol and Blackman 1991) is wrong and misleading. The reason is simple: the idea of not adhering to ethics in market transactions, usually so that companies can avoid additional transaction costs, is by itself a normative position that supports the rather disreputable ethical view of "anything goes". In other words, you cannot escape ethics; rather, the issue is what type of ethical approach companies apply and whether a company is using ethics only as a means—for example, to reduce its coordination costs—or as a true goal by implementing

DOI: 10.4018/978-1-5225-9008-8.ch009

Copyright © 2019, IGI Global. Copying or distributing in print or electronic forms without written permission of IGI Global is prohibited.

proper corporate ethical standards or adopting international standards, which can help a company boost its ethical market conduct and ultimately result in a win-win situation.

There is a difference between companies, on one hand, that do not adhere to environmental standards and poison the environment, neglect their social roles with respect to their employees, promote child labor in dangerous locations (such as mines in India), discriminate in hiring by ethnicity and sex, and exploit animals and, on the other hand, companies that apply decent ethical standards in these and other areas. Immoral and reckless behavior by companies—or even by a company's employees—presents a substantial threat to company profits. This fact can be demonstrated by numerous cases in the business world. For example, customers react negatively when a company's behavior does not live up to certain ethical standards. In that respect, it is actually in the company's interest to implement some corporate ethical standards (or to adopt respectable international standards) so as to enhance its profitability in a highly competitive market (see also Arnal 2005, 6).

To substantiate our claim, we first provide a brief analysis of the concepts of ethics and standardization in the second section of this article (immediately after this introduction). This review provides a common ground for the subsequent discussion. The third section examines the important relationship between ethics and standardization by paying proper attention to the general question of why we have (and should have) standards in the first place. Two main examples further substantiate the normative significance of standardization as a way to reduce uncertainty and build trust. Against the background of the preceding analysis, the fourth section discusses the problem of ethical standards and whether there is an ethically neutral concept of standardization. The last section offers some final conclusions.

PRELIMINARY REMARKS

To properly determine the important relationship between ethics and standardization, one first needs to know the meanings of the two concepts. In this section, we will provide two working definitions without claiming that these are the only two adequate definitions in the literature. Of course, different definitions may result in different outcomes and implications with respect to the depiction of the relationship between ethics and standardization.

What Is Ethics?

Before we can explain what ethics is, we first need to determine the relationship between ethics and morality. There are at least four different ways to determine the relationship between these two concepts: (a) ethics and morality are two different concepts, (b) ethics and morality can be used interchangeably, (c) morality is a sub-part of ethics, and (d) ethics is the theory of morality. Each relation has somewhat different implications for our normative reasoning and decision making. We will deal with each alternative viewpoint in order.

Ethics and Morality Are Two Different Concepts

According to this distinction, the concept of ethics concerns how people should live their own lives and pursue their own happiness (e.g. hedonism). What should we do to satisfy our own interests so that we can live a happy life? No duties are involved. Morality, on the other hand, concerns the interests of other people, claiming the existence of moral rules and norms as well as standards of values independent of human beings that we must take into account when we act (e.g. deontology). Habermas is one scholar who believes that ethics and morality are different concepts.

Ethics and Morality Can Be Used Interchangeably

Many scholars use the concepts of ethics and morality interchangeably without paying much attention to the long and distinctive traditions of both notions. We do not claim that they are unaware of the different meanings of the notions; rather, many use them interchangeably out of practical convenience. Other authors, however, do indeed claim that the concepts of ethics and morality are synonymous—despite their indisputably different origins—and that there is no need to make any further distinction.

Morality Is a Sub-Part of Ethics

For example, Plato, Aristotle, and in contemporary virtue ethics Williams (1985) believe that morality is a sub-part of ethics. They argue that to live a happy and fulfilled live, one must also abide by some moral standards, such as rules of justice. In other words, a happy life must also contain moral orientation. Conceptually speaking, all moral norms are also ethical norms but not vice versa.

Ethics Is the Theory of Morality

The view that ethics is the theory of morality is the standard interpretation among scholars in the field of practical philosophy. They mainly view basic ethics as a kind of general approach that provides the necessary concepts and methods for examining fundamental problems in the context of morality. In other words, ethics constitutes systematic reasoning about moral norms and values. In its narrow meaning, it contains the whole of moral rights, duties, rules, norms, value standards, and the "categorical must". In its wider meaning, it also contains advice for the individual seeking to live a happy life.

We do believe that it is of utmost importance to analyze normative problems in clear and systematic ways, as suggested by the view that ethics is the theory of morality. It seems, however, also reasonable to view morality as a sub-part of ethics when we analyze the relationship between ethics and standardization. The main reason for this combined approach is that option (d) should rather be considered the general systematic framework against which we apply our particular reading of ethics as a sub-part of morality.[1]

What Is Standardization?

Standardization, in general terms, can be defined as the process of making a standard. The aim of standardization is to establish a necessary consensus in support of a common solution to interoperability and portability. Standards therefore form a common reference point and serve as the tools that enable exchange of goods and services in anonymous (global) markets (Bousquet 2003).

The word "standard" can have different meanings, as different types of standards can be distinguished. A technical standard is an established norm or requirement with respect to technical systems. It is usually defined in a document as a set of specifications to which one must adhere (David and Greenstein 1990, 4). The International Standardization Organization (ISO) refers to standards as "documents, established by consensus and approved by a recognized body, that [provide], for common and repeated use, rules, guidelines or characteristics for activities or their results, aimed at the achievement of the optimum degree of order in a given context" (ISO 2004, 12). Thus, standards can refer not only to products but also to methods, processes and practices, in which case the word *norm*[2] can be used instead.

Among the most familiar general public standards are the paper sizes of A4 (in Europe) and Letter (in the United States). The standard (ISO 2007) prescribes specific characteristics (the dimensions) of the sheet of paper, but it does not prescribe the manufacturing method. A standard can also do the opposite; that is, it can prescribe a method of doing something without imposing any specific characteristics of the product being subjected to that method. For example, the ISO 14001 standard (ISO 2004) "specifies requirements for an environmental management system to enable an organization to develop and implement a policy and objectives" with regard to significant legal and environmental aspects.

In the modern world of increasing globalization, standardization has become a cornerstone issue for any company seeking to enter new or extend existing markets (Miles et al. 1998), whether the company is driving a market innovation or being driven by the market (Kumar, Scheer, and Kotler 2000; von Zedtwitz and Gassmann 2002). This critical role of standards holds for virtually any business operation, from the design of new products or processes (King et al. 1994) to responding to customer requirements (Fomin et al. 2005, 569) to outsourcing or devising globalization strategies (Lovelock and Yip 1996; Swaminathan 2001). Companies develop and adopt standards in numerous fields—for instance, technical design, corporate governance, financial reporting, and product development (Brunsson and Jacobsson 2000). At the turn of the millennium, standards played a role in facilitating 80% of global trade, or \$4 trillion annually (OECD 1999, 4). This shows beyond dispute that standards and standardization have effectively become an inseparable part of the wider discussion of business operations in society.

Standards typically originate from standard development organizations (SDOs) or industry consortia (Farrell and Saloner 1988; Funk and Methe 2001; Schmidt and Werle 1998), where interested stakeholders develop a standard through specified consensus mechanisms. A substantial number of the roughly two hundred thousand standards (Schepel 2005; Toth 1997; World Trade Organization 2005, xxv) in use today are set by SDOs. The most important and largest collections of standards are those of the ISO, International Electrotechnical Commission (https://www.iec.ch), and International Telecommunication Union (https://www.itu.int).

Historically, SDOs were established to develop public, technically optimal standards through collective action by technical experts (Frary 2008; ISO 2008). However, the contemporary standardization regime is dominated by private stakeholders who strive to promote their interests, such as their control over particular standard specifications or intellectual property rights. As private and public interests are juxtaposed in the standardization process, standards effectively become products of compromise, with private interests more often than not receiving greater weight than societal needs. At the same time, we also see a growing societal concern for the public good in such areas as public safety and environmental conservation.

In response to the growing demand for what can be referred to as "responsible standardization", the major SDOs have published codes of ethics (ISO 2004; ITU 2011) for their standard development processes. This move, however, has not resulted in any visible shift towards ethical standards. Besides, even "technically optimal" standards developed according to a code of ethics (ISO 2004) may be misused by the general public due to their lack of understanding of technology's inherently social and moral dimensions (Buchholz and Rosenthal 2002, 47), as there is a striking mismatch between the scale on which standards are developed and the awareness and understanding of their role in general society or even academia. Specifically, standards have received little attention from academia or the general public with regard to their development mechanisms and processes. This situation has been described as a "blurred … standardization landscape" (European Commission 2007; Jakobs and Blind 2011), due to the lack of tools or methods for "seeing through" the process (Sales et al. 2012), let alone ensuring the incorporation of ethical issues into the process of standard development.

WHAT IS THE RELATION BETWEEN ETHICS, STANDARDIZATION, AND THE MARKET?

The lack of adherence to proper standards may cause ethical problems with respect to the use and application of the products in the market. We substantiate this general assumption with two examples demonstrating that standards are well suited to reduce uncertainty and enhance trust in business relationships.

The Lack of Standardization as a Possible Source of "Failures"

The rationale for viewing lack of standardization as a possible source of various normative types of failure is relatively straightforward. If we use standards in the context of quality control to ensure that a certain product will not break after a short period of use in a particularly sensitive area (e.g., aviation operations), we need to know that the product will live up to the standards. By employing certain standards, we both reduce uncertainty with respect to the quality of a given product and build trust in the product and its underlying standards of evaluation. Therefore, standards are appropriate for fulfilling two significant tasks, as (a) guidelines as to how something should behave or be measured and (b) tools for evaluating anything that pertains to standards. For example, standards could be seen as a particular way to respond to the question of how to coordinate processes that concern the market.

Ethical standards come into play when implemented into companies as a way to coordinate processes against the background of normative considerations. As Arnal (2005, 2) has suggested:

The asset of ethical standards is that they represent a specific way of coordination. They bring positive effects such as the fall of coordination cost, or the reduction of uncertainty. Ethical standards can also be regarded by the consumer as a way to get information. Thus, ethical standards ensure information to stakeholders. … By improving information transfers, standardization constitutes an original coordination mechanism for business relationships. It helps to coordinate contractual relations with customers and shareholders. Ethical standards also reinforce the coordination process because they encourage trust among economic agents.

The academic discipline that deals with such questions is the interdisciplinary field of business ethics, which is, in turn, a part of applied ethics. One of the major questions in the field concerns the important relationship between ethics and the economy/market. The literature on this issue is legion. The spectrum of views on the ethics–economy relationship ranges from the belief that the economy/market does not need ethics (Robbins 2007/1932; Baumol and Blackman 1991) to contrary opinions, such as that of Koslowski (2013), that ethics is not only an additional factor in the market but an essential part of it (see also Arnal 2005, 3–4).

As noted above, however, normative considerations are—logically speaking—always a part of the market (or any other domain of standardization). The "anything goes" view that no ethical standards need to be applied in the market and the endorsement of high ethical standards in the market are both ethical positions. The only difference is that the latter view sets ethical limits with respect to how we should coordinate market processes and the former does not.

The prime example in recent history of the "anything goes" view concerns the financial crisis that began in 2007, during which the whole international finance system was at jeopardy. Arguably, if proper ethical standards had been followed in the first place, there had been no global financial crises. The underlying motif of "faster, higher, stronger" in the business sector should have been more strongly regulated according to a responsible pluralistic business approach that included higher ethical standards.

Cases: Standardization as a Way to Reduce Uncertainty

The International Organization for Standardization (ISO) is a worldwide organization whose membership is composed of the national societies that establish and monitor standards for commerce, trade, and communication in more than 150 countries. ISO has developed thousands of internationally accepted voluntary standards. Among these standards, the ISO 9000 series of process-oriented standards for quality management has gained more rapid acceptance than any other international standard in history (Miles, Munilla, and Russel 1997, 365).

The ISO 9000 Series

The ISO 9000 series of standards was first published in 1987 and then revised in 1994, 2000, 2008, and 2015. Next, ISO developed other management system standards (MSSs), such as the ISO 14001 Environmental Management System (EMS) and the ISO/IEC 27001 Information Security Management (ISMS) standards. All three sets of management standards have much in common (Brewer and Nash 2005, 1; Fomin, Vries, and Barlette 2008). First, they are built on the Plan-Do-Check-Act (PDCA) process cycle model, which specifies requirements and processes to enable a business to establish, implement, review and monitor, manage and maintain effective management systems, whether the specific discipline is quality, environmental, or information security management (Humphreys 2005, 15). Second, the systems are designed to complement one another in such a way that organizations can create a single, integrated management system that complies with more than one MSS (Brewer and Nash, 2005, 1). Third, the correspondence between ISO 9001 and e.g., ISO 14001 makes it easier for firms that have experience with one standard to implement another one. Fourth, all MSSs can be certified against the applicable standard. Certification is not mandatory, but most organizations that implement the standard also seek a certificate of compliance. Empirical studies have reported that achieving certification has a positive impact on business performance (Nicolau and Sellers 2002), although some authors dispute this claim (Seddon 2000). The underlying premise of ISO 9001 certification is that the process of creating products and services can be managed by using a system of standards. The inputs to and outputs from the system can be measured at various points as the system adds value (Stevenson and Barnes 2002, 696). Fifth, MSSs are applicable to any business, regardless of its size (Humphreys 2005, 16) or field of operation.

Empirical research has indicated that various benefits are associated with the adoption of an MSS. Besides the already-mentioned external benefit of an increase in the company's stock price, which may be short-lived, the implementation of a quality management system based on ISO 9001 may result in internal benefits related to production (Corbett, Montes-Sancho, and Kirsch 2005; Tzelepis et al. 2006). Overall, the positive effects stemming from certification should outweigh the high cost (Delmas 2002) of MSS standard implementation and certification, even for small and medium-sized enterprises, or SMEs (Vlachos, Michail, and Sotiropoulou 2002). Specifically, as standards are seen as tools to facilitate market transactions among anonymous market players, the use of a management system creates trust in the adopter among other market participants. Thus, the trust in the proper handling of processes is managed according to (or certified against) the MSS.

Contrary to this intended purpose, there have reportedly been instances where ISO 9001 was adopted to mislead market participants regarding a company's quality credentials (Whitney 1997). This situation embodies a mismatch between the underlying ethical philosophy of the company and the trust-building nature of the ISO 9001 standard.

The ISO 14000 Series

The ISO 14000 series of EMS standards (ISO 1996, 2004a) was introduced on the coattails of the success of ISO 9000 (Delmas 2002, 93). The United Nations' 1992 Rio de Janeiro conference on environment and development (the "Earth summit") can be seen as the starting point for the development of the ISO 14000 series of standards, in combination with the Uruguay Round of the General Agreement on Tariffs and Trade (GATT) (Gunawardena, 2006). The Rio summit focused on protecting the global environment, GATT on reducing non-tariff barriers to trade. Since the existence of different standards in different countries may create barriers to global environmental amelioration, it may be argued that an important rationale for the creation of ISO 14001 was to harmonize diverse environmental management standards and thus foster international trade by providing an internationally accepted single point of reference on such current environmental issues as pollution prevention and compliance assurance (Delmas 2002, 91–92; Miles, Munilla, and Russel 1997, 364).

When introduced in 1996, the ISO 14001 was seen as likely to "enjoy widespread adoption similar to that of ISO 9000 as organizations worldwide are encouraged by their stakeholders ... to become more environmentally sensitive" (Miles, Munilla, and Russel 1997, 365). It was expected that dominant multinational corporations would initially be affected by ISO 14000, with the impact eventually trickling down to SMEs that serve as suppliers to larger firms (Miles, Munilla, and Russel 1997, 365). As Rothery (1995) wrote:

Both ISO 9000, the quality management standard, and ISO 14000, the environmental management standard soon to be released, represent what biologists would call a dominant tendency. The spread of a standard is facilitated by its own growth, a cascade effect. The mechanism causing this biological-like growth is the customer-buyer interface. As sophisticated buyers demand standard certification from their immediate suppliers, they in turn pass on the demand to their supplies, and the standards movement cascades through the supply chain.

Indeed, the predicted cascade effect did occur in the diffusion of both the ISO 9000 and 14000 series of standards. In view of the growing concern for environmental issues in the late 20th and 21st centuries, ISO 14001 adoption can be seen as driven largely by a desire to demonstrate compliance with environmental regulations. This standard helps adopters to deal properly with requirements in environmental, health and safety, and public and product safety legislation (Rothery 1995). The early-adopting business sectors for ISO 14001 were those that tend to have the greatest environmental impact: basic chemicals/ chemical manufacturing, electro-/electronic and optical, and base metals/metal manufacturing (Mizuno 2002). In three influential Asian economies (Korea, Japan and Taiwan), government stimulated the adoption of standards (Mizuno 2002).

However, critics of the standards call ISO 14001 "a missed opportunity for sustainable global development" (Sklyarova and Kobets 2011, referring to Krut and Gleckman 1998). The ethical underperformance of the environmental system management standard may be because assurance of regulatory compliance, information disclosure to the public, legal environmental proceedings, and documentation of improvements in environmental performance are not required in the standard (Sklyarova and Kobets 2011).

Towards New Standards

Following the 2008 financial crisis, the global financial services industry has faced heightened regulatory pressure (Groenfeldt 2018). New reporting and conformance rules have been adopted to reduce the threat of new financial crises emerging unnoticed. As many financial services companies operate globally, these regulations can be seen as an international standard akin to the aforementioned ISO/IEC MSSs in that they define the content of performance quality to be attained, the frequency of verification, and the conditions for reporting.

The 2016 EU General Data Protection Regulation (GDPR), affecting the financial services industry directly but encompassing all sectors of the economy, aims to give individuals control over their personal data, in response to widespread and growing concern over unethical misuse of consumers' personal data even by industry leaders. The GDPR seeks to simplify the regulatory environment for international business by making such regulations consistent across the EU. Among other things, it sets standards on how consumer data are to be handled so as to ensure individual privacy and avert breaches.

The issue of sexual harassment in the workplace has been in the news for the last year (Weaver et al. 2018), raising public awareness regarding gender-related issues at work. Victims of sexual harassment were found not to report on the problems they faced due to psychological pressure exerted by their colleagues, especially higher-ranking colleagues. In response to these two problems—i.e. the harassment itself and the non-reporting of it—the new Labour Code of Lithuania explicitly states that sexual harassment in the workplace will not be tolerated and also requires employers to engage in active prevention of harassment.

IS THERE A MORALLY NEUTRAL CONCEPT OF STANDARDIZATION?

There are at least two main categories of standards: (a) standards pertaining to products that can be sold on the market and (b) standards pertaining to processes—e.g. defining the exchange of data, validating mechanisms, and setting reporting requirements. The processes that eventually become referred to as "standards" can emerge either organically as best practices of the market or through deliberation by SDOs. The former category of standards is referred to as "de facto", the latter as "de jure". Whichever process leads to the emergence of a standard, once implemented it is extremely difficult to change. With regard to market-driven, "unethical" de facto standards, the problem is self-evident. With regard to de jure anticipatory[3] standards, a problem arises if the development process itself does not do justice to the criteria of fairness and responsibility. Jakobs, Procter, and Williams (1998) make exactly this point, claiming that the current organizational structures and mechanisms for standards development are not designed to address matters of stakeholder representation, the interests of end users, or ethical issues.

In general, we agree with this evaluation, but we would like to restate our above-mentioned observation that "ethics" is always part of the representation in some way, simply because it is logically speaking not circumventable. It constitutes the background metaphysics underlying all human actions, regardless of whether they meet the highest moral standards or lack any moral foundation. The background metaphysics can be guided by different sources such as culture, tradition and religion, which give rise to different ethical standards. The vital point rather is that the drafters of standards are incorporating *some* ethical approach, whether or not it appears to meet the highest moral standards.

For example, the great technological developments in this century make it very likely that we will see, within the next few decades, the advent of intelligent robots that may even surpass human capabilities. One important question currently being discussed in contemporary ethics is whether we should grant such advanced intelligent and autonomous machines moral and legal rights (Anderson and Anderson 2011; Gunkel 2012, 2014). Even though the advent of such artificial beings is still some decades away, we must discuss their moral and legal status now, so that we are prepared once they emerge (Lin, Abney, and Bekey 2014). To do so requires us to contemplate proper ethical, legal and technical standards for intelligent machines, including those that may soon be outperforming us in most fields. The right choice of standards is of utmost importance since the standards will determine how human beings will treat robots in society. Should they become our slaves (Bryson 2010) or should we treat them as fellow members of our moral community (Gordon 2018)? In any case, we should intentionally seek to adhere to the highest moral standards when thinking about such important issues.

Standards and the Economy

We agree with Arnal (2005, 8), who claims that "Ethics standardization should emerge from a reflection on the links between ethics, standards and economy." The old but persistent view that the implementation of decent ethical standards in companies eventually makes them less competitive by virtue of the additional costs they incur is misleading. On the contrary, ethical standards bring positive effects: they build trust, reduce uncertainty, and can lower coordination costs.

The more interesting ethical issue here, however, concerns the problem of stakeholders' non-representation in the context of formulating ethical standards (Jakobs, Procter, and Williams 1998; Willemse, De Vries, and Dul 2006).[4] The objection is that if companies dictate ethical standards for the market without the participation of stakeholders, then they are using their dominant position to spread their particular idiosyncratic version of normative views, which is perceived as unfair. How can we solve this issue? At its heart sits the fear among stakeholders that their legitimate interests are not considered by companies and the market. There are at least three[5] main responses to this issue.

First, one could argue that the market regulates itself (by bringing forth de facto standards) and that severe shortcomings in implemented ethical standards will be revised over time in response to market pressures themselves, by virtue of the law of supply and demand. In other words, companies with inadequate ethical standards may sell fewer goods and will thus revise their ethical policy accordingly, which eventually means that the stakeholders do have a great influence on the content of the ethical standards of companies by virtue of their purchasing behavior. For example, the animal rights movement has recently been able to use market pressures to affect pharmaceutical companies' use of animals for experimentation.

Second, companies could *directly* implement the interests of stakeholders with respect to ethical standards. Of course, there may be a clash of interests between corporate profitability and consumer concerns, but it would seem possible to balance opposing interests and to arrive at solutions that may accommodate both perspectives. How to do this in practice is a matter of organization.

Third, one could also hold the view that ethical standards should be discussed, determined and disseminated for implementation by impartial experts who are very knowledgeable in the field of business ethics and who can take all perspectives equally into account without advantaging a particular party. These experts would consider the interests of all stakeholders to the same degree as they weigh the interests of the companies they represent. We do not see a principled argument against the reasonableness of this approach.

The idea of a *morally neutral concept of standardization,* which we contend is impossible, really concerns the way in which the process of moral reasoning and decision making takes place in the development of ethical standards for companies and for the market itself. As we have just delineated, there are multiple possible responses to the issue, but all of them incorporate some perspective on what is ethical. We also contend that "pure" capitalism—if such a thing has ever existed at all—will always be outperformed by an *ethically enhanced capitalism* in the long run.

Standards and Governmental Regulation

The previous sub-section briefly mentioned three ways to enrich the development of standards by implementing other groups such as stakeholders, consumers and impartial experts in the decision-making process. Most standards in our economy do not require a particular regulatory intervention (King et al. 1994) with respect to ethical considerations. However, there are many cases where one should not leave the process of developing standards up to the market. The reason is that some standards may presuppose very high ethical requirements that must be structured or strictly managed by governments and their respective institutions.

One current example, briefly cited above, is the discussion of legal rights for intelligent robots once they have reached a certain level of rationality and autonomy (see the European Parliament's Resolution on Civil Law Rules on Robotics, 2017). The discourse on implementing proper ethical standards to protect intelligent artificial beings should not take place solely in the free-market economy (where the economic exploitation of these machines is the most likely outcome). Rather, the process must unfold through international governing institutions that will set proper standards without relying solely on economic considerations. Whereas we can expect those driven by purely economic motives to have a bias in favor of lowering ethical standards on the exploitation of intelligent machines, government is generally considered less biased in that respect. This does not mean that government is not influenced at all by economic factors, but rather that these are not the only factors contributing to their moral reasoning and decision making.

On the other hand, as high-profile standardization professionals have stated, "governments have no will, interest, nor budget for significant action in [the standardization] domain" (Fomin, Pedersen, and de Vries 2008, 470). We would suggest that a possible way forward in resolving this seemingly dead-end situation involves developing some type of interfacing model, where the government establishes ethical norms to be met in the application of standardized technologies within society, and where SDOs are obligated to adhere to these norms when developing technical standards.[6] This implies the development of meta-rules regulating how standards are set or how SDOs should coordinate their efforts with government to provide assurance that the intended ethical aspect of standards is fulfilled.

CONCLUSION

Standards and standardization play a visible and important role in structuring global market interactions. Nevertheless, there is limited awareness in the general public and in academia not only regarding the importance of standards per se, but also regarding the processes that lead to the development of standards. With the growing societal concern for ethical conduct by companies and markets alike, the important relationship between ethics and standardization must be explored. In this chapter we have claimed that ethics and standardization are deeply interwoven concepts and should be seen as conjoined twins. There is no ethics without standards and there can be no standardization without ethics. To substantiate our claim, we provided a brief analysis of the concepts of ethics and standardization, and we examined a variety of standards that can contribute to more ethical market transactions by reducing uncertainty and enhancing trust among anonymous market participants. We concluded the chapter by suggesting some ways forward on how to make international standards development correspond to higher ethical norms, while recognizing the inability of governments to intervene directly in the processes that lead to the development of standards. This issue is of great importance today as emerging technology standards will be deeply interwoven into and will substantially shape daily human interactions in domains where ethics has traditionally been a high-level consideration, such as law, health, and personal privacy.

REFERENCES

Anderson, M., & Anderson, S. L. (2011). *Machine Ethics*. Cambridge, UK: Cambridge University Press. doi:10.1017/CBO9780511978036

Arnal, J. (2005). *Formalization of Ethics: The Issue of Standardization*. Retrieved from ftp://mse.univ-paris1.fr/pub/mse/cahiers2005/R05074.pdf

Baumol, W. J., & Sue, A. B. B. (1991). *Perfect Markets and Easy Virtue Business Ethics and the Invisible Hand*. Blackwell Publishers.

Bousquet, F. (2003). Dealing with Standardization: Do You Need a Guru? Paradoxes and Tricks of Standardization management. Presented at the *3rd International Conference on Standardisation and Innovation in Information Technology (SIIT)*, Delft, The Netherlands. 10.1109/SIIT.2003.1251194

Brewer, D., & Nash, M. (2005). *The Similarity between ISO 9001 and BS 7799-2*. Gamma Secure Systems Ltd.

Brunsson, N., & Jacobsson, B. (2000). The Contemporary Expansion of Standardization. In *A World of Standards* (pp. 1–20). Oxford, UK: Oxford University Press.

Bryson, J. (2010). Robots Should Be Slaves. In W. Yorick (Ed.), *Close Engagements with Artificial Companions: Key Social, Psychological, Ethical and Design Issues* (pp. 63–74). Amsterdam: John Benjamins. doi:10.1075/nlp.8.11bry

Buchholz, R. A., & Rosenthal, S. B. (2002). Technology and Business: Rethinking the Moral Dilemma. *Journal of Business Ethics*, *41*(1/2), 45–50. doi:10.1023/A:1021346021768

Corbett, C. J., Montes-Sancho, M. J., & Kirsch, D. A. (2005). The Financial Impact of ISO 9000 Certification in the United States: An Empirical Analysis. *Management Science*, *51*(7), 1046–1059. doi:10.1287/mnsc.1040.0358

David, P. A., & Greenstein, S. (1990). The Economics of Compatibility Standards: An Introduction to Recent Research. *Economics of Innovation and New Technology*, *1*(1-2), 3–41. doi:10.1080/10438599000000002

Delmas, M. A. (2002). The Diffusion of Environmental Management Standards in Europe and in the United States: An Institutional Perspective. *Policy Sciences*, *35*(1), 91–119. doi:10.1023/A:1016108804453

European Commission. (2007). *Final Report of the Study on the Specific Policy Needs for ICT Standardization.* European Commission. Retrieved from http://www.epractice.eu/en/library/281182

Farrell, J., & Saloner, G. (1988). Coordination through Committees and Markets. *The Rand Journal of Economics*, *19*(2), 235–252. doi:10.2307/2555702

Fomin, V. V., de Vries, H. J., & Barlette, Y. (2008). *ISO/IEC 27001 Information Systems Security Management Standard: Identifying Directions for Future Research.* Nice, France: International Association for Management of Technology (IAMOT). Retrieved from http://webintec.ceram.fr/euromot2008/

Fomin, V. V., King, J. L., Lyytinen, K., & McGann, S. (2005). Diffusion and Impacts of E-Commerce in the United States of America: Results from an Industry Survey. *Communications of the Association for Information Systems*, *16*, 559–603. doi:10.17705/1CAIS.01628

Fomin, V. V., Pedersen, M. K., & de Vries, H. J. (2008). Open Standards and Government Policy: Results of a Delphi Survey. *Communications of the Association for Information Systems*, *22*, 459–484. doi:10.17705/1CAIS.02225

Frary, M. (2008). *The Founding of the IEC.* Retrieved from www.iec.ch/about/history/articles/founding_iec.htm

Funk, J. L., & Methe, D. T. (2001). Market- and Committee-Based Mechanisms in the Creation And Diffusion of Global Industry Standards: The Case of Mobile Communications. *Research Policy*, *30*(4), 589–610. doi:10.1016/S0048-7333(00)00095-0

Goodpaster, K. E. (1991). Business Ethics and Stakeholder Analysis. *Business Ethics Quarterly*, *1*(1), 53–73. doi:10.2307/3857592

Gordon, J.-S. (2013). Modern Morality and Ancient Ethics. Internet Encyclopedia of Philosophy.

Gordon, J.-S. (2018). What Do We Owe to Intelligent Robots? *AI & Society*. doi:10.100700146-018-0844-6

Groenfeldt, T. (2017). Banks Turn to Technology to Cope with New Regulations. *Forbes*. Retrieved from https://www.forbes.com/sites/tomgroenfeldt/2018/03/03/banks-turn-to-technology-to-cope-with-new-regulations/#6ce9e1c85d70

Gunawardena, N. (2006). Case Study: Implementation of ISO 14000 Environmental Management System. In *Standardisation in Companies and Markets* (pp. 607–646). Hamburg: Helmut Schmidt University. Retrieved from www.asia-link-standardisation.de/

Gunkel, D. J. (2012). *The Machine Question: Critical Perspectives on AI, Robots, and Ethics*. Cambridge, MA: MIT Press. doi:10.7551/mitpress/8975.001.0001

Gunkel, D. J. (2014). A Vindication of the Rights of Machines. *Philosophy & Technology*, *27*(1), 113–132. doi:10.100713347-013-0121-z

Heath, J. (2006). Business Ethics Without Stakeholders. *Business Ethics Quarterly*, *16*(4), 533–558. doi:10.5840/beq200616448

Humphreys, T. (2005). State-of-the-Art Information Security Management System with ISO/IEC 27001:2005. *ISO Management Systems*, 15–18.

ISO. (1996). *Iso 14001:1996. Environmental Management Systems: Specification with Guidance for Use*. Geneva: International Organization for Standardization.

ISO. (2004a). *14001:2004. Environmental Management Systems: Specification with Guidance for Use*. Geneva: International Organization for Standardization.

ISO. (2004b). *ISO Code of Ethics*. Retrieved from https://www.iso.org/publication/PUB100011.html

ISO. (2007). *ISO 216:2007. Writing Paper and Certain Classes of Printed Matter: A and B Series, and Indication of Machine Direction*. Geneva: International Organization for Standardization. Retrieved from https://www.iso.org/standard/36631.html

ISO/IEC. (2004). *Guide 2: Standardization and Related Activities. General Vocabulary*. Geneva: International Organization for Standardization and International Electrotechnical Commission. Retrieved from www.iso.org

ISO/IEC. (2008). *ISO/IEC Directives, Part 1: Procedures for the Technical Work* (6th ed.). Geneva: International Organization for Standardization and International Electrotechnical Commission.

ITU. (2011). *ITU Code of Ethics*. Retrieved from https://www.itu.int/en/general-secretariat/Documents/ethics/SO-2011-002-en.pdf

Jakobs, K., & Blind, K. (2011). ICT Standardisation Policy in Europe: Recent Past, Presence, and Future. Presented at the *7th Biennial Standardisation and Innovation in Information Technology (SIIT) conference*, Aachen, Germany. 10.1109/SIIT.2011.6083611

Jakobs, K., Procter, R., & Williams, R. (1998). User Participation in Standards Setting: The Panacea? *ACM StandardView*, *6*(2), 85–89. doi:10.1145/301688.301693

King, J. L., Gurbaxani, V., Kraemer, K. L., McFarlan, F. W., Raman, K. S., & Yap, C. S. (1994). Institutional Factors in Information Technology Innovation. *Information Systems Research*, *5*(2), 139–169. doi:10.1287/isre.5.2.139

Koslowski, P. (2013). Principles of Ethical Economy (2nd ed.). Springer.

Krut, R., & Gleckman, H. (1998). *ISO14001: A Missed Opportunity for Sustainable Global Development*. London: Earthscan Publications.

Kumar, N., Scheer, L., & Kotler, P. (2000). From Market Driven to Market Driving. *European Management Journal, 18*(2), 129–142. doi:10.1016/S0263-2373(99)00084-5

Lin, P., Abney, K., & Bekey, G. A. (Eds.). (2014). *Robot Ethics: The Ethical and Social Implications of Robotics, Intelligent Robotics and Autonomous Agents*. Cambridge, MA: MIT Press.

Lovelock, C. H., & Yip, G. S. (1996). Developing Global Strategies for Service Businesses. *California Management Review, 38*(2), 64–86. doi:10.2307/41165833

Miles, G., Miles, R. E., Perrone, V., & Edvinsson, L. (1998). Some Conceptual and Research Barriers to the Utilization of Knowledge. *California Management Review, 40*(3), 281–288. doi:10.2307/41165956

Miles, M. P., Munilla, L. S., & Russel, G. R. (1997). Marketing and Environmental Registration/Certification: What Industrial Marketers Should Understand about ISO 14000. *Industrial Marketing Management, 26*(4), 363–370. doi:10.1016/S0019-8501(96)00144-7

Mizuno, K. (2002). Leading by Example. *ISO Management Systems*, 21.

Nicolau, J. L., & Sellers, R. (2002). The stock Market's Reaction to Quality Certification: Empirical Evidence from Spain. *European Journal of Operational Research, 142*(3), 632–641. doi:10.1016/S0377-2217(01)00312-5

OECD. (1999). *Regulatory Reform and International Standardization (Working Party of the Trade Committee No. TD/TC/WP(98)36/FINAL)*. Paris: Organization for Economic Cooperation and Development. Retrieved from https://www.oecd.org/tad/benefitlib/1955309.pdf

Robbins, L. (2007). *An Essay on the Nature and Significance of Economic Science*. Macmillan and Co. (Original work published 1932)

Rothery, B. (1995, November). Why ISO 14000 Will Catch ISO 9000. *Manufacturing Engineering*.

Sales, Darmois, Papadimitriou, & Bourse. (2012). A Systematic Approach for Closing the Research to Standardization Gap. *The Future Internet*, 18–29.

Schepel, H. (2005). *The Constitution of Private Governance: Product Standards in the Regulation of Integrating Markets* (Vol. 4). Oxford, UK: Hart Publishing.

Schmidt, S. K., & Werle, R. (1998). *Coordinating Technology. Studies in the International Standardization of Telecommunications*. Cambridge, MA: MIT Press.

Seddon, J. (2000). *The Case against ISO 9000*. Oak Tree Press.

Sklyarova, M., & Kobets, T. (2011). *Eco-efficiency for Sustainability: IKEA's Environmental Policy in Russia* (Master's thesis). Gotland University. Retrieved from www.diva-portal.org/smash/get/diva2:420853/FULLTEXT01.pdfEco-efficiency

Stevenson, T. H., & Barnes, F. C. (2002). What Industrial Marketers Need to Know Now about ISO 9000 Certification: A Review, Update, and Integration with Marketing. *Industrial Marketing Management, 31*(8), 695–703. doi:10.1016/S0019-8501(01)00180-8

Swaminathan, J. M. (2001). Enabling Customization Using Standardized Operations. *California Management Review, 43*(3), 125–135. doi:10.2307/41166092

Toth, R. B. (1997). *Profiles of National Standards-Related Activities*. National Institute for Standards and Technology. Retrieved from http://ts.nist.gov/Standards/Global/upload/912intro.pdf

Tzelepis, D., Tsekouras, K., Skuras, D., & Dimara, E. (2006). The Effects of ISO 9001 on Firms' Productive Efficiency. *International Journal of Operations & Production Management, 26*(10), 1146–1165. doi:10.1108/01443570610691111

Vlachos, N. A., Michail, C., & Sotiropoulou, D. (2002). Is ISO/IEC 17025 Accreditation a Benefit or Hindrance to Testing Laboratories? The Greek Experience. *Journal of Food Composition and Analysis, 15*(6), 749–757. doi:10.1006/jfca.2002.1097

von Zedtwitz, M., & Gassmann, O. (2002). Market Versus Technology Drive in R&D Internationalization: Four Different Patterns of Managing Research and Development. *Research Policy, 31*(4), 569–588. doi:10.1016/S0048-7333(01)00125-1

Weaver, M., Hern, A., Bekiempis, V., Hepler, L., & Fermoso, J. (2018). Google Walkout: Global Protests after Sexual Misconduct Allegations. *The Guardian*. Retrieved from https://www.theguardian.com/technology/2018/nov/01/google-walkout-global-protests-employees-sexual-harassment-scandals

Whitney, A. M. (1997). *The Ethical Implications of ISO 9001 Implementation Practices* (Master's thesis). San Jose State University. Retrieved from http://scholarworks.sjsu.edu/etd_theses/1613

Willemse, H., de Vries, H. J., & Dul, J. (2006). Balancing Stakeholder Representation: An Example of Stakeholder Involvement in Ergonomics Standardization. In *Handbook of Standards and Guidelines in Ergonomics and Human Factors*. Mahwah, NJ: Lawrence Erlbaum Associates.

Williams, B. (1985). *Ethics and the Limits of Philosophy*. Cambridge, MA: Harvard University Press.

World Trade Organization. (2005). *World Trade Report 2005: Exploring the Links between Trade, Standards and the WTO*. Geneva: World Trade Organization. Retrieved from www.wto.org/english/res_e/booksp_e/anrep_e/world_trade_report05_e.pdf

ENDNOTES

1 For a detailed discussion of the history, concepts, and different meanings of ethics and morality, see Gordon (2013).

2 It is not by coincidence that we introduce this synonym to the word standard, but to reinforce the relationship between ethics and standards through the generally accepted concepts of "ethical norm" and/or "moral norm".

3 Anticipatory standards, as contrasted to de facto standards, are developed to bring new standards to the market; that is, they are expected to result in new processes or products, thus effectively changing the market.

4 One classical source of stakeholder analysis in support of ethical considerations in decision making by businesses is Goodpaster (1991). For a more recent approach that is critical of the concept of stakeholders in the context of business ethics, see Heath (2006).

5 The following alternatives are not new but have been articulated previously by several different scholars.

6 Besides this option of a prominent, controlling role for government, another commonly practiced, softer form of government intervention in promoting specific kinds of standards is to mandate procurement policies favoring government-backed standards (Fomin, Pedersen, and de Vries 2008, 469).

Chapter 10
Managing Responsible Standardization of Smart Infrastructures and Applications

Kai Jakobs
RWTH Aachen University, Germany

ABSTRACT

Interoperability standards are a sine-qua-non for smart applications and the underlying smart communication infrastructure. This chapter looks at two issues that are associated with the standardization of such smart systems and the ramifications they may have for standardization management. These issues include, on the one hand, the necessary multi-disciplinarity of standards setting and the resulting diversity of stakeholders to be involved. On the other hand, they also include the need to standardize responsibly (i.e., to appreciate that various societal aspects also need to be taken seriously and to be integrated into the process). The complexity of proper standardization management will increase because of these needs.

BACKGROUND

Smart Systems

Smart systems are a fairly recent trend that is increasingly gathering momentum. Thanks to the convergence of Information and Communication Technologies (ICT) and 'traditional' technologies smart applications possess advanced control and amenability functions previously available only in the virtual world. Prominent examples include the Smart Grid, Smart Manufacturing, Intelligent Transport Systems, Smart Homes and Smart Cities. To offer the user 'smart' applications, these systems require a communication infrastructure which, in turn, will typically be based on the Internet of Things (IoT), and Cyber Physical Systems (CPSs). Forecasts indicate anything between 20 and 50 billion IoT devices for the year 2020 .

DOI: 10.4018/978-1-5225-9008-8.ch010

Copyright © 2019, IGI Global. Copying or distributing in print or electronic forms without written permission of IGI Global is prohibited.

Interoperability is the key requirement for all smart systems. To achieve interoperability between an extremely broad spectrum of devices and applications, internationally agreed standards are indispensible. For individual smart systems, these standards have been, and are still being, developed by different groups of stakeholders in different Standards Setting Organisations (SSOs). Taken together, these standards will eventually enable the technical development of smart systems towards true ubiquity.

Today, the 'ubiquity' (anywhere, anytime, any device) of the Internet refers only to its accessibility. In contrast, the IoT's billions of sensors of will collect data and make them available for users of smart applications. A considerable part of this data will be personal or private. Moreover, the results of the analysis of this massive amount of data may have major economic, ecological and other ramifications and directly impact citizens and businesses alike. Accordingly, potentially severe policy and ethical issues need to be addressed in the context of smart systems and their underlying standardization processes. Perhaps most prominently, these must include security and privacy aspects of both data and communication.

That is, for policy and, specifically, ethical issues to play a role already during smart systems standards development initiatives, overarching 'Responsible Standardisation' (RS) guidelines are needed at European and/or the global level. They would ensure that standardisation initiatives take into account internationally agreed non-technical (specifically ethical) aspects to be associated with a certain technology.

Standardisation of smart systems has started only comparably recently, with its focus still largely on the communication infrastructure. Giving the complexity of smart systems, their broad variety of stakeholders and the resulting multi-disciplinarity of both the systems design and the underlying standardisation process it should still be possible to introduce RS in the field. However, the sooner action will be taken the better.

Looking specifically at Research and Innovation (R&I) and Responsible Standardisation (RS) in smart technologies yields the model depicted in Figure 1. It shows that R&I on the one hand trigger standardisation in the field, mostly through their need for interoperability. On the other hand they also generate the need to consider ethical aspects to cover security and privacy issues and to adequately address the fact that smart technologies will eventually be truly all-embracing. Taken together, this yields the need for a responsible standardisation of smart technologies.

Standardisation Management

Basically, corporate standardisation management is the grand total of a firm's activities that aim at deploying standards and at influencing the standards setting process, typically in the firm's best interest. Figure 2 shows a very simple model.

Figure 1. The need for responsible standardisation

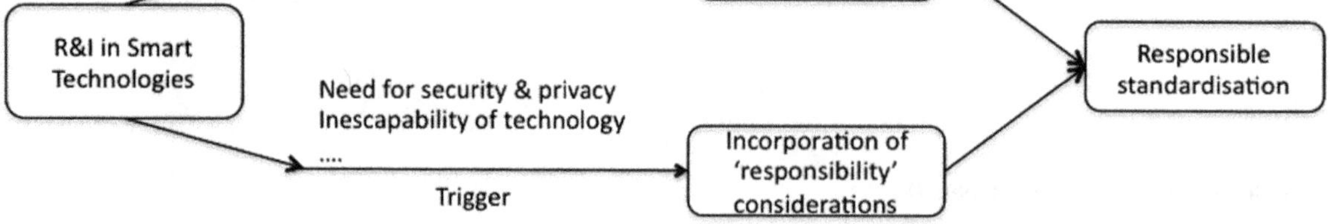

Figure 2. A Very simple view of what influences a standard
(adapted from Jakobs, 2015)

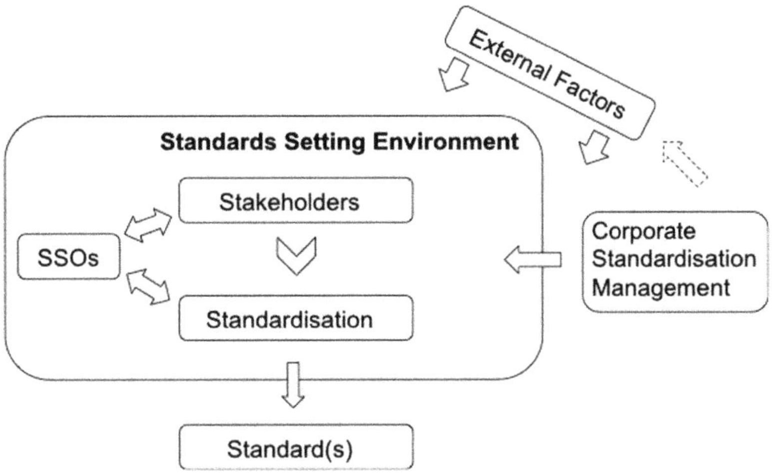

Trying to influence the external factors will be extremely difficult and perhaps next to impossible in most cases. These factors include, for example, regulatory aspects, technical progress and societal values.

Things look different for the individual elements within the standard setting environment (in Fig. 2). Firms typically represent the most powerful class of stakeholders. That is, at least large firms may have the power to influence the standardisation process (e.g. by assuming leading roles and/or by having their position represented by knowledgeable people) and thus its final outcome, the standard. Similarly, a firm may be able to influence e.g. the rules and bylaws of an SSO, including, for example, the implementation of a more favourable (from the firm's point of view) IPR (Intellectual Property Rights) regime.

As noted above, people play a decisive role. After all, those who populate an SSO's working groups and committees will eventually define the functionality and characteristics of a standard, not least including the incorporated IPR, which may well be an important source of future revenues for a company. Accordingly, hiring experienced, knowledgeable and well-respected people for standards setting, training them and generally keeping them sweet may well pay off nicely.

The above holds for all fields of standards setting (perhaps with varying levels of importance of IPR, which is currently of the highest relevance in the telecommunication sector). It also holds for the standardisation of smart systems. However, here, a number of additional factors also need to be considered. For one, applications' 'smartness' is the result of the integration of ICT into 'traditional' technologies (see also above). Yet, ICT standards are developed mostly by engineers and computer scientists. For smart, converging technologies, such 'mono-disciplinarity' will be inadequate. Accordingly, in most such cases a company will need to send multi-disciplinary teams of standards-settters to WG meetings in order to be able to adequately address the diverse technical challenges. This is a new requirement that will not be that easy to meet, certainly for most ICT companies.

Multi-disciplinarity is a defining characteristic of smart systems and, specifically, of smart applications. Accordingly, not just people from different backgrounds need to co-operate, but also different SSOs; no current single SSO has the expertise and the resources to cover all highly diverse aspects of smart systems. Yet, co-operation of SSOs from different sectors, with e.g. different cultures, traditions and technology life cycles represents another new problem that will need to be taken into account also by firms' standardisation management.

Last, but most definitely not least, the far-reaching societal implications smart applications will have triggers the need for a more 'responsible' process. That is, not unlike responsible research and innovation (RRI) standardisation will need to take into account societal, ethical and other decidedly non-technical aspects. At least for most ICT companies this is a completely new aspect and thus another issue to be dealt with by standardisation management.

The following sections will discuss the current state-of-the-art in the standardisation of smart technologies, and in responsible standardisation. The final section will briefly address some of the ramifications systems' smartness will have for corporate standardisation management.

STANDARDISATION OF SMART TECHNOLOGIES[1]

General

Standards for a smart communication infrastructure typically target (power-)constrained devices. Relevant activities in this field are ongoing in e.g. oneM2M, where standards for a common Machine-to-Machine (M2M) Service Layer are being developed. Within the European Telecommunications Standards Institute (ETSI), the 'Smart M2M Communications' committee works on the interface between the service layer and the application layer. Other ETSI Technical Committees (TCs) as well as groups of the Institute of Electrical and Electronics Engineers (IEEE), the International Telecommunication Union (ITU) and several other SSOs work on wireless applications. Within the Internet Engineering Task Force (IETF), several Working Groups (WGs) focus on constrained devices.

According to the International Organization for Standardization (ISO), over 900 IoT-related standards had been developed by late 2016. Of those, around 140 came from the IEEE, 200 from ITU and 300 from the joint committee for ICT standardisation of the ISO and the International Electrotechnical Committee (IEC; ISO/IEC JTC1). However, most of these are rather more generic standards in the field of wireless communication systems that were not necessarily developed specifically for the IoT but may well be deployed by it as well.

The number of entities that are devoted to the standardisation of a particular technology may be seen as an indicator of the increasing perceived (market) relevance of this technology. For a smart infrastructure and for several smart applications this number has skyrocketed over the past eight years (Jakobs, 2018).

Convergence of formerly separate technologies has been an ongoing trend over several decades. The – almost completed – integration of (tele)communication and information technology led to ICT. More recent examples of smart application areas include, among others, Intelligent Transport Systems (Transport Telematics, Traffic Engineering, Power Engineering, Automotive, ICT), Smart Manufacturing (Production Engineering, Robotics, Control Engineering, ICT) and the Smart Grid (SG; Power Engineering, ICT).

Cyber-security and privacy are other important fields of standards setting in which a vast array of SSOs are active (including e.g. ITU, ISO, IEC, CEN, ETSI, W3C, OASIS and the IETF). Security encompasses a set of services, including authentication, authorisation, integrity and confidentiality. Moreover, privacy needs to be guaranteed and, ideally, mechanisms to support the development of a certain level of trust between parties should be provided.

Virtually all smart application areas have strong security requirements; accordingly, industry concerns also very much focus on this aspect (Li et al., 2015). These concerns as well need to be addressed by standardisation. Security and privacy issues also have major legal ramifications. Stuurman (2017l discusses these issues against the background of the European General Data Protection Regulation (GDPR; EU, 2016).

Security and privacy concerns are not unique to smart systems – a large number of protocols to ensure them already exist. Accordingly, one might be tempted to think there is no real need to design new, dedicated security protocols for a smart infrastructure (Keoh et al., 2014). Yet, the major issue that stands in the way of a one-to-one adoption of existing protocols is – again – the power-constrainedness of embedded 'smart' devices (like sensors and actuators), which will represent the vast majority of smart infrastructure nodes. As a consequence, additional efforts will need to go into the adaptation of existing protocols to the limited capabilities of these devices. This may well amount to the development of dedicated, IoT-specific security mechanisms (see e.g. Keoh et al., 2014; Sicari et al., 2015).

Multi-Disciplinarity

Until not so long ago standardisation was mostly a rather 'mono-disciplinary' activity. More recently, convergence of formerly separate technologies has been an emerging development. For instance, the integration of (tele)communication and information technology led to ICT. The integration of ICT, in turn, instils smartness into more 'traditional' applications. Examples of resulting smart application areas are given in Table 1.

In a way, Smart Cities represent the ultimate smart application, being more or less a superset of the others. Here in particular, the development of meaningful standards, i.e. standards that are not just technically sound, but also economically viable, sustainable and of societal value (see also below) will necessitate the participation of an extremely wide range of stakeholders. In addition to representatives of the numerous technical disciplines listed in Table 1 these also include other groups that are not normally represented in standards setting like citizens, NGOs, unions and perhaps also politicians, sociologists and philosophers.

This involvement may materialise in different forms. Joint participation in one WG would be one option. In this case, major problems likely to be encountered may be expected to relate to the actual active involvement of the more 'exotic' (non-technical) stakeholders. If a realistic way to achieve this can be found, the lack of a common ground and of mutual understanding will have to be overcome before meaningful standardisation work may commence. This is a problem generally encountered in multi-disciplinary co-operation (see e.g. Bruce et al., 2004) and standardisation is no exception.

Table 1. Disciplines involved in different application areas (no claim for completeness)

Industry 4.0	Intelligent Transport Systems	Smart Grid	Smart Cities
Production Engineering Tele-communication Computer Science Robotics Control Engineering	Transport Telematics Traffic Engineering Power Engineering Automotive Computer Science, Tele-communication	Power Engineering Computer Science Tele-communication	The grand total of the others plus City planning Economics Environmental studies .....

Close co-operation between different more or less 'mono-disciplinary' WGs would be another option. In this case, the issue of broad stakeholder involvement would still persist. In addition, the problem of different boundary conditions of the different WGs would play a role. The boundary conditions in ICT standardisation are different from those in most other areas. These reasons include, for example, ICT's typically short technology life cycle, the importance of Intellectual Property Rights (IPR) and generally the amount of money that may be at stake. Different standardisation 'cultures' represent a related problem. In practice, these differences result, on the one hand, in the particularly formal processes and procedures of, for example, the ITU and on the other hand in the rather more 'chaotic'[2] approach of e.g. the IETF.

The standardisation environment in the ICT sector is rather unique, not least due to the importance of private standards consortia whose time-frames, rules, processes and by-laws may differ considerably from those of the formal Standards Developing Organisations (SDOs). These differences will not exactly help to simplify co-operation either.

Virtually all smart applications have strong security and privacy requirements. These requirements also need to be addressed by standardisation. Ideally, approaches like 'privacy by design' (see e.g. Langheinrich, 2001) should be adapted to – and adopted by – standards setting.

RESPONSIBLE RESEARCH AND INNOVATION

Research and innovation (R&I) need to be guided to address the various challenges society faces. This holds all the more for R&I in smart applications. Responsible Research and Innovation (RRI) provides guidelines to address these challenges. V. Schomberg (2013) defines RRI as "*a transparent, interactive process by which societal actors and innovators become mutually responsive to each other with a view to the (ethical) acceptability, sustainability and societal desirability of the innovation process and its marketable products (in order to allow a proper embedding of scientific and technological advances in our society)*".

Stilgoe et al. (2013) propose four dimensions of RRI. These dimensions also emerged as the result of an in-depth literature review (Burget et al., 2017). They include

- **Anticipation:** To adopt a forward view that takes into account opportunities, risks, environmental concerns, etc.
- **Inclusion:** To enlist 'new voices' that may challenge long-standing approaches.
- **Reflexivity:** To put research into context through regular questions regarding norms and values.
- **Responsiveness:** To adapt as experience is gained and knowledge is built.

That is, not just technical and economic, but also e.g. societal, ethical and environmental aspects shall be taken into account during the innovation process. This, in turn, means that a broad range of stakeholders has to be involved in the process, notably those that are not normally involved in R&I (e.g. consumers, NGOs, etc.).

V. Schomberg (2103) identifies four types of irresponsible innovation:

- Technology push;
- Policy pull;
- Negligence of fundamental ethical principles;

- Lack of precautionary measures and technology foresight.

The latter implies that e.g. technology assessment needs to be applied in order to detect potentially undesired outcomes of the deployment process and to take appropriate counter-measures as early as possible. This holds particularly for innovations in new and hardly understood technologies such as nanotechnology and smart technologies, for which standards are essential not only as technical 'guarantors' of interoperability, but also as socio-ethical frameworks.

Using ICT as an example, Jirotka et al. (2016) first note that applicable professional guidelines and codes of conduct have been in place for a while, but question their relevance and suitability for future developments. They also develop an adaptable framework (the AREA Plus Framework) that shall enable and support expert discourses on RRI.

All this may also be said about standards setting (see also above). Therefore, responsible standardisation is something that needs to be introduced. After all, standardisation represents (one of) the earliest design stage(s), during which a future technology is shaped (Williams & Edge, 1996).

Wickson & Forsberg (2015) refer to standardisation as a "*...kind of interstitial space because it effectively occupies a location somewhere between what are currently recognized as key domains, e.g. those of science, policy, civil society and industry*". This space, or rather its output, has a tremendous albeit usually overlooked impact in almost all sectors. The at one time popular perception that standards largely hamper innovation has recently been disbanded. (Swan & Lambert, 2010) and (Swann, 2010), for example, show that standards can do both, hamper and enable innovation and that the latter effect is much more pronounced. Blind (2013) highlights the fact that both standardisation and standards can be used to promote innovation, especially in relation to research, IPR and public procurement.

Three orthogonal types of approaches to link RRI to standardisation may be identified:

- To deploy standardisation to strengthen RRI.

(Jacob et al., 2013) observe that one option would be "*... linking research projects with standardisation activities, because national and European standardisation bodies provide the platform for the involvement of all interested stakeholders to participate in the development of standards, which reflect not only the interests of industry and research, but also representatives of societal interests, ...*".

- To develop Standards *for* RRI.

A number of standards have been developed that could be of relevance for RRI. At the more general level, these include e.g. the ISO 26000 series on Corporate Social Responsibility and the ISO 31000 series on Risk Management. Closer to the field of smart systems, (ITU-T, 2015), for instance, offers an in-depth discussion of the roles of the different groups of stakeholders in the standardisation of smart cities. Moreover, a number of ITU-T Technical Reports discuss aspects relating to sustainable cities.

- To apply RRI principles in standards setting.

Applying RRI principles not just in innovation but also in standards setting (which may well be a very early stage in an innovation process) is perhaps the most important aspect and should help make standards more credible and legitimate.

This holds particularly with respect to the involvement of the widest possible variety of stakeholders, both technical and societal. Sadly, this is not normally the case in the ICT sector (see above and e.g. Werle & Iversen, 2006). Here, SMEs (Small and Medium-sized Enterprises), users, consumers, NGOs and other societal stakeholders are dramatically under-represented (forming the 'Third Estate' in standards setting; Jakobs, 2005).

SOME BRIEF CONCLUDING REMARKS

From a standardisation management point of view the issues sketched above create a number of challenges. For one, the need to standardise smart systems is likely to bring about changes in the standardisation environment. Specifically, these changes will be triggered by the increasingly emerging need for multi-disciplinary standardisation on the one hand. On the other hand, the societal ramifications smart systems may have are currently entirely unclear. To change that situation and to at least try to make sure that these new technologies are actually beneficial to the widest possible range of stakeholders – particularly including societal ones – adequate forecasting exercises should be incorporated already into the earliest stages of research and innovation, notably including the developments of standards.

Regarding the former, standardisation management will need to cope with an increasingly complex environment, with new players emerging at an almost alarming rate (see e.g. Jakobs, 2018). The relevance of these players will have to be thoroughly evaluated; membership may have to be applied for and active participation be started if need be.

This brings us to the latter aspect. The merger of ICT with many different 'traditional' technologies implies that contributions from both sides will be essential for meaningful standards for smart systems. Moreover, the fairly close integration to be expected implies that representatives from both sides will need to co-operate very closely. In addition, a good understanding and appreciation of the associated ethical issues would be highly desirable. That is, ICT experts should also have some expertise in the respective application domain, and vice versa. Last, but definitely mot least and related to the previous point, representatives should also have a reasonable mutual understanding of the problems and requirements of the respective other side. From a standardisation management perspective, this implies the need for new and more diverse internal expertise, probably including the need to hire people to provide it.

The above is mostly due to the likely future true ubiquity and inescapability of smart applications. To actually reach the necessary levels of credibility and legitimacy for these technologies RRI principles will need to be applied to their standardisation. Along similar lines, these technologies not just need to be technically sophisticated and economically viable but first and foremost be sustainable and of societal value. To this end, both individuals and the various SSOs, from very different backgrounds and sectors, respectively, will need to co-operate very closely.

Again thanks to the ubiquity of smart applications this process will have to involve all stakeholders. This need, in turn, is highly likely to affect individual SSOs, the links that exist between them and thus the standardisation landscape as such.

REFERENCES

Blind, K. (2013). *The impact of standardisation and standards on innovation*. Retrieved from http://www.innovation-policy.org.uk/share/14_The%20Impact%20of%20Standardization%20and%20Standards%20on%20Innovation.pdf

Bruce, A., Lyall, C., Tait, J., & Williams, R. (2004). Interdisciplinary integration in Europe: The case of the Fifth Framework programme. *Futures*, *36*(4), 457–470. doi:10.1016/j.futures.2003.10.003

Burget, M., Bardone, E., & Pedaste, M. (2017). Definitions and conceptual dimensions of responsible research and innovation: A literature review. *Science and Engineering Ethics*, *23*(1), 1–19. doi:10.100711948-016-9782-1 PMID:27090147

EU. (Ed.). (2016). *Regulation (EU) 2016/679 – General Data Protection Regulation (GDPR)*. Retrieved from http://ec.europa.eu/justice/data-protection/reform/files/regulation_oj_en.pdf

ITU-T. (2015). *Focus Group on Smart Sustainable Cities – Technical Report – Setting the stage for stakeholders' engagement in smart sustainable cities*. Retrieved from http://www.itu.int/en/ITU-T/focusgroups/ssc/Documents/website/web-fg-ssc-0113-r9-SSC-stakeholders.docx

Jacob, K. (2005). The Role of the 'Third Estate' in ICT Standardisation. In S. Bolin (Ed.), *The Standards Edge: Future Generation*. The Bolin Group.

Jakobs, K. (2015). Standardisation Management – Some Lessons to be Learnt. In K. Bergh Skriver, K. Jakobs, & J. Jerlang (Eds.), *The Role of Standards in Transatlantic Trade and Regulation. EURAS contributions to standardisation research* (Vol. 9). Mainz Publishers.

Jakobs, K. (2018). Standardizing the IoT and its Applications – Learning from the Past?! In *Internet of Things – Concepts, Technologies, Applications, and Implementations* (pp. 191–218). IEEE. doi:10.1002/9781119456735.ch7

Jakobs, K. (2019). Responsible Standardisation of 'Smart' Applications. In *Proc. 17th Int. Conf. on e-Society*. IADIS.

Jirotka, M., Grimpe, B., Stahl, B., Eden, G., & Hartswood, M. (2016). Responsible research and innovation in the digital age. *Communications of the ACM*.

Keoh, S. L., Kumar, S. S., & Tschofenig, H. (2014). Securing the internet of things: A standardization perspective. *IEEE Internet of Things Journal*, *1*(3), 265–275. doi:10.1109/JIOT.2014.2323395

Langheinrich, M. (2001). Privacy by design – principles of privacy-aware ubiquitous systems. In *International conference on Ubiquitous Computing* (pp. 273-291). Springer. 10.1007/3-540-45427-6_23

Li, S., Tryfonas, T., & Li, H. (2016). The Internet of Things: A security point of view. *Internet Research*, *26*(2), 337–359. doi:10.1108/IntR-07-2014-0173

Sicari, S., Rizzardi, A., Grieco, L. A., & Coen-Porisini, A. (2015). Security, privacy and trust in Internet of Things: The road ahead. *Computer Networks*, *76*, 146–164. doi:10.1016/j.comnet.2014.11.008

Stilgoe, J., Owen, R., & Macnaghten, P. (2013). Developing a Framework for Responsible Innovation. *Research Policy*, *42*(9), 1568–1580. doi:10.1016/j.respol.2013.05.008

Stuurman, K. (2017). The Digitisation Driven Impact of Data Protection Regulation on the Standardisation Process. In *Digitalisation: Challenge and Opportunity for Standardisation. Proc. 22nd EURAS Annual Standardisation Conference. EURAS contributions to standardisation research* (vol. 12). Mainz Publishers.

Swann, G. M. P. (2010). *The Economics of Standardization: An Update*. Report for the UK Department of Business, Innovation and Skills (BIS). Retrieved from https://www.gov.uk/government/uploads/system/uploads/attachment_data/file/461419/The_Economics_of_Standardization_-_an_update_.pdf

Swann, G. M. P., & Lambert, R. (2010). Why do Standards Enable and Constrain Innovation? In *Services Standardisation. Proceedings of the 15th EURAS Conference. EURAS contributions to standardisation research* (vol. 2). Mainz Academic Publishers.

Von Schomberg, R. (2013). A vision of responsible innovation. In R. Owen, M. Heintz, & J. Bessant (Eds.), *Responsible innovation: Managing the responsible innovation of science and innovation in society* (pp. 51–74). Wiley. doi:10.1002/9781118551424.ch3

Werle, R., & Iversen, E. J. (2006). Promoting legitimacy in technical standardization. Science. *Technology and Innovation Studies*, *2*, 19–39.

Wickson, F., & Forsberg, E. M. (2015). Standardising responsibility? The significance of interstitial spaces. *Science and Engineering Ethics*, *21*(5), 1159–1180. doi:10.100711948-014-9602-4 PMID:25344842

Williams, R., & Edge, D. (1996). The social shaping of technology. *Research Policy*, *25*(6), 865–899. doi:10.1016/0048-7333(96)00885-2

ENDNOTES

1 This section and the subsequent ones are based on Jakobs (2019).

2 Not meant in any derogatory way.

Section 4
Legal Aspects

Chapter 11
Licensing Terms for IoT Standard-Setting:
Do We Need "End-User" or "License for All" Concepts?

Matt Heckman
Zuyd University of Applied Science, The Netherlands & Maastricht University, The Netherlands

ABSTRACT

The development of 5G and IoT standards requires an active participation of small and medium-sized companies (SMEs). These SMEs do not always have the resources and expertise to participate in the work of standard development organizations (SDOs). The valuation of the patents in standards can be based on "license for all" or "end-user" concepts. A specific choice for use-based licensing terms by an SDO might drive SMEs more towards standard-setting in consortia. The chapter will discuss the competition law aspects of both licensing concepts for SMEs and the recent communication in this field by the EU Commission.

INTRODUCTION

The intersection of standard setting, IPRs and competition law has become more and more complex in recent years. In a way, standards have some of the same characteristics as IP rights. From an economic perspective, they both produce increased welfare through product improvement, not a process which decreases the marginal costs of the product. Standardization increases the societal value by improving both the horizontal and vertical compatibility of products and thereby also creating a downstream market. Standardization also makes products available at a fair price to producers and consumers. This standardization eco-system strongly depends on the willingness of companies (e.g. SMEs) to participate and share their proprietary solutions. The management of standardization and the treatment of intellectual property rights is therefore a crucial factor in the decision-making process of companies. Research shows that the IPR-policies of standardization bodies is a crucial element for the decision whether to invest and participate in standard setting activities.

DOI: 10.4018/978-1-5225-9008-8.ch011

Copyright © 2019, IGI Global. Copying or distributing in print or electronic forms without written permission of IGI Global is prohibited.

In the present standard-setting environment, patents are still a predominant feature, despite the rise of open source development. Companies like IBM publicly favour open source development of their technology but they carefully administer and manage their patent portfolios. A patent portfolio illustrates the innovativeness of a firm and can be reflected in a specific marketing policy. The use of patents in a proposed standard can suggest and underline the exclusivity of the related product or service and can directly exclude competitors from using the standard. More importantly, patents are used as trade tools to do business with competitors via cross-licensing. The role of patents in a standard-setting context is of growing concern for competition authorities. A patent will automatically involve a certain amount of coordination between the patent holder and the implementer of the technology. The high number of patents in a standard will automatically lead to intense contacts between various firms in different stages of the commercialization of products and or services. Some scholars argue that a patent licensing agreement constitutes by nature a settlement of a dispute on intellectual property rights. The licensing agreement royalty rate is heavily influenced by the technical ability of the licensee to develop possible alternative technologies. If the licensee can use alternative technologies, this reduces his dependence on the patents of the licensor. Even the instrument of cross-licensing, which is very common in the standard- setting process, is dictated by the weight of the respective IP portfolios of the different participating companies. The economic value of the IPRs in mergers and acquisitions and the strategic management thereof also requires careful consideration.

The intersection of standard setting, IPRs and competition law has become more and more complex in recent years. In a way, standards have some of the same characteristics as IP rights. From an economic perspective, they both produce increased welfare through product improvement, not a process which decreases the marginal costs of the product. Standardization increases the societal value by improving both the horizontal and vertical compatibility of products and thereby also creating a downstream market. At the same time, standard setting facilitates exclusion (a common feature of patent rights) and collusion. As a result, antitrust authorities should identify the circumstances that lead to anticompetitive effects of the use of standards and pay special attention to these circumstances, possibly addressing them through their regulatory frameworks.

PATENTS INCLUDED IN STANDARDS AND COMPETITION LAW CONCERNS

The registered patent gives the patent owner the right to exclude others from using his technology. The patent owner can give other firms access to his inventions via the method of licensing. Licensing can create more revenues for the patent owner and leads to increased diffusion and dissemination of the innovative goods. The economic impact and contribution to competitiveness is mostly determined by the licensing terms. Patent owners can license individual patents or, more often, use package deals which offer a lower royalty fee than the total sum resulting from all the individual pa- tents. Two or more firms holding substantial IP portfolios (or even a firm just holding one essential patent to the technology), use cross-licensing to exchange their valuable IP-assets. In the case of cross-licensing, all companies are entitled to use each other's patents, often without charging any reciprocal royalties.

From the perspective of competition policy enforcers, this is almost ideal, since there is dissemination and diffusion of the patented technology without any increase in the marginal costs of the firms involved. At first sight it looks like cross-licensing should not involve any antitrust concerns, but in the case of probabilistic patents, invalid patents or patents of bad quality, the barter-trade assumption upon which the cross-license is based is no longer valid and could lead to competition policy concerns. In the case of Non-Practicing Entities (NPEs), cross-licensing is much more complicated, since these firms only monetize their intellectual property rights and are not actively involved in innovative efforts themselves.

Making general statements in this field can be hazardous, since the specific characteristics of individual markets dictate their preferences in relation to the handling of IPRs in standards and, accordingly, competition authorities should also distinguish their enforcement approach. In the case of the Internet of Things (IoT) concepts such as switching costs and lock-in effects must be evaluated in relation to the special dynamics of the relevant market. For this market, the switching costs do not only apply to the purchase of the original (primary) good but also to the purchase decisions relating to complementary (secondary) goods in the downstream market. The definition of secondary markets within the recent rate of development in telecommunications is not easy and the case law in the three different jurisdictions (especially in the US) has so far been contradictory. Most SDOs require their members to disclose intellectual property rights and licensing terms. The traditional answer has been that essential patents must be licensed on FRAND terms. This has led to a global debate on the precise content of the FRAND conditions.

THE EU GUIDELINES ON HORIZONTAL COOPERATION AGREEMENTS

Standardization agreements are regulated by the Guidelines on Horizontal Cooperation Agreements, which were adopted by the Commission in December 2010. One of the main principles is that the Commission can mandate a standard development organization (SDO) to develop a standard and use this later as a basis for a new regulation. The presence of patents in the standard changes the open standard into a closed standard protected by IPRs. Ownership of the most important patents, standard essential patents (SEPs), can confer market power on the patent owners, especially in the case of overlapping IPR ownership. In the Guidelines, the competition policy concerns start with the fact that the ownership and exercise of SEPs may give the owners control over the relevant product or service market. This control may constitute a barrier for competitors to enter this relevant market. The dominant position gives firms the opportunity to:

- Charge exceptionally and/or discriminatory royalty rates
- Refuse to license the SEPs to other firms
- Thus restrict access to the standard and, consequently, to the market for other companies.

The problem is that the level of market power can only be examined on an individual basis, so the Guidelines do not use the presumption that the ownership of SEPs automatically leads to market dominance.

The Safe Harbor Provision for Standardization Agreements

The Guidelines on the horizontal co-operation agreements provide a safe harbor exception for standardization agreements that are capable of creating market dominance but are acceptable if they meet the following criteria:

- Agreements should not have the obligation that parties must comply with the standard in question.
- Participation in standard setting must be unrestricted and accessible to all concerned parties in the relevant market.
- The selection procedure for creating the standard must be transparent.
- *Ex ante* good faith disclosure of SEPS are undertaken by the participating parties in the development process of the standard.
- Licensing is on basis of FRAND commitments. [1]

The Guidelines provide the following comments on the key provisions of para. 280,

Unrestricted Participation and Transparency: "All firms in the relevant technology market have the opportunity to participate in the formulation of the standard. Transparency must guarantee that the participating firms can get the relevant information on the standard-setting process at any moment." (European Commission, 2014, par. 280).

In reality firms do not only choose Standard Development Organizations (SDOs) as the outlet for their joint R&D efforts. Often firms use a consortia-driven standard–setting model. Lundqvist argues that the consortia-model of standard-setting also includes joint R&D as well (Lundqvist,, 2015). Competition authorities do have difficulties with the assessment of pre-standardization consortia. Baron and Pohlmann (2013) raised the concern that the establishment of pre-standardization consortia that conduct joint R&D might lead to majority voting blocks when the standard would be adopted in a SDO. The formation of consortia can have a possible anti-competitive effect when their standards creation excludes de facto competitors from entering the market with alternative standards and or technologies. The obvious reaction of consortia would be to show that they create efficiencies in joint R&D which is beneficial for consumer welfare. The efficiencies can also persuade SMEs to make a strategic choice for a consortia in relation to their standardization management. In terms of management, consortia can be smaller and more accessible than major SDOs.

The joint R&D by consortia has elements that are interesting for the competition policy discussion. The cooperation by the consortia members has to be judged by its effect on the market. One scenario could be that the consortia members hold the majority of Standard Essential Patents (SEPs) and consequently aim to replace the current standard. The EU Commission might recognize this scenario as a position of dominance. The EU R&D Block Exemption could qualify consortia members that are active on the market where the standard (by their joint R&D) was created, as competitors on this market. If the consortia members have SEPs that creates a separate market through its own technology, competitors cannot design around the SEPs resulting dominance.[2]

The 2014 Technology Transfer Block Exemption Regulation

The new TTBER was adopted on 21 March 2014 and entered into force on 1 May 2014. The TTBER includes a transitional period of one year which enables companies (if necessary) to change their agreements. It is remarkable that the new TTBER will run until 2026, which is an extension of two years above the normal duration of block exemption regulations. Especially on fast-moving technology markets, this results in both certainty but also sometimes lack of flexibility.

Regarding the main changes in the TTBER, it is important to understand that the new TTBER is subsidiary to the horizontal BERs on specialization and R&D. Because of the conflict of law rule, the application of the TTBER and the horizontal BERs simultaneously is not possible and the latter provisions prevail.

The system of the new TTBER uses the classification of hardcore restrictions and excluded restrictions. Agreements that contain hardcore provisions automatically fall outside the safe harbour. A major change was made in the field of the use of restrictions. Article 4 (2) states that licensees should be free to sell passively to any customer. Whereas hardcore restrictions have the presumption that they are negative, excluded restrictions do not affect the complete agreement. Only the restriction itself is not covered by the safe harbour, but the remaining part of the agreement is not affect- ed. A detailed reading of the new TTBER shows that the incentive to innovate is very important for the EU Commission. One example is that all exclusive grant-back provisions are now excluded restrictions. The exclusive character of the grant-back provision would mean that the licensee can no longer use his own invention. This would reduce the incentive to innovate for the licensee. Other changes relate to termination clauses that can have the same effect as non-challenge clauses. In general, non- challenge clauses may have a positive effect since they have a filtering function and can be used to distract invalid patents from technology markets. In the context of royalty negotiations for exclusive licenses between small licensors and (big company) licensees, the licensor can experience some negative effects. When termination clauses are part of non-exclusive agreements, they are classified as excluded restrictions.

The Guidelines of the new TTBER clarify the distinction between competitors and non-competitors on technology markets. The Commission paid attention to the problem of IP invalidity and the uncertainty that this creates on the market, and tried to provide more guidance. The Guidelines also clarify blocking situations with potential competitors.

The Anti-Competitive Risks of Standard-Setting by Consortia

The standard-setting by consortia bears several risks for the competitive environment. Consortia by nature, have the ability and potential to limit and restrict the access to the standardization process. Some authors also notice the risk of either over-standardization or under-standardization. Over-standardization leads to a situation wherein the very detailed character of the standard excludes other new technologies from entering the market. Under-standardization means that the depth or breadth of the standard is very narrowly defined which creates exclusive fields of use for certain patent holders. Given the size, consortia can be more transparent which provides advantages in relation to the management of the standardization process.

The most obvious concern of competition authorities is that consortia might initiate collusion in the choice of technology, resulting in sub-optimal technology to be chosen. In general the cooperation between members of the consortia enables information exchange or concerted practices that change the normal market conditions, hence violate competition law. Article 101(1) TFEU addresses the above-mentioned concerns of standard-setting by consortia. The possible exclusion of competitors from participation in consortia and the selection of sub-optimal technology will trigger the interest of the EU Commission.

The Guidelines on the Horizontal Block Exemption Regulation state that standardization agreement fall outside the scope of Article 101(1) TFEU when they meet the following conditions:

Open and non-restrictive agreements. Participation is unrestricted and non-discriminatory, with open and transparent procedures (European Commission, 2014, par. 168).

Minor agreements. Agreements that only have a negligible effect on the competition on the relevant market (European Commission, 2014, par. 164)

The Guidelines on Horizontal Agreements identify several scenario's that bring the consortia in a situation that might be caught by the prohibition of Art. 101(1) TFEU:

- It gives the consortia participants joint control over production and/or innovation.
- It limits the participants freedom to develop alternative technologies
- It may have anti-competitive effects on other markets than the product-market affected by the standard (European Commission, 2014, par. 166-167).

THE DEVELOPMENT OF 5G AND THE INTERNET OF THINGS (IOT) STANDARDS

The development of the 5G standard will see the implementation of a wide range of (consumer) products. The automotive industry, smart city development, new aircraft and household appliances will all incorporate IoT technology and standards. Implementers of this new IoT standardized technology will have to pay for the patented technology and traditionally rely on fair, reasonable and non-discriminatory (" FRAND") licensing terms. Since these new entrants to the licensing discussion come from a different industry tradition, experts expect an increase in the volume of disputes evolving on SEPs. Furthermore many of these new entrants/ implementers of the IoT-technology are small and medium-sized companies ("SMEs"). These SMEs usually do not often participate in standards development in SDOs. The development process in SDOs is a lengthy and costly process that does not match the resources and expertise of many SMEs. However a recent study shows that when SMEs do participate in the work of SDOs the acceptance rate of their technology in almost equal to that a larger companies (Gupta, 2017). A continuous and structural participation of SMEs in SDOs does not fit with their short-time objective to grow and make profit. This brings us to the heart of the discussion, how do we strike the right balance between innovators and implementers?

The Concept of "Use-Based" Licensing Terms

The European Union has expressed its intention to deploy 5G in the EU by 2025, as part of the Digital Single Market (European Commission, 2016). This objective can only be reached if the balance between innovators and implementers is reached by means of effective SEP-licensing. According to the EU Commission some of the licensing of the IoT-technology be in conjunction with non-EU based industries, which underlines the necessity to have a balanced and predictable system for SEP-licensing. The Commission identified in its recent communication, three possible challenges:

- Opaque information about SEP-exposure
- Unclear valuation of patented technologies
- Risks of uncertainty in enforcement

The EU Commission sees a clear task and role for the European Telecommunication Standards Institute (ETSI) and the European Patent Organization (EPO). At the same time the EU Commission notes that the role of SDOs in this process can only be very limited.[3] The EU Commission wants to give proper guidance on the valuation of SEPs and the practical application of the FRAND-principle. As one of the main reasons, the EU Commission explains that this guidance would encourage SMEs to increase their participation in standard-setting activities. The discussion on SEP-licensing terms has recently been divided in two different camps. The division is centered on the concept of "use-based" or "license for all" licensing terms. The "use-based" licensing concept, enables licensors to offer licensees different royalty fees that depend on how the technology is being used (Hunt, 2017). Under this approach licensors may refuse a license if the final use of the technology cannot be identified. Representatives of small and medium-sized companies claim that this approach is undermining innovation inside the EU. The "use-based" concept calculates the value of the license based upon how the technology that uses the SEP is being used in practice.[4] The SEP-holders would be able to charge different royalties depending on the application of the technology and irrespective of the value of the SEP itself. In this scenario SEP-holders would automatically receive some of the value that was created by downstream innovators. Obviously as stated before SMEs would be in a very delicate position, since they do not have the resources or expertise to engage in patent litigation, but they often do create value on the downstream market.

The "license to all" is a concept, wherein the implementer can seek a license from the SEP-holder irrespective of the downstream use of the technology. Opponents of this concept claim that this will lead to a stark increase in licensing negotiations, legal fees and delays in standard-setting. Some experts think that " license to all" will have a negative effect on innovation, the competitiveness of the EU and ultimately kill many jobs in Europe. [5]

The EU Commission short-tracked ETSI as one of the key developers of the new rules on fair licensing for 5G and the IoT. The opinions within ETSI on this subject seem to be very divided. Rosenbrock (2017) initiated the discussion by claiming that ETSI should choose the "license to all" concept. Rosenbrock refers to art.3 of the ETSI IPR policy to motivate his stand. [6] The previously mentioned Guidelines on Horizontal Agreements are also used to further underline his choice for the "license to all" principle. [7]

Another former legal expert of ETSI, Dr. Huber, counteracted with another article (Huber, 2017).

Huber states that the FRAND-commitment with ETSI's IPR policy does not extend to the electronic components of the end-product. His following comment is very interesting: "ETSI's objective is to ensure that essential IPRs are universally accessible to anyone who wants to use the standards, but not to ensure that every *individual company who seeks a license to essential IPRs is granted one. In other words, as long as an essential IPR holder does not prevent access to a standard for all, it is free to select its preferred "level" (chipset manufacturer, handset manufacturer, etc.) for licensing its essential IPRs on FRAND terms and conditions."* (Huber, 2017, p. 7). Obviously, the EU Commission stands for a daunting choice. The necessity to give guidance on SEP-licensing in the light of IoT-technology is very clear. The involvement of SMEs in the development of 5G and the IoT is strictly necessary to bring innovations to downstream markets, which will benefit consumers and increases the competitiveness of the European Digital Single Market. At first sight, SME will suffer the consequences of the adoption of the "use-based" principle. The SMEs will add value to the downstream inventions that consequently have to be shared with the holders of the patented technology. End-user licensing will increase the transaction costs for the implementer and could lead to higher royalty costs, both consequences are detrimental for the participation of SMEs in IoT standard-setting. Depending on the interpretation, end-user licensing could also include the value of other technologies that are incorporated in the product. [8]

Competition Law Aspects of the Debate on "End-User Device" vs. "License For All"

The development of the IoT-standards has put more precise focus on the discussion at which level of the value chain licensing should occur and more importantly on which legal basis. Most experts agree that the active participation of SMEs in IoT-standardization is crucial for its success. Economic literature is decisive on the positive impact of standards and SDOs on innovation. Technology firms, including SMEs may decide to reduce their participation in an SDOs and their standard-setting activities. It would be interesting to research the difference in legal treatment between FRAND commitments that are made within the context of an SDO and those commitments outside the SDO framework. If the latter commitments give firms an advantage, this will encourage the development of de facto standards. Experts hold the opinion that de facto standards are very important for both innovation and competition. The strategic choice for working in a SDO or standard-setting in consortia could be directly influenced by the choice of licensing concept. If SDOs expressly opt for end-user device licensing, this could drive especially SMEs in the direction of standard-setting by consortia. SDOs traditionally require participating companies to commit to FRAND licensing terms. The IPR-policies of the SDOs leave sufficient room for interpretation of this FRAND-commitment. In the heated debate on the licensing base, some experts see "license for all" as a movement towards compulsory licensing. Legally it in inherent to the patent right that every patent holder has the right to exclude, and choose who to license and ultimately who to sue for patent infringement.

As stated earlier par 285 of the EU Horizontal Guidelines requires firms that have agreed to FRAND-commitments to license their patents to every company that is interested. The individual choice of a company to agree to a FRAND commitment will be dictated by its market policy. The EU Commission does not often find standardization agreements anticompetitive. One clear exception would be the case where the standardization agreement leads to a reduction in product diversity. Parties must be free to develop alternative technologies which in practice is limited. The 2015 example of the change in the Institute of Electrical and Electronics Engineering Standards Association ("IEEE-SA") IPR-policy led to a reduced willingness of firms to participate in their standard-setting. In order to make IoT-standardization attractive for SMEs, SDOs must adopt an IPR-policy that fully recognizes the position of SMEs. The lack of resources and expertise of SMEs prevent an effective participation in expensive patent litigation. EU competition law demands: *"Standard-setting can, however, in specific circumstances, also give rise to restrictive effects on competition by [...] exclusion of, or discrimination against, certain companies by prevention of effective access to the standard"* (European Commission, 2014, par. 264). The participation of SME standard-setting can be increased by providing more transparency. One of the key discussions centers on methods for valuing SEPs, which explains the EU Commission eagerness to reach a consensus. A widely accepted valuing method would assist SMEs in securing early stage funding for their innovations.

An overview of recent case-law in relation to FRAND does not provide the necessary transparency for SMEs. The EU Commission clearly stated that they do not see any role for themselves in determining what reasonable royalty rates are. This function should be undertaken by national courts or by arbitrators. In the EU system, the Commission does not see a role for antitrust agencies in determining the correct level of FRAND rates. The Opinion of Advocate-General Wathelet in the Huawei preliminary ruling did not provide the necessary guidance and transparency. In general, SEP-litigation must be equally unattractive for the licensee and patentee. Nevertheless, many uncertainties remained after reading the Opinion of

Wathelet. It leaves the general question open whether there is a shift from FRAND-determined royalties to court determined FRAND damages. From a business perspective, FRAND is a peace treaty mutually determined by firms to avoid litigation. The Huawei judgment of the Court of Justice underlined the principle that patent holders should not be able to use an injunction as leverage against a willing licensee. The Court recognized the permanent character of a FRAND commitment, which is one of the reasons that the Court is willing to limit the right to injunctions. The European Union seems to show a greater willingness (compared to the US) to evaluate the level of royalties that is charged, in relation to a possible abuse of dominant position. Again the definition of FRAND licensing terms will play a crucial role in the assessment of the abuse of a dominant position. The third-party determination of FRAND rates also includes some risks. One scenario could be that the SEP holder pushes for a court determination of FRAND rates instead of private strategic negotiations. Obviously, arbitration is a risk for both parties, but it could become part of strategic behavior if the courts have different FRAND determinations.

Regarding FRAND rates, there have been interesting developments in the United States. Different calculation methods have recently emerged: the *ex ante* method, proportionality method and the regressive analysis method. One variation of the proportionality method used by Judge Robart uses patent pools as proxy for the FRAND rates. This innovative method already met with substantial criticism, but it can have interesting consequences for patent pools.

From a practitioner's point of view, the current (TTBER) safe harbour system facilitates the Commission in decreasing its heavy workload in competition law cases. The interrelation between patent law and competition law is constantly evolving and being re-designed. Although competition law takes a leading role in the standards and patents discussion, clear boundaries have not yet been established.

The ECJ tries to balance the different interests of licensor and licensee. The judgment does not provide clarity regarding the royalty rate setting or the basis thereof. For SMEs these discussions are very specialized and difficult to follow. The patent valuation guidelines of the EU Commission bear the risk of provoking SMEs to leave SDO-discussions or even refuse to agree on FRAND commitments. Again this might result in a higher participation of SMEs in consortia standard-setting. The position of SMEs in consortia is obviously even more unclear. For standards consortia, this could be a strategic opening to encourage SMEs to join their discussions and standardization.

Communication of the EU Commission: "Setting Out the EU Approach to Standard Essential Patents"

The EU Commission (2017) published in November 2017 its communication: "Setting out the EU approach to Standard Essential Patents". The communication shows that the EU Commission still allows for great flexibility regarding the valuation/ establishment of FRAND-rates. Main conclusion is that the value of the SEP should be based on the patented technology and not upon the fact that the technology is included in a standard. The value of individual SEPs should not be considered in isolation. To avoid royalty stacking parties need to seriously consider a reasonable aggregate rate for the standard based on the overall value of the added value of the technology. Most importantly the EU Commission did not express an explicit mandate for either use-based licensing or license for all concepts. The decision should be related to the individual characteristics of the case and may vary between sectors and business models. The EU Commission stated *that "[o]nce a standard is established and the holders of the SEPs have given a commitment to license them on fair, reasonable and non-discriminatory (FRAND) terms, the technology included in the standard should be available to any potential user of the standard" (i.e.*

chipset licensing still possible). And furthermore: There is no one-size-fit-all solution on what FRAND is: what can be considered fair and reasonable can differ from sector to sector and over time. Efficiency considerations, reasonable license fee expectations on both sides, the facilitation of the uptake by implementers to promote wide diffusion of the standard should be taken into account (European Commission, 2017). The EU Commission recently (July 2018) established a group of experts on licensing and valuation of standard essential patents, in order to understand all the perspectives in a better way. As the IoT emerges, the patent landscape is also evolving. New business forms like multi-sided platforms provide hubs for the connectivity of IoT devices. SMEs can be part of these platforms, but the question remains whether there is one dominant industry standard evolving. The IPRs of this standard can be controlled by an SDO or a consortium or be open source-based.

Patent Pools as a Solution to the Problem of the IoT Licensing Base?

Recently, Ericsson started a patent pool initiative named Avanci, to address the specific needs of IoT licensing. Patent pools are often named as a possible solution for SMEs to participate in IoT standard-setting. In order to evaluate the feasibility of this patent pools, a more in-depth discussion will follow below. The joint exploitation of patent rights by their owners in a collective agreement has economic benefits. Patent pools have existed for many years in the manufacturing industry, starting with sewing machines, but recently they have drawn the attention of the biomedical industry, especially in relation to AIDS/HIV-related medicine.[9] Patent pools are regarded as pro-competitive, and they provide certainty to companies that want to use the patent rights. For the inventor, the patent pool provides an incentive to bring his technology onto the market without costly litigation. The fact that the most important patents are gathered in a patent pool increases the efficiency of the technology markets.

In relation to the patent thicket problem (the situation in which multiple patentees own overlapping sets of patent rights), patent pools are often cited as the main remedy. One of the major advantages of a patent pool is its characteristic of transactional efficiency. Patent pools can clear blocking patents, limit the emergence of possible costly legal disputes and enhance network interoperability, which, in the context of standardization in the telecommunications industry, facilitates further rapid technological progress and the competitiveness of the sector.A patent pool clarifies the uncertainty of possible patent claims, the outcome of time-consuming court cases and distributes the business risks among members of the pool, thereby enabling smaller firms to share in the success of the pool, and it also counters spill-over effects.[10]

A patent pool agreement needs to be distinguished from a package license. An individual company can make the business decision to license several patent rights in a package license, without opting to combine its patents with another company's patents o establish a patent pool. In a patent pool, separate firms offer their patents under joint management, administered either on their own or by a third separate entity. Both patent pools and package licenses clear blocking patents and integrate complementary patents resolving the problem that is sometimes referred to as the "anti-commons". [11]

The Advantages of the Use of Patent Pools Within Standardization Processes

The obvious advantages of patent pools have already been discussed. Within the context of standards, patent pools can also provide a higher level of transparency for licensors and licensees and future adopters of the standard. Normally, the patent pool administrator will work for all the firms in the agreement, and decision making is done by consensus, with an equal vote for every participating licensor. A patent pool can support the adoption of a standard in a better and faster way, since it leads to more transparency and predictability for licensees.[12]

Some patent pool administrators claim that the mix of different firms results in a fairer and more market-appropriate royalty fee. The maximum return for patents policy is weakened by the different interests of the firms in the pool. The efficiency of the patent pool, therefore, would depend on the question of whether all of the licensors in the market have contributed all of the essential patents to the patent pool.

A second important condition would be the independence of the patent pool administrator. An external administrator can act more independently than an internal administrator, in the case of business or legal disputes, and can decide on the fairness and non-discriminatory level of the royalty rates. In a patent pool, royalty rates for the complete package deal can be set to encourage the adoption and growth of a standard. An attractive royalty rate will result in achieving the critical mass of followers of the standard necessary to optimize the network externalities of the telecommunications market.

A standardization body is interested in a patent pool as an instrument to facilitate the rapid technology transfer from innovation to final products and/or services. This is sometimes referred to as the shop window of technology, the fact that the collective licensing agreement speeds up the process of commercialization. The patent pool plays a role in the patent evaluation process, by evaluating the patents' essentiality, and manages the licensing administration. If an agreement on the patent pool is reached within a short time-span, this eliminates some of the deficiencies of bilateral licensing agreements. Disadvantages remain, however, such as an unbalanced negotiating position for SMEs and often time-consuming and complicated discussions. Since the patent pool has global license coverage, this minimizes the risk of expensive patent infringement actions. A reduction of internal licensing and negotiation costs also makes the patent pool attractive from a financial point of view.

These advantages can only exist when the formation of the patent pool is completed in a timely manner. For operators, patent pools have the advantage that the costs of acquiring the technology become much more market related and that, for the direction of future business policy, the essential patents have been defined, thereby reducing the burden of the essential patent portfolio management. The reduced risk in terms of patent litigation could also influence the stock market's perception of the standard. For a successful operation of the patent pool in the standardizing context, large patent holders must make the strategic decision to license their IPRs via the patent pool. Obviously, all things considered patent pools only are a feasible solution for major companies but not for SMEs.

What Will the Future Hold?

In the IoT future, there will be a stronger cooperation between the Open Source developers and standardization bodies. Open standards is a phenomenon that is here to stay. Open IoT standards are faster and more transparent. At the same time, this inevitable development also raises more questions. Two main issues need to be clarified: the adoption of open source software in the elaboration of the standard and conversely, the adoption of standards in the open source software community. Cloud computing is often developed with open source software. The 5G standard incorporates cloud computing in developing the new architecture of the core telecommunications network. What will be the impact of open source software licenses and the compatibility of FRAND be? One of the main challenges could be to ensure that the open source soft- ware license does not prevent the licensing of SEPs on FRAND terms or violates the IPR- policy of SDOs.

From a technical perspective, challenges can be found in the development of the Internet of Things (IoT). In the IoT, a lot of discussion is centered on Big Data. The IoT consists of a range of new technologies that play together. Data moves around without human intervention. Elements like cloud computing, software defined networks (SDN) and networks function virtualization (NFV) all interrelate with each other. The standardization community is still developing new standards in traditional fields. ETSI is involved in NFV standardization, but most other parts are developed by the open source community (with the ability to look at the source code). Although the open development companies sound very idealistic, 80% of the community is paid by major companies, who consequently decide whether to commercialize the open source technology or not.

Telecommunications standards will be applied in a much wider context in the future, as enabling technologies. Given the present position of SMEs this might complicate the development.

Another major influence will be the determination of the EU to stop the dominance of US tech giants. Recently, the EU Commission launched a new enforcement agenda against US tech giants. The enforcement agenda has a wide-spread coverage, from the protection of the privacy of EU citizens, to the overall control of the internet. Themes like Artificial Intelligence and the access and control of data will also have an impact on the licensing discussions. The EU and the US understand that their future competitiveness greatly depends on home-grown high technology. Within this field, IoT standards play a major role and, despite the current efforts of the relevant authorities, SMEs still have many IPR-challenges to face.

CONCLUSION

The EU Commission takes in her recent communication a holistic approach towards the basis of SEP licensing. There is no specific mandate for either use-based licensing or license for all concepts. In relation to the FRAND discussion, one option could be the development of an industry-based solution. If the major tech companies agree on a common understanding regarding FRAND and injunctions, regulators would likely follow. In the absence of an industry-based solution, it will be left to courts and arbitrators to apply and interpret the existing framework of rules. The EU Commission hopes that sectoral discussions will lead to common licensing practices. If SDOs choose for one specific license valuation base this might have direct consequences for the (necessary) participation of SMEs in the 5G and IoT standard-setting. The earlier experience with the IEEE-practices shows that this might drive SMEs towards standard-setting in consortia, if these consider a more appropriate SEP-valuation base. For many SMEs, IPR policies are at the heart of the matter of the standardization management discussion. Given the importance of the participation of SMEs in standardization for the Digital Single Market, the EU Commission and consequently the European Court of Justice could give more guidance on their preferences regarding the bases of SEP-licensing.

REFERENCES

Baron, J., & Pohlmann, T. (2013). Who Cooperates in Standards Consortia—Rivals or Complementors? *Journal of Competition Law & Economics*, *9*(4), 905–929. doi:10.1093/joclec/nht034

European Commission. (2014). *Guidelines on the application of Article 101 of the Treaty on the Functioning of the European Union to technology transfer agreements*. Brussels: Commission of the European Union. Retrieved from https://eur-lex.europa.eu/legal-content/EN/TXT/PDF/?uri=CELEX:52014XC0328(01)&from=EN

European Commission. (2016). *Speech: State of the Union address 2016: Towards a better Europe – A Europe that protects, empowers and defends Strasbourg*. Retrieved from http://europa.eu/rapid/press-release_SPEECH-16-3043_en.htm

European Commission. (2017). *Setting out the EU approach to Standard Essential Patents COM (2017) 712 final*. Retrieved from https://ec.europa.eu/docsroom/documents/26583/attachments/1/translations/en/renditions/native

Gupta, K. (2017). *The Role of SMEs and Startups in Standards Development*. Retrieved from https://papers.ssrn.com/sol3/papers.cfm?abstract_id=3001513

Heller, M. A., & Eisenberg, R. S. (1998). Can patents deter innovation? The anticommons in biomedical research. *Science*, *280*(5364), 698–701. doi:10.1126cience.280.5364.698 PMID:9563938

Huber, B. (2017). *Why the ETSI IPR-policy Does Not and Has Never Required Compulsory License to All: A Rebuttal to Karl Heinz Rosenbrock*. Retrieved from https://papers.ssrn.com/sol3/papers.cfm?abstract_id=3038447

Hunt, M. (2017). *Patent Licensing: 5G and the Internet of Things*. Retrieved from https://www.bristows.com/news-and-publications/articles/patent-licensing-5g-and-the-internet-of-things/

Lerner, U., & Tirole, J. (2007). Public Policy Towards Patent Pools. *Innovation Policy and the Economy*, *8*, 157–186. doi:10.1086/ipe.8.25056201

Lundqvist, B. (2015). *Joint Research and Development Under US Antitrust and EU Competition Law*. Edward Elgar Publishing. doi:10.4337/9781784713010

Rosenbrock, K. (2017). *Why the ETSI IPR Policy Requires Licensing to all*. Retrieved from http://www.fair-standards.org/wp-content/uploads/2017/08/Why-the-ETSI-IPR-Policy-Requires-Licensing-to-All_Karl-Heinz-Rosenbrock_2017.pdf

ENDNOTES

1 Where participation in standard-setting is unrestricted and the procedure for adopting the standard in question is transparent, standardization agreements which contain no obligation to comply with the standard and provide access to the standard on fair, reasonable and non-discriminatory terms will normally not restrict competition within the meaning of Article 101(1)."

2 This fact is also confirmed in the Google-Motorola decision.

3 It remains unclear why the EU Commission holds ETSI in a higher esteem than other SDOs.

4 See for more background: http://ipkitten.blogspot.nl/2017/11/who-is-going-to-win-big-eu-commission.html

5 https://www.iptalks.eu/news/license-to-all-is-a-license-to-kill-innovation-and-jobs-in-europe

6 Article 3 of the IPR Policy: "the ETSI IPR POLICY seeks to reduce the risk to ETSI, MEMBERS, and others applying ETSI STANDARDS and TECHNICAL SPECIFICATIONS, that investment in the preparation, adoption and application of STANDARDS could be wasted as a result of an ESSENTIAL IPR for a STANDARD or TECHNICAL SPECIFICATION being unavailable."

7 paragraph 285: *"In order to ensure effective access to the standard, the IPR policy would need to require participants wishing to have their IPR included in the standard to provide an irrevocable commitment in writing to offer to* ***license*** *their essential IPR* ***to all third parties*** *on fair, reasonable and non-discriminatory terms ('FRAND commitment');*

8 It is at the moment relatively unclear, how the different values have to be calculated.

9 See for a further discussion on public policy and patent pools (Lerner & Tirole, 2007).

10 "The pooling of patents, licensing all patents in the pool collectively, and sharing royalties is not necessarily an antitrust violation. In a case involving blocking patents such an arrangement is the only reasonable method for making the invention available to the public", *International Manufacturing Co. v. Landon* 336 F.2d 723, 729 (9th Circ. 1964).

11 See also (Heller & Eisenberg, 1998). Michelman defined the problem of the anticommons as: "a type of property in which everyone always has rights respecting the objects in the regime, and no one, consequently, is ever privileged to use any of them except as particularly authorized by others". Colangelo concludes that the patent right to exclude can lead to a situation in which the IPRs are actually underused page 61.

12 Transparency is one of the main interests of the EU Commission in relation to the management of a patent pool. See draft guidelines TTBER page 64.

Chapter 12
Customer-Driven Standardization in the Forensic Science Market in England and Wales

Karen McGregor Richmond
https://orcid.org/0000-0001-7916-2069
University of Strathclyde, UK

ABSTRACT

This chapter aims to contribute to the nascent, but expanding, body of literature concerned with sociologies of standards and standardization. Specifically, this chapter focuses on the creation of standardized forensic "products" within the marketized forensic science sector in England and Wales. This "menu" of standardized forensic products emerged during a period of significant economic and organizational disruption. The implementation of these codified products created further tensions, demonstrating the unintended consequences, which may flow from incomplete application of standards, incomplete understanding of their effect, and the instrumental use of these same standards, not to achieve efficiencies or harmonization but to affect particular institutional goals, and which are not shared across the wider community of practice.

INTRODUCTION

This chapter aims to contribute to the nascent, but expanding, body of literature concerned with sociologies of standards, and standardisation. In contributing to this field, it aims to answer Timmerman and Epstein's call 'for careful empirical analyses of the specific and unintended consequences of different sorts of standards operating in distinct social domains.' (Timmermans & Epstein, 2010). Thus, the chapter sets out to critically examine the standard-making process, emphasising the complex negotiations required. Further, it exposes the material, historical, and organisational contingencies, which led to the creation of standardised forensic products, surveys their implementation, and explores the ways in which

DOI: 10.4018/978-1-5225-9008-8.ch012

Copyright © 2019, IGI Global. Copying or distributing in print or electronic forms without written permission of IGI Global is prohibited.

these standards became subverted in site-specific contexts. The resulting analysis may be situated within a wider Science and Technology Studies *corpus*. Additionally, it is hoped that the instant case – which focusses on forensic productisation and standardisation – may resonate with socio-legal scholars.

Specifically, this chapter focusses on the creation of standardised forensic 'products' within the marketised forensic science sector in England and Wales. This 'menu' of standardised forensic products, which emerged during a period of significant economic, and organisational, disruption. The implementation of these codified products created further tensions, demonstrating the unintended consequences, which may flow from incomplete application of standards, incomplete understanding of their effect, and the instrumental use of these same standards, not to achieve efficiencies or harmonisation, but to effect particular institutional goals, and which are not shared across the wider community of practice. Ultimately, the chapter invites us to ask fundamental questions regarding the creation of informal standards within the marketplace:; who should set such standards, and whom should they serve?

The chapter follows Timmerman's recommended approach, sub-dividing the informal standardisation process into phases of creation, implementation and resistance, followed by a discussion of outcomes. The chapter utilises a case-study methodological perspective, and draws upon results gleaned from documentary analysis, and from original empirical research, conducted throughout the forensic science sector in all four corners of the United Kingdom. It is hoped that this chapter may serve to demonstrate the problems which may potentially arise when standards creation is dominated by one agency, when it does not emerge from consensus amongst stakeholders, when delivery is skewed towards the demand-side, and when those who bear the cost of implementation have little input into the standards creation process.

FORENSIC SCIENCE PROVISION IN ENGLAND AND WALES

The governance of the provision of forensic science services, and the organisational structure and management of individual forensic science laboratories, varies widely between different countries, regions and jurisdictions. Nonetheless, across this varied forensic landscape, providers face similar economic challenges. Commercial imperatives have intruded, to a greater or lesser extent, on scientific autonomy, with most forensic providers now recognising the need to demonstrate a willingness to embrace new management techniques, to internalise regulatory objectives, and to enter into rudimentary forms of competition. However, despite the increasing pressure of commercial imperatives, the overwhelming majority of developed countries still choose to deliver vital forensic services through a system of public provision.[1] The current system of forensic science provision operating in England and Wales is therefore quite, exceptional, insofar as it is achieved through a system of marketised delivery.

The development of marketised forensic provision in England and Wales mirrors similar developments across the domestic sector, where the state is no longer viewed as the only agency suitable to be tasked with the provision of services to the criminal justice system. Within the forensic science sector - as across many other domains - the limitations of the state's capacity to manage the organisational complexities of social life has been relentlessly highlighted, and long-standing institutional arrangements have been transformed through volatile patterns of policy development and innovation. Hence, what were once state-monopolised powers have increasingly been transferred to private, 'for-profit' contractors. These actors are allowed to pursue commercial interests provided that they remain within the constraints established by their contract with the government authorities (and with their private customers), and submit to various forms of monitoring and regulation.

Economic Rationalisation in the United Kingdom

The privatisation of forensic services correspond precisely to the fiscal and ideological principles of (putatively 'Thatcherite') economic rationalisation, which have affected other state institutions within the United Kingdom. The reformation of subsisting modes of production has been achieved through the creation of new ideological categories, cognate with a theory of political-economic practice which proposes that human well-being can best be advanced by liberating individual entrepreneurial freedoms and skills within an institutional framework that is characterised by strong private property rights, free markets, and free trade. The role of the state under this system is thus merely to create, and preserve, an institutional framework appropriate to such practices.

Although degrees of commercialised forensic science provision exist in the majority of developed countries, only in England and Wales have the government sought to reorganise the delivery of such services around an exclusively market-based model. However, the process of forensic market-creation (from public ownership, through a gradual blending of public and private provision, culminating in the removal of government-operated forensic science agencies), is typical of any sector which has been exposed to 'new public management' techniques, and processes of economic rationalisation.

Nor is this a recent phenomenon. The construction of consent to these processes of commercialisation began in the early-1980's, the point at which the Home Office was opened up to discourses of 'modernisation' and 'economic rationality', and its character transformed by self-negating management techniques, which valorised the concepts of 'economy, efficiency and effectiveness.' (Lawless, 2010). By the end of that decade the ethos of 'customer relations' - central to commercial organisation – had began to influence the practices of all government agencies, and the turn towards processes of economic rationalisation began to influence, and alter, the field of forensic science provision, which slowly became reconfigured around new goals, interests and incentives. Thus, the normative goals of a public sector agency – the Forensic Science Service - were gradually subsumed by the quantitative indices of marketised service delivery, marked by entrepreneurial innovation, value for money, choice, and communication between stakeholders.

The Forensic Science Service: Transition and Closure

In the decades preceding marketisation, forensic science provision in England and Wales had been achieved solely through the publicly-funded Forensic Science Service (FSS). This organisation, operating under the aegis of the Home Office, operated several facilities throughout the country; work was distributed across seven main laboratories, distributed from London to the Midlands and the North of England. The FSS provided scene-of-crime and forensic investigation services to police forces in England and Wales, as well as to the Crown Prosecution Service, HM Revenue and Customs, HM Coroners' Service, Ministry of Defence Police, British Transport Police and worldwide forensic services. It also maintained a research laboratory at Aldermaston (previously the Central Research and Support Establishment), where the FSS developed 'low copy number' (LCN) techniques, advanced DNA profiling, and established the National DNA Database (NDNAD).

From its inception, the FSS operated as a publicly-owned service. However, profound shifts in public policy and management were to bring about an emphatic reorganisation of the provision of forensic services. Further, the developing discursive framework of 'added value' service delivery - as vigorously promoted by the government's Audit Office – would carry serious implications for the governance of the publicly-funded Forensic Science Service. Prior to 1987,

…the FSS was funded centrally so the Police didn't have to pay directly for any of their requested work. This resulted in forces often submitting very large numbers of items from each case, often waiting months for results. (King et al., 2012).

In 1987 an accounting firm, Touche Ross, was commissioned to draft a report on police scientific support, concluding that police management of scientific support services was 'generally poor'. However, the Touche Ross report also explored the scope for organisational changes, and new funding methods, within the FSS. Following the recommendations of the report, the FSS introduced direct charging to police forces.

Effect on Forensic Analyses

With the advent of direct charging, the costs of forensic services thus became visible to operational forces (henceforth to be regarded as 'customers'). Further, the FSS aligned itself with a more 'business-oriented' approach to service delivery, with a particular focus on 'forensic strategy', advocating more careful triaging of submitted items, and on agreeing target dates for court reporting. Nonetheless, during this period, it was the scientists who determined what forensic examinations and analyses to make, in collaboration with the Police.' (King et al., 2012, p.5).

The majority of FSS employees interviewed were able to provide evidence to support the view that the 'pre-codification' forensic analyses carried out by the FSS were both comprehensive and contextual. A lead biologist described the process;

...essentially what would happen is that you would have almost a service provision, so in the FSS we dealt with pretty much everything...whenever there was a case that came in the door there would be a huge bag of exhibits and the police would essentially say 'can you forensic those please' and we would say "...this is the overarching strategy, we'll start with Test A, we'll do Test B,C and D" and then once we've done that, our work hasn't impacted on the work of someone else, so we then hand over the case to that individual, and they'll do their Tests 1, 2 & 3 and once they've finished that work we can then shave off part of it into toxicology, or some other department, and...after a few months of...very clever science, you write a very large report that says...we've done this to death: these are the opportunities available, these are the findings that we've got, and if necessary, if all of this falls down, we've actually retained material in these departments so we could... go down [an alternative] avenue if you wish. (Interview with Lead Scientist: Tier Two FSP, 2015)

This typical response, illustrating a standard FSS workflow, highlights the exhaustive nature of forensic investigatory processes, as carried out within the FSS. A lack of supervening concerns regarding economic costs, or value, on the part of the investigatory authorities, allowed for the submission of a large amount of initial samples. Futher, the investigation, evaluation, and reporting process, were comparatively exhaustive (to a degree which might later be conceived of as excessive, and surplus to 'customer requirements'). Another notable feature was the holistic nature of the investigation and analysis, which was not – at that time - solely dependent on DNA-profiling techniques. DNA profiling is viewed as contributing to a palette of forensic practices, with no evidence of the privileging of one method over another. The informant also highlights the possibilities for recursion and review at a later stage, in order to take account of updated contextual information. In summary, the response suggests a significant degree of forward planning, a high granularity of inference, contextual awareness, and flexibility allowing for the compilation of exhaustive reports, written by expert forensic scientists. Further, it should be noted that that the investigatory authorities did not direct the course of the FSS examination, at this time: nor did they participate directly in the formulation of a forensic investigatory strategy.

Notably absent from this expert's response were concerns regarding the over-arching importance of turn-around-times (TOTs) or the imposition of economic efficiencies. Rather, the investigation, and comparatively rigorous, forensic evaluation, appear to conform to normative representations of scientific method. They are indicative of universalism, insofar as the truth claims are subjected solely to pre-established impersonal criteria. They are communalist insofar as the 'customer' does not dictate the course of the investigation. And they are disinterested insofar as they are free from institutional motivations.

Indeed, such responses appear typical of non-marketised forensic scientific analysis. There were clear and notable similarities between the description of exhaustive forensic analysis offered above – by a former employee of the FSS - and the contemporary observations of forensic scientists working within the publicly-funded forensic sector in Northern Ireland, as indicated below:

Where I would see...the big change is in what's requested in the first place. And that's not altogether a bad thing because, back in days of yore, where the police weren't, in any sense, paying for it, a truck would hiss to a halt outside, the doors would open, a hundred items would come out, and the forensic strategy would be 'forensicate that!' 'Well, what is it you want?' 'Everything.' 'Well, that's alright for you to say but I've got another fifty cases...' And a consequence of that was that we were reporting cases months, and months, and sometimes years after they came in. And how much of that output remained valuable at that stage? Who knows. So [the introduction of pricing and an appreciation of evidential value] has focussed the police onto trying to get the best return, and, of course, DNA - bit of a buzzword - tends to be one of the things they reach for first, though actually, not always sensibly. But that's what people think... (Interview with Lead Scientist: Forensic Science Northern Ireland, 2015)

To return to the process of organisational reform within the FSS, in addition to managing internal change, the FSS' was soon faced with further challenges. Its monopoly on forensic science delivery in England and Wales came to an abrupt end when two private forensic companies (LGC, and Scientifics Ltd.) emerged, and began to compete directly for FSS' business. These companies had originated in the public sector, and were joined - in 1996 - by the first fully private company, Forensic Alliance. (Lawless, 2010).

During this period the Forensic Science Service had undergone a degree of reformation in order to bring it into line with the emergent market realities. Indeed, the FSS made it clear that the commercial considerations of the new forensic market were paramount in reshaping the relationship between FSS forensic experts and the requirements of the criminal justice system:

It is the belief of the FSS that the perception of such value for money should be that of the customer. These initiatives have the aim of not only providing better value for money, but also of achieving improvement through a genuine partnership in which the customer has a greater participation than hitherto in decisions about what work is done in the laboratory. (Cook et al., 1998).

The degree to which these changes altered the nature of FSS service delivery, and ethos, can be demonstrated by comparing the FSS 'mission statement' from 2001, in which the agency defined its role in terms of a commitment to crafting a 'safer and more just society', with later versions, which referred to the need to;

retain and reinforce our leading position as the principal provider of forensic science to the UK criminal justice system (UKCJS), and use this platform to become the leading provider worldwide, thereby enhancing long term shareholder value. (Lawless & Williams, 2010, p.737).

The alterations to policy and management – characterised by marketisation, and productisation - were accompanied by deeper structural changes. The FSS had been awarded Trading Fund status by the Government, in 1999. Thus, the service was able to recoup funds, and to declare a profit, in the short term. However, as new competitors emerged, each contributed to a reduction in the FSS' market share, and profits declined. The McFarland Review, in 2003, found that the Service was too heavily burdened by overhead costs, and was thus unable to meet clients' needs. The Review recommended a further change, to GovCo (Government Company) status, as a preliminary stage prior to restructuring as a Public-Private Partnership.

The later McKinsey Review, of 2008, examined the sustainability of the forensic science market as a whole, concluding that the market was underperforming, and was in need of urgent reform. It also noted that the costs of restructuring the FSS would be significant. As a result, the government announced its plans to wind down the FSS, following the advice of the House of Commons Science and Technology Committee in December 2010. The service was eventually closed in 2011. With the closure of the FSS, forensic science provision in England and Wales became fully marketised, with work (including the 65% market share of the defunct FSS) now to be shared between fifteen private companies.

The Forensic Science Market

The dissolution of the FSS having been completed, the forensic science sector was now left with the rudimentary market that emerged during the latter stages of FSS rundown; a market comprising a diverse number of commercial Forensic Science Providers of varying sizes, boasting varying specialisms, and displaying varying abilities. The sector was, from the outset, dominated by four large companies, who together accounted for the largest share of the market. These were Key Forensic Services[2], Cellmark[3], Environmental Scientifics Group[4], and LGC Forensics[5]. These four companies also comprised the founding commercial members of the Association of Forensic Service Providers[6], with the stated aim of furthering the interests of the forensic services industry. The four large providers offered a wide range of forensic services. The remainder of the market consisted of medium-sized, and niche, organisations, such as ROAR, Principal Forensic Services[7], Manlove Forensics[8], Randox, and Hayward Associates Forensic Science (which provides only DNA-profiling services and specialises in criminal defence work).[9] In addition, it should be noted that each of the forty-three police forces in England and Wales operated their own private testing laboratories, a state of affairs which subsists to the current day.

Procurement and the NFFA

The creation of a rudimentary forensic science market, and the introduction, by the FSS, of direct charging to customers, heralded an emphatic turn towards commoditisation of the forensic science sector. Therefore, in response to the imperatives of progressive marketisation, the FSS began to restructure service delivery. From this point forensic services began to be organised in terms of the provision of products, which began to be defined by; category of expert activity, chargeable units of time, cost, standards, and expected outcome. The demand side experienced similar commercial re-structuring, and in 2006, the government announced a pilot procurement exercise. The exercise was initially limited to three police forces. However, this pilot project quickly grew to involve fourteen police forces in England and Wales, a group which came to be known as the 'West-Coast Consortium.' The resulting SWNWW Tender (encompassing South Wales, North Wales and the West of England) established fixed prices for a range of standardised and codified forensic products, which were to be purchased from forensic science providers (FSPs) on a bulk basis. Meanwhile, on the customer side, purchasing of forensic services was shifted, from police Scientific Support Managers (most of whom had been Scene Of Crime Officers with experience of quality assurance and financial management in relation to forensic science) to police procurement departments. As will be shown, the introduction of this codified system for the purchase of fixed-price forensic products carried serious implications for the provision of forensic science services. Prior to the West Coast Consortium Tender police forces had submitted items to their forensic provider,

...in discussion with a scientist, and the scientist then decided, using their skills, independence and experience, on what items to examine, using what techniques and what analytical technique, if any. (King et al., 2012).

Following communication between the investigatory authorities, and the forensic science provider, a 'turn round time' (TRT) would be agreed, based on practical considerations (e.g. case complexity, supporting evidence, offence type, and court date). The work would then be charged on an hourly basis, with a degree of fixed-price charging in respect of analytical tasks. However, the competitive tendering process introduced by the West Coast Consortium Tender was entirely customer-led. It required FSPs to quote substantial efficiencies in the turn around times (TRTs) for both analysis, and the evaluation of forensic samples. In addition, the tendering process saw the introduction of a range of standardised forensic products. Rather than develop the codes in tandem with scientific experts, it was the police forces themselves who drew up the codes, using ex-forensic submissions administrators. Thus, under ACPO (Association of Chief Police Officers) guidance, the police created a 'menu' of forensic products, and provided forensic scientists with instructions on when and how they were to be applied.

An example is as follows:

01BF (Body Fluids) - DNA (Deoxyribonucleic Acid) Crime Scene Stains – Standard: To process recovered biological samples/material using the most appropriate means to successfully obtain the optimum Short Tandem Repeat (STR) Second Generation Multiplex Plus (SGM+) profile for:- Comparison against an individual's DNA profile and/or submission onto the United Kingdom DNA Database (NDNAD).

With the publication of the tender document, forensic providers were overnight required to reorganise their service delivery models to fit with the new regime: a process which required a thorough examination of each of the listed products, and attendant protocols, in order to determine the necessary business, and operational, restructuring in order to deliver the product in accordance with the accompanying protocol. Additionally, providers were required to ascertain an appropriately competitive price to submit for each code. The codification process thus imposed new challenges on providers, not least due to the fact that some of the products were not clearly defined, leading to diverse interpretations - and ongoing disagreements - between customers and providers. This will form the subject of further discussion, *supra*.

Returning to the initial tendering process, forensic experts began to express concerns regarding the way in which the pilot project was allowed to increase in size and complexity. Untrammelled growth presented the Consortium with significant challenges when attempting to evaluate, and compare, each of the tenders against the requirements of the fourteen individual forces involved. This led to consequent delay, and the process - which had been estimated to last a few months - took eighteen months to reach completion. During this time, providers were precluded from approaching police forces to solicit further work, and market development came to a halt, leading to increased tension between customers and providers. As the market began to stagnate, and pressures grew, commercial managers within the provider companies began to involve themselves in service delivery, taking control away from forensic scientists. This led to diminishing morale amongst forensic scientists alongside concerns over the quality of service delivery.

Contracts under the SWNWW tender were finally awarded in January 2008 with FSP's awarded contracts under a series of lots, each corresponding to a particular forensic activity (e.g. Lot 209, Questioned Documents). Under the contract, single forensic service providers were tasked with providing services to various police forces. These contracts were generally arranged on a large-scale 'volume' basis - normally in terms of tens of thousands of units, each unit corresponding to a forensic product - with the open market structure allowing forces to change providers with relative ease. Conversely, police forces might typically have contracts with a variety of providers, in order that the latter provide a range of different services. One provider may provide DNA-profiling information, another may do work relating to the analysis of footwear impressions, and a third may provide computer and telecommunications services. Thus, different elements of a complex case would inevitably be sent to different providers. Further, since the market structure actively precluded communication between rival companies, the articulation of rich contextual detail that had been shown to be essential to providing accurate results, was impacted. Whilst the productised model of delivery was limited to so-called volume crime, it is nonetheless the case that routine work on high-volume crime may throw up the same complexities and difficulties as those relating to serious crime. However, the ability to fully investigate these complexities would henceforth be determined by organisational capabilities and budgetary constraints.

Returning to the initial tender, this provided the stimulus for further restructuring of the FSS, the organisation having lost a significant amount of work to LGC Forensics and Cellmark Forensic Services. Meanwhile, Key Forensic Services[10] were tasked with providing assistance with initial resource problems across the industry. However, the previous decision to allow the tender to grow in size, and complexity, was to lead to further problems. The tender had been intended to be a small pilot, the results of which were to be analysed carefully, before the next round of tendering was instituted. Thus, improvements and modifications had been planned to be taken into account in order that lessons learned from any problems encountered during the pilot tender could be absorbed. However, due to the long delay in the tender evaluation and award process, there was insufficient time to consider operational feedback from both the forensic science providers, and the police forces, before the next round of tenders were instituted.

The NPIA/NFFA

As demonstrated above, problems became structurally embedded in the standardised procurement procedures, and were expressed in the subsequent tendering process. This later process came under the control of the National Policing Improvement Agency (NPIA) and became known as the National Forensic Framework Agreement (NFFA). The National Forensic Framework Agreement represents a government attempt to implement standardisation measures in respect of the services offered to the police by the new body of FSP's. It was launched in August 2008. The agreement sought to bring much-needed organisation to the system of police procurement of forensic services whilst ensuring compliance with overarching European Union requirements regarding transparency. A dozen FSP's including the FSS, participated in the original agreement. The structure and content of the NFFA was broadly similar to that of the West Coast tender. Thus, in August 2008, twelve FSPs - including the FSS - took part in the initial NFFA tender. The introduction of the NPIA/NFFA also allowed small private forensic science suppliers to bid for particular lots (such as DNA crime scene stains or sexual offence casework). This enabled niche providers to bid for contracts in areas, which had previously been dominated by full-service providers, whilst providing customers with a greater degree of choice and flexibility (Lawless, 2016). Whilst the government were able to introduce a level of standardised practice across the market, implementation difficulties created a further set of problems.

Forensic Productisation: Implementation and Resistance

As Lawless has previously observed, the NFFA 'placed cognitive practices of evidence interpretation alongside mechanical and technical procedures', leading to opposition, and resistance, from forensic scientists. Further, scientists raised concerns regarding the partial, and incoherent, manner in which standardisation had been implemented.

During the data collection process, a significant number of respondents highlighted the difficulties faced by FSP's, when attempting to negotiate the standardised forensic product system. In particular, they noted that whilst there had been a degree of standardisation with regard to products, the process was incomplete, and was characterised by deep meso-level diversification with regard to the application of those standards. Specifically, each of the forty-three police force 'customers' wished to apply the codes in a bespoke manner which would maintain, and serve, the latter's unique force identity.

[The codes] are broadly similar but...they're incompatible. The turn-around times, the delivery of the report, the way in which the report findings should be delivered, whether it's an SFR, an abbreviated statement, all of these change between force, even within the same consortium. So, you're effectively re-inventing the wheel for every customer. (Interview with Lead Scientist: Tier Two FSP, 2015)

[Police] procurement dictate the codes. So, for example, 'mixed sample' is A6. A6 is broken into different tiers but it's an over-simplification of the job and there are too many levels. Further, the police can manipulate the codes. So, an A6 for the Met and an A6 for Cambridge may mean different things, as they tender individually. There's no direct comparison. (Interview with Lead Biologist: Tier One FSP, 2015)

Standardisation under the NFFA, occuring at force level, led to a multitude of standards being enforced between different force areas, Forensic scientists associated such problems as being directly related to the non-unitary nature of policing in England and Wales:

The only driving force behind police forces coming together to tender for work was cost, but what they didn't do was change their own internal procedures, or lose their own force identity, because they've all got their own management, their own Chief Constable, their own ACC, their own forensic... Avon and Somerset may want an SFR sent to a CJSM account sent to an individual by post. [Conversely] if you're working in Devon you [compile] an abbreviated statement, but only for footwear... (Interview with Managing Director, Tier Two FSP, 2015)

However, the problems also extended beyond England and Wales, to allied jurisdictions within the United Kingdom.

Our product coding system is based on that original ACPO / NPIA coding system... The codes don't necessarily fit the request or the item. It doesn't easily fit the processes we do and [the product codes] have been adjusted over the years. So, each lab interprets them in a different fashion. Each lab adjusted [the codes] according to their own protocols and interpretation. (Interview with Lead Scientist: FSNI, 2015)

Further, scientists highlighted concerns relating to the ways in which productisation now afforded individual police forces with the means to direct forensic strategy within the context of a criminal investigation, often in the absence of supporting contextual information.

You might have an item from a suspect's jumper. The jumper has three obvious dark brown stains on the sleeve that appear to be blood. So the police tell you to test those stains to tie them to the victim. But the stains could be from the suspect - he may have had a bleeding nose. And beside those large stains may be a small stain more consistent with low-velocity splatter. That may be the crucial item to test that ties the suspect to the victim. (Interview with Lead Scientist: Tier Two FSP, 2015)

Biologists were especially concerned that laboratory testing processes had become visible to the police, through productisation, but that the latter lacked the necessary expertise to understand when and how to use forensic products. Conversely, scientists felt less able to approach investigations in a rigorous, scientific manner. In practical terms, this often related to a lack of provision of necessary contextual information.

In practice, the police have budgets and scientists have turnarounds. You need thinking time...or experience [to carry out a thorough analysis]. So, when time is short, the tendency is just to do what the police ask. You have targets to meet. You have to complete a number of allocations. (Interview with Lead Scientist: Tier One FSP, 2015)

Such problems were exacerbated by poor communication between forensic science providers, and the investigatory authorities, compounded by the incommensurability of each agency's role.

If you are needing further information you can only contact certain named people. Often they will be named on the contract. Ideally, you contact the budget holder, who has to sign off on the work. Otherwise you don't get paid. You have to provide an estimate. The estimate has to correspond to product codes. So the codes allow the police to control budgets and compare providers. (Interview with Managing Director: Tier One FSP, 2015)

The problem is that police procurement are monitoring for performance, and scientists are carrying out the work governed by different criteria. The key is good communication between the different layers. (Interview with Lead Scientist: Tier One FSP, 2015)

Lastly, scientists reported encountering implementation problems within the police force, directly related to the 'triaging' of forensic investigations.

The code system doesn't apply to serious crimes such as murder. They are charged under a bespoke system according to an hourly rate." You may have an item from a jumper that's been taken from a suspect in a homicide. The police may try to put that item through under a volume crime code. The police assume that it's the same test. So there has to be a triaging process of monitoring submissions from the police. (Interview with Lead Scientist: Tier 2 FSP, 2015)

This triaging process will form the subject of further discussion, *supra*.

Triaging of Forensic Investigations

Since the majority of products allotted during the tendering process were assigned a fixed price, forensic providers were forced to allocate work to their scientists as directed by the investigative authorities, categorising work according to particular product codes. Thus, the triaging of cases could be seen to be a direct response to (or was at least heavily influenced, and facilitated by) the introduction of categories defined by non-expert 'customers' from outwith the forensic-scientific domain, who themselves were propelled by financial considerations. Further, the tight turn round times associated with each product process significantly reduced the time available for expert interpretation and evaluation, whilst putting pressure on scientists to deliver particular results.[11] This reduction in 'thinking time' meant that scientists faced a significant loss in the primary resource necessary in order for them 'to use their skills and experience to look at a case and determine what techniques to use, and to carefully examine the results, interpret them and to write a clear and robust statement.' (King et al., 2012).

As demonstrated above, scientists discerned further problems related to the shift in administrative control, from the forensic-scientific expert, to the 'customer'; primarily the fact that the 'customer' was now able to dictate which product was to be used. Although the scientist retained the ability to recommend the use of alternative - or additional – products, these requests were increasingly viewed as purely advisory and were often outweighed by cost concerns. Conversely, some scientists expressed a reluctance to suggest viable alternatives, as these might diminish the provider's contracted 'turn round times'. Therefore, it may be concluded that the introduction of commoditisation led to a significant loss of independence in the setting of the forensic strategy necessary for case evaluation and investigation,[12] to that extent that larger providers increasingly began to follow customer recommendations, even where these were perceived to be mistaken, or merely inefficient.

It is dependent on the contract...the wording of that contract, what falls under [the contract], or the scientist's interpretation of what that is... some scientists previously have read a certain code to me in a source-level only interpretation...and especially because of the perceived price difference between a lower code and a higher code, they don't get that added value... I'm not going to give them that activity level interpretation because they're not paying for it, but really, my view is that [I should]. (Interview with DNA Reporting Scientist: Tier One FSP, 2015)

One interviewee (a lead biologist) discussed the ways in which commoditisation might create issues for expert forensic analysis (King et al., 2012), providing the example of a common assault, following which the police submit one blood-stained item of clothing - taken from a suspect - to the forensic science provider. The investigating authorities request that product 01BF (a DNA test for body fluids) be used. The forensic scientist examines the item, and submits one blood stain for DNA analysis. The DNA is found to 'match' that of the victim. A report is produced in those terms, stating that a DNA profile was obtained, and found to 'match' that of the victim.

Given the above scenario, the report will necessarily be limited to statements regarding the source of the material, since no parallel interpretation of the possible causes of particular blood patterns has been carried out. Therefore, the reader will not know how much - or little - blood was present on the examined item, or how it could have come to be on the item. In addition, no attempt will have been made to look for the presence of damage, or other evidence that might help the court to determine what has occurred, and which may allow the scientist to furnish propositions relating to the activity which led to the staining, as well as the source.[13]

Such limitations as may result from the sole use of product 01BF derive from the fact that this product was designed to be used in simple cases, such as burglaries - or car thefts - where answers to the question of 'who', rather than 'how', are generally sufficient. Nonetheless, this product is routinely used in more complex cases, in which the interpretation of evidential material should proceed on the basis of a more thorough, and nuanced, analysis.

In addition, it should be noted that the codification and commoditisation of forensic science under the West Coast Consortium Tender extended from substantive forensic activities such as testing and analysis, to the writing of forensic reports. The tender introduced a product called an 'abbreviated' (or 'short form') statement, for use with all forensic products.[14] This product was significantly cheaper than a full evaluative statement due to the fact that the 'short form' statement contained comparatively little information. The abbreviated statement was limited to only that information which the investigating authority, and forensic scientists, considered to be important. Hence, a complete list of case items was not provided, and interpretation of the results - if present - was not thorough. Nor was the interpretation conducted with any regard to the overall context of a case.[15]

As with the design of simple products, such statements were designed to be used in reasonably straightforward cases, such as burglaries or car thefts. In such cases, a DNA profile will be obtained and the abbreviated statement written, giving the basic DNA result (which will often be a full DNA profile attributable to a particular individual).[16] There is a section at the end of many of these abbreviated statements stating that a full witness statement should be requested prior to the case going to court. However, this requirement is frequently overlooked.

Thus, the codification process, in tandem with the introduction of short form reporting, may be seen as promoting the stratification of criminal investigations - at an early stage - into 'simple' and 'complex' cases: a division which is reflected in the pricing of forensic products, and may prove determinative when allocating resources. However, since the interposition of processes of 'triaging' may determine the amount of resources allocated to forensic investigation - thus affecting the depth of investigation, and the nature of its conclusions - the potential exists for problems to arise in relation to the initial misrecognition of cases (e.g. when the concise approach is taken to a case requiring deeper analysis and thorough evaluation). Such difficulties are compounded by the lack of availability of clear criteria with which to demarcate alternative levels of seriousness and subsequent analysis.

CONCLUSION

As the data has demonstrated, the creation of a rudimentary forensic science market, (subsequent to the introduction, by the Forensic Science Service, of direct charging to customers) facilitated the process of informal standardisation of forensic processes. Through making forensic investigatory processes visible to institutional agents within the criminal justice system, the latter became comparatively more able to dictate the course of the investigatory strategy, and to request the use of particular products, within the context of particular levels of evaluation. The standardisation, and productisation, of forensic processes thus facilitated 'triaging', and enabled criminal justice agencies to assign samples to different intensities, and modes, of forensic investigation, largely determined by the offence type. Given that each force had particular needs, this model led to perceived inefficiencies, and, allowed inexpert investigators within the CJS an inordinate amount of control over matters, which traditionally had fallen within the ambit of forensic science.

Scientists further reported that the convergence, and transplantation, of standardised products and practices had created tensions, which were overcome through the modification of subsisting practices alongside site-by-site adaptation, and the use of bridging strategies. Informant's responses demonstrated the persistence of these modified local practices, and the continued importance of tacit expert knowledge. Crucially, scientists also testified to the degree to which partial standardisation had actually created greater levels of variation, especially with regard to the delivery of the product. This flowed directly from the inability of the forty-three individual forces to agree to standard operating procedures, and protocols (allbeit that these might remain flexible enough to accommodate the particular needs of each force).

Further, informants demonstrated how the influence of codification later shaped the process of 'triaging' which set material samples on a particular evidential trajectory, and which structured the resulting analysis in terms of depth, level of expertise, and the examiner's ability to take account of contextual factors. They testified to the ways in which overarching governance structures shaped the work of expert practitioners, and considered the degree to which these influences could affect the ability of forensic scientists to carry out an exhaustive – contextually rich – evaluation, which conformed to the standard requirements of the Case Assessment and Interpretation process.

Lastly, informants illustrated the ways in which processes of standardisation and productisation articulated the concept of customer 'value', creating tensions between forensic scientists, and institutional agents within the criminal justice system, and which may carry deeper implications for both the criminal justice system, and the forensic science sector.

In closing, it is claimed that the foregoing empirical study carries significant implications for our understanding of the development of standards within emerging markets. It highlights the necessity of drafting standards as part of a comprehensive process involving all relevant stakeholders. Indeed, the empirical data raises concerns regarding the difficulties which may arise when lead agencies (or international corporations) control, and direct, the standardization process, crafting solutions – and shaping products – which are tailored to providing efficiencies to their members. Thus, it is probable that problems may be encountered when monopolies (or oligopolies) define standards in a way which delivers disproportionate benefits to one group. Such problems are amplified when the standardisation process is enacted against a background of market volatility, in the absence of formal, meso-level organisation.

The obstacles engendered by the incomplete, or partial, drafting of standards may potentially lead to further difficulties, related to implementation, and adaptation. The data from the instant study reveals the awkward complexities of implementing forensic products, intended for utilization within a structured investigatory process, which were developed in the absence of rigorous and transparent complementary protocols governing their implementation. The implications are that partial standardization does not in, and of, itself create uniformity. The outcome will depend on additional factors which relate to the ability of those tasked with implementing the standard to do so, and which will largely determine whether a standard can ultimately be followed, absent of adaptive processes.

Further, the chapter demonstrates that the subject of standards—their production, distribution, and adoption—is of central importance, not solely to Science and Technology Studies scholars, but to those from the humanities and social sciences. The study demonstrates the increasing relevance of qualitative socio-legal studies, and testifies to their capacity to unearth rich descriptions, revealing the contingency of the standardization process, and of subsequent strategies of adaptation.

REFERENCES

Cook, R., Evett, I. W., Jackson, G., Jones, P. J., & Lambert, J. A. (1998). A Model for Case Assessment and Interpretation. *Science & Justice*, *38*(3), 151–156. doi:10.1016/S1355-0306(98)72099-4 PMID:9800430

Evett. (1998). *The Case Assessment and Interpretation (CAI)*. Method.

King, D, Stangoe, C & Cooke, L. (2012). *Scrutinising Forensic Services*. CPD Presentation to 25 Bedford Row.

Lawless, C. (2010). *A Curious Reconstruction? The Shaping of 'Marketized' Forensic Science*. CARR Discussion Paper 63.

Lawless, C. (2016). *Forensic Science: A Sociological introduction*. New York: Routledge. doi:10.4324/9781315760551

Lawless, C. J., & Williams, R. (2010). Helping With Inquiries or Helping With Profits? The trials and tribulations of a technolology of forensic reasoning. *Social Studies of Science*, *40*(5), 731–755. doi:10.1177/0306312710378787 PMID:21553603

Richmond, K. (2017). Streamlined Forensic Reporting: 'Swift and sure justice'? *Journal of Criminal Law*, *82*(2), 156–177. doi:10.1177/0022018318772701

Timmermans, S., & Epstein, S. A. (2010). World of Standards but not a Standard World: Toward a Sociology of Standards and Standardization. *Annual Review of Sociology*, *36*(1), 69–89. doi:10.1146/annurev.soc.012809.102629

ENDNOTES

1 Centralisation and public ownership are common features of forensic science provision throughout Europe and across both common law, and civilian, jurisdictions: e.g. *Statens Kriminaltekniska Laboratorium* (Swedish National Laboratory of Forensic Science, SKL); Forensic Science Ireland; Netherlands Forensic Science Institute, and the *Bundeskriminalamt* Forensic Science Institute.

2 http://www.keyforensic.co.uk (in insolvency as of 2018).

3 http://www.cellmarkforensics.co.uk

4 http://www.esg.co.uk/services/forensic-services-overview/

5 http://www.lgcgroup.com/sectors/forensic-science/ (rebranded EuroFins as of 2017)

6 http://www.afsp.org.uk/node/33/
The non-commercial members are Scottish Police Authority Forensic Services and Forensic Science Northern Ireland.

7 http://www.principalforensicservices.com/
This company is noteworthy as it employs the incoming UK Forensic Science Regulator, Dr. Gill Tully.

8 Now ArroGen Forensics, merging with Forensic Access in 2018.

9 http://www.haywardforensics.co.uk/

10 Cellmark, LGC, and Key Forensic Services comprise the top tier of marketised forensic science provision in the UK.

11 Arbitrary three or four day 'turn round times' are both common in, and unique to, the UK forensic market and do not reflect the time taken for a case to reach court. Equivalent analyses may take up to ninety days in the United States.

12 Productisation might therefore be seen as having a negative impact on the scientist's ability to carry out Casework Interpretation and Analysis, given that the CAI process relies on communication and reflexivity.

13 For a discussion of the hierarchy of propositions see (Cook et al., 1998)

14 The commoditisation of forensic reports followed the introduction, by the Crown Prosecution Service, of 'staged reporting' (also known as Streamlined Forensic Reporting) for cases involving DNA. See (Richmond, 2017)

15 Abbreviated statements should be distinguished from Streamlined Forensic Reports. The latter are frequently compiled by non-experts and contain no interpretation.

16 King et al (2012) provide anecdotal evidence of problems which may arise from the use of abbreviated statements: '…we have seen examples where upon examination of the DNA profile the result is actually a mixture of DNA from which the profile of the major contributor has been deduced. In these cases there has been no comment on the presence of DNA from any other individual.'

Section 5
A Mixed Bag

Chapter 13
Predatory Strategies in Standards Wars:
On Creating Fear, Uncertainty, and Doubt

Tineke Mirjam Egyedi
DIRoS, The Netherlands

Anique Hommels
Maastricht University, The Netherlands

ABSTRACT

In standards wars, FUD (fear, uncertainty, and doubt) is sometimes created to weaken an opponent's market position. Little is known about these strategies, their use in committee standardization settings, and how to respond to them. This chapter explores this phenomenon. It (1) identifies various FUD strategies, (2) their context of emergence, and (3) their effect on the dynamics of a standards war in a historical case study: the European standards war on digital mobile radio communication in the 1990s. The study highlights the need to distinguish "FUD as perceived" from "FUD as intended." FUD strategies and case-specific characteristics of their emergence are illustrated. The chapter shows that perceived FUD polarizes and entrenches positions of warring parties thereby affecting the course of the standards war. The authors conclude that, given its impact, reflection by corporate standardization managers on (perceived) FUD, preclusion, counter-strategies, and the downscaling of standards wars is warranted.

INTRODUCTION

In the early 1990s, several European member-states decided to replace their analogue radio systems for the police, ambulance and fire brigades by advanced digital systems. Their decision coincided with the aim of the Schengen Agreement to create a Pan-European network for public safety that would allow the police to use the same handset across national networks during 'cross-border surveillance and hot pursuit' (Schengen, 1990). It also concurred with activities of the European Telecommunications Standards Institute (ETSI). Supported by the European Commission, ETSI had started work on a standard for digital mobile radio communication in 1988. One of the objectives was to define a common air interface that

DOI: 10.4018/978-1-5225-9008-8.ch013

Copyright © 2019, IGI Global. Copying or distributing in print or electronic forms without written permission of IGI Global is prohibited.

would ensure that any standard-compliant terminal (e.g., handset) could run on any European network regardless of the network supplier. A number of countries considered the Tetra standard, as it was called, to be a promising means for achieving the Schengen aims.

However, in April 1994, the period in which ETSI was approving the air interface technology (TDMA) of the Tetra standard, an incompatible competing technology (FDMA) was gaining support among European countries. The latter technology had already been developed by a French company called Matra Communications and implemented in 1992 for the French gendarmerie. To improve access to the European market, FDMA advocates also attempted to get their technology formally acknowledged as an ETSI standard. Initially they seemed to succeed. Early 1995, however, ETSI dropped FDMA from the work program. This was a conspicuous decision, according to Bekkers (2001, p. 380), given the number of suppliers supporting FDMA and FDMA being the preferred choice of a number of public safety network operators. It was the beginning of a standards war.

Standards wars are fought in markets as well as in and between standards committees (Besen, 1991). The TDMA-FDMA war foremost took place in a standardization setting. It involved a committee standard of a formal standards body (i.e., an ETSI specification based on TDMA technology) as well as a de facto standard (i.e., FDMA technology implemented in products by Matra) that later became a consortium standard (i.e., the FDMA-based technical specification of Tetrapol Forum). It was a 'rival revolutions' type of standards war (Shapiro & Varian, 1999). In such wars, two factors determine the stakes and the dynamics. First, the rival technologies are *incompatible* (Shapiro & Varian, 1999). This was the case, for example, in technology wars between Blu-Ray and HD-DVD (Gallagher, 2012), e-purse systems (de Vries, 2006) and proprietary platforms (West, 2003), to name a few de facto standards wars. Incompatible technologies were also at stake in wars between committee standards, for example, in the field of wireless telecommunication (Lee, 2006) and for DVD formats (Dranove & Gandal, 2003).

A second and related defining factor in standards wars is the effect of rival technologies on *network externalities*. The term refers to an increase in value of the network with every new connected network user (Farrell & Saloner, 1985). Rival networks based on incompatible technologies or standards cannot exploit each other's externalities. For example, owners of a certain smart phone cannot usually make use of the infrastructure of a different smart phone for spare parts and customer services. In past studies, the workings of network externalities was a main reason to presume that in IT markets only one competing technology would be able to survive ('winner-takes-all'). While more recent work indicates that there may be room for two or more standards (Singh, 2009), the presence of network externalities has been shown to heighten the stakes in standards wars. Given these stakes, "[w]hen it comes to standards wars, traditional principles of strategy, while helpful, are not enough" (Shapiro & Varian, 1999), and some companies will turn to predatory market strategies.

The predatory strategies addressed in this chapter are those that create Fear, Uncertainty and Doubt (FUD), a category referred to by Pfaffenberger (2000). To our knowledge, no other studies have as yet analyzed standards wars on the use of predatory market strategies and FUD strategies, in particular. Perhaps understandably so. The term 'FUD' is foremost referred to in business magazine and trade journal articles to capture a class of industry strategies that are perceived to be unfair and used to publicly denounce certain market practices. That is, it is used in a decidedly normative and non-scientific way. The challenge for scientific research on FUD strategies is how to take in and address the inherent subjectivity involved in attributing unfairness. This point is revisited when defining FUD strategies in the next section.

Trade literature on standards wars indicates that companies have difficulty knowing how to deal with FUD strategies. When feeling cornered, companies risk retaliating with defensive counter-strategies that are ineffective and/or may unwittingly escalate problems. Our assessment is that corporate standardization managers lack certain insights that are necessary to consider pre-emptive action and recognize alternative strategies. In the following, we hope to feed them with insights that help them in their decision making. We aim to shed more light on:

1. How may FUD strategies manifest themselves?
2. In which context do they emerge?
3. How do they affect the dynamics of standards wars?

Given the scope of these questions, we limit ourselves to studying standards wars involving committee standardization, an area underrepresented in scholarly literature. We expect the occurrence of committee standards wars to increase in tandem with the rising emergence of standards consortia (Egyedi & Hawkins, 2010). Furthermore, given the explorative nature of our questions, we present the findings of a historical case study on the use of FUD strategies in the committee standards war introduced above (Yin, 2009).

Our data were primarily gathered by means of extensive archival research on exchanged letters, policy documents, etc.[1] from three archives[2] and secondary literature. Twenty in-depth interviews with key actors were held to enrich our general understanding of the case. Five of them are referred to in this chapter as they have immediate relevance for answering our research questions and help illustrate and contextualize our archival data[3].

Below, we first review scholarly literature on predatory strategies and standards wars for insights that help define FUD behavior and its effects. Next, the case of the European standards war on digital mobile radio communication is further introduced. Used FUD strategies are identified and discussed. We conclude by revisiting our research questions and reflecting on lessons learned for corporate standardization managers.

FUD STRATEGIES IN STANDARDIZATION

In the 1970s IBM was accused of using FUD to ward off new market entrants (Pfaffenberger, 2000). Gene Amdahl remarked after he left IBM to found his own company, the Amdahl Corporation: “FUD is the fear, uncertainty, and doubt that IBM sales people instill in the minds of potential customers who might be considering Amdahl products”. Drawing a parallel with Microsoft’s reactions to the rising popularity of the Linux platform, Pfaffenberger (2000) defines FUD as “a marketing technique that a market-dominating firm employs to blunt a competitor’s first-to-market advantage”. (We will re-address his definition later on.) He lists techniques that may be part of a FUD campaign such as “press releases designed to confuse costumers about the merits of the new product, and benchmark tests – generally rigged in the market-dominating firm’s favor – that raise questions about the new product’s performance (…)” and the predatory preannouncement of vaporware (i.e., a product which does not and may never exist) “that can be timed to steal the momentum from a competitor’s technologically superior product” (Pfaffenberger, 2000).

Systematic studies of FUD strategies used in standardization settings are lacking. But, as certain parallels can be drawn with strategies used in highly competitive markets and de facto standards wars, some insight can be gained from technology management, economic, standardization and marketing literature in this field. In such situations, Shapiro & Varian (1999) recommend two basic marketplace tactics, i.e., pre-emption (being first to market and learn from positive feedback) and expectation management. Regarding pre-emption, where a committee standard is based on an existing technology, prior market experience with the technology offers clear benefits (first-mover advantage). In line, the benefit of early experience with implementing a standard tempts some companies to prematurely implement draft standards (Jakobs, 2008).

As for managing the expectations of consumers and competitors (Shapiro & Varian, 1999), this may include the use of predatory preannouncements (Haan, 2003); (Wu et al., 2004); (Bayus et al, 2001) and vaporware, tactics that also fall within the remit of FUD strategies. Product preannouncement refers to a "formal, deliberate communication that release[s] information about a product well in advance of the product's actual introduction" (Wu et al., 2004). Predatory preannouncements and vaporware can be very successful in creating uncertainty in markets among competitors and consumers(Haan, 2003;Bayus, 2001). They also play a role in standardization settings. The preannouncement of new standards or standards versions is a common occurrence. During the DVD recordables standards war, for example, both rival consortia regularly announced new standard versions with increased recording capacity and speed. This led to a race between new standards versions (Gauch, 2008). Preannouncement of a new standards version can undermine the momentum for a competitor's standard's launch. If the preannouncement signals that the newcomer will not survive competition and that customers are to 'hang on' in anticipation of a new version, it can also deter newcomers from market entry (Haan, 2003); (Bayus, 2001).

In respect to standards wars' in and between standards committees, the procedures of standard bodies and consortia, however fair and impartial, cannot safeguard against the use of predatory strategies (e.g. (Oshri & Weeber, 2006); (Wegberg, 2004). Examples of (perceived) misuse of the formal rules are staging a standards vote during the holiday season, when most participants will be absent, and defecting during the final vote after lengthy but seemingly fruitful negotiations in a situation where 100% consensus is required to proceed (http://www.noooxml.org/irregularities). Furthermore, increasingly lawsuits are used to settle standardization disputes. Fear of lawsuits sometimes paralyzes standards processes and may cause companies to withdraw from the standards process (Egyedi, 2001).

Pfaffenberger's (2000) description of FUD as "a marketing technique that a market-dominating firm employs to blunt a competitor's first-to-market advantage" assumes that FUD is intentional and therefore involves predatory strategies. However, it is often difficult to distinguish between strategic and innocent action (Haan, 2003); (Bayus, 2001). Possibly FUD is raised unintentionally. Moreover, how should one methodologically address behavior that is intended to create FUD but is not perceived as such by the targeted party? A clearer definition is needed.

Table 1. Focus of the case study is on perceived FUD strategies (A and B)

FUD Strategies	Perceived	Not perceived
Intended	A	C
Unintended	B	D

We use the word *affect*, that is, a psychological term for feeling, experience or emotion. To make possible a more systematic study of FUD, the *affect* of Fear, Uncertainty and Doubt that results from certain behavior must be conceptually de-coupled from *intentionality*. This implies two basic lines of enquiry: one focusing on the perspective of the sender ('FUD as intended' in short) and the other on the receiver ('FUD as affected' in short). In general, companies are understandably reticent about providing outsiders information on their market strategy. The same applies to their standardization strategy. In addition, the intention of creating FUD is not a societally acceptable standardization strategy, as trade journals indicate. As a result, data on intentional FUD is hard to come by. In this case study, we therefore focus on 'FUD as affected' (see instances A and B in Table 1). We only refer to 'FUD as intended' if self-reported and if perceived as such.[4]

Figure 1 illustrates that certain *behavior* may or may not give rise to the *affect* FUD, whether intended or not (see Figure 1).

Consequently, we define the strategy of creating Fear, Uncertainty and Doubt in standardization as: a market strategy *perceived* to be designed to create unease among competitors and raise concern among users about the consequences of selecting a competitor's standard, by exerting pressure - psychological, legal or otherwise – and disseminating negative and/or incorrect information about the standard, the standards process or the standard's likely market uptake, as a result of which the credibility of the competitor and/or the competing standard is undermined.

FUD strategies feed uncertainty among standardizers and market players. Typically, uncertainty undermines competition in network-based markets (Farrell & Saloner, 1986), a market to which our case also belongs. It leads to hold–ups of investments (Williamson, 1979). Producers will try to postpone investments for fear of investing in the 'losing' system and having to write off sunk costs (i.e., costs that are specific and irreversible and cannot be retrieved). The same hesitations exist on the side of consumers. They fear being stuck with an incompatible system, that is, of becoming an 'angry orphan' (David, 1987). Uncertainty arising from creating FUD in the standards setting or in the market causes market stagnation.

Figure 1. Key elements of a conceptual model for studying FUD strategies. It distinguishes behavior from how behavior is experienced (affect) and what it leads to (effect).

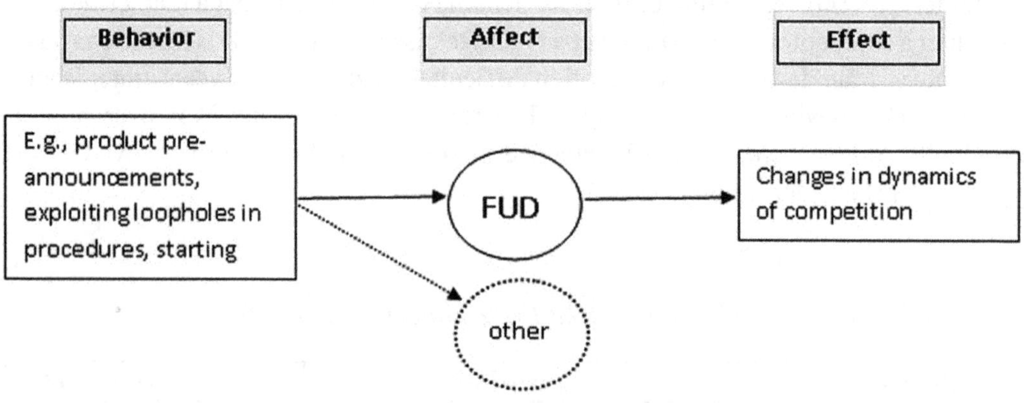

The case study's primary source for perceived FUD behavior and its effect are three public and private archives and data from interviews with former stakeholders. Key data are instances in the archived documents and interviews in which stakeholders themselves frame behavior as creating FUD. In our case, the archives almost exclusively made reference to the FUD strategies of one party - in the perception of the other party. Different causes may underlie this asymmetry. For example, methodological causes (inaccessibility of certain archives and interviewees) or case-related causes (e.g., asymmetry in *documented* FUD or different actor perceptions about what is a fair strategy). Whatever the cause(s), our aim is not to retrospectively choose sides in the standards war, but to contribute, empirically, to FUD studies by identifying (new) FUD strategies and, analytically, by exploring the conditions under which such behavior may emerge.

INTRODUCING THE CASE: TETRA VERSUS TETRAPOL

Although initially intended for a wider market (Bekkers, 2001), Tetra eventually became adopted as a standard for public safety networks in Europe under the influence of the Schengen Agreement. The police officials, who played a leading role among the potential users of Tetra, and the national governments of the - at that time five - Schengen countries (Belgium, the Netherlands, Luxemburg, Germany and France) saw it as an opportunity to meet a number of core objectives of the Schengen Agreement (signed June 14, 1985), a feeling that was shared more widely when the Schengen Agreement became officially adopted as EU policy in the Treaty of Amsterdam of 2 October 1997.

In the late 1980s, incompatible systems made direct connection between cross-border police units impossible. To overcome this, the Schengen Agreement outlined a short-term strategy (ad hoc improvements and bilateral agreements for police cooperation) and a long-term strategy aimed at developing a "uniform police radio communication system using common frequencies for exclusive use by the police" (#1).The latter required a common European communication standard like Tetra. The expectation was that "standardization would lead to a better quality of the cooperation between the emergency services, increased efficiency and increased effectiveness in case of large-scale emergencies." (#2)

The mobile digital radio system which ETSI started developing in 1988 was called MDTRS (Mobile Digital Trunking Radio System). In 1992, it was renamed Tetra (Trans European Trunked Radio, and later, when its possible use outside of Europe became clear, TErrestrial Trunked RAdio). In March 1991, the MDTRS specifications were prognosed to be ready at the end of 1992. The first tests were expected to be done in 1993/1994, and early 1995 the first systems would be operational.

The expectation of a smooth and quick standards process proved too optimistic. The first problems became apparent in 1993 and involved a competing technology that was later to be called Tetrapol. Tetrapol had been developed on request of the French government by the French company Matra Communications. Based on an FDMA access mode, this technology was the building block of the Rubis radio network for the French Gendarmerie (1992) and Acropol (1995) for the national police forces and fire brigades. The French put much effort into convincing other European countries of the advantages of the FDMA air interface technology underlying Tetrapol. But FDMA was incompatible with the TDMA air interface technology that was already being standardized in ETSI and was to be approved in 1994. Most TDMA proponents opposed standardizing two incompatible technologies. However, support for

FDMA was growing, and in 1993 a number of operators and manufacturers (Bosch, Matra, Alcatel etc.) proposed the inclusion of the FDMA standardization in ETSI's work program. FDMA was argued to be more suitable for high coverage and low traffic density areas such as the countryside. TDMA was thought to better address high density communication and low coverage typical of urban areas. Given these complementary advantages, the FDMA proponents argued, it was appropriate to standardize both air interface technologies. Intense debate among suppliers and member-state representatives followed.

The beginning of the standards war can be pinpointed to early 1995, the period in which the ETSI committee decided to drop work on FDMA. (Hence forth the TDMA and FDMA technologies are referred to as a *pars pro toto* for Tetra and Tetrapol, respectively.) Companies such as Matra and Motorola played a pivotal role in the ensuing standards war. Matra left ETSI and decided to market its system under the name 'Tetrapol'. By then, it had more than two years of experience with the network of the French gendarmerie (Bekkers, 2001) and had started rolling out Acropol for the French national police force and fire brigades. That is, it had a first-mover advantage in the market for public safety networks, which had the Schengen countries and the Police Cooperation as potential customers. In addition, the value of Matra's Intellectual Property Rights (IPRs) on the Tetrapol technology depended on the outcome of the standards war. The French government – representing a large and therefore influential member-state, geographically central to Europe and bordering with several other countries - promised to play the role of launching customer. Because it had high sunk costs and was locked into Matra's market. It had a direct stake in the standards war, even apart from having national industry interests like virtually all countries (e.g., Germany and the US).

Motorola's reasons to promote Tetra as a standard for public safety radio communication was that it wanted to re-use its technologies – and IPRs - in the development of Tetra. It had, for example, worked on a TDMA system that could serve in an adapted form as the technological base for the Tetra specification. The company already had an FDMA system in their portfolio (APCO 25), but it wanted to use this exclusively for the American market. Early on in the development of Tetra (1994), it publicly announced its intention to bring Tetra to the market. This raised the expectations of other manufacturers and end-users. It was the first company to invest heavily in Tetra and install Tetra test systems (on the Island of Jersey). In sum, both Matra and Motorola had a good starting position and ample reason to wage a war.

IDENTIFYING FUD IN THE CASE

In the following, occurrences in the Tetra-Tetrapol standards war are discussed that were perceived as creating FUD. The narratives are based on primary archival documents and, where possible, were confirmed by interviewees.

Confusion About Standards Names

In 1993, French and German technology suppliers (Bosch, Matra, Alcatel etc.), supported by the Schengen Telecom group, urged for a second, FDMA-based Tetra trajectory. The distinction Tetra 6 (FDMA) and Tetra 25 (TDMA) was introduced (i.e., based on the channel width of 6.25 kHz and 25 kHz, respectively). To outsiders, the names Tetra 6 and Tetra 25 suggested two standards options with little difference. Since both were called Tetra, the question of their (in)compatibility was not likely to be raised.

What happened before was that soon after the ETSI standards committee had renamed MDTRS to Tetra in 1992, Matra registered the name 'Tetrapol'. (Interview 5, 27-11-2007). The name appears in the archives from 1993 onwards. As support for Tetra 6 within ETSI died down and was dropped in 1994 from its work program (#3), Matra increasingly used 'Tetrapol' to refer to the Rubis and Acropol networks.

Matra had chosen this name deliberately to put the FDMA-solution on the same plane as Tetra (Interview 1, 17-4-2008). The similarity created much confusion. It positioned Tetrapol as a Tetra version developed for the police instead of a competing solution (Interview 2, 29-1-2009). Tetrapol made a 'claim by name' for a connection with Tetra (#4). By implication, ETSI, being the developer of Tetra, also sanctioned Tetrapol, which gave credibility to Matra's proprietary system. "This is deliberately misleading to users"(#5).

Over the years, the Schengen Telecom Group became an increasingly important user-player. Late 1993, it decided that an open ETSI standard would be needed to create a multi-vendor market. The Schengen Telecom group delegated, as it were, the technical decision making to ETSI. The term 'ETSI standard' became conditional for acquiring the group's support. Therefore, when ETSI decided not to pursue the Tetra 6 option, the Schengen Telecom group closed the door on Tetrapol (#6).

Confusion About the Status of Tetrapol

The Tetrapol proponents, not having achieved direct access to ETSI standardization, then explored indirect means of becoming ETSI 'accredited'. In December 1995, Tetrapol Forum expressed its wish to submit the Tetrapol technology to the so-called PAS (Publicly Available Specification) procedure in order to become a recognized ETSI standard. ETSI had introduced this procedure earlier that year "(…) to accelerate standards-making in Europe through [sic] the recognition of standards other than those produced formally within ETSI itself. (…)" (#7). Approval of Tetrapol via the PAS procedure would accredit it as an ETSI standard and provide it a status equal to that of the Tetra standard.

Tetrapol Forum submitted a formal request to ETSI on May 29 1996, and presented its specification on June 27 1996 (#8). Shortly afterwards, the ETSI Board decided that Tetrapol was eligible for the PAS procedure. Next in the PAS procedure, the ETSI committee was to evaluate if Tetrapol met the PAS criteria, one of which was that the PAS should not cover the same scope as an existing or proposed ETSI specification. (#30) An extra committee meeting was scheduled for 21-22 October 1996. But just prior to the meeting, Tetrapol Forum withdrew its request because the meeting had been announced too late and it had had too little opportunity to effectively lobby for votes (#21). Possibly it had guessed that behind the scene Tetra supporters, from government representatives to Tetra-manufacturers, had been lobbying successfully for a rejection of the Tetrapol PAS application. In a letter, Tetrapol Forum wrote:

The option of transferring the TETRAPOL P.A.S. to a Technical Specification might be more appropriate than the present proposal to transpose to an I-ETS. (…) In conclusion, we formally withdraw our request of 29 May 1996 for transposition to a P.A.S. (…) We further confirm our intention of restarting the procedure with (…) the new working rules for ETSI. (#9)

The letter created confusion and uncertainty. It unsettled ETSI members, first, because the loose use of the word 'P.A.S.' sharply contrasted with ETSI's specified use of the term 'PAS'[5] ("(…) any manufacturer or organization can publicly offer a specification and call it a PAS but this is nothing to do with ETSI." (#10)

Second, it raised the possibility of Tetrapol becoming a Technical Specification, which could create confusion and hurt the interests of TDMA proponents almost as much as a second Tetra-variant would.

With the current PAS-procedure the chances are almost zero that Tetrapol will become an EN (European Standard – the name for an open European Standard). It might sooner become a TR (Technical Report) (...). The status of a TR is low. But we are very likely to run the risk that those not well-acquainted with ETSI procedures (i.e. most people!) will not understand the difference between an EN and a TR. Matra may phrase it as that Tetrapol has been accepted by ETSI (#11)

Third, announcing that this PAS effort would not be the last one prolonged uncertainty about Tetrapol's status and Tetra's position in the market (#12).

Meanwhile, the European Commission was gradually changing its position. It started with Mr. Adoux from DG IV (Competition), noting that the Commission "(…) favor[s] competing standards but not conflicting standards. (…)." (#13)A few months later, the European Commission wanted "to speed up the standardization of telecommunications solutions which are already available on the market" (#14). This was an important impetus for Tetrapol Forum to re-start the Tetrapol PAS procedure on 21 January 1997. This time, before the voting on the Tetrapol PAS started on April 26 1999, a delegate of the European Commission informed the ETSI General Assembly that the Commission wanted to promote competition and that they should not block this (Interview 1). Nevertheless, ETSI rejected the Tetrapol PAS, with only 37.5% of the votes in favor. The Presidency of the EU Council interpreted the outcome in a way that matched the Commission's views: "Until now, attempts to achieve a Common European Standard for radio communication have generally resulted in the adoption of two basic approaches, namely the TETRA *standard* and the TETRAPOL *technology solution*, both of which will now be used in future by the Member-States." (#15) The Commission hereby recognized Tetrapol as a 'de facto' standard.

Over the years, Tetrapol's status remained a source of confusion which, according to Tetra proponents, was damaging Tetra's market position:

Members of EP TETRA remain extremely concerned over the continuing confusion in the market place surrounding the status of Tetrapol in the context of an ETSI deliverable. You will be aware of the large investment in the European Standard, Tetra, already made by manufacturers and the TETRA procurement plans of major user organizations and network operators. The confusion is undermining confidence in TETRA and creating damaging uncertainty. (#16)

Brian Oliver, chairman of the ETSI Tetra Committee, noted that although it was clear that ETSI did not want a second standard, the Tetrapol proponents repeatedly tried to label their technology as such in the years 1994 up to 2003 (Interview 5). A letter that was sent by Tetrapol Forum to Colonel Van Peer, chair of the Schengen Telecom group, dated 4 December 1995, further fuelled the confusion. Therein Tetrapol Forum called Tetrapol a Publicly Available Specification (PAS) and an open technology. "It respects the seven criteria fixed by the European Commission and approved by ETSI. The technical specifications are already available on request (…) The PAS documents and the report about compliance with the seven criteria are sent to the Director of ETSI to officially confirm that Tetrapol is already a PAS and can be transformed into an ETSI European standard." The letter implied Commission support and suggested that Tetrapol was already halfway to being accepted by ETSI. Confused, the Schengen Telecom group contacted the European Commission. In response, Mr. Richter (European Commission) denied that ETSI had received the Tetrapol PAS and that an evaluation had already taken place. He noted that the Tetrapol PAS "is clearly in conflict with the criterion four, as its scope is the same as the draft ETSI TETRA ETS, being developed under mandate from the Commission" (…) and that " it is not at all guaranteed that the proposed PAS will be presented at the next [ETSI] Technical Assembly." (#17) He ended his letter sincerely regretting that Tetrapol Forum's letter did not correctly represent known public facts.

Discrediting ETSI

Uncertainty-enhancing were also Tetrapol Forum's references to ETSI's lack of integrity. ETSI's "anti-competitive practices (…) sought systematically to prevent TETRAPOL from gaining [European] recognition (…)" (#21). Certain members were colluding "to jeopardize the chances of the PAS application getting a fair treatment." (#22) More subtly, the chairman of Tetrapol Forum wrote the following in a letter to the ETSI secretary-general with a cc to the Commission:

(…) TETRAPOL Forum suggested that ETSI proceed with a thorough and objective examination of the complementary issues between the two technologies. In this respect, it is our view that the evaluation process cannot be based on anti-competitive criteria (such as a total ban on any overlap between a PAS application and an existing or in development ETSI standard) but must be market-oriented. In particular, the standardization process cannot be allowed to result in the unnecessary elimination of a widely used and complementary technology in this particular field of telecommunications whereas, like in other telecommunications fields, valid solutions can be found that permit the continued coexistence of partly overlapping standards. (…) I am sure you will understand that TETRAPOL Forum cannot – and will not accept being involved in a standardization process unless it is fair, objective and transparent and that no unnecessary restrictions are imposed. (#23)

By discrediting ETSI, doubts were cast on its decision not to support Tetrapol, on the quality of the Tetra standard, and on the demand for and market uptake of ETSI standards.

Law Suits

Law suits took place and legal threats were made. Countries like the Netherlands, Belgium and the UK explicitly favored Tetra over Tetrapol in their procurement policy. Matra viewed this as hindering free market competition. It objected to the way the UK Home Office had handled the public procurement process for its national Public Safety Radio Communications Project (later PSRC-S or "Airwave") for emergency services in 1998 (#24). The UK had issued an open tender but had not considered bids from non-Tetra companies, according to Gary Spicks, journalist for Communications Week International. The following quote from a letter of the UK Home Office to ETSI confirms this:

The UK Home Office is currently in a procurement process for the Public Safety Radio Communications Project (PSRCP) which will provide the national, next generation emergency service radio system for England, Wales and Scotland. PSRCP is a billion UK pound procurement carried out through rigorous application of EU Procurement Procedures. Accordingly, the procurement specifies the open European Standard that meets the requirements and that standard is TETRA. (…) The introduction of a competing

ETSI standard would lead to market fragmentation, reduced manufacturing volumes, increased unit costs and reduced manufacturer viability, as well as loss of interoperability and reduced choice of terminal suppliers for users. (#25)

The Home Office chose the BT-led consortium Quadrant, which included Nokia Oyj and Motorola, "to carry out a pilot study, which if successful is likely to lead to the full contract worth 1.5- 2 billion (…) over 15 years" (#26). Matra felt that "Tetrapol manufacturers were excluded from this competition on the grounds that Tetrapol was not an ETSI standard" (#27) and started a legal case against the UK Home Office. However, Matra's case was rejected on the ground that Matra had been too late to complain (Interview 4, 27-11-2007). Whether the lawsuits and legal references (#29) were called for or not, they made people wary and cautious.

Perceived FUD Behavior and the Market

The market for European public safety networks was slow to develop. A notable cause for delay was the scope creep and increasing complexity of standards committee work in ETSI. Over the years the targeted market shifted and new requirements (e.g. of Schengen Telecom) were added (Bekkers, 2001). In addition, the emergence of a rival incompatible technology also held back market development (Shapiro & Varian, 1999). Matra, the owner of the 'proven technology', was severely side-tracked by ETSI's Tetra initiative, while Matra's Tetra-6 and two Tetrapol-PAS initiatives heavily side-tracked ETSI's Tetra committee and delayed the standard's publication. The competing technologies created uncertainty among suppliers. The implication for roaming between networks was unclear, and the fear was that the market would become too small to compete (Bekkers, 2001). Many suppliers postponed investing in commercial Tetra equipment for fear of being stuck with the 'losing' technology and/or needing to support both Tetra and Tetrapol. For the same reason, also users postponed adopting one of the digital technologies.

Market uncertainty was further fuelled and prolonged by the use of FUD strategies in the settings of standardization and government politics. The following behavior was perceived as such (see Table 2):

Table 2. Perceived FUD strategies in the Tetra – Tetrapol standards war

Behavior	Example	Affect
Procedural Pre-announcement	• Announcement of Tetrapol undergoing ETSI's PAS process	• Creating Uncertainty
Similar Naming	• Tetra 6 and Tetra 25 • Tetra and Tetrapol	• Creating Confusion
Terminology Re-interpretation	• PAS or P.A.S. • standard or technical specification	• Creating Confusion
Discrediting	• Discrediting ETSI's workings, standards and standards' uptake	• Raising Doubt
Misrepresentation	• Inaccurate account of events	• Raising Doubt
Legal Action or Pre-announcement thereof	• About breech of EU procedures	• Creating Fear • Creating Uncertainty

- Procedural pre-announcement (e.g., announcement that a technology will enter a standards process which will heighten its status)
- Similar naming (e.g., renaming a technology in a way that creates a direct - assumed positive - association with another technology)
- Terminology reinterpretation (e.g., reinterpreting a term in a different – often unintended – way);
- Discrediting (e.g., raising doubts about a competitor's integrity)
- Misrepresentation (e.g., inaccurate accounts)
- Legal action or pre-announcement thereof (e.g., about possible incorrect reference to standards in public procurement)

The delays in standardization caused by this behavior made it difficult to create momentum for the Tetra market. On ETSI's side, extra time and effort was needed to respond to disinformation and incorrect claims, and to restore trust in the Tetra standard, its standard process and its market expectations.

CONCLUSION

In this chapter a step has been taken towards a more systematic study of FUD strategies. A key element therein has been to redefine Pfaffenberger's notion of 'FUD as intended' as 'FUD as affected' to emphasize the subjective, perceived nature of FUD. This conceptual shift has immediate bearing on our answers to the three research questions and our recommendations to corporate standardization managers and Standards Development Organizations (SDOs).

Research Questions

Regarding the way (perceived) *FUD strategies may manifest themselves* in committee standards wars, FUD behavior observed in de facto standards wars also occurs in committee standards wars. Compare, for example, product pre-announcements in de facto standards wars with procedural pre-announcements in the case study, a FUD strategy specific for committee standards wars. Other FUD strategies that emerge from the study are similar naming, terminology reinterpretation, discrediting, misrepresentation and legal action (pre-announced or effectuated). The FUD strategies we have observed are case-bound and may not be evident in other committee standards wars. But the case is rich in examples, and, while new case studies are likely to extend our list of (perceived) FUD strategies, this initial list serves to help corporate standardization managers to recognize them.

In the case study, behavior associated with these FUD strategies led to confusion, uncertainty, fear and doubt. Whether the FUD that was created ('FUD as affected') was also intended, was sometimes confirmed by the stakeholders themselves. In other instances, behavior perceived as such may not have been intended. That is, unfairness is attributed to 'unintended FUD'. One may ask oneself if it is at all relevant to correctly attribute intentionality to behavior resulting in FUD since, one way or the other, the outcome is the same. Our expectation is that in most situations it is relevant. The case illustrates how unsettling FUD strategies can be if perceived as intentional by the receiving end. The documents and interviews testify that ETSI standardizers often felt cornered and forced to respond. Perceived intentionality appears to entrench positions, reduce willingness to take the opponent's perspective, narrow down perceived options for counter-strategies, hinder the identification of common interests, and cloud views on partial, intermediate and/or long-term compromises. In short, company standardizers run the risk of retaliating with defensive counter-strategies that are ineffective and escalate a standards war. That is, incorrect attribution of intentionality can be self-defeating.

In order to react in a more effective and measured manner, corporate standardization managers benefit from realizing that what may seem as a predatory strategy may be seen by others as a necessary survival strategy in a highly competitive market. To recall an earlier quote, "When it comes to standards wars, traditional principles of strategy, while helpful, are not enough" (Shapiro & Varian, 1999). A better understanding of the context in which (perceived) FUD strategies emerge reduces the chance of attributing unfairness to 'unintended FUD'.

Regarding the second research question, the *context in which FUD strategies may emerge,* FUD strategies find a fertile ground in standards wars. To recapitulate, standards wars involve incompatible rival technologies (i.e., which cannot exploit each other's externalities) in highly competitive markets (i.e., high stakes). In our case study, it started out as a war between a company with an existing market and an implemented technology, on the one hand, and a group of stakeholders that wanted to enter a new market and standardize a new rival technology, on the other. The former company feared being ousted out of the market and was perceived to use unfair FUD strategies.

Initially, both warring parties had IPRs on competing technologies and therefore incentives to exploit them. The targeted market was relatively specialized but profitable, which intensified competition. One party had a clear first-mover advantage (i.e., expertise and implementation experience) and high vested interests. Several large companies were involved that also produced for other markets (i.e. they ran businesses that were partly independent of the area standardized) *and* could survive a protracted standards war. Influential customer-users were involved, national government agencies, with high stakes in standardization (e.g. high sunk costs and crucial interests in public safety) and some with clear links to their national industry (i.e., standardizing companies).

The literature on standards wars and the case study suggest that the risk of resorting to FUD strategies will be high in highly competitive markets and standards wars. It escalates where a company's survival is at stake. Comparative research is needed to determine whether standards wars that show similar characteristics also show similar predatory behavior.

With respect to the third research question, *how do FUD strategies affect the dynamics of technology wars in committee standardization?,* the case illustrates that perceived FUD increases the number and accelerates the succession of conflicts. It polarizes and entrenches positions. It leads to competing standards and technology solutions, and to market fragmentation.

To deepen the discussion, the distinction between using FUD strategies in de facto and committee standards wars is likely to be relevant here. In the light of game theory (Axelrod, 1984), committee standardization can be viewed as a game with multiple rounds. The (formal) aim of the game is ongoing market coordination among stakeholders. Once a standard has been finalized, stakeholders are likely to meet again at a later stage to revise the standard or develop standards in adjoining areas. Using FUD strategies intentionally will affect a company's reputation and influence future standardization negotiations. This issue may be less acute in de facto standards wars, where coordination is not at stake and the game may end after one round. In these situations, intentional FUD and other short-term predatory strategies may go unpunished, but such a 'scorched earth' strategy most likely precludes future collaboration.

RECOMMENDATIONS

Why is it important for corporate standardization managers to better understand, recognize and address (perceived) FUD strategies? Because FUD strategies typically escalate and prolong standards wars. This, in turn, increases market uncertainty and possibly leads to competing standards. Corporate standardization managers will usually want to avoid these consequences. In economic terms, uncertainty about the outcome of a standards war means that producers will try to postpone investments for fear of investing in a losing system and having to write off sunk costs (i.e., costs that are specific and irreversible and therefore cannot be retrieved). For the same reasons consumers will postpone their purchases. The market will stagnate. Moreover, there is a high risk of ending up with functionally equivalent, competing standards that fragment the market. Smaller, fragmented markets are more risky for producers to enter and less worthwhile (decreased economies of scale). Competing standards also create difficulties for consumers, here: the emergency services (e.g. reduced market transparency, lack of interoperability and high transaction costs such as switching costs). (Egyedi, 2014)

Corporate standardization managers and user agencies, which are or may be on the receiving end of FUD strategies, should therefore be aware of what they entail and how they work. Insight in the context in which (intentional) FUD strategies are more likely to emerge, may aid in anticipating and precluding their emergence. Early analysis and warning allows stakeholders to explore solutions that transgress an imminent committee standards war. Is there a possibility for adequately addressing the vested interests of a company whose survival may be at stake? Can the company be compensated by means of intellectual property or other commercial assets? Or by government contracts in other areas? Is it feasible to outline long-term technology convergence and a standards trajectory? Could it be that the life-cycle of the company's and the competitor's products are so short that they will soon be by-passed by a new technology anyway?

Once FUD strategies are perceived to be used, counter-strategies will come into play. As noted, those on the receiving end of FUD need to be cautious about too easily attributing intentionality and remain aware of the existence of different perspectives and interests. 'FUD as perceived' may –but need not - equal 'FUD as intended'. FUD entrenches and polarizes positions. It deepens conflicts. Once this happens, both the contemplated range of solutions and the room for negotiation tend to narrow down to short-term defensive company interests, if our case is anything to go by. Whether there is leeway for more diverse responses requires more elaborate research.

The case study illustrates that effective counter-strategies against FUD created by, for example, similar naming, misrepresentation and legal threats are difficult to devise. This picture also emerges from descriptions of de facto standards wars. In committee standards wars, one may presume that a FUD strategy like discrediting an SDO is less likely if SDOs have a strong reputation. Transparent standards procedures and clear terminology may partly buttress an SDO against targeted misuse ('terminology reinterpretation').To our knowledge, no studies exist that address FUD counter-strategies in a systematic way, let alone strategies that down-scale standards wars and thus reduce their impact on technology development and markets. In this area more research is direly needed.

AFTERWORD[6]

Below we re-examine the above standards war from a complementary angle, i.e., using the concept of 'institutional rationality', to further contextualize and explain the emergence of predatory and cooperative behaviour. This concept is used by Arild Vatn (2005), an institutional economist, to address complex environmental issues. It highlights different mechanisms in the conflictual dynamics of this standards war. We limit our discussion of Vatn's theory to the bare essentials needed to clarify the influence of the key institutional settings of the market and standardization on strategic behaviour. In doing so, we follow Vatn's line of argument, which starts with an explanation of neoclassical economics as a point of reference.

Key to neoclassical economics is that people base their choices on maximizing their individual utility, both in markets and elsewhere. Their preferences are stable and are independent of the circumstances. That is, the individual is self-contained. To be rational is therefore to maximize one's individual utility (Vatn, 2005). In markets, private property rights are exchanged in competition. The cumulative outcome of these exchanges is market equilibrium.

Neoclassical economics has been criticized, for example, for not taking into account the effort needed to search for information and assess the quality of a product (non-transparency of markets and asymmetry of information between producers and consumers (Vatn, 2005), and the additional costs involved in transacting such as those of bargaining and drawing up contracts (information and transaction costs; e.g. (North & Thomas, 1973). Making a 'rational choice' presumes full information, but the individual does not know whether s/he has all the relevant information. In practice, therefore, people set a target and stop gathering information once the target is first met ('satisficing' rather than 'maximizing'); that is, in practice, rationality is bounded (Williamson, 1985).

These points of critique, however, still position the individual as self-contained, independent and maximizing his or her gain. A radical departure from the neoclassical tenets is made by classical institutionalists like Vatn (2005).They adhere to the social constructivist view that institutions (e.g. markets, law and family) are created by individuals, which in turn shape individual behaviour. The individual is socially formed and individual preferences are therefore (also) socially influenced. This perspective explains a broader set of behaviours than neoclassical theory. It points to multiple, context-dependent rationalities:

[T]he idea of plural rationalities is based on the observation that what is rational to do can be driven by reasons other than maximizing/satisficing individual utility. Which rationality applies, depends then on the institutional context in which one finds oneself. This implies that in some settings it is considered appropriate to take only individual interests into account. Under other circumstances this is not so. (Vatn, 2005, p.121)

That is, next to 'individual rationality', classic institutionalists identify 'social or cooperative rationality' (e.g. think of the context of the family or the community). More specifically, social rationality may consist of 'reciprocal rationality' ("propensity to respond positively to sympathetic actions and negatively to unfriendly behaviour, despite individual losses"); (Fehr & Falk, 2002) and 'normative rationality' ("norms about what is the right thing to do in certain situations (…) If norms are fully internalized, they are followed independently of whether others know and can punish those breaking the norm" (Vatn, 2005, p.123).

Although individuals differ, the institutional rationality that prevails in a specific context fosters a dominant type of behaviour (Vatn, 2005). In the case of individual rationality, a person's behaviour will be determined by utility or willingness to pay; core to social rationality is behaviour as determined by arguments in a communicative process (Vatn, 2005).

How do rationalities vary across different institutional contexts in the case we analyzed in this chapter? Let us start with the institutional context of the market for emergency communication products. In this context it is most rational for producers and consumers to get the most out of the exchange (utility maximization). For producers such as Matra Communications and Motorola the market is their natural habitat. Their individual rationality of profit maximization fosters matching strategic behaviour. In an emerging market, a company will protect its first mover advantage against newly entering competitors. Predatory behaviour falls within the scope of rational behaviour in ideal-typical markets. But note that in this market the consumers are the national emergency services. The social rationality dominant in public service provision has no place in an ideal-typical market. As consumers of emergency communication products, utility maximization entails getting the best product –i.e., the best support for (national and cross-border) quality of service – for the best price. This requires, apart from trustworthy high quality products, a common European standard for all three emergency services (police, ambulance and fire brigade) and a level playing field to help create a competitive market. In this context, coordination by means of a committee standard is preferred to a company 'de facto' standard (i.e., as the 'outcome of an emergent market equilibrium' in the wordings of neoclassical economists).

On reflection it is therefore more accurate to talk about competing standards and standard setters –with Matra Communications (c.q. Tetra Forum) and ETSI as adversaries in the standards war – rather than competing products and producers. In the institutional context of standardization, competing functionally equivalent standards constitute a standardization failure (Egyedi, 2014): the idea of a market of standards for emergency communication that one can choose among is a contradiction in terms for standardizers. It runs counter to the collective rationality of coordination that is crucial for interoperable emergency communication products. In other words, there is a clear tension between the individual rationally that is appropriate if standardization is viewed as a market (as Matra Communications saw it) and the collective rationality of standardization as market coordination (as ETSI saw it).

Lastly, the European Commission played a salient role in the standards war. Its task is to protect the public interest. Ideal-typically one would therefore expect those working in the Commission to behave according to a 'social rationality' and decide "which interests should get protection from the collective" (Vatn, 2005, p.129) based on arguments and discussion. In our case, the public interests concerned were: interoperable European cross-border emergency services and market competition. Which one to prioritize, was more difficult because "[t]wo DGs [of the European Commission] were involved in communication standards: the DG for the Internal Market and Industrial Affairs (DG III), under which standardization resided, and the DG for Telecommunications, Information Industries and Innovation (DG XIII)" (Hommels et al., 2012, pp. 11-12). The DG for Telecommunications etc. was well aware of the importance of standards for the provision of public communication services and supported ETSI's standardization initiative. In its institutional context, the argument for a single committee standard in the area of emergency communication carried weight. In contrast, the DG for the Internal Market, whose task it was to cater to the needs of European industry, had adopted the individual rationale of the market, and prioritized protecting competition in the (standards) market (Hommels et al., 2012) – i.e., on the assumption that a standard is a good like any other. To those working in this DG company strategies aimed at maximizing profit are appropriate until they overstep competition law.

What we can learn from Vatn is that "[w]hat is seen as rational, and what is to be termed irrational, may shift dramatically, depending on how we interpret the social sphere [i.e., institutional context] (…). This cannot be determined on the basis of the physical act itself." (Vatn, 2005, p.134) Applying his framework shows that predatory – and cooperative – strategies can be viewed as more or less appropriate depending on the context and rationality dominant in this context. Nevertheless, while predatory strategies may be viewed as rational in the context of the market, this institutional context also includes normative and legal rules about good business conduct (e.g. no false product claims or insider trading). However, in this respect Vatn notes that these rules "are actually counter to the basic logic of the institution." (Vatn, 2005, p.127) By this he means that the social rationale of fair play conflicts with the maximization logic of the market. Vatn's perspective thus helps to contextualize predatory strategies that do not seem to meet the norm of fair play (i.e. FUD as perceived).

ACKNOWLEDGMENT

This research was funded by the Dutch research council (NWO, project number 458-06-027). We sincerely thank the interviewees for sharing their ideas and sources with us and the holders of archives for providing us access.

REFERENCES

Axelrod, R. (1984). *The Evolution of Cooperation*. Basic Books.

Bayus, B. L., Jain, S., & Rao, A. G. (2001). Truth or Consequences: An Analysis of Vaporware and New Product Announcements. *JMR, Journal of Marketing Research*, *38*(1), 3–13. doi:10.1509/jmkr.38.1.3.18834

Bekkers, R. (2001). *Mobile Telecommunication Standards. GSM, UMTS, Tetra and Ermes*. Boston: Artech House.

Besen, S. M., & Farrell, J. (1991). The role of the ITU in standardization: Pre-eminence, impotence or rubber stamp? *Telecommunications Policy*, *15*(4), 311–321. doi:10.1016/0308-5961(91)90053-E

David, P. A. (1987). Some New Standards for the Economics of Standardization in the Information Age. In P. Dasgupta & P. Stoneman (Eds.), Economic Policy and Technological Performance (pp. 206-239). Cambridge University Press. doi:10.1017/CBO9780511559938.010

De Vries, H. J. (2006). Competing E-Purse Systems: A Standards Battle. *Journal of Cases on Information Technology*, *8*(1), 1–15. doi:10.4018/jcit.2006010101

Dranove, D., & Gandal, N. (2003). The DVD vs. DIVX Standard War: Empirical Evidence of Vaporware. *Journal of Economics & Management Strategy*, *12*, 363–386. doi:10.1162/105864003322309518

Egyedi, T. (2014). The Impact of Competing Standards: On Innovation and Interoperability for E-government. *PIK - Praxis der Informationsverarbeitung und Kommunikation, 37*(3), 211-215.

Egyedi, T. M. (2001). Why JavaTM was -not- standardized twice. *Computer Standards & Interfaces*, *23*(4), 253–265. doi:10.1016/S0920-5489(01)00078-2

Egyedi, T. M., & Hawkins, R. (2010). Standards Consortia. In W. Hesser, A. J. Feilzer, & H. J. de Vries (Eds.), *Standardisation in Companies and Markets* (3rd ed.; pp. 443–490). Hamburg, Germany: Helmut Schmidt University.

Farrell, J., & Saloner, G. (1985). Standardization, Compatibility and Innovation. *The Rand Journal of Economics*, *16*(1), 70–83. doi:10.2307/2555589

Farrell, J., & Saloner, G. (1986). Installed base and compatibility: Innovation, product preannouncements, and predation. *The American Economic Review*, *76*, 943–954.

Fehr, E., & Falk, A. (2002). Psychological foundations of incentives. Joseph Schumpeter Lecture. *European Economic Review*, *15*(4-5), 687–724. doi:10.1016/S0014-2921(01)00208-2

Gallagher, S. R. (2012). The battle of the blue laser DVDs: The significance of corporate strategy in standards battles. *Technovation*, *32*(2), 90–98. doi:10.1016/j.technovation.2011.10.004

Gauch, S. (2008). + vs. –, Dynamics and effects of competing standards of recordable DVD media. In T. M. Egyedi & K. Blind (Eds.), The dynamics of standards (pp. 47-67). Cheltenham, UK: Edward Elgar.

Haan, M. A. (2003). Vaporware as a Means of Entry Deterrence. *The Journal of Industrial Economics*, *3*(3), 345–358. doi:10.1111/1467-6451.00204

Hommels, A., Egyedi, T. M., & Cleophas, E. (2012). Policy change and policy incoherence: The case of competition versus public safety in standardization policies. *Journal of European Integration*, *35*(4), 443–458. doi:10.1080/07036337.2012.711826

Jakobs, K. (2008). The IEEE 802.11 WLAN installation at RWTH Aachen University: A case of voluntary vendor lock-. In T. M. Egyedi & K. Blind (Eds.), *The dynamics of standards* (pp. 99–116). Cheltenham, UK: Edward Elgar.

Lee, H., & Oh, S. (2006). A standards war waged by a developing country: Understanding international standard setting from the actor-network perspective. *The Journal of Strategic Information Systems*, *15*(3), 177–195. doi:10.1016/j.jsis.2005.10.002

North, D. C., & Thomas, R. P. (1973). *The Rise of the Western World: A New Economic History*. Cambridge, UK: Cambridge Press. doi:10.1017/CBO9780511819438

Oshri, I., & Weeber, C. (2006). Cooperation and Competition Standards-Setting Activities in the Digitization Era: The Case of Wireless Information Devices. *Technology Analysis and Strategic Management*, *18*(2), 265–283. doi:10.1080/09537320600624196

Pfaffenberger, B. (2000). The Rhetoric of Dread: Fear, Uncertainty, and Doubt (FUD) in Information Technology Marketing. *Knowledge, Technology & Policy*, *13*(3), 78–92. doi:10.100712130-000-1022-x

Schengen. (1990). The Schengen acquis - Convention implementing the Schengen Agreement of 14 June 1985 between the Governments of the States of the Benelux Economic Union, the Federal Republic of Germany and the French Republic on the gradual abolition of checks at their common borders. *Official Journal L 239*, 22/09/2000 P. 0019 – 0062.

Shapiro, C., & Varian, H. R. (1999). *Information rules - A Strategic Guide to the Network Economy*. Boston: Harvard Business School Press.

Singh, R. M., & Dahlin, K. B. (2009). *The winner does not take it all: Survival of niche standards*. Paper presented at the EGOS 2009, Barcelona, Spain.

Vatn, A. (2005). *Institutions and the Environment*. Cheltenham, UK: Edward Elgar.

Wegberg, M. (2004). Standardization Process of Systems Technologies: Creating a Balance between Competition and Cooperation. *Technology Analysis and Strategic Management*, *16*(4), 457–478. doi:10.1080/0953732042000295784

West, J. (2003). How open is open enough? Melding proprietary and open source platform strategies. *Research Policy*, *32*(7), 1259–1285. doi:10.1016/S0048-7333(03)00052-0

Williamson, O. (1979). Transactions-Cost Economics: The Governance of Contractual Relations. *The Journal of Law & Economics*, *22*(2), 233–262. doi:10.1086/466942

Wu, Y., Balasubramanian, S., & Mahajan, V. (2004). When is a Preannounced New Product Likely to be Delayed? *Journal of Marketing*, *68*(2), 101–113. doi:10.1509/jmkg.68.2.101.27792

Yin, R. K. (2009). *Case Study Research: Design and Methods* (4th ed.). London: Sage.

KEY TERMS AND DEFINITIONS

Affect: A psychological term for feeling, experience or emotion.

Committee Standardization: The process of developing standards in technical committees of formal standards bodies, consortia, professional organizations, (inter)governmental agencies, etc.

Committee Standards: Standards that have been created and documented for common and repeated use.

De Facto Standards: Popular products, technologies, etc. They dominate the market. Similar to popular committee standards (e.g., A4 paper format ISO 216 or Wifi IEEE 802.11g), de facto standards function as points of reference for consumers and producers; but, unlike committee standards, they were not created for that purpose.

FUD: Fear, uncertainty, and doubt. Most often used in the context of someone "creating FUD."

FUD Strategy in Standardization: A market strategy *perceived* to be designed to create unease among competitors and raise concern among users about the consequences of selecting a competitor's standard, by exerting pressure—psychological, legal, or otherwise—and disseminating negative and/or incorrect information about the standard, the standards process or the standard's likely market uptake, as a result of which the credibility of the competitor and/or the competing standard is undermined.

PAS: Publicly available specification, a term used by standards bodies for a specific, accelerated standards 'development' trajectory. The procedure allows market-relevant and mature specifications, which were developed outside of the standards body, to become a formally recognized standard.[7]

Predatory Strategies: Aggressive market strategies intended to undermine a competitor's position.

Standards War: A situation in which two competing parties with incompatible standards (i.e., committee or de facto standards) and very high stakes fight for a dominant market share.

ENDNOTES

1 Archival sources are indicated by hashtag numbers: #1 etc.. They are listed at the end of the chapter.

2 I.e., archive of the Schengen Telecom group (personal archive of H. Borgonjen), archives of the Dutch Ministry of the Interior on C2000, and the ETSI archive. They include policy reports, correspondence and minutes of meetings.

3 Interviewees are numbered: 1 etc. They are listed at the end of the chapter.

4 NB: Research question (iii) about the conditions under which FUD strategies arise, only addresses situations in which FUD-raising behavior was self-reported as intended and perceived.

5 Two days later a letter was sent by the chairman of Tetrapol to the ETSI Technical Assembly noting that "TETRAPOL remains a Publicly Available Specification; the last sections will be made public this coming December (…) (#31).

6 This Afterword was added in 2019.

7 For ETSI, see http://www.etsi.org/about/what-we-do/publicly-available-specifications-pas

APPENDIX

Interviewees

1. Chairman Tetrapol Forum (1991-present).
2. Former Head of the R&D Department of the Dutch Police, Former chairman of Schengen Telecom, former member of ETSI RES-6 representing the Netherlands.
3. Motorola Marketing department, Chairman of ETSI TC Tetra since 2002.
4. UK Home Office, Police ICT department.
5. Chairman ETSI Tetra committees between 1991 and 2002.

Archival Sources

1. Minutes of a meeting to improve cross-border communication of the police, 11 - 12 July 1989, Bonn-Bad Godesberg, p. 3.
2. Final Report initial phase C2000 (the Dutch Tetra implementation).
3. Letter from ETSI RES to Schengen Telcom Group, 15 November 1994.
4. Letter from A.N. Kent, UK Home Office to K.H. Rosenbrock, ETSI DG, 26-08-1997.
5. Letter O. Lauridsen, September 1995, TETRA MoU Chairman, to M. Bangemann, European Commission.
6. Minutes meeting Schengen Telecom, 9 May 1994, Brussels.
7. Letter from D. Kynaston, Philips, to M. Bangemann, European Commission, 20 September 1995.
8. Note from the French Delegation to WG Telecommunications, 16 October 1996
9. Letter from the chair and vice-chair of Tetrapol Forum to the ETSI DG, K.H. Rosenbrock, 9-10-1996.
10. Committee document, Motorola, J. Jensen, 14 November 1995.
11. International consultation, Police, NL, 24-11-1997, p.2 [translated from Dutch].
12. Letter from H. Borgonjen, 14-10-1996.
13. Minutes of 23/24 October meeting from J. Jensen (Motorola, MoU) to H. Borgonjen and others, 25-10-1996, p. 4.
14. Letter from H. Azémard (Tetrapol Forum) to K-H. Rosenbrock (ETSI), January 24, 1997.
15. Note from Presidency [Council of the European Union] to Police Cooperation working group, 16 November 1999 (italics added)).
16. “TETRA- the one and only European standard”, press release Nokia/Tetra, 16-9-1997.
17. Letter from Mr. Richter, European Commission, to Schengen Telecom group, 15-12-1995.
21. Letter from H. Azémard, Chairman Tetrapol Forum to F. Chumbinho, chairman of the Schengen Telecom Group, 2-4-1997.
22. Letter from H. Azémard, Chairman Tetrapol Forum to K.H. Rosenbrock (ETSI), 08-09-1997.
23. Letter from H. Azémard, Chairman Tetrapol Forum to K.H. Rosenbrock, Secretary-General of ETSI), 08-09-1997.
24. TETRA MoU document, Why is the Tetrapol PAS application contentious?, December 1998.
25. Letter from the UK Home Office to K.H. Rosenbrock, ETSI DG, 26-08-1997.
26. Letter from the UK Home Office to K.H. Rosenbrock, ETSI DG, 26-08-1997.

27. Cogent Defence System's Response to The Radio Spectrum Review Consultation Paper, 2001, p. 6.
29. Letter from the chair and vice-chair of Tetrapol Forum to the ETSI DG, K.H. Rosenbrock, 9-10-1996.
30. Letter from M. Bangemann, member of the EC, to H. Dijkstal, Dutch Minister of the Interior, 29 April 1998.
31. Letter from H. Azémard, chairman of Tetrapol to the ETSI Technical Assembly, 11-10-1996, ETSI/TA25(96)TD24.

Chapter 14
Profit Expansion Method by Standard as an Outbound Open Innovation

Manabu Eto
Hitotsubashi University, Japan

ABSTRACT

Among open innovations, standardization activities that do not cause some souse of profits, such as issuing standard essential patents for standardized technologies, can be said to be offering-type outbound open innovations. Technology providers require a careful strategy to make a profit from standardization activities. The core of this is to determine in what state the technology in the target product itself will be kept, which is the technology control strategy. What is particularly important is to determine what information will be proactively disclosed based on the theory, utility, and implementation of the technology, and what information will be kept secret. In this chapter, the author examines several cases of standardization and, by focusing on those that earned profits, presents technology management strategies that generate profits using standardization.

INTRODUCTION

Although the term "open innovation" was coined in the United States, it is widely used among Japanese companies and treated like a magical term that will reform their innovation systems. The phrase "open and close strategy" is also commonly used in Japan. Whether it is called open innovation or an open and close strategy, these are activities that many Japanese companies have been conducting actively for quite a while and are not a newly introduced type of strategy. Although Japanese companies have thus far not clarified their meaning, these concepts are actively used in corporate activities because they involve simplified technology management methods, which were previously based on know-how, successfully organized in a convincing manner.

DOI: 10.4018/978-1-5225-9008-8.ch014

Copyright © 2019, IGI Global. Copying or distributing in print or electronic forms without written permission of IGI Global is prohibited.

In this section, I focus on the activity of "standardization" that companies have been implementing for a long time. As will be described later, standardization is one of the tools that generate outbound open innovation. I reanalyze various well-known cases of standardization activities, both successful and failed, from the viewpoint of success and failure of outbound open innovation, and then attempt to sort out the roles of standardization of business strategies that utilize outbound open innovation.

OUTBOUND OPEN INNOVATION AND STANDARDIZATION

Outbound Open Innovation

Outbound open innovation has been discussed since the first paper (Chesbrough, 2003) in which Chesbrough talked about open innovation. However, inbound open innovation is more company-oriented, as open innovation and its study have progressed, while there is little research on outbound open innovation. Furthermore, regarding standardization, in the book "Open Innovation: Researching a New Paradigm" (Chesbrough, Vanhaverbeke, and West, 2006), Simcoe discussed open standards and intellectual property rights (Simcoe, 2006). However, the intensively discussed matter here is what is included in intellectual property rights, such as standard essential patents. This corresponds to "selling" in the four open innovation forms classified by Dahlander and Gann (2010) . When discussing business standardization, this issue of standard essential patents is often mentioned, but this is not a pure standardization activity. The standardization activity corresponds to "revealing" in the four open innovation forms classified by Dahlander and Gann (2010). Further, regarding outbound open innovation, it has already been pointed out that the possibility of generating profits for resource providers is low (Helfat and Quinn, 2006].

For this reason, in this section, I proceed with an analysis focusing on this "method of generating profits for resource providers." If it is not possible to earn profits as a business, there is less value for the entity holding the technical information in proactively advancing outbound open innovation.

Open Closed Strategy

The term "Open Closed Strategy is a phrase that came to be known in Japan through the books of Mr. Senoo et al. (Senoo, 2009; Ogawa, 2014; Tatsumoto, 2017). The basic line of thinking is that, by choosing to open parts, brand recognition increases, and by increasing the number of collaborators and participants, cost reductions and market expansion are achieved, and in closing-off high-selling parts, profits are ensured. In the examples presented in these prior studies, many were seen to secure profits by opening up some among many technologies, and monopolizing others.

The management of the combination of these multiple technologies is the same manner of thinking as in the open innovation shown above, and for this reason open-closed strategies were widely adopted as open innovation success strategies within Japan.

Conversely, it is well known that within original technical information there are things that should be opened and things that shouldn't be. With particular regard to patent applications, it is fundamental to intellectual property management to distinguish between the information described in application documents and the know-how that is not described, concealed information. In the examples too, within a single technology cases can be seen distinguishing between information to be opened and information not to be opened.

Open and closed forms

First, let us organize the various forms of open and closed technologies.

Black-Boxing

When technical information is created, it is usually "black-boxed" information that only the person or organization that created it knows. In some cases, the information in kept in a black box through strict information management, but in many cases, information is leaked or actively publicized, and it becomes public information. Various situations can be considered regarding the openness of technical information, from active events such as publishing academic papers to passive events such as technical content being revealed after the release of products that incorporate the technology.

Patenting

When information is released and anyone can use it, there is a high possibility that the creator of that information will be unable to expect returns, and incentives to create new technical information will be lost. The patent system is an artificial system devised to prevent this. However, the most important role of the patent system is to widely open to the public technical information that has been created in order to avoid wasteful redundant investments to produce technical information. The profits of inventors are only secured as compensation for disclosing technical information.

For this reason, from the viewpoint of managing technical information, patents involve the opening of technical information. However, from a business viewpoint, since the patent system manages the right to license and determines to whom to license the patent, it can be said that it has the function of adjusting the use of technical information for businesses between open and closed.

Disclosure

There are cases in which technology is not patented, and it is disclosed in the form of an academic paper, for example. Since many of the results of basic studies are discoveries, rather than inventions, it is difficult to patent them, and it is common for such information to be disclosed in academic journals. Further, in order to prevent other companies from obtaining a patent, technical information is sometimes made public. Preventing other companies from obtaining a patent by public disclosure is a commonly used method, particularly for small and medium-sized companies, which have difficulties covering patent costs and navigating litigation.

Standardization

When organizing the concepts in this way, the "standardization" activities discussed in this section are positioned even further toward the open side of open and closed technologies. The end point of the opening of technical information is a state in which the technical information can be used freely without requiring payment, and whether to use that technology is left to the free judgment of the user. Standardization is the activity of agreeing with other people to proactively use this technical information and to recommend using the technical information.

Rogers (1995), who can be said to be the founder of the diffusion of innovations theory, pointed out that, in order for innovation to become widespread, it is important for there to be early adopters that start using it as pioneers among the general public, and that it is not enough to just open the technology to make it available for use by anyone or to have an innovator that jumps into the new technology. It can be said that those who are involved in standardization activities are early adopters. Thus, if standardization gathers a wide range of users, such as a whole country rather than an industry, or an international audience rather than a national one, this will have a positive effect on the dissemination of that technology.

Compatibility Assessment

In the standardization activities, alongside activities to create standards, there is an activity called compatibility assessment that confirms whether products and services to be provided are compatible with the standards that have been developed and confirms the so-called third-party certification that puts this compatibility assessment into a system and makes it a business. Since this guarantees that the target technical information will be used correctly, it becomes possible for the dissemination of technology to have further positive effects.

Technical Regulations

Considering things in this way, the end point of technology dissemination is enforcing the use of technical information through technical regulation. Actually, there are very few compulsory regulations that oblige anyone to use a specific technology, but in many cases, there is no choice but to use a specific technology in order to comply with practical regulations. In other words, many compulsory regulations have the function of achieving technology dissemination by force. Rogers (1995), mentioned above, presented the case of vaccination against infectious diseases as a case study of diffusion of innovations, saying that when it was possible to choose freely, the existence of early adopters was necessary, but in present times, it is well known that immunization against major infectious diseases is mandated in many countries, and it is compulsorily implemented.

If we tabulate the forms of technical management as described above, they can be organized as shown in Table 1. A technology could be put into several states, such as "black-box," in which no information is disclosed to the outside; "patent," in which the technology can be used by paying a commission; "open," in which anyone can use the technology for free; "standardization," in which the technology is recommended to be used by everyone; "compatibility assessment," which ensure that the technology can be used, and "technical regulation," which enforces the use of the technology.

Of course, a complex technology may be in several states. For many patented technologies, it is well known that specific know-how is black-boxed so that it cannot be effectively put to practical use simply by reading the patent documentation.

Further, a transition of state always occurs. As mentioned earlier, the operation and maintenance of technical information in a black-box is costly, and, at the same time, it cannot be kept in a black-box forever, no matter how much money is spent. At some stage, it is necessary to determine whether to patent it, to disclose it, or to standardize it, and actively generate a state transition. In other words, it can be said that, among the large technology groups, the technology control strategy and intellectual property/standardization strategy indicate which technology to black-box, which parts to patent, and what to standardize.

Table 1. Classification example of technology management forms

State of technology	*Content*
Black-box	It is kept secret so that technical information does not leak to others. Usually, it is used in the implementation method of technologies. This is common in food-related recipes, such as Kentucky Fried Chicken and Coca-Cola, but, in relation to industrial products, it can be said that it is impossible to maintain a black-box state for a long period of time.
Patent	This is a system that allows exclusive use of the technology's utility, under the premise of disclosing information to realize the utility. Rights holders can control the degree of openness of the environment that uses the technical information by licensing the right and collecting licensing fees.
Open	Regarding the utility of technology, it is beneficial to actively make it public. Regarding the theory, it is often opened through a paper presentation, etc. Both the utility and its implementation method are often opened owing to the release of products that incorporate the technical information.
Standardization	When the implementation method of utility is simplified and generalized, there is a product standard that is an agreement among involved parties about using the technology, and a testing method standard that makes it possible to compare the performance of utility. Both are important in proactively disseminating technology.
Compatibility assessment/ granting certification	A system that ensures that the utility is in a state where it can be used properly, mainly by confirming the implementation method of utility. Reliability regarding the use of technology increases, and obstacles to dissemination in the market become smaller. However, there are many certification systems that do not confirm the actual utility but only the implementation process.
Technical regulation	Technical restrictions prohibit specific states of technology use, but there is an aspect of fixing the technology that can be used for that purpose and for forcing the use of that technology. It is said to have the strongest power in disseminating technical information.

Information Management for One Technology

So far, technical information has been handled as one piece of information, but, in reality, the information that is released about one technology can be broadly divided into three categories: its utility (what), implementation method (how), and theory (why). In the technology control strategy, it is necessary to strategize about how to treat each of these three categories of information separately. Then, how is each of these categories of information opened?

Information Management: Utility

The first thing that is made public is the utility of the technology. The utility of a technology, such as how the technology is useful and what kind of performance/function it has, is information that necessarily has to be opened when trying to gain profits by selling products that incorporate the technology. Such contents are often disclosed in a form that can be actively and freely used. Of course, it is also possible to actually obtain utility by purchasing products that incorporate the technology.

From the viewpoint of standardization, there are two types of standardization that can increase the impact.

First is standardization of the method to measure utility. By standardizing the method of measuring utility, the difference in performance between multiple products becomes easy for users to understand, and products can be differentiated based on performance differences. Such standardization of measurement methods should be proactively conducted and disseminated, if the company is confident about its own technical capability (capability to demonstrate utility).

The other is standardization of the interface for easy use of its functionality. Particularly, when the product is a part or material, it is important to standardize an interface through which the buyers of those parts and materials can fully utilize the functions of the products, and the market for those products can be expanded. There is standardization of interfaces even for products that are used alone in the market. This is standardization of "the way of using." If the way of using a product is standardized, and the product becomes widespread, the user will be locked into that way of using it, and the possibility that the product will be purchased continuously increases. This is also an important point of interface standardization.

Management of the Implementation Method

Next, information on how to realize the technology's utility is made public. In business, the most important thing is to determine how to manage the implementation method of this utility. There are cases where this may be disclosed as compensation for protecting the rights with patents, and so on, and there are also cases where it may be made public by analyzing the product being sold. However, important know-how is not disclosed to realize utility and, in many cases, it is devised so that the same utility cannot be realized only by looking at the patent or copying a product.

Basically, in the early days of a technology being introduced to the market, the implementation method of utility is black-boxed. However, as products go into the market, it is impossible to keep the technology hidden forever. Of course, it is necessary to patent it, and it is also necessary to incorporate leakage of the know-how into the business strategy.

Further, in order to expand the market, it is necessary to increase the number of participants in product supply. At this time, if the product differs by participant, there will be confusion in the market, and if there are defective items or low-level items, this will destroy the market. The standardization of product specifications prevents this situation. By standardizing the product specifications, it becomes possible for anyone to produce the same thing, and it can be expected that the market will be stable, and the utilization by users will expand.

Further, if the disclosure of the technology continues, the manufacturing method of the product may also be standardized. Naturally, it is possible to achieve cost reduction by standardizing the manufacturing method in-house, but it is also possible to obtain an even greater cost reduction effect by standardizing through cooperation in the same industry.

Management of the Theory

In some cases, it is unclear why utility is realized. Technology can be used if the utility can be realized constantly, even without knowing the reason. Treatments of diseases that have been passed down through the ages, for example, may be a typical case. However, if it is known why the utility is realized, it is necessary to make a strategic judgment as to whether it will be realized. If the theory is made public, the dissemination of the technology will become easier, because the credibility regarding utility will increase. For this reason, the theory is often made public in the form of paper presentations, and so on. However, disclosing the theory makes it easy for others to realize the utility, and there is a high possibility that exposure of the implementation method that should have been protected by a patent, for example, might be avoidable. For this reason, there will be a choice not to open the theory to the public.

Opening and Closing of Multiple Technologies

So far we have considered the case of one technology being opened and closed. However, it is common for multiple technologies to be used in actual products. In such a case, a strategy for managing the opening and closing of multiple technologies is also required.

Opening Complementary Products

The most effective way to control the opening and closing of multiple technologies and to increase one's own profits is to popularize and expand the market by opening the technology of products that are complementary to one's own products. Complementary products, such as contents and players, are products that mutually support each other's dissemination. In such a case, even if the information on the product's technology is kept secret, if information on complementary products is disclosed, and the number of participants increases, the market expands and one's own market also expands. In many cases, it is difficult to achieve the opening of technical information of complementary products within a single company, but if one company has many business fields, like large Japanese and European companies, it is also possible for one company to achieve this.

Opening of Non-Competing Areas

Although it is not as effective as opening complementary products, as mentioned above, achieving cost reductions by standardizing non-competing technologies of products is a practice carried out by many businesses. It is important to reduce costs as much as possible in areas that do not become differentiating factors, and standardization can exert great cost reductions. As mentioned above, in standardization of cost reduction, the first step is carried out within the company itself, but if it is a non-competing area, the industry can cooperate and achieve standardization, and the cost-reduction effect will be significant.

TYPES OF STANDARDIZATION IN OUTBOUND OPEN INNOVATION

In the following, I classify the types of outbound technologies, select 14 cases for each type, and organize the factors of success and failure in those cases. In this section, I do not pursue fairness in the selection of case examples and have selectively chosen typical cases for each type, so it is not possible to make a generalization by summarizing these cases. Nonetheless, by cross-examining many cases, it could be possible to find common success and failure factors.

In the 14 cases, as the result of analysis with products businesses wish to sell to achieve profit as its main axis, it was found that standardization activities in the 14 examples can be split into 5 patterns:

1. Standardization of product specifications of sales products
2. Standardization of the manufacturing method of sales products
3. Standardization of the sales product efficacy measurement method
4. Standardization of the sales product use method (External interface)
5. Standardization not of the sales product, but of other peripheral products

Among these, in the standardization of A, business models including standard essential patents in the standardized technical scope and using their license fees to increase profits were also observed (call B).

In addition, for F, as examples of success, cases were observed where by performing standardization of peripheral products the market for the target product was expanded, and cases where cost reduction was achieved by standardizing non-competitive areas such as shared parts used by target products (divide F&G).

For this reason, 7 patterns are ultimately shown as the results of analysis of each of the example cases.

Product Specifications

First, the basis is standardization of product specifications. The standardization of product specifications follows the standardization activity principle in such a way that patent royalties, and so on, do not exist in the standards, and anyone can adopt and use the technology as written in the standards documentation. As a result of this standardization, many companies usually enter into the deliverables supply business, and the market expands, but it may be obvious that it is difficult for only individuals who have standardized and embarked on creating technology to gain a large profit distinct from other companies, because the share of each individual participant will fall, and price competition will occur.

In addition, in order to end the competition in a specific area and to shift the competition area to another place, there are cases where a published-specifications type of standardization is conducted. This form of standardization activity focuses on the standardization function of inhibiting innovation, and since it is disconnected from the definition of "realizing innovation" in this section, I will not discuss it here.

Case 1: Bicycles

Thorough specifications for Japanese bicycles were standardized in the JIS standards. The purpose was to raise the level of technology in the Japanese bicycle industry and to cultivate Japanese bicycles as export items that could be sold around the world. As these Japanese bicycle standards were detailed and easy to use, they were adopted not only in Japan, but also around the world, and thus the bicycle specifications in Japan caused innovation around the world (Eto, 2007a). However, as a result, products in countries with price competitiveness have gained world markets, and Japanese products have been pushed out not only from the global market, but also from the Japanese market and have only a small share of the domestic and overseas markets. In other words, outbound innovation in bicycles succeeded from the social viewpoint, but it did not succeed as a business for those who provided the technology. This can be said to be a typical example of losing the market by standardizing with no black-boxed area.

Case 2: G3FAX

G3FAX technology is also a technology originally created in Japan, and there are many patents related to it, but regarding the protocol in the telecommunications business, in this era, there was a mutual understanding that patents should be provided free of charge. Further, with the strong guidance of the Ministry of Posts and Telecommunications (of that time), it was basically patent-free and standardized as a technology that anyone could use (Japanese Industrial Standards Committee, 2005).

However, in the case of G3FAX, there were not many entries, like in case 1 of bicycles, and an oligopoly by the five major companies was maintained for a long time. There are several reasons for this.

First, outside the standardized technology, there were many complex technologies, such as the feeding of paper touched up for correction, and these technologies were not disclosed. Second, when using the standardized technology, know-how other than in the technology written in the standards documentation was required, such as a method for recovering from errors, and these technologies were black-boxed and shared only among the five manufacturers that jointly conducted the standardization and connection tests. Third, the cost of the connection tests was significantly different between the standardization implementation groups that prepared only their own products and participated and the late participants that had to confirm all the interoperability of their own companies with existing models.

G3FAX technology seemed to have been released in a form that anyone could use, so it gained the confidence of the market. On that basis, because the number of participants did not increase, there was also certain success as a business. However, the reason for its success may make it difficult to consider this a case of pure outbound open innovation in that people who could use the outbound technology were limited by differences in technical capabilities, and so on.

Standard Essential Patents in Product Specifications

The standardization of product specifications mentioned above is standardization and openness that allows anyone to freely use a technology, but there is also a method of keeping the patent of a technology and acquiring the profits of innovation by controlling the use of the patent. This is the standardization form discussed by Simcoe as an open standard. Many of the patent pools based on standard essential patents aim for this form of innovation, but as mentioned earlier, such standardization belongs to "selling" among the outbound open innovations, and it is different from the standardization targeted in this section. However, recently there have been initiatives aiming at securing profits other than patent license fees by providing standard essential patents free of charge. There will be room for discussion of this in this section as well.

Case 3: Mpeg-2

Mpeg-2 has been standardized as video compression technology, and anyone can use it. However, to use it, it is necessary to pay patent royalties. Even if the specification is standardized, and it is possible for anyone to use it freely, if there is a patent and a licensing fee is introduced, it is possible to earn profits as a company. However, as mentioned above, this form is positioned as a "selling" type, not a "revealing" type in the classification by Dahlander and Gann (2010), and it is not the kind of standardization that I delineate in this section.

This business model, in which a company standardizes its own patent technology and collects license fees for standard essential patents from the users of that technology, has been followed in various ways after the success of Mpeg-2. It is well known that QUALCOMM made great profits with the basic patent of CDMA technology, which is a third-generation mobile phone technology. Further, there were many standard essential patents related to GSM, a second-generation mobile phone in Europe, mainly from Motorola. However, in the case of GSM, rather than "selling" the patent, Motorola planned a monopoly of the business, and did not license the patent. In that sense, despite being standardized, it is a rare case that can be seen only before the patent handling standard (IPR policy) was established in standards groups where the technology was outbound and not widely provided to other companies.

Case 4: Bosch's Patent Strategy

Bosch has a strong position as an auto parts manufacturer in Europe, and its main products are electronic control units (ECUs) for automobiles. This company leads the automobile industry with on-vehicle LAN technology, and it is also carrying out the standardization of FlexRay, which is currently mainstream, including CAN developed by the company, as well as the standardization of its software with a consortium organization called Autosar (Tokuda, 2008). In Autosar, patents are basically licensed for free among members. Autosar's standard essential patents are not the only patents licensed here. Bosch has numerous patents in CAN technology, which is an old on-vehicle LAN, but many of these are licensed to Autosar members for free.

Bosch's official statement is that the 80 Autosar members have contributed to patents related to Autosar, and licenses are offered free of charge because the number of licenses it obtains from members is larger than what it provides. Currently, there are overwhelmingly more members who are pure users and do not offer their patents, but on the premise that these members may offer them in the future, all Autosar member have access to patents in common. Unlike the Mpeg case mentioned above, this form is an open innovation of the "revealing" type. In the case of Bosch, there are also a lot of major basic patents, and the loss of profits by licensing free of charge, and not having royalty-bearing patent licenses, can be considered to be significant.

In Autosar, it seems that the experience with CAN dissemination had an impact on Bosch's decision to adopt a free patent strategy. CAN was widely used as a car network developed by Bosch, but because Bosch kept the patent and requested licensing fees, it remained as a "selling" type of innovation, and the cost of CAN, which was originally high, became a cost factor for other companies. There is no doubt that this situation led to the creation of the LIN standard, which can be used more cheaply, and FlexRay as the next generation standard of CAN.

The standardization carried out by Autosar, which started after the standardization of FlexRay, is the software standard of on-vehicle LAN, and its main purpose is to reduce the development cost of on-vehicle LAN. The participation of as many companies as possible, and the provision of each product in accordance with Autosar's interface standard, makes possible a cost reduction in the automobile industry as a whole. If competing standards, different from those of Autosar, emerge to create a multi-standard competitive environment, there is a high possibility that this cost reduction effect will be significantly reduced. It can be considered that, vis-à-vis Autosar, Bosch abandoned the idea of making money with patent royalties, and by making their patents available free of charge, Bosch made the business judgment that suppressing the emergence of competitive technologies was more valuable to its business than collecting patent royalty fees.

In recent years, there have been many efforts to open up patents, mainly by automobile and electronics manufacturers, such as Tesla and Toyota, but releasing a patent makes that technology de facto standardized and spread to the market, and when looking at the efforts aiming at returning the innovation effect to oneself, it is possible also to consider it a type of outbound open innovation by standardization.

Standardization of Manufacturing Equipment

In a company that manufactures products, its manufacturing technology and manufacturing equipment are parcels of know-how, and normal standardization is usually limited to internal standardization. The business model of a company that manufactures commodity-type products is to generate differences in cost and quality by using manufacturing technology and acquire market share. However, among the manufacturing technologies, if there is an area that has little know-how and does not significantly affect the product performance, but that is a major cost factor, it will naturally be made public and standardized, aiming at obtaining a cost reduction effect. Although such standardization can be said to be standardization of the implementation method of utility, it could also be considered the standardization of non-competing areas.

Case 5: Carrier Frequency Device for Semiconductor 300-mm Wafer

Investment in factories in the semiconductor industry has been rapidly expanding since the 1990s. In particular, the development cost of devices has increased sharply, and the device development costs cannot be recovered by only developing a device to be delivered to a specific device manufacturer. Performing some standardization has become an essential condition for creating an equipment market. Among these, the standardization of 300-mm wafer transfer devices was selected. It was an essential task to transfer wafers mechanically, which had been carried manually until then, by increasing the size of semiconductors; however, product prices were low because it was a technology in a non-competing area, and it was not equipment that a manufacturing company could independently develop and sell. For this reason, from 1994 to 1997, standardization of transfer devices compatible with 300-mm wafers was carried out (Tomita and Tatsumoto, 2006).

This standardization has caused several innovations. One is selection and oligopoly of transfer device manufacturers. From the standpoint of semiconductor manufacturers, various competing technologies existed related to wafer transfer devices, which is a non-competing area, and the differences in quality caused the formation of an oligopoly of transfer devices.

The other was the loss of advantage in manufacturing technology due to the change in manufacturing method. There is a clean room technology that is a specialty technology of semiconductor manufacturing factories in Japan, which made possible a high production of semiconductors. However, with the 300-mm wafer, it has become possible to lower the cleanliness level of the entire room by achieving cleanliness inside the carrier that transports the wafer. This led to the loss of the strength of the Japanese semiconductor technology.

The benefit the semiconductor manufacturers obtained through standardization of this 300-mm wafer transfer device was a reduction in the cost of transfer devices and the cost of manufacturing the semiconductor through to the use of the 300-mm wafer. However, many Japanese companies suffered in the semiconductor recession, the introduction of manufacturing equipment using 300-mm wafers was delayed, and they were not able to enjoy this cost-reduction benefit.

Case 6: Quality Management System (ISO-9001)

ISO-9001, a quality control (management) system developed by BSI in the United Kingdom and standardized by ISO, can also be considered an outbound open innovation as a form of standardization of manufacturing methods. The main merit of standardizing a quality control system lies in the visualization (understanding) of the quality control status. Originally, for this ISO-9000 series, Western European countries, which were surprised at the quality improvements of exported products during the period of high growth in Japan, organized and made public a Western-style quality control system and then standardized it in order to counter the Japanese-style quality control system, whose method and know-how could not be grasped from outside.

In this quality control system, organizing and preserving materials were thoroughly standardized, and since based on this quality control system an environment was created where organizations that manage quality could be easily compared, it became easy to compare and evaluate a supplier's quality control when procuring various purchased goods. It can be said that innovation, sophistication of quality control, has been realized by opening an outbound-type quality control system and unifying the quality control systems of suppliers.

Even in Japan, Toyota Motor Corporation, which has established its own advanced quality control system, has not introduced ISO-9001, but parts suppliers with low quality control capability may be encouraged to introduce ISO-9001 as a quality control system. In this way, it is possible to make good use of the value of ISO-9001, but in Japan, initially, under the perception that introducing ISO-9001 would produce differentiation in international trade, a formal introduction was advanced, and there were many cases where the quality control system was broken or unnecessary processes were added. It could be considered that these companies have been trapped in the outbound openness of Western quality control system technology.

Standardization of Performance Evaluation Method

Not only the technology itself but also evaluation methods and performance measurement methods for the technology are provided externally as an outbound open innovation through standardization, and efforts to differentiate companies' own technology have been actively performed recently by disseminating those methods. Of course, standardization of performance evaluation methods and measurement methods is an essential activity in the evaluation of a technology, and it is an activity that has been constantly done. However, recently, it has become strongly recognized that the standardization and dissemination of evaluation methods and measurement methods have a great effect on innovation for a company's own technology, and the standardization activities aiming for outbound open innovation are increasing. However, it is still not well known that the dissemination of technical information in this form is accompanied by significant risks for one's own business if a mistake is made.

Case 7: Liquid Crystal Panels

As an evaluation method of liquid crystal panels, the matrix-type liquid crystal display module measurement method (ED-2522), issued by the former Electronic Industries Association of Japan (EIAJ) in 1995, is a standard widely used worldwide as a method of evaluating liquid crystal panels. This standard specifies the measurement method in detail for 14 items, and it is a very high-value standard for knowing the quality of liquid crystal panels. This standard is also reflected in international standards in IEC, and Japanese liquid crystal panels evaluated by this standard have received a high evaluation in the international market.

However, it has been said that the evaluation method made a breakdown to a fine technical level and specified a detailed measurement method, making research and development of panels by latecomers much easier. In addition to being easy to conduct research and development with a specific goal, if the way of evaluating the panels is determined, it is possible to increase the evaluation of panels only by obtaining a high numerical value in that evaluation method. As a result, it can be said that this situation allowed panel manufacturers in Taiwan, South Korea, and China to catch up with Japanese liquid crystal panels.

Case 8: Photocatalyst

At the beginning of its development, photocatalyst technology took a closed-type patent strategy, and limited market development was carried out. However, since the raw material was a general-purpose product called titanium oxide, titanium oxide from many companies was used, resulting in the introduction into the market of products claiming to have a photocatalytic effect. Although the expansion of the market has advanced rapidly because of this, there are many products that have no photocatalytic effect at all or whose effect diminishes quickly, and this situation could damage the reputation of photocatalysts as a whole.

What was particularly problematic was the so-called self-cleaning function, a function that allows the item to maintain a clean state by itself, which required light and water to keep functioning. Further, a high degree of fixation technology was required to exhibit sufficient performance; however, since there was no market recognition of the self-cleaning function itself, many imitations appeared.

For this reason, an evaluation method for measuring the self-cleaning function of the photocatalyst was developed and standardized. Patented technology also existed in this measurement method, but by releasing the patents free of charge, this evaluation technology was disseminated, and many people, including users, created an environment where they could evaluate and confirm for themselves the self-cleaning function. As a result, the photocatalyst product market regained soundness, and it was possible to achieve stable growth with few imitations.

Interfaces

Although the case of optical connectors described above can be regarded as standardization of a non-competing area, it could also be regarded as standardization of an interface. Standardization of an interface means standardization of the connection part of a company's products that connects to external peripheral equipment not manufactured by the company itself; it is a method of expanding the profits from the sale of a company's own technology by enabling anyone to use technology concerning the connection method.

Case 9: IBM Personal Computers

IBM personal computers entered into the personal computer market late, and in the United States, Apple and Tandy accounted for the majority of the market, so they focused on the business market and aimed for a quick entry. For this reason, they used only general-purpose parts and released circuit diagrams and the source code of BIOS as measures to promote the entry of peripheral equipment manufacturers. This activity is not standardization, but merely opening a technology; however, the opening carried out by companies as large as IBM has its own meaning of de facto standardization. For this reason, many companies developed a variety of devices/equipment that connected to IBM personal computers and contributed to a significant expansion of the IBM personal computer market.

However, in the case of IBM personal computers, many manufactures that originally manufactured internal parts for the interface, that is, personal computers, started to make clones, which was a situation unexpected by IBM. This is the terrifying aspect of interface standardization. If it becomes possible to divide the integrated system into two, and the number of elemental technologies required for manufacturing is reduced by standardizing the interface, anyone on either side can easily enter into the market. Modularization through standardization of interfaces has the characteristic of bringing the market toward price competition.

Case 10: Interface Standard of Digital Cameras

There are three important interface standards for digital cameras. The first is the Exif/DCF standard, which stipulates the recording method (directory structure, file compression method, etc.) on the storage medium. Canon and Fujifilm jointly standardized this format, making it possible to retrieve information with the same software from the recording medium of any camera. Furthermore, the development and dissemination of the USB interface also absorbed the difference in recording media, and as long as the camera is connected with USB, it is now possible to take photos in the same way with digital cameras from any company.

The second interface standard is a digital print order format (DPOF) that allows information to be stored such as images to be printed and how many times the images should be recorded. Thanks to this standard, it is now possible to get photos at a DPE(Development Printing Enlargement) shop by choosing, at the storefront or at home, the photos that one would like to print on photographic paper. This realizes an environment where it is possible to take pictures with a digital camera and easily print them, even if one does not own a personal computer, and the same big market occupied by the optical camera was successfully acquired by making digital cameras independent from the peripheral equipment of personal computers.

The third interface is the PictBridge standard, which achieves a direct connection between the printer and the digital camera. As a result, the printer is also independent from the personal computer and gained the possibility of becoming a business alone as a peripheral device for digital cameras. Unfortunately, as the second interface that connects digital cameras with DPE shops became widespread, the market for purchasing printers exclusively for digital cameras cannot be said to have been so successful, but it can be said that it is an important example of an interface that aimed to connect with a new market.

Standardization of Complementary Products

Complementary products are related products whose functions cannot be generated unless both of them are present. Combinations of hardware and software, such as computer hardware and software, or DVD player and contents, are easy to understand, but an electric rice cooker and rice, or a flashlight and batteries can also be said to be complementary products. In many cases, complementary products have a relationship in that where and when one is sold, the other is sold too, and because of this, by extending the market by standardizing complementary products, it becomes possible to increase the sales of one's products.

Case 11: DVD Player and DVD (Contents)

The standardization activity, which is often considered as standardization of the DVD itself, did not actually standardize DVD devices, but standardized DVDs, which have the contents. With this standardization, everyone can use the procedure for reading information (contents) from DVDs if they pay the patent royalties, and many companies have entered into manufacturing DVD players.

However, video tapes and video discs, which were the previous movie recording media, failed to standardize, and based on a reconsiderations regarding market confusion, as for the standardization of DVDs, a thoroughly elaborated standardization was conducted and made public (Japanese Industrial Standards Committee, 2006). Therefore, the conditions required for the parts for reading DVDs are also standardized, so that anyone could manufacture a DVD player as long as the parts are collected and assembled. Despite attempting to standardize one side of the complementary product and trying to acquire profits on the other side, the player side was also de facto standardized, and price competition occurred as a result. After all, the biggest profit from standardization of DVDs was for Hollywood movie companies that provided content, which is a complementary product, as players expanded the market through price competition.

Case 12: QR Code

The encoding and decoding methods of the QR code, which is a two-dimensional barcode developed by DENSO WAVE, were standardized and released in the same way as for other two-dimensional codes, and anyone can freely create a QR code or make software that reads it (Kajiura and Uchida, 2005). For this reason, the QR code is widely used in various systems, and it is an important tool in electronic transactions in China.

The revenue product of DENSO WAVE is a handy reader that reads this QR code. As the QR code has become widely popular, the handy reader market has also expanded. However, naturally, competition is intense as other companies can easily enter into the QR code-reading space. The method of differentiating from other handy readers is the difference in reading error rate.

If you read a clean QR code in a bright place, you will rarely get an error, but if the code is dirty or partly missing, the success rate of reading will naturally fall. Under such conditions, DENSO WAVE utilized its technological capability to develop its own QR code-encoding technology and create an encoder software with high redundancy, and then made it available to the public. The handy reader manufactured by the company is equipped with a decoding technology that can use 100% of the know-how included in the encoding technology and achieves an overwhelmingly low error rate compared with readers from other companies. It can be said that by out-bounding the complementary product of the two-dimensional barcode (QR code) free of charge, they produced the innovation of making codes two-dimensional in the barcode area, and this is a good success example of manufacturing and selling products that are advantageous in terms of performance with black-boxed technology in them, by using outbound open innovation.

Specifications of Non-Competing Area Parts

In the case of bicycles, since the specifications of the whole product were standardized and the technology was disclosed as a standard, there was no area to be black-boxed, and it failed as a business. However, there is also a method to proactively standardize parts in a non-competing area while leaving the technology as a black-box inside the organization.

Case 13: High Speed On-Vehicle LAN

The German automaker BMW estimates that information related to video systems, as represented by back cameras that are already in widespread use, will become increasingly important for cars in the future and that the use of images will expand, especially in luxury cars; in order to overcome the insufficient FlexRay transmission speed of 10 MBps, which is a representative standard of the current on-vehicle network, they decided to equip their cars with a 100 MBps ethernet.

Users who purchase BMW cars are usually not concerned at all with the shape, protocols, infrastructure technology, and so on, of the network cable in the on-vehicle LAN. They are only interested in the information to be conveyed and its quality/use. For this reason, on-vehicle communication hardware, which is unrelated to the attractiveness of the car, is said to be a non-competing area for automobile manufacturers. It is important to reduce the cost of this part and build an environment where this can be procured externally for a long period of time. For this reason, BMW standardized this technology after collaborating with Broadcom to make this technology available to everyone. As a result, not only BMW, but also other automobile manufacturers can use the high-speed on-vehicle LAN, and innovation has been achieved in the on-vehicle LAN market by expanding the market. As a result, an environment materialized where parts for on-vehicle network equipment for in-house production vehicles can be obtained cheaply and for a long period of time. As in the Bosch example above, BMW also does not collect royalties for essential patents included in the standardized technology, and by putting BMW in the same position as other car manufactures and using technology standardized by other automakers, it was possible to eliminate anxiety or doubts that only BMW would have an advantage.

Case 14: Optical Connector

NTT and exchange system manufacturers are carrying out standardization activities of optical connectors with connector manufacturers, but the optical connector is not a business differentiation area for NTT and exchange system manufacturers. They proactively promote the standardization of optical connectors, and out-bounding of the technology of the connector's part is expanding the adoption of high-quality connectors in the market; their rationale is to enhance connectivity with their own products and avoid an increase in costs due to multiple connectors competing in the market. It can be seen that, by making public the advanced technology of the connector part, their success lay in enhancing the stability of their own equipment and system.

However, from the perspective of connector manufacturers that carried out the standardization of these connectors, this standardization is "disclosure" of "product specifications" and, as a matter of course, the profits that could have been obtained from the manufacturing of connectors cannot be expected. Actually, it can be said that connector manufacturers made corporate profits by achieving collaborative activities with procurement companies, rather than making profits from the connector itself (Eto, 2007b).

ORGANIZING THE EFFECT OF OUTBOUND OPEN INNOVATION USING STANDARDIZATION

As we have seen above, outbound open innovation can be realized by using standardization, but even when innovation was achieved in a market as a whole, it can be seen that in many cases, companies were not able to profit from the innovation. This is often caused by not having sufficiently predicted the effect of dissemination of technical information by standardization on the business and putting out excessive technical information.

Table 2 shows the effect of outbound open innovation using standardization. Here, technologies that are opened through standardization are classified into seven types, but depending on the case, multiple pieces of technical information could be out-bounded among them. It can be grasped that, among the items of technical information necessary for manufacturing and selling one product, the parts put into each state of technology 'close', and the kinds of technical information to "standardize" are important issues in business.

Firstly, although standardization of a product's specifications has the upsides of broadening its market and reducing costs, as participants increase market share will decrease, price competition will occur and the profit rate will also decline. The wider the standardized area, the fewer the number of points of differentiation, and it becomes an issue of competing by price alone.

Table 2. Business advantages and disadvantages by standardization type

Technology to open through standardization	Main advantages	Disadvantages	Technical information to be kept within the company
A:Product specifications	Market expansion Cost reduction	Difficulty to differentiate Declining shares due to expansion of participants	Product know-how
B:Standard essential patents in product specifications	Market expansion Suppressing the emergence of competing technologies (cost reduction)	Loss of patent revenue Difficulty differentiating with standard technology	Manufacturing technology
C:Manufacturing equipment	Equipment cost reduction	Loss of technical differences by equipment Cost reduction for other companies	Product internal technology
D:Performance evaluation technology	High evaluation of the company's own products High evaluation of in-house technical strength	Technology leak Easy comparison with competing products	Main product technology
E:Interface	New market development	Modularization makes it easier for other companies to enter the market	Utilization technology of patented products
F:Complementary product specification	Enjoying the benefits of market expansion due to complementary products High performance of the company's own products	Price competition by reversing position with complementary products	Systematization technology
G:Specification of non-competing area parts	Cost reduction of products/ parts	Cost reduction for competitors Exhaustion of parts industry	Non-standard technology/ product

If there are standard essential patents in the product specification, there is also a means of ensuring profits though its license fees, but as this is very popular nowadays, ensuring high-value license fees through standard essential patents is becoming difficult.

Under this kind of environment, it is important to black-box the know-how necessary to retain areas of differentiation in products. If one can secure the product manufacturing know-how to ensure that the market recognises that only your company's products offer good performance, despite fundamental standardization it can be possible to effectively utilize the market expansion and cost reduction achieved through standardization.

Although standardization of manufacturing equipment realizes cost reductions of that equipment, other companies also obtain the same cost reduction advantages, and since it is difficult to differentiate products manufactured from the same equipment, there is a high possibility of losing market share. At present the standardization of manufacturing equipment if often performed in seeking cost reduction advantages in saturated markets, but in order to ensure profits from product sales, having unique manufacturing technology that manufactures products that can be differentiated from other companies' products while using the same manufacturing equipment can be said to be essential.

Standardization of the product performance evaluation method, where the company's product has a high level of performance in practice, is a standardization that works effectively for product differentiation. However, standardization of the performance evaluation method facilitates research and development, and other companies can catch up technologically, and with low performance it is easy to be robbed of sufficient market share. It is an essential condition for standardization that there is a high level of technicality that other companies cannot emulate, and there is a market that requires it.

Standardization of the product interface makes it easier to use the products, and has the sizeable advantage of expanding the market. However, because the interface and the product's efficacy are made public, it has the disadvantage of facilitating the entry of other companies into the market. Under such circumstances, more so than for the interface, it is necessary to have strong patents for the internal parts of the company's product that other companies cannot circumvent. In monopolizing advanced technology that other companies cannot implement, where the interface can be standardized this can be said to be an ideal open-closed strategy.

Standardization not of the company's product but of surrounding products, standardization of complementary products has the greatest value. If complementary products are standardized and prices falls through competition, the market expands and with it the sales of the company's products. It is important to standardize complementary products in such a way that the company's product's performance can be displayed maximally. However, it is difficult to lead standardization of complementary products that the company does not manufacture, and complementary product manufacturers aim for standardization from their side. It is important to overcome this standardization competition strategically.

Standardization of non-competitive areas is the most effective when considering for cost reduction, however this standardization is difficult to realise where the company is not the manufacturer. In order to standardize parts that are not manufactured by the company and are in uncompetitive areas, it will be necessary for the industries using those parts to realise procurement power as one. However, in so doing, since other companies in the same industry will also achieve similar cost reduction advantages, the company will not achieve market dominance. How to make use of cost reductions in non-competitive areas in the product as a whole can be said to be an important strategy.

In any case, the most important point is that there are advantages and disadvantages in all forms of standardization, and when balancing both, it is necessary to choose which to emphasize. Whether it is possible to increase the advantages by controlling the balance is determined by the existence of valuable technological information that can be maintained within the company without standardization. While achieving market expansion and cost reduction for the part that cannot be differentiated and simultaneously expanding the technology use of the part that can be differentiated, it is necessary to create value in the market by using black-boxed technology.

As for the order of such technology strategic planning, first, it is necessary to select the technical information to be maintained within the company as a source of profit. In addition, it is necessary to examine the difference between business advantages and disadvantages when engaging in standardization for other technical information and to select a standardized form from which the greatest positive value can be obtained using the advantages.

In this analysis, as shown in Table 2, the entire business was separated into parts that should be standardized and parts that should not be. In practice however, we must not forget that this separation of use will change with time depending on the stage of the market diffusion of the product. Even for technology that is black-boxed immediately after the product's release, it will gradually become more difficult. Moreover, once standardization is done, it cannot be reversed. Therefore, choosing the timing is also an important strategy for balancing the opening and closing of technologies. In the next stage of this study, it is necessary to consider the generalization of this timing.

CONCLUSION

Standardization in actual corporate activities is conducted to increase the company's own profits. Standardization activities essentially generate outbound open innovation, but many companies have not noticed this, despite the difficulties in making profits for themselves, and the current situation is that standardization activities are being promoted by imitating successful examples. In order to overcome this situation and to position standardization activities as part of the strategy for gaining real profits, standardization activities should be positioned as a form of outbound open innovation, and it is important to organize and grasp the advantages and disadvantages and incorporate them into the business strategy.

I hope this paper will help in the consideration of the strategic use of standardization.

REFERENCES

Chesbrough, H. W. (2003). *Open Innovation: The New Imperative for Creating and Profiting from Technology*. Harvard Business School Press.

Chesbrough, H. W., Vanhaverbeke, W., & West, J. (Eds.). (2006). *Open Innovation: Researching a New Paradigm*. Oxford University Press.

Dahlander, L., & Gann, D. M. (2010). How open is innovation? *Research Policy, 39*(6), 699–709. doi:10.1016/j.respol.2010.01.013

Eto, M. (2007a). Effectiveness of standard for the competitiveness in bicycle industry. *Development Engineering*, *13*, 45–59.

Eto, M. (2007b). *Success and failure of cost reduction standardization as seen in the standardization of optical connectors*. Summary of a lecture presented at the 22nd Annual Academic Convention of the Japan Society for Research Policy and Innovation Management.

Helfat, C. E. C., & Quinn, J. B. (2006). Review: Open Innovation: The New Imperative for Creating and Profiting from Technology by Henry Chesbrough. *The Academy of Management Perspectives*, *20*(2), 86–88. doi:10.5465/amp.2006.20591014

Japanese Industrial Standards Committee. (2005). *Report of the Japanese Industrial Standards Committee*. Author.

Kajiura, M., & Uchida, Y. (2005). *Standardization of barcodes: Focusing on QR code*. Summary of a lecture presented at the 20th Annual Academic Convention of the Japan Society for Research Policy and Innovation Management.

Ogawa, K. (2014). *Open and Close Strategy: Conditions for Restructuring Japanese Companies*. Shoeisha.

Rogers, E. (1995). *Diffusion of Innovations* (4th ed.). The Free Press.

Senoo, K. (2009). *Why Japan is Losing in Business Although it Excels in Technology: Reasons that Breakthrough New Products Have Suffered Staggering Defeats*. Diamond, Inc.

Simcoe, T. S. (2006). Open standards and intellectual property rights. In H. W. Chesbrough, W. Vanhaverbeke, & J. West (Eds.), *Open Innovation: Researching a New Paradigm* (pp. 161–183). Oxford University Press.

Tatsumoto, H. (2017). *Global Strategy of Platform Companies: Strategic Utilization of Open Standards and Business Ecosystem*. Yuhikaku Publishing.

Tokuda, A. (2008). *Electronics in Automobiles and Standardization: Market of Electronic Control System in the Transition Period*. Koyoshobo.

Tomita, J., & Tatsumoto, H. (2006). *Standardization strategy in the semiconductor industry*. Summary of a lecture presented at the 21st Annual Academic Convention of the Japan Society for Research Policy and Innovation Management.

Chapter 15
Some Spanish Approaches on Standardization Management:
Discussion of the Experiences With University Students and Collaboration With Spanish Industry

María Ana Saenz-Nuño
Comillas Pontifical University, Spain

Jorge Marcos
Universidad de Vigo, Spain

María J. Fernández-Pintelos
University of Vigo, Spain

Javier Sánchez Real
Universidad de Vigo, Spain

Ana Maria Mariblanca
Asociación Española de Normalización, Spain

ABSTRACT

This chapter summarized the Spanish experience on the management of new standards including how the development of national standards has risen from needs not covered by international standards and how the collaboration with international bodies has given new opportunities of business. It will also present the problem of the gap between the needs in the industry to have people read standards versus the lack of university graduated students well prepared for that task. It will discuss the Spanish case on metrology standardization history from 1999 until now as an example of the development new standardization. It will present some new fields for standardization that are already under development in Spain related with health metrology.

DOI: 10.4018/978-1-5225-9008-8.ch015

Copyright © 2019, IGI Global. Copying or distributing in print or electronic forms without written permission of IGI Global is prohibited.

INTRODUCTION

In order to get the conditions under which the Spanish Standardization grew, It is necessary to have a look at the history. Briefly ("UNE History", n.d.), we have the following:

- 1935 Creation of the Spanish Standardization Body.
- 1939 First UNE Standard (paper formats based in DIN)
- 1946 The Instituto Nacional de Racionalización en el Trabajo (IRATRA) is founded. This was renamed in 1971 as Instituto Nacional de Racionalización y Normalización (IRANOR).
- 1986 Creation of the Certification and Standardization Body, AENOR.
- 1987 AENOR assumed the representation of Spain in ISO, IEC, CEN y COPANT
- 1987 Publication of the first UNE Standard by AENOR (UNE 36137:1987: Continuously hot-dip zinc coated unalloyed structural steel sheet and strip technical delivery conditions.)
- 1990 The Standardization Body assumed the representation of Spain in CENELEC
- 1990 First big international cooperation project (European Project in Mexico)
- 1999 The Centro de Ensayos, Innovación y Servicios S.L. (CEIS) is created.
- 2001 Creation of AENOR Internacional S.A.U.
- 2017 The Spanish Standardization Body, UNE, changes its denomination.

ISO started its work in 1947, one year before had the Spanish IRANOR, but their scope were not the same. Looking at the recent history, Spain increased its professionals from the 60's. Before that time, most of the economy was based on agriculture and some official industries, like SEAT, with a huge influence from the outside. Therefore, the lack of educated people and the fact that the standards came from the Mother Industry, was the background of Spain.

The work done between 1946 and 1976 approximately was focused into spreading the standards into the industry, educating people for allowing the industry to grow. They tried to gather to share knowledge, but there was also another problem. Not many people speak other languages from Spanish. This isolated the standardization members of the Committee. But with the 70's and the political collaboration with other countries, Spain started to be more open. People started to study languages. They had now the opportunity to learn from their European colleagues and they did. AENOR was created in 1986 and immediately Spain started to participate directly in ISO, IEC, CEN ... From 1987, when AENOR started in ISO, the Spanish Standardization Committees grew quite fast until now.

So we could say that the Standardization in Spain, as a task assumed to be relevant with an important implication in international committees, is not older than 35 years.

Among all the Standardization Committees in UNE (former AENOR), we would like to talk about the story of one of them, the AEN/CTN 82 on Metrology (Saenz-Nuno, 2003; Saenz et al, 2011). It was established from the very beginning due the needs in military institutions. They started to collect Good Practices in the Industry and developing new National Documents, most of them based on Military ones.

In 1996 the ISO standardization committee on Geometrical Product Specification and Verification, ISO/TC 213 (Marcos et al, 2012) was created. Things started to change. In the Spanish committee, AEN/CTN 82, it was decided to have a new leadership to converge faster to the International current and then is when Dr. Sáenz-Nuño, author of this chapter, together with another Professor of the Comillas Pontifical University, assumed the Technical Secretary because of her experience as researcher in the National Metrology Institution, CEM.

This Standardization Committee on Geometrical Product Specification and Verification, AEN/CTN 82/SC 2 has been developing a great effort during the past 20 years.

As it is written in the website (Marcos et al, 2012) of the ISO/TC 213 Dimensional and geometrical product specifications and verification, its scope is:

[…]Standardization in the field of geometrical product specifications (GPS), i.e. macro- and microgeometry specifications covering dimensional and geometrical tolerancing, surface properties and the related verification principles, measuring equipment and calibration requirements including the uncertainty of dimensional and geometrical measurement. The standardization includes the basic layout and explanation of drawing indications (symbols).

Excluded: the definition of the specific proportions and dimensions of drawing indications (symbols) and their execution.[…]

From 1999 until 2017, Dr. Sáenz-Nuño has been in charge of the Spanish Technical Secretary. Among the different tasks that she had to deal with, was to spread the new documents into the Spanish Industry, in order to prepare it for international business.

Nowadays, UNE is in charge of more than 30 000 Standardization documents dealing with many aspects of the daily life (Saenz et al, 2001) 217 Technical committees, 121 international responsabilities and 1800 Standardization projects for 2018. If we remember that many of the directives are based on the Standards, the implication of the work done is critical.

Meanwhile, Dr. Marcos & colleagues, has dealt with the problem of getting some of those standards and making the pre-graduated and post-graduated students to work with them.

In the following clauses, it will be shown the practical experience over the last 20 years, without mentioning any name of the Companies involved. Some of them multinational Enterprises, even from other continents, and some of them local businesses.

INTERNAL VS. EXTERNAL STANDARDIZATION IN SPAIN

We should distinguish between two cases: national Standards as a country, Standards inside the Industry even if this is part of a multinational.

National vs. International Standardization in Spain

As it was explained in the introduction, the case of a specific technical committee is going to be explained. The AEN/CTN 82/SC 2, mirror of the ISO/TC 213 has been working on a huge amount of documents. From 1999 until 2017, the number of documents worked were something from 20 even up to 50 documents per year. That means, more than one standard per month, and some cases even 1 per week.

In the website of the ISO/TC 213 (Marcos et al, 2012) is explicitly said that the Committee has:

- *Published 145 ISO Standards from 1985*. Some of them were a revision of old documents, but as there has been develop a new philosophy called GPS, all the standards has been adapted to this concept, dealing with a big amount of documents.

It is usual that each document to be under development sometime between 2 and 5 years, in which the experts participate actively in the discussions. What it was done before in Spain in the national field, allowed the experts to participate directly in the ISO field.

- *Under development 21 ISO Standards right now.* Taking into consideration that now there are around 20 members in the Spanish committee, as it will be shown bellow, that means that at least there is one expert following one Standardization document. In fact, each expert used to follow more than one standardization work, depending of his interest. Therefore, this is not a game. The participation in the Spanish Committee involves working hard. Moreover, during the life of the committee from 1999, when the Comillas Pontifical University got in charged of the Secretary, a member would be dismissed if he does not participate actively.
- *25 participating country members, out of 163 countries involved in ISO standardization activities.* And it has 28 observing members. At the end around 33% of the ISO countries close interested in the field. Therefore, we consider this committee a good example of growth of a new committee in a field of interest of the Industry, and consequently a case for learning how that information is handle in the Spanish Industry.

The Spanish Committee is the mirror one of the ISO, so it assumed the representation of Spain in that group. Therefore, the Spanish group is directly involved in the ISO Committee, following closely the Standards. In fact the structure was followed as far as it was possible.

In the following group, it is shown the Spanish Working Groups (GT) versus the ISO Working and Advisory Groups (WG and AG).

It may be noticed that there some others committees of ISO that are observed by the Spanish, because of the interest that it may have (boxes in light blue in figure 1).

Figure 1. Internal structure of the Spanish AEN/CTN 82/SC 2 versus ISO/TC 213 (at present day)

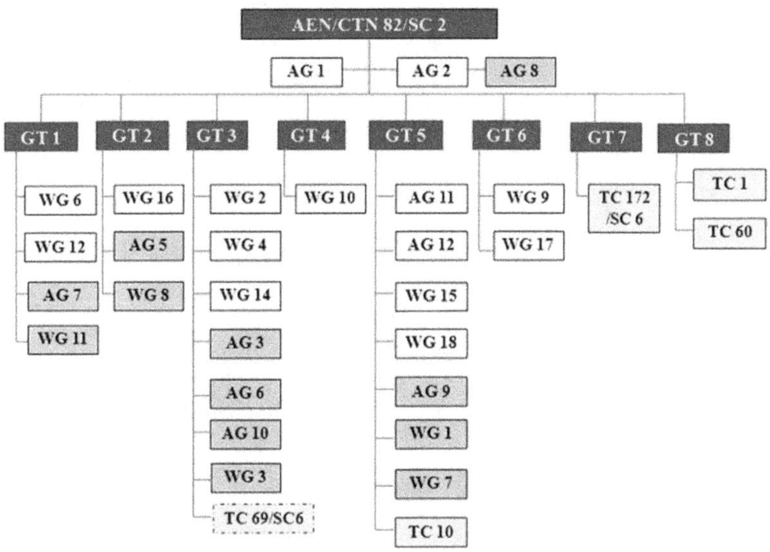

The members of the Spanish group are shown in numbers in Figure 2, the one use in each meeting for checking the attendance:

It has been considered only those years in which the Convenior and the Secretary of the Spanish committee where held by Comillas Pontifical University, in order not to introduce any undesirable perturbation to the data.

Considering that some of the initial members retired over this long period, we conclude how the new standards in Dimensional Metrology and Geometrical tolerancing arise a bigger interest in the Spanish market. This field is quite a specific one, but the interest grew. The main reason of this was due the huge effort done not only by the Secretary, but also by many of their members, who decided to prepare courses for the Industry, courses for students, Seminars, Congresses and integrated the Standards in their daily work.

It was held also three International Meetings of the ISO/TC in Madrid and Zaragoza during that time, and so was the enthusiasm, that many members joined the group.

The Spanish Industry realized that they can participate directly in the Standards that were writing. This was a huge experience. It was also remarked that some aspects, already covered, may help for the developing of the new ones, so many professionals participate in the committee. This was the reason for the growing in figure 2.

We can not get into detail of the names of the companies directly involved in the committee, but we may show in figure 4 the relation in numbers of them.

Discussing the results plotted in the figure, there are some quite important conclusions that has risen from there, from the Spanish point of view:

Figure 2. Number of members per AEN/CTN 82/SC 2meeting from 1998 until 2012

Figure 3. Poster of one of the conferences in Spain together with the ISO meeting in order to enhance the Spanish participation in standardization work

Figure 4. Number of members per meeting from 1998 until 2012 in the Spanish Standardization Committee AEN/CTN 82/SC 2, classified by their working center as High Level Research Center, University Professor or Industry Professional.

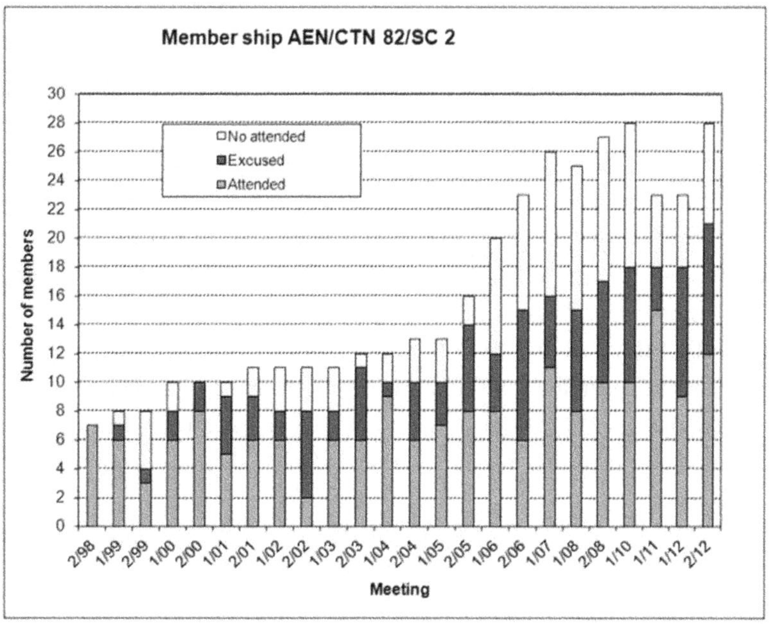

- Research Centers. The number of participants is kept in time. And if one of the researchers retired, it was immediately replaced by the new worker. The Spanish Research Centers are quite involved with Standardization. When the researchers have the opportunity to participate in committees to share their point of view and find an agreed document, they are willingly to do so. Moreover, they try to find their way to introduce their research into Standardization, if that might help the Industry. In fact, the initial core of the Spanish committee under study in fig 4, had 4 researchers (some from Military Institutions) versus 3 other professionals.
- University. Because the Spanish University is quite aware of the need for collaboration between Research and Industry, it has become a natural link between them. Therefore, although the initiative started in Research Centers, the professors involved with the Standardization GPS started to join around the group, most of the time invited by their colleagues in the research. It may seem that something happen between meetings 1/08 and 1/10, as there was a decrease in the number of professor involved. In fact, that does not happen. Numbers showed that the retirement of some professor was overcome because some other got involved. Moreover, meanwhile in some committees of the same Spanish Standardization Body is usual to find professors of the same College, even department, participating, this is not the case for the AEN/CTN 82/SC 2. Typically, in each College or Faculty, there is only one professor involved with the Geometrical Tolerancing Research. Consequently, each of the professors in that graph represents a different Univ. in any region of Spain. There were even participants from the Canarian Islands.
- Industry. The Spanish industry tends not to participate in Standardization Committee unless there is a direct benefit from their membership. This is the reason because of the slow increase in the number of professionals. But as the standard documents started to rise, together with the education initiatives of the members of the committee, they realized about the convenience for their participation.

The result of all of this was not only to participate in the development of the Standards, but to learn all the political aspects and economical interests that many times lay behind the documents, to be prepared in advance for the future Standardization under development and to get in deep detail of all the aspects involved in the business. If we might ask to the participants about this period, they will assure that it was professionally amazing.

The final result of that experience, nowadays, is a group of standardization experts that through their collaboration with the Industry and the University are willingly spreading their knowledge, that are convincing the Industry that they are not only the user of the standards, but their authors. The Spanish industry re-discovered that the Standards are done by them for them. That was a huge step. Consequently, the decision not to allow members without active work, become an avoiding tool for obstacles to the work. Probably, this was the reason that made some professionals no to continue the work done in that committee before.

On the other hand, most of these standardization participants are right now participating in Standardization Educational activities, in order to help others to work with standards.

Internal or External Standardization for the Industry

This is a problem overcome in big companies, but not in small Spanish companies. Some of them, with very few workers, tend to use their own standards, result of their experience. Some of them, when discovered by expert eyes, reveal to contain a huge amount of practical knowledge, but many times they are lost once the company closes or the worker retires. This is a problem that through the creation of a community of users in a specified technical field may be solved. Sometimes, in Professional Associations they find their way as Good Practices Books, leaflets, … but it is not easy in Spain to find it in the Technical Reports or Standards.

This does not happen in those big companies, where they might have also their own standard just in the case of a field where there is no Standardization.

On the other hand, some Spanish Industry tries to find the know-how in the Standardization. That is not the way, and from the Technical Committees we are doing a great effort in order to prepare the professionals to work with Standards in their daily tasks. The main activities are related with Seminars and courses upon demand.

Figure 5. Book about metrological management standards (ISO 10012:2003)

MANAGING MULTI-DISCIPLINARY STANDARDIZATION IN SPAIN

In Spain, vw may distinguish between Standards from different fields but the same Standardization Body, and Standards from different Organizations.

In the following lines, we will discuss the experience over the years.

Multi-Disciplinary Standardization in Spain, One Standardization Organization

This is common situation, mainly for young professionals, as the ISO standardization has become the most used. It is well known the huge effort done for developing a coherent, useful and robust system. And the users can participate in the developing procedure.

It is not easy to spread the use of Standards, if they are not known or they cannot be accessed easily. Therefore, in AENOR they have develop a AENOR+ to overcome those difficulties. It is an agile system.

But it is still necessary to teach some courses in pre-graduate Studies in the University about Standardization, or Specific Courses in the Industry to get used to work with Standardization, in the level that may be needed depending of the task of the worker in that Industry.

Multi-Disciplinary Standardization in Spain From Different Standardization Organizations

Sometimes the small company may be forced to use different standards depending on the customer to who they sell their products. This is the worst situation, as to find an expert on that standardization may not be easy. To overcome this problem, in some committees, as the AEN/CTN 82/SC 2 Dimensional

Figure 6.UNE easy access to Standards

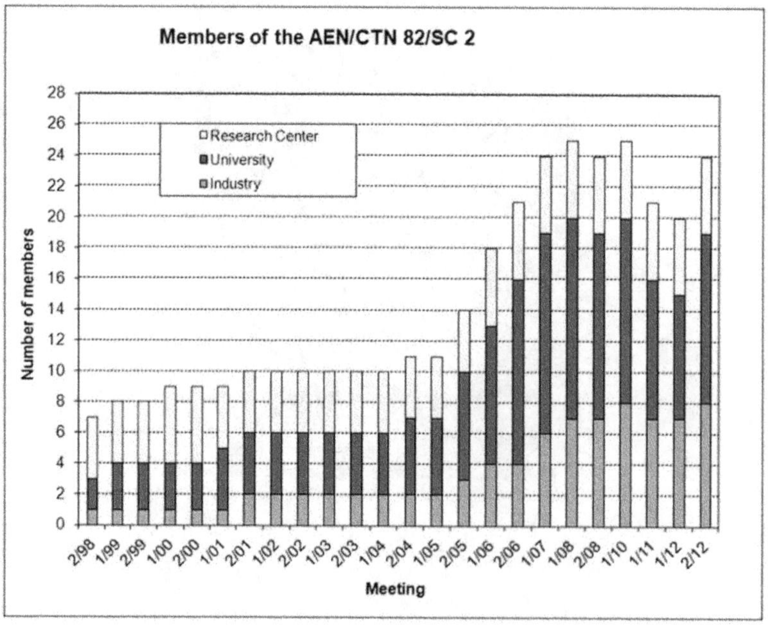

Metrology, the experts provide professional help on those cases. The experts of that committee are familiar with many of the typical standards in the field, not only UNE. That is something to be desirable.

Typically, in the AEN/CTN 82/SC 2 there are around 10 or 20 questions attended per year though UNE, and much more considering the talking given by the n experts in Seminars, Congresses, papers and so.

STANDARDIZATION AND ORGANISATIONAL LEARNING ASPECTS IN SPAIN

In Spain, the University studies has suffered a remodeling a few years ago. Many studies that were 5 years long, became 4 years long. Therefore, it has been quite difficult to include new courses that were not before. The good news are that the changes gave the opportunity to rethink the old uses versus the new ones. This, together with the new amazing technologies has lead to a new situation. Although there was little opportunity to have official courses only on Standardization, it has been included in other courses as a main part of it.

We present right here the experience in the two Spanish Universities: Universidad de Vigo and Comillas Pontifical University.

University of Vigo

Due the fact that the Standardization is very important in Engineering, the educational programs in the University of Vigo are related with this field. And many times, it is related with the content of some courses.

One of the main experiences was the joining working group of students, as the engineer students had the opportunity to work with Foreign Language Students. In Spain, the pre-graduate students tend not to share with students of other branches, as it may happen in other countries, and many times they have their own courses in specific buildings apart from each others. Therefore, it was a huge opportunity to join a mixed group of different interests and points of view, but with a quiet different and specific as-

Figure 7.

signed task that helped to share their knowledge. The students, after this teaching realized how every Standard is the result of the efforts of many professionals from quite different fields.

This activity designed in this way, may be classified as a *collaborative learning* strategy. In collaborative learning, the students must work together to get a common goal. It is a learning strategy already used for years (Slavin et al, 1987; Kagan et al, 1994; Panitz et al, 1999; Marcos et al, 2011). They have to know and understand the content of a technical document. For that they have to try that every person learns and everyone shares for the common benefit. This kind of learning is opposite to the competitive one.

The students groups were designed in the following way. Sometimes the student do not master the language knowledge, but to get over this, there has been established that each working group might be integrated by three engineering students together with a maximum of six Translation students. These translation students should be three specialized in English as first foreign language and three with French.

There has been a close collaboration with the Spanish Standardization Body, called UNE, before AENOR. This collaboration happens in several courses, that we specify bellow:

- *Fiabilidad de los Sistemas Electrónicos (FSE).* This course might be chosen by the students in the fith year of Telecomunication studies, Electronic specialization. It was taught from academic year 1998-99 until 2015-2016, that is over 18 years. The direct collaboration with UNE specifically started in the course 2010-2011. Right now, this course is not offered in the current studies, due the last changes in the Studies.
- *Ingeniería de Equipos Electrónicos (IEE).* This course might also be chosen by the students but in the 3rd year in the Telecommunication, Electronic specialization. Although this is an adapted one from the one before, its content is quite similar about Standardization matters. This course started in the University in the year 2012-2013 and from the beginning there has been a close collaboration with UNE.
- *Diseño Avanzado de Sistemas Electrónicos Industriales (DASEI).* This course might be chosen by the students in the first year of the Master on Industry Engineering Studies. This course started in the University in the year 2014-2015 and from the very beginning there has been a close collaboration with UNE.

It has been proven that the collaboration of the Spanish Standardization Body, UNE, in the teaching activities is critical. In the University of Vigo, that collaboration in particular is with the committee called *AEN/CTN 200/SC 56: Comité de Confiabilidad*, mirror of the IEC/TC 56,working directly on items of interest for those courses.

The scope of the IEC/TC56 as listed in ("International Electrotechnical Commission", n.d.) is:

To prepare international standards in the field of dependability, in all appropriate technological areas, including those not normally dealt with by IEC Technical Committees. Dependability covers the availability performance and its influencing factors: reliability performance, maintainability performance and maintenance support performance (including management of obsolescence). The standards provide systematic methods and tools for the dependability assessment and management of equipment, services and systems throughout their life cycles.

The standards cover generic aspects on reliability and maintainability programme management, testing and analytical techniques, software and system dependability, life cycle costing, technical risk analysis and project risk management. This includes standards related to product issues from component reliability to guidance for engineering dependability of systems, standards related to process issues from technological risk analysis to integrated logistics support and standards related to management issues from dependability program management to managing for obsolescence.

The application of these standards may raise safety related issues, though the standards themselves do not cover safety. They may be applied to business risk analysis but these risk areas are not dealt with by TC 56

From the beginning, the students have participated in three types of works:

- *Revision of published standards.* The scope is to prepare a report about the Spanish standard, presenting possible errors, mistakes or propose changes. In some cases, they reported some translation mistakes unnoticed before. This is not the preferred path to involve students, as the result of their work may not be considered for a while, until the official revision of the UNE or ISO standard. The length of the standard to work will be assigned with the following rule: the maximum number of pages to be revised has to be around 10 pages per student. Therefore, if the group consists of 6 students, the maximum length would be around 60 pages.
- *Revision of still non published standards.* The scope is to prepare a report about the original international standard, in French or English. Even, if it is available, the proposed Spanish Standard of the UNE Committee. This task revealed to be a quite interesting work for the students, as they were able to participate on time in the Committee meetings and develop changes that could be incorporated in the final document. The experience has shown that around 60 or 70% of the comments has been taken into consideration and resulted in modifications of the final translation. The chosen criteria is the same, 10 pages per student.
- *Translation of Standards.* The scope is to translate the ISO standards written in English or French into Spanish. This work might be an additional document for the UNE Committee for developing the final UNE Standard. The length of the standard to work will be assigned with the following rule, the maximum number of pages to translate has to be 5 pages per student. Therefore, if the group consists of 6 students, the maximum length would be around 30 pages.

After all the work done, the professor in charge of the supervision send the documents to the UNE Committee, to be taken into consideration.

The total number of participants in this work until now may summarized in Tables 1-4.

The standards on which they have worked are related with RAMS (Reliability, Availability, Maintenability, Safety) technologies. The specifica task done with each one is summarize in Table 5.

Table 1. Students work on published standards

Revision of published standards	Number of students
Documents worked: 6	Teleco. Stud.: 17 Translation Stud.: 9

Table 2. Students work on non published standards

Revision of non published standards	Number of students
Documents worked: 3	Teleco. Stud.: 17 Translation Stud.: 18

Table 3. Students work on translation of standards

Translation of Standards	Number of students
Documents worked: 9	Teleco. Stud.: 98 Ind. Stud.: 7 Translation Stud.: 54

Table 4. Summary

TOTAL	Number of students
Documents worked: 18	Teleco. Stud.: 132 Ind. Stud.: 10 Translation Stud.: 81

Table 5. Worked Standards by students

Revised Standards already published: UNE-EN 60706-3 Maintainability of equipment -- Part 3: Verification and collection, analysis and presentation of data UNE-EN 62308 Equipment reliability - Reliability assessment methods UNE-EN 61163-1 Reliability stress screening -- Part 1: Repairable assemblies manufactured in lots UNE-EN 60300-3 3 Dependability management - Part 3-3: Application guide - Life cycle costing UNE-EN 60300-2 Dependability management - Part 2: Guidelines for dependability management UNE-EN 60812 Analysis techniques for system reliability - Procedure for failure mode and effects analysis (FMEA)	6
Revised Standards non published: UNE-EN 60300-3-16 Dependability management -- Part 3-16: Application guide - Guidelines for specification of maintenance support services UNE-EN 60300-3-15 Dependability management -- Part 3-15: Application guide - Engineering of system dependability UNE-EN 60300-3-11 Dependability management -- Part 3-11: Application guide - Reliability centred maintenance	3
Translated standards: UNE-EN 61709 Electric components - Reliability - Reference conditions for failure rates and stress models for conversion UNE-EN 62502 Analysis techniques for dependability - Event tree analysis (ETA) UNE-EN 62506 Methods for product accelerated testing UNE-EN 62508 Guidance on human aspects of dependability UNE-EN 62628 Guidance on software aspects of dependability UNE-EN 62740 Root cause analysis (RCA) UNE-EN 61703 Mathematical expressions for reliability, availability, maintainability and maintenance support terms UNE-EN 61882 Hazard and operability studies (HAZOP studies) - Application guide UNE-EN 61078 Reliability block diagrams .	9

After the work was done, students were asked how did the find the experience. They found this experience:

- Very interesting because of the collaboration with the background.
- The time used quite suitable for the obtained results.
- That they will be willingly to increase their tasks in order to have the oportunity to work in some other experiences like this in Standardization.
- That the number of expected tasks like this should be around three per year,
- The engineering students preferred the revision of standards, meanwhile the students of translation preferred the task translation of Standards.

It was found that if the group worked in a collaborative way, it was able to reach higher goals than with individual and competitive work.

But when applying this collaboration learning strategy in Standardization, the following items are recommended to be considered;

- To have a motivated group to work, in order to maximize the learning of every participant.
- Every student of the group must assume their responsability.
- They have to work collaboratively. Each student of the group has to be motivated to help the others, to share and to teach, taking into account the compromise that they have with group.
- Every student has to assume the compromise to focus the effort, that means, to establish a working plan, follow it, measure the results and to establish corrective strategies.
- This kind of experiences are quite different from the others long before started, therefore, sometimes is a little time consuming to address the student to work effieciently.

But there is another relevant benefit. This quite active collaboration between students and the Standardization Body is of special interest. Meanwhile the students learn to work with the Standards, the Body has the opportunity to share the point of view of the new users.

The benefits for the students and UNE (AENOR) may be specifically at:

- The adquisition of competences in multidisciplinary environments.
- The establishment of a "business plan" and a road map to get the goals in real world.
- The group strategies to get the best of every member of the group. This usually will involve to integrate internal rules in the group agreed by everyone.
- Maybe a great strategy for the standardization Body will be join translators and experts close together in the development of Spanish standards.

The competences acquired by the students are evaluated normally in two ways:

- With an Exam:
  - The student should prepare two exercises proposed by the profesor during the course to be done by the end of the semester,
  - Laboratory sessions and the their reports, and
  - A final exam.

- Without exam:
    - The student should prepare two exercises proposed by the profesor during the course to be done by the end of the semester,
    - Laboratory sessions and the their reports, and
    - Compulsory assistance to class and two external projects in collaboration with an external Industry (Marcos et al, 2011; Martin et al, 2010; Soares et al, 2013; Marcos et al, 2009; Marcos et al, 2012). One of those two external works is with the Industry and the other directly with UNE (AENOR)

They way they are going to be evaluated, is chosen by the own student.

During the eighteen years that the FSE course were taught, 100% of the students chose an evaluation without exam.

During the four years that the EEE course were taught, 74% of the students chose an evaluation without exam. In table 6, it is shown the percentage of students that selected one option or the other along the time.

Comillas Pontifical University

We are going to specify theexpercience in Dimensional Metrology dealing with Geometrical Tolerancing. In Comillas surprisingly the students are interested once they have already finished their studies and they have started working in the Industry.

In the 90's, all the standardization efforts where focused in Quality Standards and Technical Product Documentation (TPD), but the standards on Geometrical Tolerancing where undertaught. As the studies where changed, there was an opportunity to introduce new things.

In Comillas, the standards involved with Geometrical tolerancing are taught in some courses like *Technical drawing* (slightly) in the first semester, *Manufacturing* (slightly) in the sixth and seventh semester and *Dimensional Metrology* in the seventh semester. But they do not realize about the potential of the documentation, probably because they have still not reach the Industry. Somehow, this changes

Table 6. Option selected by the EEE students during the years

Year	Total number of students	Evaluation without exam
2012-13	22	9 (41%)
2013-14	19	17 (90%)
2014-15	13	9 (69%)
2015-16	18	18 (100%)

Figure 8.

a little bit when getting involve in the Final Project of their Studies, but this depends strongly on the professor to whom they may be assigned. The situation in other Universities is worst, but we will not talked about them.

Therefore, once the education program is established, Comillas has many collaborations with the Industry. This is what may change from Universidad de Vigo.

The main motor of this was the starting active participation of some professors in some technical committees in the Spanish Standardization Body and in the ISO committee.

This direct collaboration dealt with these activities:

- National conferences about GPS Standards (Geometrical Product Specification and verification) for education of workers in the Industry.
- These conferences where held typically in National Congresses. Although the low interest for the research activity, the main scope was to get closer to the national industry, to gather around the same interests and share knowledge. For example, some of the National Congresses in which there has been many talkings about GPS standardization has been CNIM congresses (held by the Asociación Española de Ingeniería Mecánica)
- Specific courses and seminars on GPS upon demand, in collaboration with UNE and the Centro Español de Metrología (CEM). CEM is Spanish National Metrology Institution.
- Collaboration in the group of the Standardization body involved with Education in the University and the conferences organized around it.
- participation in the Standardization Body Committee in charge of assigning a prize annually to the best Spanish work of any university student, involving standardization, among others.
- Development of final grade works of Engineer Students related directly with Standards, not only using but even promoting the proposal of new ones in new fields.
- Introduction of the main Standardization concepts.

- Papers, books for workers in the industry.
- Courses under demand
- Collaboration with many other Standardization Bodies from South America, as we can share many documentations with very few effort.

There is also an initiative that will probably deal with a great opportunity for students, and it is the creation of a Spanish Standardization Committee on Health Metrology. It is 2 years old, but has already a DIS version of the UNE Standard on Health Metrology Management.

Figure 9. Poster on Geometrical Tolerancing, published by Zeiss and translated into Spanish by the AEN/CTN 82/SC 2 Technical Secretary

Universidade Vigo

Figure 10. Introductory book to Geometrical Product Specification (GPS) translated into Spanish

THE INDIVIDUAL IN STANDARDS SETTING: SELECTION, TRAINING, MOTIVATION IN SPAIN

A matter of fact is the need for training among the people working in the Spanish industry. It is now well established a formal way to work with standards in the Spanish Universities. Most of the time, it depends on the professor involved with the topic. If that professor had the opportunity to be in close contact with the Standardization, he will enhance his students with it, but unfortunately, that is not usual in Spain.

Only those professors close to standardization, because there are directly involved with technical committees, will consider Standards as references of their work.

The problem has to do also with the not official recognition to the Standardization work done by professors, who right now are pressured by many burocratic paperwork with unclear purpose.

At the end, this deals with so few university professor really involved in standardization in their courses. But they result strange even for their department colleagues.

In some universities, the professors who have worked close enough with the industry, have realized the need for standardization as one of the main items of the work. That is the experience in the Univ. de Vigo and Comillas.

CONCLUSION

The history of Standardization in Spain is the history of the political and social situation under which is has entered the XXI century. The changes in the last generations has been great, as the concepts around the Standardization.

The University is one of the main motors of the change, because of its rol as a link between the Industry and Students, enhancing the first ones to apply Standards successfully in their business and educating new pre-graduates in Standards.

The Standardization in Spain will be successful as far as the Society and the Industry feel that they are done by them for them.

Experience has shown that University is the best transmission in Spain for Standardization, as they are related with Industry and researchers.

Along this chapter, it has been presented some activities done by interdisciplinary groups from quite different Studies, Engineering and Translation. This is the situation that many of he graduated student may find in their jobs.

The activities done with students described along this chapter in Universidad de Vigo, has for them many advantages, but if had to remark the main we will say:

- They get closer to the standardization, one of the main tools for their daily work mainly in technology
- The practical development of standardization documents is understood in depth, in spite of its difficulty.

In the case of the Comillas Pontifical University the best experience with students is around the final works they have to do by the end of their studies, under the supervision of a professor really involve in Standardization.

In the Industry, the difficulty is to approach to the knowledge behind the standards. For enhancing the Spanish Industry to use the Standardization the best way results to help them to find its use and understand them. And this is done by courses upon demand, attended congresses on the topic related

FUTURE STRATEGIES

For the students in the Spanish University,

- The successful experiences of Universidad de Vigo: students of different Studies, working ogether in revision or translation of standards
- The well established experiences of Comillas Pontifical University: final project with a well funded use of Standards.

For the Industry in Spain, will be education around the Standardization and participation in the Technical Committees.

REFERENCES

International Electrotechnical Commission. (n.d.). Retrieved from: http://www.iec.ch/dyn/www/f?p=103:7:16952850021229:FSP_ORG_ID,FSP_LANG_ID:1270,25

Kagan, S. (1994). *Cooperative Learning*. Kagan Publishing.

Marcos, J., Fernández, M. J., Sánchez, J., Suárez, M., & Mariblanca, A. M. (2012). Training in RAMS in Collaboration with Industrial Companies and Institutions. *2nd International Workshop AMEST 2012 Advances Maintenance Engineering Services and Technologies*.

Marcos, J., Pérez, S., Sánchez, J., Álvarez, R., & Suárez, M. (2009). Active Learning Approach for Engineering, Collaboration with the Corporate World. *International Journal of Engineering Education, 25*(4), 777–787.

Marcos, J., Sánchez, J., Quintáns, C., & Suárez, M. (2011). *Aprendizaje activo en Ingeniería con la colaboración del entorno empresarial. In XVII Seminario Anual de Automática, Electrónica Industrial e Instrumentación.* SAAEI.

Martín, E., Lázaro, C., & Hernán-Losada, I. (2010). *Active Learning in Telecommunication Engineering: A case study.* IEEE EDUCON Education Engineering.

Panitz, T. (1999). Benefits of Cooperative Learning in relation to Student Motivation. Academic Press.

Pérez Vázquez, A., & Ruíz Rosado, O. (2005). Interdisciplinary research: A swot analysis and its role in agricultural research in Mexico. *Tropical and Subtropical Agroecosystems.*

Sáenz & Quiñones. (2001). Metrología Dimensional, Historia de un subcomité renovado. *Revista UNE, 157*, 25.

Sáenz-Nuño. (2003). La normalización en metrología dimensional. *Interempresas, 15.*

Slavin, R. E. (1987). *Cooperative Learning: Student Teams* (2nd ed.). Washington, DC: National Education Association.

Soares, F. O., Sepúlveda, M. J., Monteiro, S., Lima, R. M., & Dinis-Carvalho, J. (2013). An integrated project of entrepreneurship and innovation in engineering education. *Mechatronics (Elsevier), 23*(8), 987–996. doi:10.1016/j.mechatronics.2012.08.005

UNE History. (n.d.). Retrieved from: https://www.une.org/la-asociacion/historia

Website of the Asociación Española de ingeniería mecánica. (n.d.). Retrieved from http://www.asocaeim.es/

Website of the ISO/TC 213. (n.d.). *Dimensional and geometrical product specifications and verification.* Retrieved from https://www.iso.org/committee/54924.html

Compilation of References

Adolphi, H. (1997). *Strategische Konzepte zur Organisation der betrieblichen Standardisierung. In DIN Normungskunde* (Vol. 38). Berlin: Beuth Verlag.

AFNOR. (1967). *La normalisation dans l'entreprise*. Paris: AFNOR.

Ajzen, I. (1991). The theory of planned behavior. *Organizational Behavior and Human Decision Processes*, *50*(2), 179–211. doi:10.1016/0749-5978(91)90020-T

Alexander, E. R. (1993). Interorganizational Coordination: Theory and Practice. *Journal of Planning Literature*, *7*(4), 328–343. doi:10.1177/088541229300700403

Alexy, O., George, G., & Salter, A. J. (2013). Cui bono? "The selective revealing of knowledge and its implications for innovative activity." *Academy of Management Review*, *38*(2), 270–291. doi:10.5465/amr.2011.0193

Allen, P. S. (Ed.). (1913). *Opus Epistolarum Des Erasmi Roterodami* (Vol. 2, pp. 1517–1519). Oxford, UK: Oxford University Press.

Al-Mashari, M., Irani, Z., & Zairi, M. (2001). Business process reengineering: A survey of international experience. *Business Process Management Journal*, *7*(5), 437–455. doi:10.1108/14637150110406812

Amit, R., & Zott, C. (2012). Creating Value Through Business Model Innovation. *MIT Sloan Management Review*, *53*(3), 41–49.

Anand, B. N., & Khanna, T. (2000). Do firms learn to create value? The case of alliances. *Strategic Management Journal*, *21*(3), 295–315. doi:10.1002/(SICI)1097-0266(200003)21:3<295::AID-SMJ91>3.0.CO;2-O

Anderson, M., & Anderson, S. L. (2011). *Machine Ethics*. Cambridge, UK: Cambridge University Press. doi:10.1017/CBO9780511978036

ANSI. (2015). *Essential Requirements: Due process requirements for American National Standards*. Retrieved 15 January 2018 from https://www.ansi.org/essentialrequirements/

ANSI. (2018). *American National Standards Institute*. Retrieved from http://www.craftechind.com/ansi-standards-everything-need-know/

Argyres, N., Bigelow, L., (2010). Innovation, modularity, and vertical de-integration: Evidence from the early US auto industry. *Organization Science, 21*(4), 842-853.doi:10.1287/orsc.1090.0493

Argyres, N., Felin, T., Foss, N., & Zenger, T. (2012). Organizational economics of capability and heterogeneity. *Organization Science*, *23*(5), 1213–1226. doi:10.1287/orsc.1120.0746

Arnal, J. (2005). *Formalization of Ethics: The Issue of Standardization*. Retrieved from ftp://mse.univ-paris1.fr/pub/mse/cahiers2005/R05074.pdf

Arthur, W. B. (1989). Competing Technologies, Increasing Returns, and Lock-in by Historical Events. *Economic Journal (London)*, *394*(99), 116–131. doi:10.2307/2234208

Axelrod, R. (1984). *The Evolution of Cooperation*. Basic Books.

Backhouse, J., Hsu, C. W., & Silva, L. (2006). Circuits of Power in Creating de jure Standards: Shaping an International Information Systems Security Standard. *Management Information Systems Quarterly*, *30*(Special Issue), 413–438. doi:10.2307/25148767

Balta, D., & Krcmar, H. (2018). Managing Standardization in eGovernment: A Coordination Theory based Analysis Framework. In *Proc. International Conference on Electronic Government*. Cham: Springer. 10.1007/978-3-319-98690-6_6

Balta, D. (2016a). Stakeholder Management in Standardisation – A Framework for Analysis of Coordination Mechanisms based on Resource Dependencies. In *Enterprise Interoperability in the Digitized and Networked Factory of the Future* (pp. 52–57). ISTE.

Balta, D. (2016b). The Shape of Standardisation in the eGovernment Research Landscape. In *Enterprise Interoperability in the Digitized and Networked Factory of the Future* (pp. 66–72). ISTE.

Balta, D. (2018b). *What are the Strategies for and Benefits of Effective IT Standardization in Government? In Enterprise Interoperability: Smart Services and Business Impact of Enterprise Interoperability* (pp. 143–149). Wiley. doi:10.1002/9781119564034.ch18

Balta, D., Harders, N. M., & Krcmar, H. (2018). Managing IT Standardization in Government: Towards a Descriptive Reference Model. In *Proc. Enterprise Interoperability: Smart Services and Business Impact of Enterprise Interoperability*. London: ISTE. doi:10.1002/9781119564034.ch17

Baron, J., & Pohlmann, T. (2013). Who Cooperates in Standards Consortia—Rivals or Complementors? *Journal of Competition Law & Economics*, *9*(4), 905–929. doi:10.1093/joclec/nht034

Barzel, Y. (1982). Measurement Cost and the Organization of Markets. *The Journal of Law & Economics*, *25*(1), 27–48. doi:10.1086/467005

Basden, A. (2004). Dooyeweerd and Freedom. In *The Dooyeweerd Pages*. Retrieved January 7, 2010, from http://www.dooy.salford.ac.uk/freedom.html

Basden, A. (2010). *The Dooyeweerd Pages*. Retrieved January 7, 2010, from http://www.dooy.salford.ac.uk/index.html

Baumol, W. J., & Sue, A. B. B. (1991). *Perfect Markets and Easy Virtue Business Ethics and the Invisible Hand*. Blackwell Publishers.

Bayus, B. L., Jain, S., & Rao, A. G. (2001). Truth or Consequences: An Analysis of Vaporware and New Product Announcements. *JMR, Journal of Marketing Research*, *38*(1), 3–13. doi:10.1509/jmkr.38.1.3.18834

Beck, K., Beedle, M., Van Bennekum, A., Cockburn, A., Cunningham, W., Fowler, M., & Kern, J. (2001). *Manifesto for agile software development*. Academic Press.

Becker, M. C. (Ed.). (2008). *Handbook of organisational routines*. Cheltenham, UK: Edward Elgar. doi:10.4337/9781848442702

Bekkers, R. (2001). *Mobile Telecommunication Standards. GSM, UMTS, Tetra and Ermes*. Boston: Artech House.

Benner, M. J., & Veloso, F. M. (2008). ISO 9000 practices and financial performance: A technology coherence perspective. *Journal of Operations Management*, *26*(5), 611–629. doi:10.1016/j.jom.2007.10.005

Bentham, J. (1838). Plan of the Panopticon. In J. Bowring (Ed.), *The Works of Jeremy Bentham* (Vol. 4, pp. 172–173). Edinburgh, UK: William Tait.

Berry, T. H. (1991). *Managing the Total Quality Transformation*. New York, NY: McGraw-Hill.

Besen, S. M., & Farrell, J. (1991). The role of the ITU in standardization: Pre-eminence, impotence or rubber stamp? *Telecommunications Policy*, *15*(4), 311–321. doi:10.1016/0308-5961(91)90053-E

Besen, S. M., & Farrell, J. (1994). Choosing How to Compete: Strategies and Tactics in Standardization. *The Journal of Economic Perspectives*, *8*(2), 117–131. doi:10.1257/jep.8.2.117

Bevan, R. (2011). *Changemaking: Tactics and Resources for Managing Organizational Change*. Seattle, WA: ChangeStart Press.

Bharosa, N., Lee, J., & Janssen, M. (2009). Challenges and obstacles in sharing and coordinating information during multi-agency disaster response: Propositions from field exercises. *Information Systems Frontiers*, *12*(1), 49–65. doi:10.100710796-009-9174-z

Blind, K. (2013). *The impact of standardisation and standards on innovation*. Retrieved from http://www.innovation-policy.org.uk/share/14_The%20Impact%20of%20Standardization%20and%20Standards%20on%20Innovation.pdf

Blind, K., & Gauch, S. (2009). The Demand for E-Government Standards. In *Information Communication Technology Standardization for E-Business Sectors: Integrating Supply and Demand Factors* (pp. 9-23). IGI Global.

Blind, K., & Grupp, H. (2000). *Standards Statistics as New Indicators for the Diffusion of Technology*. Paper presented to the International JA Schumpeter Conference, Manchester, UK.

Blind, K. (2002). Driving forces for standardization at standardization development organizations. *Applied Economics*, *34*(16), 1985–1998. doi:10.1080/00036840110111158

Blind, K. (2004). *The Economics of Standards – Theory, Evidence, Policy*. Cheltenham, UK: Edward Elgar.

Blind, K. (2004). *The economics of standards: Theory, evidence, policy*. Cheltenham, UK: Edward Elgar.

Blind, K. (2004). *The economics of standards: Theory, Evidence, Policy*. Northampton, MA: Edward Elgar Publishing.

Blind, K. (2011). An economic analysis of standards competition: The example of the standardization organization ODF and OOXML standards. *Telecommunications Policy*, *35*, 373–381. doi:10.1016/j.telpol.2011.02.007

Blind, K., Gauch, S., & Hawkins, R. (2010). How stakeholders view the impacts of international ICT standards. *Telecommunications Policy*, *34*(3), 162–174. doi:10.1016/j.telpol.2009.11.016

Blind, K., & Mangelsdorf, A. (2016). Motives to standardize: Empirical evidence from Germany. *Technovation*, *48–49*, 13–24. doi:10.1016/j.technovation.2016.01.001

Blum, U. (2005). Lessons from the Past: Public Standardization in the Spotlight. *International Journal of IT Standards and Standardization Research*, *3*(1), 1–20. doi:10.4018/jitsr.2005010101

Boehme-Nessler, V. (2001). Electronic Government: Internet und Verwaltung. *NVwZ*, *374*.

Boell, S., & Cecez-Kecmanovic, D. (2014). A Hermeneutic Approach for Conducting Literature Reviews and Literature Searches. *Communications of the Association for Information Systems*, *34*(1), 257–286.

Boh, W. F., & Yellin, D. (2007). Using Enterprise Architecture Standards in Managing Information Technology. *Journal of Management Information Systems*, *23*(3), 163–207. doi:10.2753/MIS0742-1222230307

Boiral, O. (2003). ISO 9000: Outside the iron case. *Management Science*, *14*(6), 720–737.

Boiral, O. (2012). ISO certificates as organizational degrees? Beyond the rational myths of the certification process. *Organization Studies*, *33*(5-6), 633–654. doi:10.1177/0170840612443622

Boiral, O., & Roy, M. (2007). ISO 9000: Integration rationales and organisational impacts. *International Journal of Operations & Production Management*, *27*(2), 226–247. doi:10.1108/01443570710720630

Bolici, F., Howison, J., & Crowston, K. (2016). Stigmergic coordination in FLOSS development teams: Integrating explicit and implicit mechanisms. *Cognitive Systems Research*, *38*, 14–22. doi:10.1016/j.cogsys.2015.12.003

Borneman, W. R. (2010). *Rival Rails: The Race to Build America's Greatest Transcontinental Railroad*. Old Saybrook, CT: Tantor.

Borras, J. (2004a). International Technical Standards for e-Government. *Electronic. Journal of E-Government*, *2*(2), 75–80.

Botzem, S., & Dobusch, L. (2012). Standardization cycles: A process perspective on the formation and diffusion of transnational standards. *Organization Studies*, *33*(5-6), 737–762. doi:10.1177/0170840612443626

Bousquet, F. (2003). Dealing with Standardization: Do You Need a Guru? Paradoxes and Tricks of Standardization management. Presented at the *3rd International Conference on Standardisation and Innovation in Information Technology (SIIT)*, Delft, The Netherlands. 10.1109/SIIT.2003.1251194

Boynton, A. C., & Zmud, R. W. (1987). Information Technology Planning in the 1990s. *Management Information Systems Quarterly*, *11*(1), 59–71. doi:10.2307/248826

Brehm, S., & Brehm, J. W. (1981). *Psychological Reactance – a Theory of Freedom and Control*. New York: Academic Press.

Brewer, D., & Nash, M. (2005). *The Similarity between ISO 9001 and BS 7799-2*. Gamma Secure Systems Ltd.

Briscoe, J., Fawcett, S., & Tood, R. (2005). The Implementation and Impact of ISO 9000 among Small Manufacturing Enterprises. *Journal of Small Business Management*, *43*(3), 309–330. doi:10.1111/j.1540-627X.2005.00139.x

Brown, A., Van der Wiele, T., & Loughton, K. (1998). 'Smaller enterprises' experiences with ISO 9000. *International Journal of Quality & Reliability Management*, *15*(3), 273–285. doi:10.1108/02656719810198935

Brown, J. S., & Duguid, P. (1991). Organizational learning and communities of practice: Toward a unified view of working, learning and innovation. *Organization Science*, *2*(1), 40–56. doi:10.1287/orsc.2.1.40

Brown, M., Hitchkock, D., & Willard, M. (1994). *Why TQM Fails and What to Do About It*. Burr Ridge, IL: Irvin.

Bruce, A., Lyall, C., Tait, J., & Williams, R. (2004). Interdisciplinary integration in Europe: The case of the Fifth Framework programme. *Futures*, *36*(4), 457–470. doi:10.1016/j.futures.2003.10.003

Bruner, C. M. (2008). States, Markets, and Gatekeepers: Public-Private Regulatory Regimes in an Era of Economic Globalization. *Michigan Journal of International Law, 30*(1).

Brunson, N., & Jacobsson, B. (2000). The contemporary expansion of standardization. In N. Brunson & B. Jacobsson (Eds.), *A world of standards*. New York: Oxford University Press.

Brunsson, N., Rasche, A., & Seidl, D. (2012). The Dynamics of Standardization: Three Perspectives on Standards in Organization Studies. *Organization Studies, 33*, 613-632. doi:10.1177/0170840612450120

Brunsson, N. (2000). The Pros and Cons of Standardisation – An Epilogue. In *A World of Standards* (pp. 169–173). Oxford, UK: Oxford University Press.

Brunsson, N., & Jacobsson, B. (2000). Following Standards. In *A World of Standards* (pp. 125–137). Oxford, UK: Oxford University Press.

Brunsson, N., & Jacobsson, B. (2000). The Contemporary Expansion of Standardization. In *A World of Standards* (pp. 1–20). Oxford, UK: Oxford University Press.

Bryson, J. (2010). Robots Should Be Slaves. In W. Yorick (Ed.), *Close Engagements with Artificial Companions: Key Social, Psychological, Ethical and Design Issues* (pp. 63–74). Amsterdam: John Benjamins. doi:10.1075/nlp.8.11bry

Buchholz, R. A., & Rosenthal, S. B. (2002). Technology and Business: Rethinking the Moral Dilemma. *Journal of Business Ethics*, *41*(1/2), 45–50. doi:10.1023/A:1021346021768

Buckler, B. (1996). A learning process mode to achieve continuous improvement and innovation. *The Learning Organization*, *3*(3), 31–39. doi:10.1108/09696479610119660

Burget, M., Bardone, E., & Pedaste, M. (2017). Definitions and conceptual dimensions of responsible research and innovation: A literature review. *Science and Engineering Ethics*, *23*(1), 1–19. doi:10.100711948-016-9782-1 PMID:27090147

Büttner, F., Bartels, U., Hamann, L., Hofrichter, O., Kuhlmann, M., Gogolla, M., . . . Stosiek, A. (2014). Model-driven standardization of public authority data interchange. *Science of Computer Programming*, *89*(B), 162-175. doi:10.1016/j.scico.2013.03.009

Care Quality Commission. (2010). Retrieved from https://www.cqc.org.uk/sites/default/files/documents/guidance_about_compliance_summary.pdf

Cargill, C. F. (1989). *Information Technology Standardization: Theory, Process, and Organizations*. Bedford, MA: Digital Press.

Carnall, C., & Todnem, R. (2007). *Managing Change in Organizations* (6th ed.). Harlow, UK: Pearson Education.

Casadesús, M., & Karapetrovic, S. (2005). Has ISO 9000 lost some of its lustre? *International Journal of Operations & Production Management*, *25*(6), 580–596. doi:10.1108/01443570510599737

Chandler, A. D., & Hikino, T. (2009). *Scale and scope: The dynamics of industrial capitalism*. Harvard University Press.

Charalabidis, Y., Lampathaki, F., & Askounis, D. (2009). A Comparative Analysis of National Interoperability Frameworks. *15th Americas Conference on Information Systems (AMCIS 2009)*, 1-10.

Chen, J. C., & Roberts, R. W. (2010). Toward a More Coherent Understanding of the Organization–Society Relationship: A Theoretical Consideration for Social and Environmental Accounting Research. *Journal of Business Ethics*, *97*(4), 651–665. doi:10.100710551-010-0531-0

Chen, P. Y., & Forman, C. (2006). Can vendors influence switching costs and compatibility in an environment with open standards? *MIS Quarterly: Management Information Systems*, *30*(SPEC. ISS.), 541–562. doi:10.2307/25148772

Chesbrough, H. (2003). The logic of open innovation: Managing intellectual property. *California Management Review*, *45*(3), 33–58. doi:10.2307/41166175

Chesbrough, H. W. (2003). *Open Innovation: The New Imperative for Creating and Profiting from Technology*. Harvard Business School Press.

Chesbrough, H. W., Vanhaverbeke, W., & West, J. (Eds.). (2006). *Open Innovation: Researching a New Paradigm*. Oxford University Press.

Chourabi, H., Bouslama, F., & Mellouli, S. (2008). *BPMapping and UMM in Business Process Modeling for e-Government Processes.* Paper presented at the International Conference on Digital Government Research, Montreal, Canada.

Christensen, C. M., Grossman, J. H., & Hwang, J. (2009). *The innovator's prescription: A disruptive solution for healthcare*. New York: McGraw-Hill.

Clark, H. H. (1996). *Using Language* (Vol. 23). Academic Press.

Cohen, M. D., Burkhart, R., Dosi, G., Egidi, M., Marengo, L., Warglien, M., & Winter, S. (1996). Routines and Other Recurrent Action Patterns of Organizations: Contemporary Research Issues. *Industrial and Corporate Change*, *5*(3), 653–698. doi:10.1093/icc/5.3.653

Cole, R., Purao, S., Rossi, M., & Sein, M. K. (2005). Being Proactive: Where Action Research meets Design Research. *ICIS 2005 Proceedings*, 1-21.

Collis, D. J. (1994). Research note: How valuable are organizational capabilities? *Strategic Management Journal*, *15*(S1), 143–152. doi:10.1002mj.4250150910

Connor, P. E. (1997). Total quality management: A selective commentary on its human dimensions, with special reference to its downside. *Public Administration Review*, *57*(6), 501–509. doi:10.2307/976961

Contreras, J. L. (2017). *Technical Standards, Standards-Setting Organizations and Intellectual Property: A Survey of the Literature (with an Emphasis on Empirical Approaches).* Retrieved 10 January 2019 from https://papers.ssrn.com/sol3/Delivery.cfm/SSRN_ID3034557_code1335192.pdf?abstractid=2900540&mirid=1

Cook, R., Evett, I. W., Jackson, G., Jones, P. J., & Lambert, J. A. (1998). A Model for Case Assessment and Interpretation. *Science & Justice*, *38*(3), 151–156. doi:10.1016/S1355-0306(98)72099-4 PMID:9800430

Coordination Site for IT-Standards (KoSIT). (2012). *Lateinische Zeichen im Unicode Version 1.1.1 vom 27. 01. 2012.* Retrieved from http://xoev.de/latinchars/1_1/latinchars.pdfv

Corbett, C. J., Montes-Sancho, M. J., & Kitsch, D. A. (2005). The Financial impact of ISO 9000 Certification in the United States: An Empirical Analysis. *Management Science*, *51*(7), 1046–1059. doi:10.1287/mnsc.1040.0358

Craig, A., & Schriar, S. (2001). The Find-It! Illinois controlled vocabulary: Improving access to government information through the Jessica subject tree. *Government Information Quarterly*, *18*(3), 195–208. doi:10.1016/S0740-624X(01)00077-6

Cusumano, M. (2010). Technology Strategy and Management – The Evolution of Platform Thinking. *Communications of the ACM*, *53*(1), 32–34. doi:10.1145/1629175.1629189

Cyert, R. M., & March, J. G. (1963). *A behavioral theory of the firm*. Prentice Hall.

Dahlander, L., & Gann, D. M. (2010). How open is innovation? *Research Policy*, *39*(6), 699–709. doi:10.1016/j.respol.2010.01.013

Dahlgaard, J., Larsen, H. Z., & Norgaard, A. (1997). Leadership profiles in quality management: A Danish perspective. *Total Quality Management*, *8*(2/3), 16–30. doi:10.1080/0954412979659

Dale, B. G. (2007). Quality Management Systems. In B. G. Dale, T. Van der Wiele, & J. Van Iwaarden (Eds.), *Managing Quality* (pp. 279–309). Malden, MA: Blackwell Publishing.

Dale, B. G., & Cooper, C. (1992). *Total Quality and Human Resources: An Executive Guide*. Oxford, UK: Blackwell.

Dale, B. G., Van der Wiele, A., & Van Iwaarden, J. D. (2007). TQM: An Overview. In B. G. Dale, T. Van der Wiele, & J. Van Iwaarden (Eds.), *Managing Quality (5)*. Malden, MA: Blackwell Publishing.

Davenport, T. H., & Short, J. E. (1990). The new industrial engineering: Information technology and business process re-design. *Sloan Management Review*, *31*(4), 11–27.

David, P. A. (1987). Some new standards for the economics of standardization in the information age. Economic policy and technological performance, 206-239. doi:10.1017/CBO9780511559938.010

David, P. A. (1995). Standardisation policies for network technologies: the flux between freedom and order revisited. In Standards, Innovation and Competitiveness – The Politics and Economics of Standards in Natural and Technical Environments (pp. 15-35). Aldershot, UK: Edward Elgar.

David, P. A., & Greenstein, S. (1990). The Economics of Compatibility Standards: An Introduction To Recent Research. *Economics of Innovation and New Technology*, *1*(1-2), 3–41. doi:10.1080/10438599000000002

Davies, J., Harris, S., Crichton, C., Shukla, A., & Gibbson, J. (2008). *Metadata Standards for Semantic Interoperability in Electronic Government*. Paper presented at the international conference on Theory and practice of electronic governance, Cairo, Egypt. 10.1145/1509096.1509111

Davis, F. D. (1989). Perceived usefulness, perceived ease of use, and user acceptance of information technology. *Management Information Systems Quarterly*, *13*(3), 319–340. doi:10.2307/249008

Davis, F. D., Bagozzi, R. P., & Warsaw, P. R. (1989). User acceptance of computer technology: A comparison of two theoretical models. *Management Science*, *35*(8), 982–1003. doi:10.1287/mnsc.35.8.982

De Vries, H.J. (1997) Standardization – What's in a name? *Terminology – International Journal of Theoretical and Applied Issues in Specialized Communication*, *4*(1), 55-83.

De Vries, H. J. (1999). *Standardization – A Business Approach to the Role of National Standardization Organisations*. Boston: Kluwer Academic Publishers. doi:10.1007/978-1-4757-3042-5

De Vries, H. J. (2006). Competing E-Purse Systems: A Standards Battle. *Journal of Cases on Information Technology*, *8*(1), 1–15. doi:10.4018/jcit.2006010101

De Vries, H. J. (2015). Standardisation – A Developing Field of Research. In P. Delimatsis (Ed.), *The Law, Economics and Politics of International Standardsation*. Cambridge, UK: Cambridge University Press. doi:10.1017/CBO9781316423240.002

De Vries, H. J., & Slob, F. J. (2006). Best practice in company standardization. *International Journal of IT Standards and Standardization Research*, *4*(1), 62–85. doi:10.4018/jitsr.2006010104

De Vries, H. J., & Van Delden, M. (2006). How to integrate standardisation in knowledge management. *ISO Focus*, *3*(3), 37–40.

De Vries, H., Jakobs, K., Egyedi, T. M., Eto, M., Fertig, S., Kanevskaia, O., ... Scaramuzzino, G. (2018). Standardization: Towards an agenda for research. *International Journal of Standardization Research*, *16*(1), 52–59. doi:10.4018/IJSR.2018010104

Delmas, M. A. (2002). The Diffusion of Environmental Management Standards in Europe and in the United States: An Institutional Perspective. *Policy Sciences*, *35*(1), 91–119. doi:10.1023/A:1016108804453

Den Butter, F. A. G., Groot, S. P. T., & Lazrak, F. (2007). *The transaction costs perspective on standards as a source of trade and productivity growth*. Tinbergen Institute Discussion Papers, 07-090/3. Available at: http://www.tinbergen.nl/discussionpapers/07090.pdf

Dey, P. K., Clegg, B., & Bennett, D. (2009). Managing implementation issues in enterprise resource planning projects. In M. H. Sherif (Ed.), *Handbook of enterprise integration*. Boca Raton, FL: Auerbach. doi:10.1201/9781420078220-c24

Dick, G. P. M., Heras, I., & Casedesús, M. (2008). Shedding light on causation between ISO 9001 and improved business performance. *International Journal of Operations & Production Management*, *28*(9), 687–708. doi:10.1108/01443570810881811

Dokko, G., Nigam, A., & Rosenkopf, L. (2012). Keeping steady as she goes: A negotiated order perspective on technological evolution. *Organization Studies*, *33*(5-6), 681–703. doi:10.1177/0170840612443624

Dokko, G., & Rosenkopf, L. (2010). Social capital for hire? Mobility of technical professionals and firm influence in wireless standards committees. *Organization Science*, *21*(3), 677–695. doi:10.1287/orsc.1090.0470

Dooyeweerd, H. (1955). A new critique of theoretical thought. In The general theory of the modal spheres (vol. 2). Amsterdam: H.J. Paris, and Philadelphia: The Presbyterian and Reformed Publishing Company.

Dooyeweerd, H. (1957). The structures of individuality of temporal reality. In A new critique of theoretical thought (vol. 3). Amsterdam; H.J. Paris, and Philadelphia: The Presbyterian and Reformed Publishing Company.

Dosi, G., Nelson, R. R., & Winter, S. G. (2001). *The nature and dynamics of organizational capabilities*. Oxford University Press.

Dranove, D., & Gandal, N. (2003). The DVD vs. DIVX Standard War: Empirical Evidence of Vaporware. *Journal of Economics & Management Strategy*, *12*, 363–386. doi:10.1162/105864003322309518

EFFRA (Ed.). (2018). *Factories of the Future Public-Private Partnership. Progress Monitoring Report for 2017*. Retrieved from https://www.effra.eu/sites/default/files/fof_cppp_progress_monitoring_report_for_2017_online.pdf

Egyedi, T. (2014). The Impact of Competing Standards: On Innovation and Interoperability for E-government. *PIK - Praxis der Informationsverarbeitung und Kommunikation, 37*(3), 211-215.

Egyedi, T. M. (2001). Why JavaTM was -not- standardized twice. *Computer Standards & Interfaces*, *23*(4), 253–265. doi:10.1016/S0920-5489(01)00078-2

Egyedi, T. M., & Blind, K. (2008). General introduction. In T. Egyedi & K. Blind (Eds.), *The dynamics of standards*. Cheltenham, UK: Edward Elgar.

Egyedi, T. M., & Blind, K. (Eds.). (2008). *The Dynamics of Standards*. Cheltenham, UK: Edward Elgar.

Egyedi, T. M., & Hawkins, R. (2010). Standards Consortia. In W. Hesser, A. J. Feilzer, & H. J. de Vries (Eds.), *Standardisation in Companies and Markets* (3rd ed.; pp. 443–490). Hamburg, Germany: Helmut Schmidt University.

Eisenmann, T., Parker, G., & Van Alstyne, M. W. (2006). Strategies for two-sided markets. *Harvard Business Review*, *84*(10), 92–101. PMID:16649701

Elkington, J. (1997). *Canibals with Forks: The triple bottom line of the 21st century business*. Oxford, UK: Capstone.

Ellul, J. (1970). *The meaning of the city*. Grand Rapids, MI: Eerdmans.

Eto, M. (2007b). *Success and failure of cost reduction standardization as seen in the standardization of optical connectors*. Summary of a lecture presented at the 22nd Annual Academic Convention of the Japan Society for Research Policy and Innovation Management.

Eto, M. (2007a). Effectiveness of standard for the competitiveness in bicycle industry. *Development Engineering*, *13*, 45–59.

EU. (Ed.). (2016). *Regulation (EU) 2016/679 – General Data Protection Regulation (GDPR)*. Retrieved from http://ec.europa.eu/justice/data-protection/reform/files/regulation_oj_en.pdf

European Commission (Ed.). (2016). *Joint Initiative on Standardisation*. Retrieved on 12 January 2019 from http://ec.europa.eu/DocsRoom/documents/22722/attachments/1/translations/en/renditions/native

European Commission (Ed.). (2018). *Proposal for a Regulation of the European Parliament and of the Council*. COM(2018) 630 final. Retrieved 15 January 2019 from http://ec.europa.eu/newsroom/dae/document.cfm?doc_id=54252

European Commission. (2007). *Final Report of the Study on the Specific Policy Needs for ICT Standardization*. European Commission. Retrieved from http://www.epractice.eu/en/library/281182

European Commission. (2010). European Interoperability Framework (EIF) for European public services. Brussels: Academic Press.

European Commission. (2014). *Guidelines on the application of Article 101 of the Treaty on the Functioning of the European Union to technology transfer agreements*. Brussels: Commission of the European Union. Retrieved from https://eur-lex.europa.eu/legal-content/EN/TXT/PDF/?uri=CELEX:52014XC0328(01)&from=EN

European Commission. (2016). *Speech: State of the Union address 2016: Towards a better Europe – A Europe that protects, empowers and defends Strasbourg*. Retrieved from http://europa.eu/rapid/press-release_SPEECH-16-3043_en.htm

European Commission. (2017). *Setting out the EU approach to Standard Essential Patents COM (2017) 712 final*. Retrieved from https://ec.europa.eu/docsroom/documents/26583/attachments/1/translations/en/renditions/native

European Parliament and Council (Eds). (2012). *Regulation (EU) No 1025/2012 of the European Parliament and of the Council of 25 October 2012 on European standardisation*. Retrieved 22 December 2018 from https://eur-lex.europa.eu/legal-content/EN/TXT/PDF/?uri=CELEX:32012R1025&from=EN

Evett. (1998). *The Case Assessment and Interpretation (CAI)*. Method.

Farrell, J., & Saloner, G. (1985). Standardization, compatibility, and innovation. *The Rand Journal of Economics*, *16*(1), 70–83. doi:10.2307/2555589

Farrell, J., & Saloner, G. (1986). Installed base and compatibility: Innovation, product preannouncements, and predation. *The American Economic Review*, *76*, 943–954.

Farrell, J., & Saloner, G. (1988). Coordination through committees and markets. *The Rand Journal of Economics*, *19*(2), 235–252. doi:10.2307/2555702

Federal Government Commissioner for Information Technology. (2011). *SAGA-Modul Grundlagen Version de.bund 5.1.0*. Berlin: Author. Retrieved from http://www.cio.bund.de/SharedDocs/Publikationen/DE/Architekturen-und-Standards/SAGA/saga_modul_grundlagen_de_bund_5_1_0_download.pdf?__blob=publicationFile

Fehr, E., & Falk, A. (2002). Psychological foundations of incentives. Joseph Schumpeter Lecture. *European Economic Review*, *15*(4-5), 687–724. doi:10.1016/S0014-2921(01)00208-2

Felin, T., & Foss, N. J. (2005). Strategic organization: A field in search of micro-foundations. *Strategic Organization*, *3*(4), 441–455. doi:10.1177/1476127005055796

Felin, T., & Foss, N. J. (2009). Experience and Repetition as Antecedents of Organizational Routines and Capabilities: A Critique of Behaviorist and Empiricist Approaches. *SMG WP*, *9*, 2009.

Felin, T., Foss, N. J., Heimeriks, K. H., & Madsen, T. L. (2012). Microfoundations of routines and capabilities: Individuals, processes, and structures. *Journal of Management Studies*, *49*(8), 1351–1374. doi:10.1111/j.1467-6486.2012.01052.x

Flak, L. S., & Solli-Saether, H. (2012). *The Shape of Interoperability: Reviewing and Characterizing a Central Area within eGovernment Research.* Paper presented at the 2012 45th Hawaii International Conference on System Science (HICSS).

Fomin, V. V., de Vries, H. J., & Barlette, Y. (2008). *ISO/IEC 27001 Information Systems Security Management Standard: Identifying Directions for Future Research.* Nice, France: International Association for Management of Technology (IAMOT). Retrieved from http://webintec.ceram.fr/euromot2008/

Fomin, V. V., King, J. L., Lyytinen, K., & McGann, S. (2005). Diffusion and Impacts of E-Commerce in the United States of America: Results from an Industry Survey. *Communications of the Association for Information Systems*, *16*, 559–603. doi:10.17705/1CAIS.01628

Fomin, V. V., Pedersen, M. K., & de Vries, H. J. (2008). Open Standards and Government Policy: Results of a Delphi Survey. *Communications of the Association for Information Systems*, *22*, 459–484. doi:10.17705/1CAIS.02225

Fortune, A., & Mitchell, W. (2012). Unpacking firm exit at the firm and industry levels: The adaptation and selection of firm capabilities. *Strategic Management Journal*, *33*, 794–819.

Foss, K. (1996). *A transaction cost perspective on the influence of standards on product development: Examples for the fruit and vegetable market.* Working paper No 96-9. DRUID working paper series, Copenhagen.

Foucault, M. (1976). *Histoire de la sexualité I – La volonté de savoir.* Paris: Éditions Gallimard.

Foucault, M. (1977). *Discipline and Punish; Birth of the Prison* (A. Sheridan, Trans.). London: Penguin. (Original work published 1975)

Foucault, M. (1982). Afterword. The subject and power. In H. L. Dreyfus & P. Rabinov (Eds.), *Michel Foucault. Beyond structuralism and hermeneutics* (pp. 208–226). Chicago, IL: University of Chicago Press.

Foukaki, A. (2017). *Corporate Standardization Management – A Case Study of the Automotive Industry* (Dissertation). Lund University. Retrieved from http://portal.research.lu.se/portal/files/21522119/Corporate_Standardization_Management_A_Case_Study_of_the_Automotive_Industry_Dissertation_2017.pdf

Frary, M. (2008). *The Founding of the IEC.* Retrieved from www.iec.ch/about/history/articles/founding_iec.htm

Freyschuss, A. (2015). Så blev en svensk koncern världsledande med hjälp av standarder. *SIS*. Retrieved from http://www.sis.se/Global/Om%20SIS/kundseminarium%202011/camfil_ppt.pdf

Funk, J. L., & Methe, D. T. (2001). Market- and Committee-Based Mechanisms in the Creation And Diffusion of Global Industry Standards: The Case of Mobile Communications. *Research Policy*, *30*(4), 589–610. doi:10.1016/S0048-7333(00)00095-0

Furusten, S. (2000). The Knowledge Base of Standards. In *A World of Standards* (pp. 71–84). Oxford, UK: Oxford University Press.

Galasso, G., Aresu, F., Luppi, M., Campisi, C., & Garbasso, G. (2016). *Study on best practices for ICT procurement based on standards in order to promote efficiency and reduce lock-in*. PwC.

Galbraith, J. R. (1977). Organization design: An information processing view. *Organizational Effectiveness Center and School*, *21*, 21–26. doi:10.1287/inte.4.3.28

Gallagher, S. (2007). The complementary role of dominant designs and industry standards. *IEEE Transactions on Engineering Management*, *54*(2), 371–379. doi:10.1109/TEM.2007.893991

Gallagher, S. R. (2012). The battle of the blue laser DVDs: The significance of corporate strategy in standards battles. *Technovation*, *32*(2), 90–98. doi:10.1016/j.technovation.2011.10.004

Gascó, M. (2012). Approaching E-Government Interoperability. *Social Science Computer Review*, *30*(1), 3–6. doi:10.1177/0894439310392181

Gauch, S. (2008). + vs. –, Dynamics and effects of competing standards of recordable DVD media. In T. M. Egyedi & K. Blind (Eds.), The dynamics of standards (pp. 47-67). Cheltenham, UK: Edward Elgar.

Gawer, A., & Cusumano, M. A. (2008). How Companies Become Platform Leaders. *MIT Sloan Management Review*, *49*(2), 29–30.

Ghaziani, A., & Ventresca, M. J. (2005). Keywords and Cultural Change: Frame Analysis of Business Model Public Talk, 1975–2000. *Sociological Forum*, *20*(4), 523–559. doi:10.100711206-005-9057-0

Gil-Garcia, J. R., & Pardo, T. A. (2005). E-government success factors: Mapping practical tools to theoretical foundations. *Government Information Quarterly*, *22*(2), 187–216. doi:10.1016/j.giq.2005.02.001

Goldkuhl, G. (2012). Pragmatism vs interpretivism in qualitative information systems research. *European Journal of Information Systems*, *21*(2), 135–146. doi:10.1057/ejis.2011.54

Goles, T., & Hirschheim, R. (2000). The paradigm is dead, the paradigm is dead...long live the paradigm: The legacy of Burrell and Morgan. *Omega*, *28*(3), 249–268. doi:10.1016/S0305-0483(99)00042-0

Goodpaster, K. E. (1991). Business Ethics and Stakeholder Analysis. *Business Ethics Quarterly*, *1*(1), 53–73. doi:10.2307/3857592

Gordon, J.-S. (2013). Modern Morality and Ancient Ethics. Internet Encyclopedia of Philosophy.

Gordon, J.-S. (2018). What Do We Owe to Intelligent Robots? *AI & Society*. doi:10.100700146-018-0844-6

Gottschalk, P., & Saether, H. S. (2008). Stages of e-government interoperability. *Electronic Government, an International Journal, 5*, 310. doi:10.1504/EG.2008.018877

Gottschalk, P. (2009). Maturity levels for interoperability in digital government. *Government Information Quarterly, 26*(1), 75–81. doi:10.1016/j.giq.2008.03.003

Goudzwaard, B. (1979). *Capitalism and Progress: A Diagnosis of Western Society*. Toronto: Wedge.

Gouldner, A. W. (1954). *Patterns of industrial Bureaucracy – A case study of modern factory administration*. New York: The Free Press.

Gregor, S. (2006). The nature of theory in information systems. *Management Information Systems Quarterly, 30*(3), 611–642. doi:10.2307/25148742

Grimes, K. R. (2003). *ISO 9001:2000: a practical quality manual explained*. Milwaukee, WI: ASQ Quality Press.

Groenfeldt, T. (2017). Banks Turn to Technology to Cope with New Regulations. *Forbes*. Retrieved from https://www.forbes.com/sites/tomgroenfeldt/2018/03/03/banks-turn-to-technology-to-cope-with-new-regulations/#6ce9e1c85d70

Grossmann, A.-M. (2013). Suppliers' motives for applying company standards – How company standards can affect the buyer-supplier relationship. In *EURAS Proceedings 2013. The Euras board series.* Verlagshaus Mainz.

Guijarro, L. (2007). Interoperability frameworks and enterprise architectures in e-government initiatives in Europe and the United States. *Government Information Quarterly, 24*(1), 89–101. doi:10.1016/j.giq.2006.05.003

Guler, I., Guillén, M., Macpherson, J., & Guillen, M. F. (2002). Global competition, institutions, and the diffusion of organizational practices: The international spread of ISO 9000 quality certificates. *Administrative Science Quarterly, 47*(2), 207–232. doi:10.2307/3094804

Gunawardena, N. (2006). Case Study: Implementation of ISO 14000 Environmental Management System. In *Standardisation in Companies and Markets* (pp. 607–646). Hamburg: Helmut Schmidt University. Retrieved from www.asia-link-standardisation.de/

Gunkel, D. J. (2012). *The Machine Question: Critical Perspectives on AI, Robots, and Ethics*. Cambridge, MA: MIT Press. doi:10.7551/mitpress/8975.001.0001

Gunkel, D. J. (2014). A Vindication of the Rights of Machines. *Philosophy & Technology, 27*(1), 113–132. doi:10.100713347-013-0121-z

Gupta, K. (2017). *The Role of SMEs and Startups in Standards Development*. Retrieved from https://papers.ssrn.com/sol3/papers.cfm?abstract_id=3001513

Haan, M. A. (2003). Vaporware as a Means of Entry Deterrence. *The Journal of Industrial Economics*, *3*(3), 345–358. doi:10.1111/1467-6451.00204

Habermas, J. (1987). The Theory of Communicative Action: Lifeworld and System: A Critique of Functionalist Reason (vol. 2; T. *McCarthy, Trans.*). Boston: Beacon. (Original work published 1981)

Hammer, M. (1990). Re-engineering work: Don't automate, obliterate. *Harvard Business Review*, *68*(4), 104–112.

Hammer, M., & Champy, J. (1993). *Re-engineering the corporation: a manifesto for business revolution*. New York, NY: Harper Business.

Hanseth, O., & Bygstad, B. (2015). Flexible generification: ICT standardization strategies and service innovation in health care. *European Journal of Information Systems*, *24*(6), 645–663. doi:10.1057/ejis.2015.1

Hanseth, O., Jacucci, E., Grisot, M., & Aanestad, M. (2006). Reflexive Standardization: Side Effects and Complexity in Standard Making. *Management Information Systems Quarterly*, *30*, 563–581. doi:10.2307/25148773

Hanseth, O., Monteiro, E., & Hatling, M. (1996). Developing Information Infrastructure: The Tension Between Standardization and Flexibility. *Science, Technology & Human Values*, *21*(4), 407–426. doi:10.1177/016224399602100402

Harrington, H. J. (1987). *The Improvement Process*. New York: McGraw-Hill.

Haverkamp, A. (2004). *Bezint eer gij begint – Standaardisatie van werkmethoden bij Polynorm Automotive – Onderzoek op basis van een christelijk-filosofische analyse*. Rotterdam: Erasmus Universiteit, Faculteit Bedrijfskunde.

Haverkamp, A. (2006). Een veelzijdig kwaliteitsverbeteringsproject. *Synaps*, *4*(20), 21–26.

Heath, J. (2006). Business Ethics Without Stakeholders. *Business Ethics Quarterly*, *16*(4), 533–558. doi:10.5840/beq200616448

Heimeriks, K. H., & Duysters, G. (2007). Alliance capability as a mediator between experience and alliance performance: An empirical investigation into the alliance capability development process. *Journal of Management Studies*, *44*(1), 25–49. doi:10.1111/j.1467-6486.2006.00639.x

Helfat, C. E. (1997). Know-how and asset complementarity and dynamic capability accumulation: The case of R&D. *Strategic Management Journal*, *18*(5), 339–360. doi:10.1002/(SICI)1097-0266(199705)18:5<339::AID-SMJ883>3.0.CO;2-7

Helfat, C. E. C., & Quinn, J. B. (2006). Review: Open Innovation: The New Imperative for Creating and Profiting from Technology by Henry Chesbrough. *The Academy of Management Perspectives*, *20*(2), 86–88. doi:10.5465/amp.2006.20591014

Helfat, C., & Peteraf, M. A. (2003). The dynamic resource-based view: Capability lifecycles. *Strategic Management Journal*, *24*(10), 997–1010. doi:10.1002mj.332

Helfat, C., & Raubitscheck, R. S. (2000). Product sequencing: Co-evolution of knowledge, capabilities and products. *Strategic Management Journal*, *21*(10-11), 961–979. doi:10.1002/1097-0266(200010/11)21:10/11<961::AID-SMJ132>3.0.CO;2-E

Hellberg, A.-S., & Grönlund, Å. (2013). Conflicts in implementing interoperability: Re-operationalizing basic values. *Government Information Quarterly*, *30*(2), 154–162. doi:10.1016/j.giq.2012.10.006

Heller, M. A., & Eisenberg, R. S. (1998). Can patents deter innovation? The anticommons in biomedical research. *Science*, *280*(5364), 698–701. doi:10.1126cience.280.5364.698 PMID:9563938

Henderson, R. E., & Cockburn, I. (1994). Measuring competence? Exploring firm effects in pharmaceutical research. *Strategic Management Journal*, *15*(S1), 63–84. doi:10.1002mj.4250150906

Henning, F. (2016). A theoretical framework on the determinants of organisational adoption of interoperability standards in Government Information Networks. *Government Information Quarterly*.

Henningsson, S., Rukanova, B., & Hrastinski, S. (2010). Resource dependencies in socio-technical information systems design research. *Communications of the AIS*, *27*(42), 777–802.

Henson, S. J., & Hooker, N. H. (2001). Private Sector Management of Food Safety: Public Regulation and the Role of Private Controls. *The International Food and Agribusiness Management Review*, *4*(1), 7–17. doi:10.1016/S1096-7508(01)00067-2

Hesser, W. (2010). Standardisation within a Comnpany – a Strategic Perspective. In W. Hesser (Ed.), Standardisation in Companies and Markets (3rd ed.; pp. 215–258). Hamburg: Academic Press.

Hesser, W. (2010). Standardisation within a company – A strategic perspective. In W. Hesser (Ed.), *Standardisation in companies and markets* (3rd ed., pp. 215–258). Hamburg: Helmut Schmidt University.

Hesser, W., & Inklaar, A. (1997). *An introduction to Standards and Standardization, DIN-Normungskunde* (Vol. 36). Berlin: Beuth Verlag GmbH.

Hill, P. (1999). Tangibles, intangibles and services: A new taxonomy for classification of output. *The Canadian Journal of Economics. Revue Canadienne d'Economique*, *32*(2), 426–447. doi:10.2307/136430

Hofstede, G. (1978). The Poverty of Management Control Philosophy. *Academy of Management Review*, *3*(3), 450–461. doi:10.5465/amr.1978.4305727

Holmstrom, B. (1999). The Firm as a Subeconomy. *Journal of Law Economics and Organization*, *15*(1), 74–102. doi:10.1093/jleo/15.1.74

Hommels, A., Egyedi, T. M., & Cleophas, E. (2012). Policy change and policy incoherence: The case of competition versus public safety in standardization policies. *Journal of European Integration*, *35*(4), 443–458. doi:10.1080/07036337.2012.711826

Hovav, A., Patnayakuni, R., & Schuff, D. (2004). A model of Internet standards adoption: The case of IPv6. *Information Systems Journal, 14*(3), 265–294. doi:10.1111/j.1365-2575.2004.00170.x

Huber, B. (2017). *Why the ETSI IPR-policy Does Not and Has Never Required Compulsory License to All: A Rebuttal to Karl Heinz Rosenbrock.* Retrieved from https://papers.ssrn.com/sol3/papers.cfm?abstract_id=3038447

Hulstijn, J., van Wijk, R., de Winne, N., Bharosa, N., Janssen, M., & Tan, Y.-H. (2011). *Public Process Management: A Method for Introducing Standard Business Reporting.* Paper presented at the 12th Annual International Conference on Digital Government Research, New York, NY. 10.1145/2037556.2037577

Humphreys, T. (2005). State-of-the-Art Information Security Management System with ISO/IEC 27001:2005. *ISO Management Systems*, 15–18.

Hunt, M. (2017). *Patent Licensing: 5G and the Internet of Things.* Retrieved from https://www.bristows.com/news-and-publications/articles/patent-licensing-5g-and-the-internet-of-things/

IATF. (2016). Quality management system for organizations in the automotive industry. *IATF, 16949,* 2016.

Imai, M. (1986). *Kaizen – the key to Japan's competitive success.* New York: Random House.

International Electrotechnical Commission. (n.d.). Retrieved from: http://www.iec.ch/dyn/www/f?p=103:7:16952850021229:FSP_ORG_ID,FSP_LANG_ID:1270,25

International Organization for Standardization. (2015). *ISO/IEC 2382:2015 Information technology -- Vocabulary.* Fundamental Terms.

ISO. (1996). *Iso 14001:1996. Environmental Management Systems: Specification with Guidance for Use.* Geneva: International Organization for Standardization.

ISO. (2004a). *14001:2004. Environmental Management Systems: Specification with Guidance for Use.* Geneva: International Organization for Standardization.

ISO. (2004b). *ISO Code of Ethics.* Retrieved from https://www.iso.org/publication/PUB100011.html

ISO. (2007). *ISO 216:2007. Writing Paper and Certain Classes of Printed Matter: A and B Series, and Indication of Machine Direction.* Geneva: International Organization for Standardization. Retrieved from https://www.iso.org/standard/36631.html

ISO. (2008). *ISO 9001:2008 Quality management systems – Requirements.* Geneva: International Organization for Standardisation.

ISO. (2009). *ISO/TS 16949:2009 Quality management systems – Particular requirements for the application of ISO 9001:2008 for automotive production and relevant service part organizations.* Geneva: International Organization for Standardisation.

ISO. (2015). *ISO 9001:2015 Quality management systems – Requirements*. Geneva: International Organization for Standardisation.

ISO. (2018). *The ISO Survey of Management System Standard Certifications 2017*. Retrieved November 1, 2018, from https://isotc.iso.org/livelink/livelink/fetch/-8853493/8853511/8853520/18808772/00._Overall_results_and_explanatory_note_on_2017_Survey_results.pdf?nodeid=19208898&vernum=-2

ISO/IEC. (2004). *Guide 2: Standardization and Related Activities. General Vocabulary*. Geneva: International Organization for Standardization and International Electrotechnical Commission. Retrieved from www.iso.org

ISO/IEC. (2008). *ISO/IEC Directives, Part 1: Procedures for the Technical Work* (6th ed.). Geneva: International Organization for Standardization and International Electrotechnical Commission.

ITU. (2011). *ITU Code of Ethics*. Retrieved from https://www.itu.int/en/general-secretariat/Documents/ethics/SO-2011-002-en.pdf

ITU-T. (2015). *Focus Group on Smart Sustainable Cities – Technical Report – Setting the stage for stakeholders' engagement in smart sustainable cities*. Retrieved from http://www.itu.int/en/ITU-T/focusgroups/ssc/Documents/website/web-fg-ssc-0113-r9-SSC-stakeholders.docx

Jacob, K. (2005). The Role of the 'Third Estate' in ICT Standardisation. In S. Bolin (Ed.), *The Standards Edge: Future Generation*. The Bolin Group.

Jain, S. (2012). Pragmatic agency in technology standards setting: The case of Ethernet. *Research Policy*, *41*(9), 1643–1654. doi:10.1016/j.respol.2012.03.025

Jakobs, K. (2009). *Information Communication Technology Standardization for E-Business Sectors: Integrating Supply and Demand Factors*. IGI Global.

Jakobs, K. (2017). Emerging Smart Technologies and the European Standardisation System. Proc. 30th Bled eConference: Digital Transformation – From Connecting Things to Transforming Our Lives, 231 – 244. doi:10.18690/978-961-286-043-1.17

Jakobs, K. (2019). Responsible Standardisation of 'Smart' Applications. In *Proc. 17th Int. Conf. on e-Society*. IADIS.

Jakobs, K. (2005). *Advanced Topics in Information Technology Standards and Standardization Research* (Vol. 1). IGI Global.

Jakobs, K. (2007). *Standardization Research in Information Technology: New Perspectives*. Hershey, PA: IGI Global.

Jakobs, K. (2008). The IEEE 802.11 WLAN installation at RWTH Aachen University: A case of voluntary vendor lock-. In T. M. Egyedi & K. Blind (Eds.), *The dynamics of standards* (pp. 99–116). Cheltenham, UK: Edward Elgar.

Jakobs, K. (2015). Standardisation Management – Some Lessons to be Learnt. In K. Bergh Skriver, K. Jakobs, & J. Jerlang (Eds.), *The Role of Standards in Transatlantic Trade and Regulation. EURAS contributions to standardisation research* (Vol. 9). Mainz Publishers.

Jakobs, K. (2018). Standardizing the IoT and its Applications – Learning from the Past?! In *Internet of Things – Concepts, Technologies, Applications, and Implementations* (pp. 191–218). IEEE. doi:10.1002/9781119456735.ch7

Jakobs, K. (2019). *'Smart' Standardisation.* Presented at the *82nd IEC General Meeting.*

Jakobs, K., & Blind, K. (2011). ICT Standardisation Policy in Europe: Recent Past, Presence, and Future. Presented at the *7th Biennial Standardisation and Innovation in Information Technology (SIIT) conference*, Aachen, Germany. 10.1109/SIIT.2011.6083611

Jakobs, K., Procter, R., & Williams, R. (1998). User Participation in Standards Setting: The Panacea? *ACM StandardView*, *6*(2), 85–89. doi:10.1145/301688.301693

Janssen, M. (2011). Sociopolitical Aspects of Interoperability and Enterprise Architecture in E-Government. *Social Science Computer Review.* doi:10.1177/0894439310392187

Janssen, M., Charalabidis, Y., Kuk, G., & Cresswell, T. (2011). Guest Editors' Introduction: E-government Interoperability, Infrastructure and Architecture: State-of-the-art and Challenges. *Journal of Theoretical and Applied Electronic Commerce Research*, *6*(1), i–viii. doi:10.4067/S0718-18762011000100001

Janssen, M., Snijders, B., & Herkemij, F. (2011). A Reference Architecture for Interoperable and Adaptive Processes. In Y. Charalabidis (Ed.), *Interoperability in Digital Public Services and Administrations: Bridging E-Government and E-Business* (pp. 162–179). Information Science Reference. doi:10.4018/978-1-61520-887-6.ch009

Japanese Industrial Standards Committee. (2005). *Report of the Japanese Industrial Standards Committee.* Author.

Jirotka, M., Grimpe, B., Stahl, B., Eden, G., & Hartswood, M. (2016). Responsible research and innovation in the digital age. *Communications of the ACM.*

Johansson, M., & Jonsson, A. (2012). The package logic: A study on value creation and knowledge flows. *European Management Journal*, *30*(6), 535–551. doi:10.1016/j.emj.2012.04.003

Jurisch, M. C. (2014). *IT-enabled business process change in private and in public sector organizations.* Academic Press.

Kagan, S. (1994). *Cooperative Learning.* Kagan Publishing.

Kajiura, M., & Uchida, Y. (2005). *Standardization of barcodes: Focusing on QR code.* Summary of a lecture presented at the 20th Annual Academic Convention of the Japan Society for Research Policy and Innovation Management.

Kale, P., Singh, H., & Perlmutter, H. (2000). Learning and protection of proprietary assets in strategic alliances: Building relational capital. *Strategic Management Journal, 21*(Special Issue), 217–237. doi:10.1002/(SICI)1097-0266(200003)21:3<217::AID-SMJ95>3.0.CO;2-Y

Kalpakjian, S. (1995). *Manufacturing Engineering and Technology* (3rd ed.). Reading, MA: Addison-Wesley.

Kalsbeek, L. (1975). *Contours of a Christian Philosophy: An Introduction to Herman Dooyeweerd's Thought*. Toronto: Wedge.

Kanji, G. K. (1990). Total quality management: The second industrial revolution. *Total Quality Management, 1*(1), 3–12. doi:10.1080/09544129000000001

Katz, M. L., & Shapiro, C. (1985). Network externalities, competition, and compatibility. *The American Economic Review, 75*, 424–440.

Katz, M., & Shapiro, C. (1985). Network Externalities, Competition, and Compatibility. *The American Economic Review, 75*, 424–440.

Katz, M., & Shapiro, C. (1994). Systems competition and Network effects. *The Journal of Economic Perspectives, 8*(2), 93–115. doi:10.1257/jep.8.2.93

Kayworth, T., & Sambamurthy, V. (2000). Facilitating localized exploitation and enterprise-wide integration in the use of IT infrastructures: The role of PC/LAN infrastructure standard. *The Data Base for Advances in Information Systems, 31*(4), 54–81. doi:10.1145/506760.506765

Kellogg, K. C., Orlikowski, W. J., & Yates, J. (2006). Life in the trading zone: Structuring coordination across boundaries in postbureaucratic organizations. *Organization Science, 17*(1), 22–44. doi:10.1287/orsc.1050.0157

Kelly, M. (1994). Foucault, Habermas and the Self-Referentiality of Critique. In M. Kelly (Ed.), *Critique and Power – Recasting the Foucault/Habermas Debate*. Cambridge, MA: The MIT Press.

Keoh, S. L., Kumar, S. S., & Tschofenig, H. (2014). Securing the internet of things: A standardization perspective. *IEEE Internet of Things Journal, 1*(3), 265–275. doi:10.1109/JIOT.2014.2323395

King, D, Stangoe, C & Cooke, L. (2012). *Scrutinising Forensic Services*. CPD Presentation to 25 Bedford Row.

King, J. L., Gurbaxani, V., Kraemer, K. L., McFarlan, F. W., Raman, K. S., & Yap, C. S. (1994). Institutional Factors in Information Technology Innovation. *Information Systems Research, 5*(2), 139–169. doi:10.1287/isre.5.2.139

King, N. (2013). Exploring the impact of operating model choice on the governance of inter-organizational workflow: The U.S. e-prescribing network. *European Journal of Information Systems, 22*(5), 548–568. doi:10.1057/ejis.2012.47

Klein, H. K., & Myers, M. D. (1999). A Set of Principles for Conducting and Evaluating Interpretive Field Studies in Information Systems. *Management Information Systems Quarterly*, *23*(1), 67–93. doi:10.2307/249410

Kogut, B. (2000). The network as knowledge: Generative rules and the emergence of structure. *Strategic Management Journal*, *21*(3), 405–425. doi:10.1002/(SICI)1097-0266(200003)21:3<405::AID-SMJ103>3.0.CO;2-5

Kondo, Y. (1996). Are creative ability and work standardisation in contradictory relationship? *Training for Quality*, *4*(3), 35–39. doi:10.1108/09684879610125734

Kondo, Y. (2000). Innovation versus standardisation. *The TQM Magazine*, *12*(1), 6–10. doi:10.1108/09544780010287177

Koslowski, P. (2013). Principles of Ethical Economy (2nd ed.). Springer.

Kotlarsky, J., Scarbrough, H., & Oshri, I. (2014). Coordinating expertise across knowledge boundaries in offshore-outsourcing projects: The role of codification. *Management Information Systems Quarterly*, *38*(2), 607–627. doi:10.25300/MISQ/2014/38.2.13

Krcmar, H. (2015). *Informationsmanagement* (6th ed.). Berlin: Springer-Verlag.

Krechmer, K. (2000). *The Fundamental Nature of Standards: Economics Perspective*. Paper to the International JA Schumpeter Conference, Manchester, UK.

Krechmer, K. (2005). *Standards Mark the Course of Economic Progress* (Unpublished paper). Academic Press.

Krut, R., & Gleckman, H. (1998). *ISO14001: A Missed Opportunity for Sustainable Global Development*. London: Earthscan Publications.

Kubicek, H., & Cimander, R. (2009). Three dimensions of organizational interoperability. *European Journal of ePractice, 6*, 3-14.

Kuhlmann, D., Chen, L., & Mitchell, C. (2016). Trust and Legitimacy in Security Standardization–a new Management Issue? Interoperability for Enterprise Systems and Applications (I-ESA 16), Guimaraes, Portugal.

Kuldeep, K., & van Dissel Han, G. (1996). Sustainable Collaboration: Managing Conflict and Cooperation in Interorganizational Systems. *Management Information Systems Quarterly*, *20*(3), 279–300. doi:10.2307/249657

Kumar, N., Scheer, L., & Kotler, P. (2000). From Market Driven to Market Driving. *European Management Journal*, *18*(2), 129–142. doi:10.1016/S0263-2373(99)00084-5

Lagrosen, Y., & Lagrosen, S. (2005). The effects of quality management – A survey of Swedish quality professionals. *International Journal of Operations & Production Management*, *25*(10), 940–952. doi:10.1108/01443570510619464

Lam, W. (2006). Barriers to e-government integration. *Journal of Enterprise Information Management*, *18*(5), 511–530. doi:10.1108/17410390510623981

Langheinrich, M. (2001). Privacy by design – principles of privacy-aware ubiquitous systems. In *International conference on Ubiquitous Computing* (pp. 273-291). Springer. 10.1007/3-540-45427-6_23

Laursen, K., & Salter, A. J. (2014). The paradox of openness: Appropriability, external search and collaboration. *Research Policy*, *43*(5), 867–878. doi:10.1016/j.respol.2013.10.004

Lawless, C. (2010). *A Curious Reconstruction? The Shaping of 'Marketized' Forensic Science*. CARR Discussion Paper 63.

Lawless, C. (2016). *Forensic Science: A Sociological introduction*. New York: Routledge. doi:10.4324/9781315760551

Lawless, C. J., & Williams, R. (2010). Helping With Inquiries or Helping With Profits? The trials and tribulations of a technolology of forensic reasoning. *Social Studies of Science*, *40*(5), 731–755. doi:10.1177/0306312710378787 PMID:21553603

Layne, K., & Lee, J. (2001). Developing fully functional E-government: A four stage model. *Government Information Quarterly*, *18*(2), 122–136. doi:10.1016/S0740-624X(01)00066-1

Lazaric, N., & Denis, B. (1995). Routinization and memorization of tasks in a workshop: The case of the introduction of ISO norms. *Industrial and Corporate Change*, *15*(5), 873–896. doi:10.1093/icc/dth074

Lee, H., & Oh, S. (2006). A standards war waged by a developing country: Understanding international standard setting from the actor-network perspective. *The Journal of Strategic Information Systems*, *15*(3), 177–195. doi:10.1016/j.jsis.2005.10.002

Leiponen, A. E. (2008). Competing through cooperation: The organization of standard setting in wireless telecommunications. *Management Science*, *54*(11), 1904–1919. doi:10.1287/mnsc.1080.0912

Lelong, B., & Mallard, A. (1995). Presentation. *Reseaux*, *18*(102), 9–34.

Lerner, U., & Tirole, J. (2007). Public Policy Towards Patent Pools. *Innovation Policy and the Economy*, *8*, 157–186. doi:10.1086/ipe.8.25056201

Lin, Ch.-I., & Jang, W.-Y. (2008). Successful ISO 9000 implementation in Taiwan: How can we achieve it, and what does it mean? *International Journal of Productivity and Performance Management*, *57*(8), 600–622. doi:10.1108/17410400810916044

Lin, P., Abney, K., & Bekey, G. A. (Eds.). (2014). *Robot Ethics: The Ethical and Social Implications of Robotics, Intelligent Robotics and Autonomous Agents*. Cambridge, MA: MIT Press.

Li, S., Tryfonas, T., & Li, H. (2016). The Internet of Things: A security point of view. *Internet Research, 26*(2), 337–359. doi:10.1108/IntR-07-2014-0173

Liu, H., & Cargill, C. F. (2017). *Setting standards for industry: comparing the emerging Chinese standardization system and the current US system.* Honolulu, HI: East-West Center.

Li, X., & Chen, Y. (2012). Corporate IT Standardization: Product Compatibility, Exclusive Purchase Commitment, and Competition Effects. *Information Systems Research, 23*(4), 1158–1174. doi:10.1287/isre.1110.0412

Lo, L. K., & Chang, D. S. (2007). The difference in the perceived benefits between firms that maintain ISO certification and those that do not. *International Journal of Production Research, 48*(5), 1881–1897. doi:10.1080/00207540600733709

Lovelock, C. H., & Yip, G. S. (1996). Developing Global Strategies for Service Businesses. *California Management Review, 38*(2), 64–86. doi:10.2307/41165833

Lowry, P. B., Moody, G., Gaskin, J., Galletta, D. F., Humphreys, S., Barlow, J. B., & Wilson, D. (2013). *Evaluating Journal Quality and the Association for Information Systems (AIS) Senior Scholars' Journal Basket Via Bibliometric Measures: Do Expert Journal Assessments Add Value?* Rochester, NY: Social Science Research Network.

Lundqvist, B. (2015). *Joint Research and Development Under US Antitrust and EU Competition Law.* Edward Elgar Publishing. doi:10.4337/9781784713010

Lyytinen, K., & King, J. L. (2006a). Standard making: A critical research frontier for information systems research. *Management Information Systems Quarterly, 30*, 405–411. doi:10.2307/25148766

Macdonald, J., & Dale, B. G. (2007). Business Process Re-engineering. In Managing Quality (5). Malden, MA: Blackwell Publishing.

Magd, H. A. E. (2008). ISO 9001:2000 in the Egyptian manufacturing sector: perceptions and perspectives. *International Journal of Quality & Reliability Management, 25*(2), 173–200. doi:10.1108/02656710810846934

Mahadevappa, B., & Kotreshwar, G. (2004). Quality Management Practices in Indian ISO 9000 Certified Companies: An Empirical Evaluation. *Total Quality Management, 15*(3), 295–305. doi:10.1080/1478336042000183389

Malone, T. W., & Crowston, K. (1994). The interdisciplinary study of coordination. *ACM Computing Surveys, 26*(1), 87–119. doi:10.1145/174666.174668

Manders, N. B. (2015). Implementation and Impact of ISO 9001. ERIM Ph.D. Series Research in Management (Vol. 337). Rotterdam, The Netherlands: Erasmus Research Institute of Management (ERIM).

Manders, B. (2015). *Implementation and Impact of ISO 9001. ERIM PhD Series in Research in Management 337.* Rotterdam: Erasmus Research Institute of Management – ERIM.

Manders, B. (2015). *Implementation and Impact of ISO 9001. ERIM PhD Series Research in Management*. Rotterdam: Erasmus Research Institute of Management – ERIM.

March, J. G., & Simon, H. A. (1958). Organizations. Academic Press.

March, J. G., & Simon, H. A. (1958). *Organizations*. Cambridge, MA: Blackwell publishers.

Marcos, J., Fernández, M. J., Sánchez, J., Suárez, M., & Mariblanca, A. M. (2012). Training in RAMS in Collaboration with Industrial Companies and Institutions. *2nd International Workshop AMEST 2012 Advances Maintenance Engineering Services and Technologies.*

Marcos, J., Pérez, S., Sánchez, J., Álvarez, R., & Suárez, M. (2009). Active Learning Approach for Engineering, Collaboration with the Corporate World. *International Journal of Engineering Education*, *25*(4), 777–787.

Marcos, J., Sánchez, J., Quintáns, C., & Suárez, M. (2011). *Aprendizaje activo en Ingeniería con la colaboración del entorno empresarial. In XVII Seminario Anual de Automática, Electrónica Industrial e Instrumentación*. SAAEI.

Markus, M. L., & Bui, Q. N. (2012). Going Concerns: The Governance of Interorganizational Coordination Hubs. *Journal of Management Information Systems*, *28*(4), 163–198. doi:10.2753/MIS0742-1222280407

Markus, M. L., Steinfield, C. W., & Wigand, R. T. (2006). Industry-wide information systems standardization as collective action: The case of the US residential mortgage industry. *Management Information Systems Quarterly*, *30*, 439–465. doi:10.2307/25148768

Mårtensson, P., & Lee, A. S. (2004). Dialogical action research at omega corporation. *Management Information Systems Quarterly*, *28*(3), 507–536. doi:10.2307/25148648

Martín, E., Lázaro, C., & Hernán-Losada, I. (2010). *Active Learning in Telecommunication Engineering: A case study*. IEEE EDUCON Education Engineering.

Martínez-Costa, M., Choi, T. Y., Martinez, J. A., & Martínez-Lorente, A. R. (2009). ISO 9000/1994, ISO 9001/2000 and TQM: The performance debate revisited. *Journal of Operations Management*, *27*(6), 495–511. doi:10.1016/j.jom.2009.04.002

Masten, S. E. (1991). A legal basis for the firm. In O. E. Williamson & S. G. Winter (Eds.), *The Nature of the Firm: Origins, Evolution and Development* (pp. 196–212). New York: Oxford University Press.

Matutes, C., & Regibeau, P. (1996). A selective review of the economics of standardization. Entry deterrence, technological progress and international competition. *European Journal of Political Economy*, *12*(2), 183–209. doi:10.1016/0176-2680(95)00013-5

Mayer, K., & Argyres, N. (2004). Learning to contract: Evidence from the personal computer industry. *Organization Science*, *15*(4), 394–410. doi:10.1287/orsc.1040.0074

McKinnon, R. (2013). *Consent of the Networked: The Worldwide Struggle For Internet Freedom*. New York, NY: Basic Books.

Mecca, G., Santomauro, M., Santoro, D., & Veltri, E. (2016). On federated single sign-on in e-government interoperability frameworks. *International Journal of Electronic Governance*, *8*(1), 6. doi:10.1504/IJEG.2016.076684

Melin, U., & Axelsson, K. (2005). Understanding Organizational Coordination and Information Systems-Mintzberg's Coordination Mechanisms Revisited and Evaluated. *ECIS 2005 Proceedings*, 115.

Mena, S., & Palazzo, G. (2012). Input and Output Legitimacy of Multi-Stakeholder Initiatives. *Business Ethics Quarterly*, *22*(3), 527–556. doi:10.5840/beq201222333

Mendoza, R. A., & Ravichandran, T. (2011). An Exploratory Analysis of the Relationship Between Organizational and Institutional Factors Shaping the Assimilation of Vertical Standards. *International Journal of IT Standards and Standardization Research*, *9*(1), 24–51. doi:10.4018/jitsr.2011010102

Miles, G., Miles, R. E., Perrone, V., & Edvinsson, L. (1998). Some Conceptual and Research Barriers to the Utilization of Knowledge. *California Management Review*, *40*(3), 281–288. doi:10.2307/41165956

Miles, M. P., Munilla, L. S., & Russel, G. R. (1997). Marketing and Environmental Registration/Certification: What Industrial Marketers Should Understand about ISO 14000. *Industrial Marketing Management*, *26*(4), 363–370. doi:10.1016/S0019-8501(96)00144-7

Miller, D. (1996). Configurations revisited. *Strategic Management Journal*, *17*(7), 505–512. doi:10.1002/(SICI)1097-0266(199607)17:7<505::AID-SMJ852>3.0.CO;2-I

Mintzberg, H. (1993). *Structure in fives: Designing effective organizations*. Prentice-Hall, Inc.

Mione, A. (2015). The value of intangibles in a situation of innovation: Questions raised by the case of standards. *Journal of Innovation Economics & Management*, *2*(17), 49–68. doi:10.3917/jie.017.0049

Misuraca, G., Alfano, G., & Viscusi, G. (2011a). Interoperability Challenges for ICT-enabled Governance: Towards a pan-European Conceptual Framework. *Journal of Theoretical and Applied Electronic Commerce Research*, *6*(1), 95–111. doi:10.4067/S0718-18762011000100007

Misuraca, G., Alfano, G., & Viscusi, G. (2011b). A Multi-Level Framework for ICT-Enabled Governance: Assessing the Non-Technical Dimensions of 'Government openness''. *Electronic. Journal of E-Government*, *9*(2), 152–165.

Mitchell, R. K., Agle, B. R., & Wood, D. J. (1997). Toward a theory of stakeholder identification and salience: Defining the principle of who and what really counts. *Academy of Management Review*, *22*(4), 853–886. doi:10.5465/amr.1997.9711022105

Mizuno, K. (2002). Leading by Example. *ISO Management Systems*, 21.

Moen, W. E. (1994). Information technology standards: A component of federal information policy. *Government Information Quarterly*, *11*(4), 357–371. doi:10.1016/0740-624X(94)90015-9

Mom, T. J. M., Van den Bosch, F. A. J., & Volberda, H. W. (2002). Exploratie en exploitatie van kennis - Het managen van de determinanten van horizontale kennisuitwisseling. *Management en Organisatie*, *56*(5), 23–43.

Mueller, T., Dittes, S., Ahlemann, F., Urbach, N., & Smolnik, S. (2015). Because Everybody is Different Towards Understanding the Acceptance of Organizational IT Standards. *Proceedings of the 48th Hawaii International Conference on System Sciences*. 10.1109/HICSS.2015.487

Müller, J. A. (2016). Subsidiary Strategy and Importance of Standards: Re-interpreting the integration-responsiveness framework. In *Annual Conference 2016*. Verein für Socialpolitik/German Economic Association.

Myers, M. D. (1997). Qualitative research in information systems. *Management Information Systems Quarterly*, *21*(June), 1–18. doi:10.2307/249422

Myers, M. D., & Avison, D. E. (2002). Qualitative Research in Information Systems. *A Reader*, 328–328.

Nair, A., & Prajogo, D. (2009). Internalisation of ISO 9000 standards: The antecedent role of functionalist and institutionalist drivers and performance implications. *International Journal of Production Research*, *47*(16), 4545–4568. doi:10.1080/00207540701871069

Nakamura, S. (2000). *The new standardisation: Keystone of continuous improvement in manufacturing*. Portland, OR: Productivity Press.

Narayanan, V., & Chen, T. (2012). Research on technology standards: Accomplishment and challenges. *Research Policy*, *41*(8), 1375–1406. doi:10.1016/j.respol.2012.02.006

National Standards Advisory Committee, Standards Australia. (2006). Available at: http://www.standards.org.au/Pages/FAQ.aspx

Naveh, E. (2018). Standardization and Innovation: a Multipriority Approach. *Enterprise Interoperability: Smart Services and Business Impact of Enterprise Interoperability*, 125-130.

Naveh, E., & Erez, M. (2004). Innovation and Attention to Detail in the Quality Improvement Paradigm. *Management Science*, *50*(11), 1576–1586. doi:10.1287/mnsc.1040.0272

Naveh, E., Marcus, A., & Moon, H. K. (2004). Implementing ISO 9000: Performance improvement by first or second movers. *International Journal of Production Research*, *42*(9), 1843–1863. doi:10.1080/00207540410001662912

Nelson, R. R., & Winter, S. G. (1982). *An evolutionary theory of economic change*. Cambridge, MA: Belknap press/Harvard University Press.

Nelson, R., & Winter, S. (1982). *The evolutionary theory of the firm*. Cambridge, MA: Harvard University Press.

Nickerson, J. V., & zur Muehlen, M. (2006). The ecology of standards processes: Insights from Internet standards making. *Management Information Systems Quarterly*, *30*(1), 476–488.

Nicolau, J. L., & Sellers, R. (2002). The stock market's reaction to quality certification: Empirical evidence from Spain. *European Journal of Operational Research*, *142*(3), 632–641. doi:10.1016/S0377-2217(01)00312-5

Nicoloso, E. (2007). Bridging the gap between quality management systems and product quality. *ISO Management Systems*, *7*(1), 7–11.

Nonaka, I. (1994). A Dynamic Theory of Organisational Knowledge Creation. *Organization Science*, *5*(1), 14–37. doi:10.1287/orsc.5.1.14

Nonaka, I., & Takeuchi, H. (1995). *The knowledge creating company: how Japanese companies create the dynamics of innovation*. New York: Oxford University Press.

Normann, R., & Ramirez, R. (1993). From value chain to value constellation: Designing interactive strategy. *Harvard Business Review*, *71*, 65–78. PMID:10127040

Normann, R., & Ramirez, R. (1994). *Designing interactive strategy – from value chain to value constellation*. Chichester, UK: Wiley & Sons.

North, D. C., & Thomas, R. P. (1973). *The Rise of the Western World: A New Economic History*. Cambridge, UK: Cambridge Press. doi:10.1017/CBO9780511819438

OECD. (1999). *Regulatory Reform and International Standardization (Working Party of the Trade Committee No. TD/TC/WP(98)36/FINAL)*. Paris: Organization for Economic Cooperation and Development. Retrieved from https://www.oecd.org/tad/benefitlib/1955309.pdf

Ogawa, K. (2014). *Open and Close Strategy: Conditions for Restructuring Japanese Companies*. Shoeisha.

Ogilvie, S. (2004). Guilds, efficiency, and social capital: Evidence from German proto-industry. *The Economic History Review*, *57*(2), 286–333. doi:10.1111/j.1468-0289.2004.00279.x

Ojo, A., Janowski, T., & Estevez, E. (2009). *Semantic Interoperability Architecture for Electronic Government.* Paper presented at the 10th Annual International Conference on Digital Government Research, Puebla, Mexico.

Okhomatovskiy, I., & David, R. J. (2012). Setting your own standards: Internal corporate governance codes as a response to institutional pressure. *Organization Science*, *23*(1), 155–176. doi:10.1287/orsc.1100.0642

Okhuysen, G. A., & Bechky, B. A. (2009). Coordination in Organizations: An Integrative Perspective. *The Academy of Management Annals*, *3*(1), 463–502. doi:10.5465/19416520903047533

Olbrich, S. (2008). *Modellierung von E-Government-Prozessen. In Modellierung gesetzlicher Rahmenbedingungen für Verwaltungsprozesse aus dem E-Government* (pp. 47–86). Wiesbaden: Gabler.

Olian, J. P., & Ryness, S. L. (1991). Making total quality work: Aligning organizations, performance measures, and stakeholders. *Human Resource Management*, *30*(3), 303–333. doi:10.1002/hrm.3930300303

Oshri, I., & Weeber, C. (2006). Cooperation and Competition Standards-Setting Activities in the Digitization Era: The Case of Wireless Information Devices. *Technology Analysis and Strategic Management*, *18*(2), 265–283. doi:10.1080/09537320600624196

Padma, P., Ganesh, L. S., & Rajendran, C. (2008). A study on the critical factors of ISO 9001:2000 and organisational performance of Indian manufacturing firms. *International Journal of Production Research*, *46*(18), 4981–5011. doi:10.1080/00207540600793299

Panitz, T. (1999). Benefits of Cooperative Learning in relation to Student Motivation. Academic Press.

Paper, D., Rodger, J., & Pendharkar, P. C. (2001). A BPR case study at Honeywell. *Business Process Management Journal*, *7*(2), 85–99. doi:10.1108/14637150110389416

Parasuraman, A., Zeithaml, V. A., & Berry, L. L. (1985). A conceptual model of service quality and its implications for future research. *Journal of Marketing*, *49*(4), 41–50. doi:10.1177/002224298504900403

Parker, G., & Van Alstyne, M. W. (2003). Two sided networks: A theory of information product design. *Management Science*, *51*(10), 1494–1504. doi:10.1287/mnsc.1050.0400

Pawlowski, S. D., & Robey, D. (2004). Bridging user organizations: Knowledge brokering and the work of information technology professionals. *Management Information Systems Quarterly*, *28*(4), 645–672. doi:10.2307/25148658

Pérez Vázquez, A., & Ruíz Rosado, O. (2005). Interdisciplinary research: A swot analysis and its role in agricultural research in Mexico. *Tropical and Subtropical Agroecosystems.*

Perez-Aleman, P. (2011). Collective learning in global diffusion: Spreading quality standards in a developing country cluster. *Organization Science*, *22*(1), 173–189. doi:10.1287/orsc.1090.0514

Pfaffenberger, B. (2000). The Rhetoric of Dread: Fear, Uncertainty, and Doubt (FUD) in Information Technology Marketing. *Knowledge, Technology & Policy*, *13*(3), 78–92. doi:10.100712130-000-1022-x

Pfeffer, J., & Salancik, G. R. (1978). *The External Control of Organizations: A Resource Dependence Perspective*. New York: Harper & Row.

Poba-Nzaou, P., & Raymond, L. (2011). Managing ERP system risk in SMEs: A multiple case study. *Journal of Information Technology*, *26*(3), 170–192. doi:10.1057/jit.2010.34

Porter, M. (1980). *Competitive strategy*. New York: Free Press.

Porter, M. E. (1985). *Competitive advantage: creating and sustaining superior performance*. New York: Free Press.

Puffert, D. (2009). *Tracks across Continents, Paths through History: The Economic Dynamics of Standardization in Railway Gauge*. Chicago, IL: University of Chicago Press.

Radack, S. M. (1990). More effective federal computer systems: The role of NIST and standards. *Government Information Quarterly*, *7*(1), 37–49. doi:10.1016/0740-624X(90)90005-9

Rada, R., & Craparo, J. (2000). Standardizing Software Projects. *Communications of the ACM*, *43*(12), 21–25. doi:10.1145/355112.355117

Rainey, H. G., Ronquillo, J. C., & Avellaneda, C. N. (2010). Decision making in public organizations. Handbook of Decision Making, 6, 349-349.

Ralston, A., & Reilly, E. D. (Eds.). (1993). *Encyclopedia of Computer Science* (3rd ed.). New York, NY: Van Nostrand Reinhold.

Rathmell, J. M. (1966). What is meant by services? *Journal of Marketing*, *4*(4), 32–36. doi:10.1177/002224296603000407

Ray, G., Barey, J. B., & Muhanna, W. A. (2004). Capabilities, business processes, and competitive advantage: Choosing the dependent variable in empirical tests of the resources based view. *Strategic Management Journal*, *25*(1), 23–38. doi:10.1002mj.366

Reed, R., Lemak, D. J., & Mero, N. P. (2000). Total quality management and sustainable competitive advantage. *Journal of Quality Management*, *5*(1), 5–26. doi:10.1016/S1084-8568(00)00010-9

Reich, B. H., & Benbasat, I. (2000). Factors that influence the social dimension of alignment between business and information technology objectives. *Management Information Systems Quarterly*, *24*(1), 81–113. doi:10.2307/3250980

Reimers, K., & Li, M. (2005). Effectiveness of governance structures for 3G standardization and implications for China's 3G policy. In P. Cunningham & M. Cunningham (Eds.), eAdoption and the knowledge economy: Issues, applications, case studies (pp. 256-263). IOS Press.

Reinermann, H., & Von Lucke, J. (2002). *Electronic Government in Deutschland, Ziele - Stand - Barrieren - Beispiele - Umsetzung Speyerer Forschungsberichte 226*. Speyer: Forschungsinst. für Öffentliche Verwaltung.

Richmond, K. (2017). Streamlined Forensic Reporting: 'Swift and sure justice'? *Journal of Criminal Law*, *82*(2), 156–177. doi:10.1177/0022018318772701

Robbins, L. (2007). *An Essay on the Nature and Significance of Economic Science*. Macmillan and Co. (Original work published 1932)

Rochet, J.-C., & Tirole, J. (2003). Platform competition in two-sided markets. *Journal of the European Economic Association*, *1*(4), 990–1029. doi:10.1162/154247603322493212

Rogers, E. (1995). *Diffusion of Innovations* (4th ed.). The Free Press.

Rogers, E. M. (2003). *Diffusion of innovations* (5th ed.). New York: Simon & Schuster International.

Rosenbrock, K. (2017). *Why the ETSI IPR Policy Requires Licensing to all*. Retrieved from http://www.fair-standards.org/wp-content/uploads/2017/08/Why-the-ETSI-IPR-Policy-Requires-Licensing-to-All_Karl-Heinz-Rosenbrock_2017.pdf

Rosenkopf, L., Metiu, A., & George, V. P. (2001). From the Bottom Up? Technical Committee Activity and Alliance Formation. *Administrative Science Quarterly*, *46*(4), 748–772. doi:10.2307/3094830

Rothery, B. (1995, November). Why ISO 14000 Will Catch ISO 9000. *Manufacturing Engineering*.

Sæbø, Ø., Rose, J., & Flak, L. S. (2008). The shape of eParticipation: Characterizing an emerging research area. *Government Information Quarterly*, *25*(3), 400–428. doi:10.1016/j.giq.2007.04.007

Saekow, A., & Boonmee, C. (2009). A Pragmatic Approach to Interoperability Practical Implementation Support (IPIS) for e-Government Interoperability. *Electronic. Journal of E-Government, 7*(4), 403–414.

Sáenz & Quiñones. (2001). Metrología Dimensional, Historia de un subcomité renovado. *Revista UNE, 157*, 25.

Sáenz-Nuño. (2003). La normalización en metrología dimensional. *Interempresas, 15*.

Sales, Darmois, Papadimitriou, & Bourse. (2012). A Systematic Approach for Closing the Research to Standardization Gap. *The Future Internet*, 18–29.

Salop, S.C., & Sheffman, D.T. (1983). Raising Rivals' Costs. *The American Economic Review, 73*(2), 267-271.

Saltzman, J., Chatterjee, S., & Raman, M. (2008). A framework for ICT standards creation: The case of ITU-T standard H. 350. *Information Systems, 33*(3), 285–299. doi:10.1016/j.is.2007.10.001

Sanchez, R., & Mahoney, J. T. (1996). Modularity, flexibility, and knowledge management in product and organizational design. *Strategic Management Journal, 17*(S2), 63–76. doi:10.1002mj.4250171107

Sandholtz, K. W. (2012). Making standards stick: A theory of coupled vs. Decoupled compliance. *Organization Studies, 33*(5-6), 655–679. doi:10.1177/0170840612443623

Santos, F. M., & Eisenhardt, K. M. (2005). Organizational Boundaries and Theories of Organization. *Organization Science, 16*(5), 491–508. doi:10.1287/orsc.1050.0152

Schelling, T. C. (1980). *The strategy of conflict*. Harvard university press.

Schengen. (1990). The Schengen acquis - Convention implementing the Schengen Agreement of 14 June 1985 between the Governments of the States of the Benelux Economic Union, the Federal Republic of Germany and the French Republic on the gradual abolition of checks at their common borders. *Official Journal L 239*, 22/09/2000 P. 0019 – 0062.

Schepel, H. (2005). *The Constitution of Private Governance: Product Standards in the Regulation of Integrating Markets* (Vol. 4). Oxford, UK: Hart Publishing.

Scherer, S., Liotas, N., Wimmer, M. A., Tambouris, E., & Tarabanis, K. (2011). Interoperability Requirements, Recommendations and Standards in e-Participation. In Y. Charalabidis (Ed.), *Interoperability in Digital Public Services and Administrations: Bridging E-Government and E-Business* (pp. 95–117). Information Science Reference. doi:10.4018/978-1-61520-887-6.ch006

Schilling, M. (1999). Winning the standards race: Building installed base and the availability of complementary goods. *European Management Journal, 17*(3), 265–274. doi:10.1016/S0263-2373(99)00005-5

Schmidt, S. K., & Werle, R. (1998). *Coordinating Technology. Studies in the International Standardization of Telecommunications*. Cambridge, MA: MIT Press.

Schoechle, T. (2009). *Standardization and Digital Enclosure: The Privatization of Standards, Knowledge, and Policy in the Age of Global Information Technology*. Hershey, PA: IGI Global. doi:10.4018/978-1-60566-334-0

Scholl, H. J., & Dwivedi, Y. K. (2014). Forums for electronic government scholars: Insights from a 2012/2013 study. *Government Information Quarterly, 31*(2), 229–242. doi:10.1016/j.giq.2013.10.008

Scholl, H. J., & Klischewski, R. (2007). E-Government Integration and Interoperability: Framing the Research Agenda. *International Journal of Public Administration, 30*(8-9), 889–920. doi:10.1080/01900690701402668

Scholl, H. J., Kubicek, H., Cimander, R., & Klischewski, R. (2012). Process integration, information sharing, and system interoperation in government: A comparative case analysis. *Government Information Quarterly, 29*(3), 313–323. doi:10.1016/j.giq.2012.02.009

Schumpeter, J. (1934). *The theory of economic development.* London: Transaction publishers.

Schwaber, K. (1996). SCRUM development process. *Proceedings of ACM SIGPLAN on Objected-Oriented Programming, Systems, Languages, & Applications (OOPSLA '96).*

Schwaber, K., & Beedle, M. (2002). *Agile software development with Scrum.* Upper Saddle River, NJ: Prentice Hall.

Seddon, J. (2000). *The Case against ISO 9000.* Oak Tree Press.

Senoo, K. (2009). *Why Japan is Losing in Business Although it Excels in Technology: Reasons that Breakthrough New Products Have Suffered Staggering Defeats.* Diamond, Inc.

Shapiro, C., & Varian, H. R. (1999). *Information rules - A Strategic Guide to the Network Economy.* Boston: Harvard Business School Press.

Shapiro, C., & Varian, H. R. (1999). The art of standards wars. *California Management Review, 41*(2), 8–32. doi:10.2307/41165984

Sheehan, N. T., & Foss, N. J. (2007). Enhancing the prescriptiveness of the resource-based view through Porterian activity analysis. *Management Decision, 2*(3), 240–260.

Sherif, M. H., Jakobs, K., & Egyedi, T. M. (2007). *Standards of quality and quality of standards for telecommunications and information technologies. In Challenges in the Management of New Technologies* (pp. 427–447). World Scientific.

Sicari, S., Rizzardi, A., Grieco, L. A., & Coen-Porisini, A. (2015). Security, privacy and trust in Internet of Things: The road ahead. *Computer Networks, 76*, 146–164. doi:10.1016/j.comnet.2014.11.008

Simcoe, T. S. (2006). Open standards and intellectual property rights. In H. W. Chesbrough, W. Vanhaverbeke, & J. West (Eds.), *Open Innovation: Researching a New Paradigm* (pp. 161–183). Oxford University Press.

Simon, H. A. (1969). *The Sciences of the Artificial* (Vol. 1). Academic Press.

Simons, C. A. J., & De Vries, H. J. (2002). *Standaard of maatwerk – Bedrijfskeuzes tussen uniformiteit en verscheidenheid*. Schoonhoven, The Netherlands: Academic Service.

Singh, R. M., & Dahlin, K. B. (2009). *The winner does not take it all: Survival of niche standards*. Paper presented at the EGOS 2009, Barcelona, Spain.

Sklyarova, M., & Kobets, T. (2011). *Eco-efficiency for Sustainability: IKEA's Environmental Policy in Russia* (Master's thesis). Gotland University. Retrieved from www.diva-portal.org/smash/get/diva2:420853/FULLTEXT01.pdfEco-efficiency

Slavin, R. E. (1987). *Cooperative Learning: Student Teams* (2nd ed.). Washington, DC: National Education Association.

Slob, F. J. C., & De Vries, H. J. (2001). Wie die (petro)chemische Industrie von Normen profitiert. *DIN-Miteilungen*, *80*(6), 440–442.

Soares, F. O., Sepúlveda, M. J., Monteiro, S., Lima, R. M., & Dinis-Carvalho, J. (2013). An integrated project of entrepreneurship and innovation in engineering education. *Mechatronics (Elsevier)*, *23*(8), 987–996. doi:10.1016/j.mechatronics.2012.08.005

Spencer, B. A. (1994). Models of organization and total quality management: A comparison and critical evaluation. *Academy of Management Review*, *19*(3), 446–471. doi:10.5465/amr.1994.9412271807

Spivak, S. M., & Brenner, F. C. (2001). *Standardization essentials: Principles and practice*. CRC Press. doi:10.1201/9781482277388

Sprenger, C. C., & Ten Have, S. (1996). Kennismanagement als motor van de lerende organisatie. *Holland Management Review*, *51*, 69–76.

Spring, M. B. (2016). Standards management in the twenty-first century: Architectural challenges and management opportunities. *International Journal of Standardization Research*, *14*(1), 34–44. doi:10.4018/IJSR.2016010103

Srikanth, K., & Puranam, P. (2011). Integrating distributed work: Comparing task design, communication, and tacit coordination mechanisms. *Strategic Management Journal*, *32*(8), 849–875. doi:10.1002mj.908

Srikanth, K., & Puranam, P. (2014). The firm as a coordination system: Evidence from software services offshoring. *Organization Science*, *25*(4), 1253–1271. doi:10.1287/orsc.2013.0886

Stabell, C. B., & Fjeldstad, Ø. D. (1998). Configuring value for competitive advantage: On chains, shops, and networks. *Strategic Management Journal*, *19*(5), 413–437. doi:10.1002/(SICI)1097-0266(199805)19:5<413::AID-SMJ946>3.0.CO;2-C

Standardization Administration of China. (2017). *Standardization Law of the People's Republic of China*. Retrieved 12 December 2018 from http://www.sesec.eu/app/uploads/2017/09/SESEC-III-translation-China-Standardization-Law-2nd-reading-20170905.pdf

Star, S. L., & Griesemer, J. R. (1989). Institutional Ecology, 'Translations' and Boundary Objects: Amateurs and Professionals in Berkeley's Museum of Vertebrate Zoology, 1907-39. *Social Studies of Science*, *19*(3), 387–420. doi:10.1177/030631289019003001

Stevenson, T. H., & Barnes, F. C. (2002). What Industrial Marketers Need to Know Now about ISO 9000 Certification: A Review, Update, and Integration with Marketing. *Industrial Marketing Management*, *31*(8), 695–703. doi:10.1016/S0019-8501(01)00180-8

Stigzelius, I., & Mark-Herbert, C. (2009). Tailoring corporate responsibility to suppliers: Managing SA8000 in Indian garment industry. *Scandinavian Journal of Management*, *25*(1), 46–56. doi:10.1016/j.scaman.2008.04.003

Stilgoe, J., Owen, R., & Macnaghten, P. (2013). Developing a Framework for Responsible Innovation. *Research Policy*, *42*(9), 1568–1580. doi:10.1016/j.respol.2013.05.008

Strauss, D. F. M. (2009). *Philosophy: Disciplines of the Disciplines*. Paideia Press.

Stuurman, K. (2017). The Digitisation Driven Impact of Data Protection Regulation on the Standardisation Process. In *Digitalisation: Challenge and Opportunity for Standardisation. Proc. 22nd EURAS Annual Standardisation Conference. EURAS contributions to standardisation research* (vol. 12). Mainz Publishers.

Suarez, F. F. (2004). Battles for technological dominance: An integrative framework. *Research Policy*, *33*(2), 271–286. doi:10.1016/j.respol.2003.07.001

Suchman, M. C. (1995). Managing legitimacy: Strategic and institutional approaches. *Academy of Management Review*, *20*(3), 571–610. doi:10.5465/amr.1995.9508080331

Sullivan, L. H. (1896). The Tall Office Building Artistically Considered. *Lippincott's Magazine*, *57*, 403–409.

Su, S., Fortes, J., Kasad, T. R., Patil, M., Matsunaga, A., Tsugawa, M., ... Herrera, M. (2005). Transnational Information Sharing, Event Notification, Rule Enforcement and Process Coordination. *International Journal of Electronic Government Research*, *1*(2), 1–26. doi:10.4018/jegr.2005040101

Swaminathan, J. M. (2001). Using Standardized Operations. *California Management Review*, *43*(3), 125–135. doi:10.2307/41166092

Swann, G. M. P. (2010). *The Economics of Standardization: An Update*. Report for the UK Department of Business, Innovation and Skills (BIS). Retrieved from https://www.gov.uk/government/uploads/system/uploads/attachment_data/file/461419/The_Economics_of_Standardization_-_an_update_.pdf

Swann, G. M. P., & Lambert, R. (2010). Why do Standards Enable and Constrain Innovation? In *Services Standardisation. Proceedings of the 15th EURAS Conference. EURAS contributions to standardisation research* (vol. 2). Mainz Academic Publishers.

Swann, G. P. (2000). *The economics of standardization*. Manchester, UK: University of Manchester.

Swann, G. P. (2000). *The economics of standardization: Final report for standards and technical regulations directorate*. Manchester, UK: Department of Trade and Industry, Manchester Business School.

Swann, G. P. (2010). *The economics of standardization: an update. Report for the UK Department of Business, Innovation and Skills*. BIS.

Talib, F., & Zillur, R. (2010). A study of total quality managent and supply chain management practices. *International Journal of Productivity and Performance Management*, *60*(3), 268–288. doi:10.1108/17410401111111998

Tamm-Halström, K. (2004). *Organizing International Standardization – ISO and the IASC in Quest of Authority*. Cheltenham, UK: Edward Elgar.

Tanriverdi, H. (2005). Information technology relatedness, knowledge management capability, and performance of multibusiness firms. *Management Information Systems Quarterly*, *29*(2), 311–334. doi:10.2307/25148681

Tassey, G. (2000). Standardization in technology based markets. *Research Policy*, *27*, 273–284.

Tassey, G. (2000). Standardization in technology-based markets. *Research Policy*, *29*(4-5), 587–602. doi:10.1016/S0048-7333(99)00091-8

Tatsumoto, H. (2017). *Global Strategy of Platform Companies: Strategic Utilization of Open Standards and Business Ecosystem*. Yuhikaku Publishing.

Teece, D. (1986). Profiting from technological innovation: Implications for integration, collaboration, licensing and public policy. *Research Policy*, *15*(6), 785–805. doi:10.1016/0048-7333(86)90027-2

Teece, D. J. (2010). Business Models, Business Strategy and Innovation. *Long Range Planning*, *43*(2-3), 172–194. doi:10.1016/j.lrp.2009.07.003

Teece, D. J., Pisano, G., & Shuen, A. (1997). Dynamic capabilities and strategic management. *Strategic Management Journal*, *18*(7), 509–533. doi:10.1002/(SICI)1097-0266(199708)18:7<509::AID-SMJ882>3.0.CO;2-Z

Teichmann, H. (2010). *Global Standardization: Coping with Multilingualism, EURAS contributions to standardisation research 3*. Aachen, Germany: Verlag Mainz.

Terziovski, M., Power, D., & Sohal, A. S. (2003). The longitudinal effects of the ISO 9000 certification process on business performance. *European Journal of Operational Research*, *146*(3), 580–595. doi:10.1016/S0377-2217(02)00252-7

Terziovski, M., Samson, D., & Dow, D. (1997). The business value of quality management systems certification – Evidence from Australia and New Zealand. *Journal of Operations Management*, *15*(1), 1–18. doi:10.1016/S0272-6963(96)00103-9

Tether, B. S., Hipp, C., & Miles, I. (2001). Standardisation and particularization in services: Evidence from Germany. *Research Policy*, *30*(7), 1115–1138. doi:10.1016/S0048-7333(00)00133-5

Thompson, J. D. (1967). *Organizations in action: Social science bases of administration*. Academic Press.

Thompson, J. D. (1967). *Organizations in action*. New York: McGraw-Hill.

Timmermans, S., & Epstein, S. A. (2010). World of Standards but not a Standard World: Toward a Sociology of Standards and Standardization. *Annual Review of Sociology*, *36*(1), 69–89. doi:10.1146/annurev.soc.012809.102629

Tokuda, A. (2008). *Electronics in Automobiles and Standardization: Market of Electronic Control System in the Transition Period*. Koyoshobo.

Tomita, J., & Tatsumoto, H. (2006). *Standardization strategy in the semiconductor industry*. Summary of a lecture presented at the 21st Annual Academic Convention of the Japan Society for Research Policy and Innovation Management.

Toth, R. B. (1996). *Standards Activities of Organizations in the United States*. Retrieved 16 October 2018 from https://nvlpubs.nist.gov/nistpubs/Legacy/SP/nistspecialpublication806e1996.pdf

Toth, R. B. (1997). *Profiles of National Standards-Related Activities*. National Institute for Standards and Technology. Retrieved from http://ts.nist.gov/Standards/Global/upload/912intro.pdf

Tu, Q., Vonderembse, M. A., Ragu-Nathan, T. S., & Ragu-Nathan, B. (2004). Measuring modularity-based manufacturing practices and their impact on mass customization capability: A customer-driven perspective. *Decision Sciences*, *35*(2), 147–168. doi:10.1111/j.00117315.2004.02663.x

Tushman, M. L., & Rosenkopf, L. (1992). Organizational determinants of technological change: Toward a sociology of technological evolution. In L. L. Cummings & B. M. Staw (Eds.), *Research in organizational behavior* (pp. 311–347). Greenwich, CT: JAI Press.

Tzelepis, D., Tsekjouras, K., Skuras, D., & Dimara, E. (2006). The effects of ISO 9001 on firms' productive efficiency. *International Journal of Operations & Production Management*, *26*(10), 1146–1165. doi:10.1108/01443570610691111

Ulrich, K. (1995). The role of product architecture in the manufacturing firm. *Research Policy*, *24*(3), 419–440. doi:10.1016/0048-7333(94)00775-3

UNE History. (n.d.). Retrieved from: https://www.une.org/la-asociacion/historia

Updegrove, A. (2006). The Essential Guide to Standards. In *Participating In Standard Setting Organizations: Value Propositions, Roles And Strategies*. Academic Press. Retrieved from http://www.consortiuminfo.org/essentialguide/participating1.php

Vaezi, S. K. (2008). Critical Success Factors for Implementing Knowledge Based Models for Electronic Public Services (EPS). In T. Janowski & T. A. Pardo (Eds.), *ICEGOV '08: Proceedings of the 2Nd International Conference on Theory and Practice of Electronic Governance* (pp. 471–473). New York: ACM.

Van de Kaa, G., Van den Ende, J., De Vries, H. J., & Van Heck, E. (2011). Factors for winning interface format battles: A review and synthesis of the literature. *Technological Forecasting and Social Change*, *78*(8), 1397–1411. doi:10.1016/j.techfore.2011.03.011

Van De Ven, A. H., Delbecq, A. L., & Koenig, R. Jr. (1976). Determinants of Coordination Modes within Organizations. *American Sociological Review*, *41*(2), 322–338. doi:10.2307/2094477

van den Ende, J., van de Kaa, G., den Uijl, S., & de Vries, H. J. (2012). The paradox of standard flexibility: The effects of co-evolution between standard and interorganizational networks. *Organization Studies*, *33*(5-6), 705–736. doi:10.1177/0170840612443625

Van Kemenade, E. A., Hardjono, T. W., & De Vries, H. J. (2011). The willingness of professionals to contribute to their organisation's certification. *International Journal of Quality & Reliability Management*, *28*(1), 27–42. doi:10.1108/02656711111097535

Van Veldhuisen, A. (1996). *De Macht van het Systeem – Een studie naar kwaliteitssystemen gebaseerd op het werk van Michael Foucault*. Rotterdam: Erasmus Universiteit, Faculteit Bedrijfskunde.

van Wessel, R. (2010). Toward Corporate IT Standardization Management: Frameworks and Solutions. Hershey, PA: IGI Global.

Van Wessel, R., De Vries, H., & Ribbers, P. (2016), Business Benefits through Company IT Standardization. In K. Jakobs (Ed.) Effective Standardization Management in Corporate Settings (pp. 34-52). Hershey, PA: IGI Global. doi:10.4018/978-1-4666-9737-9.ch003

Van Wessel, R. (2010). *Toward Corporate IT Standardization Management: Frameworks and Solutions*. Hershey, PA: IGI Global. doi:10.4018/978-1-61520-759-6

van Wessel, R., Ribbers, P., & de Vries, H. (2006). Effects of IS Standardization on Business Process Performance: A Case in HR IS Company Standardization. *Proceedings of the 39th Annual Hawaii International Conference on System Sciences*, 6. 10.1109/HICSS.2006.141

Vandemoortele, T., & Deconinck, K. (2013). When are private Standards more Stringent than Public Standards? *American Journal of Agricultural Economics*, *96*(1), 154–171. doi:10.1093/ajae/aat064

Vatn, A. (2005). *Institutions and the Environment*. Cheltenham, UK: Edward Elgar.

Verona, G. (1999). A resource-based view of product development. *Academy of Management Review*, *24*(1), 132–142. doi:10.5465/amr.1999.1580445

VersionOne. (2018). *The 12th annual state of agile report*. VersionOne Inc. Retrieved from http://stateofagile.versionone.com/

Vlachos, N. A., Michail, C., & Sotiropoulou, D. (2002). Is ISO/IEC 17025 Accreditation a Benefit or Hindrance to Testing Laboratories? The Greek Experience. *Journal of Food Composition and Analysis*, *15*(6), 749–757. doi:10.1006/jfca.2002.1097

Von Schomberg, R. (2013). A vision of responsible innovation. In R. Owen, M. Heintz, & J. Bessant (Eds.), *Responsible innovation: Managing the responsible innovation of science and innovation in society* (pp. 51–74). Wiley. doi:10.1002/9781118551424.ch3

von Zedtwitz, M., & Gassmann, O. (2002). Market Versus Technology Drive in R&D Internationalization: Four Different Patterns of Managing Research and Development. *Research Policy*, *31*(4), 569–588. doi:10.1016/S0048-7333(01)00125-1

Walsham, G. (1993). Interpreting Information Systems in Organizations. *Organization Studies*, *15*, 269–269. doi:10.1177/017084069401500614

Wang, J., & Kim, S. (2007). Time to get in: The contrasting stories about government interventions in information technology standards (the case of CDMA and IMT-2000 in Korea). *Government Information Quarterly*, *24*(1), 115–134. doi:10.1016/j.giq.2006.04.001

Warner, A., Fairbank, J., & Steensma, H. (2006). Managing uncertainty in a formal standards-based industry: A real options perspective on acquisition timing. *Journal of Management*, *32*(2), 279–298. doi:10.1177/0149206305280108

Weaver, M., Hern, A., Bekiempis, V., Hepler, L., & Fermoso, J. (2018). Google Walkout: Global Protests after Sexual Misconduct Allegations. *The Guardian*. Retrieved from https://www.theguardian.com/technology/2018/nov/01/google-walkout-global-protests-employees-sexual-harassment-scandals

Weber, M. (1922). *Wirtschaft und Gesellschaft*. Tübingen: J.C.B. Mohr.

Website of the Asociación Española de ingeniería mecánica. (n.d.). Retrieved from http://www.asoc-aeim.es/

Website of the ISO/TC 213. (n.d.). *Dimensional and geometrical product specifications and verification*. Retrieved from https://www.iso.org/committee/54924.html

Webster, J., & Watson, R. T. (2002). Analyzing the Past to Prepare for the Future: Writing a Literature Review. *Management Information Systems Quarterly*, *26*(2), 13–23.

Wegberg, M. (2004). Standardization Process of Systems Technologies: Creating a Balance between Competition and Cooperation. *Technology Analysis and Strategic Management*, *16*(4), 457–478. doi:10.1080/0953732042000295784

Weill, P., & Ross, J. (2004). *IT Governance – How Top Performers Manage IT decision Rights for Superior Results*. Boston, MA: Harvard Business School Press.

Weitzel, T. (2003). A Network ROI", MISQ Special Issue Workshop Standard Making: A Critical Research Frontier for Information Systems. *Pre-Conference Workshop, International Conference on Information Systems*, 62-79.

Weitzel, T., Beimborn, D., & König, W. (2006). A unified economic model of standard diffusion: The impact of standardization cost, network effects, and network topology. *Management Information Systems Quarterly*, *30*, 489–514. doi:10.2307/25148770

Wenström, H., Ollner, J., & Wenström, J. (2010). *Focus on Industry and Standards – An Integrated Approach*. Stockholm: SIS.

Werle, R. (2011). Institutional aspects of standardization—Jurisdictional conflicts and the choice of standardization organizations. *Journal of European Public Policy*, *8*(3), 392–410. doi:10.1080/13501760110056031

Werle, R., & Iversen, E. J. (2006). Promoting legitimacy in technical standardization. Science. *Technology and Innovation Studies*, *2*, 19–39.

Werr, A., Stjernberg, T., & Docherty, P. (1997). The functions of methods of change in management consulting. *Journal of Organizational Change Management*, *10*(4), 288–307. doi:10.1108/09534819710175839

West, J. (2003). How open is open enough? Melding proprietary and open source platform strategies. *Research Policy*, *32*(7), 1259–1285. doi:10.1016/S0048-7333(03)00052-0

West, J., & Dedrick, J. (2006). Scope and Timing of Deployment: Moderators of Organizational Adoption of the Linux Server Platform. *International Journal of IT Standards and Standardization Research*, *4*(2), 1–23. doi:10.4018/jitsr.2006070101

Whitney, A. M. (1997). *The Ethical Implications of ISO 9001 Implementation Practices* (Master's thesis). San Jose State University. Retrieved from http://scholarworks.sjsu.edu/etd_theses/1613

Wickson, F., & Forsberg, E. M. (2015). Standardising responsibility? The significance of interstitial spaces. *Science and Engineering Ethics*, *21*(5), 1159–1180. doi:10.100711948-014-9602-4 PMID:25344842

Wiegmann, P. M. (2019). *Managing Innovation and Standards: A Case in the European Heating Industry*. Springer. doi:10.1007/978-3-030-01532-9

Wilde, T., & Hess, T. (2007). Forschungsmethoden der Wirtschaftsinformatik Eine empirische Untersuchung. *Wirtschaftsinformatik*, *49*(4), 280–287. doi:10.100711576-007-0064-z

Willemse, H., de Vries, H. J., & Dul, J. (2006). Balancing Stakeholder Representation: An Example of Stakeholder Involvement in Ergonomics Standardization. In *Handbook of Standards and Guidelines in Ergonomics and Human Factors*. Mahwah, NJ: Lawrence Erlbaum Associates.

Williams, B. (1985). *Ethics and the Limits of Philosophy*. Cambridge, MA: Harvard University Press.

Williams, C. K., & Karahanna, E. (2013). Causal Explanation In The Coordinating Process: A Critical Realist Case Study Of Federated It Governance Structures. *Management Information Systems Quarterly*, *37*(3), 933–A938. doi:10.25300/MISQ/2013/37.3.12

Williamson, O. (1979). Transactions-Cost Economics: The Governance of Contractual Relations. *The Journal of Law & Economics*, *22*(2), 233–262. doi:10.1086/466942

Williamson, O. E. (1985). *The economic institutions of capitalism: firms, markets, relational contracting*. New York: Free Press.

Williams, R., & Edge, D. (1996). The social shaping of technology. *Research Policy*, *25*(6), 865–899. doi:10.1016/0048-7333(96)00885-2

Winter, S.G., (2003). "Understanding dynamic capabilities." *Strategic Management Journal,* October Special Issue, 24, 991–996.

Wissema, J. G., Messer, H. M., & Wijers, G. J. (1991). *Angst voor veranderen? Een mythe! – Of: Hoe u veranderingsbereidheid op de werkvloer vergroot*. Assen: Van Gorcum.

World Trade Organization. (2005). *World Trade Report 2005: Exploring the Links between Trade, Standards and the WTO*. Geneva: World Trade Organization. Retrieved from www.wto.org/english/res_e/booksp_e/anrep_e/world_trade_report05_e.pdf

Wright, C., Sturdy, A., & Wylie, N. (2012). Management innovation through standardization: Consultants as standardizers or organizational practice. *Research Policy*, *41*(3), 652–662. doi:10.1016/j.respol.2011.12.004

WTO. (2005). *World Trade Report 2005: Standards, 'offshoring' and air transport*. Geneva: World Trade Organization.

Wu, Y., Balasubramanian, S., & Mahajan, V. (2004). When is a Preannounced New Product Likely to be Delayed? *Journal of Marketing*, *68*(2), 101–113. doi:10.1509/jmkg.68.2.101.27792

Yeoh, P.-L., & Roth, K. (1999). An empirical analysis of sustained advantage in the U.S. pharmaceutical industry: Impact of firm resources and capabilities. *Strategic Management Journal*, *20*(7), 637–653. doi:10.1002/(SICI)1097-0266(199907)20:7<637::AID-SMJ42>3.0.CO;2-Z

Yeung, A. C. L., Lee, T. S., & Chan, L. Y. (2003). Senior management perspectives and ISO 9000 effectiveness: An empirical research. *International Journal of Production Research*, *41*(3), 545–569. doi:10.1080/0020754021000033896

Yin, R. K. (2009). *Case Study Research – Design and Methods* (4th ed.). Thousand Oaks, CA: SAGE.

Yin, R. K. (2009). *Case Study Research: Design and Methods* (4th ed.). London: Sage.

Zink, K. J. (1997). *Total Quality Management as a Holistic Management Concept*. Berlin: Springer.

Zink, K. J. (2007). From total quality management to corporate sustainability based on a stakeholder management. *Journal of Management History*, *13*(4), 394–401. doi:10.1108/17511340710819615

Zott, C., Amit, R., & Massa, L. (2011). The business model: Recent developments and future research. *Journal of Management*, *37*(4), 1019–1042. doi:10.1177/0149206311406265

Related References

To continue our tradition of advancing information science and technology research, we have compiled a list of recommended IGI Global readings. These references will provide additional information and guidance to further enrich your knowledge and assist you with your own research and future publications.

Abtahi, M. S., Behboudi, L., & Hasanabad, H. M. (2017). Factors Affecting Internet Advertising Adoption in Ad Agencies. *International Journal of Innovation in the Digital Economy*, *8*(4), 18–29. doi:10.4018/IJIDE.2017100102

Agrawal, S. (2017). The Impact of Emerging Technologies and Social Media on Different Business(es): Marketing and Management. In O. Rishi & A. Sharma (Eds.), *Maximizing Business Performance and Efficiency Through Intelligent Systems* (pp. 37–49). Hershey, PA: IGI Global. doi:10.4018/978-1-5225-2234-8.ch002

Alnoukari, M., Razouk, R., & Hanano, A. (2016). BSC-SI: A Framework for Integrating Strategic Intelligence in Corporate Strategic Management. *International Journal of Social and Organizational Dynamics in IT*, *5*(2), 1–14. doi:10.4018/IJSODIT.2016070101

Alnoukari, M., Razouk, R., & Hanano, A. (2016). BSC-SI, A Framework for Integrating Strategic Intelligence in Corporate Strategic Management. *International Journal of Strategic Information Technology and Applications*, *7*(1), 32–44. doi:10.4018/IJSITA.2016010103

Altındağ, E. (2016). Current Approaches in Change Management. In A. Goksoy (Ed.), *Organizational Change Management Strategies in Modern Business* (pp. 24–51). Hershey, PA: IGI Global. doi:10.4018/978-1-4666-9533-7.ch002

Alvarez-Dionisi, L. E., Turner, R., & Mittra, M. (2016). Global Project Management Trends. *International Journal of Information Technology Project Management*, *7*(3), 54–73. doi:10.4018/IJITPM.2016070104

Anantharaman, R. N., Rajeswari, K. S., Angusamy, A., & Kuppusamy, J. (2017). Role of Self-Efficacy and Collective Efficacy as Moderators of Occupational Stress Among Software Development Professionals. *International Journal of Human Capital and Information Technology Professionals*, *8*(2), 45–58. doi:10.4018/IJHCITP.2017040103

Aninze, F., El-Gohary, H., & Hussain, J. (2018). The Role of Microfinance to Empower Women: The Case of Developing Countries. *International Journal of Customer Relationship Marketing and Management, 9*(1), 54–78. doi:10.4018/IJCRMM.2018010104

Arsenijević, O. M., Orčić, D., & Kastratović, E. (2017). Development of an Optimization Tool for Intangibles in SMEs: A Case Study from Serbia with a Pilot Research in the Prestige by Milka Company. In M. Vemić (Ed.), *Optimal Management Strategies in Small and Medium Enterprises* (pp. 320–347). Hershey, PA: IGI Global. doi:10.4018/978-1-5225-1949-2.ch015

Aryanto, V. D., Wismantoro, Y., & Widyatmoko, K. (2018). Implementing Eco-Innovation by Utilizing the Internet to Enhance Firm's Marketing Performance: Study of Green Batik Small and Medium Enterprises in Indonesia. *International Journal of E-Business Research, 14*(1), 21–36. doi:10.4018/IJEBR.2018010102

Atiku, S. O., & Fields, Z. (2017). Multicultural Orientations for 21st Century Global Leadership. In N. Baporikar (Ed.), *Management Education for Global Leadership* (pp. 28–51). Hershey, PA: IGI Global. doi:10.4018/978-1-5225-1013-0.ch002

Atiku, S. O., & Fields, Z. (2018). Organisational Learning Dimensions and Talent Retention Strategies for the Service Industries. In N. Baporikar (Ed.), *Global Practices in Knowledge Management for Societal and Organizational Development* (pp. 358–381). Hershey, PA: IGI Global. doi:10.4018/978-1-5225-3009-1.ch017

Ávila, L., & Teixeira, L. (2018). The Main Concepts Behind the Dematerialization of Business Processes. In M. Khosrow-Pour, D.B.A. (Ed.), Encyclopedia of Information Science and Technology, Fourth Edition (pp. 888-898). Hershey, PA: IGI Global. doi:10.4018/978-1-5225-2255-3.ch076

Bartens, Y., Chunpir, H. I., Schulte, F., & Voß, S. (2017). Business/IT Alignment in Two-Sided Markets: A COBIT 5 Analysis for Media Streaming Business Models. In S. De Haes & W. Van Grembergen (Eds.), *Strategic IT Governance and Alignment in Business Settings* (pp. 82–111). Hershey, PA: IGI Global. doi:10.4018/978-1-5225-0861-8.ch004

Bashayreh, A. M. (2018). Organizational Culture and Organizational Performance. In W. Lee & F. Sabetzadeh (Eds.), *Contemporary Knowledge and Systems Science* (pp. 50–69). Hershey, PA: IGI Global. doi:10.4018/978-1-5225-5655-8.ch003

Bedford, D. A. (2018). Sustainable Knowledge Management Strategies: Aligning Business Capabilities and Knowledge Management Goals. In N. Baporikar (Ed.), *Global Practices in Knowledge Management for Societal and Organizational Development* (pp. 46–73). Hershey, PA: IGI Global. doi:10.4018/978-1-5225-3009-1.ch003

Benmoussa, F., Nakara, W. A., & Jaouen, A. (2016). The Use of Social Media by SMEs in the Tourism Industry. In I. Lee (Ed.), *Encyclopedia of E-Commerce Development, Implementation, and Management* (pp. 2159–2170). Hershey, PA: IGI Global. doi:10.4018/978-1-4666-9787-4.ch155

Berger, R. (2016). Indigenous Management and Bottom of Pyramid Countries: The Role of National Institutions. In U. Aung & P. Ordoñez de Pablos (Eds.), *Managerial Strategies and Practice in the Asian Business Sector* (pp. 107–123). Hershey, PA: IGI Global. doi:10.4018/978-1-4666-9758-4.ch007

Bharwani, S., & Musunuri, D. (2018). Reflection as a Process From Theory to Practice. In M. Khosrow-Pour, D.B.A. (Ed.), Encyclopedia of Information Science and Technology, Fourth Edition (pp. 1529-1539). Hershey, PA: IGI Global. doi:10.4018/978-1-5225-2255-3.ch132

Bhatt, G. D., Wang, Z., & Rodger, J. A. (2017). Information Systems Capabilities and Their Effects on Competitive Advantages: A Study of Chinese Companies. *Information Resources Management Journal, 30*(3), 41–57. doi:10.4018/IRMJ.2017070103

Bhushan, M., & Yadav, A. (2017). Concept of Cloud Computing in ESB. In R. Bhadoria, N. Chaudhari, G. Tomar, & S. Singh (Eds.), *Exploring Enterprise Service Bus in the Service-Oriented Architecture Paradigm* (pp. 116–127). Hershey, PA: IGI Global. doi:10.4018/978-1-5225-2157-0.ch008

Bhushan, S. (2017). System Dynamics Base-Model of Humanitarian Supply Chain (HSCM) in Disaster Prone Eco-Communities of India: A Discussion on Simulation and Scenario Results. *International Journal of System Dynamics Applications, 6*(3), 20–37. doi:10.4018/IJSDA.2017070102

Biswas, A., & De, A. K. (2017). On Development of a Fuzzy Stochastic Programming Model with Its Application to Business Management. In S. Trivedi, S. Dey, A. Kumar, & T. Panda (Eds.), *Handbook of Research on Advanced Data Mining Techniques and Applications for Business Intelligence* (pp. 353–378). Hershey, PA: IGI Global. doi:10.4018/978-1-5225-2031-3.ch021

Bücker, J., & Ernste, K. (2018). Use of Brand Heroes in Strategic Reputation Management: The Case of Bacardi, Adidas, and Daimler. In A. Erdemir (Ed.), *Reputation Management Techniques in Public Relations* (pp. 126–150). Hershey, PA: IGI Global. doi:10.4018/978-1-5225-3619-2.ch007

Bureš, V. (2018). Industry 4.0 From the Systems Engineering Perspective: Alternative Holistic Framework Development. In R. Brunet-Thornton & F. Martinez (Eds.), *Analyzing the Impacts of Industry 4.0 in Modern Business Environments* (pp. 199–223). Hershey, PA: IGI Global. doi:10.4018/978-1-5225-3468-6.ch011

Buzady, Z. (2017). Resolving the Magic Cube of Effective Case Teaching: Benchmarking Case Teaching Practices in Emerging Markets – Insights from the Central European University Business School, Hungary. In D. Latusek (Ed.), *Case Studies as a Teaching Tool in Management Education* (pp. 79–103). Hershey, PA: IGI Global. doi:10.4018/978-1-5225-0770-3.ch005

Campatelli, G., Richter, A., & Stocker, A. (2016). Participative Knowledge Management to Empower Manufacturing Workers. *International Journal of Knowledge Management, 12*(4), 37–50. doi:10.4018/IJKM.2016100103

Căpusneanu, S., & Topor, D. I. (2018). Business Ethics and Cost Management in SMEs: Theories of Business Ethics and Cost Management Ethos. In I. Oncioiu (Ed.), *Ethics and Decision-Making for Sustainable Business Practices* (pp. 109–127). Hershey, PA: IGI Global. doi:10.4018/978-1-5225-3773-1.ch007

Carneiro, A. (2016). Maturity in Health Organization Information Systems: Metrics and Privacy Perspectives. *International Journal of Privacy and Health Information Management, 4*(2), 1–18. doi:10.4018/IJPHIM.2016070101

Chan, R. L., Mo, P. L., & Moon, K. K. (2018). Strategic and Tactical Measures in Managing Enterprise Risks: A Study of the Textile and Apparel Industry. In K. Strang, M. Korstanje, & N. Vajjhala (Eds.), *Research, Practices, and Innovations in Global Risk and Contingency Management* (pp. 1–19). Hershey, PA: IGI Global. doi:10.4018/978-1-5225-4754-9.ch001

Chandan, H. C. (2016). Motivations and Challenges of Female Entrepreneurship in Developed and Developing Economies. In N. Baporikar (Ed.), *Handbook of Research on Entrepreneurship in the Contemporary Knowledge-Based Global Economy* (pp. 260–286). Hershey, PA: IGI Global. doi:10.4018/978-1-4666-8798-1.ch012

Charlier, S. D., Burke-Smalley, L. A., & Fisher, S. L. (2018). Undergraduate Programs in the U.S: A Contextual and Content-Based Analysis. In J. Mendy (Ed.), *Teaching Human Resources and Organizational Behavior at the College Level* (pp. 26–57). Hershey, PA: IGI Global. doi:10.4018/978-1-5225-2820-3.ch002

Chaudhuri, S. (2016). Application of Web-Based Geographical Information System (GIS) in E-Business. In U. Panwar, R. Kumar, & N. Ray (Eds.), *Handbook of Research on Promotional Strategies and Consumer Influence in the Service Sector* (pp. 389–405). Hershey, PA: IGI Global. doi:10.4018/978-1-5225-0143-5.ch023

Choudhuri, P. S. (2016). An Empirical Study on the Quality of Services Offered by the Private Life Insurers in Burdwan. In U. Panwar, R. Kumar, & N. Ray (Eds.), *Handbook of Research on Promotional Strategies and Consumer Influence in the Service Sector* (pp. 31–55). Hershey, PA: IGI Global. doi:10.4018/978-1-5225-0143-5.ch002

Dahlberg, T., Kivijärvi, H., & Saarinen, T. (2017). IT Investment Consistency and Other Factors Influencing the Success of IT Performance. In S. De Haes & W. Van Grembergen (Eds.), *Strategic IT Governance and Alignment in Business Settings* (pp. 176–208). Hershey, PA: IGI Global. doi:10.4018/978-1-5225-0861-8.ch007

Damnjanović, A. M. (2017). Knowledge Management Optimization through IT and E-Business Utilization: A Qualitative Study on Serbian SMEs. In M. Vemić (Ed.), *Optimal Management Strategies in Small and Medium Enterprises* (pp. 249–267). Hershey, PA: IGI Global. doi:10.4018/978-1-5225-1949-2.ch012

Daneshpour, H. (2017). Integrating Sustainable Development into Project Portfolio Management through Application of Open Innovation. In M. Vemić (Ed.), *Optimal Management Strategies in Small and Medium Enterprises* (pp. 370–387). Hershey, PA: IGI Global. doi:10.4018/978-1-5225-1949-2.ch017

Daniel, A. D., & Reis de Castro, V. (2018). Entrepreneurship Education: How to Measure the Impact on Nascent Entrepreneurs. In A. Carrizo Moreira, J. Guilherme Leitão Dantas, & F. Manuel Valente (Eds.), *Nascent Entrepreneurship and Successful New Venture Creation* (pp. 85–110). Hershey, PA: IGI Global. doi:10.4018/978-1-5225-2936-1.ch004

David, F., van der Sijde, P., & van den Besselaar, P. (2016). Enterpreneurial Incentives, Obstacles, and Management in University-Business Co-Operation: The Case of Indonesia. In J. Saiz-Álvarez (Ed.), *Handbook of Research on Social Entrepreneurship and Solidarity Economics* (pp. 499–518). Hershey, PA: IGI Global. doi:10.4018/978-1-5225-0097-1.ch024

David, R., Swami, B. N., & Tangirala, S. (2018). Ethics Impact on Knowledge Management in Organizational Development: A Case Study. In N. Baporikar (Ed.), *Global Practices in Knowledge Management for Societal and Organizational Development* (pp. 19–45). Hershey, PA: IGI Global. doi:10.4018/978-1-5225-3009-1.ch002

Delias, P., & Lakiotaki, K. (2018). Discovering Process Horizontal Boundaries to Facilitate Process Comprehension. *International Journal of Operations Research and Information Systems*, *9*(2), 1–31. doi:10.4018/IJORIS.2018040101

Denholm, J., & Lee-Davies, L. (2018). Success Factors for Games in Business and Project Management. In *Enhancing Education and Training Initiatives Through Serious Games* (pp. 34–68). Hershey, PA: IGI Global. doi:10.4018/978-1-5225-3689-5.ch002

Deshpande, M. (2017). Best Practices in Management Institutions for Global Leadership: Policy Aspects. In N. Baporikar (Ed.), *Management Education for Global Leadership* (pp. 1–27). Hershey, PA: IGI Global. doi:10.4018/978-1-5225-1013-0.ch001

Deshpande, M. (2018). Policy Perspectives for SMEs Knowledge Management. In N. Baporikar (Ed.), *Knowledge Integration Strategies for Entrepreneurship and Sustainability* (pp. 23–46). Hershey, PA: IGI Global. doi:10.4018/978-1-5225-5115-7.ch002

Dezdar, S. (2017). ERP Implementation Projects in Asian Countries: A Comparative Study on Iran and China. *International Journal of Information Technology Project Management*, *8*(3), 52–68. doi:10.4018/IJITPM.2017070104

Domingos, D., Martinho, R., & Varajão, J. (2016). Controlled Flexibility in Healthcare Processes: A BPMN-Extension Approach. In M. Cruz-Cunha, I. Miranda, R. Martinho, & R. Rijo (Eds.), *Encyclopedia of E-Health and Telemedicine* (pp. 521–535). Hershey, PA: IGI Global. doi:10.4018/978-1-4666-9978-6.ch040

Domingos, D., Respício, A., & Martinho, R. (2017). Reliability of IoT-Aware BPMN Healthcare Processes. In C. Reis & M. Maximiano (Eds.), *Internet of Things and Advanced Application in Healthcare* (pp. 214–248). Hershey, PA: IGI Global. doi:10.4018/978-1-5225-1820-4.ch008

Dosumu, O., Hussain, J., & El-Gohary, H. (2017). An Exploratory Study of the Impact of Government Policies on the Development of Small and Medium Enterprises in Developing Countries: The Case of Nigeria. *International Journal of Customer Relationship Marketing and Management*, *8*(4), 51–62. doi:10.4018/IJCRMM.2017100104

Durst, S., Bruns, G., & Edvardsson, I. R. (2017). Retaining Knowledge in Smaller Building and Construction Firms. *International Journal of Knowledge and Systems Science*, *8*(3), 1–12. doi:10.4018/IJKSS.2017070101

Edvardsson, I. R., & Durst, S. (2017). Outsourcing, Knowledge, and Learning: A Critical Review. *International Journal of Knowledge-Based Organizations*, *7*(2), 13–26. doi:10.4018/IJKBO.2017040102

Edwards, J. S. (2018). Integrating Knowledge Management and Business Processes. In M. Khosrow-Pour, D.B.A. (Ed.), Encyclopedia of Information Science and Technology, Fourth Edition (pp. 5046-5055). Hershey, PA: IGI Global. doi:10.4018/978-1-5225-2255-3.ch437

Ejiogu, A. O. (2018). Economics of Farm Management. In *Agricultural Finance and Opportunities for Investment and Expansion* (pp. 56–72). Hershey, PA: IGI Global. doi:10.4018/978-1-5225-3059-6.ch003

Ekanem, I., & Abiade, G. E. (2018). Factors Influencing the Use of E-Commerce by Small Enterprises in Nigeria. *International Journal of ICT Research in Africa and the Middle East, 7*(1), 37–53. doi:10.4018/IJICTRAME.2018010103

Ekanem, I., & Alrossais, L. A. (2017). Succession Challenges Facing Family Businesses in Saudi Arabia. In P. Zgheib (Ed.), *Entrepreneurship and Business Innovation in the Middle East* (pp. 122–146). Hershey, PA: IGI Global. doi:10.4018/978-1-5225-2066-5.ch007

El Faquih, L., & Fredj, M. (2017). Ontology-Based Framework for Quality in Configurable Process Models. *Journal of Electronic Commerce in Organizations, 15*(2), 48–60. doi:10.4018/JECO.2017040104

El-Gohary, H., & El-Gohary, Z. (2016). An Attempt to Explore Electronic Marketing Adoption and Implementation Aspects in Developing Countries: The Case of Egypt. *International Journal of Customer Relationship Marketing and Management, 7*(4), 1–26. doi:10.4018/IJCRMM.2016100101

Entico, G. J. (2016). Knowledge Management and the Medical Health Librarians: A Perception Study. In J. Yap, M. Perez, M. Ayson, & G. Entico (Eds.), *Special Library Administration, Standardization and Technological Integration* (pp. 52–77). Hershey, PA: IGI Global. doi:10.4018/978-1-4666-9542-9.ch003

Faisal, M. N., & Talib, F. (2017). Building Ambidextrous Supply Chains in SMEs: How to Tackle the Barriers? *International Journal of Information Systems and Supply Chain Management, 10*(4), 80–100. doi:10.4018/IJISSCM.2017100105

Fernandes, T. M., Gomes, J., & Romão, M. (2017). Investments in E-Government: A Benefit Management Case Study. *International Journal of Electronic Government Research, 13*(3), 1–17. doi:10.4018/IJEGR.2017070101

Fouda, F. A. (2016). A Suggested Curriculum in Career Education to Develop Business Secondary Schools Students' Career Knowledge Management Domains and Professional Thinking. *International Journal of Technology Diffusion, 7*(2), 42–62. doi:10.4018/IJTD.2016040103

Gallardo-Vázquez, D., & Pajuelo-Moreno, M. L. (2016). How Spanish Universities are Promoting Entrepreneurship through Your Own Lines of Teaching and Research? In L. Carvalho (Ed.), *Handbook of Research on Entrepreneurial Success and its Impact on Regional Development* (pp. 431–454). Hershey, PA: IGI Global. doi:10.4018/978-1-4666-9567-2.ch019

Gao, S. S., Oreal, S., & Zhang, J. (2018). Contemporary Financial Risk Management Perceptions and Practices of Small-Sized Chinese Businesses. In I. Management Association (Ed.), Global Business Expansion: Concepts, Methodologies, Tools, and Applications (pp. 917-931). Hershey, PA: IGI Global. doi:10.4018/978-1-5225-5481-3.ch041

Garg, R., & Berning, S. C. (2017). Indigenous Chinese Management Philosophies: Key Concepts and Relevance for Modern Chinese Firms. In B. Christiansen & G. Koc (Eds.), *Transcontinental Strategies for Industrial Development and Economic Growth* (pp. 43–57). Hershey, PA: IGI Global. doi:10.4018/978-1-5225-2160-0.ch003

Gencer, Y. G. (2017). Supply Chain Management in Retailing Business. In U. Akkucuk (Ed.), *Ethics and Sustainability in Global Supply Chain Management* (pp. 197–210). Hershey, PA: IGI Global. doi:10.4018/978-1-5225-2036-8.ch011

Giacosa, E. (2016). Innovation in Luxury Fashion Businesses as a Means for the Regional Development. In L. Carvalho (Ed.), *Handbook of Research on Entrepreneurial Success and its Impact on Regional Development* (pp. 206–222). Hershey, PA: IGI Global. doi:10.4018/978-1-4666-9567-2.ch010

Giacosa, E. (2018). The Increasing of the Regional Development Thanks to the Luxury Business Innovation. In L. Carvalho (Ed.), *Handbook of Research on Entrepreneurial Ecosystems and Social Dynamics in a Globalized World* (pp. 260–273). Hershey, PA: IGI Global. doi:10.4018/978-1-5225-3525-6.ch011

Gianni, M., & Gotzamani, K. (2016). Integrated Management Systems and Information Management Systems: Common Threads. In P. Papajorgji, F. Pinet, A. Guimarães, & J. Papathanasiou (Eds.), *Automated Enterprise Systems for Maximizing Business Performance* (pp. 195–214). Hershey, PA: IGI Global. doi:10.4018/978-1-4666-8841-4.ch011

Gianni, M., Gotzamani, K., & Linden, I. (2016). How a BI-wise Responsible Integrated Management System May Support Food Traceability. *International Journal of Decision Support System Technology*, *8*(2), 1–17. doi:10.4018/IJDSST.2016040101

Glykas, M., & George, J. (2017). Quality and Process Management Systems in the UAE Maritime Industry. *International Journal of Productivity Management and Assessment Technologies*, *5*(1), 20–39. doi:10.4018/IJPMAT.2017010102

Glykas, M., Valiris, G., Kokkinaki, A., & Koutsoukou, Z. (2018). Banking Business Process Management Implementation. *International Journal of Productivity Management and Assessment Technologies*, *6*(1), 50–69. doi:10.4018/IJPMAT.2018010104

Gomes, J., & Romão, M. (2017). The Balanced Scorecard: Keeping Updated and Aligned with Today's Business Trends. *International Journal of Productivity Management and Assessment Technologies*, *5*(2), 1–15. doi:10.4018/IJPMAT.2017070101

Gomes, J., & Romão, M. (2017). Aligning Information Systems and Technology with Benefit Management and Balanced Scorecard. In S. De Haes & W. Van Grembergen (Eds.), *Strategic IT Governance and Alignment in Business Settings* (pp. 112–131). Hershey, PA: IGI Global. doi:10.4018/978-1-5225-0861-8.ch005

Grefen, P., & Turetken, O. (2017). Advanced Business Process Management in Networked E-Business Scenarios. *International Journal of E-Business Research*, *13*(4), 70–104. doi:10.4018/IJEBR.2017100105

Haider, A., & Saetang, S. (2017). Strategic IT Alignment in Service Sector. In S. Rozenes & Y. Cohen (Eds.), *Handbook of Research on Strategic Alliances and Value Co-Creation in the Service Industry* (pp. 231–258). Hershey, PA: IGI Global. doi:10.4018/978-1-5225-2084-9.ch012

Haider, A., & Tang, S. S. (2016). Maximising Value Through IT and Business Alignment: A Case of IT Governance Institutionalisation at a Thai Bank. *International Journal of Technology Diffusion*, *7*(3), 33–58. doi:10.4018/IJTD.2016070104

Hajilari, A. B., Ghadaksaz, M., & Fasghandis, G. S. (2017). Assessing Organizational Readiness for Implementing ERP System Using Fuzzy Expert System Approach. *International Journal of Enterprise Information Systems*, *13*(1), 67–85. doi:10.4018/IJEIS.2017010105

Haldorai, A., Ramu, A., & Murugan, S. (2018). Social Aware Cognitive Radio Networks: Effectiveness of Social Networks as a Strategic Tool for Organizational Business Management. In H. Bansal, G. Shrivastava, G. Nguyen, & L. Stanciu (Eds.), *Social Network Analytics for Contemporary Business Organizations* (pp. 188–202). Hershey, PA: IGI Global. doi:10.4018/978-1-5225-5097-6.ch010

Hall, O. P. Jr. (2017). Social Media Driven Management Education. *International Journal of Knowledge-Based Organizations*, *7*(2), 43–59. doi:10.4018/IJKBO.2017040104

Hanifah, H., Halim, H. A., Ahmad, N. H., & Vafaei-Zadeh, A. (2017). Innovation Culture as a Mediator Between Specific Human Capital and Innovation Performance Among Bumiputera SMEs in Malaysia. In N. Ahmad, T. Ramayah, H. Halim, & S. Rahman (Eds.), *Handbook of Research on Small and Medium Enterprises in Developing Countries* (pp. 261–279). Hershey, PA: IGI Global. doi:10.4018/978-1-5225-2165-5.ch012

Hartlieb, S., & Silvius, G. (2017). Handling Uncertainty in Project Management and Business Development: Similarities and Differences. In Y. Raydugin (Ed.), *Handbook of Research on Leveraging Risk and Uncertainties for Effective Project Management* (pp. 337–362). Hershey, PA: IGI Global. doi:10.4018/978-1-5225-1790-0.ch016

Hass, K. B. (2017). Living on the Edge: Managing Project Complexity. In Y. Raydugin (Ed.), *Handbook of Research on Leveraging Risk and Uncertainties for Effective Project Management* (pp. 177–201). Hershey, PA: IGI Global. doi:10.4018/978-1-5225-1790-0.ch009

Hassan, A., & Privitera, D. S. (2016). Google AdSense as a Mobile Technology in Education. In J. Holland (Ed.), *Wearable Technology and Mobile Innovations for Next-Generation Education* (pp. 200–223). Hershey, PA: IGI Global. doi:10.4018/978-1-5225-0069-8.ch011

Hassan, A., & Rahimi, R. (2016). Consuming "Innovation" in Tourism: Augmented Reality as an Innovation Tool in Digital Tourism Marketing. In N. Pappas & I. Bregoli (Eds.), *Global Dynamics in Travel, Tourism, and Hospitality* (pp. 130–147). Hershey, PA: IGI Global. doi:10.4018/978-1-5225-0201-2.ch008

Hawking, P., & Carmine Sellitto, C. (2017). Developing an Effective Strategy for Organizational Business Intelligence. In M. Tavana (Ed.), *Enterprise Information Systems and the Digitalization of Business Functions* (pp. 222–237). Hershey, PA: IGI Global. doi:10.4018/978-1-5225-2382-6.ch010

Hawking, P., & Sellitto, C. (2017). A Fast-Moving Consumer Goods Company and Business Intelligence Strategy Development. *International Journal of Enterprise Information Systems*, *13*(2), 22–33. doi:10.4018/IJEIS.2017040102

Hawking, P., & Sellitto, C. (2017). Business Intelligence Strategy: Two Case Studies. *International Journal of Business Intelligence Research*, *8*(2), 17–30. doi:10.4018/IJBIR.2017070102

Haynes, J. D., Arockiasamy, S., Al Rashdi, M., & Al Rashdi, S. (2016). Business and E Business Strategies for Coopetition and Thematic Management as a Sustained Basis for Ethics and Social Responsibility in Emerging Markets. In M. Al-Shammari & H. Masri (Eds.), *Ethical and Social Perspectives on Global Business Interaction in Emerging Markets* (pp. 25–39). Hershey, PA: IGI Global. doi:10.4018/978-1-4666-9864-2.ch002

Hee, W. J., Jalleh, G., Lai, H., & Lin, C. (2017). E-Commerce and IT Projects: Evaluation and Management Issues in Australian and Taiwanese Hospitals. *International Journal of Public Health Management and Ethics*, *2*(1), 69–90. doi:10.4018/IJPHME.2017010104

Hernandez, A. A. (2018). Exploring the Factors to Green IT Adoption of SMEs in the Philippines. *Journal of Cases on Information Technology*, *20*(2), 49–66. doi:10.4018/JCIT.2018040104

Hernandez, A. A., & Ona, S. E. (2016). Green IT Adoption: Lessons from the Philippines Business Process Outsourcing Industry. *International Journal of Social Ecology and Sustainable Development*, *7*(1), 1–34. doi:10.4018/IJSESD.2016010101

Hollman, A., Bickford, S., & Hollman, T. (2017). Cyber InSecurity: A Post-Mortem Attempt to Assess Cyber Problems from IT and Business Management Perspectives. *Journal of Cases on Information Technology*, *19*(3), 42–70. doi:10.4018/JCIT.2017070104

Igbinakhase, I. (2017). Responsible and Sustainable Management Practices in Developing and Developed Business Environments. In Z. Fields (Ed.), *Collective Creativity for Responsible and Sustainable Business Practice* (pp. 180–207). Hershey, PA: IGI Global. doi:10.4018/978-1-5225-1823-5.ch010

Ilahi, L., Ghannouchi, S. A., & Martinho, R. (2016). A Business Process Management Approach to Home Healthcare Processes: On the Gap between Intention and Reality. In M. Cruz-Cunha, I. Miranda, R. Martinho, & R. Rijo (Eds.), *Encyclopedia of E-Health and Telemedicine* (pp. 439–457). Hershey, PA: IGI Global. doi:10.4018/978-1-4666-9978-6.ch035

Iwata, J. J., & Hoskins, R. G. (2017). Managing Indigenous Knowledge in Tanzania: A Business Perspective. In P. Jain & N. Mnjama (Eds.), *Managing Knowledge Resources and Records in Modern Organizations* (pp. 198–214). Hershey, PA: IGI Global. doi:10.4018/978-1-5225-1965-2.ch012

Jabeen, F., Ahmad, S. Z., & Alkaabi, S. (2016). The Internationalization Decision-Making of United Arab Emirates Family Businesses. In N. Zakaria, A. Abdul-Talib, & N. Osman (Eds.), *Handbook of Research on Impacts of International Business and Political Affairs on the Global Economy* (pp. 1–22). Hershey, PA: IGI Global. doi:10.4018/978-1-4666-9806-2.ch001

Jain, P. (2017). Ethical and Legal Issues in Knowledge Management Life-Cycle in Business. In P. Jain & N. Mnjama (Eds.), *Managing Knowledge Resources and Records in Modern Organizations* (pp. 82–101). Hershey, PA: IGI Global. doi:10.4018/978-1-5225-1965-2.ch006

Jamali, D., Abdallah, H., & Matar, F. (2016). Opportunities and Challenges for CSR Mainstreaming in Business Schools. *International Journal of Technology and Educational Marketing*, *6*(2), 1–29. doi:10.4018/IJTEM.2016070101

James, S., & Hauli, E. (2017). Holistic Management Education at Tanzanian Rural Development Planning Institute. In N. Baporikar (Ed.), *Management Education for Global Leadership* (pp. 112–136). Hershey, PA: IGI Global. doi:10.4018/978-1-5225-1013-0.ch006

Janošková, M., Csikósová, A., & Čulková, K. (2018). Measurement of Company Performance as Part of Its Strategic Management. In R. Leon (Ed.), *Managerial Strategies for Business Sustainability During Turbulent Times* (pp. 309–335). Hershey, PA: IGI Global. doi:10.4018/978-1-5225-2716-9.ch017

Jean-Vasile, A., & Alecu, A. (2017). Theoretical and Practical Approaches in Understanding the Influences of Cost-Productivity-Profit Trinomial in Contemporary Enterprises. In A. Jean Vasile & D. Nicolò (Eds.), *Sustainable Entrepreneurship and Investments in the Green Economy* (pp. 28–62). Hershey, PA: IGI Global. doi:10.4018/978-1-5225-2075-7.ch002

Jha, D. G. (2016). Preparing for Information Technology Driven Changes. In S. Tiwari & L. Nafees (Eds.), *Innovative Management Education Pedagogies for Preparing Next-Generation Leaders* (pp. 258–274). Hershey, PA: IGI Global. doi:10.4018/978-1-4666-9691-4.ch015

Joia, L. A., & Correia, J. C. (2018). CIO Competencies From the IT Professional Perspective: Insights From Brazil. *Journal of Global Information Management, 26*(2), 74–103. doi:10.4018/JGIM.2018040104

Juma, A., & Mzera, N. (2017). Knowledge Management and Records Management and Competitive Advantage in Business. In P. Jain & N. Mnjama (Eds.), *Managing Knowledge Resources and Records in Modern Organizations* (pp. 15–28). Hershey, PA: IGI Global. doi:10.4018/978-1-5225-1965-2.ch002

K., I., & A, V. (2018). Monitoring and Auditing in the Cloud. In K. Munir (Ed.), *Cloud Computing Technologies for Green Enterprises* (pp. 318-350). Hershey, PA: IGI Global. doi:10.4018/978-1-5225-3038-1.ch013

Kabra, G., Ghosh, V., & Ramesh, A. (2018). Enterprise Integrated Business Process Management and Business Intelligence Framework for Business Process Sustainability. In A. Paul, D. Bhattacharyya, & S. Anand (Eds.), *Green Initiatives for Business Sustainability and Value Creation* (pp. 228–238). Hershey, PA: IGI Global. doi:10.4018/978-1-5225-2662-9.ch010

Kaoud, M. (2017). Investigation of Customer Knowledge Management: A Case Study Research. *International Journal of Service Science, Management, Engineering, and Technology, 8*(2), 12–22. doi:10.4018/IJSSMET.2017040102

Kara, M. E., & Fırat, S. Ü. (2016). Sustainability, Risk, and Business Intelligence in Supply Chains. In M. Erdoğdu, T. Arun, & I. Ahmad (Eds.), *Handbook of Research on Green Economic Development Initiatives and Strategies* (pp. 501–538). Hershey, PA: IGI Global. doi:10.4018/978-1-5225-0440-5.ch022

Katuu, S. (2018). A Comparative Assessment of Enterprise Content Management Maturity Models. In N. Gwangwava & M. Mutingi (Eds.), *E-Manufacturing and E-Service Strategies in Contemporary Organizations* (pp. 93–118). Hershey, PA: IGI Global. doi:10.4018/978-1-5225-3628-4.ch005

Khan, M. A. (2016). MNEs Management Strategies in Developing Countries: Establishing the Context. In M. Khan (Ed.), *Multinational Enterprise Management Strategies in Developing Countries* (pp. 1–33). Hershey, PA: IGI Global. doi:10.4018/978-1-5225-0276-0.ch001

Khan, M. A. (2016). Operational Approaches in Organizational Structure: A Case for MNEs in Developing Countries. In M. Khan (Ed.), *Multinational Enterprise Management Strategies in Developing Countries* (pp. 129–151). Hershey, PA: IGI Global. doi:10.4018/978-1-5225-0276-0.ch007

Kinnunen, S., Ylä-Kujala, A., Marttonen-Arola, S., Kärri, T., & Baglee, D. (2018). Internet of Things in Asset Management: Insights from Industrial Professionals and Academia. *International Journal of Service Science, Management, Engineering, and Technology, 9*(2), 104–119. doi:10.4018/IJSSMET.2018040105

Klein, A. Z., Sabino de Freitas, A., Machado, L., Freitas, J. C. Jr, Graziola, P. G. Jr, & Schlemmer, E. (2017). Virtual Worlds Applications for Management Education. In L. Tomei (Ed.), *Exploring the New Era of Technology-Infused Education* (pp. 279–299). Hershey, PA: IGI Global. doi:10.4018/978-1-5225-1709-2.ch017

Kożuch, B., & Jabłoński, A. (2017). Adopting the Concept of Business Models in Public Management. In M. Lewandowski & B. Kożuch (Eds.), *Public Sector Entrepreneurship and the Integration of Innovative Business Models* (pp. 10–46). Hershey, PA: IGI Global. doi:10.4018/978-1-5225-2215-7.ch002

Kumar, J., Adhikary, A., & Jha, A. (2017). Small Active Investors' Perceptions and Preferences Towards Tax Saving Mutual Fund Schemes in Eastern India: An Empirical Note. *International Journal of Asian Business and Information Management, 8*(2), 35–45. doi:10.4018/IJABIM.2017040103

Lassoued, Y., Bouzguenda, L., & Mahmoud, T. (2016). Context-Aware Business Process Versions Management. *International Journal of e-Collaboration, 12*(3), 7–33. doi:10.4018/IJeC.2016070102

Lavassani, K. M., & Movahedi, B. (2017). Applications Driven Information Systems: Beyond Networks toward Business Ecosystems. *International Journal of Innovation in the Digital Economy, 8*(1), 61–75. doi:10.4018/IJIDE.2017010104

Lazzareschi, V. H., & Brito, M. S. (2017). Strategic Information Management: Proposal of Business Project Model. In G. Jamil, A. Soares, & C. Pessoa (Eds.), *Handbook of Research on Information Management for Effective Logistics and Supply Chains* (pp. 59–88). Hershey, PA: IGI Global. doi:10.4018/978-1-5225-0973-8.ch004

Lederer, M., Kurz, M., & Lazarov, P. (2017). Usage and Suitability of Methods for Strategic Business Process Initiatives: A Multi Case Study Research. *International Journal of Productivity Management and Assessment Technologies, 5*(1), 40–51. doi:10.4018/IJPMAT.2017010103

Lee, I. (2017). A Social Enterprise Business Model and a Case Study of Pacific Community Ventures (PCV). In V. Potocan, M. Üngan, & Z. Nedelko (Eds.), *Handbook of Research on Managerial Solutions in Non-Profit Organizations* (pp. 182–204). Hershey, PA: IGI Global. doi:10.4018/978-1-5225-0731-4.ch009

Lee, L. J., & Leu, J. (2016). Exploring the Effectiveness of IT Application and Value Method in the Innovation Performance of Enterprise. *International Journal of Enterprise Information Systems, 12*(2), 47–65. doi:10.4018/IJEIS.2016040104

Lee, Y. (2016). Alignment Effect of Entrepreneurial Orientation and Marketing Orientation on Firm Performance. *International Journal of Customer Relationship Marketing and Management, 7*(4), 58–69. doi:10.4018/IJCRMM.2016100104

Leon, L. A., Seal, K. C., Przasnyski, Z. H., & Wiedenman, I. (2017). Skills and Competencies Required for Jobs in Business Analytics: A Content Analysis of Job Advertisements Using Text Mining. *International Journal of Business Intelligence Research, 8*(1), 1–25. doi:10.4018/IJBIR.2017010101

Leu, J., Lee, L. J., & Krischke, A. (2016). Value Engineering-Based Method for Implementing the ISO14001 System in the Green Supply Chains. *International Journal of Strategic Decision Sciences, 7*(4), 1–20. doi:10.4018/IJSDS.2016100101

Levy, C. L., & Elias, N. I. (2017). SOHO Users' Perceptions of Reliability and Continuity of Cloud-Based Services. In M. Moore (Ed.), *Cybersecurity Breaches and Issues Surrounding Online Threat Protection* (pp. 248–287). Hershey, PA: IGI Global. doi:10.4018/978-1-5225-1941-6.ch011

Levy, M. (2018). Change Management Serving Knowledge Management and Organizational Development: Reflections and Review. In N. Baporikar (Ed.), *Global Practices in Knowledge Management for Societal and Organizational Development* (pp. 256–270). Hershey, PA: IGI Global. doi:10.4018/978-1-5225-3009-1.ch012

Lewandowski, M. (2017). Public Organizations and Business Model Innovation: The Role of Public Service Design. In M. Lewandowski & B. Kożuch (Eds.), *Public Sector Entrepreneurship and the Integration of Innovative Business Models* (pp. 47–72). Hershey, PA: IGI Global. doi:10.4018/978-1-5225-2215-7.ch003

Lhannaoui, H., Kabbaj, M. I., & Bakkoury, Z. (2017). A Survey of Risk-Aware Business Process Modelling. *International Journal of Risk and Contingency Management, 6*(3), 14–26. doi:10.4018/IJRCM.2017070102

Li, J., Sun, W., Jiang, W., Yang, H., & Zhang, L. (2017). How the Nature of Exogenous Shocks and Crises Impact Company Performance?: The Effects of Industry Characteristics. *International Journal of Risk and Contingency Management, 6*(4), 40–55. doi:10.4018/IJRCM.2017100103

Lu, C., & Liu, S. (2016). Cultural Tourism O2O Business Model Innovation-A Case Study of CTrip. *Journal of Electronic Commerce in Organizations, 14*(2), 16–31. doi:10.4018/JECO.2016040102

Machen, B., Hosseini, M. R., Wood, A., & Bakhshi, J. (2016). An Investigation into using SAP-PS as a Multidimensional Project Control System (MPCS). *International Journal of Enterprise Information Systems, 12*(2), 66–81. doi:10.4018/IJEIS.2016040105

Malega, P. (2017). Small and Medium Enterprises in the Slovak Republic: Status and Competitiveness of SMEs in the Global Markets and Possibilities of Optimization. In M. Vemić (Ed.), *Optimal Management Strategies in Small and Medium Enterprises* (pp. 102–124). Hershey, PA: IGI Global. doi:10.4018/978-1-5225-1949-2.ch006

Malewska, K. M. (2017). Intuition in Decision-Making on the Example of a Non-Profit Organization. In V. Potocan, M. Üngan, & Z. Nedelko (Eds.), *Handbook of Research on Managerial Solutions in Non-Profit Organizations* (pp. 378–399). Hershey, PA: IGI Global. doi:10.4018/978-1-5225-0731-4.ch018

Maroofi, F. (2017). Entrepreneurial Orientation and Organizational Learning Ability Analysis for Innovation and Firm Performance. In N. Baporikar (Ed.), *Innovation and Shifting Perspectives in Management Education* (pp. 144–165). Hershey, PA: IGI Global. doi:10.4018/978-1-5225-1019-2.ch007

Martins, P. V., & Zacarias, M. (2017). A Web-based Tool for Business Process Improvement. *International Journal of Web Portals, 9*(2), 68–84. doi:10.4018/IJWP.2017070104

Matthies, B., & Coners, A. (2017). Exploring the Conceptual Nature of e-Business Projects. *Journal of Electronic Commerce in Organizations, 15*(3), 33–63. doi:10.4018/JECO.2017070103

McKee, J. (2018). Architecture as a Tool to Solve Business Planning Problems. In M. Khosrow-Pour, D.B.A. (Ed.), Encyclopedia of Information Science and Technology, Fourth Edition (pp. 573-586). Hershey, PA: IGI Global. doi:10.4018/978-1-5225-2255-3.ch050

McMurray, A. J., Cross, J., & Caponecchia, C. (2018). The Risk Management Profession in Australia: Business Continuity Plan Practices. In N. Bajgoric (Ed.), *Always-On Enterprise Information Systems for Modern Organizations* (pp. 112–129). Hershey, PA: IGI Global. doi:10.4018/978-1-5225-3704-5.ch006

Meddah, I. H., & Belkadi, K. (2018). Mining Patterns Using Business Process Management. In R. Hamou (Ed.), *Handbook of Research on Biomimicry in Information Retrieval and Knowledge Management* (pp. 78–89). Hershey, PA: IGI Global. doi:10.4018/978-1-5225-3004-6.ch005

Mendes, L. (2017). TQM and Knowledge Management: An Integrated Approach Towards Tacit Knowledge Management. In D. Jaziri-Bouagina & G. Jamil (Eds.), *Handbook of Research on Tacit Knowledge Management for Organizational Success* (pp. 236–263). Hershey, PA: IGI Global. doi:10.4018/978-1-5225-2394-9.ch009

Mnjama, N. M. (2017). Preservation of Recorded Information in Public and Private Sector Organizations. In P. Jain & N. Mnjama (Eds.), *Managing Knowledge Resources and Records in Modern Organizations* (pp. 149–167). Hershey, PA: IGI Global. doi:10.4018/978-1-5225-1965-2.ch009

Mokoqama, M., & Fields, Z. (2017). Principles of Responsible Management Education (PRME): Call for Responsible Management Education. In Z. Fields (Ed.), *Collective Creativity for Responsible and Sustainable Business Practice* (pp. 229–241). Hershey, PA: IGI Global. doi:10.4018/978-1-5225-1823-5.ch012

Muniapan, B. (2017). Philosophy and Management: The Relevance of Vedanta in Management. In P. Ordóñez de Pablos (Ed.), *Managerial Strategies and Solutions for Business Success in Asia* (pp. 124–139). Hershey, PA: IGI Global. doi:10.4018/978-1-5225-1886-0.ch007

Muniapan, B., Gregory, M. L., & Ling, L. A. (2016). Marketing Education in Sarawak: Looking at It from the Employers' Viewpoint. In B. Smith & A. Porath (Eds.), *Global Perspectives on Contemporary Marketing Education* (pp. 112–130). Hershey, PA: IGI Global. doi:10.4018/978-1-4666-9784-3.ch008

Murad, S. E., & Dowaji, S. (2017). Using Value-Based Approach for Managing Cloud-Based Services. In A. Turuk, B. Sahoo, & S. Addya (Eds.), *Resource Management and Efficiency in Cloud Computing Environments* (pp. 33–60). Hershey, PA: IGI Global. doi:10.4018/978-1-5225-1721-4.ch002

Mutahar, A. M., Daud, N. M., Thurasamy, R., Isaac, O., & Abdulsalam, R. (2018). The Mediating of Perceived Usefulness and Perceived Ease of Use: The Case of Mobile Banking in Yemen. *International Journal of Technology Diffusion, 9*(2), 21–40. doi:10.4018/IJTD.2018040102

Naidoo, V. (2017). E-Learning and Management Education at African Universities. In N. Baporikar (Ed.), *Management Education for Global Leadership* (pp. 181–201). Hershey, PA: IGI Global. doi:10.4018/978-1-5225-1013-0.ch009

Naidoo, V., & Igbinakhase, I. (2018). Opportunities and Challenges of Knowledge Retention in SMEs. In N. Baporikar (Ed.), *Knowledge Integration Strategies for Entrepreneurship and Sustainability* (pp. 70–94). Hershey, PA: IGI Global. doi:10.4018/978-1-5225-5115-7.ch004

Nayak, S., & Prabhu, N. (2017). Paradigm Shift in Management Education: Need for a Cross Functional Perspective. In N. Baporikar (Ed.), *Management Education for Global Leadership* (pp. 241–255). Hershey, PA: IGI Global. doi:10.4018/978-1-5225-1013-0.ch012

Ndede-Amadi, A. A. (2016). Student Interest in the IS Specialization as Predictor of the Success Potential of New Information Systems Programmes within the Schools of Business in Kenyan Public Universities. *International Journal of Information Systems and Social Change, 7*(2), 63–79. doi:10.4018/IJISSC.2016040104

Nedelko, Z., & Potocan, V. (2016). Management Practices for Processes Optimization: Case of Slovenia. In G. Alor-Hernández, C. Sánchez-Ramírez, & J. García-Alcaraz (Eds.), *Handbook of Research on Managerial Strategies for Achieving Optimal Performance in Industrial Processes* (pp. 545–561). Hershey, PA: IGI Global. doi:10.4018/978-1-5225-0130-5.ch025

Nedelko, Z., & Potocan, V. (2017). Management Solutions in Non-Profit Organizations: Case of Slovenia. In V. Potocan, M. Ünğan, & Z. Nedelko (Eds.), *Handbook of Research on Managerial Solutions in Non-Profit Organizations* (pp. 1–22). Hershey, PA: IGI Global. doi:10.4018/978-1-5225-0731-4.ch001

Nedelko, Z., & Potocan, V. (2017). Priority of Management Tools Utilization among Managers: International Comparison. In V. Wang (Ed.), *Encyclopedia of Strategic Leadership and Management* (pp. 1083–1094). Hershey, PA: IGI Global. doi:10.4018/978-1-5225-1049-9.ch075

Nedelko, Z., Raudeliūnienė, J., & Črešnar, R. (2018). Knowledge Dynamics in Supply Chain Management. In N. Baporikar (Ed.), *Knowledge Integration Strategies for Entrepreneurship and Sustainability* (pp. 150–166). Hershey, PA: IGI Global. doi:10.4018/978-1-5225-5115-7.ch008

Nguyen, H. T., & Hipsher, S. A. (2018). Innovation and Creativity Used by Private Sector Firms in a Resources-Constrained Environment. In S. Hipsher (Ed.), *Examining the Private Sector's Role in Wealth Creation and Poverty Reduction* (pp. 219–238). Hershey, PA: IGI Global. doi:10.4018/978-1-5225-3117-3.ch010

Nycz, M., & Pólkowski, Z. (2016). Business Intelligence as a Modern IT Supporting Management of Local Government Units in Poland. *International Journal of Knowledge and Systems Science, 7*(4), 1–18. doi:10.4018/IJKSS.2016100101

Obaji, N. O., Senin, A. A., & Olugu, M. U. (2016). Supportive Government Policy as a Mechanism for Business Incubation Performance in Nigeria. *International Journal of Information Systems and Social Change, 7*(4), 52–66. doi:10.4018/IJISSC.2016100103

Obicci, P. A. (2017). Risk Sharing in a Partnership. In *Risk Management Strategies in Public-Private Partnerships* (pp. 115–152). Hershey, PA: IGI Global. doi:10.4018/978-1-5225-2503-5.ch004

Obidallah, W. J., & Raahemi, B. (2017). Managing Changes in Service Oriented Virtual Organizations: A Structural and Procedural Framework to Facilitate the Process of Change. *Journal of Electronic Commerce in Organizations, 15*(1), 59–83. doi:10.4018/JECO.2017010104

Ojasalo, J., & Ojasalo, K. (2016). Service Logic Business Model Canvas for Lean Development of SMEs and Start-Ups. In N. Baporikar (Ed.), *Handbook of Research on Entrepreneurship in the Contemporary Knowledge-Based Global Economy* (pp. 217–243). Hershey, PA: IGI Global. doi:10.4018/978-1-4666-8798-1.ch010

Ojo, O. (2017). Impact of Innovation on the Entrepreneurial Success in Selected Business Enterprises in South-West Nigeria. *International Journal of Innovation in the Digital Economy, 8*(2), 29–38. doi:10.4018/IJIDE.2017040103

Okdinawati, L., Simatupang, T. M., & Sunitiyoso, Y. (2017). Multi-Agent Reinforcement Learning for Value Co-Creation of Collaborative Transportation Management (CTM). *International Journal of Information Systems and Supply Chain Management, 10*(3), 84–95. doi:10.4018/IJISSCM.2017070105

Ortner, E., Mevius, M., Wiedmann, P., & Kurz, F. (2016). Design of Interactional Decision Support Applications for E-Participation in Smart Cities. *International Journal of Electronic Government Research, 12*(2), 18–38. doi:10.4018/IJEGR.2016040102

Pal, K. (2018). Building High Quality Big Data-Based Applications in Supply Chains. In A. Kumar & S. Saurav (Eds.), *Supply Chain Management Strategies and Risk Assessment in Retail Environments* (pp. 1–24). Hershey, PA: IGI Global. doi:10.4018/978-1-5225-3056-5.ch001

Palos-Sanchez, P. R., & Correia, M. B. (2018). Perspectives of the Adoption of Cloud Computing in the Tourism Sector. In J. Rodrigues, C. Ramos, P. Cardoso, & C. Henriques (Eds.), *Handbook of Research on Technological Developments for Cultural Heritage and eTourism Applications* (pp. 377–400). Hershey, PA: IGI Global. doi:10.4018/978-1-5225-2927-9.ch018

Parry, V. K., & Lind, M. L. (2016). Alignment of Business Strategy and Information Technology Considering Information Technology Governance, Project Portfolio Control, and Risk Management. *International Journal of Information Technology Project Management, 7*(4), 21–37. doi:10.4018/IJITPM.2016100102

Pashkova, N., Trujillo-Barrera, A., Apostolakis, G., Van Dijk, G., Drakos, P. D., & Baourakis, G. (2016). Business Management Models of Microfinance Institutions (MFIs) in Africa: A Study into Their Enabling Environments. *International Journal of Food and Beverage Manufacturing and Business Models, 1*(2), 63–82. doi:10.4018/IJFBMBM.2016070105

Patiño, B. E. (2017). New Generation Management by Convergence and Individual Identity: A Systemic and Human-Oriented Approach. In N. Baporikar (Ed.), *Innovation and Shifting Perspectives in Management Education* (pp. 119–143). Hershey, PA: IGI Global. doi:10.4018/978-1-5225-1019-2.ch006

Pawliczek, A., & Rössler, M. (2017). Knowledge of Management Tools and Systems in SMEs: Knowledge Transfer in Management. In A. Bencsik (Ed.), *Knowledge Management Initiatives and Strategies in Small and Medium Enterprises* (pp. 180–203). Hershey, PA: IGI Global. doi:10.4018/978-1-5225-1642-2.ch009

Pejic-Bach, M., Omazic, M. A., Aleksic, A., & Zoroja, J. (2018). Knowledge-Based Decision Making: A Multi-Case Analysis. In R. Leon (Ed.), *Managerial Strategies for Business Sustainability During Turbulent Times* (pp. 160–184). Hershey, PA: IGI Global. doi:10.4018/978-1-5225-2716-9.ch009

Perano, M., Hysa, X., & Calabrese, M. (2018). Strategic Planning, Cultural Context, and Business Continuity Management: Business Cases in the City of Shkoder. In A. Presenza & L. Sheehan (Eds.), *Geopolitics and Strategic Management in the Global Economy* (pp. 57–77). Hershey, PA: IGI Global. doi:10.4018/978-1-5225-2673-5.ch004

Pereira, R., Mira da Silva, M., & Lapão, L. V. (2017). IT Governance Maturity Patterns in Portuguese Healthcare. In S. De Haes & W. Van Grembergen (Eds.), *Strategic IT Governance and Alignment in Business Settings* (pp. 24–52). Hershey, PA: IGI Global. doi:10.4018/978-1-5225-0861-8.ch002

Perez-Uribe, R., & Ocampo-Guzman, D. (2016). Conflict within Colombian Family Owned SMEs: An Explosive Blend between Feelings and Business. In J. Saiz-Álvarez (Ed.), *Handbook of Research on Social Entrepreneurship and Solidarity Economics* (pp. 329–354). Hershey, PA: IGI Global. doi:10.4018/978-1-5225-0097-1.ch017

Pérez-Uribe, R. I., Torres, D. A., Jurado, S. P., & Prada, D. M. (2018). Cloud Tools for the Development of Project Management in SMEs. In R. Perez-Uribe, C. Salcedo-Perez, & D. Ocampo-Guzman (Eds.), *Handbook of Research on Intrapreneurship and Organizational Sustainability in SMEs* (pp. 95–120). Hershey, PA: IGI Global. doi:10.4018/978-1-5225-3543-0.ch005

Petrisor, I., & Cozmiuc, D. (2017). Global Supply Chain Management Organization at Siemens in the Advent of Industry 4.0. In L. Saglietto & C. Cezanne (Eds.), *Global Intermediation and Logistics Service Providers* (pp. 123–142). Hershey, PA: IGI Global. doi:10.4018/978-1-5225-2133-4.ch007

Pierce, J. M., Velliaris, D. M., & Edwards, J. (2017). A Living Case Study: A Journey Not a Destination. In N. Silton (Ed.), *Exploring the Benefits of Creativity in Education, Media, and the Arts* (pp. 158–178). Hershey, PA: IGI Global. doi:10.4018/978-1-5225-0504-4.ch008

Radosavljevic, M., & Andjelkovic, A. (2017). Multi-Criteria Decision Making Approach for Choosing Business Process for the Improvement: Upgrading of the Six Sigma Methodology. In J. Stanković, P. Delias, S. Marinković, & S. Rochhia (Eds.), *Tools and Techniques for Economic Decision Analysis* (pp. 225–247). Hershey, PA: IGI Global. doi:10.4018/978-1-5225-0959-2.ch011

Radovic, V. M. (2017). Corporate Sustainability and Responsibility and Disaster Risk Reduction: A Serbian Overview. In M. Camilleri (Ed.), *CSR 2.0 and the New Era of Corporate Citizenship* (pp. 147–164). Hershey, PA: IGI Global. doi:10.4018/978-1-5225-1842-6.ch008

Raghunath, K. M., Devi, S. L., & Patro, C. S. (2018). Impact of Risk Assessment Models on Risk Factors: A Holistic Outlook. In K. Strang, M. Korstanje, & N. Vajjhala (Eds.), *Research, Practices, and Innovations in Global Risk and Contingency Management* (pp. 134–153). Hershey, PA: IGI Global. doi:10.4018/978-1-5225-4754-9.ch008

Raman, A., & Goyal, D. P. (2017). Extending IMPLEMENT Framework for Enterprise Information Systems Implementation to Information System Innovation. In M. Tavana (Ed.), *Enterprise Information Systems and the Digitalization of Business Functions* (pp. 137–177). Hershey, PA: IGI Global. doi:10.4018/978-1-5225-2382-6.ch007

Rao, Y., & Zhang, Y. (2017). The Construction and Development of Academic Library Digital Special Subject Databases. In L. Ruan, Q. Zhu, & Y. Ye (Eds.), *Academic Library Development and Administration in China* (pp. 163–183). Hershey, PA: IGI Global. doi:10.4018/978-1-5225-0550-1.ch010

Ravasan, A. Z., Mohammadi, M. M., & Hamidi, H. (2018). An Investigation Into the Critical Success Factors of Implementing Information Technology Service Management Frameworks. In K. Jakobs (Ed.), *Corporate and Global Standardization Initiatives in Contemporary Society* (pp. 200–218). Hershey, PA: IGI Global. doi:10.4018/978-1-5225-5320-5.ch009

Renna, P., Izzo, C., & Romaniello, T. (2016). The Business Process Management Systems to Support Continuous Improvements. In W. Nuninger & J. Châtelet (Eds.), *Handbook of Research on Quality Assurance and Value Management in Higher Education* (pp. 237–256). Hershey, PA: IGI Global. doi:10.4018/978-1-5225-0024-7.ch009

Rezaie, S., Mirabedini, S. J., & Abtahi, A. (2018). Designing a Model for Implementation of Business Intelligence in the Banking Industry. *International Journal of Enterprise Information Systems, 14*(1), 77–103. doi:10.4018/IJEIS.2018010105

Riccò, R. (2016). Diversity Management: Bringing Equality, Equity, and Inclusion in the Workplace. In J. Prescott (Ed.), *Handbook of Research on Race, Gender, and the Fight for Equality* (pp. 335–359). Hershey, PA: IGI Global. doi:10.4018/978-1-5225-0047-6.ch015

Romano, L., Grimaldi, R., & Colasuonno, F. S. (2017). Demand Management as a Success Factor in Project Portfolio Management. In L. Romano (Ed.), *Project Portfolio Management Strategies for Effective Organizational Operations* (pp. 202–219). Hershey, PA: IGI Global. doi:10.4018/978-1-5225-2151-8.ch008

Rostek, K. B. (2016). Risk Management: Role and Importance in Business Organization. In D. Jakóbczak (Ed.), *Analyzing Risk through Probabilistic Modeling in Operations Research* (pp. 149–178). Hershey, PA: IGI Global. doi:10.4018/978-1-4666-9458-3.ch007

Rouhani, S., & Savoji, S. R. (2016). A Success Assessment Model for BI Tools Implementation: An Empirical Study of Banking Industry. *International Journal of Business Intelligence Research, 7*(1), 25–44. doi:10.4018/IJBIR.2016010103

Ruan, Z. (2016). A Corpus-Based Functional Analysis of Complex Nominal Groups in Written Business Discourse: The Case of "Business". *International Journal of Computer-Assisted Language Learning and Teaching, 6*(2), 74–90. doi:10.4018/IJCALLT.2016040105

Ruhi, U. (2018). Towards an Interdisciplinary Socio-Technical Definition of Virtual Communities. In M. Khosrow-Pour, D.B.A. (Ed.), Encyclopedia of Information Science and Technology, Fourth Edition (pp. 4278-4295). Hershey, PA: IGI Global. doi:10.4018/978-1-5225-2255-3.ch371

Ryan, J., Doster, B., Daily, S., & Lewis, C. (2016). A Case Study Perspective for Balanced Perioperative Workflow Achievement through Data-Driven Process Improvement. *International Journal of Healthcare Information Systems and Informatics, 11*(3), 19–41. doi:10.4018/IJHISI.2016070102

Safari, M. R., & Jiang, Q. (2018). The Theory and Practice of IT Governance Maturity and Strategies Alignment: Evidence From Banking Industry. *Journal of Global Information Management, 26*(2), 127–146. doi:10.4018/JGIM.2018040106

Sahoo, J., Pati, B., & Mohanty, B. (2017). Knowledge Management as an Academic Discipline: An Assessment. In B. Gunjal (Ed.), *Managing Knowledge and Scholarly Assets in Academic Libraries* (pp. 99–126). Hershey, PA: IGI Global. doi:10.4018/978-1-5225-1741-2.ch005

Saini, D. (2017). Relevance of Teaching Values and Ethics in Management Education. In N. Baporikar (Ed.), *Management Education for Global Leadership* (pp. 90–111). Hershey, PA: IGI Global. doi:10.4018/978-1-5225-1013-0.ch005

Sambhanthan, A. (2017). Assessing and Benchmarking Sustainability in Organisations: An Integrated Conceptual Model. *International Journal of Systems and Service-Oriented Engineering, 7*(4), 22–43. doi:10.4018/IJSSOE.2017100102

Sambhanthan, A., & Potdar, V. (2017). A Study of the Parameters Impacting Sustainability in Information Technology Organizations. *International Journal of Knowledge-Based Organizations, 7*(3), 27–39. doi:10.4018/IJKBO.2017070103

Sánchez-Fernández, M. D., & Manríquez, M. R. (2018). The Entrepreneurial Spirit Based on Social Values: The Digital Generation. In P. Isaias & L. Carvalho (Eds.), *User Innovation and the Entrepreneurship Phenomenon in the Digital Economy* (pp. 173–193). Hershey, PA: IGI Global. doi:10.4018/978-1-5225-2826-5.ch009

Sanchez-Ruiz, L., & Blanco, B. (2017). Process Management for SMEs: Barriers, Enablers, and Benefits. In M. Vemić (Ed.), *Optimal Management Strategies in Small and Medium Enterprises* (pp. 293–319). Hershey, PA: IGI Global. doi:10.4018/978-1-5225-1949-2.ch014

Sanz, L. F., Gómez-Pérez, J., & Castillo-Martinez, A. (2018). Analysis of the European ICT Competence Frameworks. In V. Ahuja & S. Rathore (Eds.), *Multidisciplinary Perspectives on Human Capital and Information Technology Professionals* (pp. 225–245). Hershey, PA: IGI Global. doi:10.4018/978-1-5225-5297-0.ch012

Sarvepalli, A., & Godin, J. (2017). Business Process Management in the Classroom. *Journal of Cases on Information Technology, 19*(2), 17–28. doi:10.4018/JCIT.2017040102

Satpathy, B., & Muniapan, B. (2016). Ancient Wisdom for Transformational Leadership and Its Insights from the Bhagavad-Gita. In U. Aung & P. Ordoñez de Pablos (Eds.), *Managerial Strategies and Practice in the Asian Business Sector* (pp. 1–10). Hershey, PA: IGI Global. doi:10.4018/978-1-4666-9758-4.ch001

Saygili, E. E., Ozturkoglu, Y., & Kocakulah, M. C. (2017). End Users' Perceptions of Critical Success Factors in ERP Applications. *International Journal of Enterprise Information Systems, 13*(4), 58–75. doi:10.4018/IJEIS.2017100104

Saygili, E. E., & Saygili, A. T. (2017). Contemporary Issues in Enterprise Information Systems: A Critical Review of CSFs in ERP Implementations. In M. Tavana (Ed.), *Enterprise Information Systems and the Digitalization of Business Functions* (pp. 120–136). Hershey, PA: IGI Global. doi:10.4018/978-1-5225-2382-6.ch006

Seidenstricker, S., & Antonino, A. (2018). Business Model Innovation-Oriented Technology Management for Emergent Technologies. In M. Khosrow-Pour, D.B.A. (Ed.), Encyclopedia of Information Science and Technology, Fourth Edition (pp. 4560-4569). Hershey, PA: IGI Global. doi:10.4018/978-1-5225-2255-3.ch396

Senaratne, S., & Gunarathne, A. D. (2017). Excellence Perspective for Management Education from a Global Accountants' Hub in Asia. In N. Baporikar (Ed.), *Management Education for Global Leadership* (pp. 158–180). Hershey, PA: IGI Global. doi:10.4018/978-1-5225-1013-0.ch008

Sensuse, D. I., & Cahyaningsih, E. (2018). Knowledge Management Models: A Summative Review. *International Journal of Information Systems in the Service Sector, 10*(1), 71–100. doi:10.4018/IJISSS.2018010105

Sensuse, D. I., Wibowo, W. C., & Cahyaningsih, E. (2016). Indonesian Government Knowledge Management Model: A Theoretical Model. *Information Resources Management Journal, 29*(1), 91–108. doi:10.4018/irmj.2016010106

Seth, M., Goyal, D., & Kiran, R. (2017). Diminution of Impediments in Implementation of Supply Chain Management Information System for Enhancing its Effectiveness in Indian Automobile Industry. *Journal of Global Information Management, 25*(3), 1–20. doi:10.4018/JGIM.2017070101

Seyal, A. H., & Rahman, M. N. (2017). Investigating Impact of Inter-Organizational Factors in Measuring ERP Systems Success: Bruneian Perspectives. In M. Tavana (Ed.), *Enterprise Information Systems and the Digitalization of Business Functions* (pp. 178–204). Hershey, PA: IGI Global. doi:10.4018/978-1-5225-2382-6.ch008

Shaikh, A. A., & Karjaluoto, H. (2016). On Some Misconceptions Concerning Digital Banking and Alternative Delivery Channels. *International Journal of E-Business Research, 12*(3), 1–16. doi:10.4018/IJEBR.2016070101

Shams, S. M. (2016). Stakeholder Relationship Management in Online Business and Competitive Value Propositions: Evidence from the Sports Industry. *International Journal of Online Marketing, 6*(2), 1–17. doi:10.4018/IJOM.2016040101

Shamsuzzoha, A. (2016). Management of Risk and Resilience within Collaborative Business Network. In R. Addo-Tenkorang, J. Kantola, P. Helo, & A. Shamsuzzoha (Eds.), *Supply Chain Strategies and the Engineer-to-Order Approach* (pp. 143–159). Hershey, PA: IGI Global. doi:10.4018/978-1-5225-0021-6.ch008

Shaqrah, A. A. (2018). Analyzing Business Intelligence Systems Based on 7s Model of McKinsey. *International Journal of Business Intelligence Research, 9*(1), 53–63. doi:10.4018/IJBIR.2018010104

Sharma, A. J. (2017). Enhancing Sustainability through Experiential Learning in Management Education. In N. Baporikar (Ed.), *Management Education for Global Leadership* (pp. 256–274). Hershey, PA: IGI Global. doi:10.4018/978-1-5225-1013-0.ch013

Shetty, K. P. (2017). Responsible Global Leadership: Ethical Challenges in Management Education. In N. Baporikar (Ed.), *Innovation and Shifting Perspectives in Management Education* (pp. 194–223). Hershey, PA: IGI Global. doi:10.4018/978-1-5225-1019-2.ch009

Sinthupundaja, J., & Kohda, Y. (2017). Effects of Corporate Social Responsibility and Creating Shared Value on Sustainability. *International Journal of Sustainable Entrepreneurship and Corporate Social Responsibility*, *2*(1), 27–38. doi:10.4018/IJSECSR.2017010103

Škarica, I., & Hrgović, A. V. (2018). Implementation of Total Quality Management Principles in Public Health Institutes in the Republic of Croatia. *International Journal of Productivity Management and Assessment Technologies*, *6*(1), 1–16. doi:10.4018/IJPMAT.2018010101

Smuts, H., Kotzé, P., Van der Merwe, A., & Loock, M. (2017). Framework for Managing Shared Knowledge in an Information Systems Outsourcing Context. *International Journal of Knowledge Management*, *13*(4), 1–30. doi:10.4018/IJKM.2017100101

Soares, E. R., & Zaidan, F. H. (2016). Information Architecture and Business Modeling in Modern Organizations of Information Technology: Professional Career Plan in Organizations IT. In G. Jamil, J. Poças Rascão, F. Ribeiro, & A. Malheiro da Silva (Eds.), *Handbook of Research on Information Architecture and Management in Modern Organizations* (pp. 439–457). Hershey, PA: IGI Global. doi:10.4018/978-1-4666-8637-3.ch020

Sousa, M. J., Cruz, R., Dias, I., & Caracol, C. (2017). Information Management Systems in the Supply Chain. In G. Jamil, A. Soares, & C. Pessoa (Eds.), *Handbook of Research on Information Management for Effective Logistics and Supply Chains* (pp. 469–485). Hershey, PA: IGI Global. doi:10.4018/978-1-5225-0973-8.ch025

Spremic, M., Turulja, L., & Bajgoric, N. (2018). Two Approaches in Assessing Business Continuity Management Attitudes in the Organizational Context. In N. Bajgoric (Ed.), *Always-On Enterprise Information Systems for Modern Organizations* (pp. 159–183). Hershey, PA: IGI Global. doi:10.4018/978-1-5225-3704-5.ch008

Steenkamp, A. L. (2018). Some Insights in Computer Science and Information Technology. In *Examining the Changing Role of Supervision in Doctoral Research Projects: Emerging Research and Opportunities* (pp. 113–133). Hershey, PA: IGI Global. doi:10.4018/978-1-5225-2610-0.ch005

Studdard, N., Dawson, M., Burton, S. L., Jackson, N., Leonard, B., Quisenberry, W., & Rahim, E. (2016). Nurturing Social Entrepreneurship and Building Social Entrepreneurial Self-Efficacy: Focusing on Primary and Secondary Schooling to Develop Future Social Entrepreneurs. In Z. Fields (Ed.), *Incorporating Business Models and Strategies into Social Entrepreneurship* (pp. 154–175). Hershey, PA: IGI Global. doi:10.4018/978-1-4666-8748-6.ch010

Sun, Z. (2016). A Framework for Developing Management Intelligent Systems. *International Journal of Systems and Service-Oriented Engineering*, *6*(1), 37–53. doi:10.4018/IJSSOE.2016010103

Swami, B., & Mphele, G. T. (2016). Problems Preventing Growth of Small Entrepreneurs: A Case Study of a Few Small Entrepreneurs in Botswana Sub-Urban Areas. In N. Baporikar (Ed.), *Handbook of Research on Entrepreneurship in the Contemporary Knowledge-Based Global Economy* (pp. 479–508). Hershey, PA: IGI Global. doi:10.4018/978-1-4666-8798-1.ch020

Tabach, A., & Croteau, A. (2017). Configurations of Information Technology Governance Practices and Business Unit Performance. *International Journal of IT/Business Alignment and Governance*, *8*(2), 1–27. doi:10.4018/IJITBAG.2017070101

Talaue, G. M., & Iqbal, T. (2017). Assessment of e-Business Mode of Selected Private Universities in the Philippines and Pakistan. *International Journal of Online Marketing*, *7*(4), 63–77. doi:10.4018/IJOM.2017100105

Tam, G. C. (2017). Project Manager Sustainability Competence. In *Managerial Strategies and Green Solutions for Project Sustainability* (pp. 178–207). Hershey, PA: IGI Global. doi:10.4018/978-1-5225-2371-0.ch008

Tambo, T. (2018). Fashion Retail Innovation: About Context, Antecedents, and Outcome in Technological Change Projects. In I. Management Association (Ed.), Fashion and Textiles: Breakthroughs in Research and Practice (pp. 233-260). Hershey, PA: IGI Global. doi:10.4018/978-1-5225-3432-7.ch010

Tambo, T., & Mikkelsen, O. E. (2016). Fashion Supply Chain Optimization: Linking Make-to-Order Purchasing and B2B E-Commerce. In S. Joshi & R. Joshi (Eds.), *Designing and Implementing Global Supply Chain Management* (pp. 1–21). Hershey, PA: IGI Global. doi:10.4018/978-1-4666-9720-1.ch001

Tandon, K. (2016). Innovative Andragogy: The Paradigm Shift to Heutagogy. In S. Tiwari & L. Nafees (Eds.), *Innovative Management Education Pedagogies for Preparing Next-Generation Leaders* (pp. 238–257). Hershey, PA: IGI Global. doi:10.4018/978-1-4666-9691-4.ch014

Tantau, A. D., & Frăţilă, L. C. (2018). Information and Management System for Renewable Energy Business. In *Entrepreneurship and Business Development in the Renewable Energy Sector* (pp. 200–244). Hershey, PA: IGI Global. doi:10.4018/978-1-5225-3625-3.ch006

Teixeira, N., Pardal, P. N., & Rafael, B. G. (2018). Internationalization, Financial Performance, and Organizational Challenges: A Success Case in Portugal. In L. Carvalho (Ed.), *Handbook of Research on Entrepreneurial Ecosystems and Social Dynamics in a Globalized World* (pp. 379–423). Hershey, PA: IGI Global. doi:10.4018/978-1-5225-3525-6.ch017

Trad, A., & Kalpić, D. (2016). The E-Business Transformation Framework for E-Commerce Architecture-Modeling Projects. In I. Lee (Ed.), *Encyclopedia of E-Commerce Development, Implementation, and Management* (pp. 733–753). Hershey, PA: IGI Global. doi:10.4018/978-1-4666-9787-4.ch052

Trad, A., & Kalpić, D. (2016). The E-Business Transformation Framework for E-Commerce Control and Monitoring Pattern. In I. Lee (Ed.), *Encyclopedia of E-Commerce Development, Implementation, and Management* (pp. 754–777). Hershey, PA: IGI Global. doi:10.4018/978-1-4666-9787-4.ch053

Trad, A., & Kalpić, D. (2018). The Business Transformation Framework, Agile Project and Change Management. In M. Khosrow-Pour, D.B.A. (Ed.), Encyclopedia of Information Science and Technology, Fourth Edition (pp. 620-635). Hershey, PA: IGI Global. doi:10.4018/978-1-5225-2255-3.ch054

Trad, A., & Kalpić, D. (2018). The Business Transformation and Enterprise Architecture Framework: The Financial Engineering E-Risk Management and E-Law Integration. In B. Sergi, F. Fidanoski, M. Ziolo, & V. Naumovski (Eds.), *Regaining Global Stability After the Financial Crisis* (pp. 46–65). Hershey, PA: IGI Global. doi:10.4018/978-1-5225-4026-7.ch003

Turulja, L., & Bajgoric, N. (2018). Business Continuity and Information Systems: A Systematic Literature Review. In N. Bajgoric (Ed.), *Always-On Enterprise Information Systems for Modern Organizations* (pp. 60–87). Hershey, PA: IGI Global. doi:10.4018/978-1-5225-3704-5.ch004

van Wessel, R. M., de Vries, H. J., & Ribbers, P. M. (2016). Business Benefits through Company IT Standardization. In K. Jakobs (Ed.), *Effective Standardization Management in Corporate Settings* (pp. 34–53). Hershey, PA: IGI Global. doi:10.4018/978-1-4666-9737-9.ch003

Vargas-Hernández, J. G. (2017). Professional Integrity in Business Management Education. In N. Baporikar (Ed.), *Management Education for Global Leadership* (pp. 70–89). Hershey, PA: IGI Global. doi:10.4018/978-1-5225-1013-0.ch004

Vasista, T. G., & AlAbdullatif, A. M. (2017). Role of Electronic Customer Relationship Management in Demand Chain Management: A Predictive Analytic Approach. *International Journal of Information Systems and Supply Chain Management, 10*(1), 53–67. doi:10.4018/IJISSCM.2017010104

Vergidis, K. (2016). Rediscovering Business Processes: Definitions, Patterns, and Modelling Approaches. In P. Papajorgji, F. Pinet, A. Guimarães, & J. Papathanasiou (Eds.), *Automated Enterprise Systems for Maximizing Business Performance* (pp. 97–122). Hershey, PA: IGI Global. doi:10.4018/978-1-4666-8841-4.ch007

Vieru, D., & Bourdeau, S. (2017). Survival in the Digital Era: A Digital Competence-Based Multi-Case Study in the Canadian SME Clothing Industry. *International Journal of Social and Organizational Dynamics in IT, 6*(1), 17–34. doi:10.4018/IJSODIT.2017010102

Vijayan, G., & Kamarulzaman, N. H. (2017). An Introduction to Sustainable Supply Chain Management and Business Implications. In M. Khan, M. Hussain, & M. Ajmal (Eds.), *Green Supply Chain Management for Sustainable Business Practice* (pp. 27–50). Hershey, PA: IGI Global. doi:10.4018/978-1-5225-0635-5.ch002

Vlachvei, A., & Notta, O. (2017). Firm Competitiveness: Theories, Evidence, and Measurement. In A. Vlachvei, O. Notta, K. Karantininis, & N. Tsounis (Eds.), *Factors Affecting Firm Competitiveness and Performance in the Modern Business World* (pp. 1–42). Hershey, PA: IGI Global. doi:10.4018/978-1-5225-0843-4.ch001

von Rosing, M., Fullington, N., & Walker, J. (2016). Using the Business Ontology and Enterprise Standards to Transform Three Leading Organizations. *International Journal of Conceptual Structures and Smart Applications, 4*(1), 71–99. doi:10.4018/IJCSSA.2016010104

von Rosing, M., & von Scheel, H. (2016). Using the Business Ontology to Develop Enterprise Standards. *International Journal of Conceptual Structures and Smart Applications, 4*(1), 48–70. doi:10.4018/IJCSSA.2016010103

Walczak, S. (2016). Artificial Neural Networks and other AI Applications for Business Management Decision Support. *International Journal of Sociotechnology and Knowledge Development, 8*(4), 1–20. doi:10.4018/IJSKD.2016100101

Wamba, S. F., Akter, S., Kang, H., Bhattacharya, M., & Upal, M. (2016). The Primer of Social Media Analytics. *Journal of Organizational and End User Computing, 28*(2), 1–12. doi:10.4018/JOEUC.2016040101

Wang, C., Schofield, M., Li, X., & Ou, X. (2017). Do Chinese Students in Public and Private Higher Education Institutes Perform at Different Level in One of the Leadership Skills: Critical Thinking?: An Exploratory Comparison. In V. Wang (Ed.), *Encyclopedia of Strategic Leadership and Management* (pp. 160–181). Hershey, PA: IGI Global. doi:10.4018/978-1-5225-1049-9.ch013

Wang, F., Raisinghani, M. S., Mora, M., & Wang, X. (2016). Strategic E-Business Management through a Balanced Scored Card Approach. In I. Lee (Ed.), *Encyclopedia of E-Commerce Development, Implementation, and Management* (pp. 361–386). Hershey, PA: IGI Global. doi:10.4018/978-1-4666-9787-4.ch027

Wang, J. (2017). Multi-Agent based Production Management Decision System Modelling for the Textile Enterprise. *Journal of Global Information Management, 25*(4), 1–15. doi:10.4018/JGIM.2017100101

Wiedemann, A., & Gewald, H. (2017). Examining Cross-Domain Alignment: The Correlation of Business Strategy, IT Management, and IT Business Value. *International Journal of IT/Business Alignment and Governance, 8*(1), 17–31. doi:10.4018/IJITBAG.2017010102

Wolf, R., & Thiel, M. (2018). Advancing Global Business Ethics in China: Reducing Poverty Through Human and Social Welfare. In S. Hipsher (Ed.), *Examining the Private Sector's Role in Wealth Creation and Poverty Reduction* (pp. 67–84). Hershey, PA: IGI Global. doi:10.4018/978-1-5225-3117-3.ch004

Wu, J., Ding, F., Xu, M., Mo, Z., & Jin, A. (2016). Investigating the Determinants of Decision-Making on Adoption of Public Cloud Computing in E-government. *Journal of Global Information Management, 24*(3), 71–89. doi:10.4018/JGIM.2016070104

Xu, L., & de Vrieze, P. (2016). Building Situational Applications for Virtual Enterprises. In I. Lee (Ed.), *Encyclopedia of E-Commerce Development, Implementation, and Management* (pp. 715–724). Hershey, PA: IGI Global. doi:10.4018/978-1-4666-9787-4.ch050

Yablonsky, S. (2018). Innovation Platforms: Data and Analytics Platforms. In *Multi-Sided Platforms (MSPs) and Sharing Strategies in the Digital Economy: Emerging Research and Opportunities* (pp. 72–95). Hershey, PA: IGI Global. doi:10.4018/978-1-5225-5457-8.ch003

Yusoff, A., Ahmad, N. H., & Halim, H. A. (2017). Agropreneurship among Gen Y in Malaysia: The Role of Academic Institutions. In N. Ahmad, T. Ramayah, H. Halim, & S. Rahman (Eds.), *Handbook of Research on Small and Medium Enterprises in Developing Countries* (pp. 23–47). Hershey, PA: IGI Global. doi:10.4018/978-1-5225-2165-5.ch002

Zanin, F., Comuzzi, E., & Costantini, A. (2018). The Effect of Business Strategy and Stock Market Listing on the Use of Risk Assessment Tools. In *Management Control Systems in Complex Settings: Emerging Research and Opportunities* (pp. 145–168). Hershey, PA: IGI Global. doi:10.4018/978-1-5225-3987-2.ch007

Zgheib, P. W. (2017). Corporate Innovation and Intrapreneurship in the Middle East. In P. Zgheib (Ed.), *Entrepreneurship and Business Innovation in the Middle East* (pp. 37–56). Hershey, PA: IGI Global. doi:10.4018/978-1-5225-2066-5.ch003

About the Contributors

Carl Cargill is a Standards Consultant at large, specializing in standardization strategy creation and management. Carl has been a leader in standardization – both in practice and in theory – for over thirty years. He has written two books (*Information Technology Standardization: Theory, Process, and Organizations* and *Open Systems Standardization: A Business Approach*), multiple chapters in other books on the subject, and the "Standards" entry in the Third Edition of Van Nostrand Reinhold Encyclopedia of Computer Science. He was the Editor-in-Chief of "StandardView", ACM's journal of Standardization, and has written extensively on the subject of standardization and its practical applications. He has testified several times before Congress, and has been on Office of Technology Assessment and General Accounting Office panels as an expert on standardization. He was a Principal Scientist at Adobe specializing in standardization strategy. Before that, he was Sun Microsystems' Director of Corporate Standards. He was also the Director of Standards at Netscape and a standards strategist at both Sun and Digital Equipment Corporation. While at Sun, he founded and funded the *Standards Edge* series of books and conferences, which were instrumental in changing the understanding of standards and standardization. He holds a Bachelor in Arts from the University of Colorado in Medieval European History (1969) and a Masters in the Science of Administration (Management Engineering) from the George Washington University (1975).

Alice de Casanove is in charge of innovation culture in Airbus, where she fosters the relevant mind set to accelerate future businesses. Alice plays a pivoting role in the publication of the ISO referential on good practices in innovation management (ISO 50500 series). Indeed since 2013 she is chairing the international committee gathering 52+ countries in close coordination with WTO, OECD, WIPO and World Bank. Alice has started her career in a video deep tech start up then she joined Sagem to manage and develop the value of the Innovation portfolio of the French telecom manufacturer. She has joined the entrepreneurial adventure of Actimagine to develop video technologies on handled device (video games consoles and smartphones). Actimagine became Nintendo Europe R&D center after being bought by NINTENDO. Alice graduated Telecom Paristech.

Matt Heckman has been teaching European law and economics of European integration for 31 years at various universities in the Netherlands. He was Director of International Affairs for 14 years at a Dutch University and is currently teaching at various graduate programs (both MBA and MA) in the Netherlands, Finland, UK and the USA. Presently he works as senior researcher and principal lecturer graduate programmes. He was external examiner at DIT Dublin for four years and still acts as a consultant to both public and private companies. Matt is also a founding member of the research center on innovative entrepreneurship and risk management at the Zuyd University for Applied Sciences. Currently he is also a senior researcher at a research center for International Trade. At Maastricht University he teaches at the Center for European Studies and is an external fellow of the Institute for Globalization and International Regulation (IGIR). His recent activities also include the active involvement in university knowledge transfer. He supports start-ups in relation to the intellectual property aspects of bringing new university research to the market. He studied at the University of Maastricht, the University of Lancaster and the Vrije Universiteit Brussels. He holds a bachelor degree and a master degree in International and European Law and gained working experience at the Commission of the EU. His main research interests are in the field of intellectual property law and competition policy. His PhD-dissertation discussed the strategic use of patents in standardization in relation to US, European and Chinese competition law. Recent publications focus on legal aspects of standardization, artificial intelligence and technology licensing, comparing the jurisdictions of the USA, EU and China.

Brian McAuliffe is a master technologist in HP's CTO office responsible for standards strategy on new products & technologies in support of HP business strategy. He manages HP's engagement in multiple SDOs, fora/consortia, and industry associations and is HP's standards lead on 3DP/Additive Manufacturing. Previous to HP, Brian has worked for many years in standardization - in large technology-focused multinationals, with compliance testing laboratories (both private and government) and for a time as a self-employed product compliance consultant.

Henk J. de Vries is Professor of Standardisation at the Rotterdam School of Management, Erasmus University, Department of Technology and Operations Management, and Visiting Professor at the Faculty of Technology, Policy and Management of Delft University of Technology, the Netherlands. His research and teaching focus on standardization from a business perspective. Henk is President of the European Academy for Standardisation EURAS. He is author and co-author of 380 publications in the field of standardization. See http://www.rsm.nl/hdevries.

Robert M. van Wessel holds a Master in Electrical Engineering from Twente University and a PhD in Business Administration from Tilburg University (Department of Information Systems and Management). He is associated with Rotterdam School of Management, Erasmus University. Robert's research interests relate to the interaction of Business and Information Technology, in particular Business performance and the Value of IT, Enterprise Architecture, Data Management, IT Governance, Portfolio Management, Privacy and Information Security Management and IT Standardisation and Standards. Robert is currently Business Architect at a Dutch government agency and founder of ApexIS, a firm providing consultancy services to companies in his areas of research.

Index

T

V

W

Purchase Print, E-Book, or Print + E-Book

IGI Global books are available in three unique pricing formats:
Print Only, E-Book Only, or Print + E-Book. Shipping fees apply.

www.igi-global.com

Recommended Reference Books

ISBN: 978-1-5225-2016-0
© 2017; 375 pp.
List Price: $200

ISBN: 978-1-5225-0886-1
© 2017; 251 pp.
List Price: $160

ISBN: 978-1-5225-2075-7
© 2017; 2,266 pp.
List Price: $185

ISBN: 978-1-5225-1865-5
© 2017; 443 pp.
List Price: $200

ISBN: 978-1-5225-19614-4
© 2017; 365 pp.
List Price: $210

ISBN: 978-1-5225-1005-5
© 2015; 370 pp.
List Price: $205

Do you want to stay current on the latest research trends, product announcements, news and special offers?
Join IGI Global's mailing list today and start enjoying exclusive perks sent only to IGI Global members.
Add your name to the list at **www.igi-global.com/newsletters.**

Publisher of Peer-Reviewed, Timely, and Innovative Academic Research

IGI Global DISSEMINATOR OF KNOWLEDGE

www.igi-global.com Sign up at www.igi-global.com/newsletters facebook.com/igiglobal twitter.com/igiglobal linkedin.com/igiglobal

Ensure Quality Research is Introduced to the Academic Community

Become an IGI Global Reviewer for Authored Book Projects

The overall success of an authored book project is dependent on quality and timely reviews.

In this competitive age of scholarly publishing, constructive and timely feedback significantly expedites the turnaround time of manuscripts from submission to acceptance, allowing the publication and discovery of forward-thinking research at a much more expeditious rate. Several IGI Global authored book projects are currently seeking highly qualified experts in the field to fill vacancies on their respective editorial review boards:

Applications may be sent to:
development@igi-global.com

Applicants must have a doctorate (or an equivalent degree) as well as publishing and reviewing experience. Reviewers are asked to write reviews in a timely, collegial, and constructive manner. All reviewers will begin their role on an ad-hoc basis for a period of one year, and upon successful completion of this term can be considered for full editorial review board status, with the potential for a subsequent promotion to Associate Editor.

If you have a colleague that may be interested in this opportunity, we encourage you to share this information with them.

IGI Global
DISSEMINATOR OF KNOWLEDGE
www.igi-global.com

Celebrating 30 Years of Scholarly Knowledge Creation & Dissemination

InfoSci®-Books

A Collection of 4,000+ Reference Books Containing Over 87,000 Full-Text Chapters Focusing on Emerging Research

This database is a collection of over 4,000+ IGI Global single and multi-volume reference books, handbooks of research, and encyclopedias, encompassing groundbreaking research from prominent experts worldwide. These books are highly cited and currently recognized in prestigious indices such as: Web of Science™ and Scopus®.

Librarian Features:

- No Set-Up or Maintenance Fees
- Guarantee of No More Than A 5% Annual Price Increase
- COUNTER 4 Usage Reports
- Complimentary Archival Access
- Free MARC Records

Researcher Features:

- Unlimited Simultaneous Users
- No Embargo of Content
- Full Book Download
- Full-Text Search Engine
- No DRM

To Find Out More or To Purchase This Database:

www.igi-global.com/infosci-books

eresources@igi-global.com • Toll Free: 1-866-342-6657 ext. 100 • Phone: 717-533-8845 x100

IGI Global
DISSEMINATOR OF KNOWLEDGE
www.igi-global.com

IGI Global Proudly Partners with

eContent Pro International

Expert Copy Editing

eContent Pro International copy editors, with over 70 years of combined experience, will provide complete and comprehensive care for your document by resolving all issues with spelling, punctuation, grammar, terminology, jargon, semantics, syntax, consistency, flow, and more. In addition, they will format your document to the style you specify (APA, Chicago, etc.). All edits will be performed using Microsoft Word's Track Changes feature, which allows for fast and simple review and management of edits.

Additional Services

eContent Pro International also offers fast and affordable proofreading to enhance the readability of your document, professional translation in over 100 languages, and market localization services to help businesses and organizations localize their content and grow into new markets around the globe.

IGI Global Authors Save 25% on eContent Pro International's Services!

Scan the QR Code to Receive Your 25% Discount

The 25% discount is applied directly to your eContent Pro International shopping cart when placing an order through IGI Global's referral link. Use the QR code to access this referral link. eContent Pro International has the right to end or modify any promotion at any time.

Email: customerservice@econtentpro.com

econtentpro.com

Are You Ready to Publish Your Research?

IGI Global
DISSEMINATOR OF KNOWLEDGE

IGI Global offers book authorship and editorship opportunities across 11 subject areas, including business, healthcare, computer science, engineering, and more!

Benefits of Publishing with IGI Global:

- Free one-to-one editorial and promotional support.
- Expedited publishing timelines that can take your book from start to finish in less than one (1) year.
- Choose from a variety of formats including: Edited and Authored References, Handbooks of Research, Encyclopedias, and Research Insights.
- Utilize IGI Global's eEditorial Discovery® submission system in support of conducting the submission and blind-review process.
- IGI Global maintains a strict adherence to ethical practices due in part to our full membership to the Committee on Publication Ethics (COPE).
- Indexing potential in prestigious indices such as Scopus®, Web of Science™, PsycINFO®, and ERIC – Education Resources Information Center.
- Ability to connect your ORCID iD to your IGI Global publications.
- Earn royalties on your publication as well as receive complimentary copies and exclusive discounts.

Get Started Today by Contacting the Acquisitions Department at:

acquisition@igi-global.com

IGI Global
DISSEMINATOR OF KNOWLEDGE
www.igi-global.com

Available to Order Now

Order through www.igi-global.com with **Free Standard Shipping**.

The Premier Reference for Information Science & Information Technology

100% Original Content
Contains 705 new, peer-reviewed articles with color figures covering over 80 categories in 11 subject areas

Diverse Contributions
More than 1,100 experts from 74 unique countries contributed their specialized knowledge

Easy Navigation
Includes two tables of content and a comprehensive index in each volume for the user's convenience

Highly-Cited
Embraces a complete list of references and additional reading sections to allow for further research

Included in:
InfoSci®-Books

Encyclopedia of Information Science and Technology Fourth Edition

A Comprehensive 10-Volume Set

Mehdi Khosrow-Pour, D.B.A. (Information Resources Management Association, USA)
ISBN: 978-1-5225-2255-3; © 2018; Pg: 8,104; Release Date: July 2017

For a limited time, receive the complimentary e-books for the First, Second, and Third editions with the purchase of the *Encyclopedia of Information Science and Technology, Fourth Edition* e-book.*

The **Encyclopedia of Information Science and Technology, Fourth Edition** is a 10-volume set which includes 705 original and previously unpublished research articles covering a full range of perspectives, applications, and techniques contributed by thousands of experts and researchers from around the globe. This authoritative encyclopedia is an all-encompassing, well-established reference source that is ideally designed to disseminate the most forward-thinking and diverse research findings. With critical perspectives on the impact of information science management and new technologies in modern settings, including but not limited to computer science, education, healthcare, government, engineering, business, and natural and physical sciences, it is a pivotal and relevant source of knowledge that will benefit every professional within the field of information science and technology and is an invaluable addition to every academic and corporate library.

Scan for Online Bookstore

Pricing Information

Hardcover: **$5,695** E-Book: **$5,695** Hardcover + E-Book: **$6,895**

Both E-Book Prices Include:

- *Encyclopedia of Information Science and Technology, First Edition E-Book*
- *Encyclopedia of Information Science and Technology, Second Edition E-Book*
- *Encyclopedia of Information Science and Technology, Third Edition E-Book*

*Purchase the Encyclopedia of Information Science and Technology, Fourth Edition e-book and receive the first, second, and third e-book editions for free. Offer is only valid with purchase of the fourth edition's e-book through the IGI Global Online Bookstore.

Recommend this Title to Your Institution's Library: www.igi-global.com/books

www.igi-global.com/infosci-ondemand

InfoSci®-OnDemand

Continuously updated with new material on a weekly basis, InfoSci®-OnDemand offers the ability to search through thousands of quality full-text research papers. Users can narrow each search by identifying key topic areas of interest, then display a complete listing of relevant papers, and purchase materials specific to their research needs.

Comprehensive Service

- Over 110,800+ journal articles, book chapters, and case studies.
- All content is downloadable in PDF format and can be stored locally for future use.

No Subscription Fees

- One time fee of $37.50 per PDF download.

Instant Access

- Receive a download link immediately after order completion!

"It really provides an excellent entry into the research literature of the field. It presents a manageable number of highly relevant sources on topics of interest to a wide range of researchers. The sources are scholarly, but also accessible to 'practitioners'."

- Lisa Stimatz, MLS, University of North Carolina at Chapel Hill, USA

"It is an excellent and well designed database which will facilitate research, publication and teaching. It is a very very useful tool to have."

- George Ditsa, PhD, University of Wollongong, Australia

"I have accessed the database and find it to be a valuable tool to the IT/IS community. I found valuable articles meeting my search criteria 95% of the time."

- Lynda Louis, Xavier University of Louisiana, USA

Recommended for use by researchers who wish to immediately download PDFs of individual chapters or articles.

www.igi-global.com/e-resources/infosci-ondemand

IGI Global
DISSEMINATOR OF KNOWLEDGE
www.igi-global.com

www.ingramcontent.com/pod-product-compliance
Lightning Source LLC
LaVergne TN
LVHW062120300926
849161LV00010B/2507